Massive Small *NOUN*

1 constructive activism for bottom-up urban change

2 a practical alternative to ‘bigness’

3 the collective power of many small ideas and actions to build urban society

4 a way of delivering radical incrementalism

5 the enabling protocols, conditions and behaviours needed to help form urban neighbourhoods

PRAISE FOR **MAKING MASSIVE SMALL CHANGE**

...a stunningly curated Kama Sutra *for city-making...*

—Edgar Pieterse

'Bigness has grown out of control—in our cities and in our life-critical systems—but here's the good news: small actions are the best way to cut bigness down to size, and this compendium contains a thousand different ways to start.'

—John Thackara, founder of Doors of Perception; author of *How to Thrive in the Next Economy*

'Kelvin Campbell has done it again. Starting with a broad understanding of how urban change happens and needs to happen—less through top-down command-and-control methods, more through *massive small* interventions—he guides us through a rich compendium of tools and strategies. His section on process tools (what he calls "activators") is particularly helpful—covering asset-based community development, participatory budgeting, and other crucial modifications of the malfunctioning "operating system for growth". The compendium is richly illustrated with case studies and simple takeaways, like his "Ten Things to Do" and "Ten Things Not to Do". They are eminently sensible, raising the question, Why are they still done and not done? The answer might be that Campbell's book has not yet come along to give such a clear picture! Campbell says the book is only a beginning, and we look forward to more of his insightful work in the future. Meanwhile, this delightful book deserves a spot on the bookshelf next to *The Death and Life of Great American Cities*, *A Pattern Language*, and other icons of fine-grained, process-based development.'

—Michael Mehaffy, PhD, executive director of Sustasis Foundation; coauthor of *Design for a Living Planet*

'This powerful and highly engaging book is an inspiring call for all of us to start making a difference tomorrow. I have always believed that more than hope driving action, it is action that drives hope. Read this book, be inspired by its stories of change from modest beginnings, and get working for a better world.'

—Matthew Taylor, chief executive of the Royal Society for the Encouragement of Arts, Manufactures and Commerce

'What a beautiful bastard this book is: a hybridised glossary, dictionary, manual, playbook, catalogue, manifesto, polemic and so much more. It is a stunningly curated *Kama Sutra* for city-making—inventive and seductive. If you have any connection with urban transformation, in any capacity, scale or setting, spend quality time with this book and engage with its many provocations.'

—Edgar Pieterse, director of the African Centre for Cities; author of *New Urban Worlds*

'The urban neighbourhoods we know and love have evolved over generations with successive contributions from countless people. They have shaped buildings, streets and spaces as well as activities and processes. Today the way we build places is simpler, quicker and courser with fewer people involved. The principles and approaches in *Making Massive Small Change* reflect how we can empower people to once again participate in shaping our communities whilst creating more successful places.'

—Ben Derbyshire, president of the Royal Institute of British Architects

'*Making Massive Small Change* is part of a growing movement that recognises the value of small, incremental development for our cities, our economies and our citizens. The systems that shape our communities have been distorted to privilege bigness—big companies, big projects, big budgets and big plans—while small actors face disproportionate burdens or outright exclusion from building their homes, businesses and communities. Just as urbanists reclaimed the lost knowledge of traditional design, we must now rediscover the value of incrementalism, of many small projects done by many hands, of enabling local residents and businesses to participate in community development. As a leading urban theorist, Kelvin Campbell recognized this early on, and with *Making Massive Small Change* has created this thorough compendium to address it. The thinking builds on good design to consider how the systems should be restructured—from closed to open, from centralized to local, from top-down to bottom-up—to enable small. And it provides new and collected tactics and tools to make it happen. *Making Massive Small Change* is a valuable contribution to the movement.'

—Brian Falk, director of the Project for Lean Urbanism

'*Making Massive Small Change* is a passionate, heartfelt plea for a new approach to urban development, but it is also much more. Campbell presents evidenced arguments and highly innovative solutions from leading-edge, organised complexity research concepts, from his own four decades of practice, and from tactics of change-makers across the world. The Massive Small project is the culmination of a decade-long search for better, alternative ways to meet our city challenges from dialogues reaching out to practitioners, academics, and community activists across a wide network. Campbell's call is for a renewed social movement—using an innovative framework of ideas, tools and tactics—to leverage the *small*-scale ideas and efforts of citizens, professionals and progressive governments into a collaborative urbanism that could have a *massive* positive impact on our current broken systems of urban development. These are important ideas—and an urgent call to action. Jane Jacobs would be overjoyed to see a designer finally turning her recommendations about organised complexity—made over fifty years ago—into a practical framework and toolbox for transformative action. It is a timely and major achievement.'

—**NezHapi Dellé Odeleye,** PhD, course leader, department of Engineering and the Built Environment, Anglia Ruskin University

'Finally a book that offers abundant evidence that a built environment is an organism composed of living cells. Kelvin Campbell demonstrates that professionals can learn from such evidence and find ways to contribute to the organism's health.'

—**John Habraken,** author of *Supports* and *The Structure of the Ordinary*

'*Making Massive Small Change* is everything its author declares. That means it is an up-to-date sourcebook and vocabulary as well. My reading and re-reading list has been substantially updated. Kelvin's comprehensive compendium is an ideal reference for all seeking patterns of sustainable and therefore bottom-up placemaking and management. The emerging paradigm, so clearly illustrated in this book, highlights the fact that only peoples' local capacities can provide the vital variety of requirements for human and natural life.'

—**John F.C. Turner,** architect; author of *Freedom to Build* and *Housing By People*

'*Making Massive Small Change* is an extremely valuable new handbook for urbanism that brings together the most pertinent, current, tested ideas and strategies for a better future.'

—**Kristien Ring,** founding director of the German Centre for Architecture; author of *Selfmade City*

'An extremely valuable new handbook of urbanism—it's the beauty of simplicity and small actions that can provoke a positive start. Wise urban acupuncture and co-responsibility for incremental change.'

—**Jaime Lerner,** architect and urbanist; author of *Urban Acupuncture*

'One quote from E. F. Schumacher that immediately comes to mind when reading *Making Massive Small Change* is: "Any intelligent fool can make things bigger and more complex...it takes a touch of genius—and a lot of courage—to move in the opposite direction". This book does have more than a touch of genius and is massively courageous. This is an essential book for anyone involved in systems thinking, complexity and design. Aimed primarily at urban development it also applies to all aspects of human endeavours—all our institutions, governance, economics and trade emerge from the world we build around us and we need this message of small beginnings for massive system change.'

—**Ian Roderick,** director of the Schumacher Institute

This is an essential book for anyone involved in systems thinking, complexity and design

—Ian Roderick

'Transforming cities is highly complex, and the challenge can often feel overwhelming. Large, sexy, iconic projects can be big targets and quite polarizing, which means they often don't get delivered, creating layers of mistrust and frustration. *Making Massive Small Change* by urban maestro Kelvin Campbell shows us another way: that change doesn't have to take decades to realise or even to be gold-plated. It shows us that small done well can actually be the most powerful change agent on the planet because it can mobilise a whole city or community, allowing the goodness to creep up. With cities, small can be mighty. Read this and make that change.'

—**Ludo Campbell-Reid,** urbanist; Design Champion for Auckland, New Zealand

Great acts are made up of small deeds.

—Lao Tzu

WITH SINCERE THANKS TO OUR KICKSTARTER BACKERS:

The game-changer: *Larry Rosner@TheSocietyProject.org.* **The enabler:** *Architecture & Design Scotland.* **The accelerator:** *Urban Initiatives Studio, Urban Movement, Priya Prakash, Louise Reid.* **The generous donor:** *Sean Monahan, Archie Smith, Justin Wilde, Eve Denney, Grant Gerald, Annick De Swaef, Naomi Rohwer, Sam Golding, Will Alsop@aLL Design, David Prichard.* **The collector:** *Tom Bloxham MBE, Mike Rawlinson, Jon Andrews, Tony Reddy, Rick Robinson, Dan Hill, Paul Dodd, Briony Turner, Catja de Haas, Andrew Frey, Kay Pallaris, Piers Gough, Luke Tozer, James Soane, Jason King, Joe Headon, Max de Rosee, Graeme Monk, Ram Hardy, Barra Mac Ruairi, Zaven Gabriel, Lauren Bigelow, Grahame Edwards, Marc Dorfman, Paul Plak, Hans Peter Sommer, David Bishop, Shannon Basham, Leni Schwendinger, Michael Owens, Arthur Frontczak, Alan Leibowitz, Sean McCann, Lyn Fenton, Tyler Moorehead, Zane Prodahl, Shujaat Ali Mohammed, Mesh Chhibber, Daniel Bessant, Andreas Taylor, Lucy Weldinger.* **The urban pioneer:** *Andy Reeve, James Pargeter, Nicole White, Susan Frank, Blair Francey, Tine Saint-Ghislain, Jeroen Thibaut, CJ Livingston, C Jugendstil, R.J. Success, Karen Schubert. Mauro Di Tanna, Holger Weinecke, Andrew Budgen, Damian Williams, Wolfgang Sperrer, Santiago Garcia, Craig Grocke, Sheri Hachey, Steve Dixon, Martin Helm, Robert Hoogenboom, Charles Landry, Brose Hagerman, Katherine Roberts, Kate Wagner, Chris Fredericks, Hugo Gagnon, Sander Baumann, Rob Collinson, Amy Buerk, Nicolas Bauer.* **The giver and getter:** *Conor Moloney, Jonathan Bannister, Richard Tracey, Dan Pearce, Dan Hill, Colin Fairweather, Justin Varney, Stephen Taylor, Greg Keeffe, Eileen Flatley, Cany Ash, Lauren Ugur, Emma Ibbetson, Ben Derbyshire, Andrew Boraine, Kobus Mentz, Clementine Cecil, Dick Gleeson, Martin Harradine, Patrick Bellew, David Rudlin, Nino Rajic, Dinah Sanders, Sara Lappi,Delle Odeleye, Nick Churchouse, David Mathew, Jana Wisniewski, Ingrid Jones, Benoit Naturel, Manny Hernandez, Christer Ljungberg, Justin James Walsh, Jurie Lombard, Geoffrey Rosen, David Kaplan, Sean McCullagh, Michela Ventin, Roger Estop, Frank Sazama.* **The giver:** *Sophie Paton, Roger Connah, Hiddo Huitzing, Chris Romer-Lee, Finn Harries, Clara Sousa Silva, Lorna Prescott, Tim Pope, Katie Wallace, Lennart Bueth, Pieter Herthogs, Jon Irwin, Rachel Godfrey, Paul Ducker, Scott Elliott Adams, Hannes Couvreur, Franklin, Michel Wolfstirn, Juliet Bidgood, Matthew Mullan, Claudio Sarmiento-Casas, Philip Singleton, Daniel Teoh Yong Liang, Darshana Gothi Chauhan, Aoife Reid, Liz Thomas, Preeti Tyagi, Finn Williams, Niels van Dijk, Kayla Friedman, Ming Cheng, Jo Lees, John P. Houghton, Khalifa, Amanda Gore, Joseph Burgum, Helen Gordon, James Donnelly, Florie Salnot, Adrian Cull, Philippa Wilkin, Rebecca Barrett, Siobhan Adeleke, David Geering, Rob French, Zbadi Ilham, Josh Acurio, Rebecca Taylor, Jonathan Bretherton, Ivor Chomacki, Paul Bowker, Adrian Cull, Matthias Bauer, Christiaan Weiler, Matthew Hardy, Philip Cave, Wayne Hemingway, Dave Adamson, Jaime Parsons, Julian Dobson, Alex Gavozdea, Ivan Tennant, Deborah Nagan, Riccardo Bobisse, Neil Barker, Maija Meuller, Chloe Clay, Stephanie Cole, Stuart Croucher, Alice Eggeling, Melanie Forster-Nel, John Alderson, John Lord, Amira Osman, Matthew Riley, Julian Cottee, Justine Daly, Euan Mills, Toby Fox, Gabriel Greeff, Natalia, Annette King, Gabor Sooki-Toth, John Rundle, Beth Kay, Claire Curtice, Tricia O'Donovan, Rex Curry, Jan Starcevic, Holger Wessels, Kelvin Mason, Mary Margaret Kirby, Tameca Miles, J. Kim,Brandon Wheat, Nicolas Grangier, Dana Wendt, Golden Family Company, Judy Rahn, Vika Golovanova, Duane Oen, Jennifer Morone, Sebastian Arrese, Thed Weller, Thomas Kim, Russell Wayne Franklin, Kathleen Kirkpatrick, Johgn Wilgus, Christoph Lokotsch, Jane Halsey, Yao Yue, Daniel Nephin, Taylor Rankin, Anthony Kimpton, Gustavo Gonzalez, Tom Martin, Jessica Bader, Humberto Godinez,, Glen Liberman, Colin Krasnozon, Phyllis Hoyte, Maire Dekle, Stephanie Nieto, Herman Yueh, Chuck Cammarata, Jesse Hamlet Han, Roland Karoliny, Elizabeth Wallace, Sharon Ede,Matthew Morse, Sandra Scott, Jason Diceman, Charles Morris, Shannon Hong, Jean-Michel Gillet, Madeleine Beart, Jiang, Howard Goldkrand, Tomi Schuetz, Sampath Ramanujan,, Justin Gathright, Trung Thai Truong, Chris Rumbell, Marc-Oliver Paux. The giver: Ana Luisa Ramirez, Bogomil Kohlbrenner, Thorsten Bruns, Jean-Luc Geronimi, Oona Strathern, Richelle Lockett, Hilary Kemp, Chris Benfield, Bettina Gies, Gareth Evans, Cali Livingstone, Jaroslaw Paluch, Christian Tilleray, Scott Smith, Tim Pinder, Tomasz Szreder, Kellya Clanzig, Csaba Szigetvari, Suzette Jackson, Maciej Folta, Jon Smith, Richard Vahrman, Rob Allport, Eric Treske, Katherine Garzonis, Andrea Zampiva, Matthew Young, Atam Verdi, Kim Vo, David Moberly, Dennis Straub, Elizabeth Reynolds, Ludovic Coutant, Ramon Barturen, Dave Ong, Francesca Vergani, Daniela Fuentes, Dave Wastall, Leonor Vanik, Shelley Chevalier, Jorge Gil, Sean Cleary, Martha O'Toole, Juho Kostet, Matt Mendenhall, Adrian Richardson, Tabi Joy, Alexandros Daniilidis, David Rosenthal, A.T. Ferweda, Michael Wild, Henrique Prata, Sonny Masero, Nancy Stone, Katie Sickman, Ingo Lantschner, Mark Cellura, David Jacquet, Antoniya Statelova, Alma Erfurt, Lorien Goodale, Paul McGarry, Sean Furey, Francesca Froy, Johannes Treytl-Hartmann, Alex Fuller, Daniel Partridge, Georgia Butina Watson, Henry Winter, Emily Crompton, Stephan Erfurt, Rasheed Barnes, Peter Reay, Bo Hansen, Nicholas Colello, Thomas Schmidt, John Kelly, Jacques Gerber, Ulrich Lott, Helen Ruisi, James Tanner, Riel Sibley, Thomas Davis, Luke Archer, Charlie Peel, Peter Dodds, Jiri Koten, Mandi Pretorius, Patti Shook, Ros Percy, Peter Ellis, Alison Peters, Stephen Rose, Chris Gill, Guillermo Palacios, Andrew Williamson, Irina Torelli, Hayrettin Gunc, Michael Visocchi, Diana Reis, Rona Suzuki, Armelle Fustec, William Neher, Fabrizio Lepore, Brian Cuiffo, Linda Smiley, Francisco Machado, Karen Frederiksen, Chris Butler, Sadie Moseley, David Godfrey, Ken Chiang, Philippa Hamill, Jimmy Ray Tyner, Juanjo Amate, Bruce Bean, Mingjia Chen, Mike Sakony, Federico Manuri, Michelle Paganini, Robert Pierre Otte, Martin van Elp, Catherine Fillmore, Anthony Pickering, Rene Castro, Szymon Nogalski, Arturo Elenes, Dirk Dresch, Mandar Puranik, Jeffrey Moses, Jeff Carrell, Megan Elmore, Nick Pearson, Hanyan Shi, Eliot Rosenbloom, Austin J. Austin, Joao Antunes, Louise Armstrong, J Calicutt, Caroline Pitt, James Wheeler, James Goodman.* **The seeker:** *Julian Buckle, Nehaa Bhavaraju, Maria-Elena Petrescu, Jaime Arredondo, Lia Ghilardi, Alexander Valbjorn Nielsen, Tim Abrahams, Andrew Reynolds, Clare Flatley, Benjamin de la Pena, Craig Campbell, Belinda Campbell, Martin O'Rourke, David Dewar, Gillian Meyer, Rod Gurzynski, Jim Colleran, Chuck Wolfe, Peter Driver, Isobel Knapp, Isabella Wagner, Filipa Wunderlich, Jimmy Campbell, Clare Darling, Honore van Rijswijk, Ross Ingham, Thomas Whitley, Ian Leete, Paul Sagor, Doru Calangea, Ian Cameron, Peter Kylin, Chris Ramirez, James Beaumont, Ronan Loughney, Paul Stephenson, Clement Delort, Maarten Beisterveld, Vanessa Eghardt, Christophe Duquesne, Marc Furnival, Anke Schuettemeyer, Peter Lawrence, Danny McKendry, Hakan Agca, Scott Gillespie, Andrew Sheldon, Gina Skinner, Laurent Puissant, Betty Cherniak, Jovin Hurry, Adrian Monzon, Jack Bodger, Jane Kim, Romain Piasecki, Mahesh Thadisena, H Werkheiser, Civic Works, Michael Clark.* **The difference-maker:** *Dan Dubowitz, Leci, Zach Van Stanley, Shruti Shankar, Peter Main, Karen Reid, Martin Curran, Graham Smith, Joshua Finn Weddle, Chris McCormick, Jamie Macleod, Aimee Marie Jackson, Anouska Warner, Isabella Beebee, Neha Kandwal, Annie Eby, Ivan Olsen, Allister Long, Grant Campbell, Sonja Long, Naomi Campbell, Roxy, Gwyneth Caldwell, Andrew Hilton, Lauren Hermanus, Jane Jones, Sulabh Goel, Bruno Postle, Rick Cody, Nicolas Tsaoushis, Brittany Wallace,Jorge Gerini, Oli, Maiken McCormick, Dominic, Jason Orozco, Beezhan Tulu, Chelle Destefano, Lynn Ross, Keryna Johnson, Tom Joncret, Yashshri, Kathleen Reed, Daniel Bissonnette, Jaime Crossier, Alan Stevenson, Csaba Kocsis, Dorothy Hollingsworth, Nicodemus Bouck, Emily Catedral, James Poulette, Riccardo Sartori, Hamza Boutaleb, Lee-Rae Rodwell, Stacey Roos, Katayha Watson, James Tyler, Venka Michaela Zimmer, Louise McCulloch, David Head, Bernd Hauser, Trevor Pedley, Steven Meulemans, Alexi Wheeler, Ina Dimireva, John Sleeman, Lorenz Zahn, Oonagh, Christopher Stieha, Alexandre Chabot-Leclerc, Dana Freeman, James Parkinson, Malcolm Odekele, John Goodchild.*

KICKSTARTER

MAKING MASSIVE SMALL CHANGE

SHELTER

KELVIN CAMPBELL

MAKING MASSIVE SMALL CHANGE

BUILDING THE URBAN SOCIETY WE WANT

CHELSEA GREEN PUBLISHING
WHITE RIVER JUNCTION, VERMONT
LONDON, UK

Imaginary Stories Editor: Rob Cowan
Project Manager: Patricia Stone
Copy Editor: Deborah Heimann
Proofreader: Angela Boyle
Indexer: Shana Milkie
Design: Christopher Freeman, conductdesign.com
Design Support: Andrew Campbell, Massive Small Collective, massivesmall.org
Matthias Wunderlich, Urban Initiatives Studio, uistudio.co.uk
Adam Samuel, Renderworx, renderworx.co.za

Printed in the Czech Republic.
First printing August, 2018.
10 9 8 7 6 5 4 3 2 1 18 19 20 21 22

Our Commitment to Green Publishing
Chelsea Green sees publishing as a tool for cultural change and ecological stewardship. We strive to align our book manufacturing practices with our editorial mission and to reduce the impact of our business enterprise in the environment. We print our books and catalogs on chlorine-free recycled paper, using vegetable-based inks whenever possible. This book may cost slightly more because it was printed on paper that contains recycled fiber, and we hope you'll agree that it's worth it. Chelsea Green is a member of the Green Press Initiative (greenpressinitiative.org), a nonprofit coalition of publishers, manufacturers, and authors working to protect the world's endangered forests and conserve natural resources.

Library of Congress Cataloging-in-Publication Data
Names: Campbell, Kelvin, author.
Title: Making massive small change : building the urban society we want / Kelvin Campbell.
Description: White River Junction, Vermont : Chelsea Green Publishing, 2018.
Identifiers: LCCN 2017061272 | ISBN 9781603587754 (paperback)
Subjects: LCSH: City planning. | Cities and towns—Growth. | Land use—Environmental aspects. | BISAC: ARCHITECTURE / Urban & Land Use Planning. | POLITICAL SCIENCE / Public Policy / City Planning & Urban Development. | POLITICAL SCIENCE / Public Policy / Regional Planning.
Classification: LCC HT165.5 .C36 2018 | DDC 307.1/216—dc23
LC record available at https://lccn.loc.gov/2017061272

Chelsea Green Publishing
85 North Main Street, Suite 120
White River Junction, VT 05001
1 (802) 295-6300
chelseagreen.com

MIX
Paper from responsible sources
FSC® C004378

CONTENTS

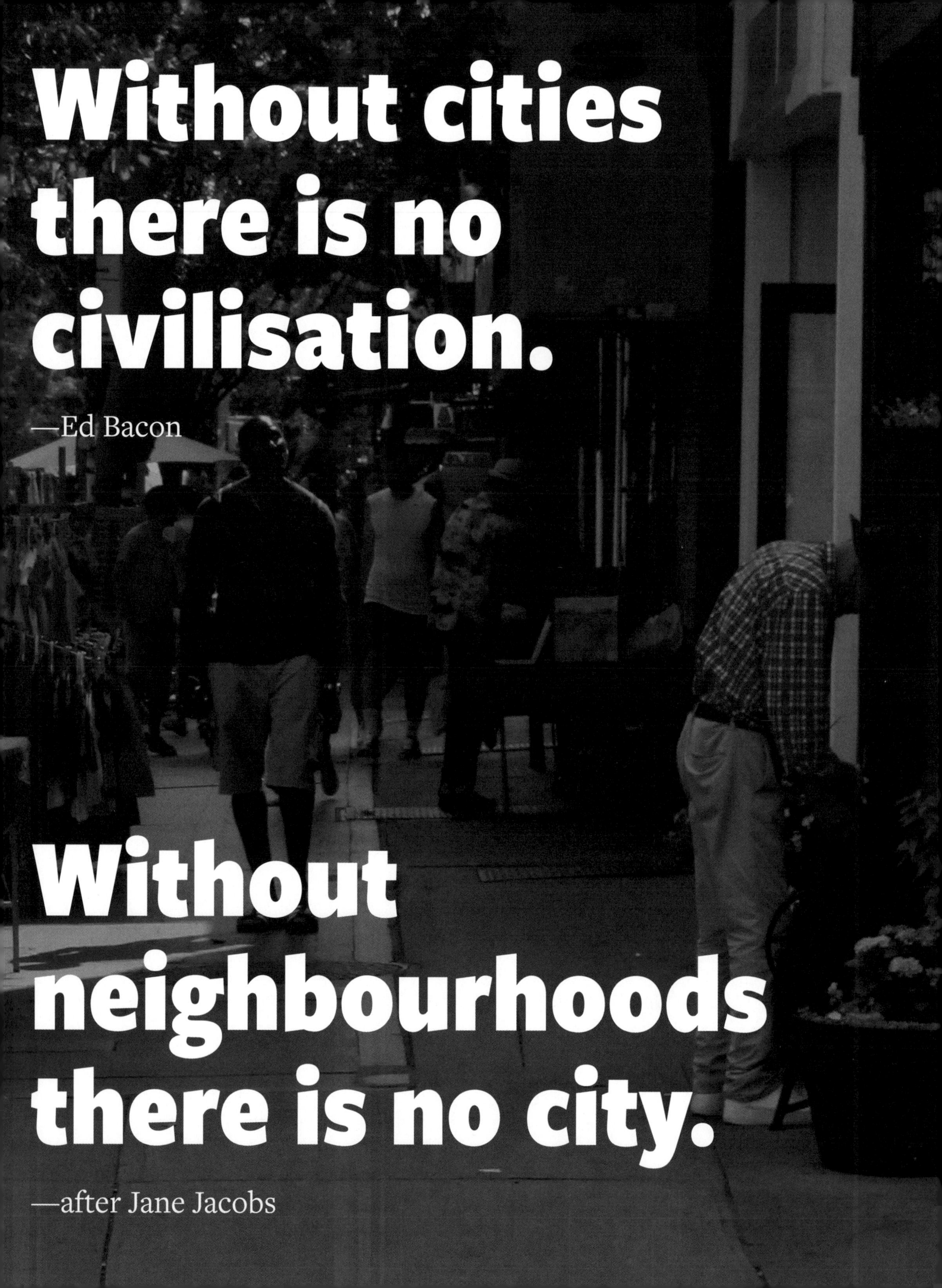

Without cities there is no civilisation.

—Ed Bacon

Without neighbourhoods there is no city.

—after Jane Jacobs

If your heart doesn't break at the state of urban society in the world today, then stop reading now. This is for those who want to make a big difference but don't know where to start. Because even though the difference-makers didn't get us into this mess, we are the ones with the drive and belief to get us out of it.

[a million dabs on the canvas]

PROLOGUE

Jane Jacobs

ORGANISED COMPLEXITY

PUT DEMOCRACY BACK INTO URBANISM

small actions
×
lots of people
=
BIG CHANGE

BUILD A NEW MODEL

BE A RADICAL INCREMENTALIST

XXS
MAKE MASSIVE SMALL CHANGE

ACTIVE CITIZENSHIP
A FORCE FOR CHANGE

BIGGEST IMPACT
LIGHTEST TOUCH

BUILD COMMUNITY

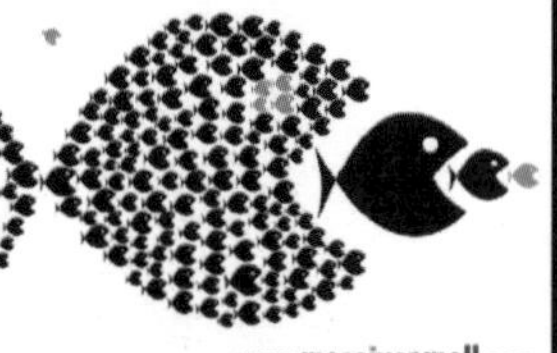
www.massivesmall.com

NOW,

MANAGE IN THE PRESENT

URBANISATION
GOVERNMENT EFFECTIVENESS

URBAN ETHICS

BOTTOM-UP MEETS TOP-DOWN

SCALABILITY

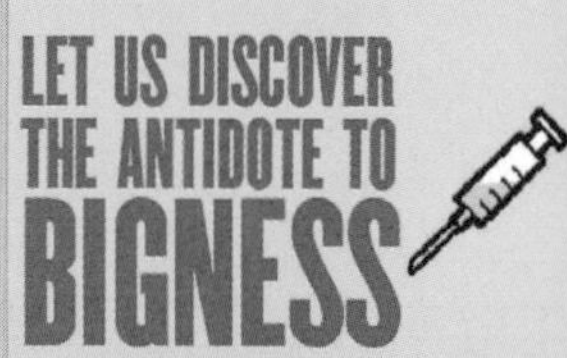
LET US DISCOVER THE ANTIDOTE TO BIGNESS

PEOPLE CAN BE TRUSTED

LOCAL

REDUCTIONISM
A CRIME AGAINST URBANITY

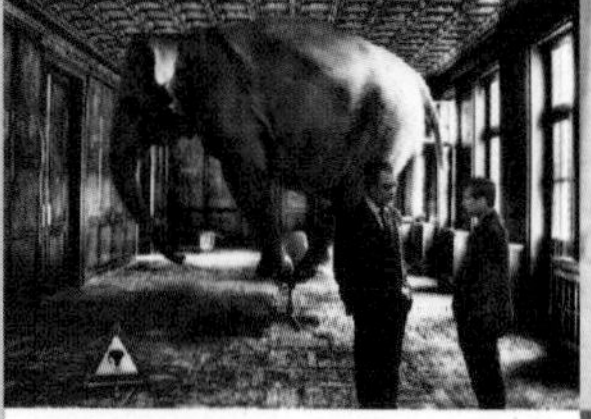

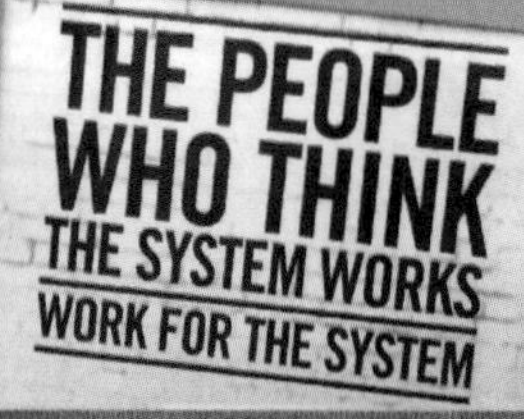
THE PEOPLE WHO THINK
THE SYSTEM WORKS
WORK FOR THE SYSTEM

HOW DID WE THINK WE COULD CONTROL SOMETHING AS COMPLEX AS A CITY?

VIVA LA EVOLUTION

City superstar

MULTIPLICITY
MULTIPLICITY

CIVILIA

www.massivesmall.com

THINK OPPOSITE

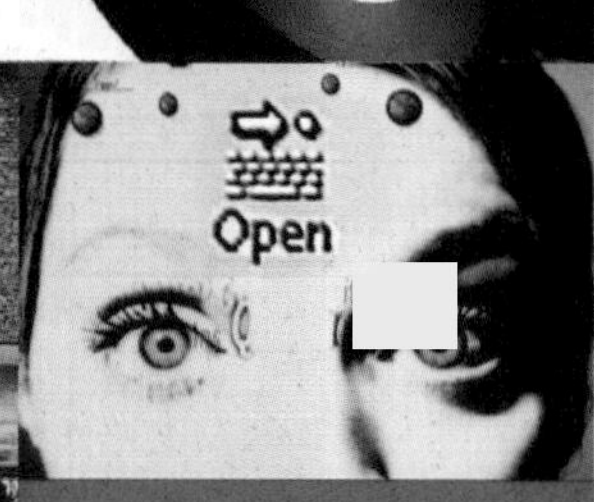
Open

SHOW THE WAY

SYSTEMS THEORY

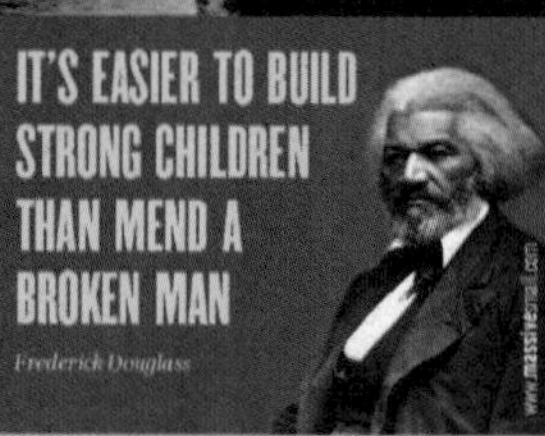
IT'S EASIER TO BUILD STRONG CHILDREN THAN MEND A BROKEN MAN
Frederick Douglass

RESISTANCE

EMERGENCE*

[noun] 1. Coming into existence
2. Early stages of development
3. Becoming manifest or known

SMART CITIZENS MAKE SMART CITIES

LIMITING CHOICE: INFINITE POSSIBLITIES

DO.LEARN.INFLUENCE

It is not the strongest species that survive, nor the most intelligent, but the ones most responsive to change.
- Charles Darwin

In an increasingly complex and changing world, where global problems are felt locally, the systems we currently use to plan, design and build our urban neighbourhoods—the vital building blocks of our towns and cities—are doomed to failure.

For three generations, governments the world over have tried to order and control the evolution of cities through rigid, top-down action. They have failed dismally. Everywhere masterplans lie unfulfilled, housing is in crisis, the environment is under threat, and the urban poor have become poorer.

All around we see the unintended consequences of governments' well-intended actions. Our cities are straining under the pressure of rapid population growth, rising inequality, inadequate infrastructure—all coupled with our governments' ineffectiveness in the face of these challenges and their failure to deliver on their continued promises to build a better urban society for all of us. Everything we see out there is the outcome of the system. We struggle to point to any new viable and decent urban neighbourhoods anywhere in the world that we have created in the last three generations. The system is not broken: it was built this way.

Governments alone cannot solve these problems. But there is another way. This compendium, expressed through the lens of complexity thinking, shows a way: by changing thinking, practices and language to enable governments and people to work together to achieve the urban transformation that neither could achieve alone.

We call it making Massive Small change.

Whenever something is wrong, something is too big.

—Leopold Kohr

ALL GUNS BLAZING

In the spirit of Jane Jacobs, this work is an unashamed, all-guns-blazing attack on the way we plan, design and develop our cities. It is an attack not on the people but on the system that forces us all down narrow alleys to places we do not want to be. It is an attack not against private development that curates a long-term managed view of the neighbourhood but against the quick in-and-out, big-capital development model—fostered by the system—that kills places at the outset. It is an attack not against informality but against the system that traps people in this state and never fosters social mobility or improvement. It is an attack not against the essential role of governments in delivering good urbanism but against the rigid, command-and-control models they use to shape our cities.

We do not want governments to get out of the way; we want them to refocus their efforts to where they will make a difference. This is not a neo-liberal rant demanding laissez-faire deregulation; it is a plea for stronger action by all scales of government in certain areas, and a lighter approach in others.

It recognises that active citizens are our best shot at creating a more equitable urban society, but they are frustrated by the rigidly deterministic practices the system imposes. It recognises that many urban professionals came into this world to make it a better place, but their best efforts and ideas are suspended in the false utopian dreams that the system professes to deliver. It recognises that civic leaders have the best intentions to lead us to a better place, but they do not have the tools or tactics to take us there. The system holds us all to ransom. Cities and their neighbourhoods pay the price.

There is no better time to focus on these matters than now. In many places, people are dreaming about a new post-capitalist society that is much more equitable and rewarding for its citizens; about a localist model that maintains the wealth and assets of a community in the community; and about a future where we break free from the shackles of our narrow, outdated, single- or two-party political views of our world that reduce all debate to mindless rhetoric and to bland solutions that do not work for people.

Finally, this is not the wishful thinking of a single hero; it is the work of many great minds and committed neighbourhood-builders who over the centuries have created places we love and showed us the way. This work attempts to bring their bold efforts together to make common sense.

GIANTISM IS THE FIRST SIGN OF FAILURE

For over 300 generations, cities evolved as rich tapestries of life, each stitch the result of an individual action, collectively making a story of urban civilisation. For the last three generations, we have lost the art of urban evolution. What we now see is the efforts of big governments, big corporations and big plans that suck the life from urbanity. Bigness has become the problem.

'Wherever something is wrong,' wrote the economist and political scientist Leopold Kohr, 'something is too big.' Kohr thought that the problems of urban society were caused not by particular forms of social or economic organisation but by their size. Things work at a scale at which people can play a part in the systems that govern their lives. At a larger scale, all systems become oppressive.

> *The central disease of our time is not ugliness, poverty, crime or neglect, but the ugliness, poverty, crime and neglect that comes from the unsurveyable dimensions of modern national and urban giantism.*
>
> —Leopold Kohr

Kirkpatrick Sale takes giantism to task in his book *Human Scale Revisited* and looks at how the crises that imperil the world are the inevitable result of bigness grown out of control. He carefully argues for bringing human endeavours back to scales we can comprehend and manage—whether in our built environments, our politics or our business.

Like Kohr, Sale believes that when buildings were scaled to the human figure, democracies were scaled to the societies they served and enterprise was scaled to communities, things were more resilient. The bigger-is-better paradigm that has defined modern times has brought civilisation to a crisis point.

> *Retreating from our calamity will take rebalancing our relationship to the environment; adopting more human-scale technologies; right-sizing our buildings, communities, and cities; and bringing our critical services from energy, food, transportation, health, and education back to human scale as well.*
>
> —Kirkpatrick Sale

Here human scale is the main idea in sustainability: a vision 'not only of appropriate technologies, but of participatory dwelling, in which creaturely being is prized, nothing is merely a resource and the environment is deemed beyond further compromise'.

Like *Small Is Beautiful: Economics as if People Mattered* by E. F. Schumacher, *Human Scale Revisited* is a classic of modern decentralist thought and communitarian values—a key tool in the kit of those trying to localise, create meaningful governance in bioregions, or rethink our reverence of and dependence on growth.

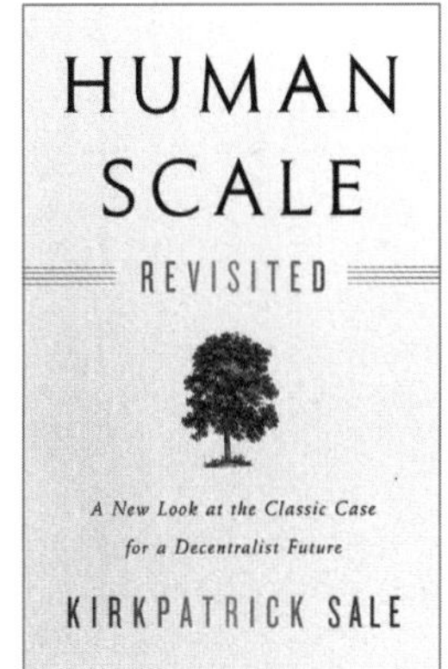

The theory underpinning this compendium provides an antidote to the bigness that has become the standard fare for building our towns and cities. It does this by showing how we can move back to the idea of the urban neighbourhood as a distributed system made through an infinite number of small efforts that add up to making a big picture. We express this as 'making a million dabs on a canvas' rather than making a few big splashes. This can also be seen as many small fishes, working collectively, becoming stronger than the biggest fish.

> *Big fish eat small fish.*
>
> —African proverb

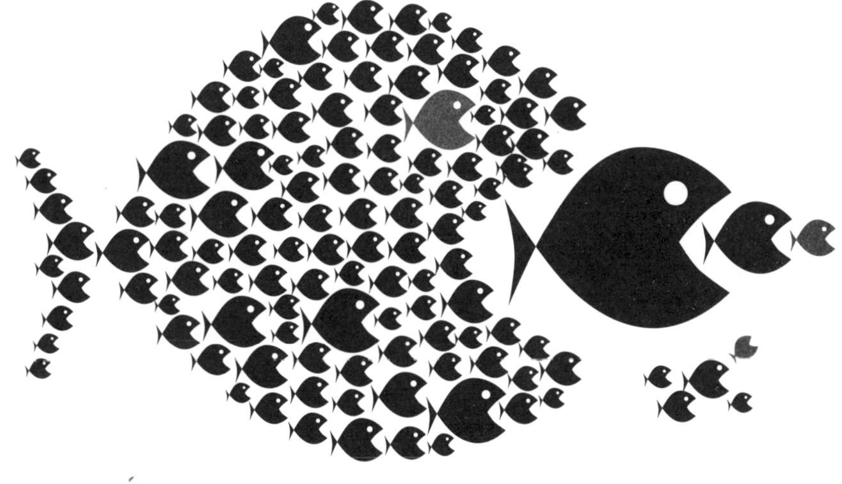

WHAT IS MASSIVE SMALL?

The *Massive Small* project has its roots in Smart Urbanism, an urban research and development initiative led by the author. The project's aim is to reconcile the conflicts and potentials that exist between top-down and bottom-up systems of urban planning, design and development in our increasingly upside-down, local, informal and complex world.

The name was first coined in his book *Massive Small: The Operating System for Smart Urbanism*. Published as an open source, beta version of this book to stimulate debate around the subject and develop an online community on LinkedIn, it posed the view that the solution to building a better urban society lies in mobilising people's latent creativity. As an antidote to bigness, it looks to harness the collective power of many small, bottom-up ideas and actions to shape urban neighbourhoods.

The Massive Small project has evolved into a viable proposition. With the support of the Royal Commission for the Exhibition of 1851 and University College London, it has developed a range of ideas, tools and tactics that show practical ways of reforming our current top-down systems. This project demonstrates how people and governments can work together to shape new and existing environments to meet the needs of future generations.

This work has been underpinned by a collective body of knowledge that comes from a wide range of sources: from the old urban theorists and contemporary thought leaders; from constructive activists to rational optimists; from self-help projects, non-governmental organisations, creative commons, social innovation hubs, peer-to-peer workers, self-organised groups, bottom-up initiatives, and civic and sharing economy programmes. The list grows.

The project is aimed at active citizens, civic leaders and urban professionals: anyone who wants to make a difference but may not know where to start. Our companion book, *The Radical Incrementalist: How to Build Urban Society in 12 Lessons*, written by this book's author Kelvin Campbell and edited by his long-time collaborator Rob Cowan, tells inspirational stories through the eyes of imaginary citizens from different parts of the world, showing governments and people successfully working together to make amazing things happen that neither could have achieved alone. *The Radical Incrementalist* and this book were made possible by a successful Kickstarter crowdfunding campaign, supported by the Royal Society of Arts, Impact Hub, Alan Baxter, the Geovation Hub and our part-time volunteers.

Although making Massive Small change is the sharp point of this project, it is framed within the larger challenges that our towns and cities face. It stems from the context of increasingly falling government effectiveness in addressing these challenges—all made worse by the intentions of many governments worldwide to 'do more with less' and expressly withdraw from solving the full spectrum of urban problems. It is also set within the growing realisation that our current systems of planning, design and development have to change.

So the project forms part of a larger systems change perspective—how we need to move from restrictive top-down policies to generative urban protocols that release the potential of bottom-up action; how we need to move from deterministic practices that envision perfect end states to establishing the initial conditions for new urban vernaculars to emerge; and how we need new behaviours that move from our old, rigid, command-and-control processes to enabling and managing responsively in the present.

Why does Massive Small work?

Thousands of small-change projects are being carried out by people—active citizens are taking the initiative, helping each other, helping themselves or using technology to engage with one another. We look around and see their energy. Someone is struggling to build a shack in an informal settlement. Someone else is trying to make a new use in an underused building. A community group is reclaiming a local street. A local civic leader is stepping outside the mainstream. An urban professional is exploring new ways of changing the world.

Things happen despite government not because of it. Instead of waiting for the authorities or established organisations to act, people are getting going themselves. This process is innate. It cannot be taught. It cannot be coerced. So how can we harness this latent energy to build urban society?

Too often, people's energy is obstructed by our top-down systems. Most people can be trusted to do the right thing, but they are too rarely given a chance. The system works against them, stifling their initiative and knocking them back. Some battle through, but most fall by the wayside. Many small projects fizzle and die, or they rely on the efforts of a few people to keep them alive, and because these projects fail to grow and mature, their lessons never benefit other places.

Most people are in some way creative. They want to make a big difference to their communities. With the right tools, they can solve urban problems. Amazing things happen whenever people take control over the places they live, adapting them to their needs and creating environments that are capable of adapting to future change. When many people do this, it adds up to a fundamental shift. It is what we now call making Massive Small change, or radical incrementalism at work.

RADICAL INCREMENTALISM

> *We need to act spontaneously, to improvise and to build in small increments. Spontaneity, as a quality of practice, is vital because most problems and opportunities appear and disappear in fairly random fashion and need to be dealt with or taken advantage of accordingly.*
>
> —Nabeel Hamdi

For some, radical change is the only way to deliver real change. 'Do it big once and get it over with', they say. Some would say this is too risky. Others gain an advantage by building on incremental improvements. 'Small progressive changes will get us where we need to go'. Some would say progressive change is not quick enough and doesn't have the same impact.

In juxtaposing radical with incremental change, a common assumption is that the two are mutually exclusive. Seeing the two concepts, incremental and radical, as being different can be psychologically satisfying—it's either this or it's that—but by consciously pursuing incremental changes with a radical goal, one can ultimately bring about something far more transformational.

It's called 'radical incrementalism'.

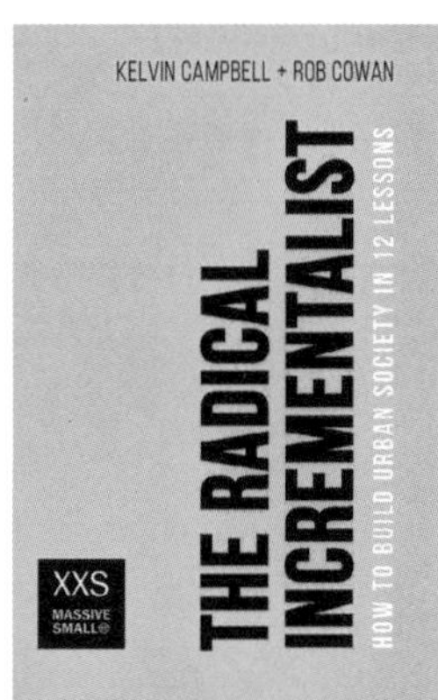
KELVIN CAMPBELL + ROB COWAN
THE RADICAL INCREMENTALIST
HOW TO BUILD URBAN SOCIETY IN 12 LESSONS
XXS
MASSIVE SMALL

> *In real life, people make a series of small steps over time that adds up to larger, more profound change. Sometimes early successes build momentum for bigger changes that previously were viewed as too radical or risky. Alternatively, incremental successes can build courage and internal support, stimulating requisite imagination and energy to design more radical and innovative changes.*
>
> —Creative Commons

We have used the term *radical incrementalism* to describe a deliberate strategy in urban planning, design and development, in which a series of small changes are enacted one after the other, resulting in radical cumulative changes in the formation of neighbourhoods. While you should have a shared vision of where you want to go, the incremental steps to get there necessarily shape the course. The feedback you get along the way will initiate, accelerate and modify your next actions. It is iterative and adaptive learning at its best—governments and people gain knowledge along the way, better informing their future decisions.

SELFCITY BXL
LET'S MAKE
OUR
OWN CITY

Top left: A community-based urban agriculture project as part of the SelfCity Initiative, Brussels.

HOW DO YOU TRANSFORM ONE HUNDRED DISUSED PUBLIC SPACES ACROSS FORTY-PLUS CITIES IN 150 DAYS?

THE ANSWER IS SIMPLE: AN INTERNATIONAL DESIGN COMPETITION IN SCALING UP MASSIVE SMALL CHANGE

While most academic-based design competitions focus on futuristic conceptual solutions, the Westminster Design Competition (South Asia) takes a different direction, with a vision to give underappreciated urban zones a new lease of life. Part of the wider Latitudes Network at the University of Westminster in London, and co-sponsored by Smart Urbanism [Massive Small], the competition was inspired by the Clean India Mission. Darshana Gothi Chauhan, founder of the competition, explains: 'The intention of the competition has always been to inspire and bring together the creative energy of students and local communities to work towards a common vision, use design as a catalyst of change and scale up the impact of small but effective local transformations to make a massive difference.'

The competition invited students from eighty-seven architecture colleges in South Asia to transform their neighbourhood—as the brief states, '...a competition strictly for doers, creators, change makers; initiate ideas, change will follow.' The result was the transformation of one hundred disused public spaces—across forty-two cities and towns—by over 1,500 local undergraduate architecture students. The public spaces brought back into active use through the design-and-build solutions, mostly through clever use of recycled materials, stretched across 3,000 kilometres (1,864 miles) from Quetta to Madurai and Jaipur to Visakhapatnam. The range of revamped public spaces include a number of children's play areas in Noida, Madurai, Nagpur, Bengaluru and Pune; flyover undercrofts in New Delhi, Calicut and Sonipat; public spaces along train stations in Mumbai and Chennai; pedestrian footpaths in Jabalpur, Jaipur and Hyderabad; and village streets in Jammu. Dynamic pop-up transformations such as an open-air public library in a Delhi bazaar and a recreational space along Elliot's Beach in Chennai proved to the masses the potential of urban spaces.

The participating students were tested on their creative as well as entrepreneurial skills by having to navigate through the challenges of working on publicly owned land, seeking permissions from local authorities and stakeholders and raising funds for their projects, as well as bringing together local communities to build their designs. This hands-on approach to design saw the students engaging with the local populace—sometimes even facing opposition or apathy—trying out different design interventions and improvising along the way.

Take, for instance, the four-member team from the Measi Academy of Architecture, Kulam. Nostalgia surrounding a historic lake that was once thriving with life, but later was neglected, forced the young students to take action. Located in Panaiyur, Chennai, the forty-foot-deep lake was used by the locals for irrigation, drinking water and cooking; but in the course of time, the lake became a residential waste dump. 'Rapid urbanisation had made the lake into a dump yard. We [took] the initiative to clean the lake as well as design the space around the lake to make it an interactive public space for the local villagers,' stated the design team. Their drive initially met with very little support. Undeterred, they decided to still go ahead and began cleaning the lake and its surroundings. Eventually, media coverage of their initiative led to support from the locals as well as the authorities—giving the project a big boost. To maintain the integrity of the lake and its surroundings, the team made some necessary additions: a fishing deck, a carrom station, plantations, seating made from dead palm trunks, and a *kabaddi* court for the state team (who were without a practice space). So profound was the impact that the village performed a ritual celebrating the rebirth of the lake. For their incredible effort and result, the students received the Radical Incrementalist Award, sponsored by Massive Small.

Through the Brick by Brick project, the winning design team from Visvesvaraya National Institute of Technology, Nagpur, saw a unique opportunity. 'Observing several user groups and their access to public spaces, we inferred that an urban pocket adjacent to a deaf and dumb school and surrounding neighbourhood is in an appalling condition. We intended to provide the kids in this area with a space of which they were deprived, breaking the barrier between the abled and differently abled', stated the team. The neglected plot began to take shape as a kids' playground marked with a creative zone, self-exploration zone, play area and Green clean zone—using scrap, recyclable materials to create sensory and sturdy play structures. The team even conducted a post-occupancy evaluation after a month and made some additions/changes to their design based on the feedback.

The fact that the competition managed to instil a passion for public urban space in the students and the local communities is a big win in itself. And it has got better. The latest round of the competition, run by the students, has produced truly remarkable results: 379 transformed spaces, in 50+ cities and towns, in 150 days.

BEFORE

AFTER

Top Row: The Kulam Lake Initiative, Panaiyur. **Second Row:** Brick by Brick Project, Nagpur. **Third Row:** The Slats Project, Chennai. **Bottom row:** The Vann Way, Jabalpur.

MASSIVE SMALL DECLARATION

The urban antidote to bigness

These declarations define and govern the Massive Small Project. They outline the thinking, principles and behaviours needed to meet the future challenges of urban society. They are mutually reinforcing: each point should not be considered in isolation to the others. They will evolve as new challenges arise.

A NEW COLLABORATION

Putting democracy back into urbanism

Governments alone cannot effectively tackle the increasingly complex problems of rapid urbanisation. We must mobilise people's latent creativity, harnessing the collective power of many small ideas and actions to make a big difference. To release this potential, we must trust people to do the right thing. By adapting their environments to their needs, people form the building blocks of urban society – our neighbourhoods, districts and quarters. Using protocols that generate simple rules; putting in place essential conditions; and, providing enabling leadership, governments can show the way. We need to renegotiate the social contract between government and its citizens – between top-down and bottom-up systems, developing more democratic processes that will foster an open and collaborative relationship.

RADICAL INCREMENTALISM

Managing in the present

In an uncertain future, we must stop fixating on the visual form of the city and specific imposed end states. Rather, we need a clear vision of our goals. We will achieve these by focusing on catalysts and small beginnings, intervening in a precisely targeted way that will stimulate growth and change. Our approach to urban governance should involve rapid and continuous feedback loops. This will inform, alter and accelerate our next actions. This is iterative and adaptive learning – one gains knowledge along the way that affects future decisions.

FREEDOM WITHIN CONSTRAINTS

Limiting choice to create infinite possibilities

We must define clear and simple boundaries within which people are free to organise and improvise. This means providing the enabling conditions within which endless potentials emerge. Structured choices enable the growth of highly responsive environments and provide a place's inhabitants with a full progression in life. Our top-down urban planning, design and delivery systems must evolve to offer a common platform with an equitable framework of choices - design options, procurement routes and entry levels to the system - for the individual, collective or institutional builder. We advocate a range of defaults and catalysts for urban change to help this process.

A WHOLE-WORLD VIEW

Towards urban viability and resilience

We understand that the human habitat exists as a dependent sub-system of the environment. It cannot be isolated from the natural habitat. We must build the foundations for viable urban life and a responsible urban society that takes us to a point where we are no longer destabilising this encompassing system. We must not be caught up in a narrow, prohibitive top-down view of the problem but rather we must see the relationship between urban interventions and the global system. Enabling people to control their own habitat is an essential part of building the resilience that will be needed as we enter a period where global issues are increasingly felt locally.

COLLECTIVE WISDOM

Smart citizens make smart cities

We believe that data and technology should augment human intelligence, not seek to replace it. We must trust intuitive wisdom, avoiding the twin traps of reductionism and determinism. We must see the urban system as a network of interrelated spectrums, not polarities. We must recognise the city as a constantly changing organism, not a mechanistic model capable of highly processed control. Rather than seeking reassuring ideologies and absolutes, we should rely on collective intelligence to find our 'timeless way of building'.

OPEN TO CHALLENGE

Operating in the sweet spot of creativity

We must never allow our thinking to freeze into a static doctrine. No group or individual can possess the complete view needed for working with complexity. Our thinking is structured to avoid the danger of group-think and the myth of the single hero. Our theory is compatible with and fosters diversity, complexity and change, makes use of conflict and paradox constructively, and embeds self-analysis and correction at its very core, by always being open to challenge. It freely treads the fine line between chaos and order – the place where innovation flourishes and we leverage the power of complex systems. Our theory embraces feedback from different sources, integrating new perspectives, enhancing itself over time. It never parts from the reality of the city and people's experience of it. The focus is always praxis: where theory meets practice.

EVOLUTION NOT REVOLUTION

Small changes make a big difference

We must rediscover the art and process of urban evolution, harnessing the collective power of people and unleashing the potential of billions of bottom-up actions. We do not need to start again – we just need to begin balancing the roles and responsibilities of all people, building on their strengths. In some instances this means a far greater involvement by governments. In others cases, it means some simplification and streamlining to allow people to take greater responsibility in the system. Above all this must never justify unbridled laissez-faire approaches and unprincipled deregulation.

ENABLING LEADERSHIP

From command-and-control to facilitation

We must challenge and reform the rigid command-and-control systems that inhibit people's ability to adapt their place to their needs. This depends on new forms of leadership that can work in the interface between top-down and bottom-up systems. A new generation of civic leaders and professionals must see their responsibility as agents of urban change, building social capital and promoting self-organisation at every opportunity. In the public sphere, responsibility and accountability must be devolved to the lowest levels - fundamentally changing the scope and purpose of practice from reaction to strategic enabling.

A CODE OF ETHICS

Responsibility to your charge

True professionalism and civic leadership must be built on trust and commitment to do the right thing. Like any calling that fundamentally affects the lives of others, any member of the urban professions, any elected official and anyone in a position of authority in the city, must be bound by commonly accepted behaviours. In time this should be defined by the collective creation of code of ethics equivalent to the medical profession's Hippocratic Oath or its Declaration of Geneva. In signing up to these principles, they accept their duty and responsibility to the present and future well-being of the inhabitants of the city they have charge over.

A COMMON PLATFORM

Rational discourse based on shared understanding

We advocate a common language for collaborative knowledge sharing and joint action by all people in the system. This common platform will provide a basis for cross-sectoral collaboration between all the urban professions and their institutions; between civic leaders and their agencies; and between active citizens and their communitiess. Using this shared language, we must promote openness, shared working and joint ownership of ideas and solutions across the sectors. Let us start by starting; try by not being scared to fail; and, learn by experimenting.

ENDORSED TO DATE BY THE FOLLOWING LEADING INFLUENCERS AND THOUGHT LEADERS:

Rob Adams, Monica Albonico, Christopher Alexander, Mike Batty, Alan Baxter, Kelvin Campbell, Rob Cowan, Rex Curry, Arunava Dasgupta, Julio Davila, Dave Dewar, Dan Dubowitz, Toni Griffin, John Habraken, Nabeel Hamdi, Inderpaul Johar, Julia King, Michael Mehaffy, Amira Osman, Alessandra Orofino, Klaus Overmeyer, Himanshu Parikh, Karl-Henrik Robert, Jason Roberts, Kristien Ring, Judith Rodin, Saskia Sassen, Barbara Southworth, Matthew Taylor, Jeremy Till, John FC Turner, Vanessa Watson

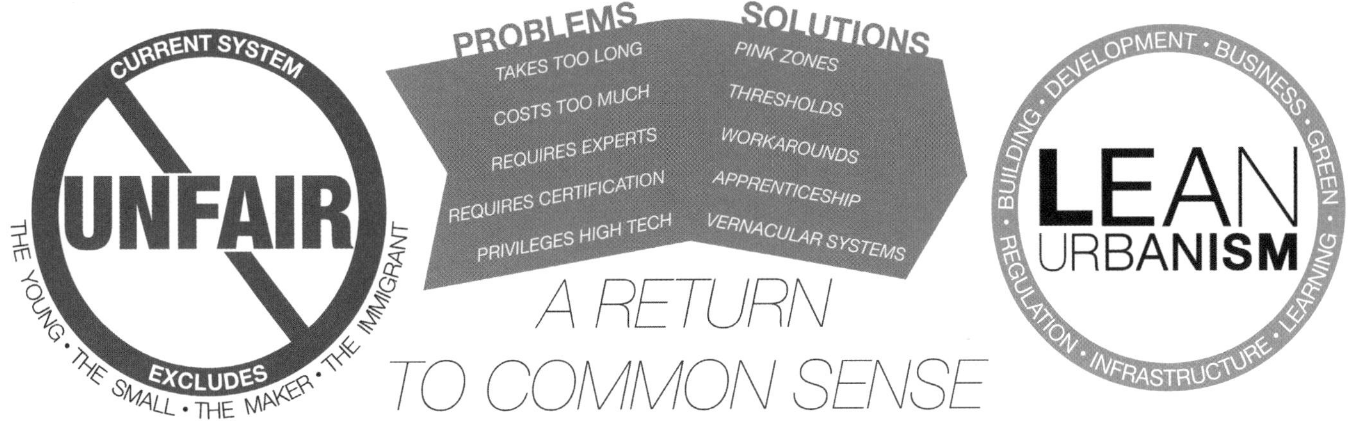

ITS TIME HAS COME

Making Massive Small change is a growing idea worldwide. The principle of 'micro-massive' underpins many social change efforts today. People are thinking about alternatives to bigness and now *scaleability* has become the watchword. Crowdfunding and crowdsourcing initiatives are the best manifestations of this. Organisations are built around the subject, books are written about it and people are excited about its prospects.

Our Massive Small declaration—seen on the opposite page—started the movement, and has been endorsed by the world's leading urban thinkers. People such as John F. C. Turner, Christopher Alexander, Nabeel Hamdi, Saskia Sassen, Jeremy Till, Inderpaul Johar, Edgar Pieterse, Matthew Taylor and John Habraken, to name just a few, have lent their support to this initiative. A full copy of the declaration is included in Chapter 3.0: CHANGE, page 301.

The belief in small-scale is getting bigger

The Project for Lean Urbanism, promoting incremental small-scale change, occupies 'the emerging seam between the demonstration projects of Tactical Urbanism and the policy-focused agenda of Smart Growth and New Urbanism'. Jason Roberts and his Better Block Foundation educates, equips and empowers communities to reshape and reactivate their built environments to promote the growth of healthy and vibrant neighbourhoods. They are doing it by just starting. Roberts says, 'Let's go out and break every rule this weekend', capturing the spirit of the organisation.

John Anderson and Jim Kumon from the Incremental Development Alliance are running small developer training workshops across the United States to develop local capacity in this field. Now many cities are doing it. Andrew Frey of the Townhouse Center, a longtime advocate for small-scale development, sees it as a way to recharge Miami's urban neighbourhoods, developing Little Havana with narrow-fronted, flexible townhouse models. Jim Heid is writing about it in *Building Small*.

Small-scale housing delivery is now a recurring theme in the Royal Institute of British Architects' agenda for change, with new president Ben Derbyshire calling for a Big Small summit. Increasingly, we see initiatives such as the Rational House, WikiHouse and the Naked House projects emerging. Architects, having shied away from the term for ages,

MAKING SMALL POSSIBLE

The Project for Lean Urbanism program is a movement of builders, planners, architects, developers, engineers, activists, nonprofits, municipalities and entrepreneurs, working to lower the barriers on community-building, to make it easier to start businesses, and to provide more attainable housing and development.

Savannah was selected as one of five US cities to participate in a pilot project to identify viable, short-term, incremental improvements and the talent and resources needed to make these improvements: develop mechanisms for getting past blockages and barriers, and develop an action plan for implementation by local people.

Some of the criteria considered when selecting a pilot project includes:

- → Empty buildings, older neighbourhoods and declining shopping streets that can be assets rather than liabilities when creativity and incrementalism are applied.
- → Municipal leadership supporting the need for reducing process burdens for small enterprise, development, self-building and retrofit.
- → An engaged base of local support among businesses, homeowners and residents, and organisations such as business improvement districts and community nonprofits.
- → Willingness to tap into the energy of minorities, millennials, makers and downshifting baby boomers, among others. It views diversity as an asset.

Plan for what will be difficult while it is easy. Do what is great while it is small.

—Sun Tzu

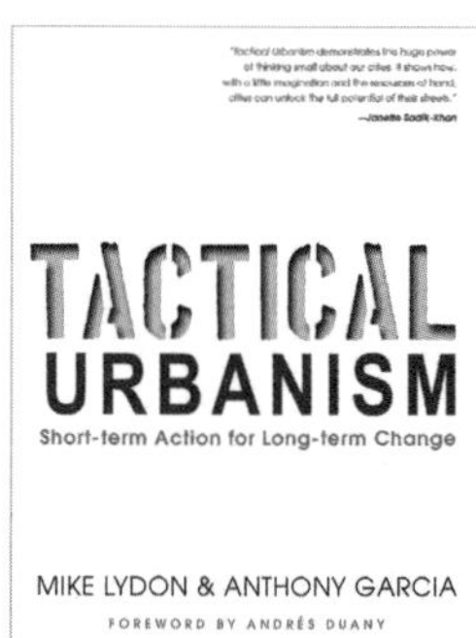

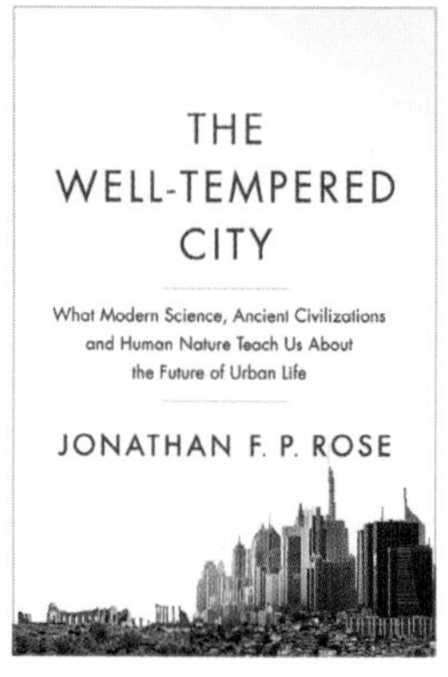

are now talking about an urban *vernacular* again. We now see articles in leading online channels calling for a return to fine-grained urban development. Dan Parolek of Opticos Design calls it the search for 'housing's missing middle'.

It's getting organised

In recent years the Small-Scale Urbanism Summit has been held in the United States, attended by representatives of Massive Small. Its purpose was to discuss the emerging trend, its importance, the different perspectives on it, and how to cooperate to maximise impact and change.

A joint statement was prepared:

We, the participants of Small-Scale Urbanism Summit 2015, agree that:

- → *Scale or grain is an independent variable of urban buildings and neighbourhoods.*
- → *Scale or grain that is small has many benefits, faces barriers, and needs support.*
- → *Groups that we are part of have missions that implicate small, thus it is a shared value.*
- → *Our groups can provide support for small.*
- → *Summit participants will use best efforts to encourage our groups to support small.*
- → *Such support will primarily continue existing group strengths but with a focus on small.*
- → *Such support may involve new dedication of resources (money, time, etc.).*
- → *To achieve maximum benefit, groups should continue to communicate and cooperate.*

The summit, joint statement and ongoing cooperation can lead to a significant increase in top-down support for small-scale urban buildings and fine-grain urban neighbourhoods.

Designing for social change

Social enterprises like Oi Polloi—an innovation think-tank and socioeconomic movement hitting the reset button in Greece—are setting new agendas. Because with Trump, Brexit, and who knows what else, the world needs a new model for urban society and practical hope more than ever. Oi Polloi does it by leveraging the power of the arts and philosophy to tackle unemployment, cultural stagnation and the paralysing sense of citizen helplessness. Their founder, Mary Valiakas, says, 'Think of us as the Uber or Airbnb of social change'.

> *Who says change has to come from the top? We're creating a new model of civilisation, because the world needs hope, along with positive solutions.*
>
> —Mary Valiakas

Even the smart city movement is breaking away from its traditional top-down approaches. Priya Prakash, founder of Design for Social Change (D4SC) helps people create better neighbourhoods, using technology to create a 'citizen-centric' approach to urban design. While the theory of 'co-creation' is often spoken about in smart city projects, in reality bringing top-down and bottom-up systems in real-time is rarely practised. Rather than treat citizens and local businesses as consumers, one of their tools, Citizen Canvas, invites them to be active architects of the changes they want to see and make them inherently resilient. Tech is becoming more responsive to society's needs, not the other way round.

A changing mood: a growing realism

We see in recent books, blogs, talks and lectures a reaction to the static urban design approach that has been the standard fare of modern urbanists. People are tired of the narrow, top-down Krier versus Koolhaas 'big architecture' battles, seeing both of them as part of the same problem. People are writing enthusiastically about *DIY urbanism, handmade urbanism, open-source urbanism, urban commons* and *self-made city*, to name just a few, with a burning belief that everything is now possible in a precarious, post-industrial economy. There is a desperation for new thinking out there.

In his book, *The Well-Tempered City: What Modern Science, Ancient Civilisations and Human Nature Teach us about the Future of Urban Life*, we see a developer, Jonathan Rose, recognising that in order to survive, we need to balance prosperity and well-being with efficiency and equality in ways that continually restore the city's social and natural capital.

Mike Lydon and Anthony Garcia's book *Tactical Urbanism: Short-term Action for Long-term Change* has captured people's imagination and inspired a new generation of engaged citizens, urban professionals and civic leaders to become key actors in the transformation of their communities.

People are rediscovering old ideas from earlier urban thinkers. Robert Kanigel's biography, *Eyes on the Street: The Life of Jane Jacobs*, has exposed a new breed of constructive activists to Jane Jacobs's concept of 'organised complexity'.

Concepts such as *plural urbanism*—multifaceted, multiple actioned and incremental—expressed in David Crane's idea of a 'city of a thousand designers'; or in Edmund Bacon's support for the 'dynamic city as people's art'; and some of Kevin Lynch's notions of 'an ideal city', are regaining traction. Somehow, in whole or part, they make more sense today.

Brent Ryan's book *The Largest Art: A Measured Manifesto for a Plural Urbanism* examines the influence of these earlier thinkers and shows a way forward. His book is a shot across the bow of the urban design profession. It promotes a declaration of independence for urban design by distinguishing urban design from its sister arts through its pluralism: plural scale, ranging from an alleyway to a region; plural time, because it is deeply enmeshed in both history and the present; plural property, with many owners; plural agents, with many makers; and plural form, with a distributed quality that allows it to coexist with diverse elements of the city. Ryan concludes his manifesto with three considerations that urban designers must now acknowledge: eternal change, inevitable incompletion, and flexible fidelity. Cities are ceaselessly active, perpetually changing. It is the urban designer's task to make art with aesthetic qualities that can survive perpetual change. This is an important message for the professions.

Cities are doing it

No city is doing Massive Small better than Berlin at the moment. Kristien Ring's work on *Selfmade City*, as interpreted in the Berlin Townhouse Project and numerous other schemes, shows us a new way. Here we are seeing far better social outcomes, space standards and property values on schemes delivered quickly and well below cost to the occupants. This is big talk.

Curitiba in Brazil, through the targeted actions of its dynamic mayor, Jaime Lerner, has a long history of successful small-scale urban interventions—or, as he calls them, *urban acupuncture* projects. Many other cities are following in his path.

Hamilton in Canada has become a Massive Small city. Their campaign #coollittlethings, headed by Jason Thorne, focused on many small interventions in the city—the types of seemingly small urban interventions which can add up to a happier and more liveable city. Even the tiniest bureaucratic changes were deployed in a delightful way. Some of the ideas ended up making a larger statement about the city as well. What's most astonishing in looking at Hamilton's accomplishments are the speed and flexibility with which they were implemented. Now even Auckland in New Zealand is recognising the power of many small interventions.

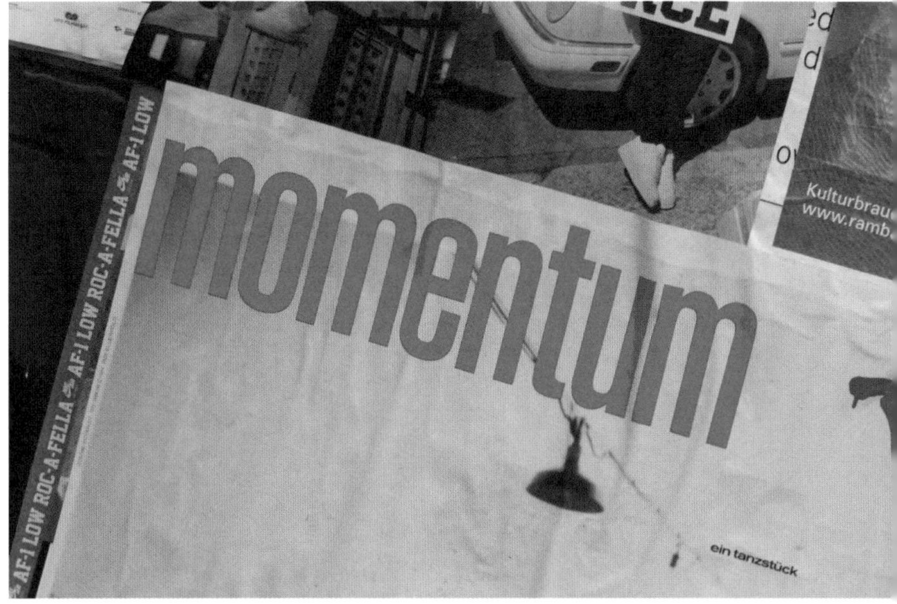

It's gaining momentum

Massive Small principles are taught at University of Oxford in their Masters in Sustainable Urban Development course. It is now an established part of the postgraduate programme and many students have been exposed to many of its concepts. It has been researched, peer-reviewed, applied in a number of postgraduate dissertations, and its principles have been found to be robust.

It has formed the basis of many mayoral leadership programmes, change-maker labs and advanced urban design masterclasses. It has featured in keynote lectures to the United Nations and at numerous international conferences and seminars. It has been road-tested in numerous housing development programmes and neighbourhood expositions—winning awards and commendations. There is no better example of proof of concept than in Darshana Gothi Chauhan's public-space improvement projects in India—featured as an inspiring case study on page 14—or in Andrew Lamb's work with Engineers Without Borders, where he led with the slogan 'Making Massive Small Change', which has now been taken forwards in his disaster recovery work for Field Ready. Both show the power of scaling up small ideas and actions to make a big difference worldwide.

As we can see in Alex Steffen's *Worldchanging: A User's Guide for the 21st Century*, we need a wildly optimistic imagining of the culture of sustainable prosperity, of design, urbanism and social innovation that increases our happiness and opportunities. Massive Small could be just that imagining.

It seems like its time has come.

URBAN SOCIETY: WHAT IS IT?

The good we secure for ourselves is precarious and uncertain until it is secured for all of us and incorporated into our common life.

—Jane Addams

URBAN SOCIETY evolves when the city and its citizens come together to create urbanism that is relevant to the time and needs. It is a complex and dynamic interaction between the physical form of the city and the collective will of active citizens to build their urban habitat. In an evolved urban society, the urban neighbourhood is its best manifestation and still the most successful example of this habitat. Its success is dependent on high degrees of two essential qualities: COMPACT URBANISM and SOCIAL CAPITAL. They are like the hardware and the software of urban civilisation. The evolution of our cities and their neighbourhoods has shown that if you can use this social capital to build a compact form of urbanism, you have a place that far exceeds all expectations.

WHAT IS COMPACT URBANISM?

Urbanism is the condition of living in a city and for most of our world represents a predominant way of life. It is within the context of the city that urban neighbourhoods, as geographically identifiable social units, become the building blocks of our cities. The term *urbanism* generally denotes the diffusion of urban culture and the evolution of urban society about its urban fabric. As urban society evolves, it reaches a state of civilisation we call 'urbanity'—a state where people and place are in perfect harmony.

In an urban context, *compactness* means something joined together or united, where the social and economic benefits of proximity provide added value to all in the neighbourhood. So *compact urbanism* is based on people living adjacent to others at an optimal urban density with a mix of land uses to enable a viable urban society to start, flourish and mature. It creates a highly inclusive community, mutually sharing in the benefits that closeness brings and expressing the way they build the neighbourhood as a collective act of will. Where one person's home abuts another's, this proximity or immediate adjacency demands a clear negotiation and agreement between neighbours, but this is usually established by a set of simple rules, evolved over time, to clarify this interface. These simple interface rules are the single defining characteristic of compact urbanism. Here people have to work together to co-exist. This is distinctly different to the exclusiveness that one finds in suburbia where individual expression is the defining characteristic and the interface is determined by rigorous setbacks and boundary rules. In suburbia, people can exist alone without any form of negotiation with neighbours.

Compact urbanism can take many different forms but is often narrowly defined by urban professionals in terms of density alone. This is too limiting. Although density does contribute to urban success, it is best seen as an outcome of places as they evolve over time, not a determinant at the outset. So compact urbanism does not automatically assume that high density is a prerequisite but assumes instead that it is the consequence of progressive urban change, finding its balance at every stage of its development.

WHAT IS SOCIAL CAPITAL?

> *A culture is like the upright strands that you begin with in basket-making, round which you wind the texture of the basket itself: no sticks, no basket; no culture, no community. It is the grammar, the story, humour and good faith that identifies a community and gives it existence. It is both the parent and child of social capital. And the social capital of a community is its social life—the links of cooperation and friendship between its members. It is the common culture and ceremony, the good faith and reciprocal obligations the civility and citizenship, the play, humour and conversation which make a living community, the cooperation that builds its institutions. It is the social ecosystem in which a culture lives.*
>
> —David Fleming

URBAN SOCIETY
= COMPACT URBANISM
+ SOCIAL CAPITAL*

Social capital is the cement of an urban society's goodwill—it creates a cohesive urban society, it builds community, and it facilitates collective action for mutual benefit.

Although there are many definitions of *social capital*, it is most clearly defined by the Organisation for Economic Co-operation and Development (OECD) as 'networks together with shared norms, values and understandings that facilitate co-operation within or among groups'. In this definition, we can think of networks as real-world links between groups or individuals. According to Wikipedia, 'Social capital is a form of economic and cultural capital in which social networks are central; transactions are marked by reciprocity, trust, and cooperation; and market agents produce goods and services not mainly for themselves but for a common good'. In urbanism, it has been used to explain the improved performance of diverse groups, the value derived from strategic alliances and evolution of communities.

Social capital recognises the inherent creativity and community of common interest that exists in people to solve urban problems. It implies that people working together with a collective self-interest can come up with solutions that individuals or governments working alone might never consider. It also recognises that people can be trusted and will conform by matching evolved attitudes, beliefs and behaviours to group norms. Some call it 'herd instincts'. Philip Ball in his book *Critical Mass: How One Thing Leads to Another* believes that this represents the 'science of society' that can be described using a few simple postulates. Here we see implicit, specific rules shared by a group of individuals that guide their interactions with others. This tendency to conform occurs in small groups and society as a whole and may result from subtle unconscious influences, or direct and overt social pressure. Regardless, it represents an important part of how people interact in working together to form their neighbourhoods.

So there are many distinct factors that give rise to social capital:

→ Sharing a common purpose and commitment to public good
→ Using collaborative intelligence and shared learning by doing
→ Harnessing collective action for mutual interest
→ Operating with high levels of trust and concern for others
→ Having agreed rules of engagement, behaviour and acceptability

Although we can see signs of social capital in many projects initiated by communities—from local small-change initiatives to larger informal settlements—it is also fair to say that much new urban development ignores this latent potential and energy in people and even chooses to suppress it. That is why we are not building stable and effective communities anymore.

Of course, we can always add social capital to established places, but we believe that if governments use the inherent social capital that exists in urban society to build compact urbanism, we stand a far better chance of forming viable, resilient, and socially and economically diverse urban neighbourhoods.

Civilisation rests on the fact that most people do the right thing most of the time.

—Lewis Mumford

Doornfontein, an inner city neighbourhood in Johannesburg, South Africa, has all the basic conditions in place for growth and change.

WHAT IS A NEIGHBOURHOOD?

Neighbourhoods are the coalfaces of urban society: that critical coming together of people and place to build civilisation. As the building blocks of our towns and cities, they are the single most important unit of social, cultural and local economic development.

Neighbourhoods provide sufficient scale of human settlement where collective social capital can be developed and harnessed to achieve a greater whole. They are places where wounds can be mended and new relationships can be built, where social integration, social transformation and social advancement can flourish. They are the hotbeds of innovation and the springboards of evolution. They are too important to ignore in building viable cities. Like family and friends, they are all we have.

I have an affection for a great city. I feel safe in the neighbourhood of man, and enjoy the sweet security of the streets.

—Henry Wadsworth Longfellow

Neighbourhoods, then, are types of urban fabric in which face-to-face social interactions occur—the personal settings and situations where people living near one another seek to realise their common values, socialise, and maintain effective social control. In this sense, they are larger versions of households.

We know that a neighbourhood is a localised community within a city and is largely residential. Urban researchers have not agreed on an exact definition of a neighbourhood, but it is often defined as a specific geographic area with a set of social networks. Walkability has been used to define the optimum scale of the neighbourhood, but this is not a determinant, just a measure of success.

Neighbourhoods do have boundaries, and these boundaries play an important role in determining the identity of each neighbourhood. However, boundaries are not clearly defined in their nature or their place. Quite often this identity is established by its main streets, its history or its dominant uses—not its edges. The vitality of a neighbourhood will be enhanced if we do not try too hard to fix its boundaries. Rather, we should allow for their constant renegotiation.

> *Neighbourhoods, in some primitive, inchoate fashion exist wherever human beings congregate, in permanent family dwellings; and many of the functions of the city tend to be distributed naturally—that is, without any theoretical preoccupation or political direction—into neighbourhoods.*
>
> —Lewis Mumford

Neighbourhoods in many preindustrial cities often had some degree of social specialisation or differentiation. Ethnic neighbourhoods were important in many past cities and remain common in cities today. Specialist businesses, including craft producers, merchants, and others, could be concentrated in neighbourhoods. In societies with diverse religions, neighbourhoods were often characterised by religion. One factor contributing to neighbourhood distinctiveness and social cohesion in emerging cities is the role of rural to urban migration—something that still prevails today in many growing cities.

> *But we propose a discipline of urban design, which is different, entirely, from the one known today. We believe that the task of creating wholeness in the city can only be dealt with as a process. It cannot be solved by design alone, but only when the process by which the city gets its form is fundamentally changed.*
>
> —Christopher Alexander

Neighbourhoods cannot be created by design alone. They are formed by the individual responsive actions of many acting in the collective interest of a place and for their own needs. Successful urban neighbourhoods arise from continuous bottom-up action by people working within strong normative constraints or pressures that give rise to a continuously emerging urban vernacular. Here *vernacular* is not seen from a historicist viewpoint but is defined as 'the best outcome that can be achieved within the constraints or pressures of the time'. It is the right thing to do—the way, the custom, the norm, the tradition.

These actions emerge from the conditions that give rise to a neighbourhood—its networks, blocks, platforms, defaults and activators. More importantly, they emerge from the collective goodwill, creativity and sense of community of its inhabitants.

History has shown us that for compact urban neighbourhoods to be truly successful, they must display five qualities. All are essential, and places suffer if one or more are not evident:

1. **They must be comfortably FAMILIAR.** Successful neighbourhoods must be made up of many similar, recognisable, normative elements. These reflect the accepted rules and norms of urban society at the time—its typologies, regularities and practices. So they must be made up of many 'ordinary' things that become the backdrop to the 'extraordinary'.
2. **They must be socially INCLUSIVE.** Successful neighbourhoods must be made of all walks of society and cater for all their citizens as they negotiate the full ladder of life, going up or down.
3. **They must be functionally DIVERSE.** Successful neighbourhoods must be made of many uses at every scale to cater for the richness of urban activity and respond to local everyday needs.
4. **They must be highly ADAPTIVE.** Successful neighbourhoods must be capable of responding to rapid and continuous change as social, economic and technological conditions change. Urban resilience is dependent on places bouncing back from the effects of abnormal external factors.
5. **They must be formed by MULTIPLE small actions.** Successful neighbourhoods must be made by many hands, all operating openly and independently within a clear urban structure set within a framework of simple rules, to reflect the immediate needs of people as they make structured and unpredictable choices and scale these up over time. They are distributed systems, not centralised functions of big government or big business.

> *Neighbourhoods cannot be created by design alone. They are formed by the individual responsive actions of many acting in the collective interest of a place and for their own needs.*
>
> —Massive Small Manifesto

Although we can find many examples of compact urbanism built in recent years, it is fair to say that much of our new urban development displays few or even none of the qualities listed above. That is why we struggle to find examples of successful new urban neighbourhoods built in recent decades. This project shows how we can create the conditions for these qualities to flourish again through making more robust hardware, software and operating systems to enable healthy urban neighbourhoods to be formed from the outset.

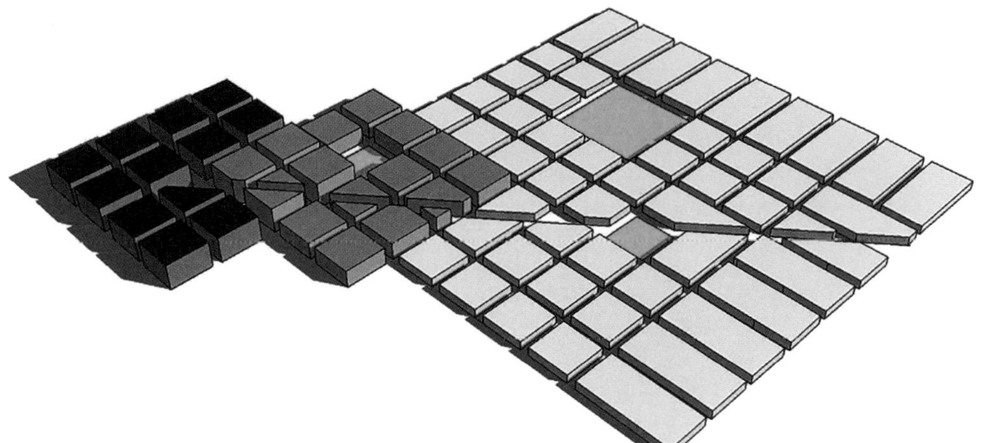

Urban centres, quarters and neighbourhoods all have a strong relationship with one another and, in many instances,can be part of each other.

OUR NEIGHBOURHOOD PLEDGE

1

EVERYONE CAN START
BUT FROM DIFFERENT STARTING POINTS.

2

EVERYONE CAN FIND THEIR OWN WAY
BUT BY DIFFERENT ROUTES.

3

EVERYONE CAN REACH THE SAME PLACE
BUT AT DIFFERENT TIMES.

THE COMPENDIUM

WHOLE EARTH CATALOG

access to tools

Fall 1968

$5

IT'S NOT HOW GOOD YOU ARE, IT'S HOW GOOD YOU WANT TO BE.

The world's best-selling book by PAUL ARDEN.

Above: These three ground-breaking books provide the inspiration for this compendium. They are all of their time but made a significant impact in communicating complex ideas in simple ways.

Opposite page: The table provides a simple and navigable structure for the compendium. It gives a summary of each section, the mechanisms employed and the key elements of the Massive Small proposition. It concludes with a list of concepts covered in each section.

 Ideas

 Tools

Tactics

The Massive Small compendium is a sourcebook of ideas, tools and tactics to help build viable urban neighbourhoods; it works in tandem with our online information-sharing platform: www.massivesmall.com/pendium

As a bold and ambitious project aimed at 'changing hearts and minds', it has many sides to it:

→ It is a compilation of KNOWLEDGE and WISDOM on a complex matter that affects all of us, pointing to many sources of information on the subject and backed up with relevant CASE STUDIES. It is a starting point, providing the prompts, potentials and examples to show how governments and people can work together to make Massive Small change. The examples are here to give proof of concept only; not to be blindly followed. Each place has to find its own way. It is not an academic tome—it does not set out to predict the outcome of a declared hypothesis and provide endless justifications of its truth—so it is always open to challenge. It is a new beginning, not an end.

→ It is based on the emerging science of COMPLEXITY, which is more concerned with how we start, how we learn from starting, and how we evolve to a better place—so it is about organising complexity. It is about SYSTEMS THINKING, and systems change—so it shows how this can happen. It borrows from many places, so it is not original—its originality lies in how it is assembled. It recognises that people will search Google to find its quotes and sources—so it does not slavishly reference every point.

→ It shows how governments can put their effort into shaping the earliest stages of the development process and sow the seeds for people (in all sectors) to grow their own environments. This means that the role of governments is to provide the ENABLING MECHANISMS for this growth and change to happen—by organising complexity. Here people play an influencing role in the process, providing informed feedback and responding to small changes made. We call these enabling mechanisms our 'starter conditions'.

→ It is a practical, rigorous and progressive USER MANUAL to show how these starter conditions can be applied in all likely circumstances. It offers a set of tools that act at the interface of each of the starter conditions, showing how these conditions can be effectively implemented, managed and reviewed over time. It is supported by a collection of ESSAYS, gleaned from our online blogs and articles. Our online platform provides the means of updating information and evolving the Massive Small project.

→ It demonstrates how Massive Small principles can be applied in an imaginary urban neighbourhood, LOCALIA, taking us through the STARTER CONDITIONS, step by step, to shape the built environment and allow incoming citizens to form their own neighbourhood.

→ It is also a compilation of INSPIRATIONAL STORIES that elucidate and expand on the narrative of the theory. These stories, based on those in *The Radical Incrementalist*, are told through the eyes of imaginary citizens from different parts of the world. They show governments and people successfully working together to make amazing things happen that none could have achieved alone. The stories are fiction, based on reality. Woven into imaginary plots are the narratives of some real people with real projects in actual places. They could be anywhere. These stories are not proof of concept, just an illustration of the 'sense of the possible'. Real proof of concept lies in over 300 generations of neighbourhood building that happened before we created the current system.

→ It concludes with how effective SYSTEM CHANGE can be initiated and accelerated by changing our ideas, tools and tactics at the national level through to metropolitan, city and town levels and down to the neighbourhood level. It gives us many clues as to how we can get back onto this path of EVOLUTION by harnessing the potentials and conflicts that exist between our bottom-up and top-down systems and build a better urban society worldwide.

SUMMARY	SECTION	MECHANISM	ELEMENT	CONCEPT

This opening section identifies the problem, talks about new thinking needed and sets up the Massive Small proposition. It looks to clarify the conflicts in the dynamics of urban change and shows how our top-down systems need to be evolved to release the potentials for greater bottom-up activity.

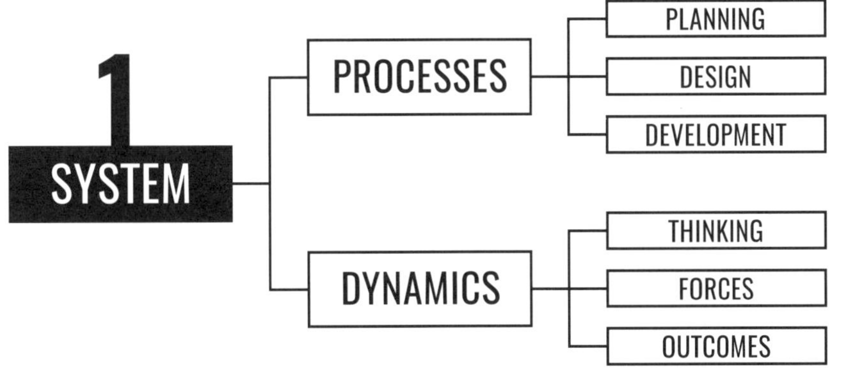

- Centralist vs. Localist
- Utopia vs. Evolution
- Paradigms: shift happens
- Failure of bigness
- Formal vs. Informal
- Refocusing government

- Organising complexity
- Bottom-up needs top-down
- Government vs. People
- Old science vs. Complexity
- Viablity vs. Resilience
- Bigness vs. Massive Small

This section, which represents the substance of the Massive Small proposition, shows how we can reconcile the conflicts and potentials that exist between our top-down and bottom-up systems. To build viable urban neighbourhoods, we must move our IDEAS from complex policies to simple protocols; our TOOLS from fixed end states to starter conditions; and our TACTICS from command-and-control to enabling behaviours.

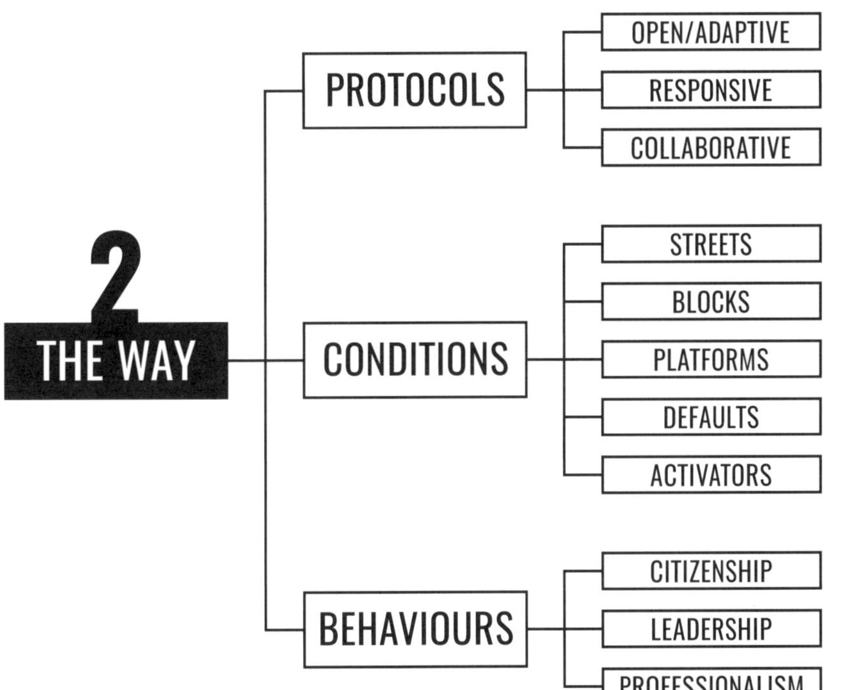

- Radical incrementalism
- Open standards
- Light touch: big impact
- Simple rules/instructions
- People can be trusted
- We will if you will

- Boundary conditions
- Balancing constraints
- Condition-making
- General plan and regulations
- Mountains to molehills
- Thinking in levels
- The Neighbourhood Model
- The invisible chassis
- Emergent vernacular

- Constructive activism
- Collaborative leadership
- Managing in the present
- Urban ethics
- Building consensus
- Urban ethics

System change is the emergence of a new pattern of organisation or system structure that brings about different outcomes. This section of the compendium shows how you could start the process of change by focusing on the basics of change, the leverage points of change and the agency needed to bring about system change.

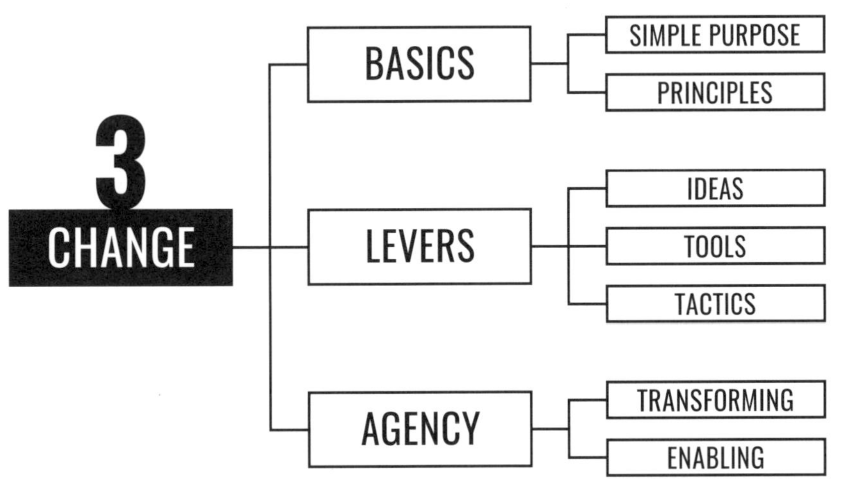

- Find your own way
- Building shared visions
- Collaborate to innovate
- Mobilise your assets

- Unleash your people
- Focus on the many small
- Start by starting
- Learn by doing
- Build a common platform
- Try, test and experiment

- Act, wait and watch
- Run in parrallel
- Operate at all scales
- Row, steer and cheer

[*bottom-up versus top-down*]

1

SYSTEM

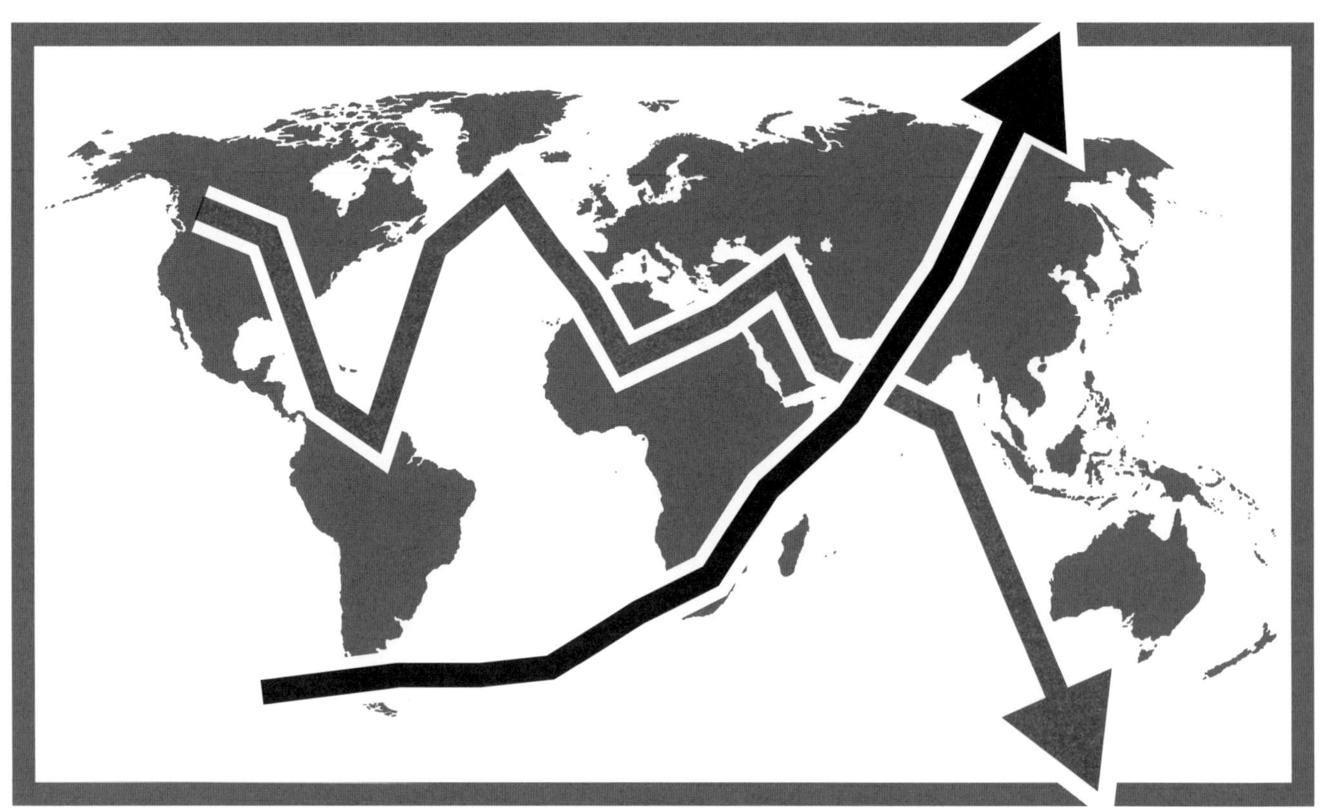

System *NOUN*

A ***closed system*** is a system with clearly defined boundaries, in which every input is known and every resultant is known (or can be known) within a specific time. It is isolated from its surroundings so it does not interact with its environment.

An ***open system*** is a system with clearly defined but permeable boundaries that permits interaction across its boundaries, through which new information or ideas are readily absorbed, allowing for the incorporation and diffusion of viable, new ideas.

This part of the compendium identifies the problem, talks about new thinking needed to address the problem and sets up the Massive Small proposition. It looks to clarify the conflicts in the dynamics of urban change and shows how our top-down systems need to be evolved to release the potentials for greater bottom-up activity.

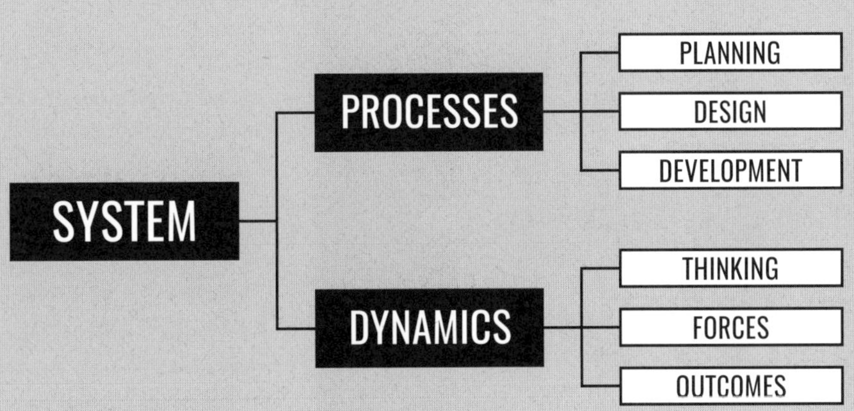

WHY DO SYSTEMS FAIL?

Is the system going to deny us our humanity, or are we going to be able to make use of the system to the attainment of our human purposes?

—Joseph Campbell

People wonder why our current systems fail to deliver the urban society we need. Why in the developing world have the natural processes of urban development so often stalled, despite the human ingenuity and energy that is available to build places? Why, even in the developed world, do we fail to build the neighbourhoods we want and need, despite the enormous amounts of money that are spent on housing? Why do we fail to build attractive places, despite all the efforts spent on the processes of planning, design and development of our cities?

These questions have as much validity in the slums of Mumbai as they do in the boroughs of London; the favelas of Rio de Janeiro or the suburbs in Paris; the informal settlements of Nairobi or the neighbourhoods of Detroit. The issues are universal; the mechanisms that can tackle them are largely the same.

Most governments have lost the battle to deliver on their promises to meet society's needs. For many, the problem is too big, so they turn a blind eye. Others tinker with the system, shifting deckchairs on the Titanic.

We know our systems do not work. They treat cities as things that are ordered and mechanical, as problems to be solved, not as complex places of rich and diverse possibility where people use their ingenuity and energy to make things happen. The applied processes of urban development have failed. The more that governments try to solve the problem, the less effective their efforts seem to be.

> *The master's tools will never dismantle the master's house.*
>
> —Audre Lorde

These processes come under even greater strain as more people move to cities. People challenge conventions and look for alternatives. Even in booming London, the most common new house type is the unfit, unserviced, back-garden shack. Things happen despite government, not because of it.

Governments say we must do more with less, but they don't know how. They talk about devolution but insist on acting big. The established thinking is deeply ingrained in all our institutions, but it doesn't work. Those who think the system works work in the system.

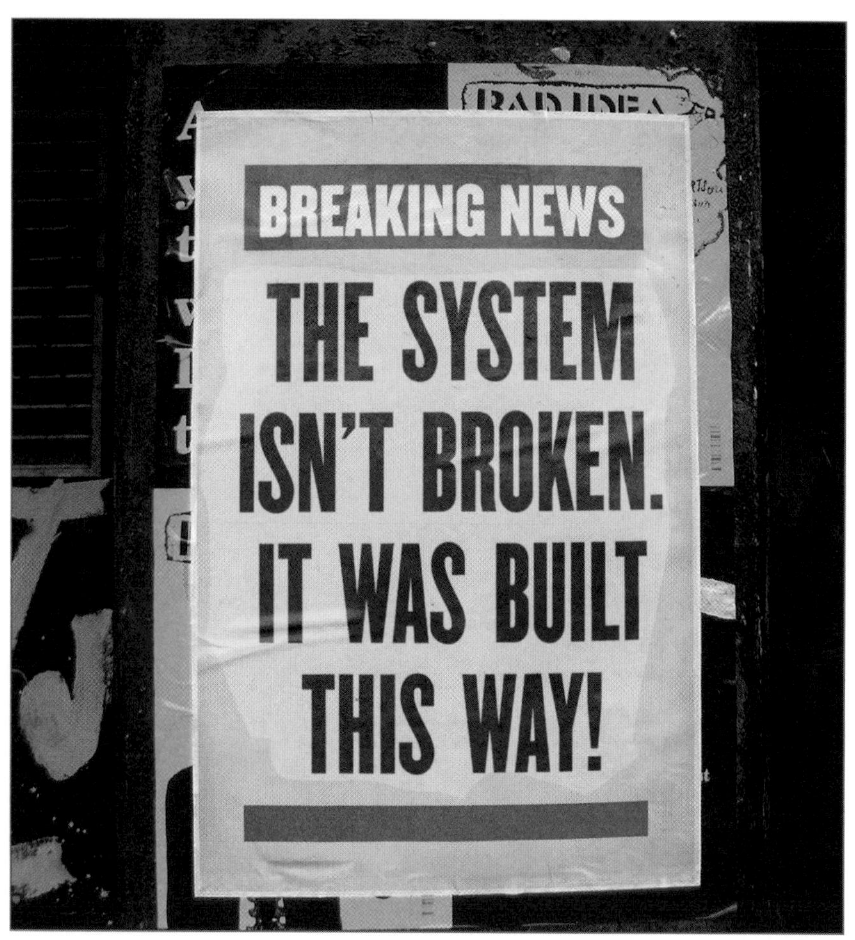

IS THE SYSTEM BROKEN?

This question has been asked by many in the know. Some would blame the recent worldwide recession for breaking the system. 'It will all get better,' others say, 'when confidence returns.' Some would say the system was broken long before the worldwide crisis. The unfortunate reality is it will only get worse, especially if we continue on the path we follow today. So what are the facts to support this?

1 We start from a losing position

A worldwide crisis now exists in the provision of housing and decent settlements for all. This problem started some decades ago when the falling graph of government effectiveness crossed with the rising graph of rapid urbanisation. We failed to see this problem at the time, and now we just cannot catch up.

2 The new numbers are against us

The graph of rapid urbanisation is set to rise even further: every expert has a different view of the numbers, but the fact remains that averaged projected growth of our urban population, currently sitting at 50 per cent of the world's inhabitants, shows rises to 75 per cent by 2050. Even without a rapidly growing population, this is an astronomic shift in thirty-five years. If we haven't been able to solve the problem today, how are we going to solve it in the future?

3 More of us will be outside the system

According to UN-Habitat, as we stand today, the bulk of new employment opportunities are to found in the informal sector, and even more will be found there by 2050. As a result, fewer people pay taxes and governments have less money to spend. Immigration in most parts of the world is fuelling this economy and the xenophobia that comes with it. This relationship is even reflected in places like London and Paris, where we have seen the rise of informal housing to meet the needs of this new population.

4 Some call it austerity

We live in the narrative of our times, and fewer taxpayers and more spending cutbacks are features of most governments worldwide. For everyone chanting for government to take the lead three generations ago, there is now an equal number clamouring for big government to get out of the way. Regardless of this, we will have less government funding to solve urban problems. We have to think smart about how these resources are deployed.

5 Supertankers are difficult to turn

We start with no solutions. If we think we have time to go back to first principles to build a new system, we are lost. The inertia needed by governments to turn things around is tremendous. We have to realise that we just need to start doing something different and learn from it. And then we must do something different and learn from it again and again and again. This is the time for the light touch of enlightened leadership and not just strong hands on the wheel.

HOW DID WE GET HERE?

It is important to understand where we came from and how we got to where we are today. One simple way is to understand the systems at work. Over the past sixty years we have seen the three distinct operating systems that have emerged for different reasons. In simple terms these are:

1 A distributed system (evolved urban vernacular)

In the interwar years we still saw the remnants of a distributed system of neighbourhood formation and city building in most parts of the world. There was no central controller. People built in the manner that evolved over time. They shared ideas, learnt from others and got better at doing it. The system was bottom-up, highly local, resilient, open and adaptive. Top-down controls focused on building and health acts, which were largely concerned with preventing the spread of fire and disease in densely built up areas. The construction industry consisted of many small tradesmen and craftsmen building from traditional pattern books with simple rules. There was no planning system. There were no big developers. Government had little or no role in housebuilding. In the United Kingdom alone, the system built four times as many houses during these years than at the peak of its most recent housing boom.

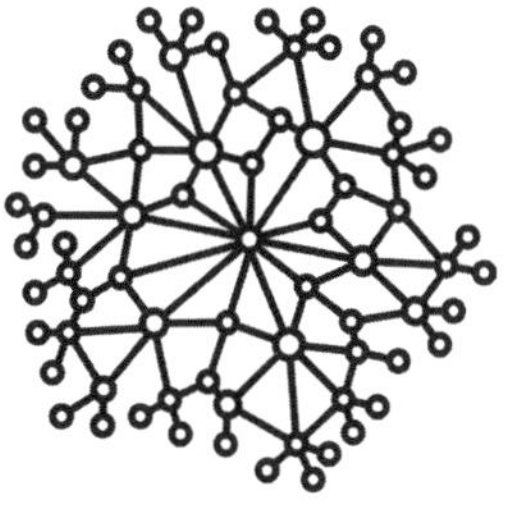

A classic distributed system of neighbourhood formation where everyone learnt from others.

2 A centralised system (big government)

Postwar reconstruction in Europe and returning servicemen in many parts of the world promised a brave new world. Solutions lay in concerns developed over the previous half-century in response to industrialisation and urbanisation. The particular concerns of the time were pollution, urban sprawl, and ribbon development. These concerns were expressed through the work of thinkers such as Ebenezer Howard, the modernists and the philanthropic actions of the big industrialists of the time. Political ambitions towards social reconstruction and better opportunities for the working classes saw government taking responsibility for things people and communities would traditionally have done for themselves. In these postwar years we saw the centralisation of power around health, education and housing, to name just a few. The central controller emerged as government promised to house, heal and teach all its citizens, building a planning system to reinforce their utopian dreams of a better society.

A centralised sytem imposed in the 1950s saw a concentration of power and responsibility for delivering utopian ideals.

It was a fragile system that was dependent on the will of government.

Damaged buildings were torn down, and council housing estates emerged in many cities. Slum clearances coupled with new towns became the norm in many countries. New suburbs fuelled the needs of burgeoning families. Large rebuilding programmes required large contractors and we saw the birth of 'bigness' in the construction sector. Big government got bigger, but housing numbers shrunk.

3 A centralised system (big private)

Towards the end of the last century we saw a growing belief that governments alone could not solve the needs of their citizens and we saw a growing move for privatisation of state industries, calls for outsourcing and pressure placed on the private sector to help. The problem was that big government found it difficult to deal with a distributed construction industry, which was progressively shrinking, so we saw the emergence of the big developer or housebuilder that matched big government. Big contractors that served big government were primed to step in, and we saw the rise of the big developer. To this day governments see the big private sector as the saviour of the centralised system. They want to become smaller but they cannot think beyond this. They still want to be in charge.

What we have now is a big private sector that shadows a big public sector.

The new problem for government is that the housing crisis worldwide is deepening. They are building far less, and the big guys do not see their role as solving the government's housing crisis. The big guys are looking after their shareholders. Housing numbers are now at their lowest levels, and the crisis continues to deepen. In many parts of the world, housing is now considered to be in a permanent crisis. The fragility of the system is apparent. Many would say it is reaching breaking point.

WHERE CAN WE GO?

The experience of city living is valued more than ever. In most parts of the world, cities are the product of an industrial society. Postindustrial society may not create urbanism in any familiar way, but it needs it more than ever. With capital and knowledge increasingly mobile, and technology allowing people to work and live apart, urbanism provides the means of bringing us together.

The more our lives are lived through the global information network, the more we want to feel we belong to actual, physical neighbourhoods to which

we can contribute as citizens. The new wealth-creators will move to, or stay in, cities or neighbourhoods whose built and natural environment offers them what they see as an attractive quality of life and a place that meets their changing needs.

Neighbourhoods are constituted from complex and diverse human interactions. Neighbourhoods are where the potential for conflict must be resolved, and much of their creative energy flows from this fact.

We need a new philosophy to guide practice and education in how to make great cities and neighbourhoods for the twenty-first century. Otherwise, we will continue to make do with nothing more than patching up what we have or slavishly reproducing past forms. Without a philosophy to underpin good urbanism, governments will be frustrated in their attempts to implement their social, economic and environmental policies.

The established thinking is deeply ingrained in all our institutions, but we must think and act differently, now. So is this a time to reflect and change our approaches, or is a paradigm shift upon us whether we like it or not?

The answer to both questions is 'Yes'.

A Massive Small system: top-down/bottom-up

System change is difficult to swallow. So what do we tell big government and what would a new system look like?

Clearly we are not going to move away from some form of top-down authority in the short term, nor is such a move entirely necessary. We will also find it difficult to get back onto the path of evolution that a bottom-up distributed system gave us in past generations. And we recognise that centralised control gives us benefits if used wisely, but we also recognise that we need to bring back the rich and varied benefits that a distributed system can offer us. Paradoxically, the solution lies in harnessing both systems. We must shift our centralised system from its top-down command-and-control processes to operating in a more enabling role. At the same time we must shift to dovetailing this with an evolving distributed system. Governments must set up the preconditions and behaviours for such a system to take root and evolve. In this way governments can share in the learning that a distributed system offers and harness the collective creativity of many people. The challenge lies in how we shift paradigms to kick-start the evolution.

THINKING POSITIVELY

> *A wide range of voices that call for change and transformation have focused on the problems of legacy language: Orwell, in his well-known work on bureaucratic-political language, pointed to how words and their meanings come to be intertwined with purposeful distraction and how this exhausts the language.*
>
> —Marc Ventresca and Rachel Sinha

It's quite obvious that political systems thrive on their polarities—regulation versus deregulation; libertarianism versus paternalism; big government versus big society; centralism versus localism; and so on. Quite often, in the feverish pursuit of change, politicians tend to throw the baby out with the bathwater, and we lose some of the best things. Reform to the system often amounts to tinkering with the mechanics rather than facing up to the need for fundamental change. We need reform, but further progress depends on fundamentally changing the operating system. Like Apple, we need to 'Think Different', but also like them, our mantra should be 'Evolution, Not Revolution'. Small changes can make enormous differences.

A distributed system fused with a centralised system offers a potential way forward.

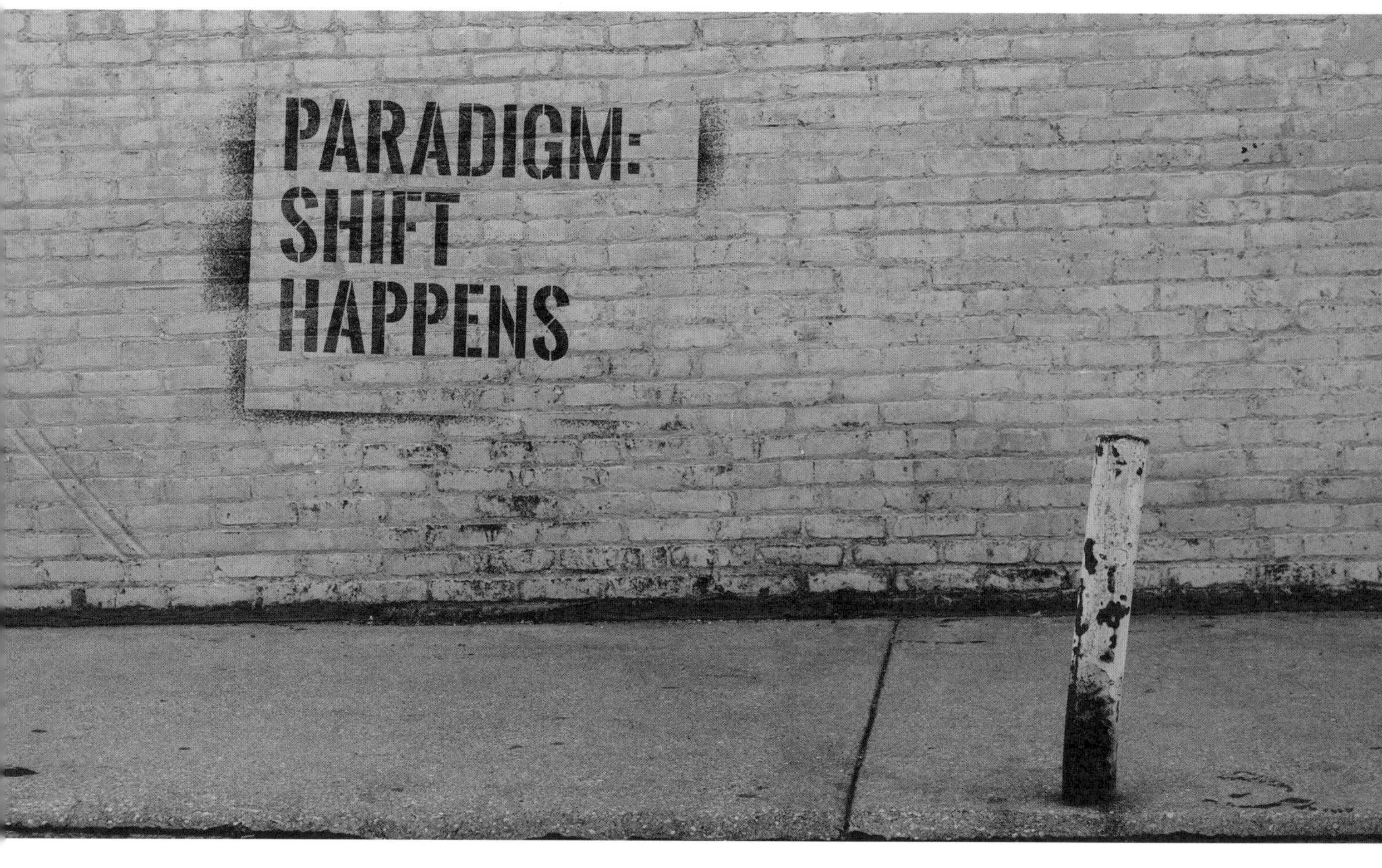

WELCOME TO THE NEW, NEW NORMAL

Usually the first problems you solve with the new paradigm are the ones that were unsolvable with the old paradigm.

—Joel Barker

'Paradigm, shift happens'. This tongue-in-cheek slogan, written on a wall in Shoreditch in East London, captures in a few words the realities we face today. There is an implied slant to it: that things are not working and are changing whether we like it or not. It also recognises the pain and challenge of change. We are all knee-deep in it!

We often talk about a paradigm shift, but most often it is wishful thinking—like hoping that the weather will change for the better. Real shifts stall because interests are not aligned. The Haight-Ashbury movement of the 1960s pointed to a time where social and economic concerns were at a heightened state; political concerns were not. The oil crisis of the 1970s gave us an opportunity to address the environmental concerns of the time. But instead of change, apathy happened!

In the same way, we could have shifted our planning, design and development paradigms with the urban renaissance agenda of the early 2000s. We just ended up wasting a good word. *Sustainability*, not being dealt with seriously enough, is suffering a similar fate.

> *Apathy can be overcome by enthusiasm, and enthusiasm can only be aroused by two things: first, an ideal, which takes the imagination by storm, and second, a definite intelligible plan for carrying that ideal into practice.*
>
> —Arnold Toynbee

Thomas Kuhn has a lot to say about how you achieve *paradigm shift*, a term he coined in *The Structure of Scientific Revolutions*. In his view, in a nutshell, you keep pointing at the anomalies and failures in the old paradigm, you keep coming yourself, loudly and with assurance, from the new one. You insert people with the new paradigm in places of public visibility and power. You don't waste time with reactionaries; rather you work with active change agents and with the vast middle ground of people who are open-minded.

Systems champions would say you change paradigms by modeling a system, which takes you outside the system and forces you to see it whole. We say that because our own paradigms have been changed that way.

New normal is a term often used by McKinsey and other leading economists to define the conditions in a new post-credit crunch economy. It recognises that things will never be the same as before, and for the doom-and-gloom merchants, the trend suggests two things: lowered expectations for economic activity and a climate of austerity. Both are now true in most parts of the world. The question is: what will normal look like? No one can say how long the trends will last, so what we find on the other side will not look like the normal of recent years. The new normal will be shaped by a confluence of powerful forces—some arising directly from the trends and some that were at work long before they began. For those who have recognised the power of the new economy with all its potential, it means more start-ups, fewer giants and infinite opportunity.

As Chris Anderson, the editor of *Wired* magazine, states:

> The result is that the next new economy, the one rising from the ashes of this latest meltdown, will favour the small. Involuntary entrepreneurship is now creating tens of thousands of small businesses and a huge market of contract and freelance labour. Many will take full-time jobs again once they become available, but many others will choose not to. The crisis may have turned our economy into small pieces, loosely joined, but it will be the collective action of millions of workers hungry for change that keeps it that way.

The fragmentation of our economy points to a completely new way of looking at the pattern, grain and usage our cities. Small pieces fit within a big idea.

A combination of neo-liberal policies and changing businesses have produced a huge and growing number of people with enough common characteristics to be called an emerging class, the 'precariat' or members of the 'gig economy'—people across the world living and working precariously, usually in a series of short-term jobs, without recourse to stable occupational identities or careers, stable social protection or protective regulations relevant to them. They include migrants but also locals.

Guy Standing, in his book *The Precariat*, argues that this class of people could produce new instabilities in society. They are increasingly frustrated and dangerous because they have no voice, and hence they are vulnerable to the siren calls of extreme political parties. He also outlines a new kind of good society, with more people actively involved in civil society and the precariat re-engaged.

Kevin Kelly, author of *New Rules for the New Economy*, recognises a new emerging socialism at work in his 2009 article 'The New Socialism: Global Collectivist Society Is Coming Online':

> Nearly every day another startup proudly heralds a new way to harness community action. These developments suggest a steady move toward a sort of socialism uniquely tuned for a networked world.... While old-school socialism was an arm of the state, digital socialism is socialism without the state. This new brand of socialism currently operates in the realm of culture and economics, rather than government—for now.

FROM BIG TO SMALL GOVERNMENT

In some countries, we hear about the move from big government to small government, which is the philosophical drive towards devolution of power to the local level. It is a form of localism that looks to alter the relationship between the individual and the state (often coupled with words such as *efficiency* and *cost-savings*). In the United Kingdom this was expressed as a move 'from big government to Big Society'.

David Snowden says, 'We live in the narrative of our times', so in our neo-liberal world this means governments getting out of the way, devolving responsibility to the local level and making sure that planning is more permissive—adopting a more flexible approach. But for the majority of governments, it is the dawning realisation that the problem is too big for any government to deal with. They need another way, but they find change difficult to articulate in any new way.

Small government, in contrast, is government that minimises its activities, so it is not really about size. The notion of small government is an economic philosophy that emerged amongst European liberal scholars in the 1930s to define a 'third' or 'middle way' between the conflicting philosophies of classical liberalism and socialist planning. The impetus for this thinking arose from a desire to

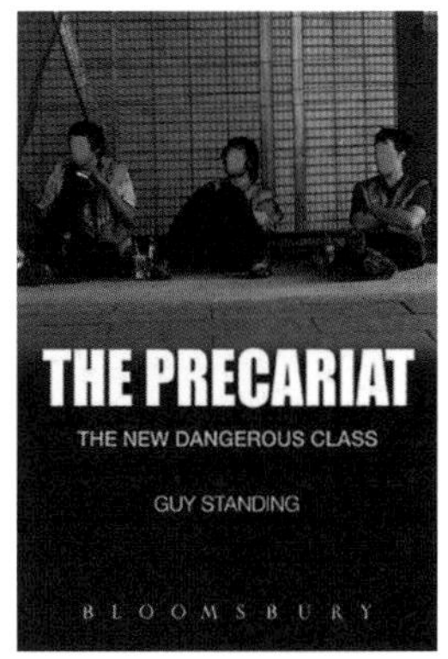

WHY BIG PLANS FAIL

'Make no little plans. They have no magic to stir men's blood and probably themselves will not be realised' is Daniel Burnham's rallying cry that urbanists love hearing.

Burnham's rebuilding of Chicago is so far from where we are today in many parts of the world. Where we used to have to do more with less, exactly the opposite is now true. Many big plans don't just stir the blood, they clog the arteries. So what we need to understand is how the big plan now needs to work in established complex environments and especially in an increasingly bottom-up world—where the focus is much more on enabling than controlling.

> *But in practice master plans fail—because they create totalitarian order, not organic order. They are too rigid; they cannot easily adapt to the natural and unpredictable changes that inevitably arise in the life of a community.*
>
> —Christopher Alexander

Many things need to be conceived of at scale; there is nothing wrong with having big ideas or big plans. Big ideas do not means big solutions in the same way that big plans do not mean radical or wholesale change. The Birmingham Big City Plan, prepared for Birmingham City Council by consultancy Urban Initiatives in 2010, directed its efforts to releasing the potential of a 'city of a thousand designers', the 'city of a thousand trades' and the place of multiple interventions all set within an enabling vision for the city. It was determined to build the fine-grained fabric of the city. Here *big* meant *lots*!

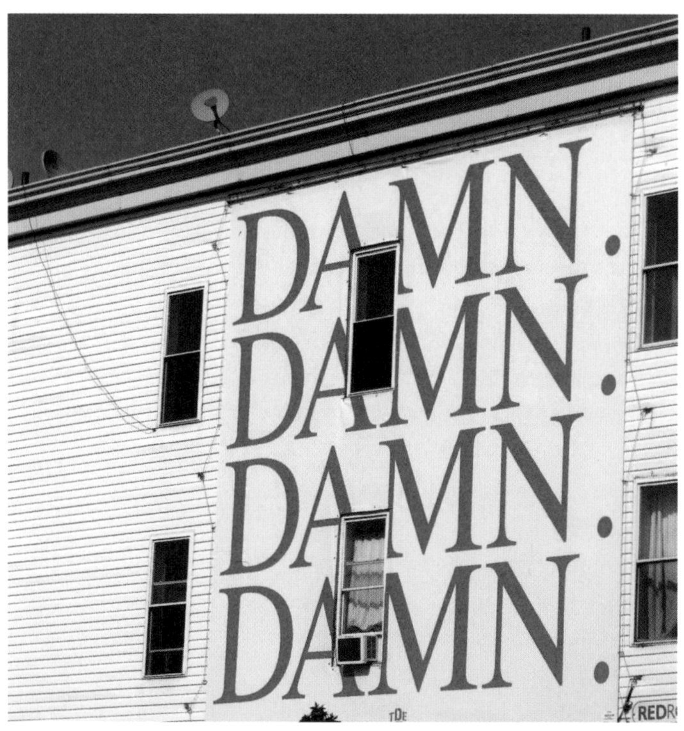

SO WHAT TYPE OF BIG PLANS FAIL?

1 **Big plans that present only a static view**

The world is littered with big plans that cannot change unless you go back to first principles. Because we have no interim step to bed down urban structure, it is always possible to start again...and so we do! All of this points to plans that have the fixed qualities of robustness, responsiveness and resilience. They can adapt to changing circumstances and do it well.

2 **Big plans that require big leaps**

Many big plans cannot start or are dependent on something else happening before they can start or get on with action. The first step is often a jump too far. Plans need quick wins to build confidence (and perhaps even meanwhile uses or interim strategies). Plans need to be broken into bite-sized chunks that can be scaled up or scaled down. Lots of smalls add up to something big! Independent timelines allow us to get on with other things if some stall.

3 **Big plans that need big players**

The classic de-risk formula is to put all your problems in a problem basket and get a big player to sort it. The country is littered with failed schemes where the big player has walked away after a big procurement process. The biggest risk is nothing happens. All the eggs are in one basket. Plans need to allow for small changes to make a big difference, widening choice and delivery for many from the individual to the collective to the corporate. Not just the corporate.

4 **Big plans as big architecture**

In our world there is constant pressure to deliver radical change and quickly—'Give us something different, a big bang', the city fathers say. 'Can we show it at MPIM or the Venice Biennale?' This problem arises when the plan is defined by the big architectural solution that holds a place to ransom. Urban design is not architecture. It creates the medium in which exciting architecture can flourish, releasing the potential of the unexpected and providing the backdrop for where the everyday meets the extraordinary.

5 **Big plans that demand big outcomes**

Many big plans demand change to happen quickly. If change isn't fast, confidence sinks. Their expectations suck the oxygen from the room. Some of our biggest sites are in the hands of the biggest players and very little is happening. We also know that excellent places take a long time to evolve and mature.

So...we still need big shared visions, but they must be capable of releasing the collective power of many small ideas and actions that will add up to make a big difference.

Indira Gandhi said, 'Have a bias toward action—let's see something happen now. You can break that big plan into small steps and take the first step right away.' She had it right.

avoid repeating the economic failures of the early 1930s. These failures were mostly blamed on the economic policy of classical liberalism, which advocated a specific kind of society, and government as a direct response to the industrial revolution and urbanisation. Classic liberalism drew on the economics of Adam Smith and on a belief in natural law, utilitarianism and progress.

In the decades that followed, the use of the term *neo-liberal* referred to theories that contrasted with the more laissez-faire doctrines of classical liberalism. It promoted a market economy under the control of the state. This model came to be known as the 'social market economy'. The essence of the social market economy is the view that private markets are the most effective allocation mechanism, but that output is maximised through sound state macroeconomic management of the economy. In recent years, neo-liberalism's return to a more classical focus—the pursuit of the free market—has produced a contemporary theory that links economic theory and political life. Economic strength is the overriding and decisive basis for political power today.

> *While democracy has advanced, the part we ordinary citizens have played in the making and sustaining of the places and communities we live in has diminished. Never has so much been decided for so many by so few.*
>
> —David Fleming

CENTRALIST VERSUS LOCALIST

John Atkinson of the UK's Local Government Leadership, in his article 'Centralist v Localist', shows that localism only works in certain sectors of government, and for many, local government is not the natural home of localism. He puts two opposing forces on two axes to show that where people work (central or local) and their natural tendency (to centralise or localise) gives us different categories of behaviour—from centralising centralists to localising localists and various shades between.

Governments find it difficult to give away power. In many instances, things that are devolved to the local level are still controlled at the central level. Here, their relationship with local democracy is not clear and, robbed of local feedback loops, the pressure for change remains from the centre and, with this, the risk of continued central control. In other instances, we just see central bureaucracy re-created locally.

When it comes to neighbourhood formation, the category of 'localising localists' is the most interesting. According to Atkinson, these are people who are not by nature involved in the major local organisations but are active in their communities. This form of localism takes us beyond the scale of the local authority to communities of all shapes and sizes. Here we find people who do not wish to take on the existing functions of the state but instead do those things that they, with all their desires and concerns, consider necessary. At its best, this sort of behaviour leads people to act in the collective interest of their community.

> *We end up with a patchwork of different localisms knitted together and, confusing as it may seem, it is a messy solution to a messy problem, and that is probably what we need.*
>
> —John Atkinson

He is right. An ideology of one simple methodology for running a country isn't tenable: urban society is too complex and too adaptive for one size to fit all. And we must remember that just devolving activity is by no means more efficient or cheaper if it is not accompanied by a change in behaviour that allows the devolution of trust and responsibility. Simply re-creating centralised processes at a more local level only adds another level of bureaucracy and cost. Equally, devolving power to local democratic bodies, especially those not equipped with an understanding of how to act in the collective interest of their community, is just as bad. We need to recognise that we need a spectrum of central and local, building capacity at the local level to act proactively. Local alone will always find it difficult.

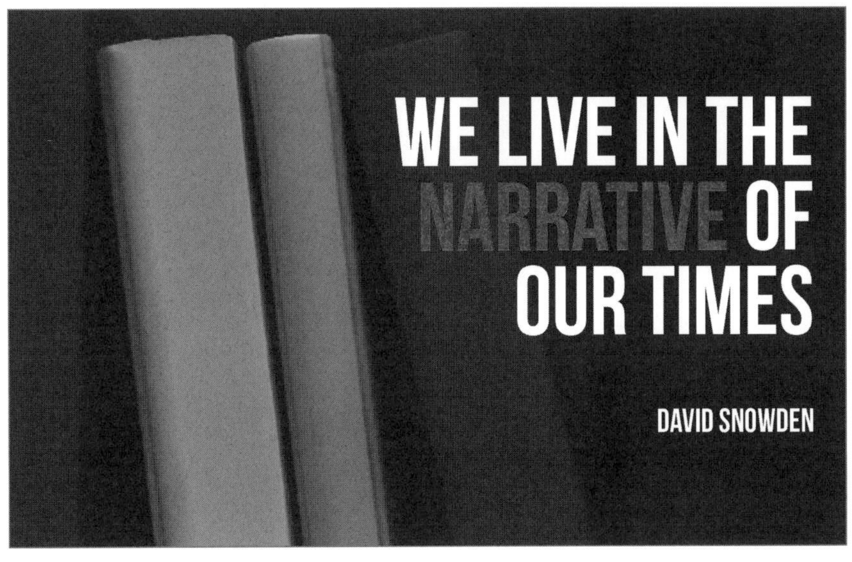

WE LIVE IN THE NARRATIVE OF OUR TIMES
DAVID SNOWDEN

Localisation stands, at best, at the limits of practical possibility, but it has the decisive argument in its favour that there will be no alternative.

—David Fleming

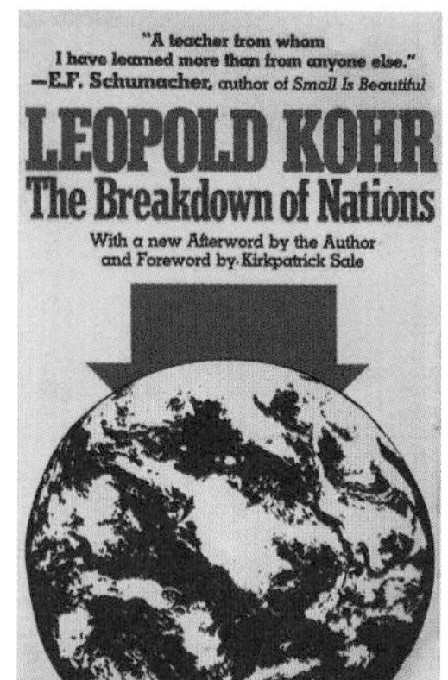

BIG SOLUTIONS ARE LAZY WAYS OF SOLVING COMPLEX URBAN PROBLEMS

Leopold Kohr claims that society's problems are not caused by particular forms of social or economic organisation but by the size of solutions. Any system could work well on what he calls 'the human scale'. It is at this scale that people can play a part in the systems that govern their lives. But once scaled up, all systems will dominate people. Changing the system alone will not prevent that oppression—as any number of revolutions has shown. We need to return to that human scale captured so well in Kirkpatrick Sale's writings.

Neo-liberal policies remain embedded in the psyche of policymakers, despite a multitude of modern failings. The adoption of these ideals has, without a doubt, made the wealthy wealthier but this, as we all know, has not come without consequence. When it comes to cities, the real failings of the policies are that they have bred bigness—the big players call the shots, the boundaries between the big players and governments has become blurred, and the big are too big to fail. All of this is at odds with local.

> *A culture is unsalvageable if stabilising forces themselves become ruined and irrelevant. The collapse of one sustaining cultural institution enfeebles others, makes it more likely that others will give way...until finally the whole enfeebled, intractable contraption collapses.*
>
> —Jane Jacobs

Why is it that the machinery of urban regeneration and development is directed so emphatically to site assembly? Are we so convinced that putting more land under the control of fewer people is always a good thing?

Urban development does not warrant the sheer scale of the effort we see in many places towards consolidation and bigness—the loss of finer grain of ownership, management, design and variety that so damages our cities. This consolidation changes historic patterns of use and ownership just as much as a tall building might, yet it is somehow seen as more acceptable to spread large buildings across an entire city block rather than let a building rise higher from a smaller footprint. Temple Bar in Dublin shows how the cumulative effect of countless small carefully designed interventions adds up to a far bigger picture than any single solution.

Consolidation sterilises entire city blocks, rendering them less capable of responding to changes in markets or technology and requiring bigger, more costly, more dramatic interventions of change in the future. It curtails movement, the permeability of the city that might otherwise offer choice of routes and encourage us to wander in the city, confident that if we explore an unknown route we can easily find our way back. It creates a megastructure that distorts development as well as long-term influences on neighbourhood development that is disproportionate to its physical size. When megastructures fail, they fail disastrously. The solution: replace them with even bigger megastructures.

Big sites should not, however, be confused with 'big pictures'. Every place needs a big picture to guide its future growth and change, but big pictures need big walls. Successful cities and towns create the 'galleries' for these big pictures—their own city or town plans.

Typical stages in the evolution of incremental housing in Savda Ghevra, Delhi, India.

ANSWERING THE NEW URBAN QUESTION

If the new normal is driving our thinking on a changed economy and a professed move to localism is driving our thinking on changed governance of society, what are the new questions we should be asking?

Andy Merrifield, in his book *The New Urban Question*, is concerned that contemporary urban studies have become 'politically disengaged and overrun with empiricism', not least because of the constant need to demonstrate impact through the media hype about exploding urban populations. He believes we need to dispense with the old chestnuts between global North and global South, between developed and undeveloped worlds, between city and suburb. He is right. We are all in the same boat.

Merrifield suggests that urban professionals—planners, city managers and economists—see the global city as a 'growth machine', while ignoring the pandemic that is rapidly overwhelming urban life. What is evident is the big question on how we want to live in the future. We know that modern democracy is riddled with faults. We grin and bear it, come what may; as individuals and communities, inventing our truths along the way, we get on with life as best we can. Occasionally we feel that democratic lack weighing down on us too heavily and decide to do something about it. We take to the streets and organise ourselves into a social movement that struggles for real democracy.

> *We need to build a social movement to resolve the problem of the urban. Those struggling with local concerns (those that are now common global concerns) need to make themselves more important than they actually are.*
>
> —Andrew Merrifield

The 2014 Scottish independence referendum showed how it is possible to mobilise the whole of the population to talk about what sort of society they want to live in. For the first time in years we have seen an intelligent debate about the role of democracy at every level. This is the type of debate we need about our urban society worldwide. Whatever happens, we need to put the democracy back into urbanism.

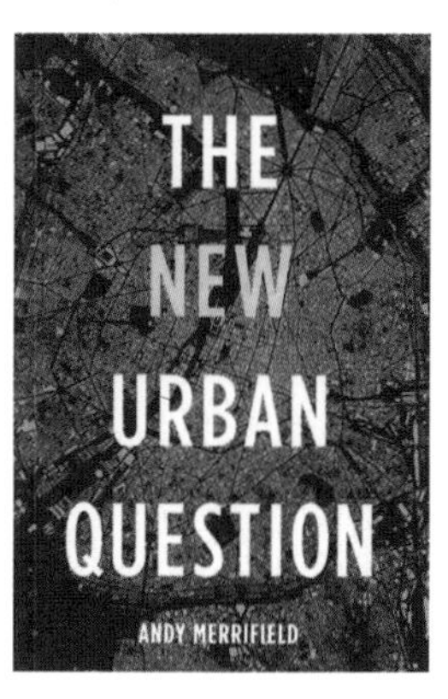

It ain't what you do, it's the way that you do it—and that's what gets results.

—Ella Fitzgerald

OUR PLANNING, DESIGN AND DEVELOPMENT **PROCESSES**

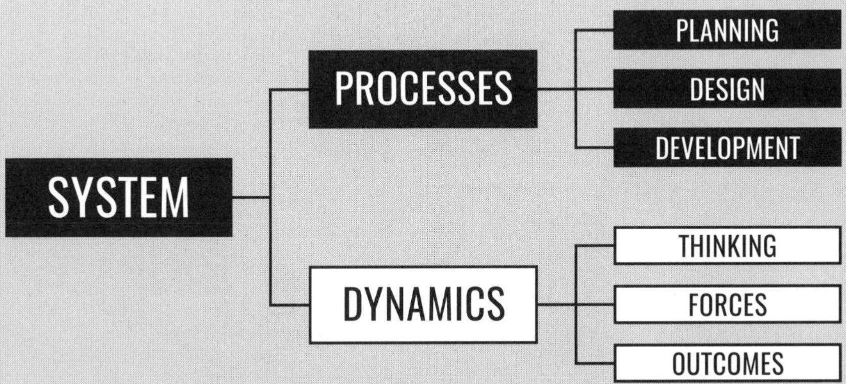

The system we use to shape our urban society has three discrete but interrelated parts: urban planning, urban design and urban development. Together they add up to how places are shaped over time. But the way in which we plan, design and develop our cities is the product of thinking that emerged from postwar reconstruction throughout the world. The top-down, command-and-control system has now become the predominant way of doing things throughout the world.

> **Process** *NOUN*
>
> a series of actions or steps taken in order to achieve a particular end
>
> SYNONYMS
> procedure, operation, action, activity, set of tasks, undertaking

Civic leaders and urban professionals believe that they can control something as complex as a city, and they set forth their utopian plans, complex policies and bureaucratic practices precisely in a centralised regulatory system to do so. In our pursuit of certainty, we built the system this way. It was put in place in a different time, when governments believed they had to lead the process, deliver the homes and build the perfect urban society. How things have changed since those heady days.

For years since that time we have relied on 'fixes' to deal with the inadequacies of the system. Shifts towards sustainability, smart cities and urban resilience have become some of the patches we have made to its operations to hopefully make it work better. Every week we hear of a new government announcement, made from a speechwriter's familiar script—new promises made, new solutions found and new targets set. Most trend and then fail like most top-down strategic initiatives that have been tried and have failed in so many parts of the world.

In truth, the system can't be fixed. The bugs lie too deeply buried. The system has to be upgraded.

There is no absolute truth and that is the absolute truth.

—Batman

UTOPIA

ON URBAN PLANNING

Planning systems throughout the world share the same characteristics. They are all obsessed with providing certainty and constantly looking to define ways forwards through complex policies. They all have the same problems.

> *Rationalism, that bright dream of figuring out everything in advance and setting it forth precisely in a centralised regulatory system, has made us blind. Obsessed with certainty, we see almost nothing.*
>
> —Philip Howard

The main instruments of urban planning are long-term strategies based on predict-and-plan models: mechanistic methods intended to deal with complex problems. They are justified by looking backwards at piles of evidence. The bigger the pile, the better the evidence, or so it seems.

Many plans are out of date before their ink is dry. They are written to keep the big players at bay and end up creating a game where only the big players can play. It is a closed system, not open to challenge. Most plans evolve into standard operating procedures for places, as one plan copies another. They fail to create a vision of a place, except for a few vaguely expressed, generic goals. Despite few people having any faith in these instruments, we blindly plough on.

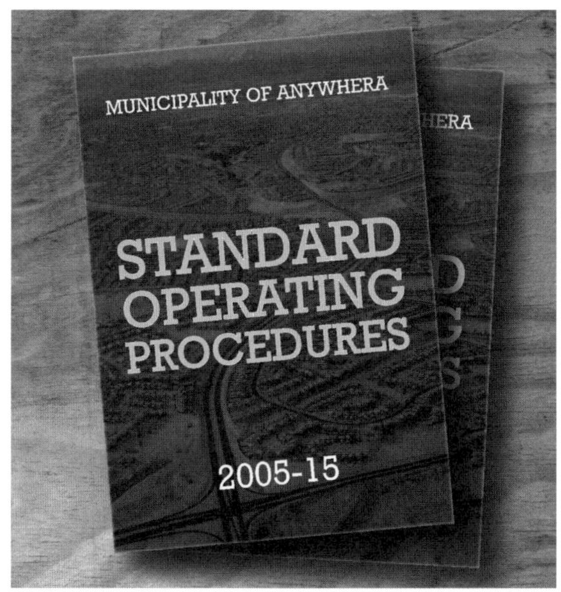

WEAKNESSES IN THE SYSTEM

The growing search for new, more effective ways of approaching and shaping the future of cities flows from the recognition of planning weaknesses in dealing with the complex challenges posed by the contemporary world. These are:

> *Uncertainty is an uncomfortable position. But certainty is an absurd one.*
>
> —Voltaire

1 Planning stifles evolution

Planning cannot duck the fact that so much out there is a result of the system. The restrictive nature of the system has prevented the ability to learn by trying. This was a natural process of urban evolution that is denied to many today. By trying to predetermine where things go we have denied the natural forces that shaped the city so well in the past. Blind adherence to zoning, an abject fear of ribbon development and an obsession with preventing coalescence of different settlements have perpetuated urban sprawl. Utopia and evolution are uncomfortable bedfellows. The first imposes; the second emerges.

2 Planning prevents sustainability

No matter how hard the planning system seeks the truth, it fails. Places that guarantee to be more sustainable are most often less sustainable. Density is never a guarantee of urban life. Mixed use is never a guarantee of socially diverse neighbourhoods. Good design is not a guarantee of good quality of life. Good intentions fail, and we don't know why. The lobby groups that seek to protect our natural environment have missed the point. The pursuit of compact urbanism and the building of a viable human habitat are denied. More pressure is piled on the natural habitat. What they are promoting is a double loss. Nobody wins.

A PREDICT-AND-PLAN model looks to review and update a five- to ten-year development plan only when the time comes.

A model using a CONTINUOUS FEEDBACK loop gets regular feedback and reviews issues when they arise. There is no fixed period for this type of plan.

Both have long term strategic visions that influence the preparation of the development plan.

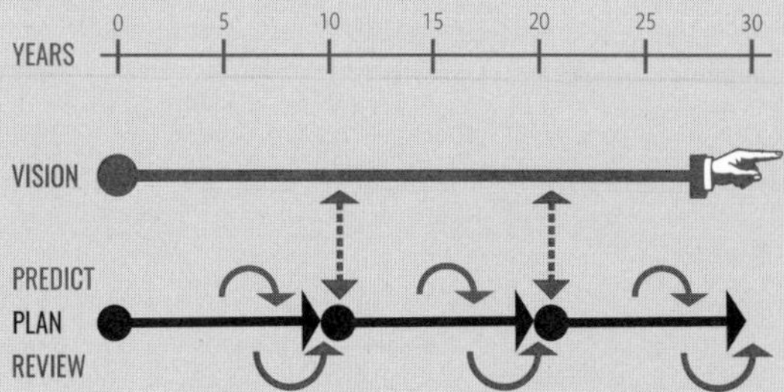

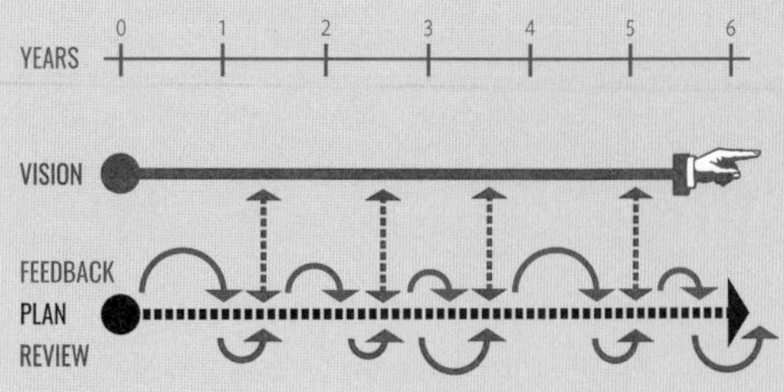

On planning: if it ain't broke, we'll fix it until it is.

—Mark David Major

3 Planning contradicts complexity

Planners, operating in complex environments, use traditional planning techniques that do not have the flexibility needed to address multifaceted and rapidly paced urban change. Like a user interface on a computer, the planning function sits on top of a flawed and outdated operating system. In recent years, what we know as urban design has been adapted as the friendly interface to the planning system. Although this has been a big step forwards, it has disguised the true source of the problem. Further progress depends on evolving the operating system.

4 Planning uses the wrong metrics

How can we measure the performance of our communities? This may seem like a strange question. After all, communities are organic and ever-evolving entities, are they not? Much of the research surrounding social and community problems in rapidly growing communities has been based on objective indicators such as assessments of housing shortages, crime, and educational attainment. The use of these metrics tends to produce a limited view of possible social problems. We need to accept that there are intangibles that we cannot measure easily, such as sense of community and degree of social capital, well-being and happiness. These intangibles are what any sophisticated planning system fails to deliver. Given that these metrics are not just simple performance indicators to be measured by some bureaucrat in some dusty office, the real question lies in how we create the conditions to allow these intangibles to flourish.

5 Planning creates wrong outcomes

We constantly see the outcomes of the planning process resulting in something we don't like. Despite all the policies, design guidance, negotiations and responses, we end up with schemes that fail to offer the quality of life we demand for our citizens—places with no soul, places locked in transition, places that lack a sense of belonging. Good design is seen as the antidote to bad planning. Efforts all end up in endless design reviews, with one expert's view pitted against another. Despite this, the outcome is never better design. It is just more of the same with better details.

6 Planning looks for the next new thing

Spatial justice, smart cities, urban resilience, biodiversity, social inclusiveness, urban renaissance... this list goes on. All brave concepts that are going to save the system. The trouble is, by the time they get shaped into urban policy, they becomes worthless. Just look at what we have done with urban sustainability. In planning, this monstrously ill-defined, abstract concept is likely to be masking the incompetent application of some half-formed idea vaguely related to the use of resources. Freedom and justice are noble concepts and useful words. It is just that history teaches us not to accept them at face value. Sustainability can be a useful concept, and the word can be called into service as a convenient chapter heading. But we are deluded if we believe that there is a simple thing called sustainability that, by merely invoking the word, can be made to infuse a planning policy or development concept with unchallengeable virtue.

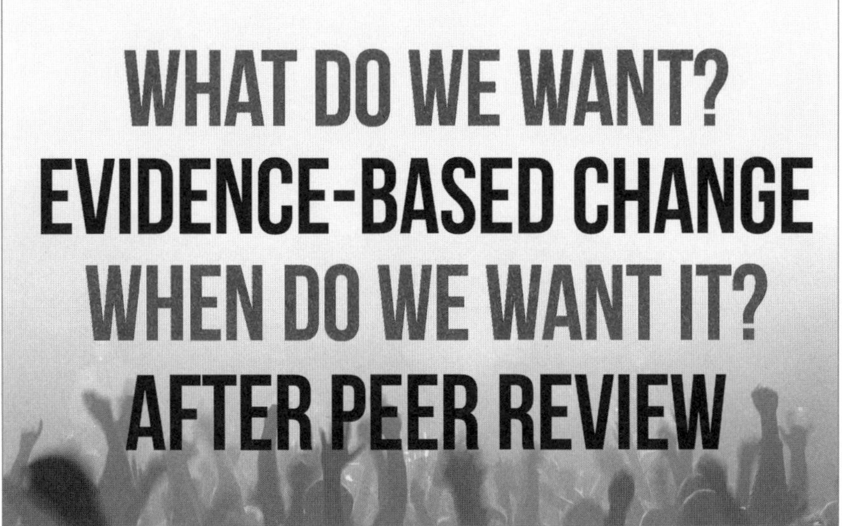

Looking backwards to look forwards

In recent years, little has been offered in the way of providing a robust and adaptable model of neighbourhood building that is capable of guiding growth and change to create high-quality environments. The unthinking application of limiting rules or theories dictates fixed end-state conditions. The one-size-fits-all approach has never worked for us. There is nothing wrong with rules or theories, but we need the right ones. Complex choices have to be structured, but the structure must allow for infinite possibilities.

Evidence-based decision-making, or in its latest reincarnation, data-driven decision-making, is seen as a prerequisite for more responsible and effective urban planning. Commitments to this kind of process acknowledge that future development needs to take into account the past and react in an iterative and progressive way to its findings.

However, three main problems emerge from this limited approach:

1. Firstly, the assumption that we humans are rational beings who, upon being given new information, will act logically as a result.
2. Secondly, that evidence, or data, is essentially 'the absolute truth', and that making decisions based upon it is always a route towards better decision-making.
3. Thirdly, we often collect evidence based on justifying policies that we want to prove, and generally we end up using the wrong metrics.

An old adage is, 'Sometimes when you look through the rear view mirror, you just see dust'.

RISING TO THE CHALLENGE

If a command-and-control model does not work, neither does a predict-and-provide one. Instead we need a new approach: a system that is both progressive and enabling—a system that embraces continuous feedback as a core operating principle.

Rather than being scared of physical planning because of previous failures, we need to invest a new confidence in the process: this time, rooted in a clear understanding of how cities evolve. We need to embrace complexity and see the city in the context of a complex adaptive system and not in terms of utopian dreams that will never be realised.

In the sequence of plan, design and develop, planning must come first. It has to become relevant again to give the others any chance of success.

Never look back unless you are planning to go that way.

—Henry David Thoreau

ON URBAN DESIGN

Many modern cities have seen the destruction of the elements that once made them successful: the street, the urban block, the discrete public space and the differentiated private place. If we are to rebuild those elements we must understand how they fit into spatial framework that will allow the city to change. Although many architects claim to value the traditional city with its streets, blocks and urban grain, too many of them continue to see that structure as a problem.

> *Too often the issues are presented as battles of architectural styles. Take your choice: the new-urbanist, traditional urbanism of Leon Krier; or the modernist, post-urbanism of Rem Koolhaas. That false polarity neatly diverts the discussion up a fetid cul-de-sac of architectural introspection. Enthusiastic coteries join their heroes at the extremes, in glorious isolation from any possible collective view of the future of cities.*
>
> —Re:Urbanism

Successful cities and their neighbourhoods have a coherence above and beyond the individual expression of particular buildings. The special is complemented by the ordinary, the city's essential fabric. Some of the best new urban architecture, particularly in Holland, Ireland and Scotland, is reinventing the traditions of the terrace and the tenement. Designers in the modern idiom are inspired, not intimidated, by the past: it just makes good sense. Architects may complain that the constraints of urbanism compromise their artistic integrity. So why is it that the best designers perform so brilliantly when the brief sets particularly challenging constraints?

The last time we saw radical architecture was in the 1960s and 1970s: a time of architecture without architects, community architecture, and self-help challenging the role of the designer. Since then, architecture has retreated from any overt political or social agenda. Instead of being radical in any real sense, the most it can be is avant-garde. For-

mal, technological and mechanistic inventions are its only innovations. Subsumed to marketing and branding, architecture offers only novelty rather than any challenge to the status quo or any alternatives for change. The rise of the megaconsultancy and the starchitect has seen the rise of the grand vision, multiplied across all parts of the world—cities all striving to be distinctive: to be the next new thing. The shock of the new has been replaced by the consumption of the new because architecture has now become fully assimilated into the society of the spectacular.

However, the architectural establishment in practice and academia cannot see the irony of all this. The fact that anything so stylistically regressive might be considered radical is beyond their comprehension. Here we see another, hidden, unchallenged 'truth'—that architecture has become obsessed with product. Only innovation of the product is legitimised. Radical approaches, radical reframing of professional roles is ignored. In part, this is to do with architecture's anachronistic idea of the architect as the romanticised model of the artist.

Urban design is still rooted in its top-down traditions of city beautiful, based on the conviction that good urban design can become the essential antidote to bad buildings. It believes that its vision of 'place-making' will prevail in the face of the architect's view that good design will emerge only from their own best devices. Contrary to the impression given by the masterplan, the aim of urban design is not to visualise—and then to achieve—a permanent end state. Every place is always changing, either for the better or for the worse. Unless we accept that fact, we will succeed neither in managing decline in the places where that is appropriate, nor in supporting success in the places where there is the most potential for that.

Our urban design education has grown from a utopian townscape tradition and, as a result, we have not tackled the issue of complexity in our cities. Most courses have been grown from within a modernism and garden city tradition and both are buried deep in the DNA of planning or architecture. Most courses have tried to bolt on sustainability but have not been able to apply it in real-life conditions. In reality, there is a disconnect between sustainability, change and urbanism in most courses. Even those teaching sustainability have failed to make the link that good urbanism should equal good sustainability. Moreover, we need to be able to move beyond single-focus approaches. An excellent way of doing this would be through embracing the interface between urban design and urban living, cultural and business assets, political and social needs, financial drivers and value, innovation and creativity.

Design is a word that's come to mean so much that it's also a word that has come to mean nothing.

—Jonathan Ive

So urban designers plough on, developing design principles, design codes and design guidance to help shape their view of the perfect end state. They use lazy tools such as walk bands, axes, vistas and sustainable add-ons to justify their work. There is no guarantee that any of these will produce the complex and socially diverse neighbourhoods that Jane Jacobs strived for. They fail as well.

> *But in practice master plans fail—because they create totalitarian order, not organic order. They are too rigid; they cannot easily adapt to the natural and unpredictable changes that inevitably arise in the life of a community.*
>
> —Christopher Alexander

Christopher Alexander's *A New Theory of Urban Design* amounted to a gauntlet thrown down to conventional urban design, not unlike that thrown down by Jane Jacobs three decades earlier.

A New Theory of Urban Design
Christopher Alexander Hajo Neis
Artemis Anninou Ingrid King

VENUS AND MARS

Michael Mehaffy, writing in the *Journal of Urbanism* on 'Generative Methods in Urban Design', raised important but significant differences between Christopher Alexander's thinking and Andres Duany's new urbanist movement.

The most notable example of an effort to implement Alexander's ideas—and Jacobs's in equal measure—has been the new urbanism movement but, in Mehaffy's words, it 'accelerated the kind of segregation and top-down formalism in city-planning that both Jacobs and Alexander decried. By contrast, the New Urbanism is explicitly about mixed use, and, its proponents would argue, about process.'

For Alexander, the process is a laudable effort at reform that is still woefully inadequate for the challenge. Most importantly for Alexander, the process builds structures that are not at all generative but are based upon standardised templates, 'with the result that they feel lifeless and unsuccessful. They may have the outward appearance of a more organic neighbourhood, but they are, in the end, standardised reproductions.'

For Andres Duany, the figurehead for the New Urbanists, 'Alexander's critique misses a key point. Yes, there are standardised templates within The New Urbanism—as, for example...basic plan drawing of the scheme. But that structure can then be adapted and allowed to serve as a skeletal form for more organic growth. In effect, it can serve as a kind of well-designed 'trellis' on which organic growth can self-organize. Duany notes that such combinations of the standard and the contextual are common in nature.

'Duany and others point to Alexander's own patterns as typological structures that are, in part, standardised elements within his own design system (though a networked one, and not a strict hierarchy). They are then adapted to the specific context, and used in a kind of flexible grammar. Duany believes he is doing something very similar (and indeed, often using Alexander's own patterns). 'I am the best Alexandrian', he recently told [Mehaffy].

'Moreover, Duany believes Alexander is failing to come to terms with a core reality of modern technological society: that large numbers demand top-down management methods. In a mass society, the norm quickly reverts to chaos and kitsch. In order to implement Alexander's methods, this demands expert, top-down leaders for the design and construction process.'

For the New Urbanists, 'Alexander's proposal is to return to a painstaking one-off process of organic design, which is simply not up to the scale of the present challenge. Rather, we must create more automatic processes that generate the same result, like seeds that generate vast numbers of living structures....

'So Duany and other New Urbanists have turned to a new project: the development of codes that replace the old, destructive protocols with new ones that allow good urbanism to flourish, as if on well-constructed trellises. The "SmartCode" is a form-based code that replaces the segregated "Euclidean" zoning of an earlier era with a series of parametric specifications designed to ensure coherent streetscapes and public realms. The code uses a "transect" system to organize contextual responses to the urban condition, from the most intense urban setting to the most pristine natural environment....

'Duany's SmartCode...has begun to take on some stepwise layout guides very similar to Alexander's.... Duany argues that his code also incorporates many other aspects of generativity.' But for Alexander, 'this kind of code does not address the core prerequisite of generativity, and without such guidance for growth the result is still likely to be well-aligned, lifeless junk. It prescribes a series of static parameters within which generative events may occur, but it does not in any way facilitate or guide their generation. Moreover, even to specify such parameters is to constrain the emergence of organic wholes, which require an environment in which adaptation of form can occur as needed.'

'Alexander has now proposed an alternate kind of code, based explicitly upon rule-based, generative processes of the kind outlined in *A New Theory of Urban Design*. Alexander's "generative code" addresses not physical parameters of the built environment, but steps that the participants should take together in laying out and detailing a given structure. Alexander likens it to a recipe, or a medical procedure, in which the steps always follow a logically similar pattern, but the actual actions continuously adapt to the context—the taste and texture of the food in the case of a recipe, or the condition of the patient's tissues in a medical procedure. But in this case, the "recipe" or the "procedure" guides the unfolding of environmental form.

'In its fullest form, this kind of generative code can be thought of as a design-build system, addressing all of the conditions of building—financing, ownership, management, sourcing, and, crucially, changes to the design along the way.

'For Alexander, the issue of cost control is a manageable process, and indeed, is done regularly within existing design-build approaches. He points out that much of the direction of technology is today aimed favorably for such an approach—one-off manufacturing, customization, niche marketing, and so on. He is convinced of the possibility and even the inevitability of this transformation of technology, in a more adaptive, and ultimately, a more organic direction.'

'Duany's discussion of the "problem of large numbers" would find a sympathetic audience with the architect and theorist Rem Koolhaas... For Koolhaas—perhaps representing many other contemporary "neo-modernist" architects—the modern city is simply too complex to yield to a reform agenda like that of the New Urbanists. In the face of sheer quantity, architecture is powerless to change the direction of the urban wave, and therefore is wiser to seek merely to surf that wave with skill.... Koolhaas challenges Duany's faith in planning, and suggests that urbanism is now the art of accommodating generativity, rather than the futile attempt to "design" it...

'For all their disagreements, the cross-fertilizations between Alexander's process advocates and the New Urbanists continue, with constructive results. The topic of generative urbanism continues to loom large.'

The key theoretical points on which his methodology differed from conventional practice include:

→ Urban design must not be an act of tabula rasa imposition of a form designed remotely, based upon an abstract programme. It must understand, respect, and seek to improve the existing conditions.

→ Urban design must incorporate the decisions and needs of the local stakeholders, as a matter not only of fairness but also of the intrinsic quality of the result.

→ Above all, urban design must be a generative process, from which a form will emerge—one that cannot be imposed but will of necessity be, at least in some key respects, local and unique.

Mehaffy's paper confirms the belief that the new urbanists and the neo-modernists use the same thinking but with different slogans on their T-shirts, even though Koolhaas professes differently. No matter how hard we try to reconcile the differences between Alexander and the collective force of the two movements, we recognise that two fundamentally different thought processes are at work. One is from Venus and the other from Mars. The former has its roots in bottom-up individual response and the latter in top-down physical determinism. The former resonates with the self-builders, the latter with the established building industry. Most civilisations use standardised approaches: they call it vernacular. Most civilisations recognise individual expression, but within defined constraints. Both Alexander and Duany recognise the need for putting in place the preconditions for responsive environments. They just disagree on how far you need to go.

In order for design to become more relevant to urban society, it has to see itself in a different light. Design is not the mark of the single hero—the Robert Ruark of Ayn Rand's *The Fountainhead*. It is not about all the elements of control that urban designers strive for. It is also not the product of mindless design reviews that all go back to first principles to define the meaning of *good design*. Good design emerges through continuous evolution of an urban vernacular—the best thing we can do in this place at this point in time. Good design emerges from balanced constraints. It is not forced. It just gets better.

Making the simple complicated is commonplace; making the complicated simple, awesomely simple, that's creativity.

—Charles Mingus

Formality meets informality in Mumbai, India.

ON URBAN DEVELOPMENT

Most governments recognise that expanding housing supply and building effective neighbourhoods are priorities for urban society. It has been known for some years that housing shortages are now intensifying and growing bigger worldwide. There is no bigger crisis in most parts of the world than the housing crisis.

HOUSES AND SHACKS: ALL THAT LACKS!

Two models largely predominate in most parts of the world—the big-developer house-building model and the informal shack-building model. In between is a sprinkling of social and affordable housing, which, as many goverments promote austerity, is not being delivered in sufficient numbers. Both models occupy different ends of the market spectrum and both are characterised by how governments see them as solving the problem. Both fail to deliver the qualities of life expected in successful urban neighbourhoods. Both are failures of our systems.

Both models involve the contesting of land: the formal looks to grab market advantage through seeking a consent on secured land to boost value (and then sitting on it); the informal looks to grab land in order to secure survival (and then resist intervention). Both models are opportunistic. Both could be improved by governments taking a stronger lead in shaping future development by reducing the constraints on delivery of development land in places that lead to better urbanism. Without a clear direction, cities will continually face the great twin threats—unbridled market pressures from developers and uncontrolled occupation of land by the disenfranchised—and invariably will lose.

There is now a sheer lack of imagination about what a city's rich urban fabric might be. Worldwide, the big guys are producing housing as distinct products, not as the fine-grain building blocks that integrate to form socially diverse urban neighbourhoods. The system has to change.

MODEL 1. BIG DEVELOPMENT

In this model, every scheme appears to be a victim of bigness—bloated behemoths. Every scheme calls for a unique brand. Every scheme is a 'Square', a 'Quarter', or a 'Village'. Nothing adds to a unique character. Nothing hangs together.

The housing development market has now polarised into two dominant solutions: the high-density, low-family model (typified by large apartment blocks); and the low-density, high-family model (as can be seen in sprawling, gated, suburban developments). Both promise false ideas of sustainable development. The former has been translated into 'super density' as cities seek to drive up their housing numbers in the hope of delivering some form of affordable housing as planning gain. The latter still offers the hope of some sort of social utopia, which never seems to materialise.

Super dense thinking

In London, we saw the disastrous effects of super density when former mayor Ken Livingstone set the trend for megadevelopment. Livingstone told developers, 'I don't care how big it is, as long as 50% is mine for social and affordable housing.' He single-handedly moved housing from a failing social utopian model to being the sideline of a booming real-estate market. The standard investment-led, one- and two-bedroom apartment block was spawned. Money was cheap and given away easily. With buildings aiming for the sky, space standards plummeted—and urban quality fell even further. We saw the emergence of the transient community with little commitment to the place. Housing became reduced to a commodity. Later mayors came into power at a time when the Livingstone model had collapsed under the weight of the global banking crisis. But, as we found out, the banks (and the big housebuilders they were in bed with) were too big to collapse. This issue meant one thing. Drop the social and affordable housing requirement and plough on. London needs housing. Keep building. The big guys know best.

When the housing crisis deepens, where does the mayor go for advice? Of course, those who have a vested interest in the status quo—the big guys and their megaconsultants. It is like the foxes and the weasels advising the farmer on pest control. The status remains quo.

Today New York is toying with this model.

HOUSEBUILDING BLUES

Armed with the hope of a new urbanism, suburbia soldiers on. Design codes promise better design. Walkability promises healthy living. Community promises better values—social and land. The romance with the past evokes memories of a perfect vision of young Timmy riding his bike down a tree-lined avenue flanked with ideal homes. With sweeping swales, green roofs and hyperinsulated buildings, these places offer the dream of sustainable development. Today, still branded as garden cities or eco-towns, they provide the tantalising thought of a perfect place for the perfect family. Didn't Ebenezer Howard also promise this? Guess what Jane Jacobs said about him:

> His aim was the creation of self sufficient small towns, really very nice towns if you were docile and had no plans of your own and did not mind spending your life with others with no plans of their own. As in all Utopias, the right to have plans of any significance belonged only to the planner in charge.

The predominant model in formal housebuilding worldwide, the turnkey real-estate model, encompasses all phases of the housebuilding process and sells into a formal market through formal processes. It has only emerged as a significant industry within the last few generations as governments have moved from the central position in the housebuilding process to a bit-player in the process. The crisis in the formal housebuilding industry, as the subprime mortgage debacle in the United States has shown us, is resulting in significant changes to the way new properties are financed, built and planned. The consequence could be that traditional volume housebuilders could play a smaller role in the delivery of homes in the future and different routes could open up. In most countries the formal house-

Suburbia is a collection of private benefits and public nuisances.

—Anonymous

building model is still seen as the government's preferred choice as they retreat from active involvement in the housebuilding process, but they are being held to ransom by the industry as monopolies emerge and supply is controlled to maximize profits. In many parts of the world, formal housing is still promised and promises are broken. Big sites continue to be sold to big housebuilders, but they are not moving. Whatever the reason, market conditions or not, they are not the agents of bottom-up change, and something has to be done to come up with better practices to both avoid strategic land banking and mitigate the extreme damping effect big sites have on the market. At the same time we need to keep up the steady flow of better housing. If there is one model that is fundamentally broken, it is the volume housebuilding market.

Yet we still persist with this model.

Little boxes on the hillside, and they are all made out of ticky-tacky.

—Malwina Reynolds, *Little Boxes*

THE MISSING MIDDLE

The flexible, midrise, medium-density housing models that served our cities so well are missing from the big developers' toolkit. These are the small tenement blocks that we see in the East Village of New York; the havelis of New Delhi; the five-storey townhouses of London that can be occupied individually or subdivided for a mix of uses; the courtyard houses that we find in the hutongs of Beijing; or the pension blocks of Paris. Every city has its models that have endured, and we value the process of urban neighbourhood building. These are the typologies that Dan Parolek of Opticos Design calls the 'missing middle' because 'very few of these housing types have been built since the early 1940s due to regulatory constraints, the shift to auto-dependent patterns of development, and the incentivisation of single-family home ownership.' In Europe, the shift to state-led housing estates effectively eliminated the fine-grained, middle housing models, replacing these with the tower block and low-rise terrace.

A common characteristic of these housing types are small- to medium-sized building footprints, with the largest of these types having a typical frontage width of about 15 metres (50 feet). This characteristic makes them ideal for urban infill, even in older neighbourhoods that were originally developed as single-family housing but can easily evolve with slightly higher intensities.

Rediscovering the art of middle housing is the focus of this compendium.

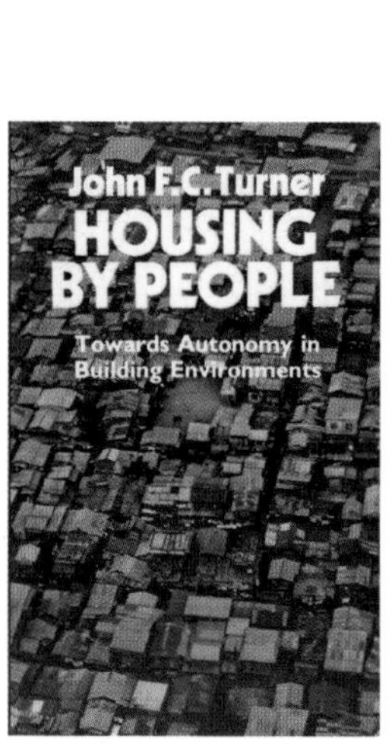

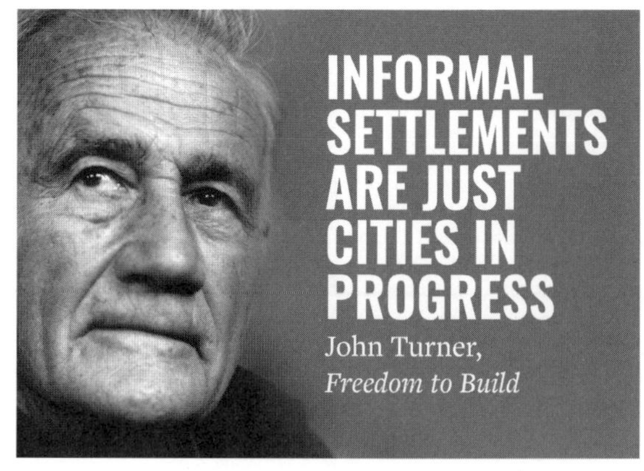

INFORMAL SETTLEMENTS ARE JUST CITIES IN PROGRESS
John Turner,
Freedom to Build

MODEL 2. INFORMAL SHACK-BUILDING

The other, and more significant model, is the informal shack-building model, which predominates in most parts of the world, even creeping into well-developed parts of the world as the system fails. For many, informality is a state that provides the first foothold in a city. Sometimes it allows progress to the next level, but in most instances it traps people in a permanent state of urban malaise and prevents transition. This is not just a crisis of finance or confidence, but a crisis that has emerged from initial conditions. In this crisis, people have not started well, so they find it difficult to move up. As a result, they are not able to translate their efforts into realisable assets and are trapped in a cycle of poverty. This is a problem shared by many in social housing estates, where the next step up the ladder is too difficult to achieve.

It is this sector that is growing rapidly worldwide, and we need a different understanding of its potential in order to harness it. Many governments see informal housing as a problem in isolation: a problem that needs its own special solution.

Capturing the 'ordinary' nature of informality

Despite years of research and policy development, the gaps in current urban theory and a limited understanding of the real nature of informal urban settlements means that they are often treated as being outside 'normal' urban considerations—or as aberrations. According to Melanie Lombard in her paper 'Constructing Ordinary Places', we see informal settlements not only as 'a manifestation of poor housing standards, lack of basic services and denial of human rights, [but] also a symptom of dysfunctional urban societies where inequalities are not only tolerated but allowed to fester.' This concern by governments has led to mass evictions, slum clearances and ill-considered rehousing solutions, leading to the stigmatisation, discrimination and displacement felt by millions of urban dwellers today.

Lombard says, 'Most prominent depictions of informal urban settlements have tended to conceptualise them in overriding negative terms. It is hardly surprising given the very real inequalities and injustices that occur daily in these settings, and the fact that such accounts of informality are frequently motivated by an underlying ideological concern with social justice.'

By capturing the messy, dynamic and context-driven processes that shape informal urban settlements as places, Lombard believes that we need to capture the 'ordinary' nature of cities, imagining these informal places differently so that we can realise their potential contribution to the city as a whole. So how do we build on their positive qualities and not impose a jaded development view on them? It is here that a new leap of faith is needed.

Somewhere between

In most parts of the world, affordable housing, open-market housing and informal housing are treated as three separate staircases, each going to a different level of the metaphorical house and with no other way of moving from one level to another. People taking one route may want to transfer to one of the others when their personal circumstances change, through economic conditions, family changes, the cycles of life, or anything else. But it is rarely possible. Governments' solutions to informal housing are often part of a system that, while meant to help the urban poor, ends up making the poor even poorer.

Governments carry the can, whatever

Governments always pick up the responsibility of sorting out the problems facing informal settlements—problems that arise not only from the much higher costs in upgrading these places but also from related issues such as greater health, fire prevention and crime costs, to name a few.

Unless there is some form of basic land subdivision system that will allow a place to evolve, governments will be continually faced with putting their fingers in the dyke to stem the sheer volume of secondary problems that emerge in unconstrained urban development.

'Is it cheaper to prevent a slum than to fix one?' is a question asked by many. The Inter-American Development Bank (IADB) has attempted to answer this in their report *Room for Development*. With a focus on housing development in the Americas, it shows that many slum-upgrading programmes have not proved useful in providing basic infrastructure to informal settlements in the long-run, for a number of reasons.

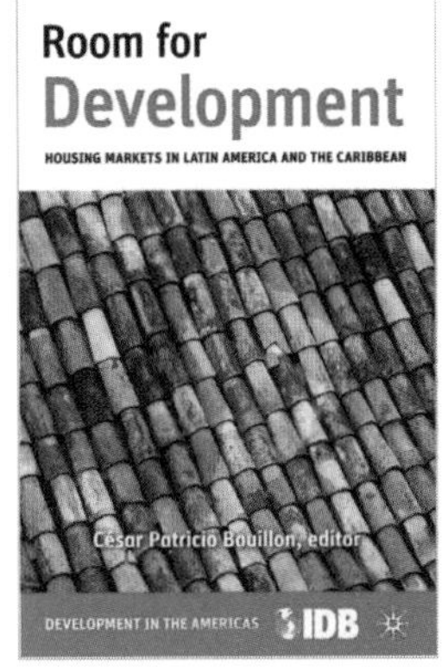

As shown in the figure below, providing basic infrastructure in a slum can cost up to eight times more than providing it on serviced land that has not yet been developed. According to IADB, research from the United States Agency for International Development (USAID) into comparative costs for upgrading settlements shows that if the relative cost factor for unserviced, subdivided blocks and plots is 0.6, then for serviced land it rises to 1.6. This means that, like in Villa El Salvador in Peru, if land is efficiently laid out, it can be easily serviced later, as

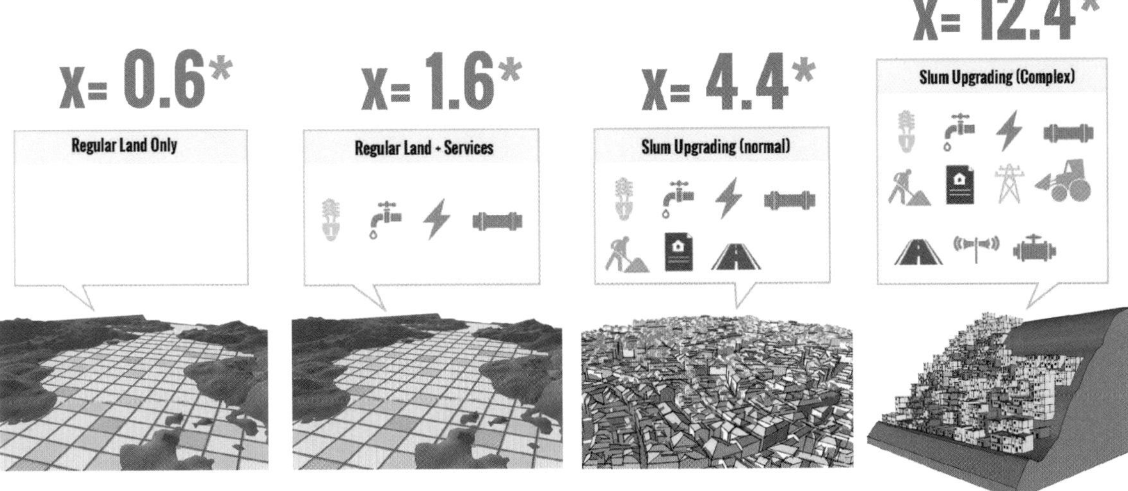

Comparative costs from USAID for ugrading settlements based on different layout and topographical conditions.

Housebuilders are market-takers not market-makers.

—Yolanda Barnes

was the case where the World Bank funded a services programme some years after this land was occupied.

If urban land is not efficiently laid out, the relative cost factor for upgrading services on flatter 'normal' terrain rises to 4.4, and on steeper 'complex' sites, a feature of many Latin American favelas, it could be as high as 12.4. Governments carry the can.

The IADB believes that in order to be cost-effective, governments should also develop strategies and offer subsidies to increase the supply of efficiently laid out urban land, at least, and prevent the formation of slums in the first place.

Boom and bust doesn't build trust

We have tried to replace the role of the big public sector with that of the big private sector, and in doing so we have limited the true potential of the private sector to operate effectively at all levels. Also, somewhere along the line, governments moved from thinking like the public sector to acting like the private sector. Our development models have become shaped around issues of risk and investment and structured around some form of contribution to the public good.

Steve Tolson, in his paper 'The Regeneration Crisis', says that the average competitive dialogue tendering process costs the same as building seventy-five houses or one primary school. Philip Howard in *The Death of Common Sense: How Law Is Suffocating America* says that in America one-third of the capital cost of a project is spent on procurement. With so much focus on reducing risk, the biggest risk is nothing happening.

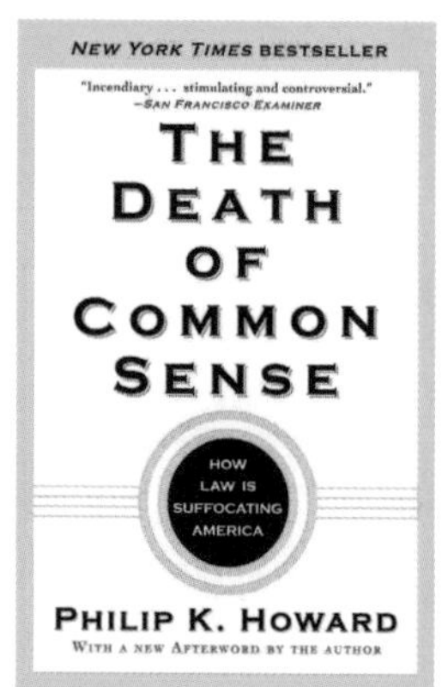

These are universal models that have developed as governments tried to offset their promises to their citizens when times were good and government was big. Today, market forces shape our neighbourhoods as governments retreat. Growth is the measure of success, particularly short-term growth.

But success and failure of urban transformation processes cannot be measured by short-term growth alone. A booming economy with an over-inflated property market can banish all creative energy from the city, making it impossible for young and weak economies to thrive, potentially endangering what one might call 'a sustainable mix'. Both scenarios reveal a crisis in our current top-down systems, which fail, to different degrees, to initiate and direct successful urban change.

While traditional state-initiated planning, design and development is no longer affordable, the radical shift to neo-liberal thinking fails to offer inclusive models that will deliver to our three accepted measures of urban change—competitive cities, stable communities and sustainable development.

Boom and gentrification can lead to social exclusion and an increasingly divided urban society, while the failure of market-driven development to adapt in the context of economic collapse has led to apathy and stagnation. Both wholesale renewal and neglect are symptoms of our crisis.

NEW MODELS FOR TOMORROW'S URBANISM

One of the key drivers of developing new urban models is promoting diversity of provision in our cities, towns and neighbourhoods today. Diversity does not happen by chance but is a result of the nature of housebuilding, entrepreneurship and competition, and of the environments in which they exist. The diversity of provision gives benefits to urban dwellers in a wider range of choice across the full spectrum by offering different routes to solving their housing needs.

Yolanda Barnes, of UK property agency Savills, has undertaken new research into different types of housing provision. In her paper 'New Business Models for Tomorrow's Urbanism', she shows how the top-down 'big capital' concentration model of development is far less successful than the bottom-up landownership and management model. Case studies internationally show the latter achieving up to 30 per cent greater property values. This makes a convincing case for fine-grained neighbourhood formation which is 'varied and messy'.

Barnes's paper also demonstrates how the market is being shifted by changing demographics. The rising economic group of millennials, largely characterised as being members of the new precariat or gig economy, will by 2025 form half the world population and 75 per cent of its workforce. These millennials do not want to live in suburban housing, work in business parks and play out their lives in shopping malls. They are looking for fine-grained, 'varied and messy' neighbourhoods that have authentic, diverse, connected communities, with all the opportunities that come with them. If this is so, why are we still building the unwanted models? As Barnes says, 'Housebuilders are market-takers not market-makers'. The established models of risk and reward are so buried in the banking, public sector procurement and construction industries that, in the absence of being shown any viable alternatives, they will plough on until they fail.

The Berlin townhouse projects, which have their roots in the concepts of Kristien Ring's *Self-made City: Self-Initiated Urban Living and Architectural Interventions* and are based on the disposal of narrow-fronted plots in the city for multi-occupancy buildings, show an alternative. By cutting out the middleman, it is reputed that housing is being delivered much quicker and at a much lower cost than the traditional developer model.

On top of this, it has had far greater social outcomes, better space standards and higher property values. Because of this success, private developers are increasingly using this model as successful low-risk solutions in places like Mitte in central Berlin.

These are models that Barnes's report says we need to scale up and invest in. They build neighbourhoods that people want.

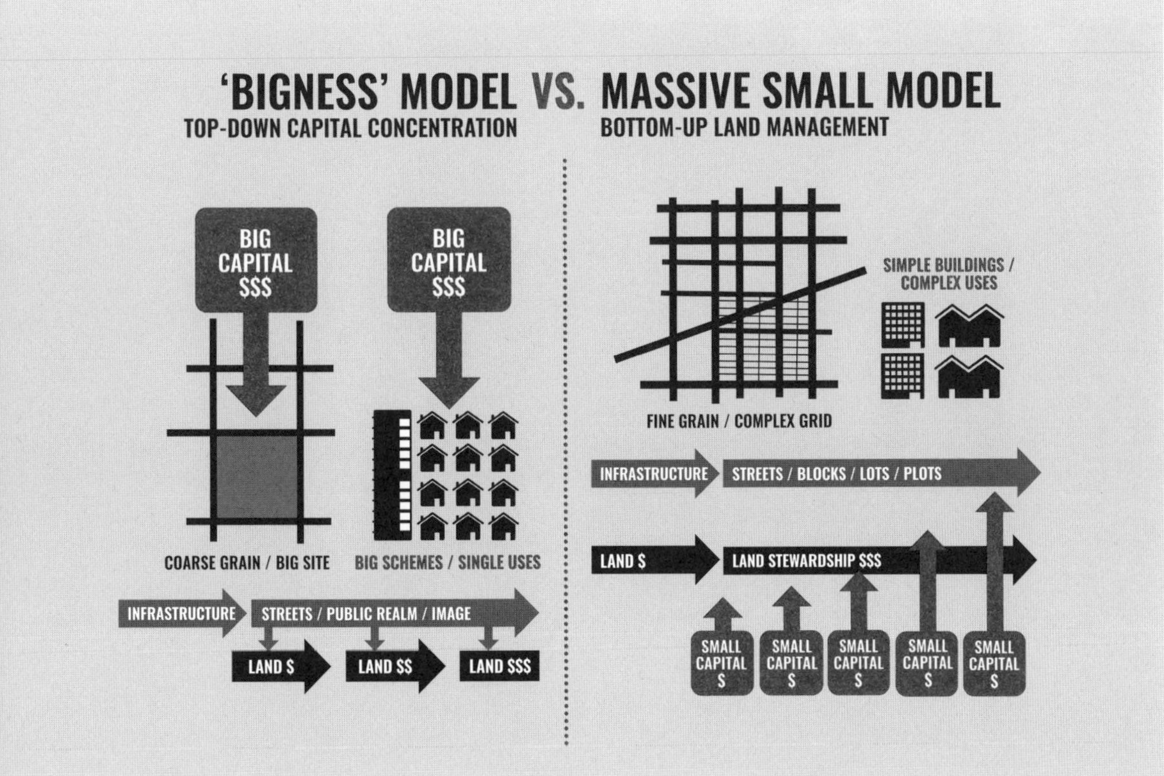

Top: The Berlin townhouse project in Berlin-Mitte, Germany, provides a valuable case study for fine-grained, mixed-use urbanism, delivered by private investment. **Bottom:** Two different models with two different outcomes for urban society.

If we always do what we've always done, we will always get what we've always got.

—Albert Einstein

UNDERSTANDING OUR URBAN **CHANGE DYNAMICS** 1.2

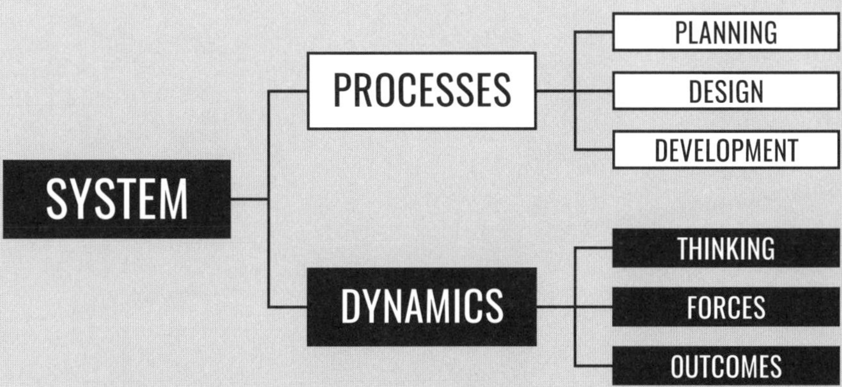

When our footloose forefathers decided to live together and not move on, a process of evolution was set in motion that has led to the most complex of social phenomena: the formation of our urban neighbourhoods, districts and quarters. Underpinning this evolution are basic human dynamics by which people look to provide safety and shelter, to co-exist and to flourish as a community.

> **Dynamics** *NOUN*
>
> 1 the properties that stimulate growth, development or change within a system or process
>
> 2 the various outside forces—physical, social, economic—operating in any field
>
> 3 the way such forces shift or change in relation to one another

The best cities are rich tapestries of urban life, made by many hands. For 300 generations we built places that served us well. In the last three generations we have lost the art of urban evolution. Humans have lived in planned settlements for a long time, so we have a great deal to learn about how they did it, how they learnt from their mistakes and how they became even better at doing it. We have valued this past and look to protect its memory, but we have stopped learning from its experience. Although in many countries this evolution can still be seen, it is happening by default, not by intention.

In exploring the dynamics of urban change, we see three distinct processes that influence how our neighbourhoods are shaped over time:

1. The THINKING that gives rise to our understanding of how we deal with the city as a complex adaptive system
2. The FORCES that act on the system as a result of this thinking, and the complex interrelationship between these forces
3. The OUTCOMES of applying this thinking in the context of any an increasingly bottom-up, local and complex world

Cities are not problems. They are solutions.

—Jaime Lerner

IT'S NOT THAT WE THINK, IT'S HOW WE THINK!

Everything we hear is opinion, not fact. Everything we see is perspective, not truth.

—Marcus Aurelius

So how did we think we could control something as complex as a city? In our developed world over the past three generations we have arrested the process of urban evolution. We have forgotten how to do it for ourselves. So we have lost the ability to build successful human habitats. Our current plans treat the city as an ordered, mechanical system where every variable must be entirely understood and managed, painstakingly controlled and legalistically prescribed for.

REDUCTIONISM—A CRIME AGAINST URBANITY

Cities are victims of outdated thinking. Narrow reductionist thought processes linger under the influence of the pseudosciences, drawing from past philosophies that have little relevance today. We celebrate the good intentions of the two movements that in the twentieth century set about reshaping urban life—garden cities and modernism. We mourn their faded dreams and regret the malign influence they exert from beyond the grave.

Ebenezer Howard's garden city movement wrote off the Victorian industrial city as a dead end. Howard's big—and brilliant—idea was to create new settlements whose people would themselves, collectively, benefit from the increased land values that urbanism brings to rural sites. As for the physical form of garden cities, Ebenezer Howard looked to them to be clean, green and airy, in contrast to the old industrial cities he abhorred. Low densities and the separation of industry from housing would do the trick. Within a few years the garden city movement had grown into the town planning movement, its founder's visionary hopes of radical land reform forgotten. Ever since, the residual suburban vision has remained one of the planners' favourite templates.

CIAM (Congrès Internationaux d'Architecture Moderne) and the garden city movement served as the foundations for a succession of ideological

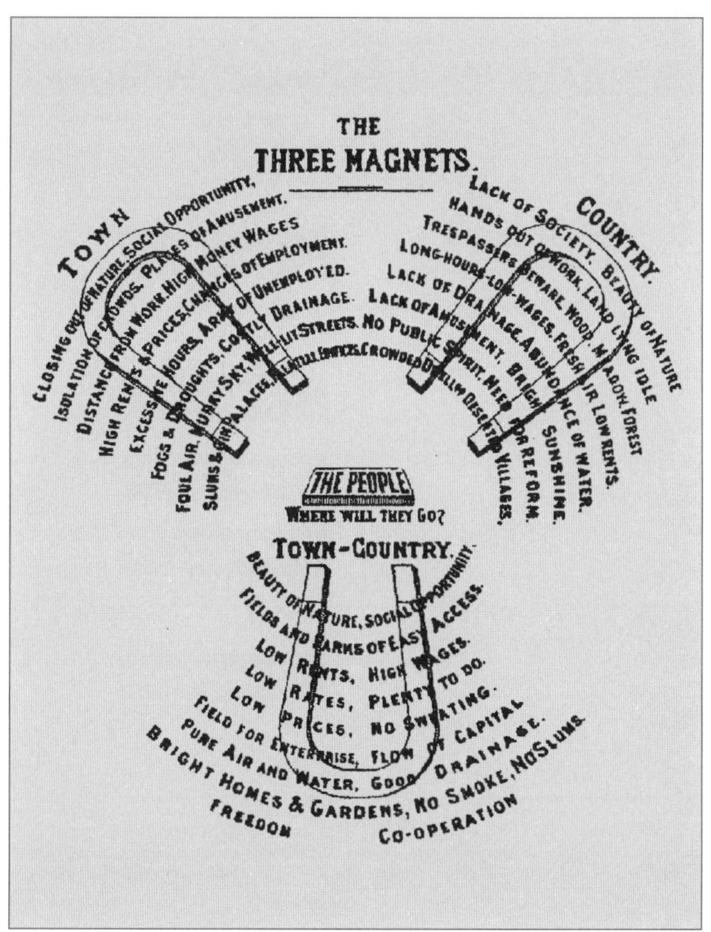

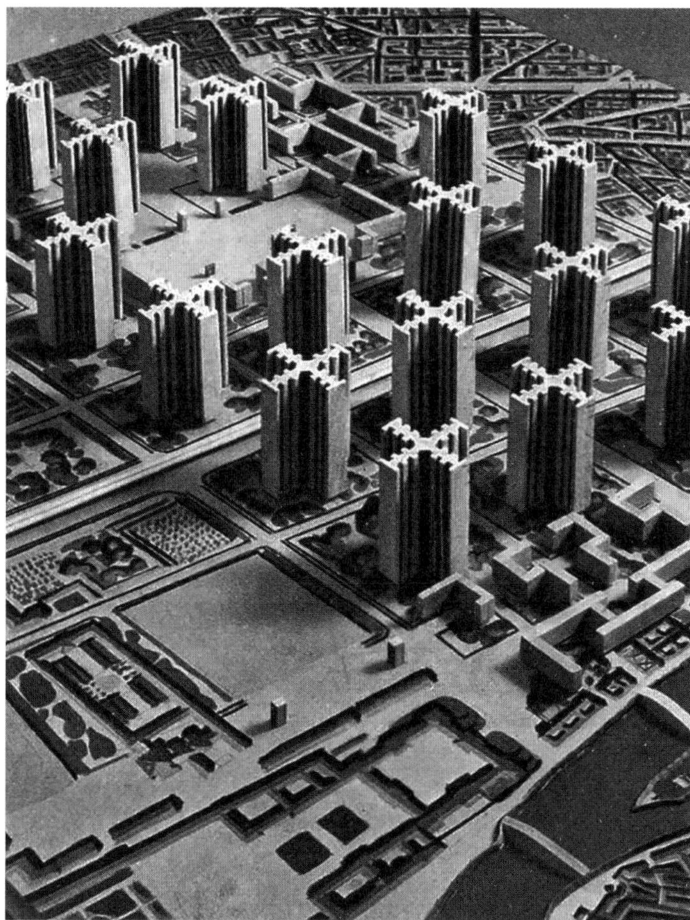

This page, left: Ebenezer Howard's three magnets diagram that defined the garden city. **Right:** Le Corbusier's plan for Voisin, Paris.

battles over the years. Modernists against traditionalists. Architects against planners. Grid layouts against meandering roads. Ideological? Perhaps not. For all their vehemence, these were family squabbles. CIAM and the garden city movement were two sides of the same coin. Both had it in for cities, and with them our urban neighbourhoods.

The two movements shared a conviction that the street-based city with districts of mixed uses had no future. Yet for both of them the concept of the city did mean something important. Ebenezer Howard called for 'garden cities', not garden suburbs. Le Corbusier called his concept the 'radiant city', not the radiant parkscape. For all their hatred of the cities they saw around them, both CIAM and the garden city movement valued something in the concept of the city. Unfortunately, that something was the baby they threw out with the bathwater.

Cities have a wonderful ability to renew themselves—if we let them. For a hundred years we have handicapped them in our search for utopian forms, whether garden city or modernist. Rationalism, scientific reasoning and abstract thought have let us down. In the words of Vaclav Havel: 'The era of absolutist reason is drawing to a close. It is high time to draw conclusions from that fact.'

Every theory claims its own truths, even if it is not very different from last year's theory. Indoctrinated by the scientific method, we pose hypotheses, analyse, apply our new theories and synthesise. The absolute truth provides an unshakeable basis for practice—until the next theory comes along. We cannot follow this traditional scientific model or,

Reductionism *NOUN*

In PHILOSOPHY and related subjects, the process whereby CONCEPTS or statements that apply to one type of entity are defined in terms of concepts, or analysed in terms of statements, of another kind, normally one regarded as more elementary or more basic. Reduction is seldom an uncontentious activity, and to list some of the many varieties of reductionism (which may be contrasted with HOLISM) is to list a series of controversies. The reductionist sometimes justifies his activity as a principle of economy in EXPLANATION, a principle that has obviously paid off in science.

—From *The Dictionary of Modern Thought*

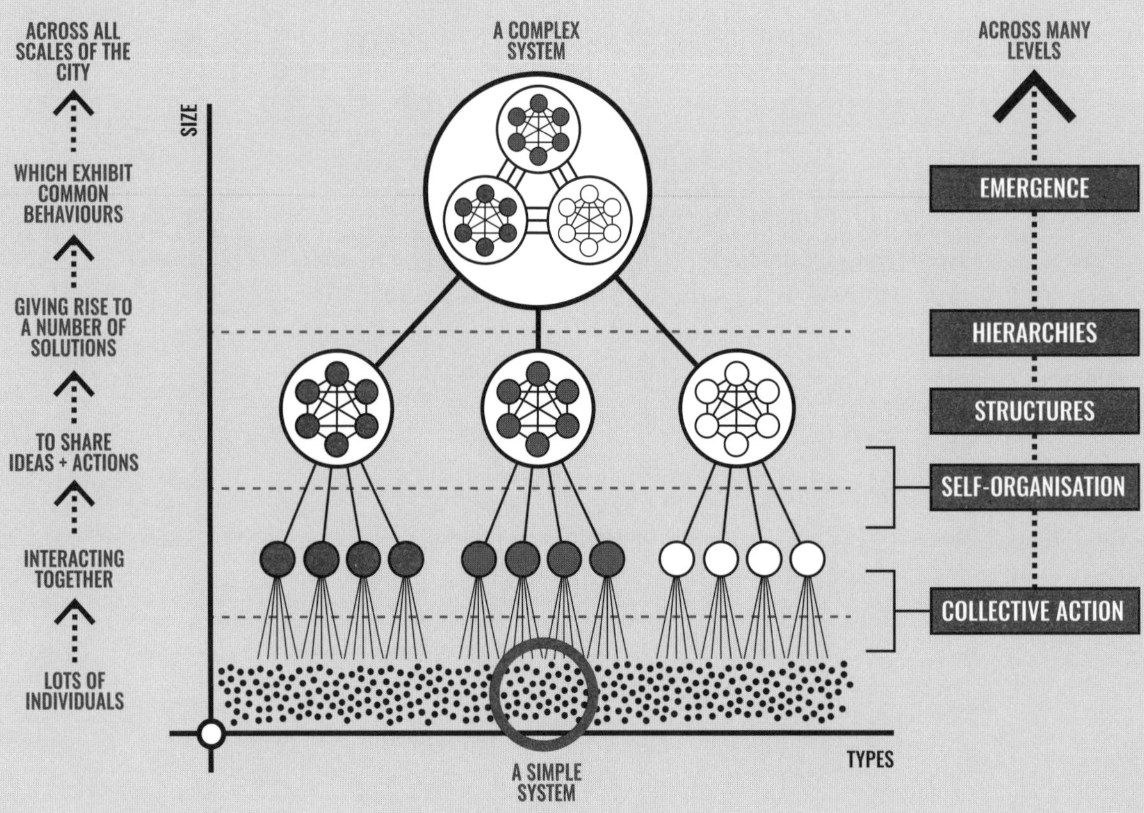

in our world, the predict-and-provide approach to shaping our urban end states. The idea that we can deal with complexity by setting different trajectories to catch up or influence physical outcomes in cities has never worked. As soon as we implement a new fix, it is out of date.

> *Every civilisation has had its irrational but reassuring myth. Previous civilisations have used their culture to sing about it and tell stories about it. Ours has used its mathematics to prove it.*
>
> —David Fleming

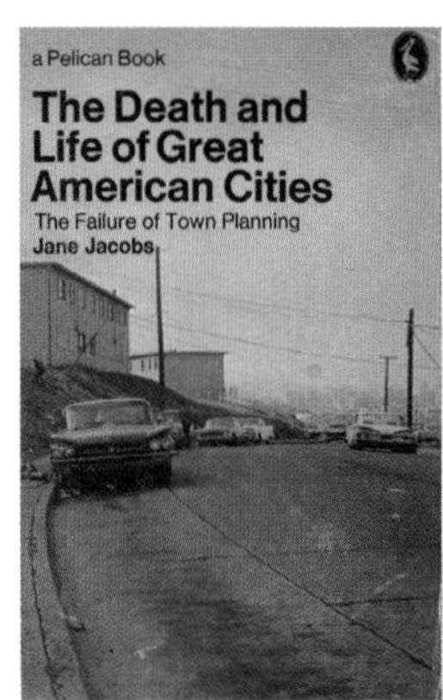

Creating good urbanism is not a matter of connecting isolated sets of abstract theories or rules. It is about seeing the whole picture and rediscovering the art of building cities. It depends on recognising cities as complex, highly evolved and open/adaptive, responsive and collaborative environments. Their inevitable conflicts do not always need to be resolved: good urbanism is a matter of managing their interaction.

PROBLEMS IN ORGANISED COMPLEXITY

Cities consist of vast numbers of interrelated agents and factors. These create an unrivalled richness and diversity of possibilities, but also—like all complex systems—situations that are highly unpredictable and hard to manage. So how did we think we could control something as complex as a city?

> *Cities [are] problems in organised complexity, like the life sciences...city areas with flourishing diversity sprout strange and unpredictable uses and peculiar scenes. But this is not a drawback of diversity. This is the point...of it.*
>
> —Jane Jacobs

A classic exposition of the implications of the phenomenon of 'organised complexity' for city planners and urban designers was made by Jane Jacobs in her landmark book *The Death and Life of Great American Cities*. It is difficult to overstate its influence on the planning discipline in general, and on subsequent thinking about generative processes in particular. As Michael Mehaffy says, 'When you are looking for a great quote, the great old lady is always there to oblige.'

In talking about 'the kind of problem a city is', Jacobs lucidly analysed the implications of the scientific advancement—in particular, the understanding of complex systems in which some factors were interrelated into an organic whole. This was important for urbanists because they needed to be sure they were thinking about the right kind of problem and using the right tools to solve it.

Organising complexity is now a growing subject. In many spheres of life, new research and development have given us different ways of looking at complex issues—giving us new ideas, tools and operating systems to deal with their complexity. In areas such as business, economics, computational studies and social networks, we can see how multiple agents, working collectively within a framework of simple rules, can bring about phenomenal change. We can draw on principles from other complex phenomena—from how Ebola spreads, how traffic works in Delhi, how fans behave at football matches or how stock markets behave.

There is far more outside the discipline of urbanism than we could ever imagine. We just have to learn how we can apply these essential principles to neighbourhood formation.

In defining the term *complexity*, theorists often refer to systems that are composed of many parts. It is certainly true that complexity usually arises when a system consists of many interconnected parts. However, the number of parts is not an absolute guide. Large systems are sometimes very simple in their structure and behaviour. On the other hand, some systems with very simple structures behave in very complicated and unpredictable ways.

Here are three different descriptions of complexity from three different people:

1 The state of being composed of many interconnected parts

> *In a complex system, a large number of independent elements interact. The system acquires collective properties of its own—a life of its own, you might say—through those elements clashing with or accommodating each other. As the system becomes more complex, new collective properties emerge, and new ways of understanding them need to be found. Small events can result in unexpectedly large changes. It is the structure of the networks that we must understand, not their details. The structures can be understood only as being constantly in transition as they respond to ever-changing conditions. Influencing complex systems is a matter of managing change, not of achieving equilibrium. A system in equilibrium is one in which its elements have ceased to interact. Apart from somewhere like Pompeii, that is a condition not found in cities.*
>
> —Rob Cowan

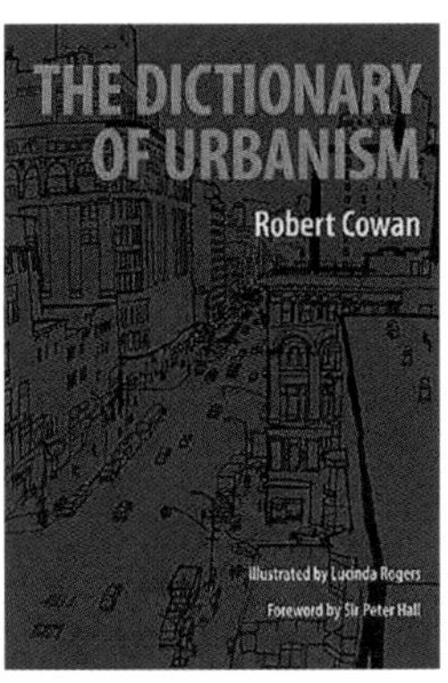

2 A global order built out of local interactions

> *Complexity is a word that has frequently appeared in critical accounts of metropolitan space, but there are two kinds of complexity fundamental to the city, two experiences with very different implications for the individuals trying to make sense of them. There is, first, the more conventional sense of complexity as sensory overload, the city stretching the human nervous system to its very extremes, and in the process teaching it a new series of reflexes—and leading the way for a complementary series of aesthetic values which develop out like a scab around the original wound. But complexity is not solely a matter of sensory overload. There is also the sense of complexity as a self-organising system. This sort of complexity lives up one level: it describes the system of the city itself and not its experiential reception by the city dweller. The city is complex because it overwhelms, yes, but also because it has a coherent personality, a personality that self-organises out of millions of individual decisions, a global order built out of local interactions.*
>
> —Steven Johnson

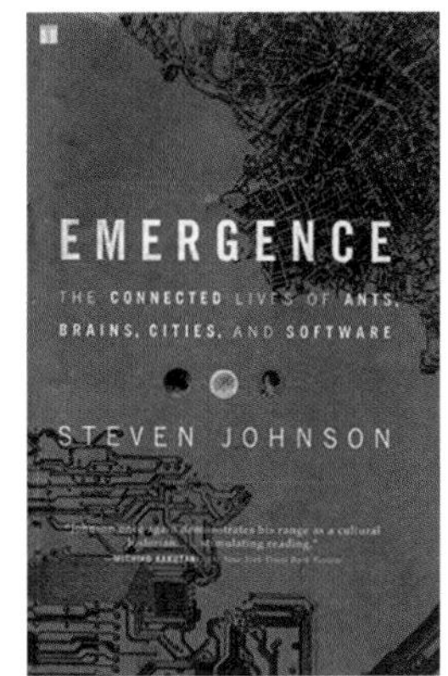

3 Complex contexts: the fertile domain of emergence

> *In a complicated context, at least one right answer exists. In a complex context, however, right answers can't be ferreted out. It's like the difference between, say, a Ferrari and the Brazilian rainforest. Ferraris are complicated machines, but an expert mechanic can take one apart and reassemble it without changing a thing. The car is static, and the whole is the sum of its parts. The rainforest, on the other hand, is in constant flux—a species becomes extinct, weather patterns change, an agricultural project reroutes a water source—and the whole is far more than the sum of its parts. This is the realm of 'unknown unknowns,' and it is the domain to which much of contemporary business has shifted.*
>
> —David Snowden

EMERGENT SYSTEMS

A lot has been written in recent years about emergence. Some regard it as a pseudoscience, a kind of hippy invention to tear down the walls of the establishment's reductionist ivory towers. Certainly, evidence shows that many articles have been written that start well but, challenged with showing how emergence can be applied, dissolve into soft, fuzzy focus and dodgy architectural constructs. Some have even said that emergence undermines the meaning and agenda of the science of complexity, which is a real science. They are probably right, and we have been so caught up in the metaphors and psychedelia of the fractal geometries, the kaleidoscopic patterns and the sinister slime moulds that characterise emergence that we cannot see its true worth in influencing how we think of cities and their districts, neighbourhoods and quarters. We are wasting a good science.

Out of intense complexities, intense simplicities emerge.

—Winston Churchill

Others have used emergent thinking in urban design theory to meaningfully explain unintended consequences and novel patterns of city growth and neighbourhood formation, but much of this lies in the academic cyberspace. For many theorists, such as Christopher Alexander, it has been used to explain the evolution of spontaneous settlements in third world conditions, to good effect. Whatever the perspective, the fact remains that not much has been written about the application of emergence in the first world, other than with regard to historical processes. This does not mean that emergence is not relevant to the first world. Its scarcity is most likely because the first world has had the most evolved top-down systems of control, which has prevented any form of emergence. There was no audience. A move to localism opens up the potential for a change towards emergence.

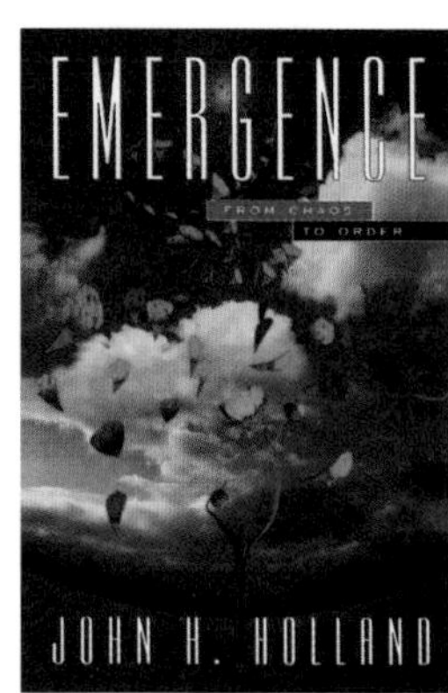

What are the qualities of emergent systems?

1 Emergent systems can be good innovators

It is now well recognised that emergent systems tend to be more adaptable to sudden change than our more rigid hierarchical models. These qualities make the possibilities of bottom-up intelligence tantalising for towns and cities struggling to keep up with rapid change. Bottom-up systems lend themselves to adaptive self-organisation, and we can learn from some sources where this has been effective—from cities and nature to the Web.

2 Emergent systems are unpredictable

Emergent systems display fluctuating outcomes. They can give rise to 'perpetual' or 'radical' novelty, a property that displays new features not previously observed. This makes sense—if you allow for an individual response, prepare to be surprised. We should not be scared of these outcomes but embrace them. Unpredictability is where innovation happens.

3 Emergent systems create regularity

On the other hand, something else arises that totally contradicts what might be expected from this freedom of expression—that of 'regularity', a property characterised as having persistent, recurring structures, patterns and themes. This contradiction could be explained in informal squatter settlements where, despite having the freedom to build what they want, people build remarkably similar things in conventional ways. In fact, many squatter settlements display a dominance of regularities. So in emergent systems, freedom is not always freely taken.

4 Emergent systems are hierarchical

Another important contradiction and consequence of emergence is the tendency of individuals to group into hierarchical organisations. John Holland, in his book *Emergence: From Chaos to Order*, cites this as one of the important conditions needed to foster emergence. Hierarchies are common in complex systems. They usually arise either from the organisation of systems on different scales (for example, in communities) or from interactions that impose order on the agents that comprise a system. Hierarchies ensure total connectivity but limit interactions (and hence complexity) between links up and down the hierarchy. So, in urban design, this means that hierarchical spatial structures and networks are preconditions to organic growth and change.

5 Emergent systems have generative rules

Traditional science has tended to focus on simple cause-effect relationships. Complexity science posits simple causes for complex effects. At the core of complexity science is the assumption that complexity in the world arises from simple rules. However, these rules (which are termed *generative rules*) are unlike the rules (or laws) of traditional science. Generative rules typically determine how a set of agents will behave in their virtual environment over time, including the interaction with other agents.

The emergence of places showing horizontal growth followed by vertical growth.

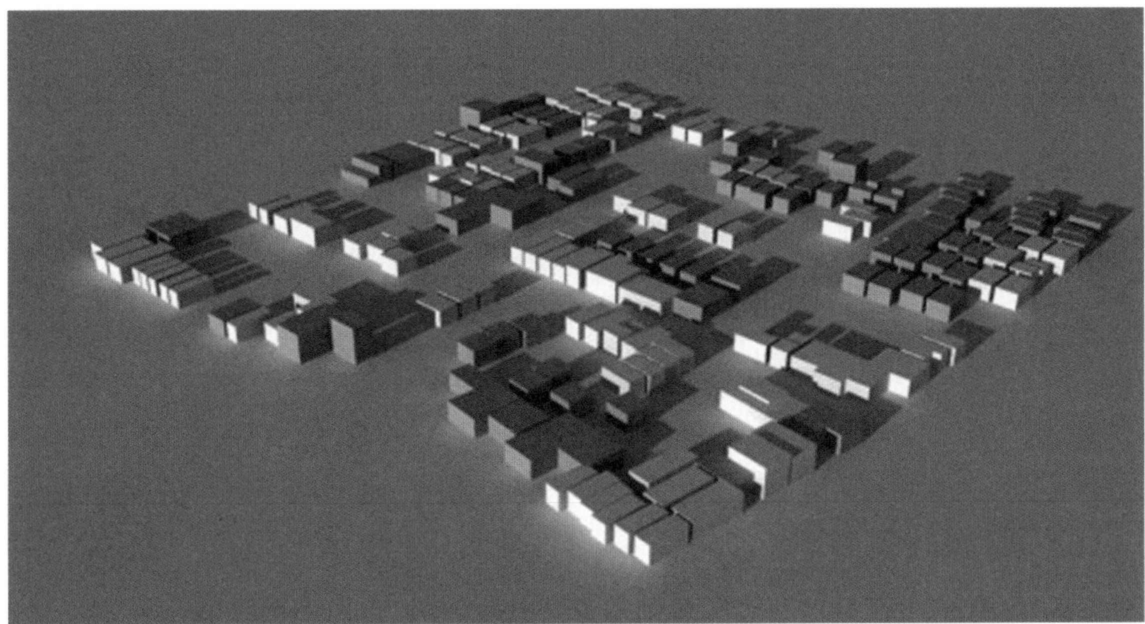

Think of cities not as artefacts, but as systems built more like organisms than as machines.

—Michael Batty

6 Emergent systems use feedback loops
Unlike traditional science, emergent systems do not predict an outcome for every state of the world. Instead, generative rules use feedback and learning to enable us to adapt to our environment over time. The application of these generative rules to a large population leads to emergent behaviour that may bear some resemblance to real-world phenomena. Finding a set of generative rules that can mimic real-world behaviour may help scientists predict, manage or explain hitherto unfathomable systems (such as cities and their districts, neighbourhoods and quarters).

Urbanists and software designers have been experimenting with models that can simulate the ways that cities self-organise themselves over time. While actual cities are heavily shaped by top-down forces, such as planning policy and planning committees, we have long recognised that bottom-up forces play a critical role in city formation, creating distinct neighbourhoods and other unplanned demographic clusters. In recent years, some theorists have developed more precise models that re-create the neighbourhood-formation process with some precision.

LEAN THINKING

David Fleming in his dictionary, *Lean Logic*, defines lean thinking as a frame of reference for enabling people to join together in the shared aim. People are set up with the necessary resources, the skills and equipment, a common purpose, and the freedom to apply their judgement. The threads running through every entry are Fleming's analysis of how our present market-based economy is destroying the very foundations—ecological, economic and cultural—on which it depends, and his core focus: a compelling, grounded vision for a cohesive society that might weather the consequences. A society that provides a satisfying, culturally rich context for lives well lived, in an economy not reliant on the impossible promise of eternal economic growth.

Lean thinking brings to life the imagination and tenacity of the people; it transforms the quality of decisions; it is flexible; it sets out conditions for alert feedback: it makes the needs of the system quickly apparent, responding to the local and real rather than to a distant caricature.

—David Fleming

SO WHAT DOES THIS MEAN?

The greatest practical problem in dealing with complexity is how to analyse, interpret and manage real systems. Complexity theory does provide some sobering lessons that planners need to heed. One lesson is that complex processes are often inherently unpredictable. This makes it difficult to anticipate the precise effects of many planning strategies. Moreover, unexpected events become highly likely. It also means that the world can no longer afford ad hoc approaches to planning and development.

Traditional methods of analysis and interpretation do not work for complex systems. The need to understand and manage complex systems has led to many active areas of research that attempt to devise methods for dealing with them. These new methods constitute entire new paradigms. An important part of this process is using effective mechanisms to narrow choices—something evolved societies have always done. Without a limiting of choice, self-organisation stalls.

Dee Hock shows a diagram of two overlapping circles arranged on a spectrum from chaos to order—one end has 'destructive despair' and the other, 'stifling control'. At the overlap is the 'sweet spot of generative emergence'.

We are not starting from a clean slate. In most of the world, urban society is not operating in a state of 'destructive despair', or if it is, it does not stay like this for long. Our systems have evolved to a point where some form of order has emerged. In other places, we have gone well beyond this to Dee Hock's 'stifling control'. Rigid conformity—or 'stifling control'—has now become a dominant characteristic of our current processes of planning, design and development worldwide, and this constrains creativity, innovation and evolution.

The real prospects of change lie in moving our thinking back to the 'sweet spot of generative emergence', which lies at the overlap of chaos and order.

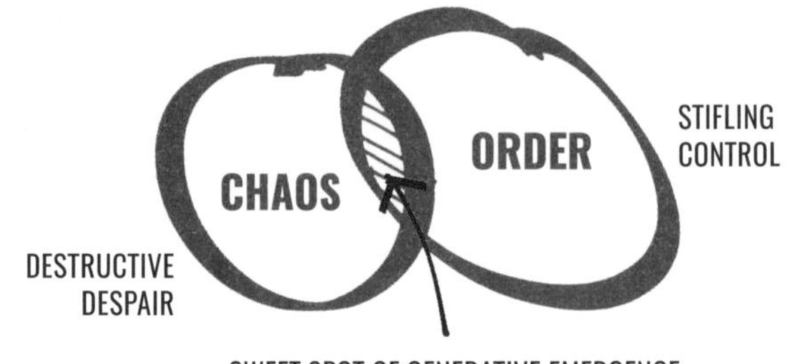

Researchers have used simulation games to explore further the idea that spatial laws shape behaviours through self-organisation processes. This is perfectly evident in, say, traffic movement in places like Delhi, India.

THE FORCES ACTING ON URBAN CHANGE

The ways in which neighbourhoods form, cities are shaped, and urban society evolves can be seen in the complex interrelationships between three different elements of change and the forces they exert on and use to influence each other:

1. **PURPOSE (what we are looking to achieve?)**
2. **INTELLIGENCE (what are the accepted ways of doing things?)**
3. **POWER (where does the act of will lie to make it happen?)**

Each of these elements has varied dimensions that are often projected as opposing forces with extreme positions being taken to demonstrate a theory, but this projection is wrong. In being presented like a pendulum, only swinging left or right, each becomes a destructive force when it reaches its extremes. We tend to choose to look only at a few of these dynamics and discard others and then wonder why all goes wrong. We forget the interrelationships of these elements and the effect they have on each other. They are often mutually supporting, and we will often need a dose of each. We need to shift from pendulum thinking to seeing the solutions within a spectrum of possibilities. These elements are perspectives or dimensions within the same sphere of influence, and we can view them in different ways. One way is to see them as three sliders on a graphic equaliser, instead of as on/off buttons. As we slide the control towards one end, we are reducing the impact of the other side. We are not switching it off, and, as is true in most good music, we have elements of both sides of the equaliser. We can also see a number of further perspectives acting like forces on these dimensions and jostling for superiority.

Or we can see them as invisible magnets that get charged up as ideas, philosophies and policies shift, unpredictably pulling the sliders in different directions. They raise many questions, which this project will attempt to answer, over time.

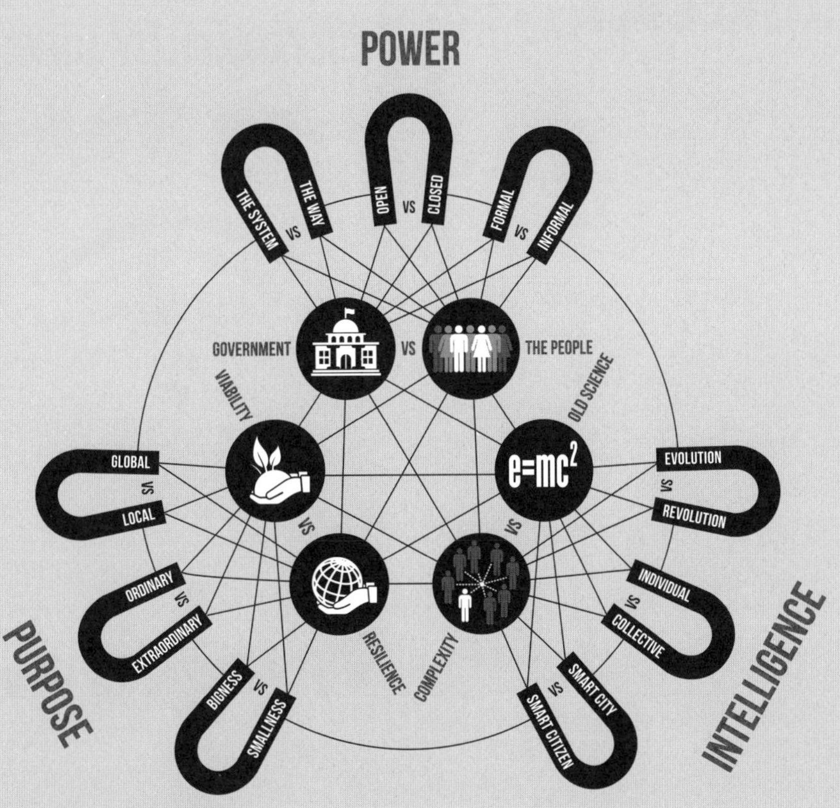

The diagram alongside displays, as an illustration, many of the dimensions and perspectives that act on the formation of neighbourhoods. If any magnet gets stronger, it exerts stronger forces on the others creating an imbalance in the system.

Let us look at each of these dimensions and these perspectives in more in detail.

1 PURPOSE

The purpose in making urban change lies somewhere within the dimensions of VIABILITY and RESILIENCE, and each of these raises further questions. Are we building something new (a viable human habitat) or are we fixing something that is broken (a better human habitat to withstand the shocks of change)? In the words of Frederick Douglass, are we 'building strong children or mending broken men'? In most places we are working somewhere within the spectrum of both—making things both viable and resilient.

The further perspectives that act on viability and resilience are:

a **Global versus local.** What is our viewpoint of the problem? Are we looking from out there or from down here? We often hear the adage, 'think global, act local'. Sometimes thinking about it from so far away means you do not know how to act at the other end of the spectrum.

b **Ordinary versus extraordinary.** What do we hope to do? Is this about building the ordinary or making the special? If everything is special, everything becomes ordinary. We need to focus on how we can structure the ordinary so we can create the conditions for the special.

c **Bigness versus smallness.** What is the scale of action? Are we looking to make a major change or is it about a minor change? Or are few doing it for many or many doing it for fewer? For us, big can also be the combination of many small actions. That is why we call it Massive Small.

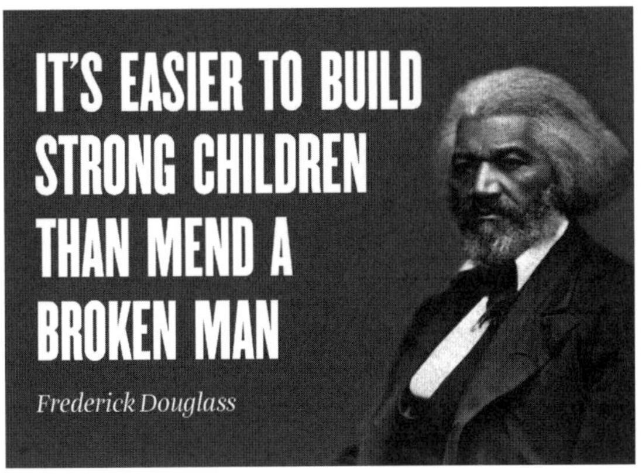

IT'S EASIER TO BUILD
STRONG CHILDREN
THAN MEND A
BROKEN MAN
Frederick Douglass

VIABILITY AND RESILIENCE IN A COMPLEX WORLD

THINK LOCAL, ACT LOCAL: THINK GLOBAL, ACT GLOBAL

The Massive Small project is set within the agenda of promoting urban sustainability. This agenda suffers from being driven by a top-down perspective. Here, our governments and corporates are our prime targets, and we are encouraged to 'think global, act local'. Unfortunately, promoting urban sustainability has little or no traction when it touches on the behaviour of the individual. This is because it uses abstract and emotive models that start with the planets and are then beamed downwards through a filter of environmentalism. By the time the signal reaches the individual, it is distorted or lost. There is too much noise. As thinking takes place at the 'global' level, we just don't know how to 'act local'. So we get frustrated, resort to partial approaches or continue to behave in the same bad old way, sometimes just offsetting our bad actions with something good. The planning system, which seeks to influence how we 'act local', also finds it hard to respond, so it resorts to technical fixes, demanding some form of mitigation, or it applies ineffectual policies—often blindly promoting other policies that work against the overriding purpose of sustainability. Considering it is such an important issue, we are struggling to find a way!

This project looks to provide a counterpoint to the 'sustainability' agenda by putting the human element at the heart of the discussion. Most people wish to live their lives in a better way: travelling less, buying local, saving resources, having a greater sense of community and a greater control over their future. With the right tools, people acting in a collective bottom-up manner can be our prime agents of change. At the local level, the behaviour change signal will be strong. Through the filter of successful compact urbanism (our cities and towns and their neighbourhoods), we can then beam the message upwards to the wider environment. We 'think local and act local', and in this way we 'change global'. We call this the 'viability' agenda. In this context, a viable system is any system organised in such a way as to meet the demands of surviving in the changing environment. One of the prime features of systems that survive is that they are adaptable and are capable of maintaining themselves or recovering their potentialities. All we need to do is focus on creating the conditions that will enable a viable human habitat to emerge and the desired outcomes will flow for our natural habitat and for our planet.

Put the 'sustainability' and 'viability' agendas together and we have a powerful signal across the full spectrum from local to global. Abstract models working with agent-based models will make the real difference.

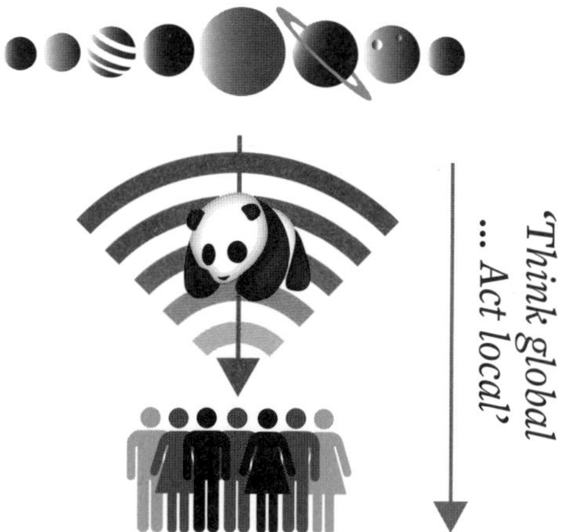

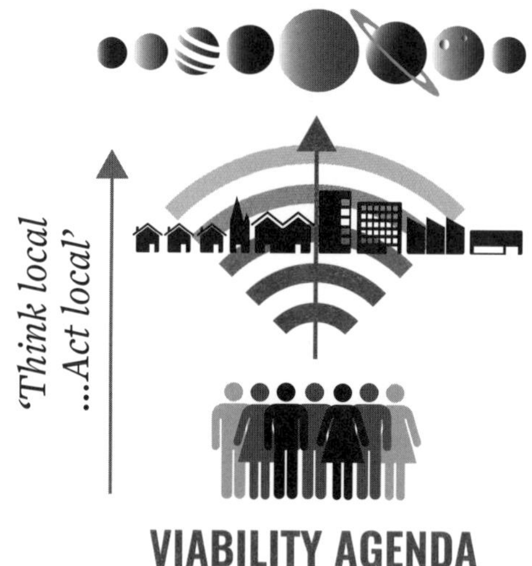

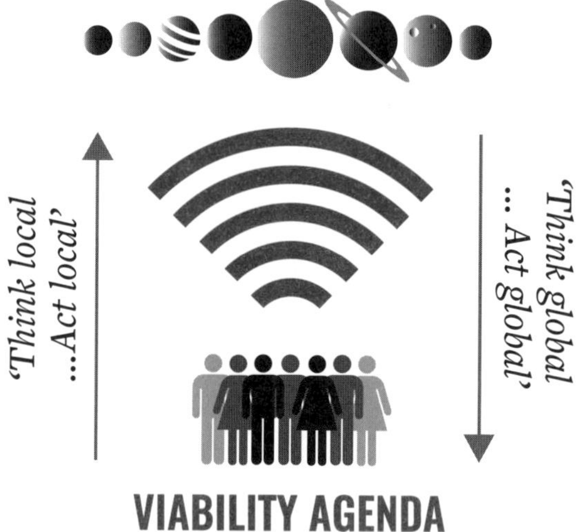

2 INTELLIGENCE

The intelligence we use to make a successful urban change (the truth we can rely on) lies somewhere in OLD SCIENCE and COMPLEXITY.

Are we talking about reductionism, where we take things to pieces and look at their parts, or is it about holism, where we see the whole as the sum of the parts? Is it about complex adaptive systems or those systems that can be perfectly rationalised? Is it about abstract models of science or agent-based models? How do we reconcile the forces of chaos and those of order? What is the truth and is it always absolute? What is the role of collaborative intelligence or collective wisdom in this process? Clearly, the truth lies in here somewhere. We need to find it.

The further perspectives that act on old science and complexity are:

a **Evolution versus revolution.** How do we see change? Is it about gradual progressive change, or do we make a wide-sweeping radical change? Do we make small shifts and continuously monitor their effects or do we make big moves and review them over a longer period? Do we start from first principles or do we start from where we are? Do we manage in the present or do we look to predict an uncertain future?

b **Open versus closed systems.** How open are we to challenge? How resistant are we to change? We know that our urban systems are closed. We cannot challenge them, we can only challenge the decisions that come from them. No system is perfectly open, so the big question is: what are the limits to openness we need to explore?

c **Smart city versus smart citizen.** Where do we invest our smartness? Do we focus on smart citizens or smart cities? Is it about technical innovation or social innovation? There is an increasing view that big data is with us to stay, so how do we harness it in different ways? Why does it always become the instrument of the big guys? Why can't it become the driver for big society?

3 POWER

Power lies in the complex interrelationship between the GOVERNMENT and the PEOPLE. This is where the act of will to create urban change lies.

The sliding switch on a graphic equaliser is never fully on 'government' and never fully on 'the people', but is somewhere in the bandwidth between. It all depends on whether the government is interventionist or noninterventionist, or whether its citizens are active or passive. Its sweet spot lies in the democratisation of urbanism—where people and governments work collaboratively in the collective interests of community: where the strengths of each are deployed for maximum effect. The further perspectives that act on governments and people are:

d **The system versus the way.** This where we get our instructions for change. Are we told how to do it (the system) or do we learn from experience (the way)? In the sphere of government, it is our top-down systems of planning, design and development that determine how we move forwards. In bottom-up activity, the ways—the norms, conventions, traditions, mores—that have evolved over time enable the way forwards. In time we need the system to *be* the way.

e **Individual versus collective.** What is our attitude to collaboration? Are we building a system that promotes the rights of the individual or the collective interests of the community? Is it about exclusivity or inclusivity? Are we going it alone or together? In the suburban condition, we can facilitate individual action. In the urban condition, the only way is collaboration. People need people.

Complexity excites the mind, and order rewards it.

—Diane Ackerman

f **Formal versus informal.** Where do we fit into the system? Are we in it or out of it? For many people worldwide, their future, socially and economically, lies outside any formal systems. As places emerge, formality creeps in. How do we deal with this transitioning process? How do we change the nature of formality to embrace the energy and creativity that comes out of informal actions? How do we fast-track informal change?

In essence, we do not have just three sliders on our graphic equaliser. We have a whole sound desk. It is like a musical cacophony of many voices and instruments that need to be finely managed to create harmony. Moving any of these sliders has an effect on the others. Some become louder, and others change the tone. In cities, this fine tuning can only be managed in the present. People make the music. Governments smooth out the inequalities in the system. Is this is what we mean by bottom-up and top-down? What is this relationship?

TOP-DOWN MEETS BOTTOM-UP

The Massive Small project focusses on the relationship between top-down and bottom-up systems of change. Ultimately it looks to show how top-down systems can be evolved to release the potential of bottom-up activity by all actors in the system.

THE OUTCOME OF THINKING AND FORCES

There is increasing understanding of how bottom-up systems, in difficult conditions of complexity, display a remarkable ability to innovate.

At the same time, top-down systems have real power to enable. We also need to recognise that bottom-up systems don't work without some form of top-down activity. The real question, in thinking differently, is what type of behaviours do we need in these top-down systems?

Top-down systems and bottom-up systems share the same structuring characteristics.

Change from the top down happens at the will and whim of those at the bottom.

—Peter Block

They both have:

→ **IDEAS.** This includes all forms of thinking, ideologies, theories and learnt pearls of wisdom that can be applied to solving the problem.

→ **TOOLS.** This includes all applications, techniques, methods and developed practices to turn ideas into action on the ground.

→ **TACTICS.** This includes all management styles, control mechanisms, agreed behaviours and organisational systems to control or enable.

WHAT IS A TOP-DOWN SYSTEM?

A top-down system has one or more agents who fully understand the system. The process starts by working from the general to the specific. These agents are capable of representing the whole system in an overall strategy that they can store as a policy or a plan, using it to take command and control the outcome. In our world, a top-down system denotes a model of

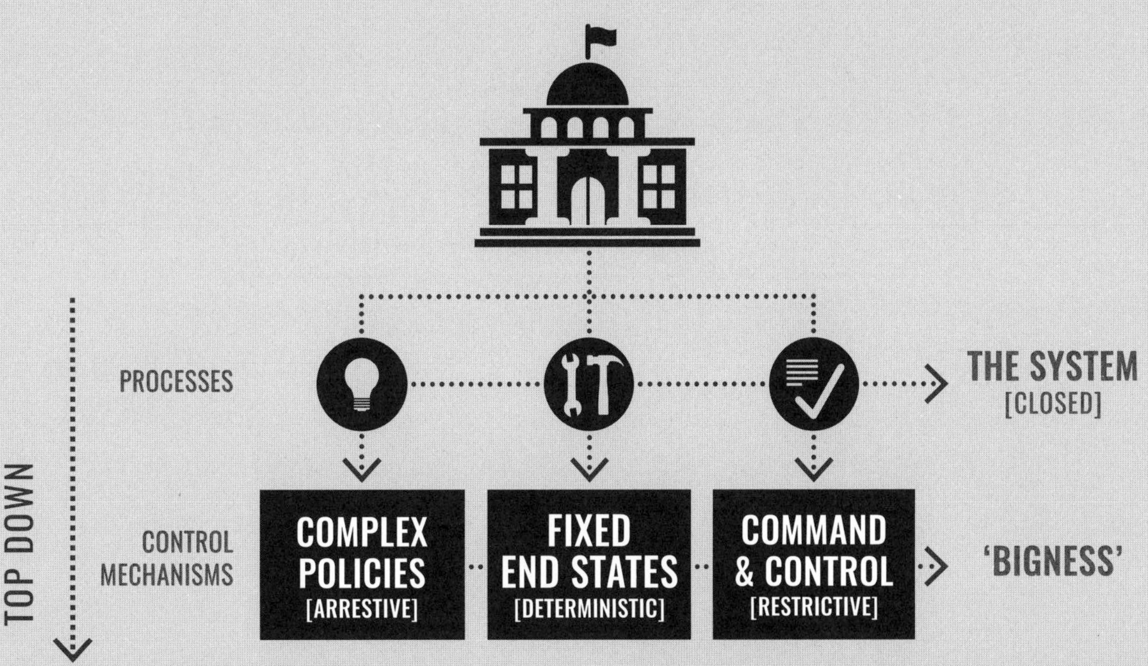

government or management in which actions and policies are initiated at the highest level and sent downwards to the lower levels of the hierarchy, who are, to a greater or lesser extent, bound by them.

→ **Top-down ideas in urbanism are largely shaped by the utopian visions of the past century and tinkered with over time as other issues such as sustainability raised their heads.** Many ideas were created at a time when big government and big thinking were thought to be needed to solve big problems of the time. Driven by these visions, they have promoted simple behaviours, treating neighbourhoods, quarters and centres as mechanistic elements of the city. This thinking is now deeply embedded in rigid definitive policies that provide a blanket approach to how we look at cities. Uniform and all-embracing, they are like the standard operating procedures for anywhere. The outcome is a set of complex policies that are difficult to comprehend and use. The rules have become so complex that they stifle innovation and arrest urban evolution.

→ **Top-down tools look to operationalise these policies and turn them into action—development frameworks, area action plans, design codes—all designed to predetermine every outcome.** Our place-making models, meant to predict and plan perfect, fixed end states with absolute certainty, force us down the narrow corridors of conformity. The outcome is fixed solutions that are rigidly deterministic and leave little wriggle room for trying different things.

→ **Top-down tactics are command-and-control, which is restrictive.** In this world, people cannot be trusted to do the right thing. There is no room for experimentation, creativity or learning. Do it our way or else! As long as you follow the rules, individualism triumphs over collective action. This system, which was developed to counter the forces of the big players, has ironically become a game that only the big guys can play. This command-and-control planning is reactive and restricting. The unintended consequence is bigness: big sites, big players, big processes, with the plans demanding big outcomes. The little guys lose.

Simplicity does not precede complexity, but follows it.

—Alan Perlis

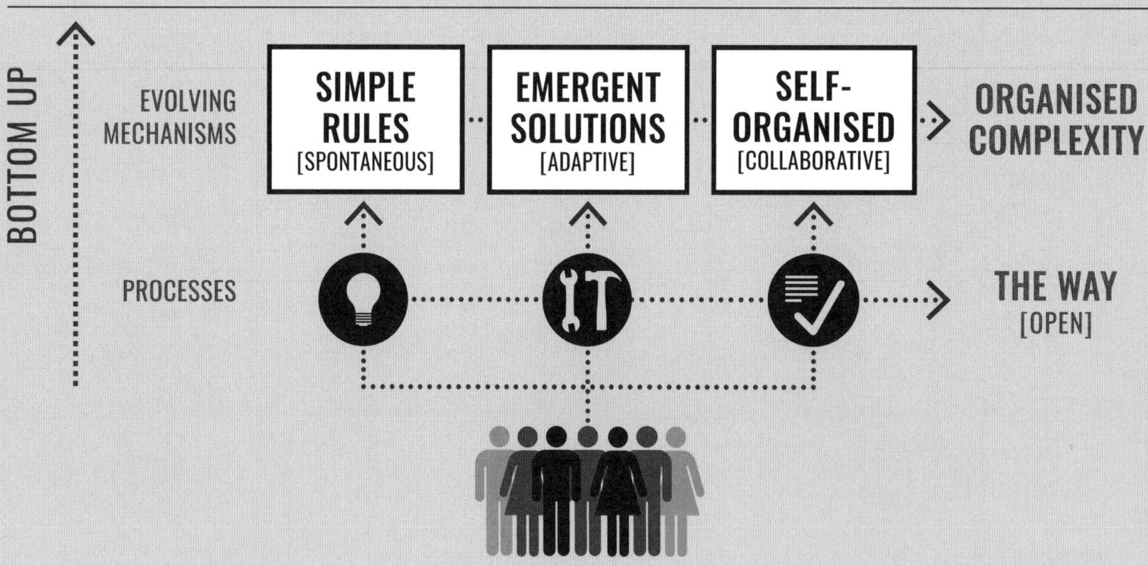

WHAT IS A BOTTOM UP SYSTEM?

Bottom-up systems are very different in nature. These are systems in which no individual understands the whole picture. They are like jazz, where each musician knows only a small part of the whole. These systems function by applying simple rules. A bottom-up approach is one that works from the grassroots—from a large number of people working collectively, causing a decision to arise from their joint involvement.

It is, therefore, a hierarchical system that emerges from multiple, small actions progressing to larger basic actions. Most living systems follow this bottom-up logic. It is innate and cannot be coerced. With our developing knowledge of emergent systems, we have a better understanding of the irreducible complexity of life that evolves from these processes: how order emerges from chaos.

Complex adaptive systems show how things work from the bottom up. This process is natural forces at work. We see it every day in informal or spontaneous settlements. At the start, informal settlements do not need top-down processes to make them happen. As the process evolves, they look for top-down leadership to take over.

Ideas, tools and tactics can evolve from the collective intelligence of many diverse agents to become the accepted way in which we plan, design and develop urban neighbourhoods, quarters and centres.

These ideas, tools and tactics translate into enabling mechanisms, which all add up to become 'the way'—the conventions, traditions and normative practices that emerge from this process.

Bottom-up systems of planning, design and development tend to be open to challenge. Each has fluid outcomes that harden up over time. The flow chart above shows how this all works.

→ **Bottom-up ideas, all informed by a common purpose, rapidly transform into simple rules.** Without these rules, action stalls. They are spontaneous and give rise to complex behaviour. Later, bottom-up ideas make demands on government to be receptive to their needs. This means providing a more open, responsive and collaborative environment to engage with top-down systems effectively.

→ **Bottom-up tools tend to be borrowed from traditional practices.** We start with what we

Informal settlements, such as this favela in Guatemala City, demonstrate self-organisation at work. People cannot build like this unless they cooperate.

know. Things are tried: some succeed; others fail. We learn and we get better at what we do. The best solutions survive. Regularities form, leading to the emergence of a vernacular: an everyday, timeless way of building. This vernacular continues to adapt, continually becoming the best solution within the constraints of its place and time. There is no central person or body in control. This is natural, human dynamics at work. There is no need to determine a future end state: we start from where we are—the present.

→ **When bottom-up tactics are used, the process of self-organisation is open and connected, relying on collaboration and on trusting people to do the right thing.** Collective action means that we rely less on individual freedoms. The outcome is that this organised complexity makes cities, towns and their neighbourhoods work inclusively and with a sense of community.

According to the book *Spatial Agency: Other Ways of Doing Architecture*, this action involves the design of processes that can enable people to transform their own environments, meaning that the mechanisms involved are embedded within their own locality and are not external to it. Since self-organised projects emerge from the negotiations of many different actors in the system, they are inherently relational practices, and point towards the collective production of space.

> *Whilst the usual frameworks of architecture and urbanism operate in ways in which local actors have little influence on their outcome, self-organised practices provide an alternate framework for the production of space. A lineage can be traced through political activism, cultural production in the form of music, art and literature, and other ways of dwelling such as squatting or autonomous communities. All demonstrate a desire to challenge the status-quo by developing fiercely independent approaches.*
>
> —*Spatial Agency*

As these bottom-up processes evolve, people demand appropriate forms of governance. They do not want to have to do everything themselves. They want to get on with their lives, to get formal jobs, to socialise, to educate their children, and so on. At this point, they need top-down.

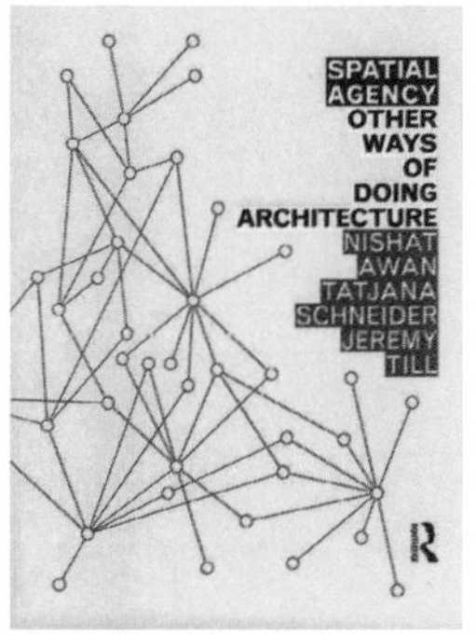

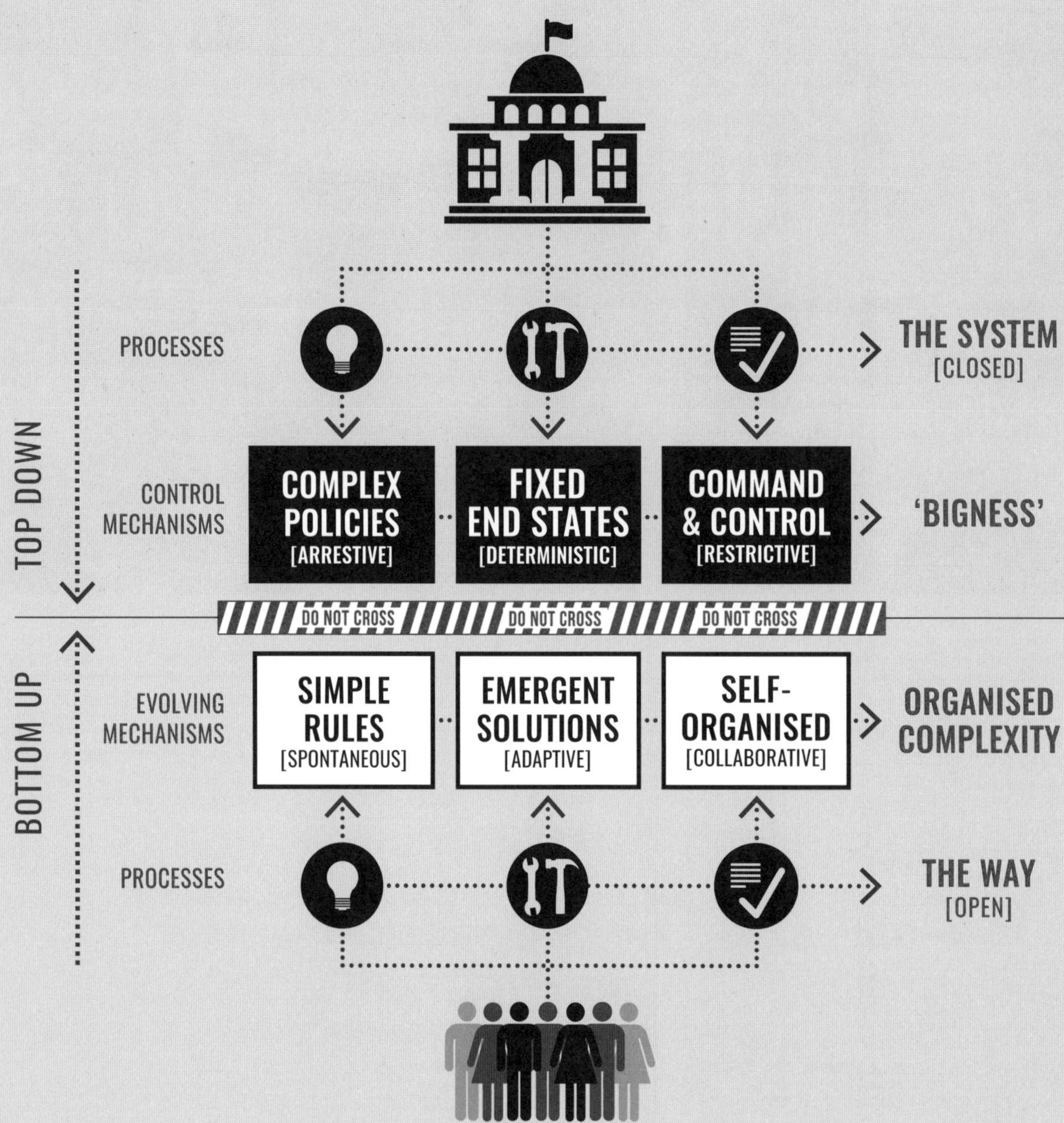

This diagram shows that when our current top-down system meets bottom-up they find it impossible to interact properly. Both systems are fundamentally opposed to one another.

> **SIMPLE RULES GIVE RISE TO COMPLEX AND INTELLIGENT BEHAVIOUR. COMPLEX RULES GIVE RISE TO SIMPLE AND STUPID BEHAVIOUR.** —*Dee Hock*

WHEN THE 'SYSTEM' MEETS THE 'WAY'

We can see that the outcomes of these models are in fundamental conflict with each other. It appears that there is a planned 'do not cross' line between them. The top-down systems that we currently have make it impossible for change to happen from the bottom-up. This is why:

→ **Complex policies vs Simple rules.** The complex policies through which our top-down systems operate don't just obstruct the development of the simple rules on which more spontaneous bottom-up action depends. They arrest all forms of spontaneity and creativity.

→ **Fixed end states vs Emergent solutions.** Our deterministic place-making tools that focus on fixed end states do not allow more adaptive vernacular ways of building to emerge from the bottom up. We are denied the chance to learn and to evolve better solutions. Innovation is stifled.

→ **Command-and-control vs Self-organisation.** The restrictive command-and-control tactics of top-down systems do not work with the more collaborative self-organisation characteristics of bottom-up approaches. Try to put command-and control together with self-organisation, and it becomes a riot.

Dee Hock is definitive on the need for a simple and clear purpose to guide strategy. Without doubt, the system we use is creating stupid behaviour. It works against the urban poor, the active citizen and the whole fabric of urban society.

We need a different way.

[*organising complexity*]

2

THE WAY

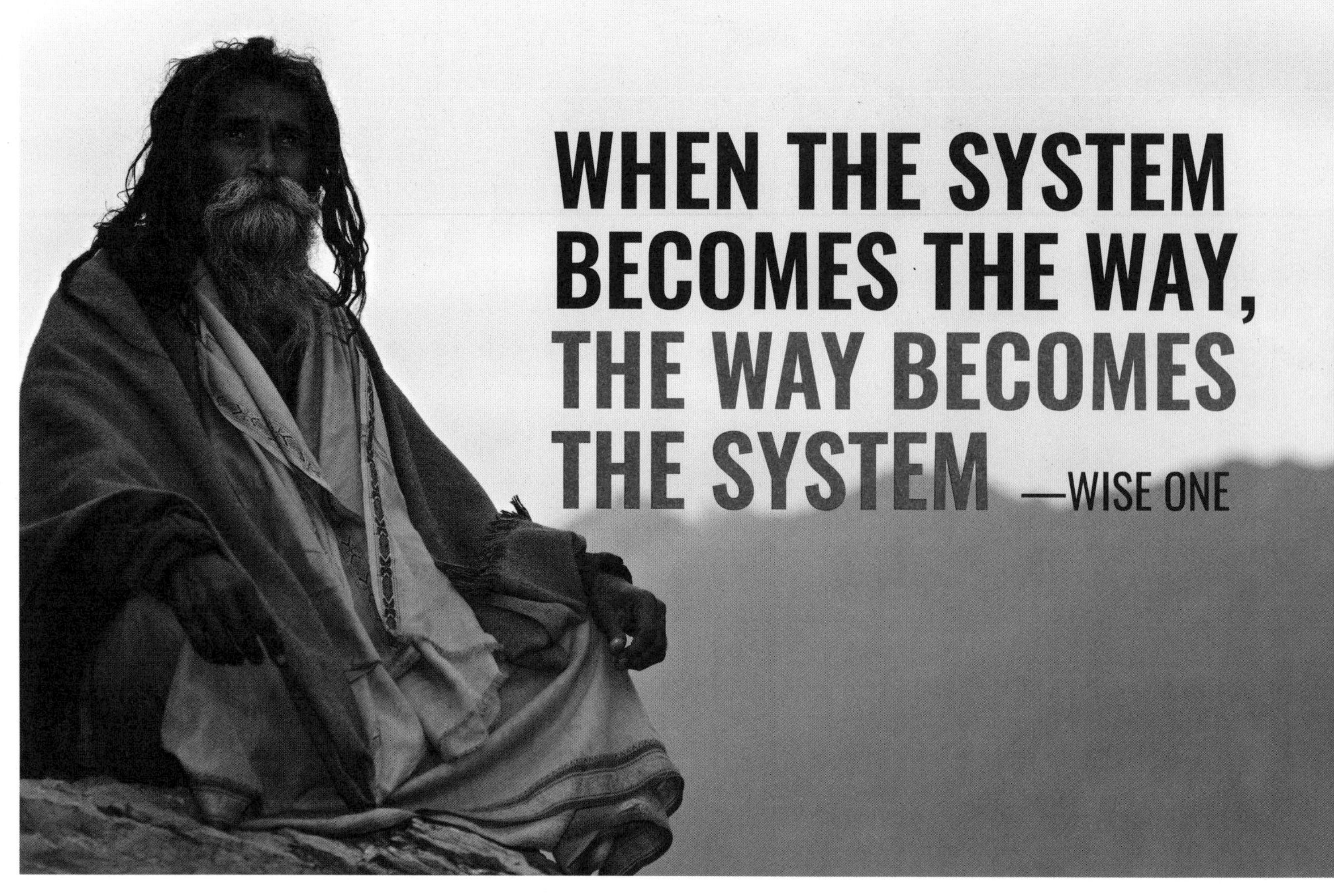
WHEN THE SYSTEM
BECOMES THE WAY,
THE WAY BECOMES
THE SYSTEM —WISE ONE

Way *NOUN*

1 a method, style or manner of attaining a goal

2 an optional or alternative form of action

3 a course (such as a series of actions or sequence of events) leading in a direction or towards an objective

4 a characteristic, regular, or habitual manner or mode of being, behaving or happening

SYNONYMS

custom, norm, tradition, mores, path, modus

How can we reconcile the conflicts and potentials that exist between our top-down and bottom-up systems? To build viable urban neighbourhoods, we must move our IDEAS from complex policies to simple protocols; our TOOLS from fixed end states to starter conditions; and our TACTICS from command-and-control methods to enabling behaviours.

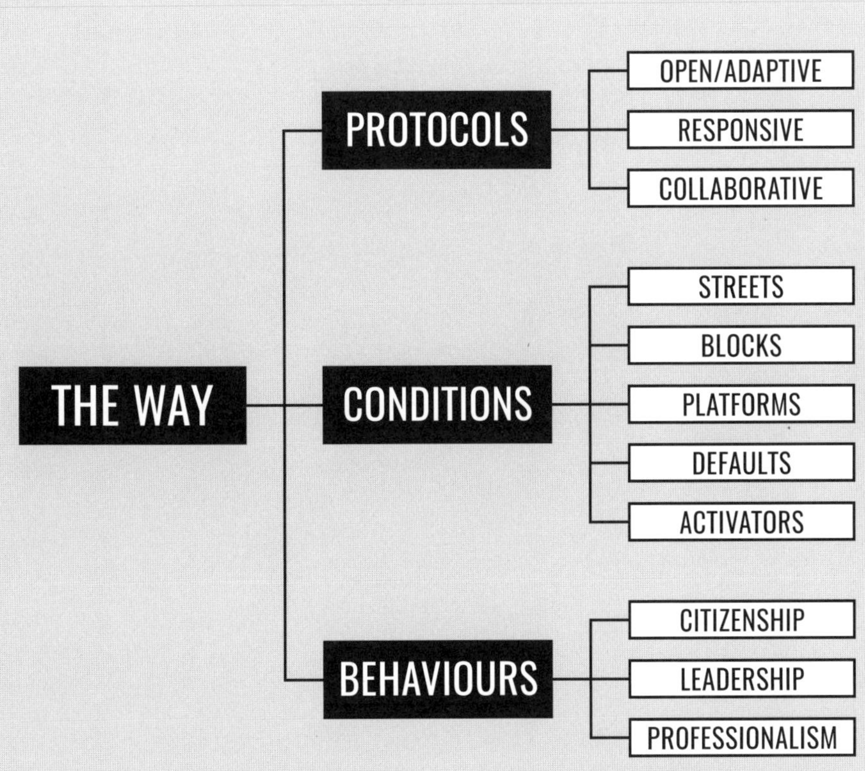

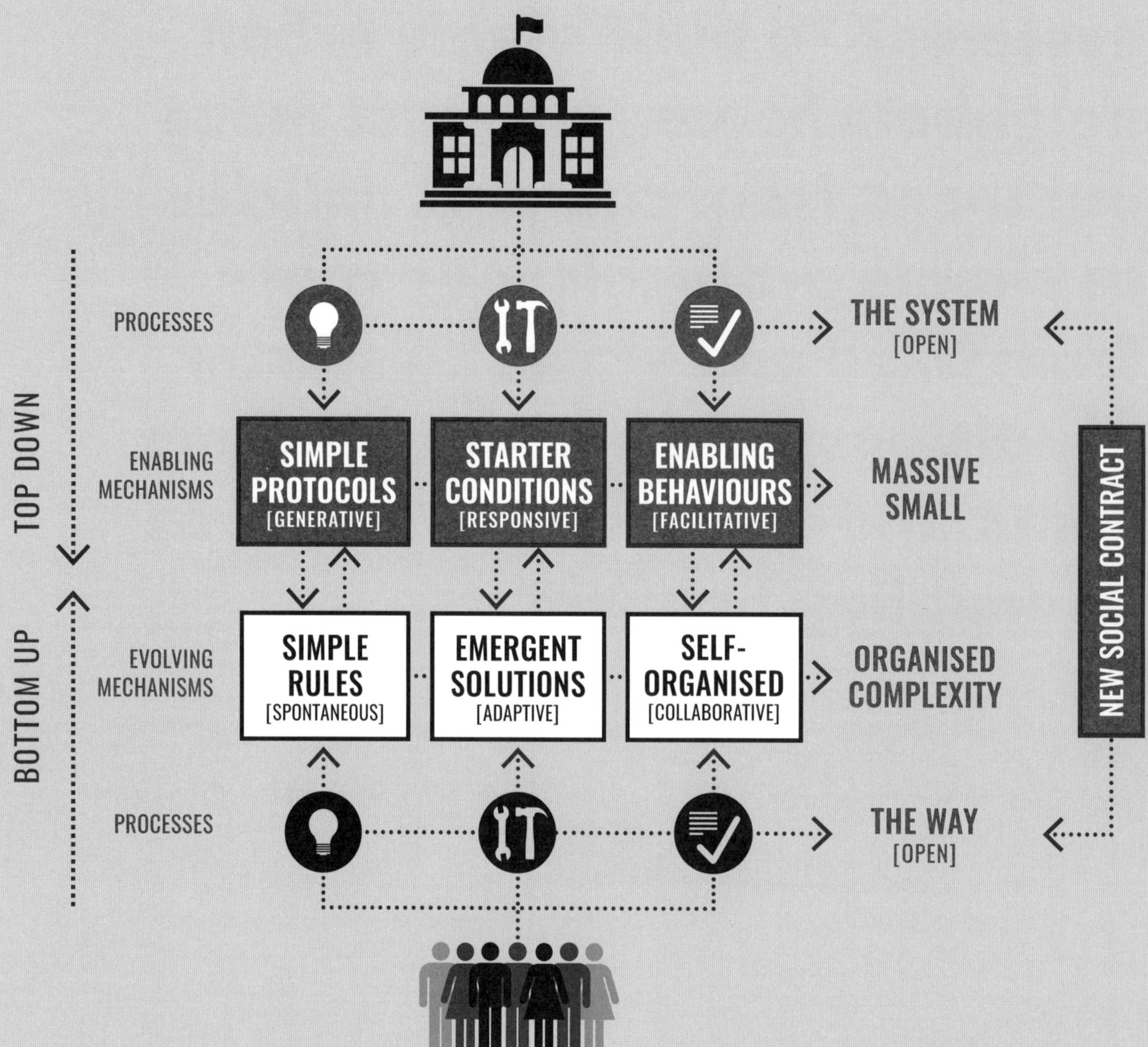

This diagram shows that in order to build viable urban neighbourhoods, we must move our IDEAS from complex policies to simple protocols; our TOOLS from fixed end states to starter conditions; and our TACTICS from command-and-control methods to enabling behaviours.

HOW TOP-DOWN SYSTEMS NEED TO CHANGE

Our existing top-down processes need to transform to allow for greater bottom-up citizen action. This means rediscovering how active citizens, civic leaders and urban professionals can work together to build a better urban society. Processes need to be more open, responsive and collaborative. Open systems recognise that uncertainty and change make traditional top-down, command-and-control ways far less effective. Instead, the aim must be to adapt continuously to the environment. Open systems are therefore organic rather than mechanistic and require a fundamentally different mindset to run them. In these conditions, strategy and feedback are more important than detailed planning.

To organise complexity and deliver Massive Small change, our top-down processes need to transition:

1 **From complex policies to simple protocols.** Complex policies, which are rigid and arrestive, need to be replaced by a range of simple protocols that are more generative, allowing simple rules and spontaneous action to emerge at the grassroots.
2 **From fixed end states to starter conditions.** Our rigidly deterministic place-making tools that focus on fixed end states will have to be replaced by condition-making tools that focus on starter conditions that create more open, responsive and collaborative environments.
3 **From command-and-control to enabling behaviours.** Our restrictive command-and-control practices will be replaced by enabling behaviours that work with communities' instincts to self-organise and collaborate.

The obsession with the end state is replaced by a focus on managing the present, using continuous feedback loops—rather than fixed long-term plans—to monitor action and results.

The new top-down processes will provide the light touch that is essential at a time when we need to do more with less. They will imply that a new social contract between government and people is agreed to do the right thing. The resultant open planning, design and development system will lead to Massive Small change and stimulate complex behaviours, replacing the closed current system that drives bigness as a consequence.

So what are the implications?

The shift—from a bigness model to a Massive Small model—will have a profound effect on how we approach planning, design and development of our neighbourhoods, towns and cities. The comparison table, overleaf, rings the differences within a range of metrics. Across the full spectrum, embracing new ideas, tools and tactics, we see how we can begin to understand and realise change. Clearly, the Massive Small model opens opportunities to us that we find difficult to realise in our current operating system. This section shows how we can mobilise a shared and common language to start unpacking these opportunities in a practical and rigorous manner.

> *To work our way towards a shared language once again, we must first learn how to discover patterns, which are deep and capable of generating life.*
>
> —Christopher Alexander

The new shared and common language will revolve around our three ways of enabling: PROTOCOLS, CONDITIONS and BEHAVIOURS. This is the start of something evolutionary! A different way.

Behind complexity, there is always simplicity to be revealed. Inside simplicity, there is always complexity to be discovered.

—Gang Yu

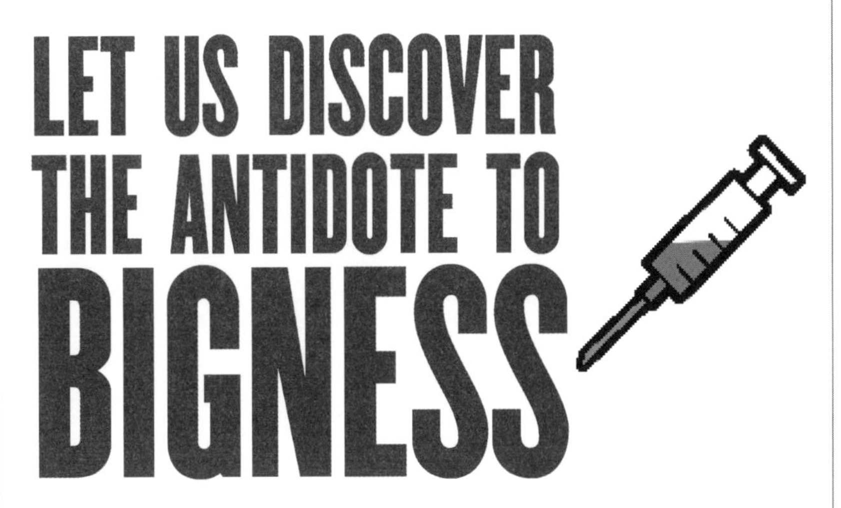
LET US DISCOVER
THE ANTIDOTE TO
BIGNESS

		BIGNESS MODEL	MASSIVE SMALL MODEL
PLANNING	High-level drivers	Single vision	Shared vision
	Planned outcomes	Social utopia	Emergent vernacular
	Approaches	Top-down commanded	Bottom-up facilitated
	Methods	Predict and plan	Learn by doing
	Tools	Arrestive policies	Generative protocols
	Controls	Restrictiveness	Responsiveness
	Community roles	Consultation	Collaboration
	People focus	The individual	The collective
	Social outcomes	Low social capital	High social capital
	Community type	Transient community	Stable community
DESIGN	Perspective	Fixed end states	Starter conditions
	Starting point	Back to first principles	Open building platforms
	Outcomes	Revolutionary design	Evolutionary design
	Guiding process	Masterplan + design codes	General plan + regulations
	Design approach	Form follows function	Long life, loose fit
	Design agency	Single hero	'School of Thinking'
	Default solutions	Big architecture	Popular typologies
	Design ambition	Perpetual novelty	Regularity/normative
	Thinking	Closed/reductionist	Open/holistic
	Design focus	'The Project'	'The Place'
DEVELOPMENT	Change agents	Few big players	Many small players
	Financial models	Big-capital model	Land management model
	Value drivers	Land value	Social purpose
	Change process	Big bang	Radical incrementalism
	Tenures	Limited range	Mixed/flexible range
	Urban solution	High density / low family	Medium density / high family
	Scale	Big block / high-rise	Plot-based/medium-rise
	Form	Closed/isolated	Open/connected
	Market	Homogeneous/zoned	Diverse/mixed use
	Brand identity	'The Scheme'	'The Neighbourhood'

Bigness: The Olympic Village in London, with its megastructural blocks, demonstrates all the qualities of bigness. it will never be a socially diverse, adaptable neighbourhood. It is trapped in transition.

Massive Small: The Berlin Townhouse project in Mitte provides an alternative to the megablock but still gives good urban density. Based on the development of single plots, with active involvement of the endusers at the outset of the project, it can change over time.

BIG
IMPACT
SMALL
ACT
WHAT'S
YOUR
SMALL
ACT OF
Walldoggie style

MASSIVESMALL

A CALL TO COLLECTIVE ACTION, AN ATTITUDE,
AN INVITATION.
CELEBRATE THE MAGIC OF THE SMALL-SCALE
AND THE IMMEDIATE. TRY OUT YOUR IDEAS.
TELL YOUR STORY. BUILD SHARED VISIONS. LEAVE YOUR
NEIGHBOURHOOD IN A BETTER PLACE THAN YOU FOUND IT.
BE FLEXIBLE.
DESIGN WITH A PASSION. TEST SOLUTIONS.
FIND UNEXPECTED OUTCOMES. TURN SPACES INTO PLACES.
CARE FOR YOUR COMMUNITY.
DO THE RIGHT THING.
START BY STARTING, EXPERIMENT, FAIL,
RECALIBRATE, IMPROVE, LEARN BY DOING.
AUTHENTICITY IS EVERYTHING.
SHARE IDEAS OPENLY AND BUILD ON THOSE OF OTHERS.
PARTNER CREATIVELY. PLAN IMAGINATIVELY.
DO IT TOGETHER.

#MASSIVESMALL
MASSIVESMALL.COM/PENDIUM

universal and discrete guiding instruments. They create an almost poetic, standardised irrationality.

—Alex Lehnerer

FROM COMPLEX POLICIES TO SIMPLE **PROTOCOLS** 2.1

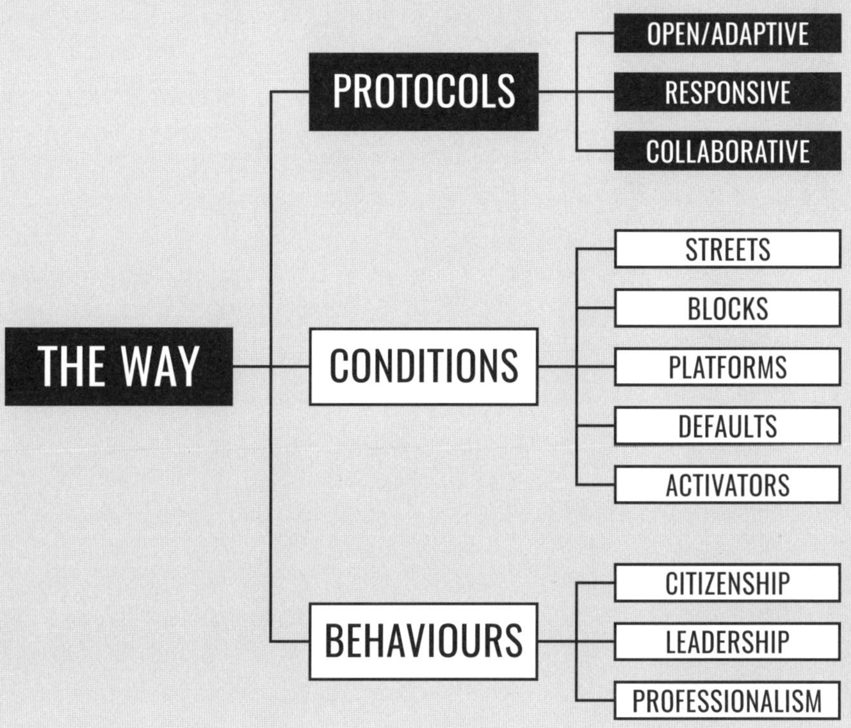

Protocol *NOUN*

the accepted or established code of procedure or behaviour in any group, organisation or situation

SYNONYMS
rules of conduct, agreement, code, custom, compact, convention, formalities, order

PROTOCOLS are enabling mechanisms that are distinct from complex policies. They define a set of operational procedures, etiquettes, codes of behaviour, rules, or practices to ensure that there is a well-defined way of doing a particular task. This is most important when the task is executed over a period when different people will be performing the task. Protocol means you do something a certain way because it has been deemed the 'most effective way' through cumulative experience. Protocols are simple rules that instruct bottom-up action.

THEORY

A protocol should not be confused with a policy, which is a set of rules designed to achieve certain blanket objectives. A policy should help in the decision-making process when there is more than one option available. Policies grow over time. They are not made at once. They grow along with governance. Policies are a fixed system of principles to guide decision-making and achieve rational outcomes. They are classic top-down instruments. Policies are more like the law. They are interpreted as: 'There may be other ways of doing this, but this is how we always do it here.'

In a world of bottom-up action, complex behaviour happens only in response to simple rules. We have developed some broad principles that will facilitate writing these rules. We call them all our 'simple protocols'. They are generative in that they provide gentle nudges in the right direction. In doing so they establish the essential ground rules for engagement between top-down and bottom-up players in the process, enabling the process of forming simple rules to be triggered and accelerated.

These protocols concern:

Rules are universal and discrete guiding instruments, and they create an almost poetic, standardised irrationality.

—Alex Lehnerer

- → the drivers of growth and change;
- → the boundaries of the system and how we manage these boundaries;
- → the codes of behaviour (ethics) for all involved;
- → the principles that help open/adaptive, responsive and collaborative environments evolve; and
- → guidance about when the rules can be broken.

It is within this context that the Massive Small project applies systems thinking to the job of creating open adaptive, responsive and collaborative environments—the protocols for urban society—which are capable of growing and sustaining urban life in continuously changing conditions.

> **Rules** *NOUN*
>
> **an agreed set of conditions, standards or required actions**
>
> SYNONYMS
> **guidelines, regulations, decrees, orders, laws, norms, standards**

RULES AS TOOLS

Rules are everywhere—they are infrastructural. They hang like a fog over our built and nonbuilt environments. They remain in force in locations that no street will ever reach. They dominate the air, just as they do the ground and that which lies beneath. They constitute a connection between built structures, land and its use. Rules are tools that can be used to guide us in structuring complex choices and achieving universal solutions. They give us our freedom within constraints. No society can manage without them. There are three types of rules as tools that concern us: *method tools, thinking tools* and *boundary tools.*

1 Rules as method (how-to) tools

We can hardly avoid acknowledging the significant role played by rules in shaping our cities, towns and their neighbourhoods. In fact, the discipline of urban design—that is to say, the linking together of shared visions through the mediation of a variety of public and private sector interests—consists more of the conscious declaring of rules than the drawing up of plans. Design codes are an example of this.

Methodological tools are well described in Alex Lehnerer's book *Grand Urban Rules*. He says that in integrated, operational tools in planning and design, rules possess special qualities. Their implementation enables the precise formulation of degrees of freedom for specified areas and for the protagonists of the planning process. These freedoms are decisive for urban diversity, differentiation and vitality. Consciously deployed freedoms, moreover, endow planning with a certain sustainability and permanence in confronting an unpredictable future.

Method rules are useful in structuring the design process and give us the means to evaluate it. They give us the design principles that can be applied to developing alternatives. They give us regularity and reliability. Some refer to norms or standards, others to procedures. Some are required minimums or maximums; others are preferred optimums. They can range from rigorous determinism to flexible interpretation.

2 Rules as thinking tools

Thinking rules are valid at the higher level and shape our thoughts before they become operational. These rules are more performance-based and enabling in nature. They are the rules that release the freedoms for multiple actions. They are an essential part of the feedback loop—constantly learning, evolving and reinterpreting.

From our understanding and thinking about emergent systems in life, business, information technology and choice architecture, we can extract certain lessons—used to derive simple thinking rules that can be applied to achieving a better urbanism.

3 Rules as boundary tools

Boundary tool rules set the boundary conditions within which innovation is channelled to enable structured choices to be made and complexity to be organised. They are not rigid but provide limits of deviation, so they need to be managed and renegotiated as circumstances warrant. Quite often it is not the rules themselves that are important but the rules to break the rules that are key.

> *The boundary between complex and complicated should at times be maintained as a semi-permanent space—something I have talked about as a grazing dynamic. We should maintain a space of partial certainties while maintaining options.*
>
> —David Snowden

Do rules constrain or help the creativity of designers to innovate? Do rules inhibit the natural evolution of cities or do we need prescriptiveness to prevent disorder? They say rules are meant to be broken but there is always a search of balance between what should be done and what works in reality. The book *City Rules: How Regulations Affect Urban Form* by Emily Talen entails the challenge of why rules, or codes, are important for city planning and how they are determined in urban development.

WHAT ARE SIMPLE RULES?

Scientists have discovered that complex behaviour can result from a few simple rules. The most creative growth and change processes have a few simple rules, which reflect shared values and guide behaviour—the fewer the rules, the higher the creativity. People are able to keep a small number of rules in mind, which helps them act on behalf of the city as its agents.

Complexity science is about finding simple rules that can generate complexity in the planning, design and development of our towns and cities. Scientists can decode simple rules from emergent systems that, even with modest means, will generate complexity and simultaneously solve a vast diversity of unique problems.

Without understanding how these rules create complexity, scientists simply repeat them after each successful experiment. This is exactly the field of work that urbanists should learn today, and from there we could allow maximum diversity in our cities without breaking their symmetry and harmony.

> *The rules may be so simple that they may be easily codified into building regulation even by the dullest bureaucrats. Then again the behaviour may be so complex (that is to say, there is emergence) that post-rationalised codification is even impossible, and the processes by which cities are governed may have to be completely reconsidered.*
>
> —Stephen Wolfram

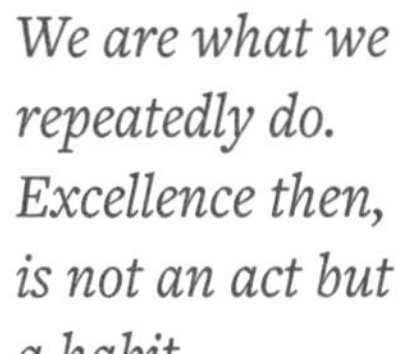

We are what we repeatedly do. Excellence then, is not an act but a habit.

—Aristotle

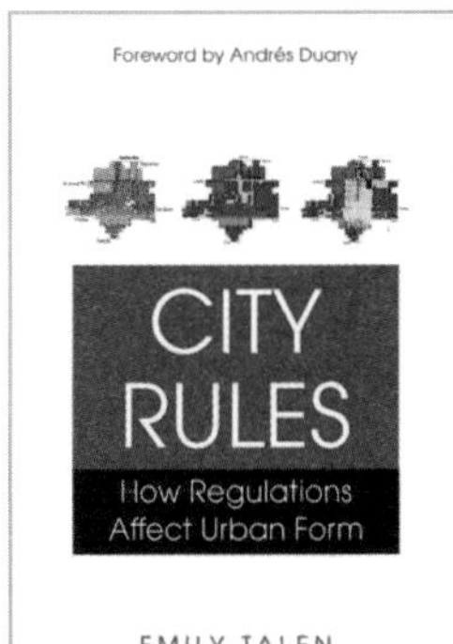

Foreword by Andrés Duany
CITY RULES
How Regulations Affect Urban Form
EMILY TALEN

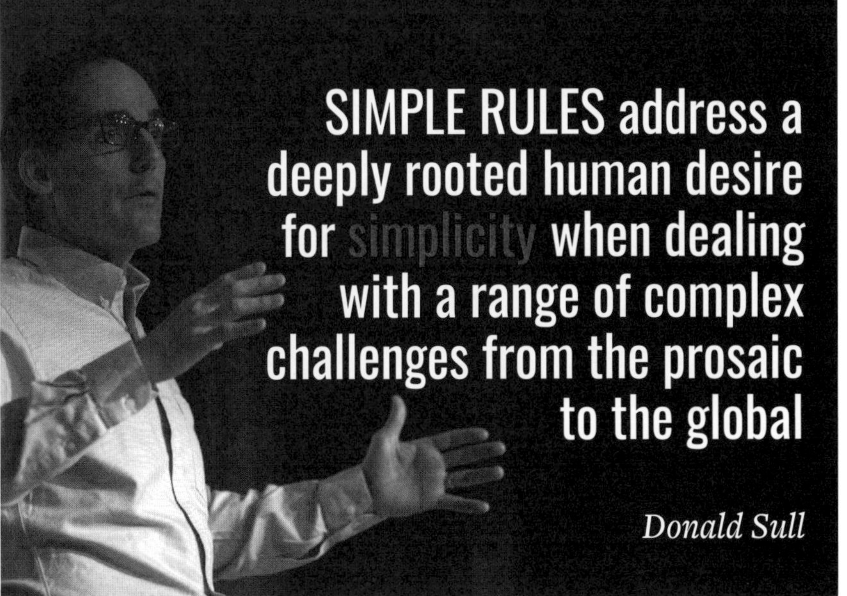

SIMPLE RULES address a deeply rooted human desire for simplicity when dealing with a range of complex challenges from the prosaic to the global
Donald Sull

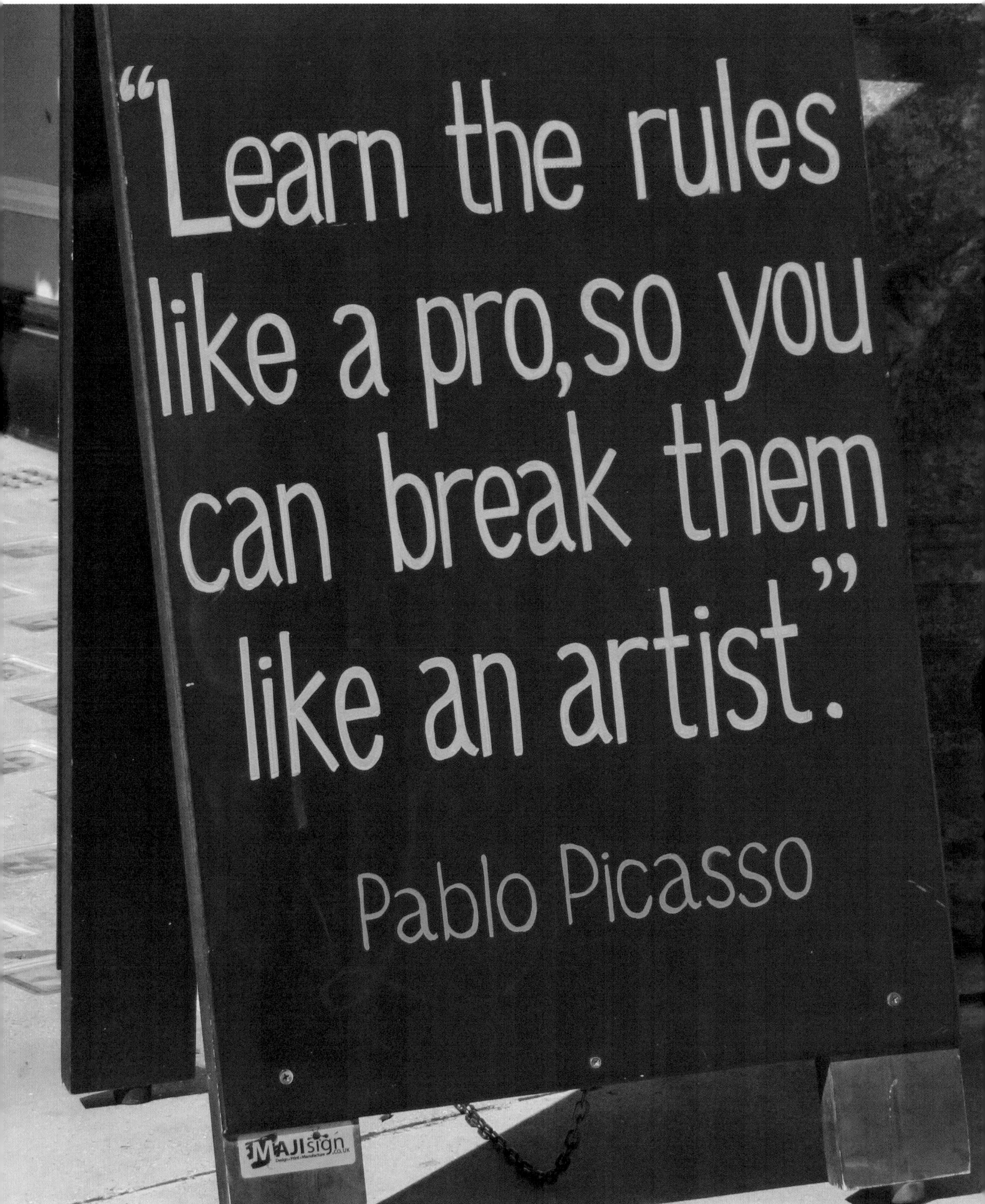

"Learn the rules like a pro, so you can break them like an artist."

Pablo Picasso

According to the findings of the Human Systems Dynamics Institute, simple rules accomplish the following:

- → Establish the conditions that give rise to patterns in the system. They can be covert agreements that emerge over time in a system, creating its culture.
- → Can be used retrospectively to understand what shaped the conditions to generate whatever patterns are currently in the system. On the other hand, simple rules can be used prospectively to shape a desired future.
- → Are different from the norms we name for short-term interactions because they are intended to be more generally applied, and not time bound. They are also different from values and beliefs because they are about action. They start with a verb, so they inform action.

The book *Simple Rules: How to Thrive in a Complex World* by Donald Sull and Kathleen Eisenhardt says that, to be effective, simple rules must meet four conditions. They must be:

- → Limited in number
- → Tailored to the people using them
- → Applied to well-defined activities
- → Open to exercising of discretion

According to Sull and Eisenhardt:

1. **Simple rules make it easier to act.** Complex situations create many possible courses of action, which can confound people on the front line. When faced with a superabundance of alternatives, people are afraid of making the wrong choice. As a result they delay decisions, default to the safest option or avoid choosing altogether. Because simple rules are easy to put into practice, they can induce action without unnecessarily limiting options.

2. **Simple rules fare better against complex models.** A growing body of evidence shows that simple rules match or beat more complicated analyses across a wide range of decisions. Simple rules outperformed state-of-the-art statistical models in forecasting and matched sophisticated algorithms in effectiveness.

3. **Simple rules differ from checklists.** Checklists for an operation are extremely helpful when the challenge is to perform a process repeatedly and efficiently. They lay out clear tasks that together constitute the steps in an optimal process. Simple rules, in contrast, are most useful when the challenge is to adapt quickly to changing circumstances. They set the boundaries of acceptable behavior while leaving ample scope for flexibility within those limits.

GENERATING THE SIMPLE RULES

An open, responsive and collaborative environment is the opposite of a closed, deterministic and restrictive one. In the former, there will be a set of conditions that help to make things happen without any attempt to determine what the precise outcome will be. Simple rules cannot be imposed. They derive from the boundary conditions that define their operating principles. We call these operating principles our protocols—the accepted or established code of procedure or behaviour in any relationship between a government and its people.

These protocols reflect and incorporate the essential qualities that are found in most complex systems: diversity, connectivity, adaptability and a multiplicity of elements working together. We have added to these and categorised them as operating principles according to our three types of environments: open, responsive and collaborative.

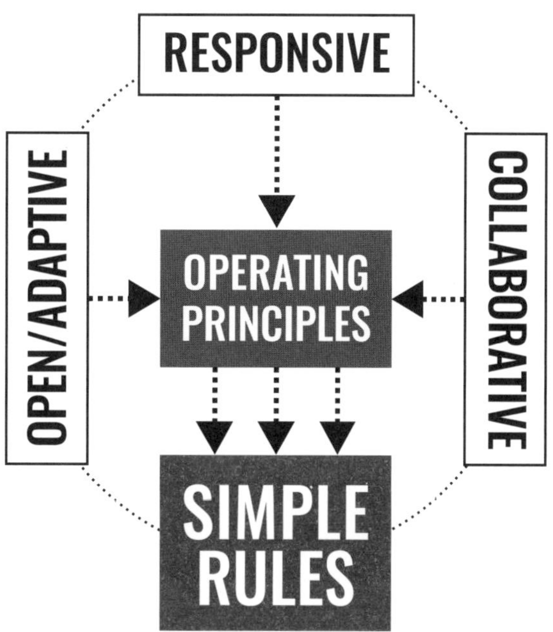

Democracy must be built through open societies that share information. When there is information, there is enlightenment. When there is a debate, there are solutions.

—Atifete Jahjaga

TYPE A: OPEN/ADAPTIVE ENVIRONMENTS

Openness is an overarching concept or philosophy that is characterised by an emphasis on transparency; free and unrestricted access to all knowledge and information; and, collaboration or cooperation in management and decision-making rather than a dependency on a central authority.

These protocols deal with how urban neighbourhoods, quarters and districts—as total systems—can grow and change by interacting with their wider external environment. This will enable them to continue to evolve successfully in changing conditions.

Rod Collins, in 'The Management Wisdom of Complex Adaptive Systems', shows that open environments share three common organising principles:

1. **Intelligence resides in the whole system.** This means that, while different individuals may hold specific knowledge or differing interpretations of a common reality, no one person is capable of processing all the information within the system. Self-organising systems produce intelligence only when they have the capacity to process the diversity of knowledge that resides within the entire system. Thus, organisations are most intelligent when they have a rich diversity of perspectives and the means to aggregate their collective intelligence.

2. **Simple rules guide complex collective behaviour.** This most important premise is completely counterintuitive to conventional wisdom. We usually think that complex structures will work only if we have detailed blueprints or a comprehensive set of rules and regulations. While this is generally true for mechanical tasks, it is not the way the open systems of biology work. In the organic world, the secret to the effective execution of complex tasks is that order is created by the collaborative application of a few simple rules rather than by compliance with a complex set of controls. Thus, one of the distinguishing features of complex adaptive systems is that responsibility for control and coordination rests with each of the individual participants rather than with one central executive.

3. **Order emerges from the interaction of the independent participants.** In open systems, there are no blueprints. Order is not preordained before the work begins but rather emerges through an iterative learning process. This is the secret to the remarkable success of Linux and Wikipedia. Because complex systems can quickly learn and adapt and are capable of efficiently aggregating the collective intelligence of their many participants, they are far better organisational models when the primary business challenge is managing innovation.

Open standards

In other industries and sectors that promote openness (also called open standards) as a key feature of their systems, such as business and information technology, some benefits are realised that could apply directly to the field of urbanism.

Benefits of open environments are:

1. Addressing broad market needs
2. Streamlining development and implementation
3. Embodying diverse perspectives
4. Reducing costs
5. Leveraging proprietary knowledge
6. Opening new markets and applications
7. Serving as a building block for innovation
8. Encouraging market competition
9. Providing interchangeability (interoperability) and scaleability
10. Driving wider innovation and advancement

There is no reason why open standards applied to urbanism cannot realise the same benefits.

PRINCIPLES

Guiding principles for achieving open/adaptive environments include:

→ **Seeing the whole picture.** Whole-systems thinking is a method to understand how things (elements and systems) are related, and how they influence one another within a whole. Seeing the whole picture enables us to transcend ideological battles and unite around shared goals.

→ **Making it work in all times and places.** Solutions, appropriate to their context, should be applicable in both the developed and the developing worlds; at the start and during the urban growth and change process; and at all scales.

→ **Thinking in spectrums, avoiding polarisation.** Urbanism has been bedevilled by the pendulum of fashion. Our actions should reflect the fact that our cities, towns and neighbourhoods are rich tapestries.

→ **Using open standards to build an invisible chassis.** An open standard is one that is publicly available and has various rights to use associated with it. It may also have different properties reflecting how it was designed (through an open process, for example). Establish a common platform (an invisible chassis, so to speak) for the shared development of ideas, tools and tactics. This will generally avoid the need to always go back to first principles.

→ **Thinking in parameters, not in absolutes.** An obsessional pursuit of certainty breeds a requirement for exactness, but exactness is difficult to predict in a complex adaptive system. Manage the boundary conditions of any system by using a range of flexible dimensions, allowing for diverse responses.

→ **Trusting people to do the right thing.** Civilisation derives from most people doing the right thing most of the time if they are trusted. This is implicit in the extent of conformity in most societies, where attitudes, beliefs and behaviours are usually matched to group norms. These norms are implicit, unsaid rules, shared by groups of individuals, that guide their interactions with others.

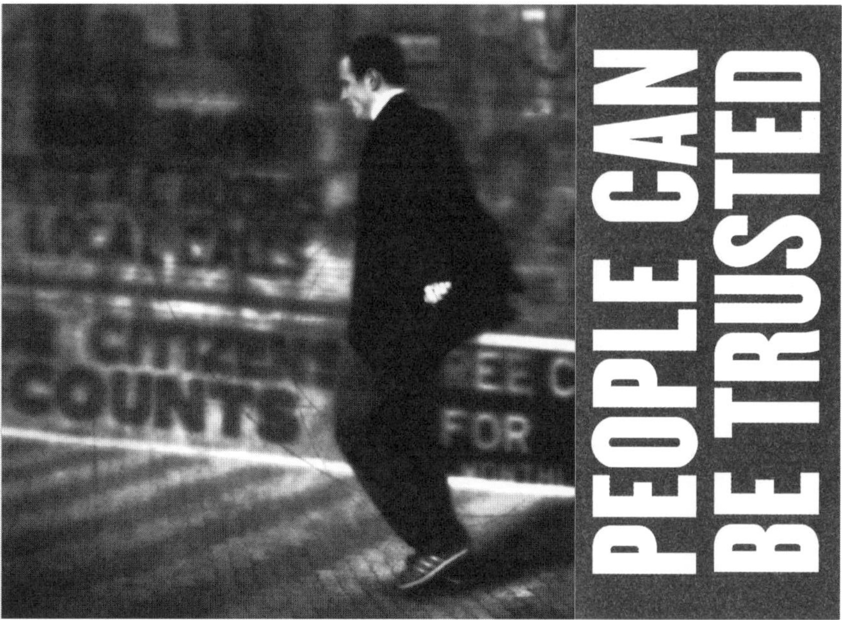

→ **Seeing informality as a stepping stone.** Ensure that the first rung of the ladder is set low, and intentionally allow things to start at the lowest levels. Turning a blind eye should sometimes be a deliberate policy. Informal systems are just an early stage in the process of making urban development viable. Formality will be needed later, as the systems evolve.

→ **Making the system work equably for the individual, the collective and the corporate.** Make sure that the playing field is level for all actors in the system. This means establishing common rules and equity for anyone entering or engaging with the system, no matter who they are or how big they are.

→ **Ensuring transparency and be open to challenge.** Being open to change means managing the boundary conditions of the system. We need to create the rules to break the rules. Evolution comes from learning. Learning comes from challenging the status quo.

→ **Developing both fast-track and conventional ways of doing things.** There are different paths to achieving the same outcome. There also are different paths to creating different outcomes. All of them may be valid. Enabling leadership can facilitate choices through establishing fast-track and short-cut methods, while still maintaining conventional or traditional methods.

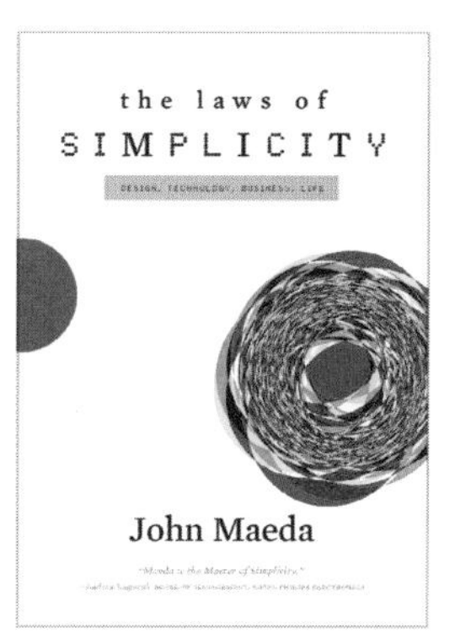

Openness simplifies complexity.

—John Maeda

We are the children of our environment; it dictates behaviour and even thought in the measure to which we are responsive to it.

—Lawrence Durrell

TYPE B: RESPONSIVE ENVIRONMENTS

Urban designers aim to create responsive environments: places that can be adapted by the people who use them and live there. This allows governments to provide the lightest touch to maximise impact by others. How adaptable a place is will be determined in large part by how it first develops.

PRINCIPLES

Guiding principles for creating responsive environments include:

1 **Establishing an underlying connected urban structure.** An open/adaptive plan will allow both regularity and novelty, encouraging responsive innovation. Any settlement evolves from this first essential action. Get it right, and we will create the conditions for other urban infrastructure to be installed later.

2 **Limiting choice to build infinite possibilities.** Narrowing down choices is a precondition for emergent behaviour (the order that emerges from a complex system). Evolved societies have always found ways of limiting choices so that decisions can be made and self-organisation can develop.

3 **Allowing for progressive change and inner growth.** Avoid using up all the space. Do not become fixated on end states. Make it possible for others to come along later and make their contributions. Encourage temporary uses.

4 **Protecting and incentivising what is small.** Create fine-grain structures and promote the concept of the 'city of a thousand designers'. The emergence of order from complex systems depends on mechanisms (building blocks, generators and agents) and what theorists call 'perpetual novelty' (a lack of equilibrium). In urbanism these conditions are provided by the pattern of the arrangement and size of buildings and their blocks, lots and plots in a neighbourhood, so we need to understand the art of subdivision. An area should be subdivided so that the smallest building blocks are available to be developed. The city's fine grain needs to be protected.

5 **Preferring 'long life, loose fit' over 'form follows function'.** Successful places are robust. Their systems adapt efficiently to rapidly changing circumstances. Create universal space rather than restricting future options.

6 **Allowing interchangeability of solutions.** Complex environments are always changing. Avoid going back to first principles by developing solutions that can be interchanged with one another. In this principle, 'plug and play' becomes a desirable construct, allowing flexibility with compatibility.

7 **Ensuring upscaling and downscaling of elements.** Avoid solutions that only work when they have achieved critical mass. Scaleability of this sort supports incremental and organic change.

8 **Structure the ordinary, and the extraordinary will follow.** To understand something as complex as our built environment, we must figure out what is common in its many manifestations. In bringing about everyday solutions, we also set the scene for the most special results.

9 **Making timelines independent and nonlinear, allowing flexibility.** The first step is often the most difficult to take. The essential structure has to be in place, but we should avoid drawing up plans that depend on following a particular sequence of actions. The best results are achieved when progress is possible on multiple fronts, allowing incremental, simultaneous, nonsequential action.

10 **Using small changes to make a big difference.** Initial conditions can have far-reaching effects, as in complexity theory's popular image of the beating wings of a butterfly creating the potential for a tornado thousands of miles away. A small number of rules applied to a distributed network can generate highly complex systems. Small 'nudges', backed by a continuous review, can lead to massive change. This is evolution, not revolution.

REMEMBER THE MANTRAS

1 **CONTEXT IS A MODIFIER, NOT A CONSTRAINT.**
Time and politics are part of context.

2 **DENSITY IS AN OUTCOME, NOT A DETERMINANT.**
It evolves as a consequence of accessibility and proximity.

3 **UNPREDICTABILITY IS AN OPPORTUNITY, NOT A THREAT.**
It is a precondition for innovation.

> *Collaboration is not just another tactic for addressing public concerns. It is a means for building social capital, sustaining a democratic society and transforming a civic culture.*
>
> —David Chrislip

TYPE C: COLLABORATIVE ENVIRONMENTS

Collaborative environments are those that freely seek partnership through co-creation, co-working and co-production as a way of achieving goals. They recognise that neither party could attain these goals alone and each party is different—providing a mutually reinforcing role in the process.

PRINCIPLES

Guiding principles for creating collaborative environments include:

→ **Fostering and accelerating basic human dynamics.** People have an innate sense and ability to solve their problems if left to their own devices. Be permissive, spontaneous and cooperative, and build capacity to accelerate growth and change. We can harness these dynamics by providing the initial conditions within which this change can happen.

→ **Agreeing on basic rules of behaviour.** Draw up a new social contract. Citizens' moral and political obligations depend on a contract or agreement amongst them to form the society in which they live. In a bottom-up world, new roles and relationships are established, requiring new social contracts between local government and community. A simple rule for emergence can be expressed as 'We will, if you will.'

→ **Delegating accountability and responsibility to the lowest level.** Allow urban professionals to act like junior doctors early in their careers: giving them wide responsibility within a framework of clearly-defined accountability. Devolve power to the lowest appropriate level and allow urban professionals to make things happen.

→ **Ensuring professionals take an ethical view of what they are achieving.** The measure of success should be how a framework of universally accepted rules and codes leads to action on the ground.

→ **Building a common language and values for cross-sector working.** If specialist terms are needed to communicate about these matters, make sure that everyone understands them. End the absurdity of different urban professions having different ways of measuring success.

→ **Sharing and developing ideas collectively.** Opening up ownership of problems and solutions to a broad group of people can make things work from the bottom up. Common intellectual property can be built through collective action.

→ **Encouraging self-organisation and peer-to-peer working.** Bottom-up working depends on limited hierarchies with flat organisational structures that foster collaboration. Nobody should be too far from the top.

→ **Building social capital at every opportunity.** The hardware of cities depends on the software of social life. Shared ownership and collective responsibility develop out of social relationships that are built through local initiatives. Every project should have the potential to bond communities by galvanising social action.

→ **Simulating strategies to envision opportunity.** This principle recognises that while we cannot predict exact end states, we can test our assumptions to gain some understanding of potential outcomes of our decisions. Use gaming theory as a tool. Allow the metrics to be set by the players.

→ **Learning by experimenting.** We learn by trying things out. Failure can be positive if the failures are small. Promote the innovators and outliers, support the urban pioneers.

LOCALia NEIGHBOURHOOD MANUAL

100 SIMPLE WAYS TO BUILD A COMMUNITY

PROTOCOLS AS SIMPLE INSTRUCTIONS

We have a lot to learn from women's magazines, car repair manuals and recipe books. All of these include classic how-to instructions—'10 tips for healthy nails', '5 steps to fixing your carburettor', 'Jamie's 15-minute meals'. Make the rules easy to follow, and people *will* follow.

Most complex policies do not endure because they are not embedded in people's awareness and understanding. They have too much jargon, too much legalese and are too abstract, so people disregard them. For protocols to be effective, they must communicate 'how-to' as simply as the examples above do. There is no reason why we cannot write simple rules with simple routines in different ways, making them relevant.

After the Vietnam War, the Vietnamese government put up inspirational posters all over towns and villages calling people to rebuild their country: 'Grow grain to feed chickens', 'Save water by using irrigation correctly', and so on. They focussed on simple messages to mobilise action. The government in Porto Allegre in Brazil painted their local budget on the wall of a public building to get the message out to the wider audience.

WikiHouse provides a simple open source platform for housebuilding. We have a lot to learn from all of these.

Have a practical neighbourhood manual that can be updated over time. Give examples of what you mean. Show progressive steps that need to be taken to achieve an outcome. Put the manual online, write an app, or even make posters. Whatever you do, inspire people to do the right thing.

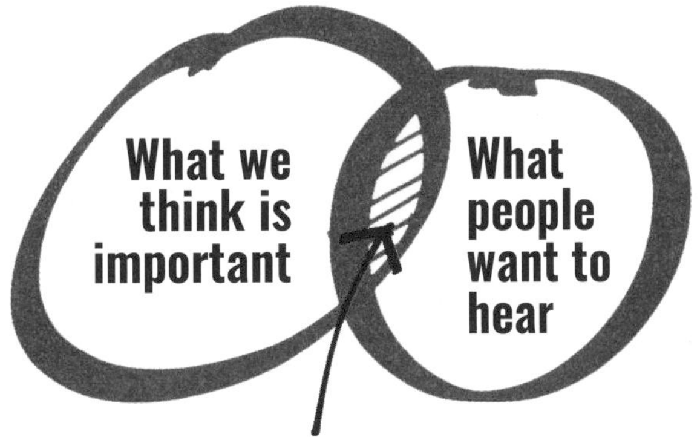

Development, like all human processes, needs designed structure with simple rules and routines... that provide a shared sense of purpose.

—Nabeel Hamdi

FROM FIXED END STATES TO STARTER CONDITIONS

2.2

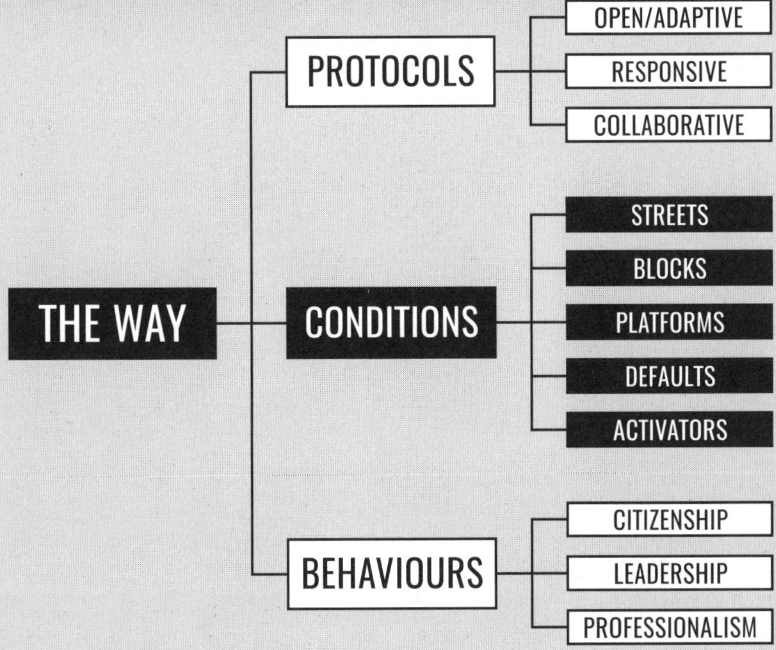

Conditions are the enabling mechanisms that are distinctive from the fixed end states and place-making agendas we use to rigidly determine our urban environments today. This chapter shows a different way of approaching the problem by focussing on the conditions that governments need to put in place to provide the medium for open, responsive and collaborative environments to start and evolve over time. Doing so opens up the potential for the widest range of bottom-up responses by many people.

Conditions *NOUN*

1 the circumstances or factors that have a significant influence on an outcome
2 the structures and limits that must exist before something can happen
3 the behaviours influencing the performance of a process

SYNONYMS
state, shape, order, constraints, boundaries

SCOPE

This chapter introduces new concepts: boundary conditions, balancing constraints, drivers of change and moving from place-making to condition-making. In combination these promise a new framework for creativity, innovation and collective response.

It sets out:

→ The complex relationships between freedoms and constraints
→ The hierarchy of levels of intervention required, providing clear roles and responsibilities for active citizens, civic leaders and especially urban professionals in dynamic urban processes
→ The hardware, software and operating system for building healthy urban neighbourhoods
→ The minimum possible level of effective intervention by governments to achieve the maximum possible outcomes by people
→ Practical tools and processes to structure, guide and enable open, responsive and collaborative action
→ Distinct roles for government and people in the process, and how they interact with one another

What's New
The new Fira Gran Via is huge
How can we support more recycling during MWC?
REIMAGINE
OUR CITY
DAG
BETTER
BLOCK
AHEAD
SELF
MADE
CITY
BEZAHLBARKEIT
COST EFFECTIVE
KINDERFREUNDLICHKEIT
CHILD FRIENDLY
BEHINDERTENFREUNDLICHKEIT
DISABILITY FRIENDLY
URBANE INTERAKTION
URBAN INTERACTION
FLEXIBILITÄT
FLEXIBILITY
QUALITÄT DER ARCHITEKTUR
ARCHITECTURAL QUALITY
jovis
vodafone
BUILDING
A BETTER
DALLAS

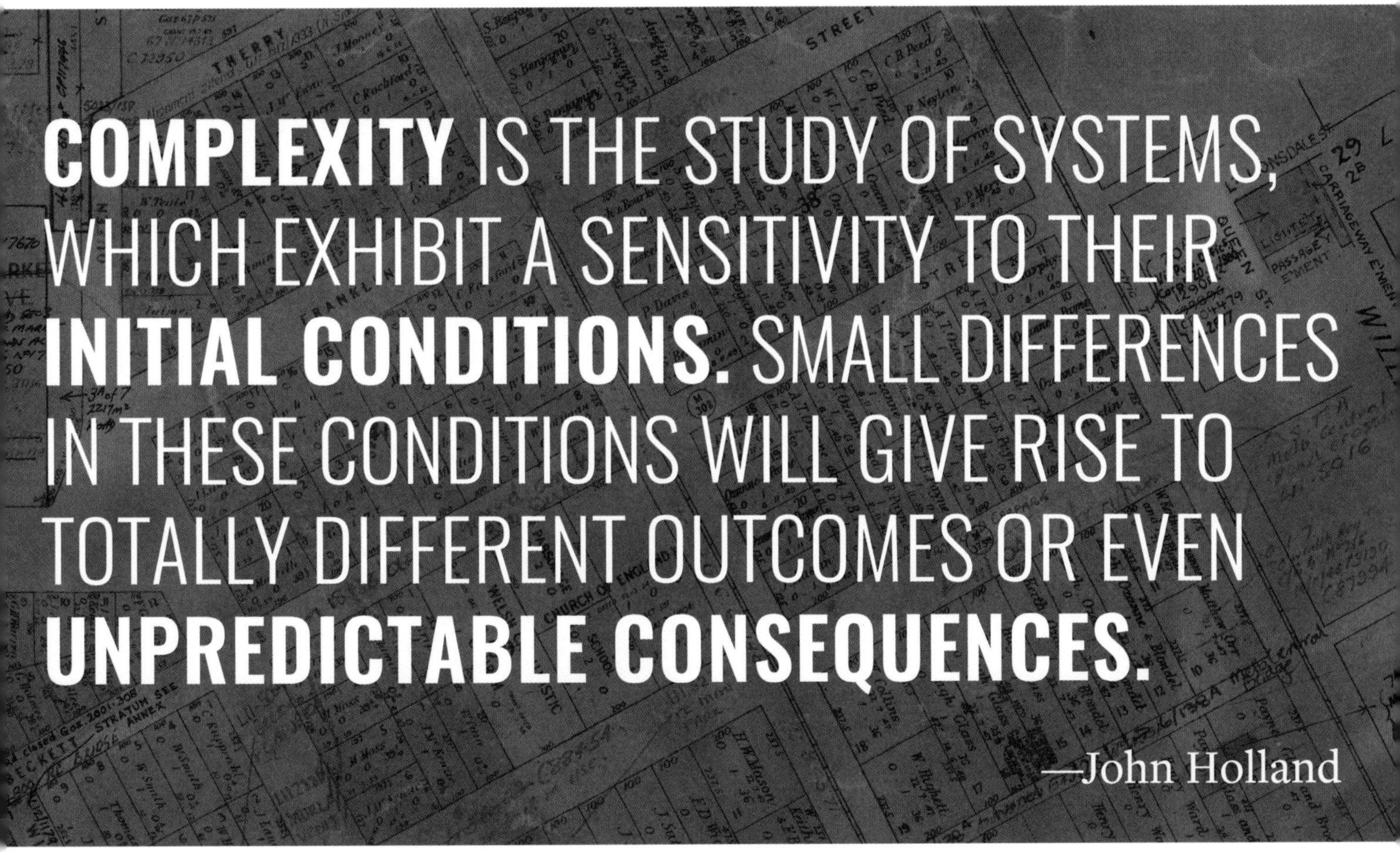

COMPLEXITY IS THE STUDY OF SYSTEMS, WHICH EXHIBIT A SENSITIVITY TO THEIR **INITIAL CONDITIONS.** SMALL DIFFERENCES IN THESE CONDITIONS WILL GIVE RISE TO TOTALLY DIFFERENT OUTCOMES OR EVEN **UNPREDICTABLE CONSEQUENCES.**

—John Holland

Clear and simple boundaries provide balanced constraints for growth and change through the application of a regular urban grid in Melbourne, Australia.

THEORY

Complexity does not arise from designed structure itself but from the extraordinary number of agents who, in response to the designed structure, cooperate towards the effect. It is this designed structure that provides the initial conditions—or starting points—for organising complexity.

There are two issues to consider when looking at these starting points: *boundary conditions* and *balancing constraints.* The one influences the other.

1 Boundary conditions

When Charles Mason and Jeremiah Dixon sailed to Philadelphia with their commission to survey America, they had the most powerful tool at their disposal: that of the boundary. Their job was to create order and with it define the new framework for response by many hands.

> *A border—the perimeter of a single massive or stretched-out use of territory—forms the edge of an area of 'ordinary' city. Often borders are thought of as passive objects, or matter-of-factly just as edges. However, a border exerts an active influence.*
>
> —Jane Jacobs

Boundary conditions are necessary to determine how people interact with the entire system. Good boundaries seem to be required for emergence to occur. These may be about the parameters of the block, lot or plot or about the relative scale of their compositions into larger chunks of the city. The common factor seems to be that there is a well-bounded space within which an emergence can occur.

It is well recognised by many researchers that the clarity of a boundary aids the process of creativity and is the essential precondition to innovation. That is, to support innovation, lay down very strict boundaries, add a clear goal and then give freedom to experiment within those parameters. It is the boundary that gives rise to the urban grain—the DNA or cellular structure of the place—by breaking down the city and its neighbourhoods, districts and quarters into fields for complexity and therefore emergence. We can see these fields as the Petri dish: the medium where we can grow life, economy and culture.

By breaking down the city into its smallest elements, we release the potential for multiple interactions and creations by many actors: making Massive Small change.

> *It was my fate from birth/ To make my mark upon the earth.*
>
> —Mark Knopfler, *Sailing to Philadelphia*

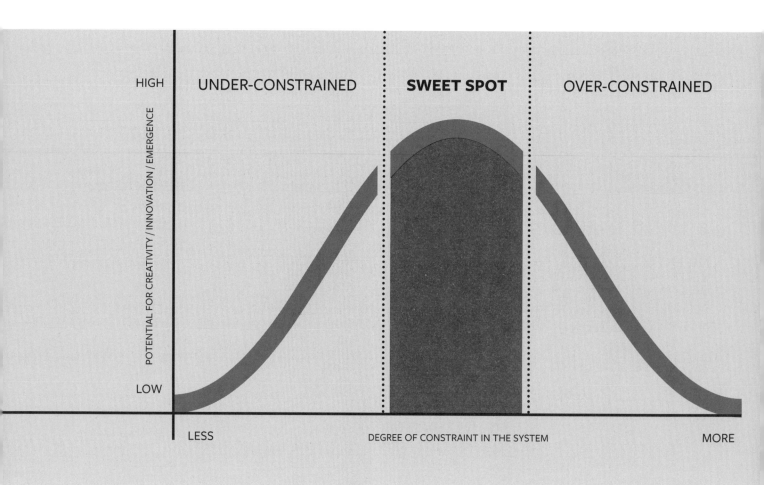

HIGH
UNDER-CONSTRAINED
SWEET SPOT
OVER-CONSTRAINED
POTENTIAL FOR CREATIVITY / INNOVATION / EMERGENCE
LOW
LESS
DEGREE OF CONSTRAINT IN THE SYSTEM
MORE

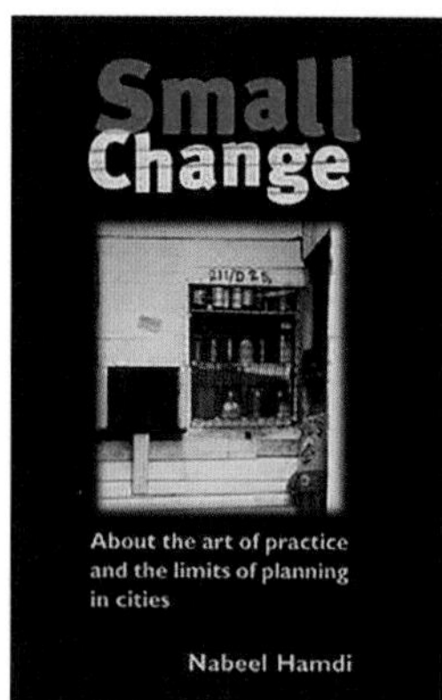

2 Balancing constraints

When Nabeel Hamdi, in his book *Small Change*, talks of the need for designed structure with simple rules and routines, he also recognises that in adopting this designed structure we 'give up some of our liberty in order to protect the rest.' The question facing practice is: 'How much structure will be needed before the structure itself prohibits personal freedom, gets in the way of progress?' Balancing and, therefore, carefully managing the constraints that this structure imposes becomes paramount to the development process.

Creativity research shows a growing interest in the fundamental interplay between constraints and creativity. Careful handling of constraints is a prerequisite for urban innovation. Balder Onarheim and Michael Biskjaer, in their paper 'Balancing Constraints and the Sweet Spot as Coming Topics for Creativity Research', provide an easier way of conceptualising this through their bell curve, which shows that the potential for creativity and innovation (also called the sweet spot of generative emergence) lies at the point of balance. If systems are underconstrained or overconstrained, it reduces this potential.

Onarheim and Biskjaer see the relationship between creativity and constraints as demonstrating the complex nature of constraints as both enabling and restraining in creative processes. This might appear counterintuitive, as one might imagine that more rather than fewer creative freedoms would consistently yield better outcomes. This is why most writings on creativity seem to focus on freedom rather than on constraints.

The importance of constraints appeals to several disciplines related to or within creativity, and none more so than urbanism. Many urbanists not only recognise constraints as lying at the core of creativity but also will argue that creativity cannot be conceptualised, applied or understood without considering the complex nature of constraints.

Our current systems of planning, design and development could be seen to be positioned in the overconstrained dimension of Onarheim and Biskjaer's bell curve or the rigid conformity extreme of Dee Hock's chaordic spectrum—both accounting for the stifling of creativity and innovation in building new urban neighbourhoods.

DRIVERS OF CHANGE

Bottom-up systems imply that they start from small beginnings and can get bigger, but this depends on the individual drivers of growth and change that allow them to flourish.

The following four drivers can be seen as working together. They are all essential. None can be disregarded in a system looking to harness bottom-up activity.

Cities, too, are constellations of networks, and laws of scalability relate with eerie precision to them.

—Geoffrey West

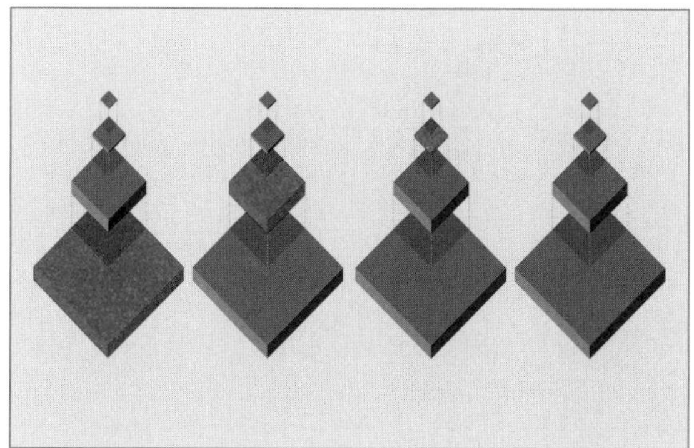

1 **Scaleability** is the ability of place (urban block or neighbourhood) to continue to function well when it (or its context) is changed in size or volume in order to meet local needs. Rescaling is usually to a larger size or volume, although it could relate to managing the decline of a town or city. The rescaling can be of the place itself—for example, the addition of a single new home to a street or the building of a new urban block. It could also be in the scaleable object's migration to a new context—for example, to a new operating system.

2 **Interchangeability**, also referred to as interoperability, is a property of a system (say, block and plot structure), whose interfaces work with other systems, present or future, without any restricted access or implementation. This occurs in situations where two or more items are so similar in their functional and physical characteristics that each is capable of replacing the other without causing a need for alteration or adjustment to fulfil the same requirement. In housing this could be seen as one house replacing another within the constraints of the same plot.

3 **Replicability** is the property of an activity, process or experiment that allows it to be duplicated at another location or time. This duplication is particularly important to the development of normative approaches where the lessons learnt can be reapplied—in network development, urban block layouts, open building systems and housing and street typologies.

4 **Diversity** is essential for emergent change to occur. The greater the diversity in a system, the greater the 'possibility space' it can explore. What is needed is diversity of all kinds. Diversity, on its own, will not give rise to emergence; in fact, it can lead to anarchy and conflict. But in combination with the other conditions, it has a vital part to play.

PLACE-MAKING TO CONDITION-MAKING

We now know that in order to facilitate bottom-up action in forming the building blocks of our cities—our neighbourhoods—we must move from deterministic place-making (where there is a focus on fixed end states) to responsive condition-making, which gives rise to emergent solutions.

CONDITIONS give us a new way of thinking about planned urbanism. Gone are the utopian visions we have used in recent decades. Gone are the old ways of believing that we can plan, design and develop successful end states through the top-down techniques that fixate on imagined end states. Gone is the single focus governments bring to the way we procure and deliver housing and neighbourhoods for people.

The theory of evolution by cumulative natural selection is the only theory we know of that is in principle capable of explaining the existence of organised complexity.

—Richard Dawkins

This shift does not mean that we do not plan, design and develop, only that we plan, design and develop differently—and with better outcomes for urban society. It is a shift from Venus to Mars. It means that we do things to liberate the latent creativity in people to contribute to solving their problems. It means we are the curator in this process and not the dictator. Our role becomes enabling, not limiting. In this shift, we move to our new dimension:

1 **From viewing the city as a mechanistic model to viewing it as a complex adaptive system.** This demands a better understanding of how complexity can be organised.

2 **From seeing urbanism as a closed set of rules to seeing it as an open system that continuously interacts and evolves with its environment.** This is one that is not restricted by abstract urban planning notions and demands a better understanding of open standards principles and the role they play in the evolutionary process.

Cities are just problems in organised complexity.

—Jane Jacobs

3 **From physical determinism to establishing highly responsive urban places that offer choice to all their constituents, from the individual to the collective, to form their living environments.** This demands an understanding of the generators and accelerators of urban form.

4 **From constantly going back to the first principle in the pursuit of the next best thing to establishing the common platforms from which innovation can spring.** This demands a better understanding of scaleable, interchangeable and replicable processes that act as an invisible chassis to stimulate and shape urban development at all levels.

5 **From a view of places as idealised organic representations of 'townscape' to the regularity and order that urban systems require for the development of an urban vernacular.** This demands a better understanding of the nature of typologies across the whole scale of cities—from streets, blocks, lots and plots to buildings and their parts.

6 **From bigness to Massive Small change, where the focus is on multiple actions by many small actors rather than on single actions of the big few.** This demands a better understanding of behavioural dynamics, social systems and collective action.

7 **From single, fixed end states to radical incrementalism, where the focus is on small beginnings and intervening occurs in a precisely targeted way to stimulate growth and change.** This demands a better understanding of long-life, loose-fit solutions that are highly adaptive to changing conditions.

8 **From seeing cities as a static set of visual artefacts to working with them as a living organism that will deliver remarkable results if treated in a genuinely democratic and ethical way.** This demands a better understanding of open systems theory, organisational dynamics, urban resilience and sustainable development.

Ultimately condition-making is a better way of thinking and acting for all actors in the system. Fixed masterplans that sit on dusty shelves will be replaced by dynamic tools and processes, which will lead to spontaneous and continuously evolving places. The best qualities of urbanism will emerge as we get better at doing it. Best of all, we will have the organised complexity that Jane Jacobs described.

We know that emergence cannot be controlled, predicted or managed. There are no magic levers that can be pulled to give us a particular kind of emergent result. But we also know that emergence can be facilitated and influenced. In other words, while you cannot create complexity, you can put in place certain conditions for it to emerge.

MASTERPLAN VERSUS GENERAL PLAN

Faced with a big problem, city fathers commission yet another masterplan / strategy / action plan / framework to plot a realistic way forwards. Using this approach, the scale of the problem mountain remains huge and is only resolved when action occurs—and inevitably it does not occur.

The standard plan-making process is long, extended and arduous. There are big brief-writing processes, followed by big procurement processes to get big names to come up with big ideas. What follows is the traditional early consultation / evidence collection / policy review / ideas generation / more consultation / draft planning / viability assessment / even more consultation / final plan process. This could take up to three years from inception to completion, and by the time the process has been completed, the brief is well out of date.

As a linear sequence of events, the entire process is deeply flawed and holds cities to ransom as it plods on. When it fails to come up with the right answers, yet another masterplan / strategy / action plan / framework process is commissioned. And so we go back to first principles again and again.

Cities and their neighbourhoods are complex systems that must be responsive to changing times. With the masterplan approach as we know it today, most aspects of the city, from the larger to the smaller scale, are defined by a single big vision at a particular moment of time. Most are out of date before they start, and they require big players to implement them.

> *The general plan requires the least amount of government intervention.... With its addressed surveyed plots, it gives low-income families the greatest freedom to build, at their own pace and responding to their own needs.*
>
> —John F. C. Turner

According to UN-Habitat in their paper 'Planned City Extensions: Analysis of Historical Examples', when a neighbourhood is defined as the combination of a general plan and regulations, we have the best possible outcomes:

1 A general plan—best demonstrated in places such as Barcelona, New York and Savannah—delineates the underlying distribution of public and private space (such as streets and blocks) and defines the hierarchy of streets and open spaces. It also establishes the subdivisions of urban blocks into lots and plots. It can be a very simple document that sets the base of the urban fabric. It prevails through time and must be designed with the future in mind.

2 Regulations define all the desirable aspects of buildings and public spaces and establish city form. They are the 'generators of urban fabric'. They can be consolidated into four main groups: construction, vicinity, public ornament and hygiene. Regulations are defined by a variety of actors and are a representation of the culture of the city and its time. Regulations tend to evolve through time, reflecting the changing needs of the population and altering the city.

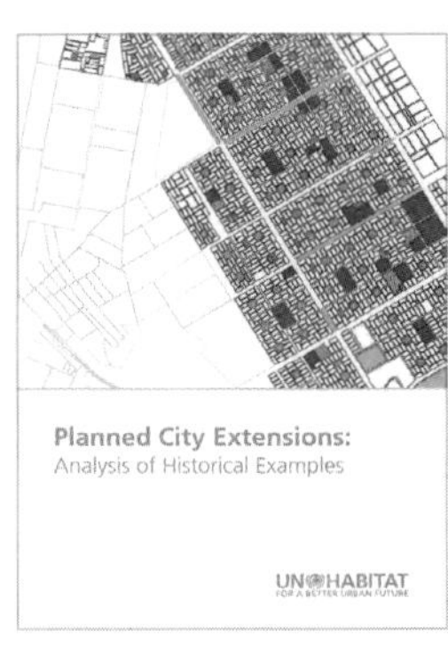

The general plan and regulations approach provides a flexible framework for the creation of the city and its neighbourhoods.

THINKING IN LEVELS

John Habraken, in his book *The Structure of the Ordinary: Form and Control in the Built Environment*, proposed the process of designing and building on environmental levels as a way of breaking the problem mountain down into problem molehills. The idea of environmental levels is not new, but his explicit formulation of the principle of levels is rather new.

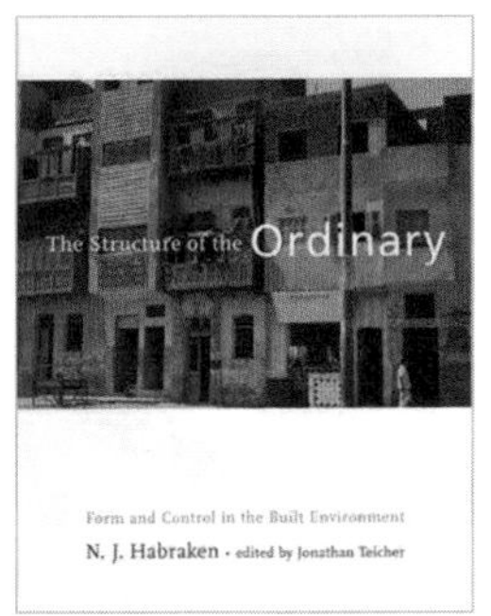

The design professions have evolved naturally in correspondence to the behaviour of environmental levels: urban planners, engineers, urban designers, architects and interior architects each operate according to a certain level of intervention.

These levels, according to Habraken, represent distinct spheres of control in the built environment—'a hierarchical structure in which higher levels serve as the setting and context in which lower levels operate. As such, higher levels exercise dominance over lower levels, while lower levels are dependent on higher-level structure.' Innovation takes place within each of these levels, and they evolve as self-learning feedback loops, avoiding the need to always go back to first principles.

Urban Code: 100 Lessons for Understanding the City, by Anne Mikoleit and Moritz Purckhauser, gives us another way of understanding the forces that shape a place. By uncovering the syntax of one hundred familiar patterns of life in neighbourhoods—through maxims, observations and bite-sized truths—they reveal its inherent logic and language.

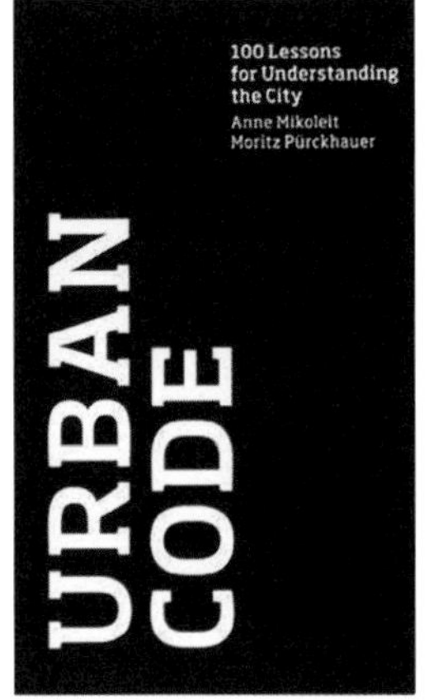

PROBLEM MOUNTAINS INTO MOLEHILLS

In breaking down the scale of the problem, we can identify two distinct and progressive stages: one that is the dominant domain of government and another for the people. These stages, starting with the 'invisible chassis' and ending with the 'emergent vernacular', overlap at their crossover point and are described as follows:

1 The invisible chassis

> *Order is not sufficient. What is required, is something much more complex. It is order entering upon novelty; so that the massiveness of order does not degenerate into mere repetition; and so that the novelty is always reflected upon a background of system.*
>
> —Alfred North Whitehead

We all know that places are susceptible to their early conditions, and urban neighbourhoods are the most complex places we know. We also know that you cannot design complexity, but you can put in place the preconditions for complexity to emerge and be organised.

So the invisible chassis exerts its influence on all aspects of a neighbourhood's future outcomes. It is a way of organising complexity and moves us from our current position where we only see the city as a mechanistic model. The invisible chassis provides future urban neighbourhoods with a set of balanced constraints within which creativity and innovation flourish.

Under the seeming disorder of the old city, wherever the old city is working successfully, is a marvelous order for maintaining the safety of the streets and the freedom of the city. It is a complex order.

—Jane Jacobs

Invisible chassis is the name we have given to that simple 'essential urban order' that needs to be put in place by governments at the start to enable people to respond effectively in shaping the future life and evolution of their own urban neighbourhoods. This works in combination with the generators of urban fabric, such as standards, codes and regulations that initiate and accelerate development. It can be seen as the lightest touch that will ensure the maximum impact by creating the early top-down interventions that will trigger subsequent bottom-up responsive action.

The essential urban order and the generators of urban fabric are both enabling mechanisms that give structure to the city and its neighbourhoods, providing the necessary framework for public action that will generate private reaction. These gestures in the public domain need to be fundamental and, coupled with an apparent general direction, recognise that a framework of well-considered constraints provides the medium for creative response. This process cannot be completely rationalised or determined by analysis: its intention is, using synthesis, to create an environment that will always contain aspects of accident and disorder within its framework. It is not necessary to determine where to locate the pub, or how much retail space is required to sustain the local community. A successful urban fabric needs no functional programme. In fact, diversity within a complex, multiuse urban grain becomes the ideal substitute for formal land-use planning. Alternative responses are then merely influenced by proximity of location or variety of place.

If we balance these constraints carefully, we can operate within the sweet spot of generative emergence—the point at which people can continually explore, experiment, learn and evolve. We must manage this process in the present, getting rapid and continuous feedback and making small changes to achieve a better balance.

We must make a million dabs on a canvas, rather than a few big splashes.

2 Emergent vernacular

Emergent vernacular comes out of collective action by people responding to the invisible chassis. Working within these balanced constraints—in combination with the resources of the place and the skills of the citizens—solutions emerge. Things start and people learn by doing. Things adapt, and people get better at doing them. These solutions become embedded as the way of doing things, and they continually evolve as circumstances change. These solutions feedback to the invisible chassis, and it evolves as well. This is emergent vernacular at work.

THE NEIGHBOURHOOD ENABLING MODEL

To break down the sheer scale of complexity into manageable phases, we have adapted the Habraken model to work with our starter conditions. We call it a NEIGHBOURHOOD ENABLING MODEL, and it has the following qualities:

1 **Discrete levels.** The starter conditions can be seen as levels that are separate but interlinked stages in the formation of the localities of towns and cities—neighbourhoods, districts and quarters. As in Habraken's model, this creates a hierarchical structure that can be easly understood by all the players in the system.

2 **Sequential layers.** Using the Kelly analogy, the model is 'built up out of modules that work perfectly, layered one over the other'. It uses a sequential approach from the strategic to the local (neighbourhood to home) and from the collective to the individual.

3 **Active interfaces.** The model uses a series of development tools that act as switches or interfaces between each of the levels to help evolve the conditions. As a result, the model remains stable while innovation happens progressively at these interfaces.

4 **Combined qualities.** Each of our starter conditions draws together combinations of the universal qualities, characteristics and features that give rise to emergent urbanism. These build on the new science of cities and include, in many instances:

   a **Scale:** scaleability, interconnectivity, diversity, multiplicity
   b **Form:** regularity, self-similarity, clear boundaries, interoperability
   c **Context:** openness, lack of inhibitors, self-organisation, spontaneity
   d **Choice:** intentionality, conformity, coherence, replicability, interchangeability
   e **Dynamics:** unpredictability, rate of flow, perpetual novelty, continuous feedback

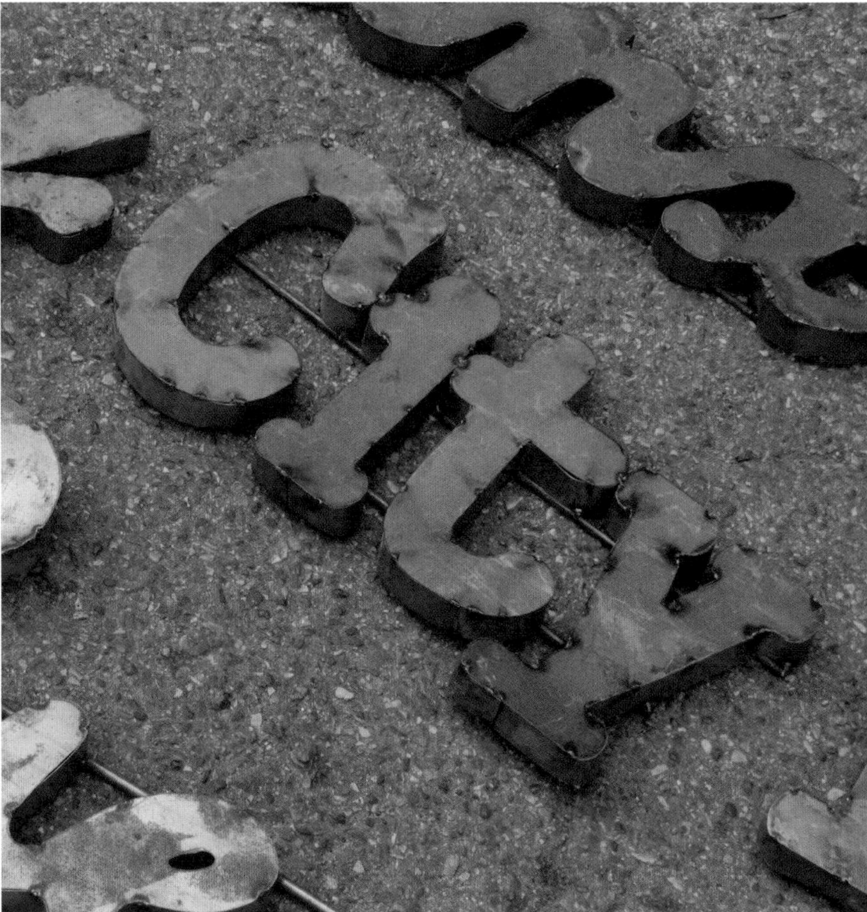

5 **Clear roles and responsibilities.** Each of the starter conditions shows the boundaries of individual and collective roles and the responsibilities of government and people within top-down and bottom-up systems of planning, design and development. Each starter condition has different strengths, but any desired outcomes will not be realised unless they all work together.

6 **Feedback loops.** The model provides a mechanism for providing rapid and continuous feedback loops through the active interfaces. These feedback loops enable targets and trajectories to be monitored, outcomes to be assessed and remedial action to be taken.

Complexity that works is built up out of modules that work perfectly, layered one over the other.

—Kevin Kelly

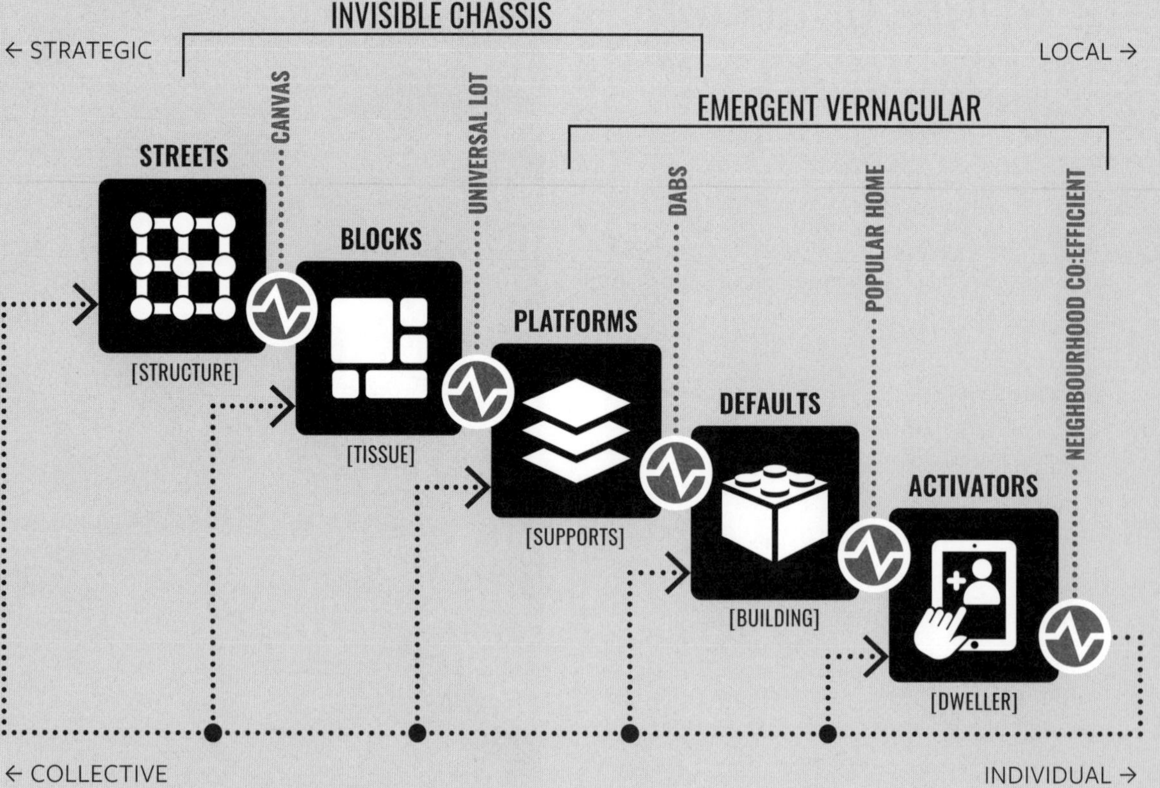

COMPONENTS OF THE MODEL

The two core components of the NEIGHBOURHOOD ENABLING MODEL, starter CONDITIONS and development TOOLBOX, are described overleaf.

1 Starter CONDITIONS

The structure and relationship of these five conditions remain relatively static and intact, only evolving slowly as the system is tested and learns. The conditions, which are widely principle-based and have been structured to establish the balanced constraints and provide the medium for innovation, creativity and emergence, include:

1 **STREETS:** creating open and adaptive urban networks to enable progressive evolution of urbanism at the outset

2 **BLOCKS:** establishing a scaleable and responsive urban fabric by defining clear and regular parameters for parcelling land

3 **PLATFORMS:** developing common springboards for continuous innovation in order to generate and accelerate urban growth and change

4 **DEFAULTS:** defining evolving sets of structured choices that offer infinite possibilities and promote constant evolution of urban typologies

5 **ACTIVATORS:** providing the triggers to build human social capital through creating compact urbanism in every possible instance

When a city is defined by an essential urban order and fixed with a general plan—what we refer to as a combination of STREETS and BLOCKS—the result is more flexible and neighbourhoods can evolve through time. When we add to these the generators of urban fabric—what we call PLATFORMS—then we have the invisible chassis. This is the minimum input required by governments to lever action by others to form urban neighbourhoods.

The MODEL identifies the first three conditions (shown as the invisible chassis) where the role of government is dominant and the last three (shown as emergent vernacular) as the predominant domain of the people. This means the roles of government and the people overlap at the PLATFORM condition—the point at which top-down and bottom-up systems operate in the closest collaboration.

2 Developmental TOOLBOX

These tools provide the active interface between each of the levels. Each place will be able to develop their tools to suit local circumstances, so the tools are identified as our way and provide a prompt only. They include:

1. **CANVAS:** a grid-based simulation tool for facilitating layouts and testing the metrics for a full range of development scenarios—from suburban intensification through to urban renewal and new urban extensions
2. **UNIVERSAL LOT:** a parametric method for parcelling land, testing capacity and providing a regular, orthogonal framework for further subdivision and consolidation
3. **DABS (dweller adaptive building systems):** an open building platform and generative framework to initiate and accelerate built form, providing the springboard for innovation
4. **POPULAR HOME:** a parameter-based approach to developing standard building typologies across the full spectrum of the neighbourhood
5. **NEIGHBOURHOOD CO:EFFICIENT:** a citizen engagement tool to build social capital, which provides a catalogue of potential catalysts to be employed across the full spectrum of starter conditions

These all work together to make complex processes manageable. The model can be adopted, adapted or reinvented as necessary, but it provides a starting process that we have found very useful as an organising device to think differently and act differently, quickly.

the Beauty Parlor

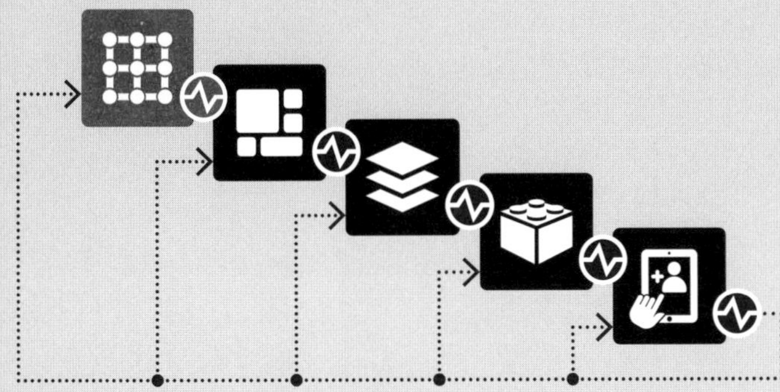

STREETS

AS OPEN ADAPTIVE NETWORKS

STREETS as urban networks, our first condition, are enabling mechanisms that give rise to the coarse web that provides us with the essential structure of our cities and their neighbourhoods. Street networks, as conduits for movement and locations for social interaction, give us the sticky lattice of urban life. They act as motherboards, giving us the basic circuitry and components of city processes. Without them, urbanism finds it difficult to take root and evolve.

Streets *NOUN*

1 The channel for flows of movement and associated stopping that breathes economic life and reason into places

2 The focus for responsive action by people, providing the primary generators of urban form

3 The first point of social interaction, forming the foundation of community life in neighbourhoods

4 Urban networks, which are shown to be any interconnecting structure or pattern that is intricately formed or complex

SYNONYMS
arteries, ways, boulevards, avenues, lanes, mews

SCOPE

This section introduces three main theories: the plan as a motherboard for growth and change, street networks as complex systems, and emerging hierarchies. These theories all influence how we look at urban networks in a neighbourhood context. It then shows how these theories are reflected in the desired qualities of openness and adaptiveness, considering two issues: trees versus webs, and smart networks and how they relate to the design of networks.

The main content of this section includes:

1 **The grid as the primary generator of urban form:** showing examples and describing the regular urban grid and adapting the grid to a place

2 **Urban streets:** showing examples and describing types of city streets and local streets

3 **Development tools:** using the example of CANVAS, a grid-based modelling tool that can be used to test urban capacity and simulate new neighbourhoods

4 **Localia urban neighbourhood:** designing a neighbourhood network, showing an imaginary example of this process

URBAN NETWORKS AS COMPLEX SYSTEMS

Networks are complex adaptive systems and have an underlying order. This order is embodied in the patterns of interactions between the components of the network—its streets, spaces, activities and services. Networks are a simplified schematic view of cities, capturing a large part of their structure and their organisation. They contain a significant amount of information about the deep underlying and universal rules at work in their formation and evolution.

According to Wikipedia, a *complex adaptive system* is a 'complex macroscopic collection' of relatively 'similar and partially

connected micro-structures'—formed to adapt to the changing environment and increase its survivability as a macro-structure.' In cities, *macro-structure*, also called the *primary urban structure*, corresponds to the overall organisation of urban society, described at a rather large-scale level by the arrangements of neighbourhoods, districts and quarters and their respective properties and relationships to one another. *Micro-structures* are the connected networks of local streets and spaces that provide the medium for neighbourhood formation and social interaction to flourish. Although we may move to more local and independent systems, networks impose a regulating order that's hard to overcome and exert a strong influence on the shape of our urban fabric.

We can't get away without defining any order. Even relational systems need some structure and rules. Nor should we be scared of imposing order. Traditional societies have done this well: clearly defining freedom within constraints and limiting choice, which gives rise to infinite possibilities. So, the success of any incremental transformation will depend on the creation of a significant and essential order—an urban network imbued with choices at a variety of levels. Some of the structures within this order can be stable and long-lived while others can be volatile and ever-changing in quality and function. We find structure at all scales. To see how difficult it is to grasp the nature of this order, it is necessary to look at the boundaries of complex systems, and to the role of hierarchies within them.

EMERGING HIERARCHIES

Since cities have structure, they inevitably have hierarchies. We will not understand the city if we do not allow for the role of these hierarchies, but we have to remember that, depending on the nature of the urban structure, they are often not clearly determined and they often overlap with one another.

> *Hierarchy is a natural ordering that is initially based on size.*
>
> —Michael Batty

Hierarchies are an important outcome of the evolution of cities and are commonly found in complex systems. They usually arise from the organisation of systems at different scales and their connectedness. Neighbourhoods are a good example of this. They can also arise from simple rules, norms and mores that impose order on these communities—the main street, the civic spine, the neighbourhood streets and traffic-managed zones. They form in the early stages and are transformed over time.

> *Although hierarchies are necessary to generate frameworks of meaning in the system, they cannot remain unchanged. As the context changes, so must the hierarchies. Some hierarchies may be more long-lived than others, but it is important to perceive of hierarchies as transformable entities.*
>
> —Paul Cilliers

Edinburgh New Town is a complex grid that is both regular and connected, but it is also carefully planned with a hierarchical system of streets and lanes, deliberately devised to reflect the social hierarchy of the times. This plan can be compared with the more open, democratic, orthogonal gridiron of Glasgow from a similar period, which is similar to what we find in many American cities like Houston and Chicago. These plans develop hierarchies as they evolve. More complex grids such as Savannah in Georgia are imbued with a hierarchy at the outset. We have to remember that hierarchies themselves have a complex structure and they can be managed. In a viable system, such as a city, it will be possible to transform existing hierarchies into different ones, but not to eliminate them.

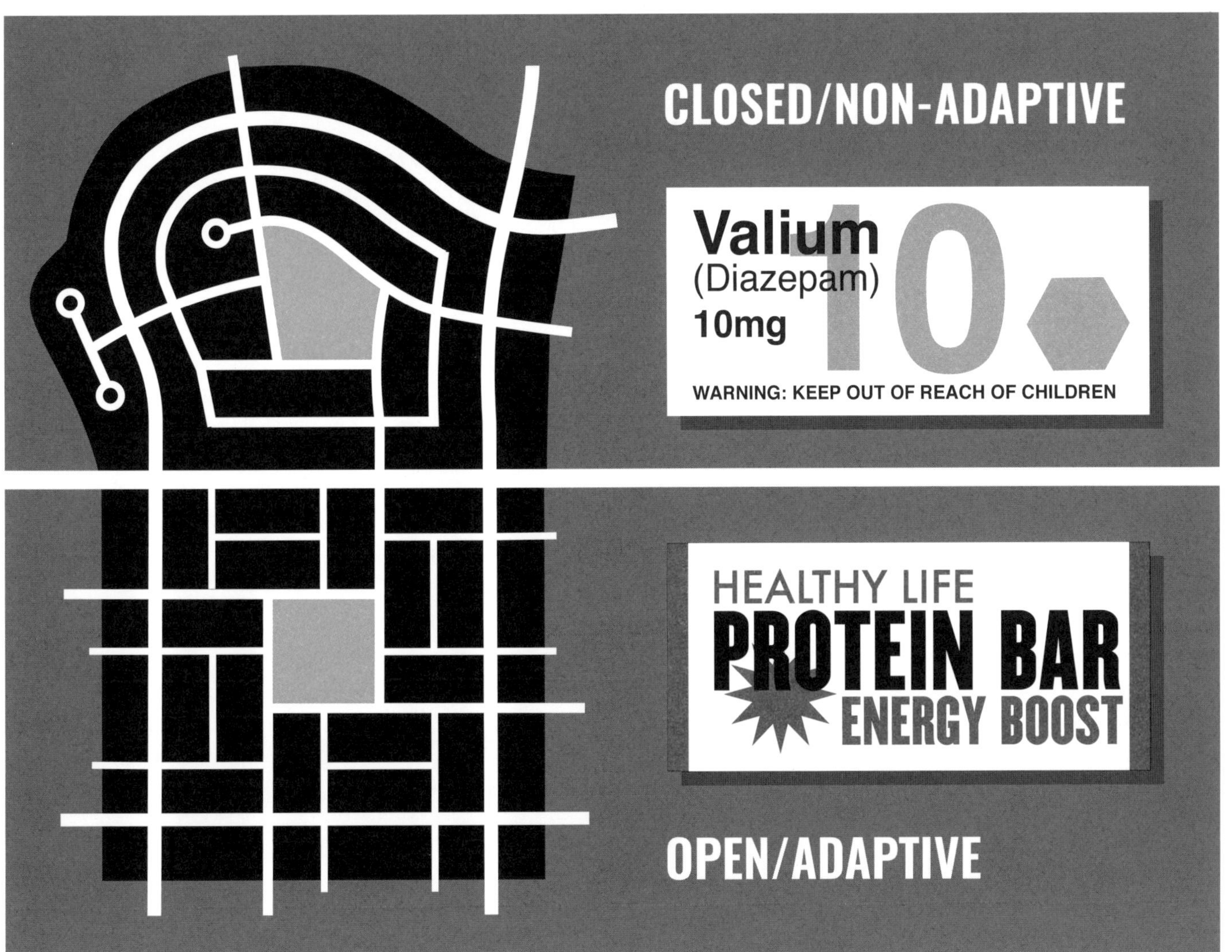

QUALITIES OF STREETS

Whatever order the street network of the city takes—regular or distorted, orthogonal or radial, celebratory or modest—it must at least have the qualities of openness and adaptiveness. These qualities are essential for fostering complexity and structuring complex choices. In planned urbanism, we cannot re-create the organic nature of the village, but we can create the conditions that give rise to organic transformation. If we wish to design for diversity, however, we have much to gain from learning to recognise nuances in traditional planned cities and towns: their origins and initial intents.

This means we need to understand how differences in them have developed; how our building and environmental management policies may, in turn, affect them; and how we can better respect or enhance differences that already exist between one area and another. We can learn to see street layouts not merely as roads diagrams but as responsive environments—city streets and local streets—that reveal the processes of urban building.

Trees versus webs

The design of street patterns in towns and cities has long been a contentious subject. The battle still rages.

In *A City Is Not a Tree*, Christopher Alexander shows that successful social and economic networks form complex web-like, lattice patterns, but that reductionist thinkers limit their interpretations to a simple mathematical tree of segregated parts and subparts, eliminating many connections in the process. The same can be said for movement systems. In attempting to plan for urban structure, a single human mind falls back on tree diagrams to maintain their conceptual control of the plan, thus computing well below the level of spontaneous urban complexity.

Traditional engineering design still argues for a hierarchical, treelike street pattern, particularly in new suburban environments. It is a traffic planning technique for laying out road networks that exclude through-traffic from developed areas. At the lowest level of the hierarchy are cul-de-sac streets. Treelike structures reflect the standard road hierarchy approach that is adopted in most countries, some more rigorously than others.

Sometimes they are referred to as tributaries, a similar analogy to the branching tree. In the tree example, you can only go from the trunk to the big branch to the smaller branch and finally to the leaf. Then you can only go back again following the same rules. So once you fix a place with a treelike street pattern, it's hard to reverse or open it up later to be a more connected system.

Many traffic engineers argue that there are some benefits to a hierarchy of streets in that it:

→ Aggregates traffic to correspondingly larger routes so there can be economies of scale in construction and operation
→ Separates access from movement functions to reduce conflict, making both potentially safer
→ Keeps residential neighbourhoods quiet
→ Reduces network redundancy

Proposals for open, adaptive grids draw strong opposition from old-school, die-hard traffic engineers, but many urban designers propose a flatter, weblike pattern of streets, with *connectivity* and *permeability* as their watchwords. They see the present traffic-planning system as being dominated by the pseudoscience found in the current closed and nonadaptive hierarchy of roads policy. For them, the treelike street diagram does not easily offer different interpretations. It is a reductionist construct that stifles urban life at the outset. In their demerits column, a treelike hierarchy:

→ Increases travel distance
→ Puts pressure on limited specific points in the system
→ Requires a fixed, never-changing set of design parameters
→ May be less legible (Lynch, 1960) in that it increases difficulty in navigation compared with flat networks.

By contrast, many regular, traditional grids are laid out as city streets (e.g., main streets, avenues and boulevards) connected at regular intervals to local streets. They are by their very nature open but can still be managed to achieve many of the professed advantages of treelike structures and changed back again as needs arise. The strategy in Barcelona to break down the continuous street grids into environmental cells of nine grid squares to limit through traffic and thereby reduce pollution is a case in point.

For us to move on, this conflict in thinking needs to change, and this is not just a matter of narrowly defining hierarchies through reference to factors other than just traffic. It will require us to recognise that the nature or character of any given street can vary significantly along its length and is likely change over time.

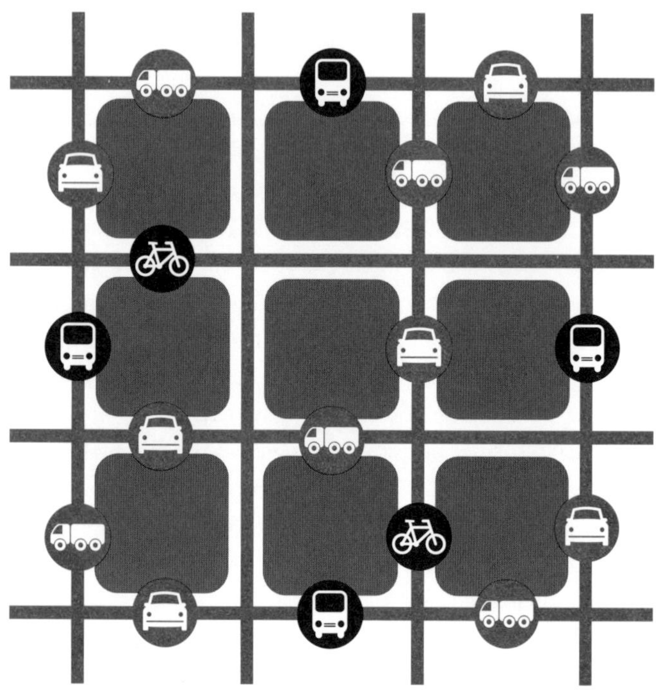

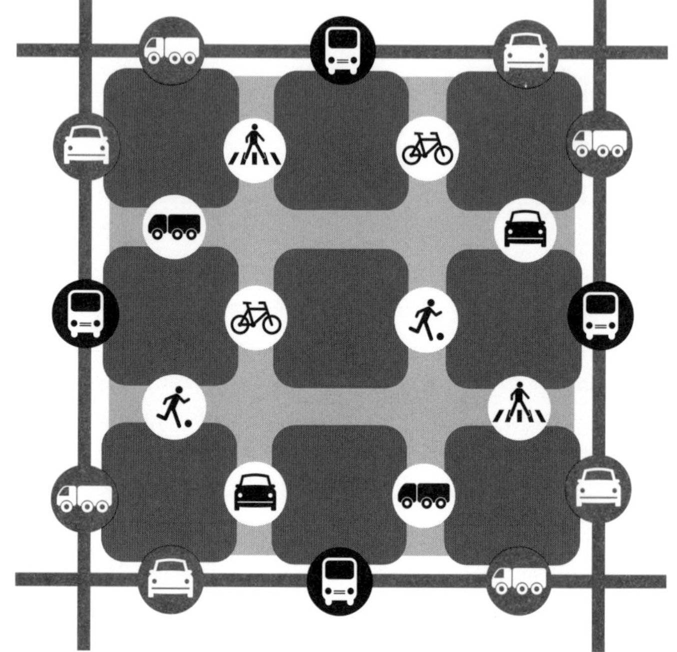

This page, left: Current layout of urban blocks in Barcelona, Spain. **Right:** Proposals to incorporate nine city blocks into a traffic calmed zone. **Opposite page:** Night view of Phoenix, Arizona by NASA.

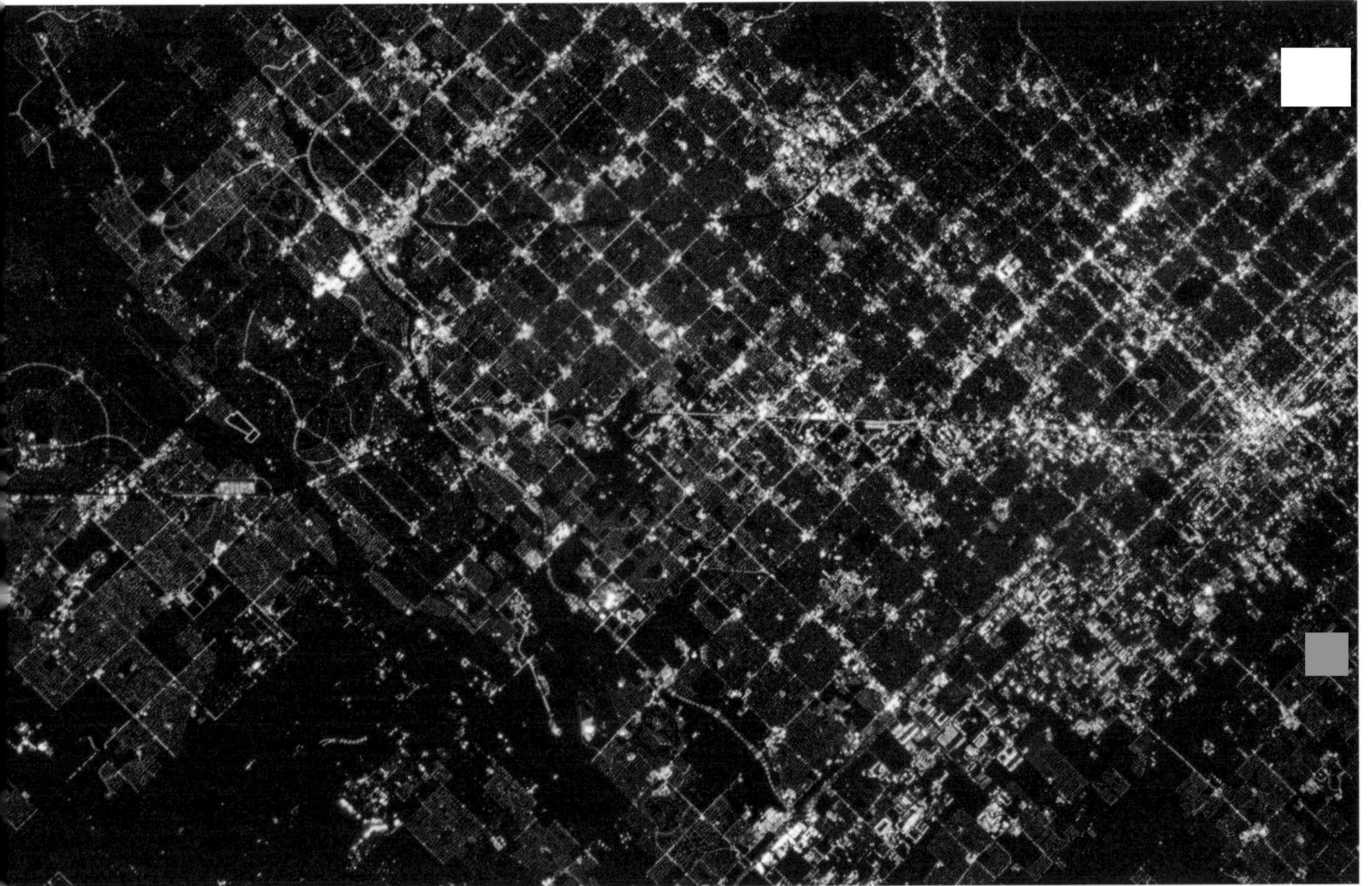

SMART NETWORKS

Smart has become the umbrella term for making the best possible use of new technologies and new ideas to make life better in urban areas. Whether it is London's Oyster Card, sustainable housing, low-carbon schemes or the targeted delivery of public services online to save energy and time, innovation can create intelligent networks for all.

A smart grid is a form of intelligent network utilising digital technology and is being promoted as a way of addressing complex energy dependence and resilience issues. It thrives on a lattice formation. Its principles can be applied to local energy networks, water management and information technology. Recognising that traffic models cannot deal with the complexity of urban traffic-monitoring and management systems, engineers are now exploring the potential for grids to take on the principle of self-learning, with traffic controls adjusting to peak flow conditions in intelligent ways.

A smart city is an open city. It runs on data, so public bodies need to demonstrate a presumption of openness, making data freely available online in an accessible format. Data connectivity needs to be seen as a right, not a privilege, and as ubiquitous as water from the tap.

Technology cannot replace common sense, as most of the challenges are social, not technical. You need a critical mass of people creating ideas and solutions.

> *Do not turn to futurologists with glib visions.... The smart city is about connectivity: connectivity of systems, devices, data, people, and organisations. Connectivity between all kinds of things, on all kinds of levels. To those charged with creating the smart cities of the future are this: invest in connectivity (and bandwidth) and build up your social capital—trust, intelligence, and opportunity. The community is king.*
>
> —Drew Hemment

The community is the long game because active and engaged communities build sustainability into the system. Local authorities need to shift out of a top-down service delivery mindset to let the new smart ecosystem evolve, rich in complexity. It is going to be built by many people, working in different ways and on different levels.

Cities will be key drivers for this agenda, and there is a sweet spot between cities that are small enough for coordinated action and broad enough to achieve a critical mass. But it is around neighbourhoods, with their efficiencies of scale and their relative fleetness of foot, that the lasting effects of change will be realised and happen quickly. A city can be defined as 'smart' when investments in human and social capital and traditional and modern communication infrastructure fuel sustainable economic development and a high quality of life, with a wise management of natural resources, through participatory governance.

The fundamental question is: do intelligent networks demand a new urban form or configuration for the city or does conventional urbanity still prevail? It would appear that at city scale, technology does not shape; it is a servant to the plan. At neighbourhood scale, the situation is slightly different. Utility networks do impose a rigour on the plan, but these can be readily accommodated within the open hierarchical system.

GENERATIVE URBANISM

We know that if we can get the structure of a place right, we can use different techniques to generate urban form and even give us clues to transforming neighbourhoods. This is not necessarily as end states but rather to anticipate outcomes such as how much land we need and the nature of infrastructure investment or provision of local services. The tools could test such variables as public transport accessibility to determine the nature and extent of services over time. They could be used to identify thresholds for energy networks or carbon footprinting. They could also be used to determine thresholds for the provision of public services and model public good outcomes. They could even be used to simulate neighbourhood formation.

SimCity offers us some clues as to how we could do this, but it is still not a generative model. It follows relatively simple rules and projects these rules out over an infinite number of interacting agents. At present, it is still difficult to model the whole city, given its sheer complexity, but given enough interactions, and given the right simple rules, the simulated idea of a neighbourhood can emerge.

Urban designers and local authorities could benefit from further research into the most appropriate norms in this domain, thus moving it from the realms of gaming to real-life applications. Generative urban design needs the development of a design system or process rather than a single design solution. The answer lies in an amalgamation of systems. Geographic information systems (GIS) are very powerful systems for accessing large-scale urban data; hence, they play a significant role in urban planning as an analytical tool. However, they were conceived as interactive maps, and so they lack capacities for designing. On the other hand, computer-aided design (CAD) systems are very powerful drawing tools and fit for design practice.

In urban design, the linking of GIS to CAD tools becomes an important goal, as this will allow designing directly on the GIS data. This design process uses preexisting GIS data as a starting point, and the generation of designs will involve the application of the rules codified in patterns. Moreover, this toolkit will allow the designer to create designs that respect these patterns rather than simply repeating them.

MANIPULATING COMPLEXITY

Bill Hillier and his colleague at University College London, Mike Batty, have developed a number of methodologies to analyse and manipulate complexity in our towns and cities. Their insights clearly draw from the rapid developments in complexity science in general. Investigators have been able to identify with mathematical precision the processes that give rise to complex structures from an apparently simple set of rules, with useful implications for game theory, economics, biology, physics, meteorology and many other fields. In the fields of planning and urban design, the insights can be used to understand the relationship between complex urban form and relatively simple generative rules—like those followed by a group of actors in a building process. The significance of Hillier's and Batty's tools is that they have applied these insights to the urban toolkit available to practitioners, in effect regenerating the urban complexity that previously existed or could potentially exist, with desirable results. Hillier's analytical technique, Space Syntax, in particular, has been put to the test a number of times with notable success.

Technology gives us the ability to be flexible, to give us infinite possibilities to forward-fund projects against later revenues. We need to make good decisions that get us the good public outcomes we are trying to achieve. What we need to do is see our city and neighbourhood plans as our motherboards, enabling places to go through change but still have a fundamental order—plug-and-play comes to mind. In this way, we can wire up our cities to suit, add new processors and memory, and boot up.

Space Syntax map of Central London, showing how many other streets are connected to each street, with blue representing simple streets with few connecting streets and red representing complex streets with many connecting streets.

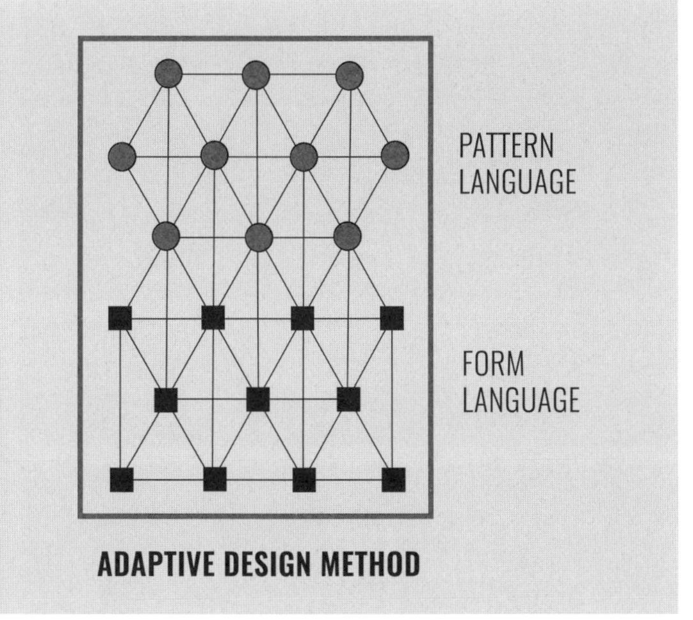

PATTERN LANGUAGE AND FORM LANGUAGE

In his paper 'Adaptive Design Method: Pattern Language, and Form Language', Nikos Salingaros says, 'Design in architecture and urbanism is guided by two distinct complementary languages: a pattern language, and a form language.'

1 **The pattern language** contains rules for how human beings interact with built forms—a pattern language codifies practical solutions developed over millennia, which are appropriate to local customs, society and climate.

2 **A form language**, on the other hand, consists of geometrical rules for putting matter together. It is visual and tectonic, traditionally arising from available materials and their human uses rather than from images. Different form languages correspond to different architectural traditions or styles.

Every adaptive design method combines a pattern language with a viable form language, otherwise it inevitably creates alien environments.

In Alexander et al.'s *A Pattern Language: Towns, Buildings, Construction*, each pattern is an individual entity that identifies a recurrent problem in our environment and points out the solution to that problem in such way that it can be used many times without having the same outcome. Alexander et al. propose the idea that patterns can be modified and refined according to specific situations and environments: opening a full field of concepts for exploring design. Furthermore, the idea provides the possibility of creating new patterns for new districts, neighbourhoods and quarters. The proposed patterns were criticised for their lack of precision or structure at a finer level, but this was at a time when we did not have the power of computers to assist us.

Generative models

Beirão, Duarte and Stouffs, in their paper 'Structuring a Generative Model for Urban Design', see urban design as the result of applying a set of urban patterns and 'method' rules that can be applied at four different scales or development phases, separately or together.

→ Rules based on a city scale, through an analysis of the existing settlement, establish the relevant clues for the definition of the plan's structural geometries.

→ The urban grids or city tissue lay down the remaining features of the street structure.

→ The norms of the place determine the characteristics of the urban elements, such as the neighbourhoods, blocks, lots and plots.

→ The detailing of the urban space defines its material aspects, ambiences and the like.

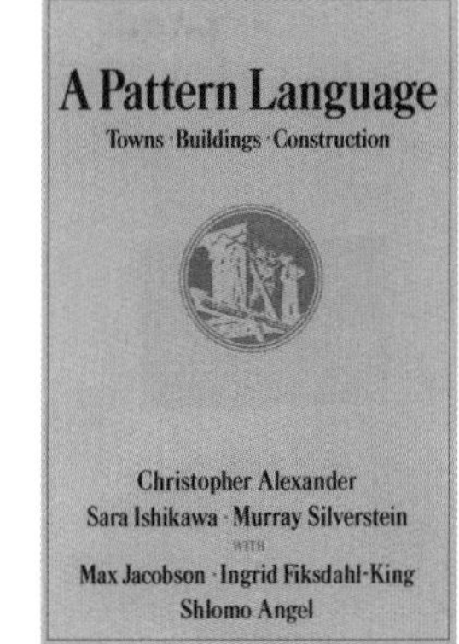

A set of urban patterns sets out a vision for a particular scale of the urban design problem. Each urban pattern may produce different 'method' rules, meaning each designer will define his own interpretation for that pattern based on his preferences.

To allow a suitable structure for computing, Beirão, Duarte and Stouffs proposed a refined pattern structure to solve specific design problems and make design solutions more flexible and reusable. Their approach uses the same principles as any programming language. This upgrade to the pattern language theory points a way of linking a mostly theoretical side of a really good pattern concept developed by Alexander to a precise structure, suitable for computational purposes.

To build up an active, generative tool for urban design purposes, we need to refine this approach into one better adapted to design rather than analysis, or where analysis is part of the continuous feedback process. This is the golden egg of urban design. We are not there yet, but we are getting close.

MOTHERBOARDS FOR GROWTH AND CHANGE

We have a long history of formal plan-making throughout civilisation that has served us well. A history where city streets have been repetitively laid out in highly efficient patterns that reflect vernacular traditions and the higher order needs of the place and society. These traditions and needs are our standard motherboards on which we can build urban society.

This tradition, at a mass scale, is best seen in the Roman *castrum* plan, whose standard, off-the-shelf imprint still exists in many European and North African towns and cities. The Roman grid is characterised by a near-perfect orthogonal layout of streets, all crossing each other at right angles, and by the presence of two main streets, set at right angles from each other and called the *cardo* and the *decumanus*. At its intersection lies the forum, the heart of the place. In simple terms, this is the main public space at the junction of two main roads, which gives us our networks. The urban blocks give us our fields.

Since then we have seen endless grids—formal, modified or distorted to suit the topography of the place (some even disregarding it)—produced on vellum or using Chinese inks in smoky plan-makers' offices in government buildings or royal palaces. Rolled up, they have been dispatched to surveyors to colonise the old and new world. These grids have given rise to the best and most enduring examples of planned urbanism we have ever seen:

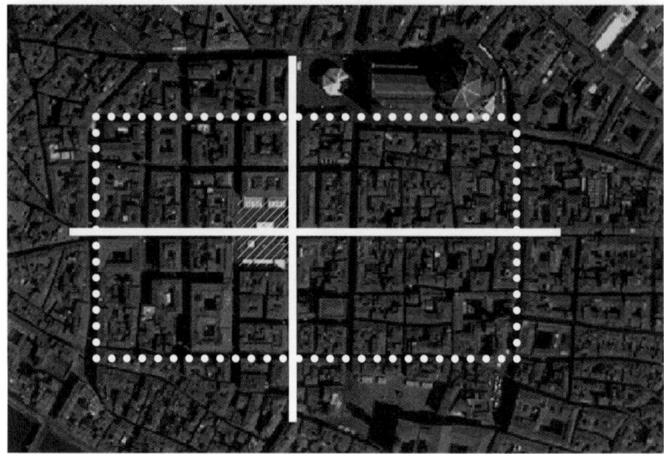

→ The nine-square grid plans of Jaipur are based on ancient Hindu planning principles, also used later by Balkrishna Doshi for its expansion a few decades ago.

→ The mediaeval bastides of southern France were planned as fortified towns with a grid layout of intersecting streets, with wide thoroughfares that divide the town plan into insulae, or blocks, through which a narrow lane often runs, and a central market square surrounded by arcades (covered) through which the axes of thoroughfares pass.

→ In the Spanish colonisation of South America, King Phillip II's Laws of the Indes specified the requirement for a square or rectangular central plaza with its eight principal streets running from the plaza's corners. Hundreds of grid-plan communities throughout the Americas were established according to this rigid pattern, echoing the practices of earlier Indian civilisations.

→ The Portuguese downtown plans for Lisbon were rebuilt after the 1755 earthquake, largely according to the plans of the Marquess of Pombal. Instead of rebuilding the mediaeval town, Pombal decided to demolish the remains of the earthquake and rebuild the downtown by modern urban rules. This plan with its rules was used as a template for Lourenço Marques (now known as Maputo) in Mozambique and many other Portuguese colonial settlements.

→ The tradition of Scottish town-making created the formal grids of Inverary, Cullen, Stonehaven (well-illustrated in Thomas Sharp's *The Anatomy of a Village*) and the supergrid of Glasgow, which was the template for many North American and Canadian cities.

→ Victorian town plans became standard fare for the colonisation of the Empire. You can see the same DNA of the plan in towns in Australia, New Zealand, Africa and the West Indies. All show the same orthogonal approach with the town hall or church as the centrepiece to the place—urban blocks, lots and plots meticulously pegged out by the surveyors using chains.

→ The great grids of America...and so on.

Without a doubt, the three masterpieces of planned urbanism are the old-world examples of Edinburgh New Town and Jaipur Pink City in India, and the new-world example of Savannah in Georgia, which are all described in more detail later. All demonstrate the idea of repetitive elements of streets and blocks. All are open and hierarchical within a logical framework.

All demonstrate a remarkable robustness to accommodate new forms of living and working. Edinburgh New Town has adapted well to the flight of its banking industry to leafy business parks. Jaipur, although it has a focus on tourism, still accommodates a rich mix of uses at street and building levels. Savannah has evolved into a place where each central square has taken on a different personality to reflect its surrounding land uses. All are classical cities as 'patterns in time', like universal motherboards just waiting to process urban life.

More recently the Dutch have been showing us how to do it in places like Ijlburg in Holland. There you see the evolution of the trimmed plan to the modified grid and the new urban structure. Nothing complicated: simplicity giving rise to complexity. It is the sequence of the designer overlaying a standard repetitive grid plan on the site and trimming it to fit that is meaningful. We have always done this—dropped a plan in a context and modified it to fit the vagaries of the place. The plan of Mayfair in London shows where the legacy of the lost rivers of London is still reflected in narrow winding Marylebone Lane that breaks the formal grids. This inconsistency introduces the delight of thc uncxpcctcd. Nowhere is this delight more evident than in the plan of San Francisco, which begs the question, did the plan-makers ever visit the site? Thank goodness they didn't. Otherwise, Steve McQueen's car chases in the film *Bullitt* would never have been the same.

The steep slopes of San Francisco have modified the plan. The grid plan, in turn, has altered the place. There, context is a modifier, not a determinant. 'Push and push back', the essential conditions for emergence, have happened to the benefit of both sides.

Plan-making is not difficult. So why are our urban designers making it so difficult? Why does everything have to start from first principles? If we are to offer anything to the evolution of our cities and towns and their districts, neighbourhoods and quarters, we have to understand the tools of our craft better. Idle technocratic solutions or abstract clichés won't help. Looking to our past achievements and picking up the threads of this experience will.

Opposite page: Florence, Italy, showing the Roman *castrum* plan embedded in its DNA with its two main streets, the 'cardo' and the 'decumanus', and the 'forum' at their intersection. **This page, top left:** The regular urban grid of Barcelona, Spain. **Top middle:** Edinburgh New Town. **Top right:** The Pink City, Jaipur. **Bottom left:** Savannah, Georgia. **Bottom middle:** Marylebone in London, showing the weaving route of the underground Tyburn River. **Bottom right:** The grid of San Francisco laid over its rolling hills.

THE GRID AS THE GENERATOR OF FORM

> *The philosopher Hippodamus was the first city planner, initially proposing a grid pattern and zoning scheme, as well as a central agora open square, that beloved place of gathering and assembly so precious to democracy. We know how Plato, in the* Republic, *said much about how cities relate to democracy.*
>
> —Andy Merrifield

The grid as a basic organisational structure has proved valid and useful in the development of cities and their neighbourhoods all around the world in all places and times:

→ The rational organisation of streets in a geometrical network eases the complex process of neighbourhood formation.
→ It allows the urbanisation of vast areas with a single identity and a coherent image.
→ It becomes a device that is understandable and that can be embraced by all urban actors, providing a functional, cohesive and readable city.
→ It optimises infrastructure.
→ Its primary virtue is its simplicity.

The open, hierarchical grid has long been advocated as providing the necessary framework for urban variety. It need not be monotonous. Variety can be introduced in subsequent phases, through hierarchy or with the definition of smaller scale elements. Our most successful models for planned growth are those where the positive qualities of the grid have been exploited in combination with squares, mews and boulevards. Most successful planned cities are collisions of minigrids or combinations of formal grid patterns. Some are regular grid patterns laid out in rigorous orders across the town or city.

There are examples we can see around us every day in great cities and their districts, neighbourhoods and quarters: the supergrids of New York and San Francisco; the regular hierarchical Georgian grids of Mayfair or Fitzrovia in London; the highly evolved complex grids of Edinburgh New Town, Savannah, Jaipur, Lima and Beijing. All of these demonstrate the potential to accommodate urban variety at a number of scales and have served us well, adapting to change over the years and perpetually expressing regularity and novelty. They can take the extraordinary and the normal. They are both the foreground and the background of an essential order.

THE PRO-GRID CREED OF FAITH

To dispel many of the myths propagated by the garden city movement, Paul Groth refers to the following articles of the 'pro-grid creed of faith':

> Article 1: The grid can be a symbol of positive and human values. The grid historically has been a common symbol not for greed but rational urban life, symbolising the achievement of relative egalitarianism.
>
> Article 2: Viable human settlements with a proper sense of community can thrive on a grid plan as well as any other form and, for the newcomer, the comprehensibility of the grid can be a source of security.
>
> Article 3: Grids do not necessarily create mechanical monotony in urban design and may, in fact, be the best possible provision for organic growth in a city's future. Further, the grid has adapted itself well to long periods of growth and change.
>
> Article 4: The grid allows but does not cause high density. Grids are indeed the most efficient forms of compact settlement, but the decision to build compactly should be seen as policy, not as a result of street form.

To this we can now add:

> Article 5: The grid, when having the qualities of an open hierarchical network, provides the essential order for emergence. Hierarchical redesign of grids is, therefore, a diversifying process.

It is the processes of change—design, initial settlement, social specialisation, accretion, traffic management and evolution of infrastructure systems—that give the grids their subtle but real variety. Although only one of many formal and social contexts in which urban architecture can take place, the open hierarchical grid is nonetheless the most robust and adaptable form of physical structure. So it is not remarkable that many spontaneous urban settlements—given the total freedom to arrange themselves how and where they want—organise themselves into open hierarchical systems that endure well into their formalisation as neighbourhoods, districts and quarters of the city or town. Most are complex social, economic and movement networks. Most are regular street grids.

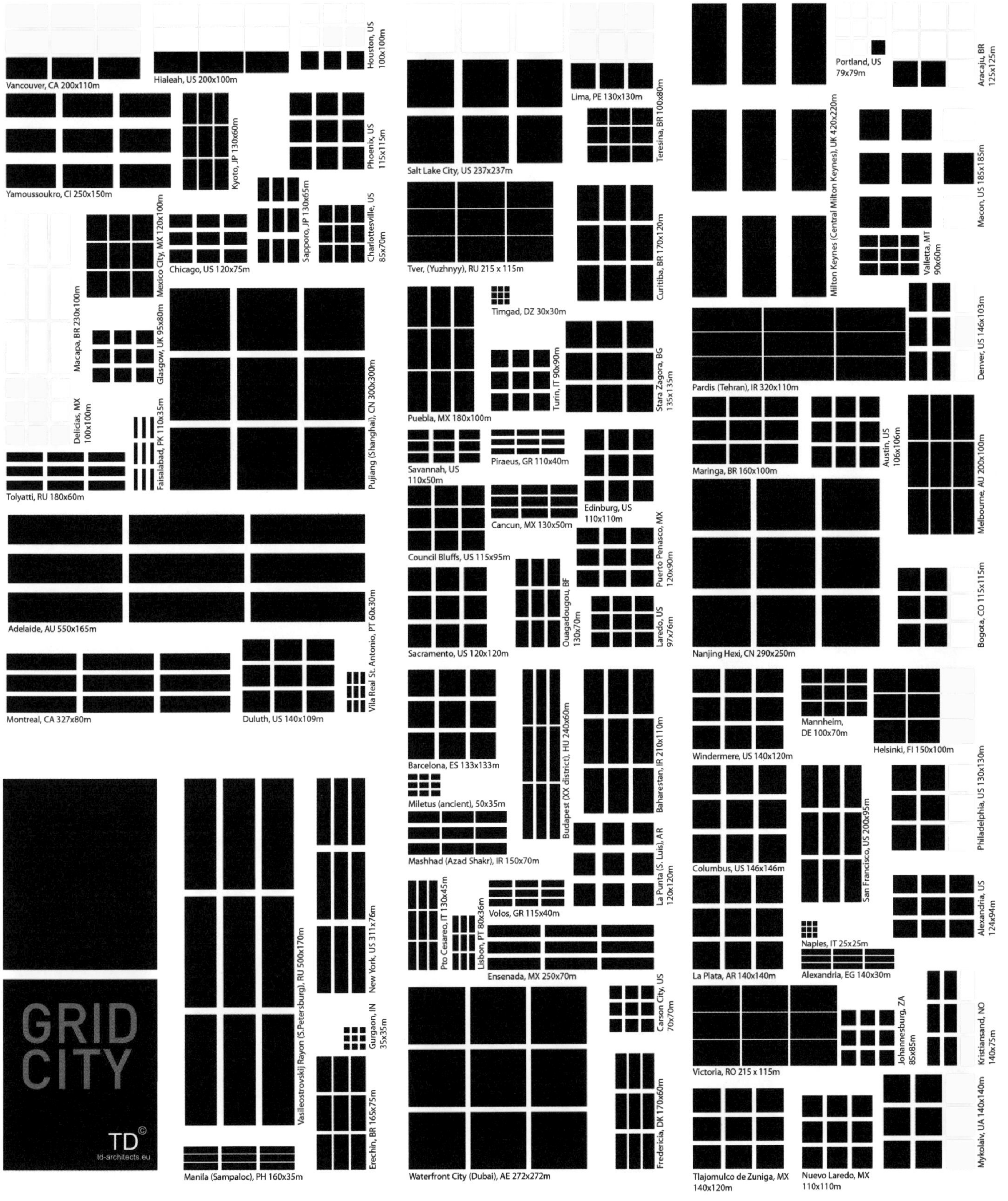

An extract from Grid City, an analysis of different grids by Theo Deutinger Architects, Netherlands. Grid sizes, proportions and repetitions have varied extremely throughout time, proving the grid's longevity and flexibility.

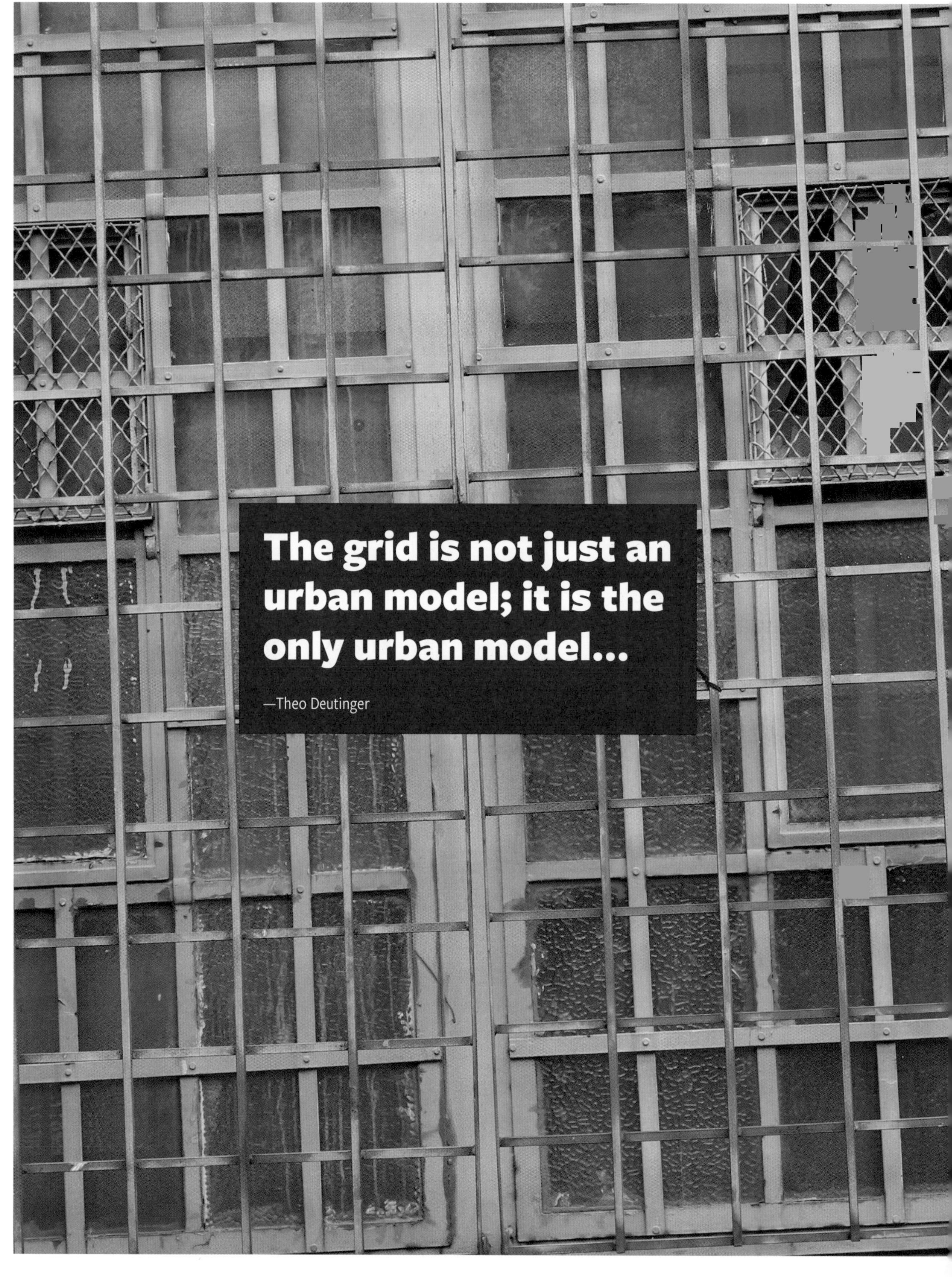

The grid is not just an urban model; it is the only urban model…

—Theo Deutinger

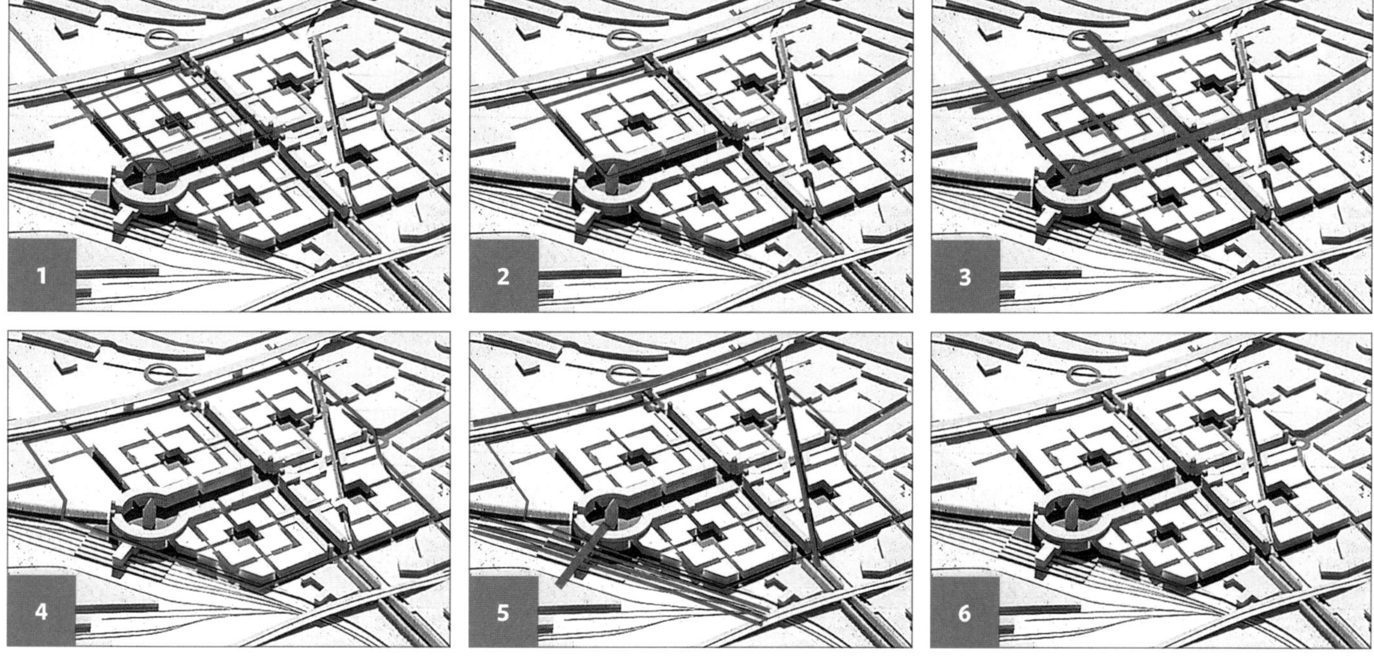

THE REGULAR STREET GRID

Regular street grids as networks come in many sizes and configurations and can be recognised by their scale (minigrids to megagrids), their form (regular to irregular) and their nature (simple to complex) and can be categorised in the following ways:

1 **Grain:** These range from a coarse grid of regular streets, which are then broken down more informally like the Jaipur or Barcelona grids, to a finer grain of regular streets that can be found in many Victorian and Parisian plans. The scale of streets is perfectly aligned to the pattern of built development, with little wastage.

2 **Module pattern:** How grids are composed and assembled to form distinct units (or modules) of development will have an effect on how people respond. These range from composite patterns of regular street blocks that can be replicated easily, such as the Philadelphia grid, to more sophisticated arrangements of regular composite street blocks, including open spaces and social structures, such as the Savannah grid.

3 **Hierarchy:** How streets are differentiated from one another will have a fundamental impact on how hierarchical systems will evolve. Some will find it easier to evolve than others. At one end of the spectrum these types of street grids range from a rigid gridiron pattern where streets and blocks are laid out in a monocultural single pattern with a flat hierarchy. At the other end, they could be more complex arrangements, which have a hierarchy of different street and block assemblies such as 'tartan' grids or use offset street patterns at the lowest scale to discourage unnecessary through-routing.

4 **Extent:** To this, we can contrast the continuous area of the street grid. How far it extends could exert an influence on the sense of identity or perceived boundaries of the neighbourhood. Street grids could roll out over large areas—like many of the American grids—or could be collections of colliding minigrids with open spaces, which are more typical of many European cities. In New York the grid of the West Village collides with that of the Manhattan gridiron, creating the distinct West Village neighbourhood.

5 **Contextual:** How a street grid responds to the nature and topography of a place will have an effect on its responsiveness. It could be as acontextual as the San Francisco grid, which is laid across the hillsides with little regard to topography (and creates its unique quality) to the Jaipur grid, which is cut away to give primacy to the sloping hills where the grid meets them.

6 **Urban condition:** Where a street grid is located is also a defining factor. Clearly, a street grid in a compact urban condition will have a different effect on its urban form to that in a suburban location. Street grids are well-suited to urban neighbourhoods.

Clearly, the ranges expressed in all of the above categories are valid. The design and layout of a settlement lie in structuring the choice of a network (or combination of networks) that provides the best possible responsive environments for the place and its culture.

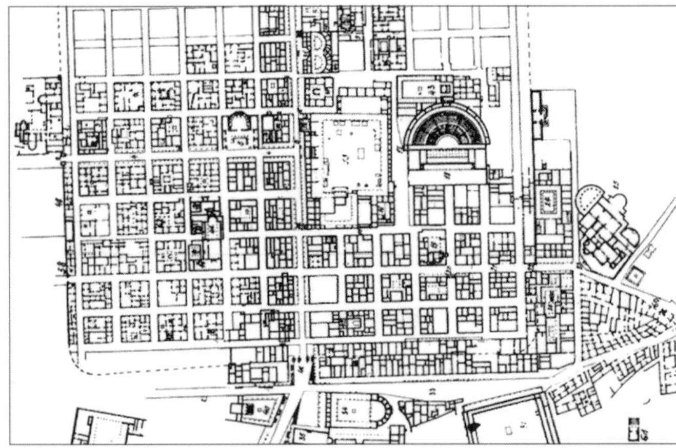

ADAPTING THE STREET GRID TO THE PLACE

Street grids represent universal solutions that can be adapted to the particular qualities of a location. As such, they can even be overlaid over existing informal development that can be restructured over time to allow its transition to more formal development. In responding to the location, the unique qualities of the place emerge and create their own special identity. The ways in which these street grids could be adapted include:

→ **They could be aligned with local topography and natural features, existing development and established movement routes.** Many Roman settlements emerged from Roman camps that were planned along key military routes and at river crossings.

→ **They could be clipped along their edges to accommodate existing natural features such as rivers, sharp changes in topography or protected greenspace.** Ilburg in the Netherlands and Graaf-Reinet in South Africa are good examples of this.

→ **They could accommodate diagonal routes that collide with the regularity of the grid to create special architectural conditions.** Broadway in New York and the Diagonale in Barcelona are the best examples of this.

→ **They could respond to organic and formal features internal to the grid, such as historical assets, water bodies, streams or other natural elements.** The Marylebone grid in London shows the accommodation of an underground river.

→ **The grid could be split apart or rotated to create collisions with other grids to accommodate irregular internal open spaces that deal with changes in alignment of the grid.** Woodstock in Cape Town, and Berlin and London are good examples of this.

→ **The grid could be distorted to align with existing road patterns.** Tel Aviv and Chandigarh have minor shifts in the primary street pattern but still maintain an overall gridlike quality.

→ **The grid could utilise willful intervention, including the introduction of special urban design features such as formal crescents, ovals or offset urban squares.** Georgian Bath and the Edinburgh New Town are good examples of this in the United Kingdom.

→ **The grid could respect local cultural norms and traditions such as orientation, historical axes and views.** Jaipur shows how this is done using Vastu Shastra, a traditional Hindu system of architecture, which translates to 'science of architecture that describes principles of design, layout, measurements, ground preparation, space arrangement and spatial geometry'.

However a grid is adapted, it is the definition of a grid that will primarily define the city shape. The particular procedure of each designer finds different ways of applying a grid by basing decisions on various criteria. Decisions on grid dimensions come from experience and tacit knowledge. Certain patterns relate grid dimensions with the characterisations of the types of urban blocks and neighbourhoods, producing different links for future phases of design. Chosen patterns generate designs for transportation and street networks and movement systems.

Use the centreline of the street as the starting point

The logic of movement and access is the most obvious reason to take the street as the module. Karl Kropf makes a good case for this:

> At a primitive level, once there is a line of movement there is a line of centrality—you are at the centre. It establishes the axis and opens up the land either side. The street space and land either side are stitched together by the shortest movements in and out. It is usually a street or combination of streets—typically a functional and visual hierarchy of the main street and side streets. The hierarchy is reinforced by the reciprocal relationship between form, use and movement. Both uses and building types tend to cluster along the lines of movement.

It is always best to start with a grid based on the centreline of the street, with an offset on both sides defining the width of the street. The centreline always remains constant.

Opposite page, top: Early example of Roman town planning in Timgad, Algeria, 100 CE. **Upper middle:** The town of Graaff-Reinet, South Africa, set in an oxbow river. **Lower middle:** Cerda's Eixample, Barcelona, showing the Diagonale. **Bottom:** Marylebone, London showing winding route of underground Tyburn River. **This page, top:** Colliding grids in Woodstock, Cape Town, South Africa. **Upper middle:** The distorted grids of Tel Aviv, Israel. **Lower middle:** The structured grids and crescents of Craig's Edinburgh New Town, Scotland. **Bottom:** The historical axis that runs through the Pink City in Jaipur, India, with its supergrids that provide the primary urban structure.

LEARNING FROM HISTORY

UN-Habitat has produced a valuable compendium of grid-based plans in their publication 'Planned City Extensions: Analysis of Historical Examples'. From their analysis of cities that have been built in the historic past or recent history that have evolved in many different ways, we can learn things that only the passage of time can provide. These lessons are useful in guiding future urban growth, particularly in countries where urban life is not predominant.

> *The urbanisation process should be planned for the long-term; it should provide an essential structure, the spine, the matrix, the pattern of how the city will expand. Over time, economic activities and the various social needs will change the shape, and urban land uses, but not the pattern. This essential element must be defended and protected by the local authority, the repository of political legitimacy, and the rule of law.*
>
> —Jean Clos, Executive Director, UN-Habitat

Drawing from their lessons and adding others, we can learn how places with a grid-based layout—set in a physically rational plan—have evolved over time and adapted to changing needs. The ten case studies presented here, which include five from the UN-Habitat report, are different from one another—they are in developed or developing countries; they were built in different centuries; they are neighbourhoods or complete places; they house the rich or the poor—and yet they can all be classified as general plans with clearly defined street and block structures. However, they also have common aspects that serve to identify and explain an approach that can guide future urbanisation so as to generate cities that are sustainable, socially inclusive, and economically viable. They include:

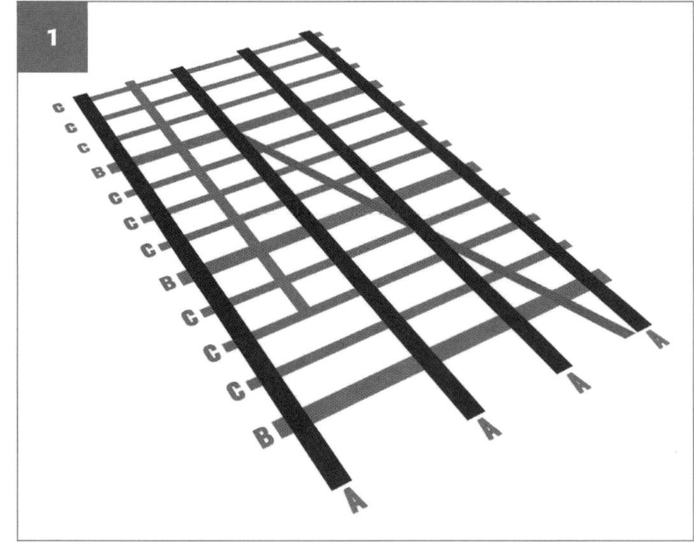

1 **Manhattan in New York** has a regular gridiron pattern that derives from the Commissioners' Plan of 1811. Often referred to as the 'greatest grid on Earth', its avenues extend through the peninsula in a direction that is parallel to the Hudson and East Rivers. Manhattan's grid has two main factors that create variety: street widths and block dimensions. Although block widths are constant, block lengths vary. The road network operates at two scales: the territorial and the local. The 30-metre-wide (100 feet) avenues and major cross streets provide the territorial scale. The 18-metre-wide (60 feet) standard cross roads provide the local point of reference. Broadway, as the single disruptive element, collides with the grid. Hilary Ballon's book, *The Greatest Grid: The Master Plan of Manhattan 1811–2011*, provides a valuable insight into the development of the plan.

Manhattan's grid gives rise to the following qualities:

→ It provides a simple, clear and flexible grid structure, within a limited city extension area defined by the river.

→ The grid has proved extremely flexible by offering value to the original 1811 plan without losing its essence, including the introduction of elements such as Broadway and Central Park.

→ It is global project understood at different scales—city scale and local scale—with a street hierarchy composed of a territorial scale of avenues and boulevards and a basic street grid.

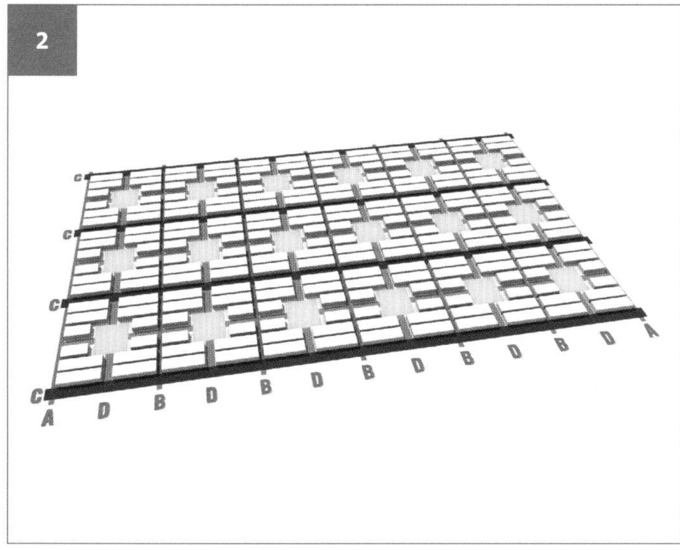

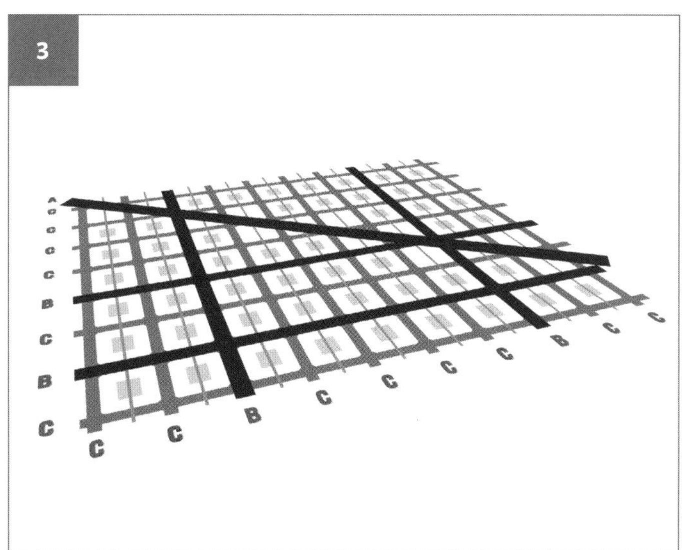

2 **Savannah, Georgia,** laid out in 1733 by General Oglethorpe, has a modular grid that runs parallel to the riverfront; it is a remarkable example of colonial planning. Savannah's hierarchically structured city plan is distinguished from those of previous colonial towns by its repeated pattern of connected neighbourhoods, multiple squares, streets, and designed expansion into lands held by the city (the common). The basic plan unit is a ward, laid out with standard dimensions. Streets and blocks are organised around a central open space or square. The streets bounding the wards allow uninterrupted movement of traffic. Internal streets are interrupted by squares to create a pedestrian-friendly scale that has adapted well over time. Savannah's plan reflects political and organisational considerations of the day with the repetitive placement of wards, squares, and equal-sized lots pointing to the egalitarian ideals of the Quaker colony. Its qualities are summed up as follows:

→ The simple nature of the general plan creates a legible and well-organised street structure.

→ The neighbourhood units provide public spaces and facilities at the local scale.

→ The idea of the modular arrangement of the block and its capacity to generate neighbourhood life has provided inspiration for many urban plans since.

→ The modular arrangement introduces a larger urban scale that breaks the monotony of a simple grid and can be repeated, facilitating urban growth.

→ The proximity of the urban squares with wider streets linking them results in a network of interconnected public spaces.

3 **Example in Barcelona** is defined by its bevelled-corner grid squares, an important feature of the Cerda General Plan of 1860. The grid extends in directions that are parallel and perpendicular to the sea. The grid can be read at different scales, with the avenues representing the territorial scale. The streets that define the local scale are 50 per cent dedicated to pedestrian use and 50 per cent to vehicular traffic. Generous dimensions of streets and avenues have created the flexibility to allow them to adapt well over time:

→ It has resulted in a responsive and evolving city centre.

→ It has evolved into a variety of street sections, ranging from the mainly vehicular street to the pedestrian promenade.

→ It has permitted the adaptation to new ways of urban transportation (car, tramway) and urban infrastructure that was not common practice when the plan was designed.

→ It allowed the creation of a variety of public spaces.

→ It has created a street hierarchy with the superposition of fast vehicular routes over the homogeneous city grid.

→ It is evolving into a system of neighbourhood units as some streets are being traffic-calmed within a nine-grid-square arrangement.

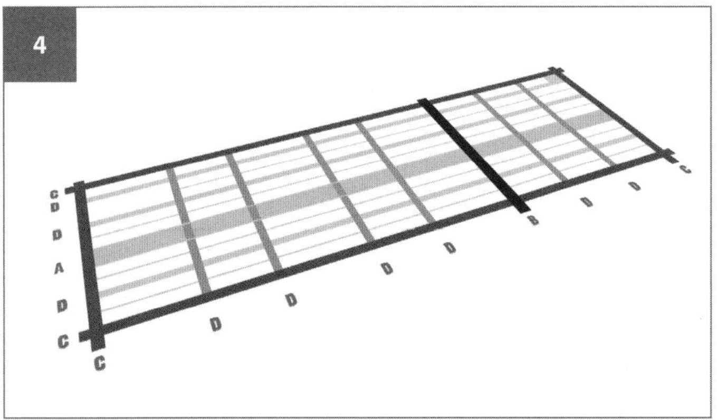

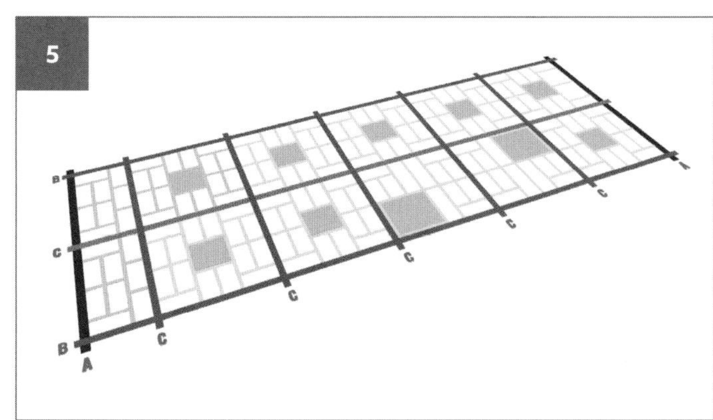

4 **The Back Bay in Boston** was planned by Arthur Gilman in 1856 for the Commonwealth of Massachusetts when they reclaimed part of the Bay area for development. The grid orientation is adapted to the natural features of the city, with the longitudinal and central direction of the grid arranged parallel to the tidal lines of the Bay. The street grid has a clear and well-organised structure. Major streets that surround the neighbourhood and connect it to the city-wide street grid are 26 metres (85 feet) wide. Neighbourhood streets are 21 metres (70 feet) wide and provide internal circulation. Commonwealth Avenue, at 60 metres (200 feet) wide, is the core of the neighbourhood—a central linear open space around which the neighbourhood is built. Qualities of the Back Bay grid include:

→ Open spaces are a key feature of the plan, with the grid based on the voids rather than on the built-up spaces. Considerable importance is given to streets as the primary components of the public space network.

→ The quality of the streets is ensured by designing their sections with adequate height/width proportion. Narrow service lanes resolve many of the functional requirements of housing (garbage collection, services and deliveries), removing these from the main streets.

→ It has a cohesive image that generates neighbourhood identity.

5 **Villa El Salvador in Peru** is based on the plan prepared by architect Miguel Romero Sotelo in 1971 for the Junta Nacional de Vivienda. Based on a modular pattern of neighbourhood units, it draws inspiration from Savannah. The physical form (with its neighbourhood modules) is easily replicable and scaleable. A very distinctive street hierarchy is put in place with 50- to 70-metre-wide (165 to 230 feet) avenues dedicated to vehicular traffic, with narrower inner neighbourhood streets of 10 to 14 metres (33 to 46 feet). The simple plan allows for coherent growth in a period of rapid urbanisation.

6 **New Town in Edinburgh**, planned by James Craig for the city fathers of Edinburgh in 1768, who were concerned about the poor health conditions in the old town, is a high point in Georgian rationalism in both architecture and planning. It has a clear hierarchy of streets and squares. In the initial phase of New Town, a series of street blocks (or neighbourhood subunits) set on a grid of approximately 160 by 210 metres (525 × 690 feet) line both sides of the central George Street, which is 30 metres (100 feet) wide. Cross streets are 24 metres (80 feet) wide. These street blocks are made up of local streets of 10 metres (33 feet) wide and service lanes of 7.5 metres (25 feet) wide.

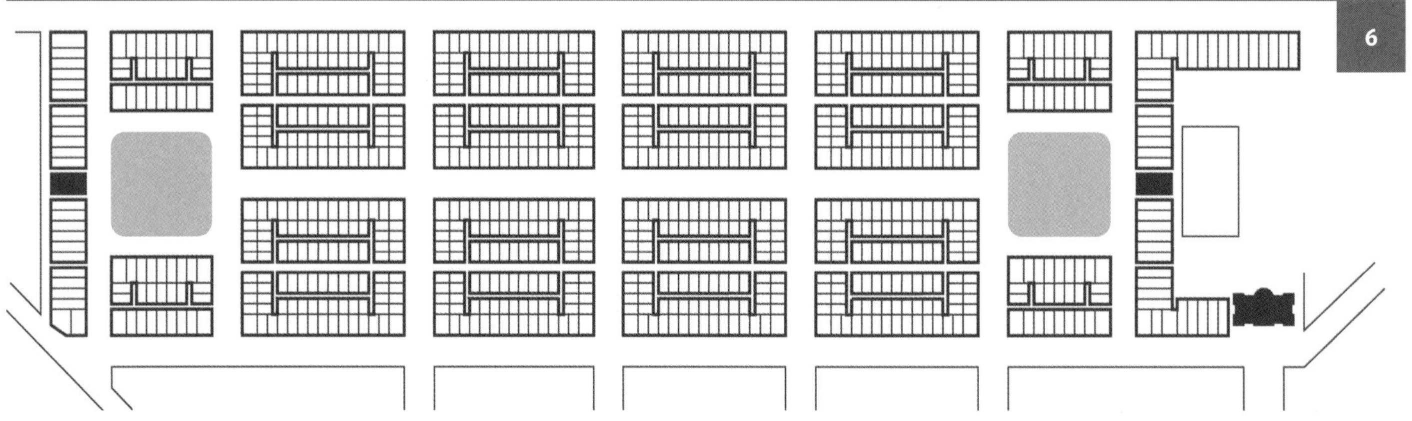

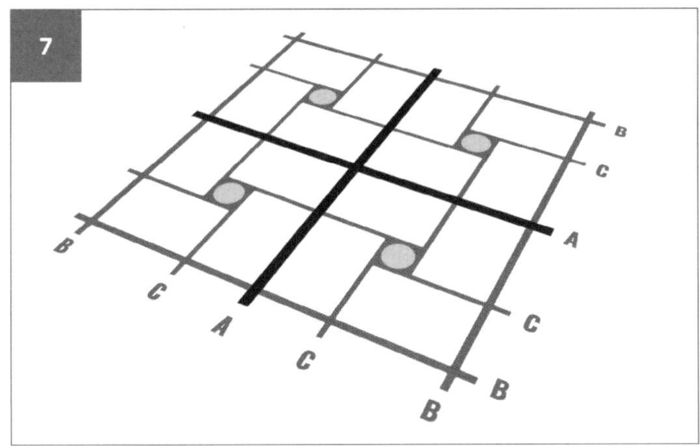

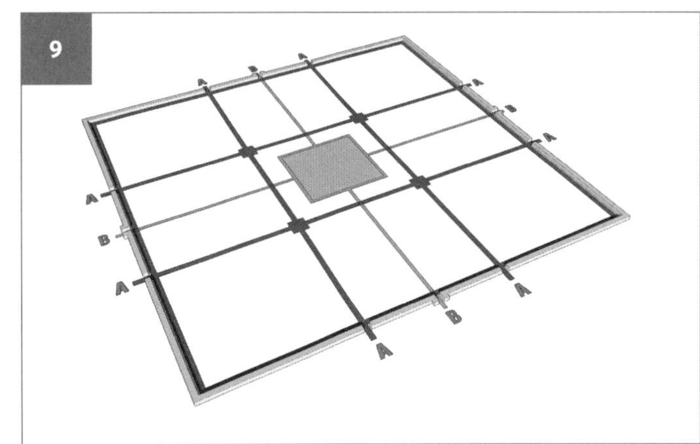

7 **Belhar, Cape Town**, planned by urbanist Roelof Uytenbogaardt in 1978, is a basic grid pattern with residential cells bounded by collector roads of 12 to 15 metres (40 to 50 feet) wide. The residential cells, which are located around a series of public open spaces or community facilities, are arranged on a pinwheel concept. Each cell was made up of four street blocks comprising three regular blocks arranged in a *T* shape around a shared-surface playstreet. Out of the centrally located central squares, four roads of 9 metres (30 feet) wide radiate outwards, interlocking with the adjoining cells. This solution was an inspired way of allowing permeability through the neighbourhood and still traffic-calming internal streets.

8 **Haveneiland in Ijlburg, Holland**, is a grid-based urban development district in the eastern part of Amsterdam. Frits Palmboom produced the initial urban design in 1996. Development on Haveneiland is dense, mainly flatted and has been developed through a series of 100- by 200-metre (330 × 660 feet) street blocks that have some shared surface internal streets. Most neighbourhood streets are 22 metres (72 feet) wide. Haveneiland is an excellent example of the creation of a 'good ordinary' neighbourhood that the Dutch do so well. They start with an ordering grid and then evolve it to respond to topographic and civic design considerations.

9 **Jaipur Pink City in India** was planned under the architectural guidance of Vidyadhar Bhattacharya in 1726 and was designed on ancient Hindu planning principles, known as Vastu Shastra. These texts set out rigorous standards that govern the design of cities—site analysis; dimensions and patterns of towns; locations of temples and bazaars, circulation routes and axial arrangements. The general plan of Jaipur is based on three by three grids, or mandalas, each 800 by 800 metres (875 × 875 yards) wide. Their composition has been amended to reflect topographical constraints and form the nine quarters of the city. The central quarter houses the palace and civic functions. Jaipur has a clearly defined road hierarchy with major streets, called *rajmarg*, that bound the quarters and link to the city gates, 33 metres (110 feet) wide. At the junction of each of these major streets is a *chaupar*, or civic square. The internal road network comprises 16.5-metre-wide (55 feet) streets linking the inner areas of the quarters with the major streets. Smaller streets of 4 and 8 metres (13 and 26 feet) wide break the quarters down into the *prastara* chessboard pattern called *mohallas*. Seen above is a stylised plan of the Pink City, with the palace at the centre, before the plan was adapted to the site and rearranged significantly.

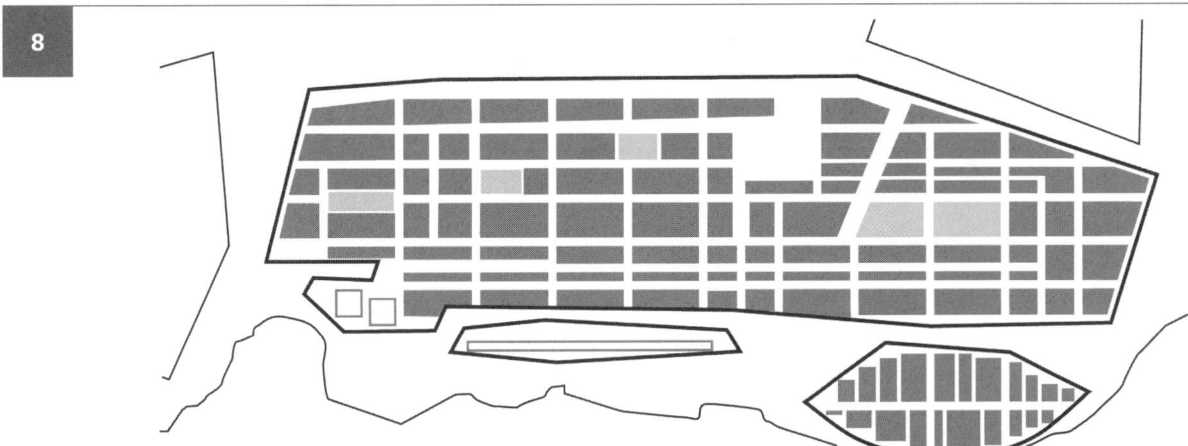

URBAN STREETS

Some urban researchers believe that cities have fingerprints or DNA that can be deduced from the pattern of street networks. Without doubt, many cities display unique characteristics. Many cities are also made of neighbourhoods, districts and quarters—built at different times—with different street patterns, but many show remarkable similarities, and a set of underlying principles can be deduced from most places. These principles revolve around the nature of the street and the role it plays in the neighbourhood.

An urban street is a public thoroughfare in a city, usually with sidewalks or pavements. It is, therefore, public space, one of the few shared between all sorts of people and vehicles, a place where people may freely assemble, interact, and move about. It is a public parcel of land adjoining buildings in an urban context. As a subset of the built environment as old as our first human habitats, the street sustains a range of activities vital to civilisation. Its roles are as many and diverse as its ever-changing users.

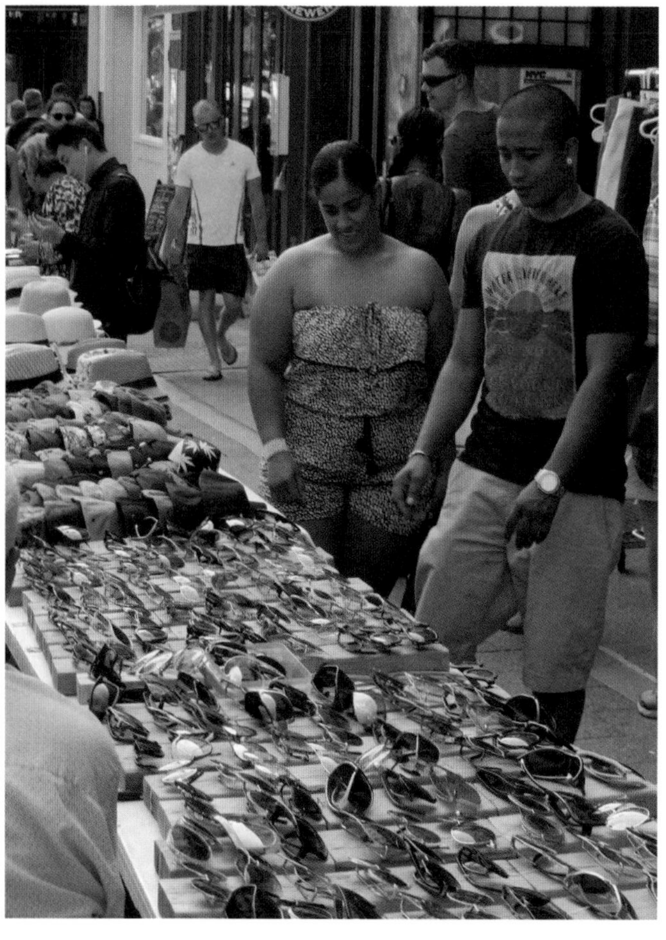

TYPES OF STREETS

At the neighbourhood level, the street is the primary generator. The fundamental configuration of a street—a movement axis lined by buildings with their entrances facing each other—is not in the first instance derived from issues of style or tradition. It is the result of an emergent order derived from inherent qualities of geometry that maximise integration of movement patterns and thus maximise the potential for human interaction. This potential is why the street can be found across a range of cultures and throughout history.

Every street needs a function that contributes to the accretion of urban fabric. Movement is like a channel of glue. It is not the flow down this channel that sticks things together; it is the action of stopping that does it. Thus, in the early formation of a neighbourhood we cannot waste any adhesiveness, never mind the energy and costs, on roads that have no function other than to bypass.

Streets can be loosely categorised as city streets and local streets but can have even lower order routes such as service lanes or mews, which could be public or private.

CITY STREETS

City streets are important streets, such as main streets, avenues and boulevards, and are usually wider, with a relatively high level of movement activity. Commerce, civic expression and public interaction are more visible on city streets, and vehicles may use them for longer-distance travel. In many instances, they are also the focus for higher order public transportation and can be associated with transit corridors and the location of underground stations, where they integrate with other lower order public transport systems, such as buses and streetcars.

City streets are strong manifestations of top-down action, operating as they do in the collective interest of the whole city as useful hierarchies.

Main streets

Main Street, called *High Street* in other parts of the world, is a generic phrase used to denote a primary civic and shopping street of a neighbourhood, district or quarter.

It has the following qualities:

1 It always starts and thrives on the most connected through route that has the greatest level of continuity and critical mass of community and is, therefore, dependent on:

- → Passing trade (the flow of pedestrians in the area and the ability of through traffic to stop and access the street)
- → Public transport accessibility and stopping points
- → Its catchment of people (those living, working or visiting the locality)

2 It is usually a focal point for local shops, markets and higher order civic and cultural uses and is most often used in reference to trading, living over the shop, socialising and celebrating.

3 It is the street most responsive to change as accessibility, markets and social conditions change. It is always in a constant state of reinvention.

4 Its qualities are driven by a combination of:

→ Its essential functions (such as civic buildings, health facilities, learning institutions and financial services)
→ Its attractors (such as its social and cultural activities, nighttime uses and public events)
→ Its public spaces (such as civic squares, parks and marketplaces)
→ Its strong degree of enclosure (usually defined by higher building frontages)

5 Its activities demand the highest degree of frontage relationship between building access and the street. A successful main street has many doors at frequent intervals and multiple layers of interface between public and private. They are best served with rear service lanes which could evolve over time into a rich mix of uses, as Rose Street does on the Edinburgh New Town.

Main streets can be typological or bespoke, and in many cities they can be the primary public space in the neighbourhood or city centre.

Boulevards

Boulevards carry the highest level of through traffic but still offer high levels of frontage access. Local traffic is segregated from strategic traffic by slip roads on both sides of the main through route such that vital traffic is allowed to flow freely. Boulevards offer good alternative through-routeing and generally run parallel to main streets.

Avenues

Avenues are also higher order streets that carry high levels of traffic but still preserve the strong frontage relationship between building access and the street—without slip roads. Buildings are generally set back slightly further from the front building line of the site and sidewalks are more generous and accommodate tree planting and on-street parking. Avenues work well when they link main streets with boulevards.

Top: New York pedestrian crossing. **Upper middle:** Marylebone High Street, London. **Lower middle:** Paris Boulevard. **Bottom:** Jaipur Avenue, also called a *rajmarg*.

LOCAL STREETS

Local neighbourhood streets are quieter, often residential in use and character, providing primarily local access, although they still allow general traffic to filter through. They are sometimes managed to reduce the impact of through traffic.

Local streets are more typological than main streets and can be developed within a standard street range that takes on different hierarchies.

Residential streets

Residential streets are the predominant street type in the neighbourhood and provide continuous frontage to housing and related uses. As such they have sidewalks (that could accommodate street trees) and continuous on-street parking. Standardising the street means you can regulate the underground servicing arrangements.

Shared-surface streets

These streets are like residential streets but downgraded to become shared-surface environmental cells, similar to the Dutch *woonerven* or playstreets. The entrance to these streets can be narrowed to form gateways identifying these as streets where motorists need to behave differently. They have no sidewalks and parking is arranged informally.

Service lanes and mews

The lowest order of vehicular streets, service lanes and mews provide service access to rear of properties. Over time they can evolve into new frontage development and have the highest potential for mixed use.

Alleys and arcades

Alleys and arcades are the lowest order of pedestrian streets in a neighbourhood and could be covered or open. They provide direct frontage to small shops, residential units or other uses.

Top: Brooklyn Heights street, New York. **Upper middle:** Shared surface (*woonerf*) street, Holland. **Lower middle:** Back lane mews, Marylebone, London. **Bottom:** Pedestrian alley, Melbourne, Australia.

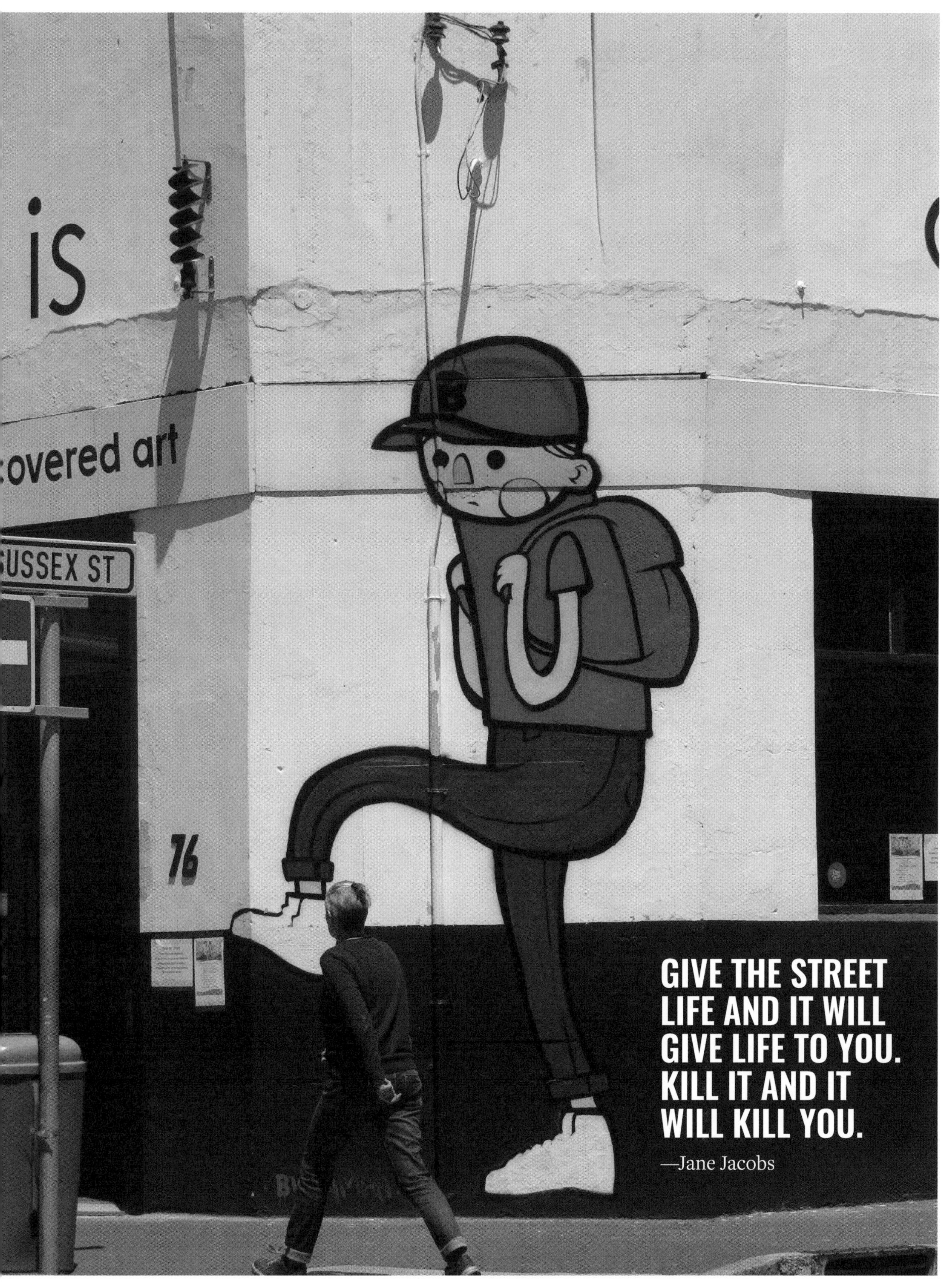

GIVE THE STREET LIFE AND IT WILL GIVE LIFE TO YOU. KILL IT AND IT WILL KILL YOU.

—Jane Jacobs

THE STRATEGIC INNOVATOR

HOW SIMPLE RULES GAVE INFORMAL SETTLEMENTS A SECURE FUTURE

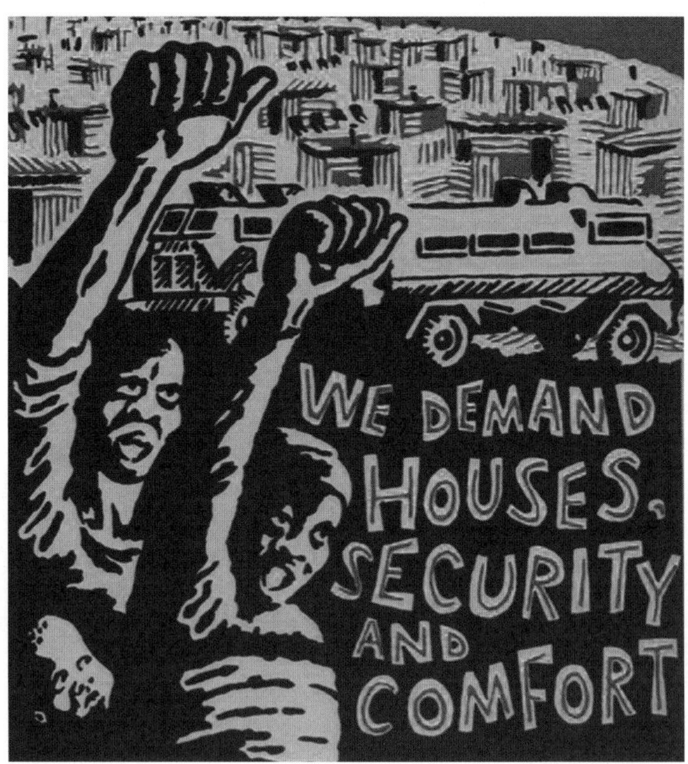

Katerina, head of sustainable settlements at the provincial authority in Cape Town, South Africa, is in charge of urban policy. She has a master's degree in strategic sustainability from a leading Scandinavian university. Sustainability is one of the most important planks of her department's settlements policy.

Katerina recognises that the sustainability agenda suffers from being driven from a top-down perspective. It adheres to the old adage 'think globally, act locally'. Unfortunately the debate has too little influence on the behaviour of people at a local level. This is because the experts use abstract and emotive models that start with the planets and are beamed downwards through the distorting filter of the environmental movement.

The result is that people who believe in the cause get frustrated, respond only in limited ways, or continue to behave in the same bad old ways, sometimes just offsetting their negative impacts with something that seems positive. The planning system, which seeks to influence how we act locally, finds it hard to respond. Too often it resorts to technical fixes, demanding some form of mitigation or applying ineffectual policies, while blindly promoting other policies that work against the overriding purpose of acting sustainably.

Africa has been the most rapidly urbanising region on the globe over the past half-century, and Cape Town has witnessed the full force of immigration from all parts of Africa. This urbanisation has been seriously dysfunctional. While a functional city provides people with both better employment opportunities and a better quality of life than rural areas do, the settlements that Katerina's authority has been creating generally provide neither.

They do little to create jobs, as they lack the density of settlement and the supporting infrastructure that would support local economic activity. The housing is squalid and lacks basic public services. These deficiencies did not just happen, nor are they an inevitable consequence of poverty. They result from errors in housing policy, or a lack of any formal policy at all.

Katerina is working in an environment where central government has promised everyone a house. It is the ruling party's big policy story, building on Nelson Mandela's vision of building a million new homes in South Africa, so few people speak out. The bad old regime put people in small houses designed for the typical small family, based on the UK's Parker Morris standards. These homes were rolled out with surprising efficiency across the outskirts of many towns and cities.

The new government has come up with a different housing solution. Called the RDP house, it comes out of the policies of the government's Reconstruction and Development Programme—a radical programme to redress the inequalities of society. The trouble is that the RDP house is almost identical to the previous government's small house: a single dwelling sitting on a plot, built in a suburban setting where most people do not want to be.

Katerina knows that the dream of new homes for everyone is impossible to fulfil: the demand can never be met. The government lost that battle a long time ago when it started to see housing as a numbers game. Many people might still get a government house eventually, but they might have to wait up to fifteen years. What do they do in the interim?

The majority of people now realise that they obtain rights if they squat in places illegally, often close to their place of work, and the local government is obliged to provide them with local services. They build their shacks but still hold out for a new house somewhere else. This, Katerina's big problem, is one that the government is firmly committed to eradicating.

Marie Huchzermeyer, a leading South African academic who challenges the dominant perceptions of informal settlements, points out that 'informal settlements occupy contested spaces in our cities—physically, legally and in public discourse', while playing an important role in shaping South African cities. 'This form of land occupation is driven by human needs, rather than the market processes that determine formal urban development patterns', she writes.

In many parts of South Africa, informal settlement eradication is often justified with reference to the Cities Without Slums campaign of the Cities Alliance, a joint programme of UN-Habitat and the World Bank. Huchzermeyer sees glaring inconsistencies in this international campaign. Its official target of 'significantly improving the lives of at least 100 million slum dwellers by 2020', if reached (which is unlikely), would affect only 10 per cent of the world's growing slum population, and it would not create cities without slums.

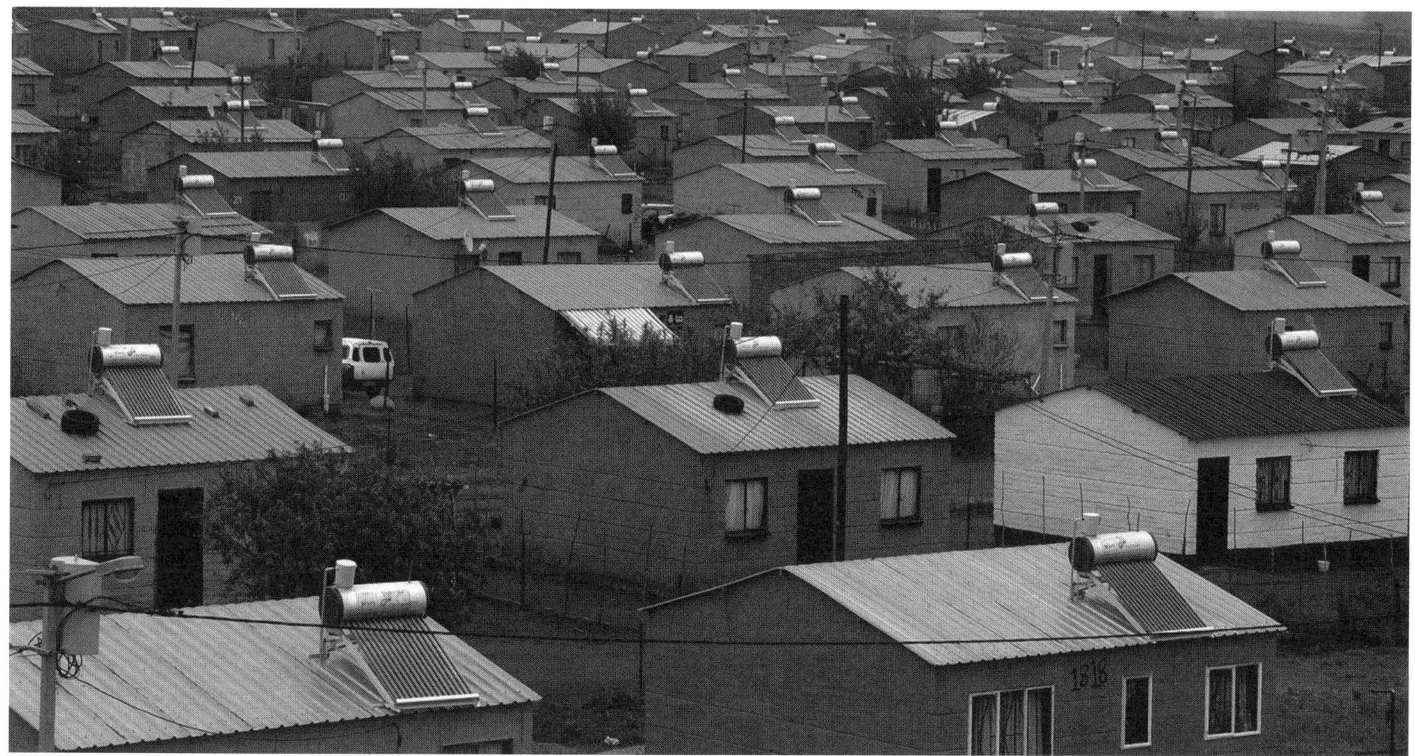

The governments of several countries interpret the goals of the Cities Without Slums campaign to mean the eradication of slums, rather than merely the improvement of the lives of those living in them. Huchzermeyer writes:

> While perhaps well intentioned by governments, the eradication process is feared by slum residents and often results in worsened life conditions. This thinking is distant from contemporary policy in Brazil, a country to which the South African government, business and academia looks for south-south comparison, inspiration and partnership. In response to market-driven fragmentation of its cities, Brazil has embraced informal land occupation as a process that yields desirable results in terms of land utilisation and land distribution. Though far from ideal, Brazilian cities are visibly shaped by informal processes driven by the poor, as much as by the market.

Katerina has to deal with the problem of informal settlements as well as the challenge of building new housing. She must get more urban land ready and make the system more inclusive.

Meanwhile, the provincial government commissions a new report from a leading consultancy. More complex diagrams and matrices are presented. More acronyms are offered, shortcutting difficult concepts. More conflicting urban policies, funding routes, development options and executive actions are put forwards, adding to the pile of other conflicting urban policies, funding routes, development options and executive actions—but without getting rid of the old ones. It moves nothing forwards. She knows that she cannot win using the systems and thinking that are prevalent today. She has to get back to her simple purpose.

Katerina sees the failure of the system as the following:

→ The old system's inequality has been perpetuated and the official processes and solutions add to the problem.

→ Although everyone knows the scale of the problem, politicians think they may lose votes if they tell the truth.

→ Many politicians promise housing to their constituents to gain votes, but they often fail to deliver. Katerina gets the blame.

→ Because new housing is promised, the informal settlements remain in a state of limbo. Threatened with eradication, they do not transition into normal bits of town like similar settlements in places like South America. They seem frozen in a permanent state of informality, which many people accept as the best they can ever achieve within their means.

→ The informal settlements are managed with the aims of preventing fire and the spread of disease, but little else.

→ The formal process to release urban land for development takes seven years. It is a hangover from the old bureaucratic system that requires a protracted proclamation process. This is unreasonable. In the meantime people squat and the government has to cope with the consequences.

KATERINA COMES UP WITH A SOLUTION

Pravin Gordhan, the ousted finance minister, challenged leading city officials to 'Think differently; act differently. Now!' Katerina rises to the challenge. She recognises that her department has to provide a counterpoint to the 'sustainability' agenda by putting the human element at the heart of the discussion. Most people would wish to live their lives differently: travelling less, buying locally, saving resources, and having a greater sense

of community and greater control over their future. With the right tools, people acting collectively from the bottom up can be our prime agents of change, helping to create successful cities, towns and their neighbourhoods, and shaping the wider environment. We 'think local and act local' and in this way we 'change global'.

Katerina thinks of this in terms of viability. In this context, a viable system is one that is organised in such a way as to be able to survive in changing conditions. To survive, a system must be adaptable, capable of maintaining itself or recovering its capabilities. This is not happening in Katerina's settlements. She is determined to focus on creating the conditions that will enable a viable human habitat to emerge, with beneficial results for the natural habitat and our planet.

The premier of the province announces a drive towards innovation, recognising that thinking must change. Bright people in Cape Town have been showing the way for years, but the politicians were not listening. Now the young guard are to be given a chance. Katerina is given the task of coming up with a new settlement strategy.

Katerina sees a study undertaken by USAID that shows that the cost of installing infrastructure is between four and ten times more if the land has not been laid out efficiently to accommodate it. In most informal settlements the process of occupying the land produces no definable urban structure. There are no streets: almost every scrap of land is built on.

This is very different from some places in Lima, where massive spontaneous settlements are laid out using simple grids. As a result the Lima settlements transition over time to become normal parts of town, whereas those in Africa without any initial structure seem to be locked in their informal state. Getting land laid out in a regular, structured pattern is crucial to the process.

Katerina learns more from a conference paper, 'Incremental Housing: The Past and Future Dwelling Solution for the Poor', by Roberto Chávez. It shows how in the early 1970s the government in Peru built large-scale, least-cost housing solutions in and around Lima. This research demonstrates that incremental housing with surveyed plots can work in different countries with different cultures, and that they are extremely resilient in the face of economic and political change. Over time these settlements tend to transition into cohesive communities with the most appropriate housing. They also seem to be well suited for incremental improvements in infrastructure and services at all scales. The most affordable and cost-effective service network of all service networks is regular urban blocks and subdivisions with a simple relationship to the street network. This network system has the greatest impact in terms of sense of identity, community organisation and municipal management.

Regular surveyed plots give low-income families the greatest freedom to build, at their own pace and responding to their own needs, as John F. C. Turner has shown us. They require the least amount of government intervention and financial support. As opposed to South Africa's one-size-fits-all approach of conventional low-income housing, regular subdivisions allow for a full spectrum of responses by the informal sector, generating jobs and giving the poor more options to choose from.

Compared to conventional sites-and-services or other public housing projects, surveyed plot projects seem to be more amenable to being scaled up to meet the enormous demand of rapid urbanisation in least-developed cities. The main obstacle, aside from agreed practices and political will, has been and will be the availability of an adequate supply of urban land in the system.

Given a new freedom to innovate by her superiors, Katerina recognises that both Marie Huchzermeyer and Roberto Chávez have given her much food for thought. Working with the African Centre for Cities at Cape Town University, Katerina's development unit undertakes research into urban grid patterns throughout the world.

They realise that the most successful cities have open, adaptive grid patterns that are almost standardised in nature. Such patterns are seen in the camps of the ancient Romans, the early colonial plans in South America, the structured grids of Savannah in the United States, and Jaipur in India. Katerina learns that in the early 1980s a simple pinwheel grid layout was successfully implemented at Belhar, near Cape Town, by the urbanist Roelof Uytenbogaardt. There is no reason why the development unit should not develop its own standard plans.

Katerina and her colleagues design a standard range of block plans, all based on a universal lot principle: a regular urban block with a length-to-width ratio of 2:1, subdivided into 15-metre-wide (50-foot) development lots. This establishes the potential for multiple street arrangements and structure choices for the application of a range of multiple plot layouts and building types. They also introduce a simple range of streets and lanes to cater for every condition. This enables a range of regular street blocks and superblocks, similar to the 400- by 400-metre (1,300 ×

1,300 feet) Villa El Salvador grid, to be applied to any site and modified where necessary. They test these layouts in a variety of situations, and they seem to work. Critics warned that they would be boring and monotonous, but they do not seem to be. They are rich in potential and allow for a full range of responses by everyone. Coupled with the simple set of rules, they are available to all local authorities in an easy-to-use CAD (computer-aided design) format.

The pattern book of plans becomes known as CANVAS (computer-aided neighbourhood vision and structure). The government adopts these as its urban standard.

Every development site, no matter how big or small, uses a fragment or combination of street blocks. In one week, more than thirty sites are laid out. The national executive uses the emergency powers to proclaim these as new settlements. They offer those waiting for new houses the prospect of owning plots. If people take up this right, they forego their right to a new RDP house. This gets the government off the hook to some extent.

The development unit tries a range of different starting points that enable new urban dwellers to get on with building their own homes. It does this by trying different responsive elements that will trigger growth and change—from building corner blocks that set the standard for the street, to building terraces of standard buildings that they have evolved, to setting up a programme to build party walls on the side boundaries of every lot (based on the accelerator site concept developed by housing architect Daniel O in Nairobi).

These are all called dweller-adaptive building systems (DABS). The local authority responds by trialling a range of incremental housing solutions built on these systems. Innovation flourishes.

KATERINA REPORTS TO THE NATIONAL EXECUTIVE:

1. The regularity of the plans allows for the development of the full range of building types and site layouts. Individuals respond by creating their own types of building. The local shack-building industry and formal housing contractors develop their own prototypes. Everyone wins.

2. The standard block layouts give rise to infinite possibilities. They do not limit responses by individuals, collectives or large contractors. They provide a framework for diversity.

3. CANVAS allows for a simple, regular pattern of development that anyone can use. It is now easy to cost infrastructure and find ways of reducing costs. Full infrastructure can be put in later as the settlements grow.

4. To avoid continued reliance on emergency powers, Katerina proposes a new fast-track process of proclaiming land, using CANVAS. The fast-track process makes it possible to reduce the time taken from seven years to one.

5. The regularity of the layout and experimentation with new housing types (by both the local government and the people) enable many of the new settlements to become fully fledged neighbourhoods, with development rising up to three storeys in many places. These neighbourhoods create the conditions for urban viability, and within a short space of time places begin to support their own local services and economy.

6. The million-house programme is now called the million DABS on the CANVAS. It is now—in more ways than one—a big picture.

Katerina is still passionately committed to the cause. 'We understand that the total human habitat exists as a dependent subsystem of the environment,' she writes. 'It cannot be isolated from the natural habitat. Accordingly we must build the foundations for viable urban life and a responsible urban society that takes us to a point where we are no longer destabilising this encompassing system.

'In doing so, we must not be caught up in a narrow, prohibitive top-down view of the problem but rather we must see the relationship between urban interventions and the global system. Enabling people to control their own habitat is an essential part of building the resilience that will be needed as we enter a period where global issues are increasingly felt locally.'

We now know that urban design processes need to adopt flexible and adaptive procedures to respond to the evolving demands of the contemporary city. To support these dynamics, as well as monitor conditions, we need specific design methods and the tools to help them. Urban designers have some tools at their disposal. However, these are certainly lacking in usefulness and meaning in complex urban environments—for example, using a 400-metre (1,300-foot) walk band as a determinant. This tool is classic reductionism: the great unchallenged truth in urban design that fails to acknowledge the complexity of the city. What is missing is a process tool that offers design information as well as feedback, the essential ingredient for bottom-up approaches.

The framework plan for the expansion of Ashford in the United Kingdom used CANVAS as a development tool to test various expansion options against agreed criteria.

USING CANVAS

We know that if we can get the structure of a place right, we can use different techniques to generate urban form and it can even give us clues to transforming neighbourhoods. Canvas is not used to determine end states but rather to anticipate outcomes such as how much land we need, the nature of infrastructure investment or provision of local services. The tools could test such variables as public transport accessibility to determine the nature and extent of services over time. They could be used to identify thresholds for energy networks or carbon footprinting. They could also be used to determine thresholds for the provision of public services and model public good outcomes. They could even be used to simulate neighbourhood formation. For some time we have been experimenting with a development tool called CANVAS (computer aided neighbourhood visualisation and simulation), which could be incorporated into a simple operating manual.

Canvas is an integrated spatial model for measuring and delivering the urban networks at a range of settlement scales and links back to the NEIGHBOURHOOD CO:EFFICIENT development tool described later in the section on ACTIVATORS (page 260). CANVAS looks to basic forms of simulation, using simple rules to assist the community in making complex decisions around trade-offs—having armed them with a number of 'rules' they can control. This is an iterative process and is not intended to gives us a final outcome but rather to chart a course of action that we can monitor for feedback and adapt over time.

It is also a simple geo-design application, bringing GIS and design processes together with the qualities of land-use mix, accessibility and land value as part of an integrated process for spatial planning and urban design at multiple scales. The system allows users to test development scenarios, giving real-time data on the development performance. This reduces project time and risk, and offers clients a more responsive approach to large-scale urban design and spatial planning projects. It can be used by all built environment professions, often working best as a collaborative project tool.

Through the 'neighbourhood game' interface, the system can be employed as part of community or neighbourhood planning events and is therefore ideally suited to the new localism agenda. For large-scale engagement, the tool can be used as a physical gaming board and screen projection. It operates across a range of urban scales from the whole town or city through to district and neighbourhood and has been designed to test the implications of large- and medium-scale urban changes. At a large scale, CANVAS can test the effects of urban extensions, mixed-use development, public transport corridors, brownfield development and town centre redevelopment. At a medium scale, the system can assess the implications of new social infrastructure such as schools or hospitals, as well as areawide transport strategies.

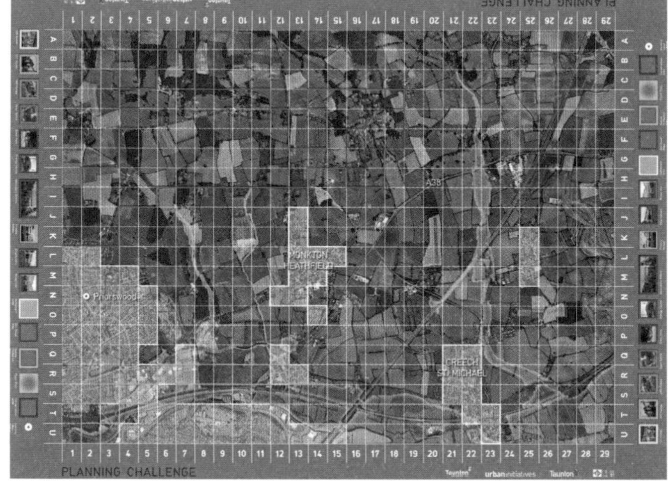

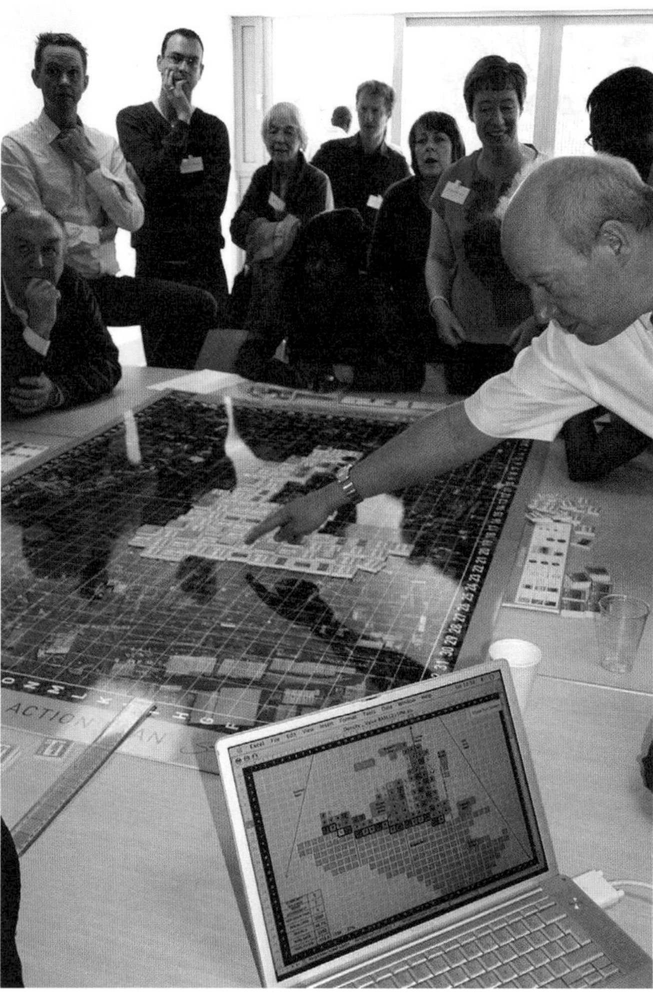

To simplify data entry, data is managed through a grid-and-tile system. The approach works across a number of scales and allows grids to be tailored to the study area. At whole-town or -city scale, we often adopt a 500-metre (1650-foot) tile, which equates to 25 hectares or 62 acres. For projects focussing on urban extensions, a 200-metre/660-feet tile (4 hectare / 10 acres) is used. At the neighbourhood level or for smaller settlements, smaller grain tiles of 100 metres / 330 feet (1 hectare / 2.5 acres) are best.

Localia, our imaginary case study shown on the following page, uses 75 metres (250 feet) as a square grid layout module. It would be good to choose this scale or multiples of this—say, a 150- or 300-metre (500- or 1,000-foot) grid—to maintain an understanding of scale throughout the whole process.

Moving Forward

Canvas brings social, economic and accessibility considerations together, allowing a more joined-up view of the world. By doing so, it offers a new way of looking at our neighbourhoods, towns and cities—providing a fresh perspective on urban form, street networks and viability. This collateral approach helps create more positive planning decisions and enables the designer and community to model and test a range of different scenarios.

Canvas doesn't design—good designers do that. It's more about setting a direction at an early stage, or at any stage if things don't seem to stack up. It helps set project tone and direction through a better understanding of scale, land-use mix, density, social infrastructure, accessibility, value and sustainability choices. It can be used over time to chart plan progress; coordinate infrastructure delivery; and provide continuous feedback to enable early decisions to be made. It can be used to test new development, reconsider planned but yet undelivered development or seek to optimise existing places through small-scale and incremental change. It breaks the big down into the smaller and makes it comprehensible.

Top left: The game board laid out with grid squares. **Right:** Example of spreadsheet on computer showing where tiles have been played on the game board. **Bottom left:** Playing tiles with different land uses and densities.

LOCALIA URBAN NEIGHBOURHOOD

DESIGNING A NEIGHBOURHOOD NETWORK

Localia is an imaginary example of a new urban neighbourhood in a new urban extension, located on the site of a former airfield, industrial area and redundant farmland. It could be on the outskirts of Johannesburg, Lima or Delhi, so its demographics reflect a poorer population with lower to middle income earnings. There is strong demand for people who want to build their own homes. The city authorities are leading a neighbourhood planning process with existing landowners and adjacent communities.

The context of Localia is typical of many sites one would find in established urban environments:

- → It has a pattern of active main routes that cross the site and connect to places further afield, but these roads would have to be rebuilt.
- → The public transport network runs along these main routes, and there is a heavy railway line with sidings for a container depot adjacent to the site. It has the potential for opening up a new station to serve Localia.
- → There are potential connections to surrounding areas.
- → The boundary conditions are established by a combination of forested areas, a river and existing urban development.
- → The topography of the site is generally flat, but a steep hill forms a corner of the site.
- → It has a number of features that could be retained, such as some former industrial buildings that could be reused.
- → Primary utility infrastructure runs along the rail line, but there is one major overhead power line that runs across the site.

The street network has three stages of evolution from its initial definition of its structure, through its development of the grid, to its adaptation and mobilisation as an efficient and functioning system. Here is a simple way of showing how we can design a new urban network using an imaginary case study.

The imaginary site is on a disused airfield and farming land at the edge of the city. It has a powerline running accross the site and local indusries are served by a station.

STAGE 1: DEFINING URBAN STRUCTURE

Stage 1 gives the essential diagram of the place: the ten strokes of a pen on a plan—the backbone of major city streets—locating public transport infrastructure, the institutions for civic life, and zones of development and urban edges. At a city scale, this background plan is the first trigger for an emergent urbanism. Some uses aggregate to accessibility, others to similar uses and yet others to the need for some form of prominence. At a neighbourhood scale, it is the high street, the market, the station precinct and the civic spaces. It also includes defining the boundary conditions, the site constraints and its relationships to its surrounding areas.

STAGE 2: EVOLVING THE GENERIC NEIGHBOURHOOD GRID

This stage involves gaining an understanding of the scale, modularity and hierarchy extent of the generic neighbourhood grid and what its contextual response will be to the site conditions. In considering how Localia might evolve as a neighbourhood, this includes:

1 **Choosing the grain of the grid**

We have chosen a finer grain 75- by 75-metre (250 × 250 feet) layout grid that provides us with:

→ The potential centrelines for our local street network
→ A 60-metre (200-feet) deep urban block structure by offsetting the block boundaries by 7.5 metres (25 feet) from the centrelines
→ The potential to aggregate two grid squares together to create a rectangular block structure, opening up a wide range of urban block arrangements and still having an effective block length
→ In the case of more space-extensive land uses, such as schools, the potential to aggregate further by combining four of them to create a larger urban block

2 **Exploring a modular pattern**

We have chosen a six by six grid square arrangement that provides us with:

→ A ward block (subneighbourhood module) of, say, 450 by 450 metres (1,500 × 1,500 feet), which could be grouped around an internal public space
→ The potential for myriad internal street and block arrangements
→ The potential to create an 'environmental cell' with traffic-calmed or shared-surface streets

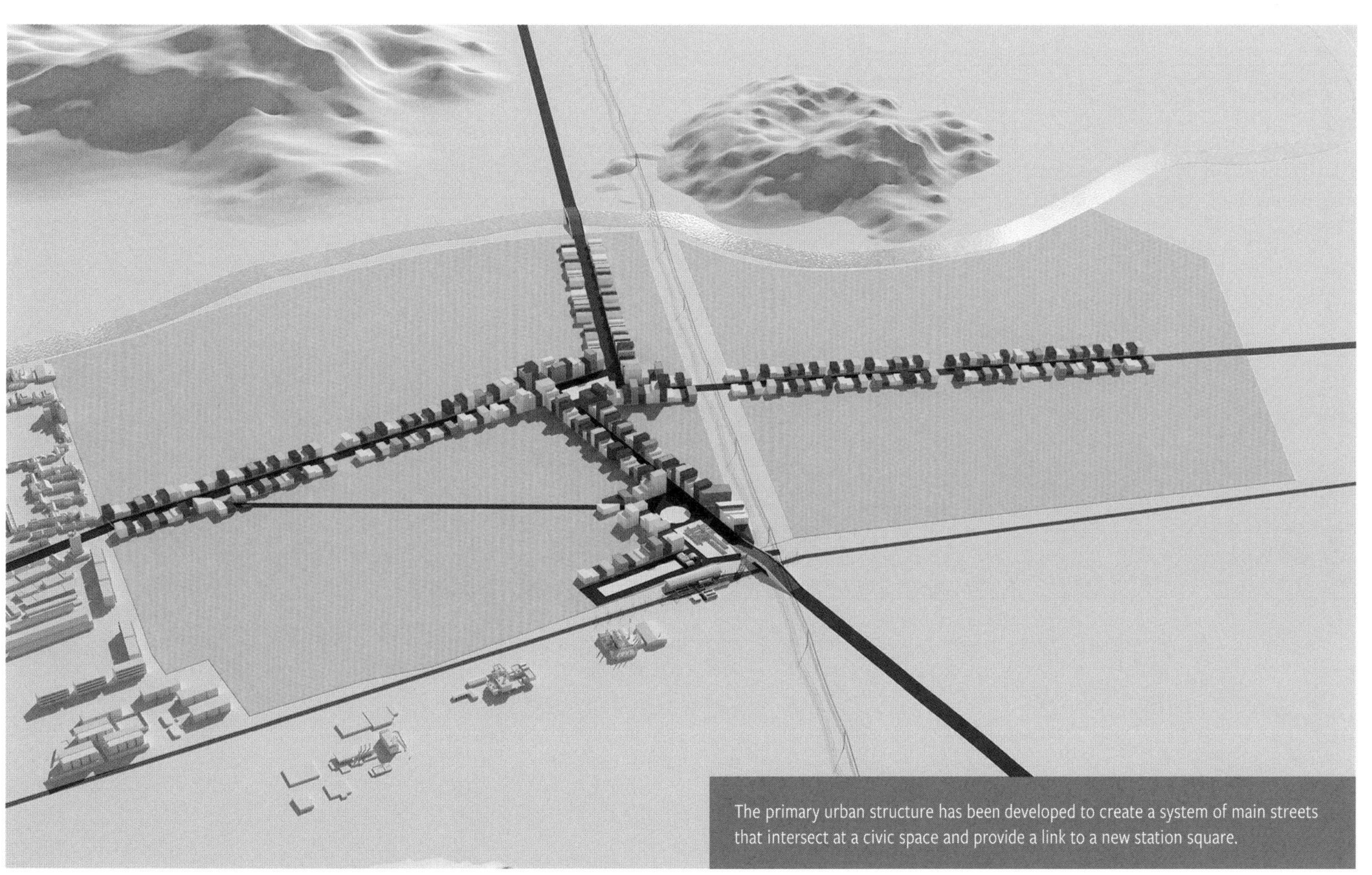

The primary urban structure has been developed to create a system of main streets that intersect at a civic space and provide a link to a new station square.

3 **Developing a grid hierarchy**

We have chosen to arrange the ward blocks with a tartan pattern of city streets with a distinct hierarchy that provides us with:

- → A main street structure that follows a central route through the area, giving full potential for local economic activity to flourish
- → A parallel network of generous boulevards that provide alternative through-routing in the future
- → A transverse pattern of wider avenues that link main streets and urban boulevards

Note that we have chosen to keep the six by six grid square module intact to maintain the integrity of the block structure and the dimensions of local streets. In the case of wider streets, we have pulled the modules apart to give, in effect, two centrelines.

4 **Considering the extent of regularity**

We have chosen to maintain a regular tartan grid arrangement across the whole site. This provides us with:

- → A strong identity for the area based on its consistent pattern of urban streets and ward blocks
- → A typological neighbourhood plan that could be used elsewhere as a model
- → The possibility that future urban extensions will shift the alignment of the grid to avoid a continuous spread

5 **Considering your contextual response to site**

We have chosen to allow the pattern of regular blocks and ward blocks to dominate the area. This provides us with:

- → A normative model that can provide the backdrop to retained features
- → A regular plan that is contained by its natural boundaries and rail infrastructure
- → A plan that accommodates colliding city streets, such as the existing diagonal route down to the station, and sets up richness and variety as a result of this

STAGE 3: ADAPTING THE GRID TO THE CONTEXT

This stage involves laying the generic neighbourhood grid over the urban structure and adapting either grid or structure as necessary to create a viable plan. In considering how Localia might evolve as a neighbourhood, this includes:

1 **Aligning the dominant tartan grid pattern over the site**

We have chosen to:

- → Orientate the proposed main street to the major movement networks
- → Locate the centre of the neighbourhood at the junction of two main roads
- → Adapt overlaid grid to accommodate existing routes and retained features and trim plan to natural boundaries

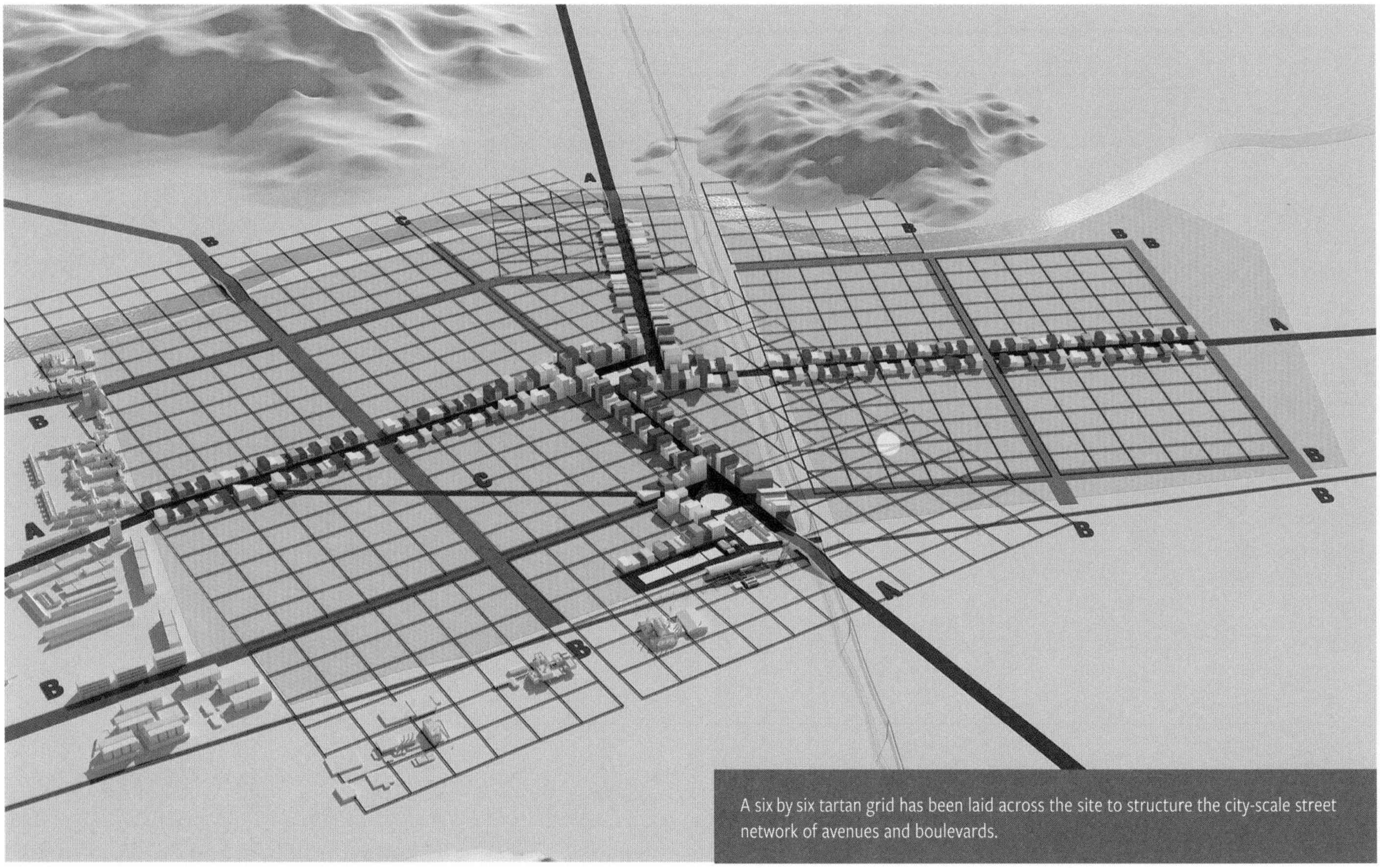

A six by six tartan grid has been laid across the site to structure the city-scale street network of avenues and boulevards.

2 **Developing a new public transport infrastructure network**

We have chosen to open up a new station on the line of the avenue linking to the centre, which will:

→ Create a secondary mixed-use axis along this route
→ Focus bus activity at the interchange
→ Create a focus for a network of local bus services

3 **Establishing a public open space network**

We have chosen to develop a network of primary and secondary spaces to include:

→ A central civic square at the junction of the two main roads to create a civic heart to the area
→ Space for a street market on the route down to the station
→ Creation of a new station square to serve buses and taxis
→ The location of public spaces within each of the ward blocks

4 **Establishing social infrastructure**

We have chosen to locate the following:

→ Schools within each of the ward blocks or along avenue frontages to provide easy access to public transport
→ Larger space-extensive uses, such as urban agriculture and playing fields, along the periphery of the neighbourhood
→ Primary social and civic infrastructure along main streets and central civic square

5 **Mobilising the street pattern**

We have chosen the following catalogue of urban street typologies:

City streets

→ Main street: 30 metres (100 feet) wide
→ Boulevards: 45 metres (150 feet) wide

Local streets

→ Residential streets: 15 metres (50 feet) wide
→ Local service lanes and mews: 6 metres (20 feet) wide

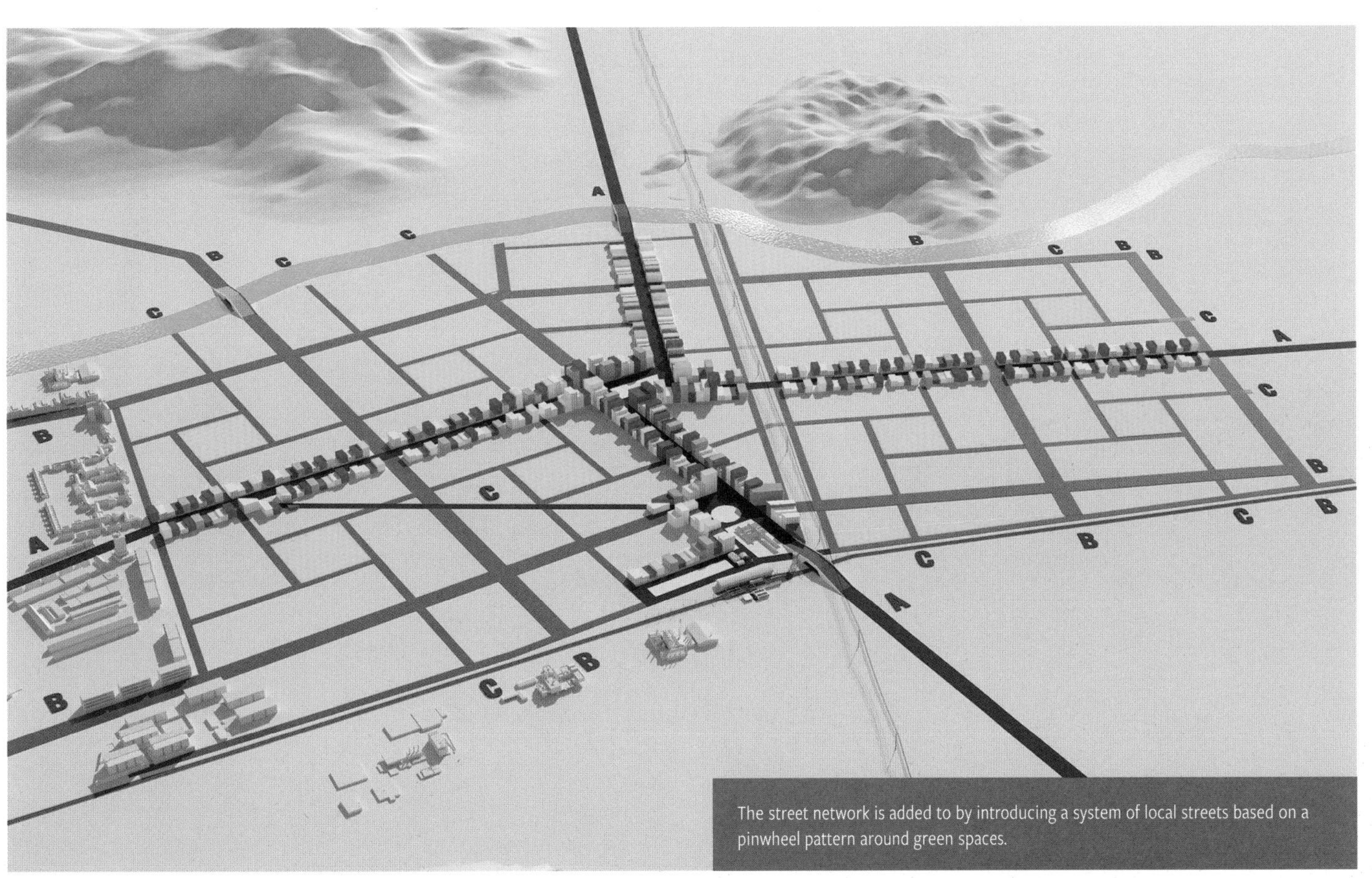

The street network is added to by introducing a system of local streets based on a pinwheel pattern around green spaces.

BLOCK

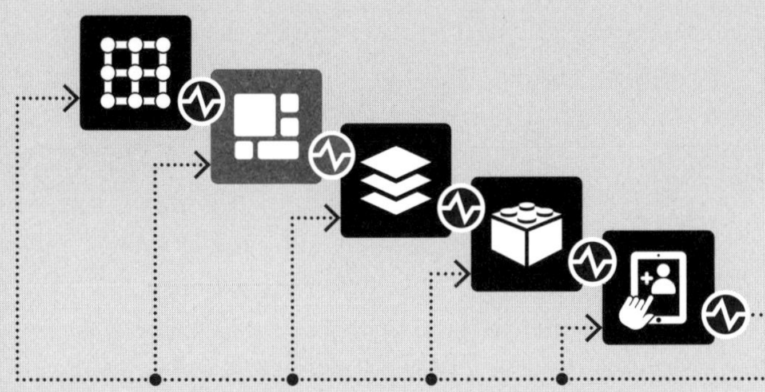

BLOCKS

AS FERTILE FIELDS FOR EMERGENCE

The urban BLOCK is a central element of urban planning, design and development and plays a key role in breaking down the big into the smaller. As the second essential condition for the invisible chassis, blocks are critical enabling mechanisms in the structuring of responsive urban environments. They provide the balanced constraints within which structured choices can be made by the individual, the collective or the institutional agents in the system. As regular shapes, they form the standard building blocks of a neighbourhood, define the primary patterns of settlement and accommodate a wide range of uses at all scales. As social units, they structure groups of citizens into democratic hierarchies and promote self-organisation at various scales.

Blocks *NOUN*

1 the smallest area of urban land that is bounded by streets

2 regular-shaped parcels of land that can be divided into smaller parcels of land

3 the basic units of urban development that can be arranged to assemble the urban fabric of the neighbourhood

SCOPE

This section introduces a number of theories around the complex interrelationships between streets and blocks; around blocks as nested systems; on continuity of urban enclosure; and on scaleable systems—examining the role of the superblock as a viable urban model. It shows the qualities necessary for the formation of an urban block structure. It then goes on to develop the content of this condition:

→ **Building blocks:** define the regular urban block and how it can be scaled up to street blocks, to ward blocks and to neighbourhood assemblies

→ **The art of subdivision:** looks at the relationship of the lot (a collection of plots) and the plot as a vehicle for fine-grained urbanism

→ **Innovative land-release strategies:** look at ways of facilitating compact urbanism through different approaches to accretion, choice and progressive change

→ **Developmental tools:** describe how generative modelling techniques can be used to simulate future urban neighbourhoods and introduces the concept of the universal lot

→ **Localia urban neighbourhood:** breaking the big down to the small takes us through a series of steps to layout the block structure and subdivision of these blocks to form an imaginary urban neighbourhood

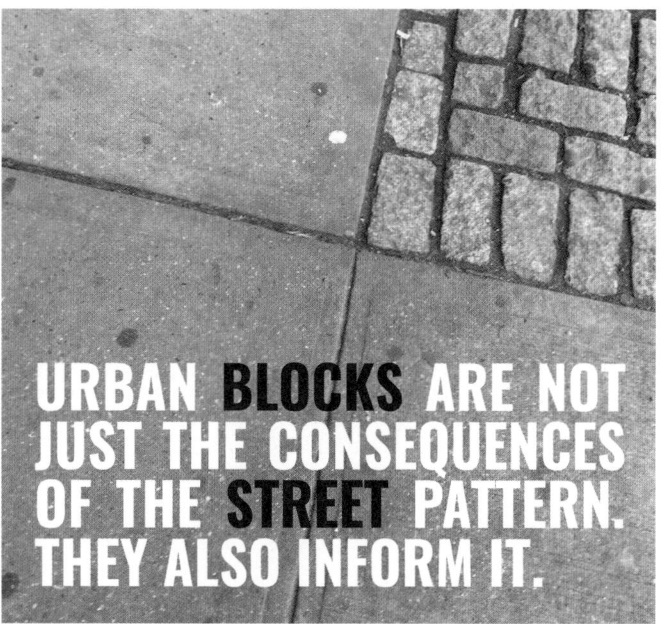

The regular supergrid structure of the neighbourhood of Ecatepec de Morelos, Mexico City.

The building of cities is one of man's greatest achievements. The form of his city always has been and always will be a pitiless indicator of the state of his civilisation.

—Edmund N. Bacon

STREETS AND BLOCKS: YIN AND YANG

Block design is an area of urban design theory and practice that has been overlooked in recent years—an understanding of the efficiency of the block in all its forms and its applications. Many urban design educators, particularly in the United Kingdom, see the urban block as the consequence of the street pattern without any reference back to it. The urban block is often discarded as a typological solution. In other words, once the street pattern is laid out with its desired lines, hierarchy and street types, the urban form flows into the spaces left over. Coupled with the fact that a formal subdivision process is not required, this leaves reduced chances for a regular urban vernacular to emerge. In many ways, this is a hangover of the effects that Gordon Cullen's book *Townscape: The Language of Place* had on the birth of the profession and the later effects that techniques, such as Space Syntax, had on the design of street patterns.

The urban block can take many forms:

- → The regular (orthogonal and linear) block with clearly defined back-to-back relationships that becomes the building block of urban fabric
- → The soft-centred block that can accept later inner growth and change
- → The superblock or street block that can be an arrangement of regular blocks into full neighbourhood assemblies or subassemblies
- → The dual aspect block that has its frontage to the street and its service functions in a back lane
- → The mews block that has buildings separated from the street frontage buildings and accessed from a back lane—they could be under the same ownership as the frontage buildings or under different ownership

All of these are valid. All can accommodate a wide variety of typologies at various scales. Many great examples of planned urbanism show the urban block itself as a typological solution, and none more so than the those of the Victorians, who built efficiently on a vast scale. But this does not mean that we look at the block as an architectural solution in isolation, something we are constantly guilty of doing. To understand the complex relationship between the street and the block, we must look at it from both sides. This relationship cannot be separated—urban structure can be explained as the interrelationship between streets and blocks. They are like the negative and the positive space and can be seen in both ways. The one forms and informs the other.

1 **Streets** form a network where nodes are intersections and links are the roads between. They can easily be seen as piping diagrams where flows can be regulated. It is this potential that has excited engineers over the years and created the greatest conflict with urban designers.

2 **Blocks** can usually be defined without ambiguity as being the smallest area delimited by streets. In urban areas they can be seen as parcels of land where clear boundaries are contained and do not leak out. They are assembled to make up frameworks for responsive action. They are the motherboards that allow different things to be plugged in. They provide the essential and simple order for urban life.

Both streets and assemblies of blocks (those that make up the definable areas of the city with distinct identities) are organised hierarchically. Road networks have local streets at the base of the hierarchy, serving primarily to enable land access at low speeds and low levels of traffic, and city streets serving high volumes of longer-distance movements. Definable areas that are organised hierarchically range from the street block to neighbourhoods, districts and quarters through to whole towns or cities.

Urban structure is formed by the complex interplay between streets and blocks. In well-structured cities, they are like yin and yang—both forming and informing one another by their relative typologies, their regularities and their frontage conditions within the system.

URBAN BLOCKS AS NESTED SYSTEMS

The urban block has been a fundamental element of the form of a neighbourhood since the beginning of cities, and people have found different ways of arranging these into hierarchical structures as urban society has evolved. The best example of this can be found in early Chinese cities, which looked to arrange urban blocks into hierarchies to create the ideal city form. Michael Weinstock, in his book *The Architecture of Emergence: The Evolution of Form in Nature and Civilisation*, shows how even in places such as early Beijing we saw the evolution of the nested grid and courtyard system with blocks of houses on 150-metre-wide (500 feet) hutongs, nested in 1-kilometre (0.62 miles) superblocks inside megablock districts, including the enormous Forbidden City.

Many systems are made of smaller systems, and most systems are nested within other systems. In general, something that is nested is entirely contained within something else of the same kind. This is what we mean when we talk of 'self-similarity'.

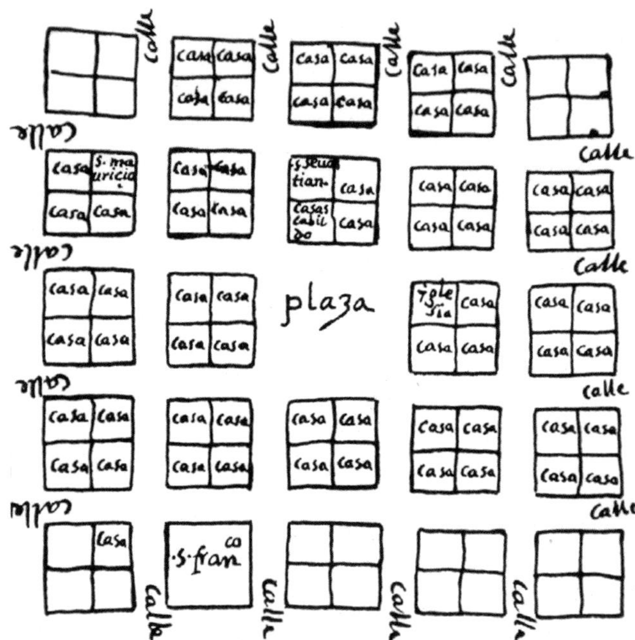

The first map of Caracas in Venezuela (1578) showing its regular block structure around a civic plaza.

Ever since we have planned and organised cities and their localities, we have been striving to understand the nature and scale of this block hierarchy. The Spanish Law of the Indes of 1573, governing colonial settlements in Latin America, provided a regular size and arrangement of urban blocks surrounding a main public square to create a perfect town. Cerda, the planner of Barcelona's 1860 extension, designed the ideal industrial city block of 113 metres (370 feet) with a central garden all arranged within a regular superblock arrangement.

According to David Graham Shane's 'Block, Superblock and Megablock: A Short History', 'The nesting of blocks provided a potent system of urban organisation that only changed when the development of linear sequencing and channelling of flows allowed for the creation of new hierarchies.'

In recent decades the superblock and megablock have become shorthand for this kind of early thinking but with different results. In many instances, the urban block has been lost at the smallest scale in the system as the treelike structures have predominated. In Chandigarh, Le Corbusier planned a 1.6-kilometre (1 mile) grid scaled to the car that contained seventeen superblock neighbourhood sectors containing several 'urban villages' of 150 families. The last British new town, Milton Keynes, has a 1-kilometre (0.62 mile) grid similar to Brasilia. Three or four suburban-density residential superblocks are nested within this megablock grid. Both lost the smaller urban block as a fundamental part of the nested system.

We need to rediscover the full spectrum again.

CONTINUITY OF URBAN ENCLOSURE

An urban block built up on all sides is referred to in urban design circles as a perimeter block. Perimeter blocks are an important feature of many European cities and are seen by urban designers as an urban form that allows very high urban densities to be achieved without resorting to high-rise development. They can be seen in two ways: one is as continuous buildings such as in the classic Parisian pension blocks or as in Rob Krier's larger Berlin blocks that enclose a private or semiprivate space. In this case the building becomes the block. Another way is as a response to the nature of movement and other activity on the street. In this case the enclosure of the street on both sides becomes the important point. The street becomes the reason why the buildings evolve in the form they do.

Although the perimeter block principle is important to urban design theory, it also has become a lazy way of thinking about making built urban blocks. As top-down determinism, many urban designers resort to drawing '10-metre sausages' of buildings around the street boundaries to represent the urban form. They then try to subdivide it to give it the appearance of urban grain. The standard template of urbanism generated by the perimeter block not only is oversimplistic but also it creates a set of problems. It can lead to places that are not responsive to change. It undermines legibility and reduces variety. It also works against the development of a hierarchical structure of streets and spaces. A block without reference to this kind of structure becomes arbitrary and contributes to a disorienting public realm.

Top: Aerial view of neighbourhood in Amsterdam, showing the continuity and enclosure of urban blocks made up out of many buildings.

Karl Kropf, in his hard-hitting critique 'Against the Perimeter Block: A Morphological Critique', says:

> The perimeter block is held up as a defence against a range of ailments: the destructive extremes of Modernist urbanism, mindless cul-de-sac sprawl, arbitrary ego-maniacal expressionism and general ineptitude. But as a cure, it is like a harsh emetic or laxative. It induces a complete evacuation of alternatives. Once purged, we are left with a safe and simple play-school stamp. Without much skill and without the danger of going too far astray, the invalid can produce a satisfying but ultimately crude simulacrum of urban form.

He refers to it as perceptual seduction—something that at face value seems right but masks its reductionist tendencies to see the urban block as an architectural problem in isolation.

Kropf argues that if you simply outline blocks, you learn very little about a town. If, in contrast, you start looking inside blocks at plot and buildings patterns, it soon becomes evident that the similarities of pattern attach to the street, not the block. Continuity of pattern runs along streets.

If you want to outline the area of similar plot series, in most cases you have to split a number of blocks along the back boundaries of plots. To do so is essentially to outline the full, double-loaded street. Even in gridded towns, there is variation in the patterns within the block around its fronts (Savannah, New York, San Francisco). That variation is not *caused* by the streets; it *is* the streets, each making its contribution. If there is no variation, it is not because the block is separate but because it is a part of several streets. The 'street effect' is a similar but less well known phenomenon where the change or alteration of one property is copied by others along the same street. Examples include not just positive changes such as frontage improvements, conversions or paint colours but also dereliction. Towns are abandoned and decay street by street.

The exercise of outlining common patterns of plots and buildings makes it clear that the block is the result of connecting streets. The block only comes into being when streets are connected. The perimeter block only arises when streets are connected and well defined by buildings. They are made up of more complex building arrangements and typologies that derive from the type of subdivisions of the block, and in response to the nature of the street that they front onto. When narrow-fronted homes locate along the street frontage, they automatically contain the block. Continuity and enclosure of the urban block are therefore a consequence of lining the street, not a determinant. Corners become a special response to where the streets sit in the hierarchy. The definition of the block and its subdivisions merely becomes a place-holder, allowing buildings to respond to the street on both sides.

QUALITIES

In addition to our main drivers of change—scaleability, interchangeability and replicability—most complex adaptive systems also display features of self-similarity, which gives us a significant clue to how we introduce scaleability into the development of our urban fabric. A self-similar object is exactly or approximately similar to a part of itself (i.e., the whole has the same shape as one or more of the parts). In our world, this raises some questions: how does a lot fit into a block, or a plot fit into a lot? Regular subdivision rules are a powerful technique for building self-similar objects. The ability to adapt depends on the scale and granularity of the subdivision.

Always consider a brick in a wall, a wall in a room, a room in a house, a house in a street, a street in a neighbourhood, and a neighbourhood in a city.

—after Eliel Saarinen

Top: The regular block structure of Woodstock in Cape Town, South Africa, provides the underlying structure for developing a strong urban vernacular.

THE URBAN BLOCK AS A SCALEABLE SYSTEM

Blocks start as two-dimensional plan objects and, when viewed as individual units or composite groups, are the first level of parcelling urban land into the urban fabric. As these blocks, to varying degrees, are built-up around their edges, they clearly define the primary boundaries between public and private space. They can either be seen as the physical containers of private space or as definers of public space, particularly the streets they give frontage to. It is the regular nature of the urban block that enables it to be subdivided into any number of smaller regular lots (a collection of plots) or individual plots—usually in private ownership or other forms of tenure.

Most cities are composed of a variety of sizes and shapes of the urban block. Many preindustrial cores of cities in Europe, Asia and the Middle East tend to have irregularly shaped street patterns and urban blocks, while planned cities based on grids have much more regular arrangements. Blocks can be arranged in a wide variety of different composite subassemblies that can be treated as typological arrangements and further scaled up.

The scales of subdivision of the neighbourhood are the block, the lot and the plot—units laid out in an orderly manner. Each unit plays an essential role in their formation. Each is mutually supportive. The block is the subset of the neighbourhood. The lot is the subset of the block. The plot is the subset of the lot. All are essential. We need to understand this complex relationship.

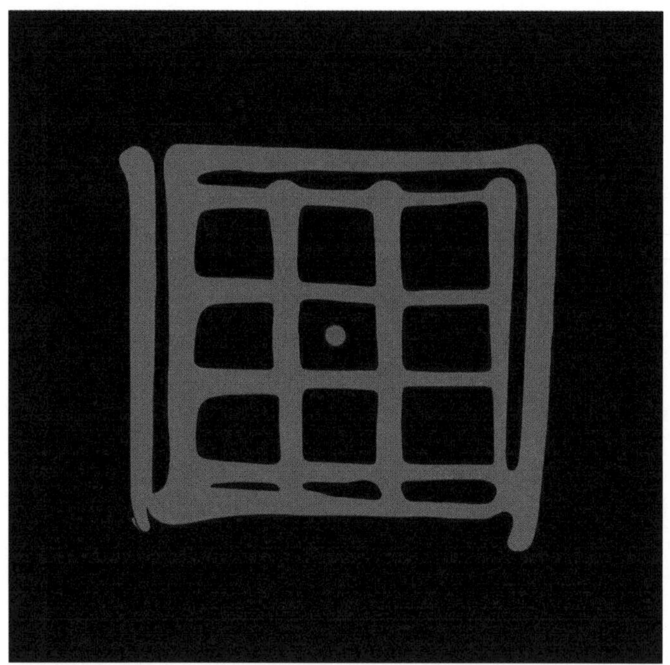

THE SUPERBLOCK AS A SCALEABLE SOLUTION

A superblock is an example of a subassembly: a collection and arrangement of multiple urban blocks, street blocks, open spaces and other uses. It is typically bounded by city-scale streets—main streets, avenues, boulevards or arterial routes—rather than by local streets. In some examples, it is treated as a unified plan and generally closed to vehicular through traffic. In others, it is a simple grid of secondary streets and spaces allowing traffic to filter through indirectly and slowly. The superblock provides the strongest clue to the structure of the urban network, with its city-scale streets providing the primary urban structure. This concept was well developed in Villa El Salvador in Lima, Peru, where the 400- by 400-metre (1,300 × 1,300 feet) supergrid structure containing a soft-centred superblock became the main structure of the new settlement.

The earliest examples of superblocks can be found in the hutongs of Beijing and in the streets and blocks of Jaipur. Jaipur is a model of town planning—the first planned city in India. It followed the principles prescribed in the Vastu Shastra. According to this text, the site should be divided into superblocks or mandalas of equal proportions. Planned according to the prastara type of layout, which gives prominence to the cardinal directions, Jaipur is an arrangement of nine superblocks (three by three) defined by the city's main streets. The renowned Indian architect, Balkrishna Doshi, who worked with Le Corbusier on Chandigarh, went on to use this traditional Hindu system in his plan for the expansion of Jaipur. Other examples in the new world include Penn's early plan for Philadelphia and Oglethorpe's plan for Savannah, both of which show superblocks at various scales.

Superblocks as reductionist models

Superblocks were popular during the early and mid-twentieth century, fuelled by modernist ideas in architecture and urban planning. Planning in this era was based upon the distance and speed scales for the car and discounted the benefits of pedestrian and cyclist modes. Accommodating the car is where urban designers have put their efforts in recent decades, but have they just missed the point?

Superblocks are often found in planned cities where a tree-like street hierarchy replaced the traditional grid. In these cities, the interior of the superblock is typically served by discontinuous dead-ended or looped streets. The discontinuity inside the superblocks forces dependency on the car, discourages easy walking, and forces more traffic onto the fewer continuous streets, increasing demand for through streets, which leads ultimately to these streets having more travel lanes added for cars, thereby making it more difficult for any pedestrians to cross such streets. In this way, superblocks cut up the city into isolated units, expand vehicle dominance, and make it impossible for pedestrians and cyclists to get anywhere outside of the superblock. The new towns of Chandigarh in India and Milton Keynes in the United Kingdom are prime examples of this approach and are based on Clarence Perry's idea of a 'neighbourhood unit'.

A recent example of a superblock can be found in Peter Calthorpe's pedestrian pocket concept. Similar to the plan of Jaipur in that it is also composed of nine normal city blocks, it is clustered around a light rail station and a central open space. Its circulation pattern consists primarily of a dense pedestrian network, which is complementary to but independent from the car. Access by car is provided using three loops. This superblock differs from Perry's concept in that it makes it impossible for cars to cross the full length or breadth of the block. The pedestrian pocket idea makes no sense. Why bury your most accessible point of public transport in your least accessible location? Surely we know that we put our stations at the highest point of road accessibility, in other words at the crossroads of higher order streets. This means we get the benefits of interchange and locate public transport at the point where commercial and civic activity is most likely to occur.

In 2003, Vauban (a rail suburb of Freiburg, Germany) was constructed with a similar goal. It has a superblock arrangement with a central pedestrian spine and a few narrow looped and dead-end streets. In all instances, pedestrian segregation is seen as another branch of the tree that operates in isolation to the street.

Good urbanism always loses.

Top: The nine-square block structure used in Jaipur, India, is based on the principles prescribed in the Shilpa-Shastra, an ancient Indian treatise on architecture.

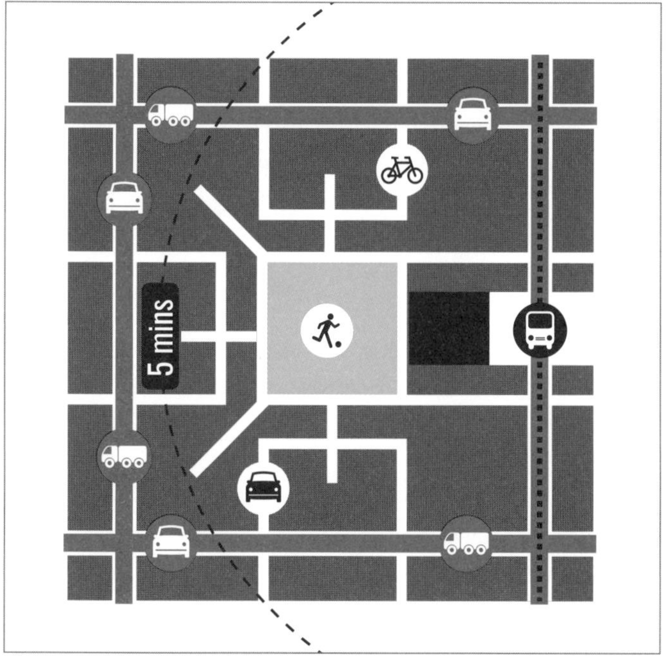

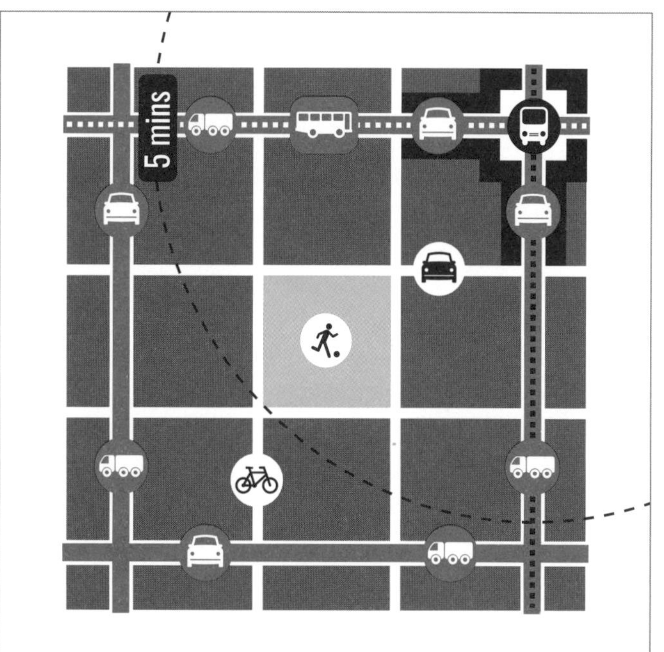

The way forwards for the superblock

Urban planners and designers, today, now know that the discontinuity of the street and the limited-access roads associated with superblocks have reduced pedestrian and bicycle use wherever this 'sprawl' pattern is present. The traditional urban block networks spread traffic onto several narrower roads at slower speeds. This more finely connected network of narrower roads better allows the pedestrian and cyclist realms to flourish.

Virtual, unplanned superblocks have been created in many cities as the result of continuous modifications to streets and increased traffic management. Most such superblocks have occurred in older cities where the street network originates in earlier times. Not only is the street pattern tortuous, but many streets are not capable of accommodating passing cars. Such constraints, along with deteriorating air quality, forced many cities to remove car traffic from such streets. Good examples are Soho in London and Bremen in Germany.

There is no reason why a superblock cannot have the benefits of the larger main street structure for high volumes of through movement and still have an internal structure that spreads slower traffic flow through the superblock at the outset. As the place emerges and different pressures arise, the internal street structure can be managed to limit through traffic. In this way, it has the best of both worlds. Over time, the superblock remains accessible on foot or bicycle, retaining its design intentions.

It all depends on how these urban blocks are arranged. The combination of the irregular pattern with the standard blocks results in a more differentiated series of urban spaces.

Top left: Calthorpe's pedestrian pocket concept. **Top right:** A superblock that puts its primary activities at the point of highest accessibility. **Bottom:** Clarence Perry's superblock.

LEARNING FROM HISTORY

Which block sizes, shapes and plot configurations can most flexibly accommodate a variety of building typologies? This question is fundamental to urban design and planning because it decides whether the network of streets and blocks can act as the stable framework for the growth and change of land uses over time. We can learn a lot from block typologies that have been employed in some of our great urban neighbourhoods and cities. Supplemented with other research, UN-Habitat's *Planned Urban Extensions* gives us some valuable information.

Each of the case studies represents different hierarchies of block subdivision and different arrangements—simple gridiron structures to neighbourhood submodules—each offering benefits of regularity and form.

1 **Manhattan, New York,** uses the simple regular block that is fixed in its width of 60 metres (200 feet) but varies in its length from 125 to 288 metres (410 to 950 feet). The width allows the introduction of a service lane along the midblock. Blocks are subdivided into 5- or 6-metre-wide plots with 30-metre depths (16- or 20-feet-wide with 100-foot depths).

2 **Eixample, Barcelona,** has square blocks with chamfered corners and sides of 113 metres (370 feet). Plots are 9 to 15 metres (30 to 50 feet) wide.

3 **Savannah, Georgia,** has neighbourhood units of 180 by 200 metres (590 × 660 feet). These are broken down into two block types: tything blocks that are 25 metres wide by 80 metres long (85 × 265 feet) subdivided into 16-metre-wide (52 feet) plots, and trust blocks that are 25 metres wide by 50 metres long (85 × 165 feet) subdivided into 25-metre-wide (85 feet) plots.

4 **Back Bay, Boston,** has a simple block structure with a rear service lane. Block depths are generally 75 metres (250 feet) wide and 114 to 208 metres (375 to 680 feet) long. Blocks are subdivided into 7-metre-wide (23 feet) plots.

5 **Villa El Salvador, Peru,** uses neighbourhood units of 288 metres (950 feet) square. These are broken down into standard blocks that are 40 metres wide by 89 metres long (130 × 290 feet) subdivided into 7.5-metre-wide (25 feet) plots and larger corner plots.

6 **Jaipur, India,** uses an 800 by 800 metre (2,625 × 2,625 feet) mandala as a neighbourhood subunit. Each of these mandalas is subdivided differently, but these are generally broken down into street blocks that range from 120 to 270 metres long (390 to 885 feet) and generally are 100 metres (330 feet) wide. Narrow streets and pedestrian lanes break down these blocks into an infinite arrangement of subblocks. Plot sizes vary, as they have been subdivided further over the years to create a rich compact environment.

7 **Montagu Square in Marylebone, London,** uses a combination of square and rectilinear street blocks with internal mews. They range from 92 to 132 metres (300 to 430 feet) in length and are generally 92 metres (300 feet) wide. They are split along their length with a 7.5-metre-wide (25 feet) mews service lane. The predominant plot subdivision is 7.5 metres (25 feet) wide with varying depths.

8 **Belhar, Cape Town,** uses T-shaped street blocks of 108 by 170 metres (350 × 560 feet) made up out of three regular blocks measuring 108 by 48 metres (350 × 160 feet) assembled around a shared-surface street space. Plots are 24 metres (80 feet) deep and 7.5 to 9 metres (25 to 30 feet) wide.

9 **Borneo Sporenburg, Amsterdam,** uses a number of different-sized street blocks. They range from 75 to 240 metres (250 to 800 feet) long and are mainly 24 metres (80 feet) wide, allowing for back-to-back housing. They are subdivided into development lots ranging from 5 to 25 metres (16 to 80 feet) wide. Waterfront plots are 5 metres (16 feet) wide.

10 **Edinburgh New Town** has predominant street blocks of 180 metres long by 64 metres wide (590 × 210 feet). These are broken down by internal service lanes. The plot width range appears to be 10 to 15 metres (33 to 50 feet) wide.

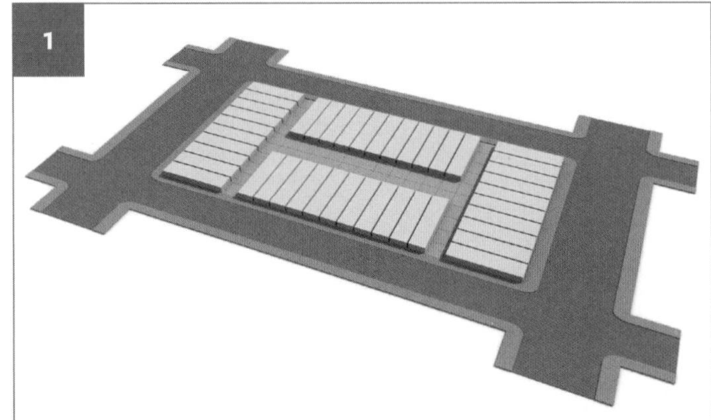

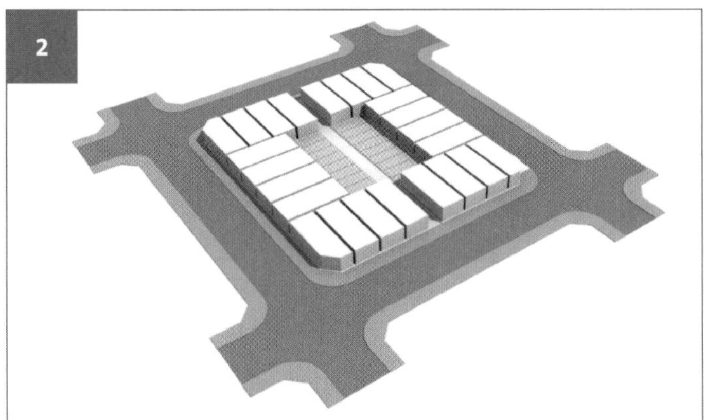

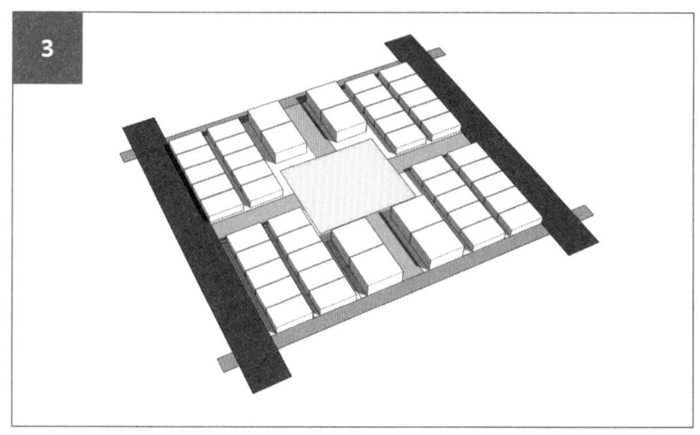
3

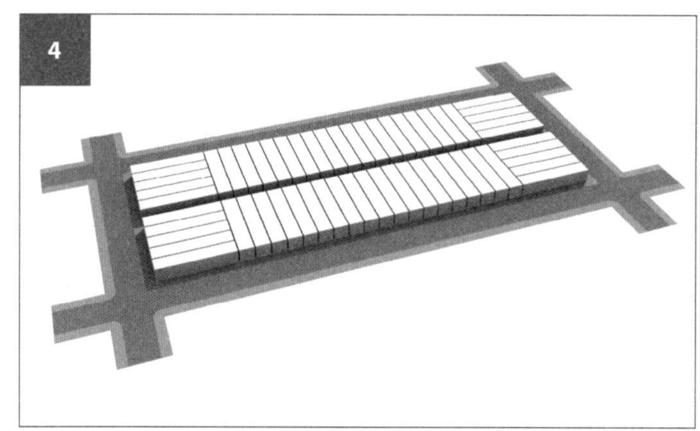
4

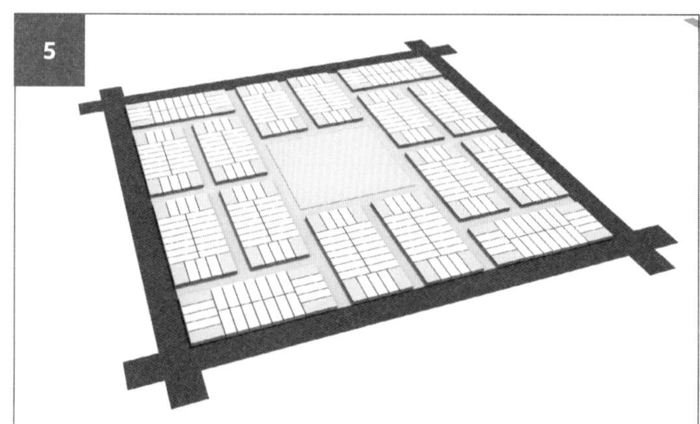
5

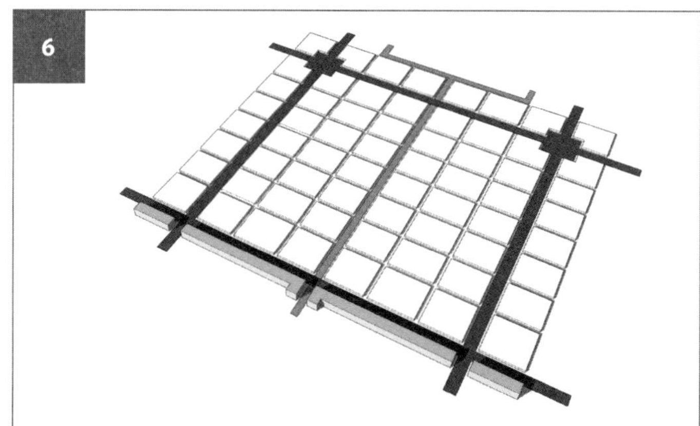
6

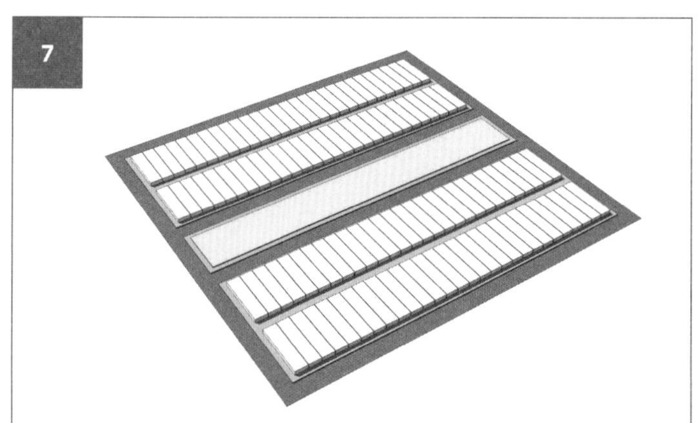
7

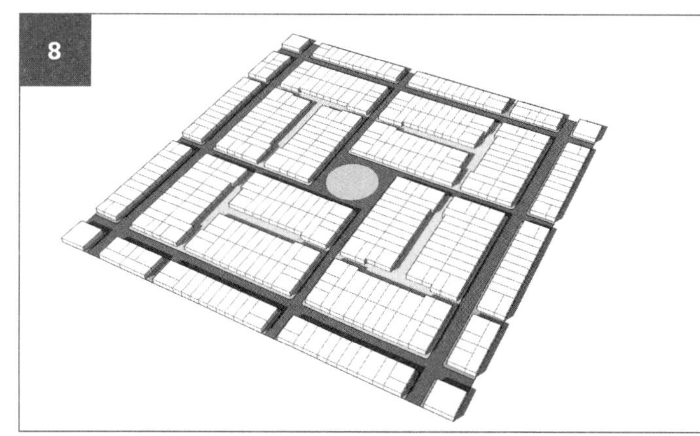
8

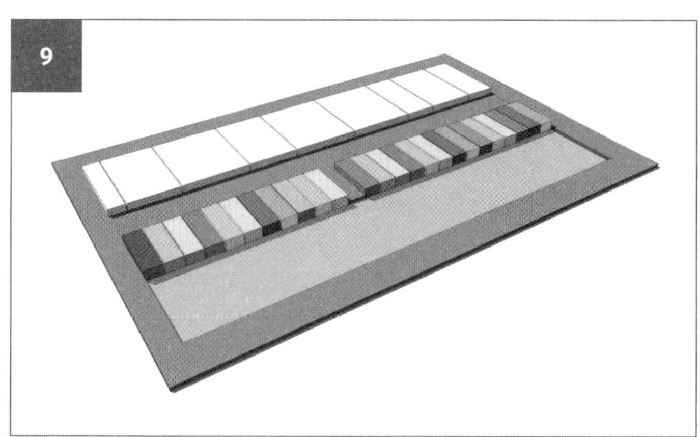
9

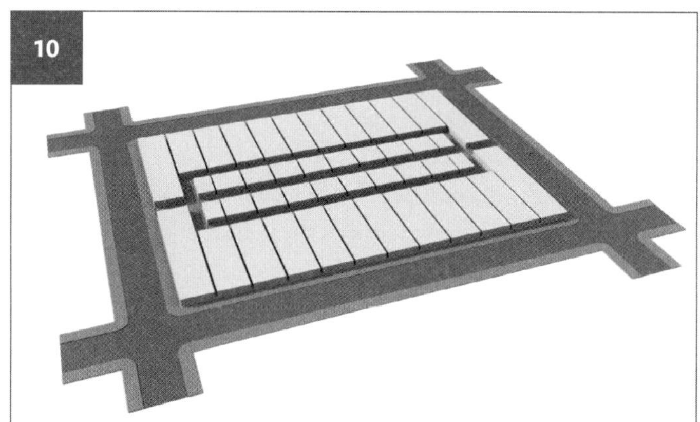
10

BUILDING BLOCKS

It is the combined pattern and varied arrangement of the streets, blocks, lots, plots, open spaces, and their boundary conditions—called the *urban fabric*—that:

→ Provide the medium for the growth and change of the neighbourhood, acting as the seedbed for community life to take root and flourish

→ Provide a complex underlying structure that gives rise to a place's diversity and future growth and change

→ Allow typological solutions at a variety of scales to be developed and a local urban vernacular to emerge

→ Exert a fundamental influence upwards on the structure and pattern of our urban networks

→ Give us the physical boundary constraints within which the built urban fabric of our neighbourhoods, districts and quarters forms

Urban fabric can be interpreted as an exercise in assembling a neighbourhood out of tried and tested, regular, standardised urban blocks. The concept is not new. Famous cities such as Paris and Barcelona have successfully conformed to their typology and become the most celebrated examples of planned urbanism in the world. The best of these bring together the strict order of the urban block with the diversity of individual infill buildings, thus creating a timeless and lively urban neighbourhood. Sometimes new infills appear and old ones disappear. Lots and plots are consolidated or subdivided further, but the urban block endures.

The degree to which an area's pattern of blocks and their subdivisions is respectively small and frequent is called *fine-grain fabric*; large and infrequent is called *coarse-grain fabric*. It is the process of breaking down the big into the small that gives us clues to how we deal with our large sites, either inner city or, more particularly, on the fringes of many of our towns and cities. In this process we can find solutions to the problem of monopolising practices that offer only single-formula approaches and open up the housing market to a wider range of responses. Breaking the big into small units also enables us to assemble them again to make up the identifiable social and economic localities of the city: its neighbourhoods, districts and quarters.

THE REGULAR BLOCK

A regular (or standard) block is fully surrounded with roads and contains single or multiple uses, accommodated in subdivisions. It is classically a perimeter block with uses lining the street. Opportunities for inner growth and change exist in the intensification of frontage development and limited rear yard infill. An important feature of a regular block is its consistent scale and proportion. The more regular it is, the easier it is to provide the smallest unit of a neighbourhood assembly. Square blocks and rectilinear blocks are easy to assemble, with square blocks best suited for city centre fabric, where the pattern of streets and blocks is far tighter.

According to the Calgary Greenfield Tool Box, there are several rules of thumb for defining appropriate block and lot standards in a new development. Some of these include:

→ Block dimensions should balance all modes of transport, including walking.
→ Block sizes and lots of modular units or flexible scales should be able to be assembled or subdivided to meet future needs and market demands.
→ Block and lot standards should result in a street network with high connectivity and meet objectives for street network and block density.
→ Blocks should be able to support a range of building types for all neighbourhood uses.
→ Blocks should be able to support a range of housing formats.
→ The configuration of blocks should account for access to services, such as rear lanes for access to parking and utilities.

Simple ways in which we can understand and manipulate the regular block to create greater urban opportunities include:

1 The urban block as a 'brick'

In a neighbourhood, the best way of seeing an urban block is in the proportion of a 'brick'. A brick can build a wall, in a house, on the street, to make a block to form a neighbourhood. Bricks can be arranged in endless patterns to create endless forms. Brick proportions allow two bricks laid on end (with a joint) to be equal to one brick laid along its length. If we can get the same proportions for the block (roughly 2:1), then we can arrange blocks in similar endless patterns. For example, two blocks laid out along their lengths with an internal street become a square block.

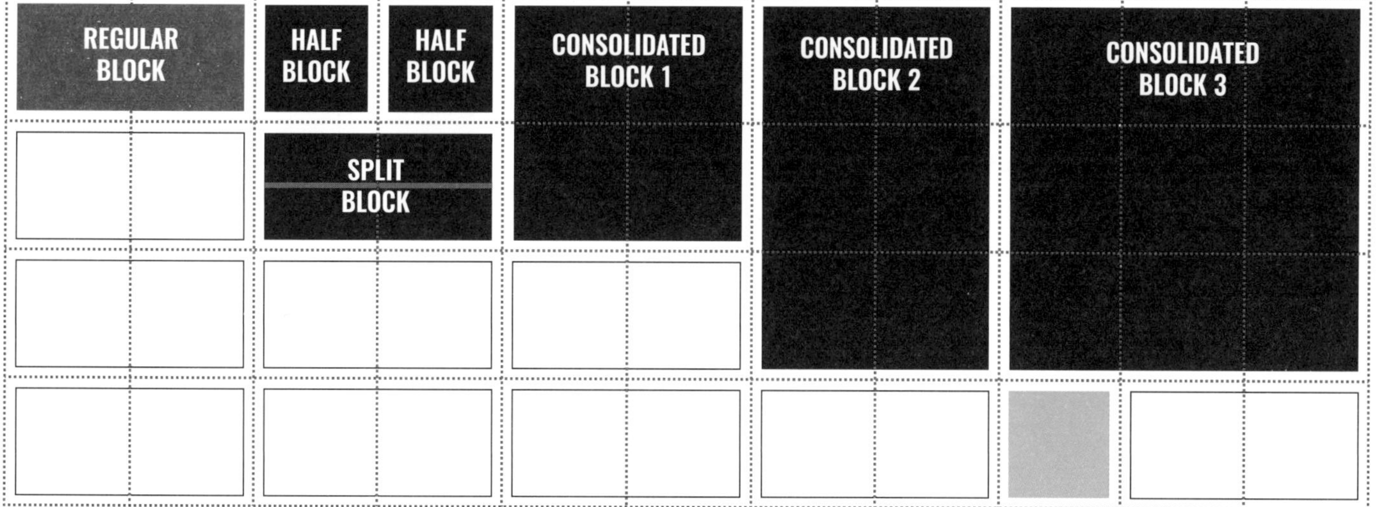

2 Dimensioning a block

Efficient dimensioning and design of the block derives from a strong understanding of building typologies and their complex interrelationship with the street and plot. This is the reason why in places such as Cadogan Square in London or in the pattern of many Parisian blocks we see such successful urbanism. It is not just because of their great architecture; it is because these places demonstrate the efficiency that lies in a highly evolved urban solution. Street, lot, plot, building and block become entwined—no waste, easily replicable.

There is no magic formula for determining the optimum dimensions of an urban block. Each place must look to its history—the answers may lie buried in previous experience—or find a possible solution and try it. For example:

→ The American Planning Association in their Planning and Urban Design Standards give the dimensions for a connected street pattern of blocks as 120 to 180 metres (390 to 590 feet) between junctions. So 150 metres (500 feet) is the midpoint of this range.

→ Portland, Oregon, has a 75-metre (250 feet) square grid, measured from its street centrelines. Although this is seen as a successful city centre scale, it does not work for neighbourhoods, as too much road space is required. A solution could be to combine two blocks for neighbourhood blocks (giving 150 × 75 metres / 500 × 250 feet) and allow for subdivision in more central or main street locations.

→ The Cerda grid in Barcelona is approximately 140 metres (460 feet) square, measured from its street centre lines, and this has served the city well.

3 A split block to enable inner growth

A split block is a subdivision of a regular urban block with a new service lane (or mews) along the centre of the block, which is similar to the Boston Back Bay example. The service lane starts as a private access route shared by the occupants of the block and later can be adopted as public space and can take many forms. It represents the lowest order of public access to the rear of private properties, providing opportunities for dealing with parking and servicing issues in the short term and allowing the potential for later inner growth and change through opportunities for new frontage development along the lanes. The lanes, because they evolve over time, represent the greatest potential for fine-grain, mixed-use urban activities to serve the neighbourhood.

4 The half block as the main street solution

There are two ways of addressing the composition of urban blocks along main streets. One body of opinion suggests that regular urban blocks should be presented 'end-on' to main streets, giving more corners for commercial activity and improving walkability to a wider catchment. If these blocks are then put together, the shared-surface streets could be developed for street markets, events spaces, parking areas, and so on.

The other body of opinion suggests that blocks should be arranged lengthwise along the main street, putting the service lane along the midblock and avoiding the number of crossings a shopper has to make.

5 Consolidating blocks for larger land uses

There are good reasons to merge urban blocks to accommodate such uses as schools, hospitals, open spaces and so on. There are also good grounds for these consolidated blocks to be later subdivided as these uses go away. For example, the Cerda grid in Barcelona allows open space and facilities to be spread out throughout the city and integrated into the grid design using the block as a basic compositional unit. The combination of several block units (two, four, six and nine units) has created areas of various dimensions that accommodate parks, hospitals, universities and even industrial zones.

THE LOST ART OF SUBDIVISION

Understanding the initial design of a city is important, but the first settlement within the land subdivision is even more crucial, as the dominant process is the adjustment of block size and plot and lot dimensions to actual use. In general, the plot is more permanent than either the building or the street.

> *You always have to look at the relation between the collective to which these people adapt to, on one hand, and the freedom within the constraints of the system on the other hand. For me the plot is extremely important in that sense.*
>
> —Kees Christiaanse

The block is the assembly of a number of plots or lots and provides an essential ordering device for districts, neighbourhoods and quarters. Efficient dimensioning and design of the block derives from a strong understanding of building typologies and their complex interrelationship with the street and plot. This is the reason why in places such as Cadogan Square in London or in the pattern of many Parisian blocks we see such successful urbanism. It is not just because of their great architecture; it is because these places demonstrate the efficiency that lies in a highly evolved urban solution. Street, plot, building and block become entwined—there is no waste and they are easily replicable.

All vernacular starts with the plot and defining its relationship with the building and the street, something we did very well in the past. Many of the successful models hinged around the narrow-fronted plot with the frontage dimension becoming the key indicator of wealth and social standing.

Booth's plan of London is a poverty map. It is also a map of plot frontages—the narrower the plot frontage, the lower the pecking order.

1 The lot

The lot, defined as a collection of plots, is an intermediate unit of subdivision of the block. It provides a more flexible way of breaking down the neighbourhood into smaller parcels of development. If you go directly from the block to the plot subdivision, you tend to overconstrain development. The lot provides for a fuller range of structured choices but still gives sufficient constraints. It allows scaling up or scaling down. In other words, we can join two lots together, or we can subdivide these lots further.

So, the relationship between the block and the lot is fundamental. The scale of the block informs how lots can be subdivided. The optimum size and number of the lots have an influence on the scale of the urban block.

We need to experiment to find the optimum lot size, looking at the close relationship between:

- → Frontage to depth ratios
- → Building typologies
- → Design coding and guidance
- → Delivery models
- → Development control

The use of the lot gives us the first clue to setting potential default conditions that could give us ways of dealing with different forms of permitted development.

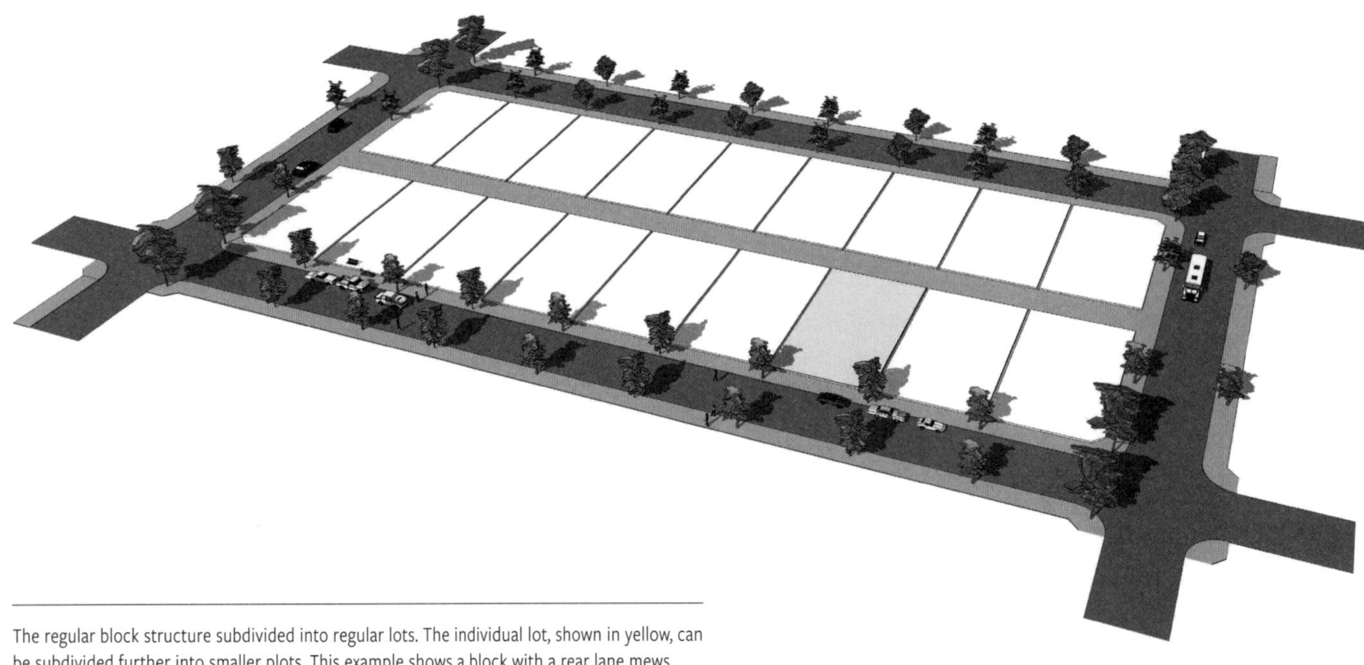

The regular block structure subdivided into regular lots. The individual lot, shown in yellow, can be subdivided further into smaller plots. This example shows a block with a rear lane mews.

2 The plot

The plot is the smallest unit of mixed use and the smallest, and therefore the most achievable, unit of delivery. It provides an opportunity for independent timelines and introduces the possibility for individual responses—the preconditions for richness, variety and uniqueness. The plot only comes about through subdivision: the breaking up of the problem mountain into pebbles. The plot and building relationship have always been interdependent, so we need to rediscover subdivision alongside the development of new building typologies. Many countries require plotting plans—some require very formal processes before development can happen. In Spain, they call it an *urbanizacion*; in the new world, a township plan. The problem with defining the plot as the only granular method is that it can become too limiting if its dimensions are fixed at the outset and cannot be easily changed. Of course, you could release plots of land based on variable frontage dimensions. In other words, if you only want six metres, you only buy six metres. This is like organic village growth. It works well for one-off, bespoke projects, but is less flexible for releasing larger chunks of land. It also does not readily facilitate regularities and promote default conditions.

Ombretta Romice and Sergio Porta at the University of Strathclyde in Glasgow see plot-based (or fine-grained) urbanism as a form of urban resilience where relatively small components can easily adapt, assemble and reassemble over time. Resilience then depends on a system of units that maintain their own identity even when combined into greater wholes. These wholes then accrue their character while changing, in complexity and functionality.

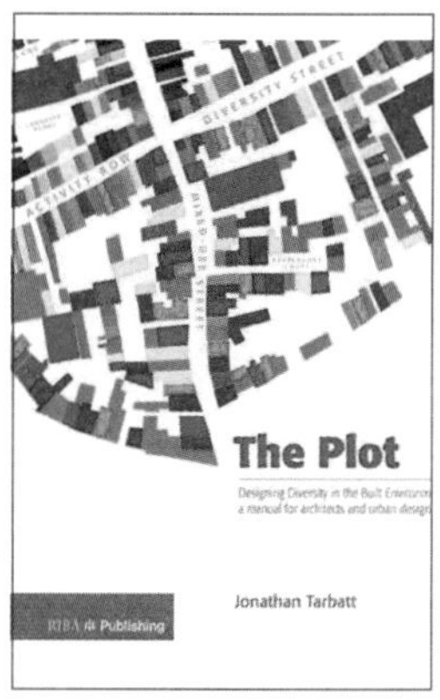

In Jonathan Tarbatt's book, *The Plot: Designing Diversity in the Built Environment*, the plot is a reliable component of greater wholes and a scaleable entity capable of being seen on its own or together with others. It is consistently recognised as a feature of the built environment across time and, as such, has attracted consensus as a robust and meaningful unit of development for the next generation of urban neighbourhoods.

Andrew Price, writing in *Thoughts on Building Strong Towns, Volume III*, sees fine-grained urbanism as preferable because it implies:

→ **Diverse ownership:** Each individual plot typically has a different owner.

→ **Lower cost of entry:** It costs less to build a home on a small, narrow plot than building an entire apartment complex.

→ **More destinations within walking distance:** There are a greater number of doors on a street.

→ **Greater resistance to bad buildings:** Poor architecture can make less of an impact when buildings are limited in size.

The plot may or not coincide with ownership subdivision: it is of crucial importance, in fact, to distinguish the unit of development from the unit of ownership, as fine-grained development must—and can in fact—be made compatible with large land ownership in processes of urban regeneration.

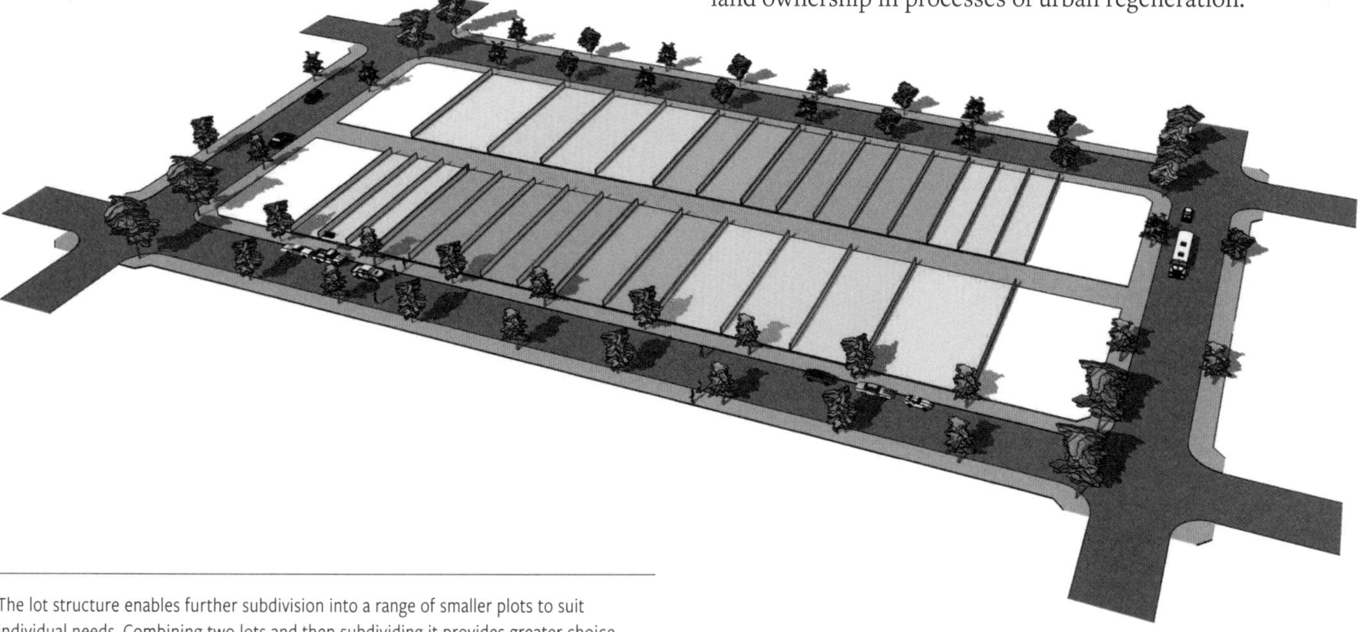

The lot structure enables further subdivision into a range of smaller plots to suit individual needs. Combining two lots and then subdividing it provides greater choice.

ADDRESSING THE PLOT

CREATING A FRAMEWORK FOR EVERYONE TO TRANSITION TO FORMALITY

Research has shown that incremental housing with surveyed plots can work in different countries with different cultures, and that surveyed plots are extremely resilient in the face of economic and political change. Over time these settlements tend to transition into cohesive communities with the most appropriate housing. They are also well suited for incremental improvements to infrastructure and services at all scales. The most affordable and cost-effective service network of all service networks is regular urban blocks and subdivisions with a simple relationship to the street network. This structure has the greatest impact in terms of sense of identity, community organisation and municipal management.

Regular surveyed plots give low-income families the greatest freedom to build, at their pace and responding to their needs, as John F. C. Turner has shown us. They require the least amount of government intervention and financial support.

Roberto Chávez's conference paper 'Incremental Housing: The Past and Future Dwelling Solution for the Poor' shows how in the early 1970s the government in Peru built large-scale, least-cost housing solutions in and around Lima. Chávez writes:

> The National Social Mobilization System, SINAMOS, organized low-income communities and groups of squatters, transported and settled them in vast tracts of empty land to the south and north of the capital city. These settlements consisted of nothing more than organized communities with surveyed plots and virtually no urban services. This was one step down from the Bank-supported sites and services projects that usually included core dwelling units and communal water points. In the sites and services projects, the object was to provide 'affordable' housing to low-income households, which usually put them out of reach of many of the poorest urban dwellers. The objective of the surveyed plots was to provide housing solutions for the greatest number of poor households who were streaming into the cities from the countryside.
>
> Both the sites and services and the surveyed plots programs were inspired by the work and research of a British architect, John F. C. Turner...[who] observed that when left to their own devices people produce the most efficient possible housing solutions for themselves, over time and through self-help and mutual aid. From his observations came his well-known, 'Freedom to Build'.

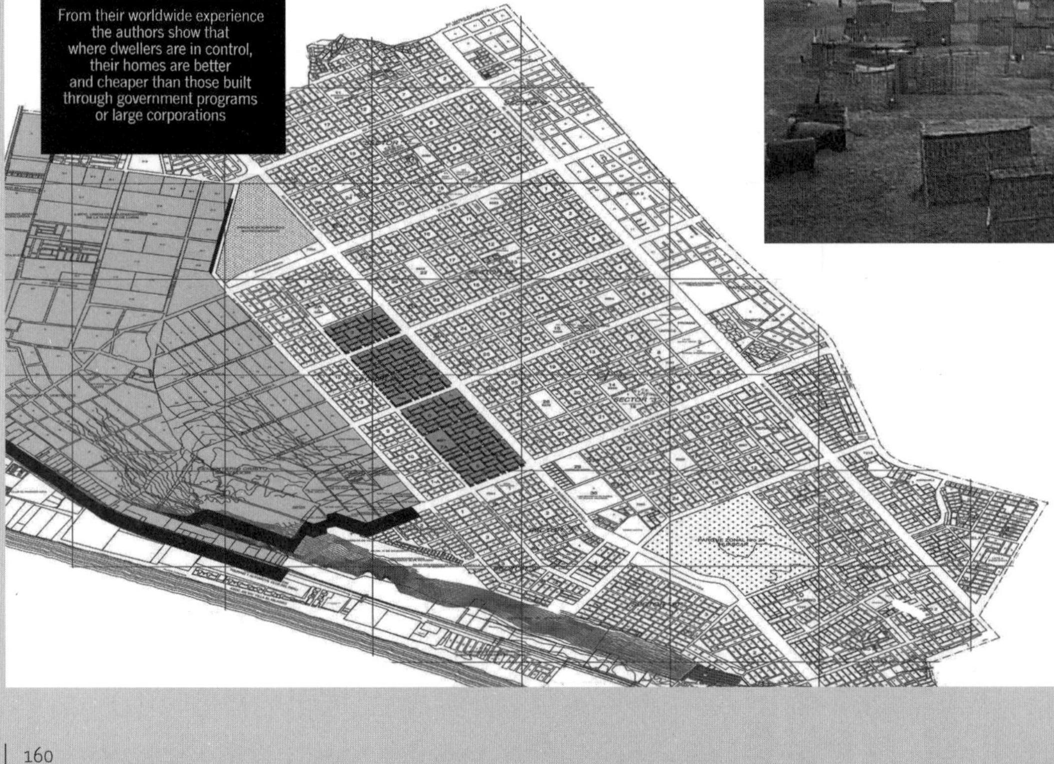

Left: The SINAMOS plan of Villa El Savador, Lima, showing its regular block structure.
Above: The regular urban structure enabled its early settlement of the site.
Opposite page: Villa El Savador as it is today, showing how incremental housing on surveyed plots can lead to transition from informality to formality over time.

The first SINAMOS settlement was Villa El Salvador, which initially consisted only of surveyed plots. The design was a large-scale grid of adjoining neighbourhoods of 400 by 400 metres (1,300 × 1,300 feet). At the heart of each of these was an area reserved for community facilities. At the beginning, Villa El Salvador was a vast stretch of desert dotted with plastic and cane shanties almost as far as the eye could see. SINAMOS coordinated the delivery of water by tanker trucks, and the military established a number of field clinics to provide essential health services to the population. Another important feature of Villa El Salvador was that it was built on the considerable social capital generated by the worker self-managed economy model....

The World Bank was invited to upgrade some of these settlements in 1975. It was agreed that Bank-supported Sites and Services project would provide water and electricity....

Forty years later, Villa El Salvador has become the second largest city in Peru, [joined up] with Lima at the southern end of the extended urban region. The shanties have evolved into one to three storey, brick and mortar dwellings, often with a small business on the ground floor. The communal areas in the middle of each barrio have evolved in different ways. In most cases, they hold a school or a health center, and they almost always serve as a playground. Contrary to other parks and public spaces in Lima,... these areas are free of urban crime and violence since they are surrounded by residential areas with a strong sense of community and are under the watchful eyes of their occupants.

Other examples of successful surveyed-plots programmes supported by the World Bank took place in Africa: Ouagadougou, Burkina Faso, in the mid-1980s and Nouakchott, Mauritania, in the 1990s.

In the case of Ouagadougou, there was an important innovation to the surveyed plots program. In addition to the surveyed plots, a street address was also provided. This was an important improvement, as it allowed the government to collect a very small tax ... which was enough to cover the cost of operating and maintaining the street addressing system. But perhaps more importantly, the street address gave the new residents a sense of belonging....

[In Nouakchott,] the agreed option was a radical upgrading, where a 400- by 400-metre (1,300 × 1,300 feet) grid would be overlaid on the squatter settlement, and the main avenues would be bulldozed through the community. An interesting feature of the project was that in the interior of the grid, the organic layout of the plots of varying sizes would be maintained. This design worked because the [community water-supply points] would be located only in at the intersections of the streets. The electrical network initially would consist only of public lighting along the street network.... The dwellings that were removed from the main thoroughfares were relocated to an adjoining surveyed-plot area, continuing the [grid system], and linking the squatter settlement to the formal road network of the city....

[C]ompared to conventional sites and services or other public housing projects, surveyed plot projects seem to be more amenable to going to a large enough scale to meet the enormous demand of rapid urbanisation in the least developed cities....

The main obstacle, aside from know-how and political will, has been and will be the availability of an adequate supply of land. Polices that have been discredited by the development banks and bilateral agencies, such as land banking and urban planning, need to be revisited. In the meantime, policies that tend to increase pressure on the supply of land, such as destruction and relocation of slums and squatter settlements must be permanently discarded in favour of urban upgrading in situ. Slum upgrading and slum prevention must be addressed simultaneously on a global scale, and from the bottom up, with all hands on deck, at the local level. The dawn of the twenty-first century may be our last chance to get it right.

THE SUBASSEMBLY

All of these blocks can be assembled in different ways to create subassemblies of the neighbourhood's urban fabric. All can accommodate a wide variety of typologies at various scales. These subassemblies could include the following.

THE STREET BLOCK

A street block is a composite arrangement of regular or lane blocks to create smaller environmental cells, where the internal streets can be treated as shared-surface spaces, *woonerven*, or limited-access play spaces. The concept is a safer street where children can play but where vehicles can still traverse slowly. A good example can be found in the street blocks of Belhar in Cape Town, where there is a shared-surface internal street formed by three regular blocks. The entrances to the shared-surface street have been necked to form a gateway to the quieter interior.

There are other examples of street block arrangements:

1. In the **square block**, two regular blocks are arranged along their lengths to become an equal-sided composition. The internal street is downgraded from a residential street to a shared-surface solution with gateway treatments at their entrances to signal a different domain. Square blocks provide an easy way of laying out a regular square grid pattern.

2. In the **T block**, three regular blocks are arranged to create a T-shaped rectilinear composition with an internal shared-surface street.

3. In the **H block**, four regular urban blocks are arranged in a larger rectilinear arrangement with a 2:1 length-to-depth relationship.

4. In the **pinwheel block**, four regular urban blocks are arranged in a pinwheel shape around an internal open space or community facility to create a square composition.

Each of these blocks can be used alone or in combination with each other (and in combination with the regular urban block) to create a larger assembly.

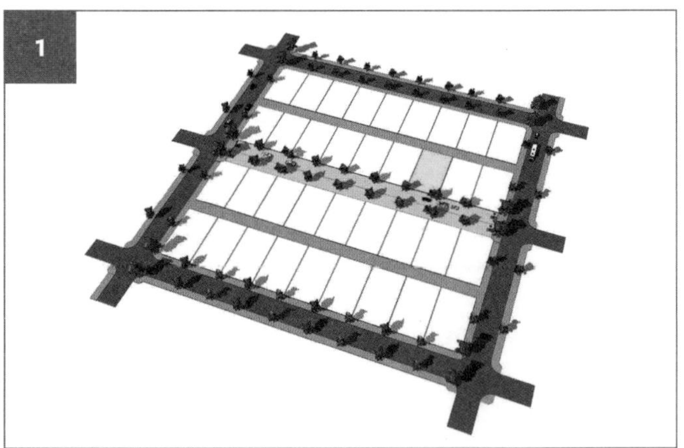

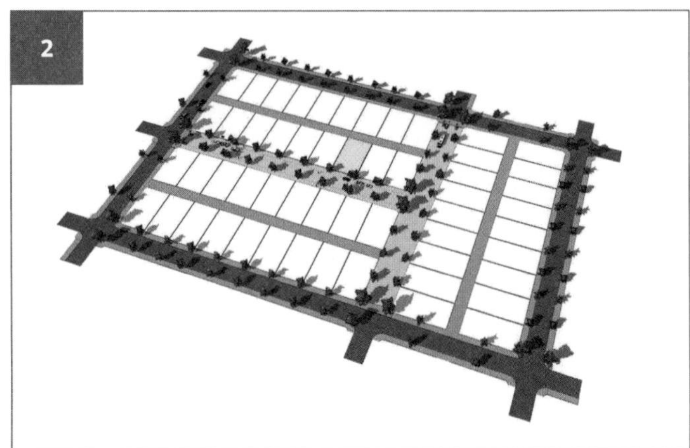

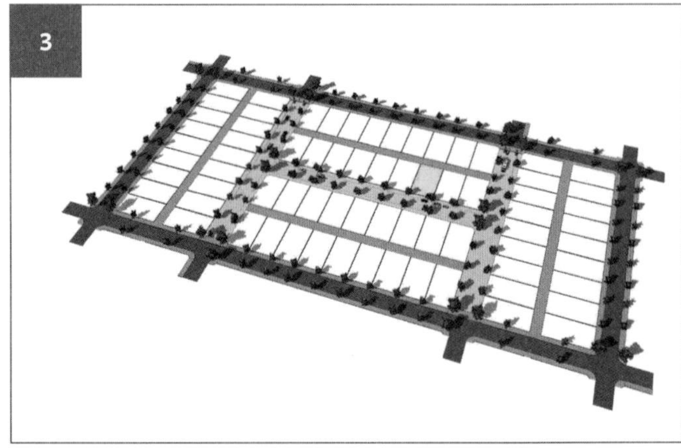

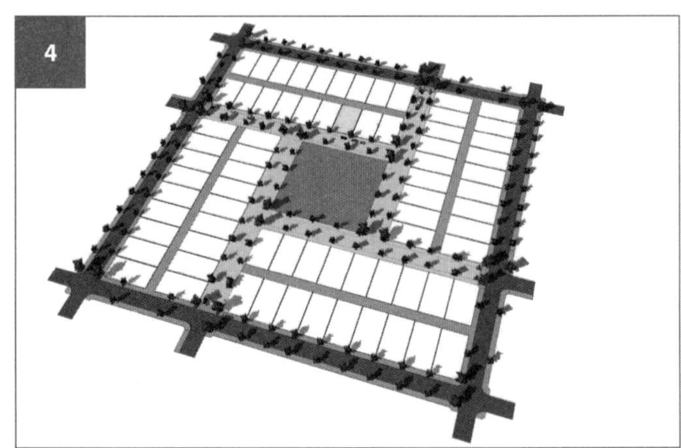

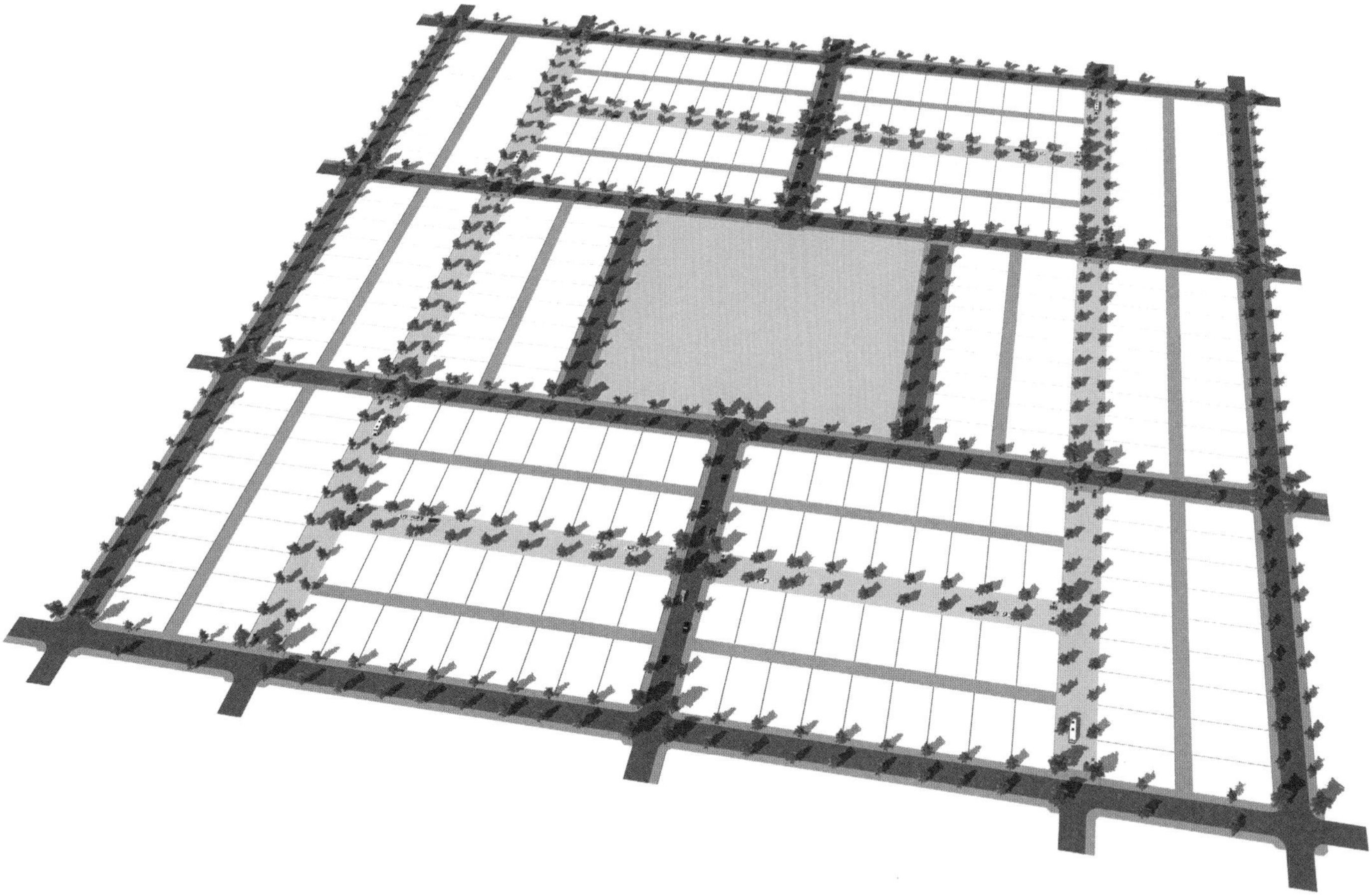

THE WARD (PRECINCT) BLOCK

This is an arrangement of regular or street blocks to create subneighbourhood modules or superblocks. The neighbourhood can be incorporated with other uses, such as open space, schools and so on, to form a defined unit of delivery that can be replicated. A good example of this arrangement can be found in the Savannah urban block (also called a ward block), which hosts some regular blocks arranged around a central communal space. We can also call it a precinct block because it makes up a unit of development that when assembled with other precincts can make up a neighbourhood. It is also a good scale to promote more effective local democracy.

Taking our clues from the work of others, we believe that the optimum external dimension of the ward block is within the range of 300 to 600 metres, (1,000 to 2,000 feet) wide in either a square or rectilinear arrangement of street blocks. The Savannah ward block scale of 400 by 400 metres (1,300 × 1,300 feet) has been a favoured option for many, and the Villa El Salvador settlement plan in Lima, Peru, is a more recent example of this scale.

The ward block structure as a subneighbourhood unit in Savannah, Georgia, provided the model for neighbourhood democracy.

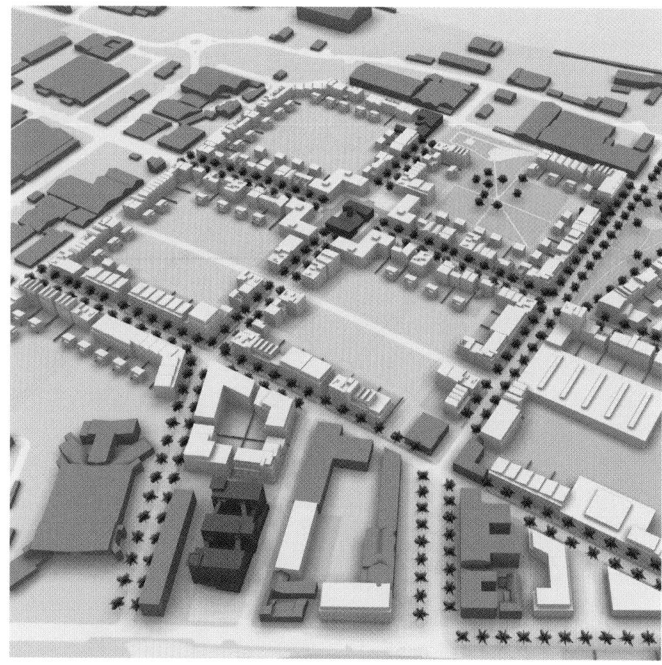

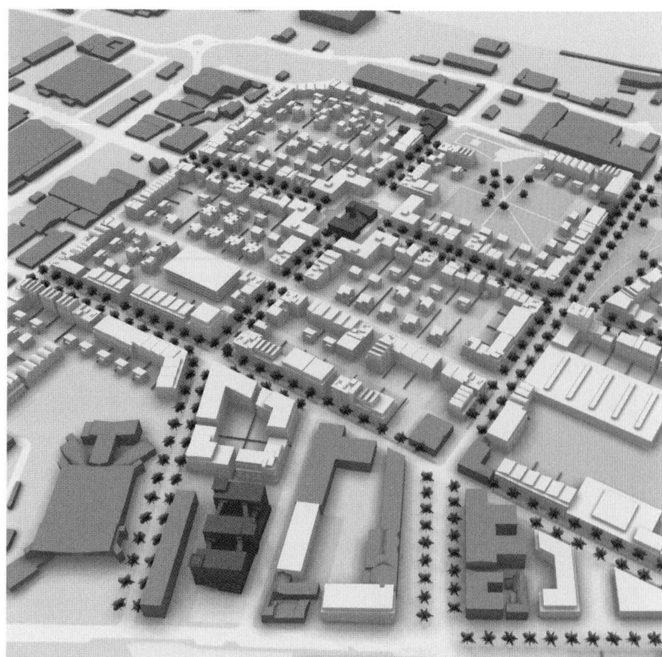

Soft-centred ward blocks as incremental solutions

The soft-centred block is one where the larger composite block, such as the ward block, is physically contained along its principal city streets by varied development, allowing for inner growth and change to occur over time. In the interim, the soft centre of the larger block can accommodate a range of internal uses such as urban agriculture or temporary uses, allowing for new activities to emerge over time and for places to find their purpose. This central space can be formalised as open space or held in a trust for future generations. The best example of this solution can be seen in the regeneration of the historic Middlehaven Quaker settlement in Middlesbrough, where the centre of the larger block has been left as a potential for later inner infill and growth.

Boosters and reducers

Boosters and reducers are ways of changing the width of streets and lanes without tampering with the integrity of the overall grid layout. The block dimensions are increased along street boundaries to narrow the street or are set back to widen the street. Streets can have a combination of boosters and reducers along the same length of road, such as in shared-surface streets where the entrance of the streets can be 'necked down' and the internal street space widened to create a more useful shared space. The same could apply to rear service lanes.

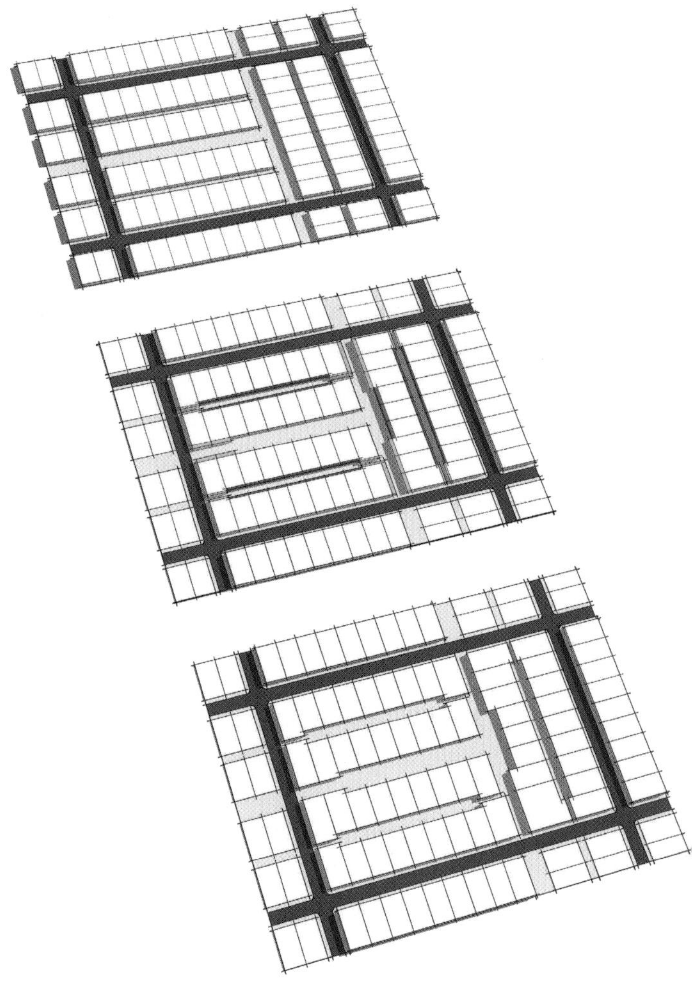

Top left: Middlehaven renewal strategy in Middlesbrough, England, showing soft-centred urban block. **Top right:** Soft centres infilled over time. **Bottom:** Boosters and reducers showing the evolution of a standard T block to a block structure with shaped streetspaces.

THE NEIGHBOURHOOD

An assembly of ward blocks and street blocks working in concert with a city street hierarchy establishes the structure for the likely formation of the neighbourhood. We know that neighbourhoods do have boundaries, and these boundaries play a major role in determining the neighbourhood identity. However, boundaries are not clearly defined in their nature or their place. Quite often neighbourhood identity is established by main streets, history or dominant uses and not edges.

Neighbourhoods can and do vary in size. Sometimes they are identified in terms of administrative functions. Sometimes they rely on people's perceptions of their extent. What is more, large and small conceptions of neighbourhoods can be considered as complementary. According to the Young Foundation in *How Can Neighbourhoods Be Understood and Defined?*, some analysts have suggested a layered understanding of community, under which neighbourhoods of several thousand people bring together several smaller areas. These 'proximity neighbourhoods' are streets or estate areas where neighbourliness is personal; people know one another as individuals. This approach is informed by anthropological evidence that a human group finds it hard to coordinate to reach decisions if its population is above a range from 500 to 1,500. Neighbourhood management is a function that seems to work well when grounded in smaller-scale neighbourhoods.

But a neighbourhood of 5,000 to 10,000 inhabitants is large enough to include a primary school, park and playground space, a doctor's surgery, library or leisure centre, and some shops and offices. This scale of neighbourhood usually provides a range of services and activities within walking distance of home and presents common issues that require a more strategic response.

Some geographic prescriptions for the size of neighbourhood draw on social criteria, such as the old town planners' rule of thumb that the overall size of a neighbourhood should be dictated by 'the maximum walking distance for a woman with a pram', or the new urbanist argument that you should be able to walk across a neighbourhood in five minutes. Dominant urban design thinking uses 400-metre (1,300-foot) walk bands (equivalent to five minutes of walking) as a measure of the size of the neighbourhood. This type of thinking is more suitable for the planning and design of suburban neighbourhoods.

Urban neighbourhoods are different:

→ Accessibility in urban neighbourhoods is not determined by walking alone. Often walking in combination with cycling and public transportation opens up far greater possibilities of travelling reasonable distances to meet daily needs.

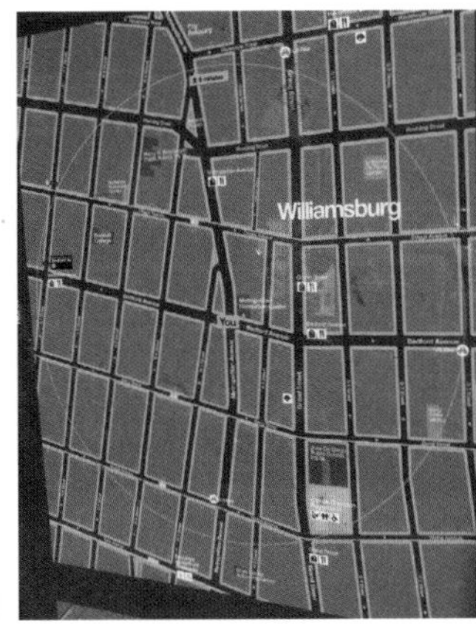

→ Destinations today are not distributed in single points, so other than such destinations as stations, single-centred walk bands do not apply. Most uses are distributed along streets, so accessibility diagrams look more like sausages than circles.

→ The destination in a modern urban neighbourhood is not as important as it used to be for daily survival, as many basic services are distributed to the home. So the reason to travel to chosen destinations in a neighbourhood is driven by other needs, such as social interaction and choice.

→ Walkability has been loosely used to define an optimum scale of the neighbourhood, but it is not a determinant—just one measure of success.

Considering an optimum size of a neighbourhood

Brooklyn Heights in New York is often noted as a good example of an urban neighbourhood. It has a population of 20,000 people in an area of less than 1 square kilometre (0.39 square miles). Williamsburg, an adjacent successful neighbourhood, has a population of 125,000 people in an area of 5.64 square kilometres (2.2 square miles). Both have strong identities.

Although there is no fixed size for an urban neighbourhood, we can still have a real fix on a size that would optimally work. Using some measure of walkability and combining this with local facilities and public transport, it is realistic to estimate that a neighbourhood's main street could serve an area up to 1,350 metres (4,430 feet) wide. As the main street is a linear element, the neighbourhood could extend up to 1,800 metres (5,900 feet) along the main street alignment and still be well served. This neighbourhood would give us an area of 2.2 square kilometres (0.85 square miles), well within the Brooklyn Heights / Williamsburg range.

This neighbourhood could involve up to twelve ward blocks. Each ward block could accommodate 4,000 to 12,000 people, giving us a potential population of 50,000 to 150,000 people.

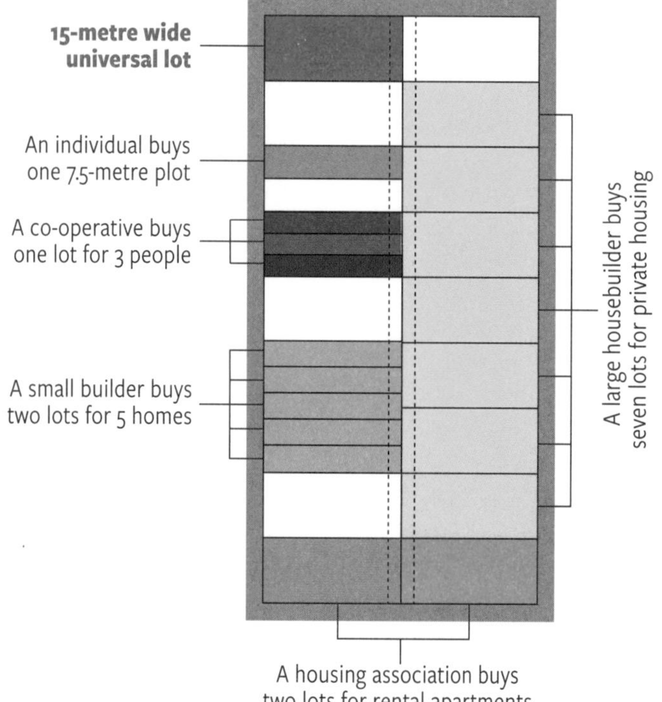
15-metre wide universal lot
An individual buys one 7.5-metre plot
A co-operative buys one lot for 3 people
A small builder buys two lots for 5 homes
A large housebuilder buys seven lots for private housing
A housing association buys two lots for rental apartments

Top: Homerus quarter in Almere, Holland, which looks to dispose plots of land to individual self-builders. **Bottom:** A regular urban block showing a variety of subdivisions and land parcels to suit all actors in the development process.

INNOVATIVE LAND-RELEASE STRATEGIES

Building compact urbanism requires clear and simple rules when consenting and releasing land for development. This is particularly important in countries where formal planning processes have tried to drive the shape of neighbourhoods—with limited success.

Ways of facilitating this accretion, choice and progressive change could include:

1 The mixed bag method

Like in Schumacher's concept of 'smallness in bigness', not everything needs to be small, but larger things should start from an agglomeration of the small. In other words, once we have a plot, we can combine this into a lot, a block or even a whole phase of development, but we can always go back to the plot.

This concept has implications for land release from the smallest scale to larger chunks. In the default condition, agglomeration does not imply consolidation into larger chunks that allow the underlying fine grain to be lost. Where land is controlled by the public sector, the combination of the elements allows different levels of entry and intervention by various players: individual, collective or corporate.

This method accommodates the full range of procurement options from individual self-build through to self-procurement, shell construction or full completion by any of a range of smaller local to larger contractors.

For any scheme, there should be a proportion of land given over to each and every one of these activities, with the larger option ideally being seen as a fallback position. Local authorities could use parametric approaches to set and manage the percentage mix for each option, and this could be monitored and adjusted based on relative success and take up of any option.

All of these procurement options should allow for example:

- → The individual self-builder building his own home and operating at the plot scale
- → The collective, for example, three individuals who purchase a lot for the development of a small scheme of three units
- → A local builder purchasing two lots, who wants to build five homes every year
- → A local housing association, who wishes to build a small apartment building of no more than twenty units, purchasing two lots
- → A national housebuilder who buys off-plan as a normal course of practice to keep cash flowing, purchasing a whole phase of development comprising ten lots

There could be a combination of these land release strategies in each urban block to promote the widest level of diversity.

2 Inner growth

The importance of the plot, lot and block relationship allows us to develop some methods to facilitate this process over time. This particular mechanism deliberately addresses the issue of accretion and evolutionary change. It gives rise to the potential for long-life, loose-fit buildings to be delivered as needs change and for an increase in densities over time.

It comes into play in the following ways:

- → The expansion of the building to allow for it to be vertically subdivided into smaller units
- → The long, deep plot or lot that allows access down the side for different forms of backland development
- → The mews block that allows for backland development to be separated with its front door from the mews or lane
- → The soft-centred block that reserves the right for the introduction of a new lane or alley to allow access to infill development at the rear of the plot or lot—in this condition, the soft centre is used for planting or shared recreation and takes on the qualities of a superblock

Inner growth is an option that implies that the neighbourhood will be developed on a managed-estate basis and is a good way for the estate to take out future receipts by allowing later development, much in the same way that landlords in large London estates manage their properties.

3 Neighbourhood land dividends

This mechanism overcomes the single-formula offers that are the volume housebuilders' stock-in-trade. It applies in large urban extensions where the private sector is the only player. Rather than the full standard social housing contribution, an option could be framed to contribute a portion of the total land (say 30 per cent) to the local authority or through a community land trust, allowing the mixed bag method to be applied to this portion of land and introducing the necessary richness of mix and variety. The portion of land could be agreed in advance with the applicants or could be determined as a proportion of each phase. If the housing market stalled, the local authority could still be experimenting with other forms of delivery.

4 Slow land-release method

This method mediates the single big-bang approach to development and looks to open up more fronts in areas to allow small incremental change. As such, it is a way of local authorities hedging their bets. It could relate to the careful phasing of schemes to ensure that we have progressive, slow, but continuous release of sites by a number of players, including the land captured through the neighbourhood land dividend scheme (see above). This method gives local authorities a chance to monitor the effects of change, report on these effects and take different courses of action if necessary.

5 Target-driven consents

This method is a way of preventing landbanking by linking planning consents to agreed delivery targets. In other words, if the housebuilder does not deliver on the agreed programme, local government can take various actions:

- → Give someone else a chance to take up the target and, using the slow land-release principle, carefully phase the process
- → Increase the share of the total land consented to boost the neighbourhood land dividend, or let consent lapse
- → Purchase the land

Each of these options could be trialled. They need to be tested against established practices and policy constraints and may not be difficult to implement. They require considered thinking. Some might require new legislation. In all the land-release options, everyone has a bite of the apple. Timelines are independent. Complex choices can be made. Massive Small change can happen.

THE WISE COUNCILLOR

HOW A CIVIC LEADER CHANGED THE GAME IN HOUSING RENEWAL

Mahmoud is a local councillor in a suburban Paris commune. Four thousand families, who were moved there by inner city renewal, live in a Brutalist housing project of sixteen-storey blocks. A visit by the French president, following the killing of a young immigrant, led to renovation grants, architectural competitions, the dynamiting of one of the blocks and a momentary glare of publicity. But the policies and actions that followed brought little change to the estate's decaying fabric and social problems.

The government sees the solution as being to replace one big scheme with another. It sets a brief specifying that the density of development in the area should be doubled to pay for improvements, and that the social mix of the area should be changed by bringing in 'aspirational families'. Preferred developers will be asked to bid on development parcels. One large contractor, armed with its bespoke building system, has already approached the government to be allowed to do the whole job and take on all the risk.

The redevelopment will be successful as long as it is well designed, the government says. It has appointed a well-known, international, multidisciplinary urban design company to prepare a masterplan for the whole place. Their team includes five of the biggest names in architecture.

One specialises in very tall buildings. Another does wacky public buildings. The housing project has been divided into five large chunks, with each of the architects in charge of one of them. A branding company has already prepared a brand for the project, ready for a glitzy launch at the international property show at Cannes next year.

Mahmoud knows that the demolition of the estate and its replacement with a large scheme based on the conventional real-estate development model will not solve the problems of the area. He sees the system failing on several fronts:

→ Everything the government does seems to make the poor poorer. Good intentions have unintended consequences.
→ Big solutions are the lazy way of dealing with complex, urban problems. It seems easier to run a big procurement process and give it to someone else to sort out than for the government to take the lead. Government has lost confidence in its ability to make a difference.
→ Big architecture has never solved this sort of problem, even when the design is of a high standard. Cities need the richness that a fine urban grain delivers. Big-name architects don't create social diversity.
→ Big visions can hold places to ransom for long periods. The world is littered with big plans that were never implemented.
→ The real-estate-led approach will deliver more transient communities and lead to speculation. The original population is likely to be priced out. The developers tend to find ways of reneging on their promises.
→ La Courneuve is in danger of becoming a clone of any other place where this sort of approach has been used. It deserves much better.

MAHMOUD FINDS THE TIPPING POINT

The renewal of new towns in the suburban quarters of Paris is the goal of Banlieues 89, a collaborative enterprise launched under the patronage of the French president. Led by the architect Roland Castro and a number of social entrepreneurs and political appointees, the enterprise draws its inspiration from the French Revolution tracts of 1789 affirming the rights of all citizens.

The goal is to find 'new ways of enhancing the fabric and image of neglected areas' and of 'reuniting the amorphous, sprawling suburban zones with the vital heart of the city'. La Courneuve was seen as a prime candidate for this project. The trouble with this approach is that it has been implemented from the top down.

Mahmoud hears about the mayor of Berlin's project to build townhouses in the centre of Berlin. Paris has a strong tradition of terraced building types and blocks of pensions that have served the city well over the years. It is not essential to build tall in order to achieve sufficient densities to make the neighbourhood work. He takes a delegation to see the Mitte townhouse projects in Berlin. The group is shown around Berlin by Kristien Ring, the author of *Selfmade City*. She explains that these projects are undertaken by *baugruppen*, small groups of people who come together with a common purpose of housing themselves. In this instance they have the support of local government. They want to build not just housing but also social capital. That is what La Courneuve needs as well.

Mahmoud learns about the urban designer David Crane's call for a 'city of a thousand designers'. That's what we need, he thinks, instead of one big masterplan and five big names. Mahmoud arranges a public meeting and brings along a shredder. The masterplan is ceremoniously shredded.

This act is a symbolic declaration that the commune will never be held to ransom by one single vision or by the hands of so few. Instead it will be built on a collective vision and on the actions of many. The shredded plan is displayed in a glass box in the lobby of Mahmoud's public office for all to see, like a Damien Hirst artwork. A national newspaper writes that Mahmoud is 'ahead of his time'. That's strange, he thinks: aren't we just building cities the way we used to before utopian visions became fashionable? He recalls that Le Corbusier said: 'Kill the street.' Yes, the street was killed. And the community as well.

The newly formed project team identifies thirty sites of varying sizes. Mahmoud hears about the universal lot that is being promoted in the Massive Small project. His team starts by subdividing all the sites into 15-metre-wide (50 feet) lots. This 'framework for diversity', as he and his colleagues call it, allows many people to become involved in the project, rather than just a few big players. Except in certain locations, the lots may be subdivided further. Two lots can be consolidated to make a larger lot, which allows more flexibility for subdivision. The 15-metre-wide lots will accommodate 5-, 7.5-, 10- or 15-metre-wide frontages. The double (30-metre) lots will accommodate 5-, 6-, 7.5-, 10-, 15- or 30-metre-wide frontages (the 30-metre frontage might be an apartment block, for example). But no more than two lots may be consolidated. To get the ball rolling, they settle on the 7.5-metre-wide (25-feet-wide) plot as a default option. This can be used to create homes with two rooms across the front of the building. These homes can be for single or multiple occupancy.

A design code is created, setting out a handful of simple rules that should be followed. These specify that buildings must be five or six storeys high; that any setback of the roof should be done in a specified way; that the frontage of each building should be positioned in a certain relationship to the street; that the ground floor of homes should be raised from the street to provide privacy; and that the ground floor of shops or other uses (or buildings that might later be used for such uses) should be at street level.

There could have been a few more or less rules, but those are the ones that were chosen. This design code is for the default option. People can build something that does not comply with that option if they want to. If so they will have to comply with some other rules, which are not quite so straightforward.

Working with a large building contractor, the project team develops an open (freely accessible) building concept that includes a structural system for the buildings. The standard unit has party walls and three, four or five floors. The contractor reckons that in most cases savings of around 30 to 40 per cent of the cost of building can be achieved if the standard structural option is chosen. The La Courneuve open standard is open for anyone to use.

The first site is laid out with eleven standard plots and two special corner plots. Local people are invited to come forwards with proposals of how they would develop the plots. La Courneuve Council will sell them plots at current market value, and buyers have up to ten years in which to pay. If buyers want to sell before the ten years is up, they have to pay the council a proportion of the market value of that time (the proportion diminishes as the ten-year limit approaches). The aim is to avoid speculation and to build a stable community.

People unite like the German *baugruppen*, each group working with its architect to develop solutions to suit their needs. Some groups choose to put more communal space in the building, some choose to create some office space. One proposes a daycare centre on the ground floor. Some are trying to help others who are less fortunate. People arrange financing in the form of mortgages or subsidies. Eventually the first five schemes are built, and they prove successful. Momentum gathers: more than 500 sites are now under construction, providing 2,700 new homes.

MAHMOUD TELLS OF HIS SUCCESS

Mahmoud is interviewed about the project for a newspaper. These are the main points he makes:

1 People are producing homes that are on average 45 per cent cheaper than if they were bought from developers, as there is no developer's profit to be paid.
2 The La Courneuve open standard has provided a common platform from which most of the housing has been built. It has provided the benefit of mass construction techniques without the stigma. Competition between contractors has meant that the costs of the structural system have been driven down even further.
3 The use of a default did not lead to monotony, as each building was different, tailored to particular people's needs. You could not tell by looking that each was built according to the same underlying standard.
4 Being involved in the process has given people a strong sense of ownership of the solution, and the community seems to have become far more settled. People see a long-term future in La Courneuve. Local rates are paid sooner, and the commune is prospering.
5 People have taken on the job of providing some local services and are managing some of the streets. There is a greater sense of trust between them and the authorities.
6 The project is developing in ways that could not have been predicted. La Courneuve stands the chance of becoming a real piece of the city rather than a failed housing estate, just as Banlieues 89 had hoped.
7 This project can be scaled up. Its principles are transferrable, and there is great potential for further developing the La Courneuve open standard.

The approach to urban governance should always involve rapid and continuous feedback, learning from the outcomes of every decision. This feedback will inform, alter and accelerate the next steps. This is adaptive learning: one gains knowledge along the way that affects future decisions. When we live in an uncertain future, there is no reason to fixate on what our neighbourhood will look like in twenty-five years. Rather, we need a clear vision of our goals. We will achieve these by focusing on catalysts and small beginnings, providing clear constraints within which people can innovate and intervening in a precisely targeted way that will stimulate growth and change.

— Mahmoud M, France

THE **UNIVERSAL** BLOCK|**LOT**|PLOT

[STRUCTURING VARIETY OF CHOICE]

The universal lot is an approach developed through work by Urban Initiatives in 2010 for the proposed Scotswood Housing Expo in Newcastle, United Kingdom. It was based on a methodology for parcelling development land into bite-size chunks using a progressive modular approach to trigger drivers of change: interchangeability, scaleability, flexibility and the variety of response.

As a fundamental concept, the universal lot lies in using a standard module of 15 metres (50 feet) wide as the basic unit of development. This can be subdivided into two, three or four plots or doubled and split into five plots as defined by common party walls. Along with the height of the building, these define the maximum building envelope and therefore the volume of each unit.

The 15-metre (50 feet) dimension was settled on after testing a range of lot dimensions with street and housing typologies. It is not the only way, but it seems to work best. Detailed architectural testing by a panel of excellent architects and the results of many successful solutions from the Scotswood Expo international architectural competition showed the robustness of the frontage dimension to accommodate the desired variety. Developing different dimensions to the depth of the block accommodates a wider range of building typologies. In this way complex choices are structured, retaining the benefits of the plot but still allowing greater flexibility with the lot.

The 15-metre-wide lot allows for the following:

→ A single lot can be for single or collective use, such as a 'family' of buildings, compounds or housing cooperatives.

→ A single lot can be subdivided into four 3.75-metre- (12-foot), three 5-metre- (16-foot), or two 7.5-metre-wide (25-foot) plots to create narrow-fronted developments.

→ Two lots together create three 10-metre- (33-foot) or five 6-metre-wide (20-foot) plots, or they can be used together to get a larger plot for, say, an apartment or courtyard building.

→ Variable dimensions can be used within the widths of the one- or two-lot combinations.

These plot dimensions accommodated a wide range of housing and mixed-use building typologies, from the mews cottage to the townhouse to living over the shop to the semidetached to even the detached house. The London Popular Home Initiative—a research project undertaken with five London boroughs, housing developers and contractors—road-tested these dimensions against simple rules for apartment buildings, looking at optimum social dynamics within buildings, lengths of corridors and viability, and found them to be remarkably robust.

Single Lot: 15m wide

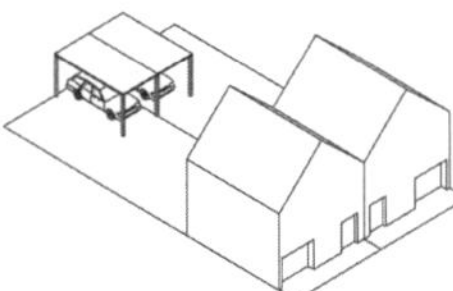

Front: 2 townhouses
Rear: 2 car ports

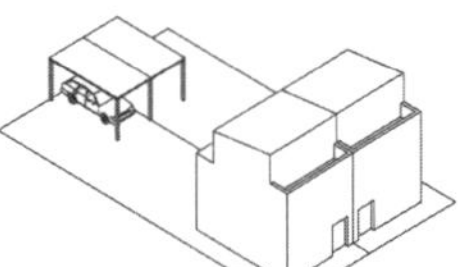

Front: 2 semi-detached houses
Rear: 2 car ports

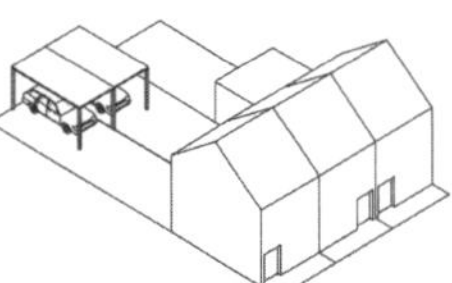

Front: 3 townhouses
Rear: car ports / rear extension

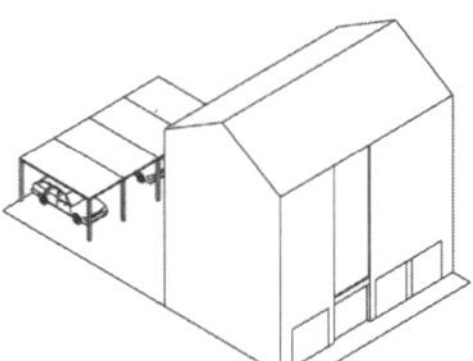

Front: 1 apartment building
Rear: car ports

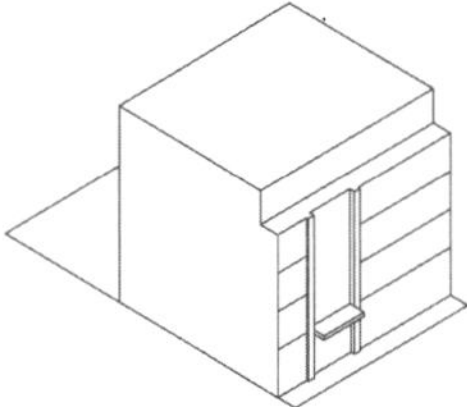

Front: 1 office or mixed-use building

Two Lots: 30m wide

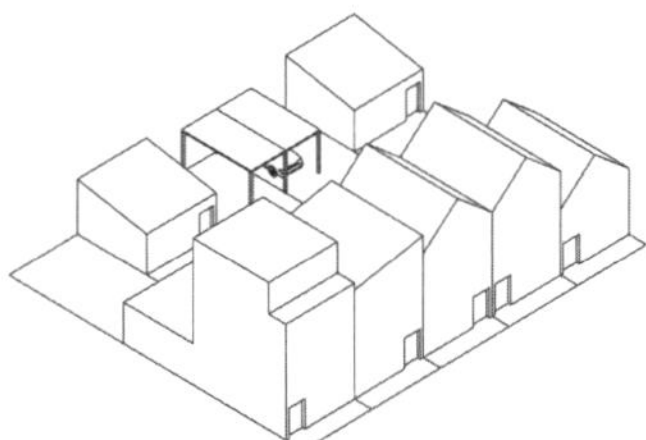

Front: 5 terraced houses
Rear: outbuildings / garages / car ports

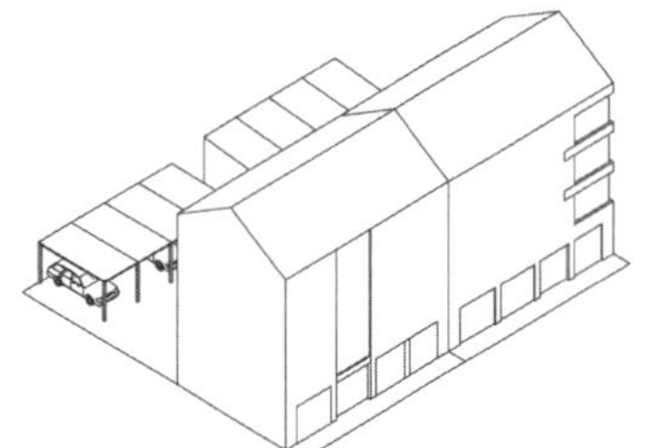

Front: 2 apartment buildings
Rear: garages / car ports

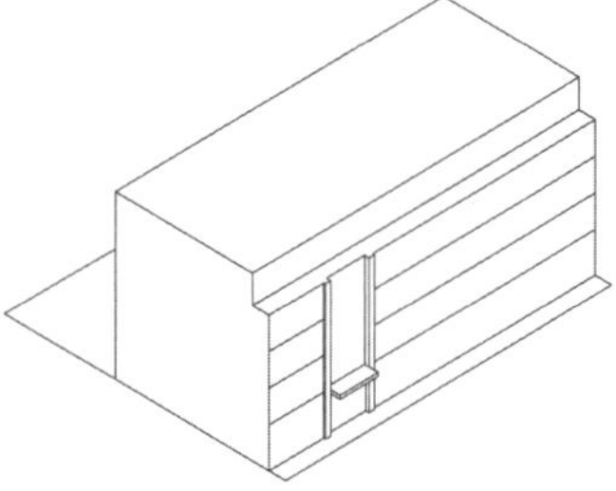

Front: 1 large office, mixed-use building or hotel

LOT/PLOT WIDTH

LOT/PLOT DEPTH

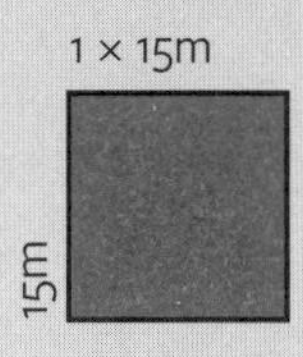

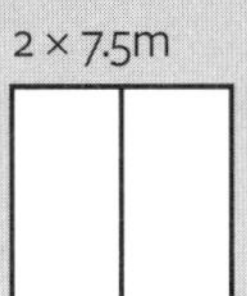

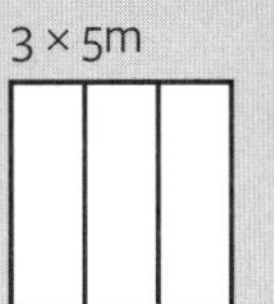

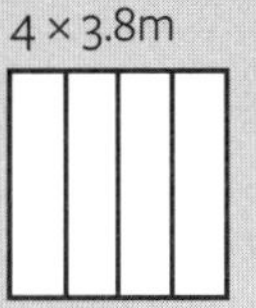

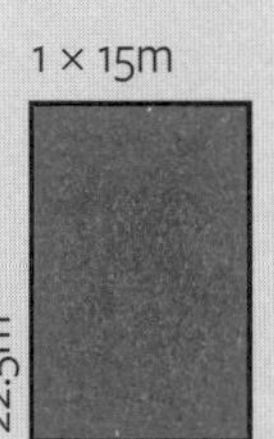

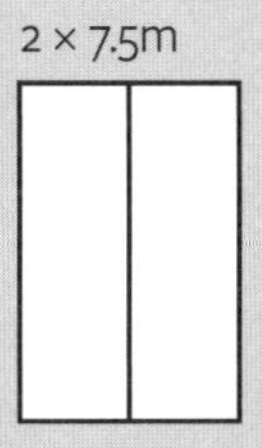

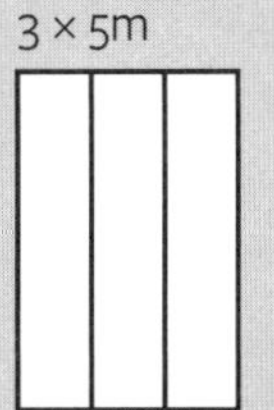

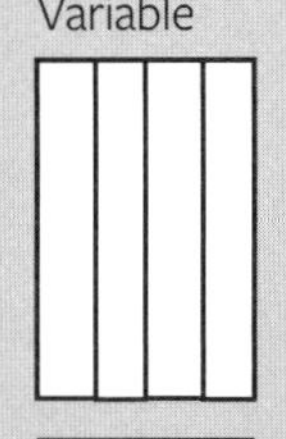

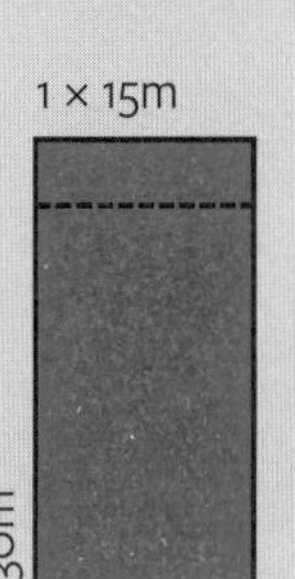

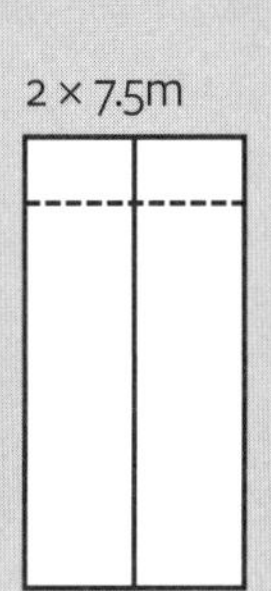

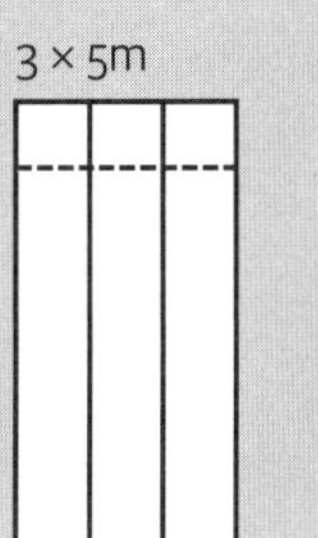

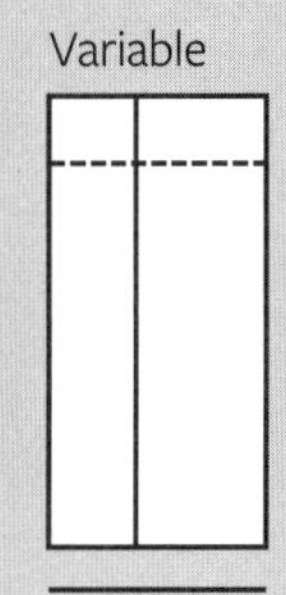

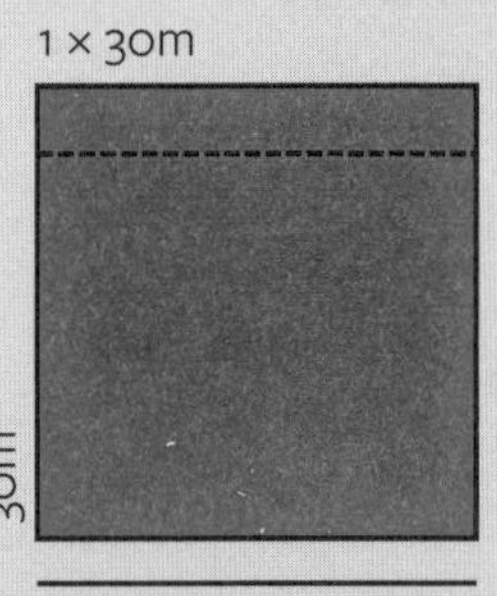

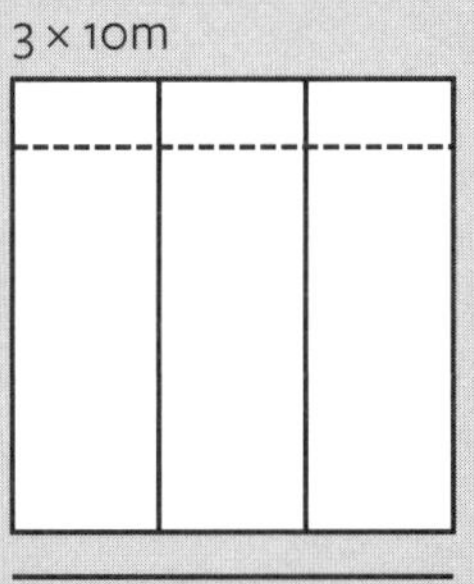

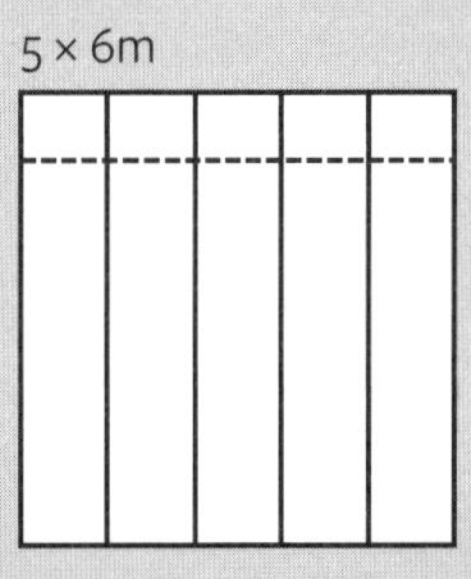

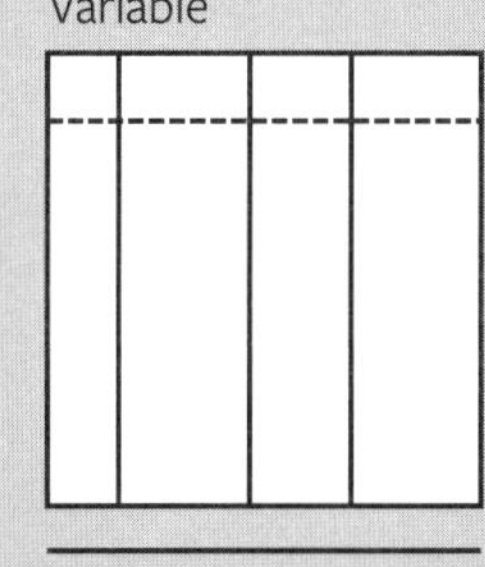

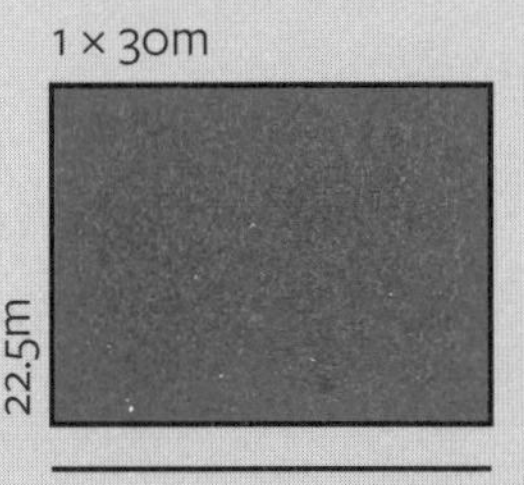

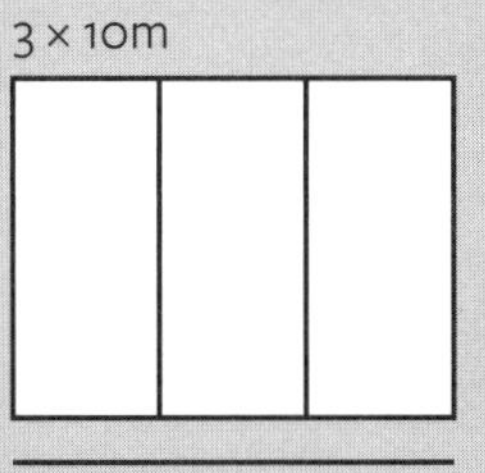

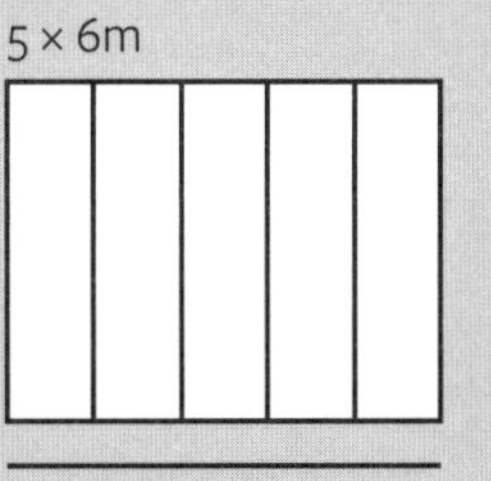

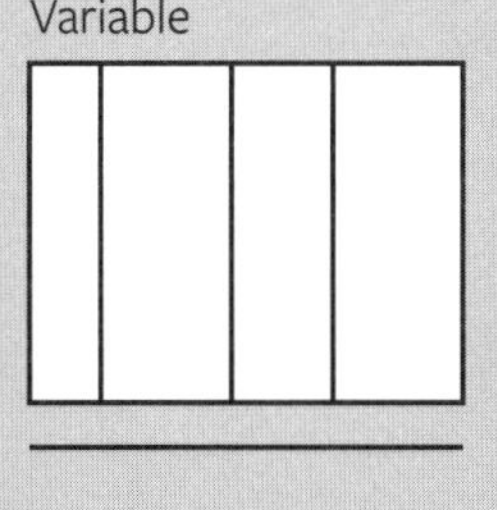

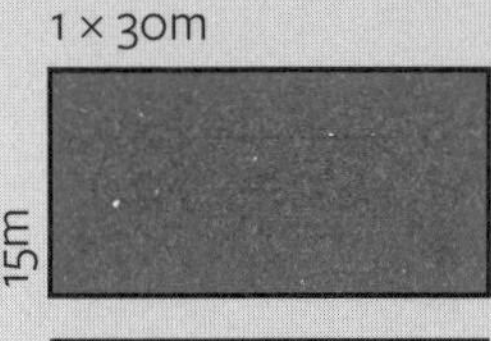

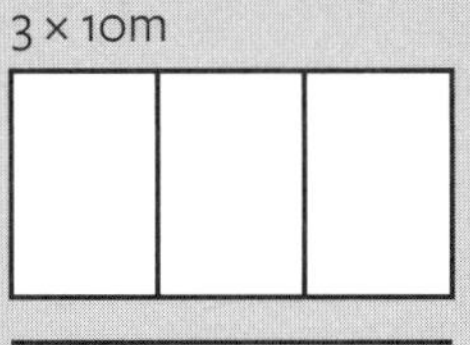

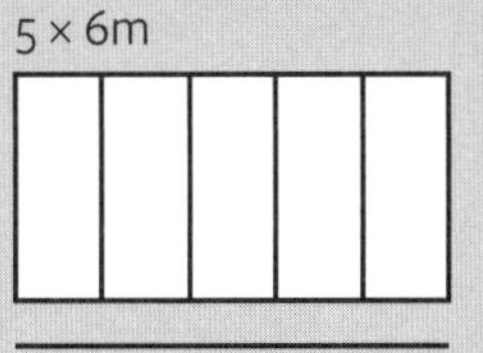

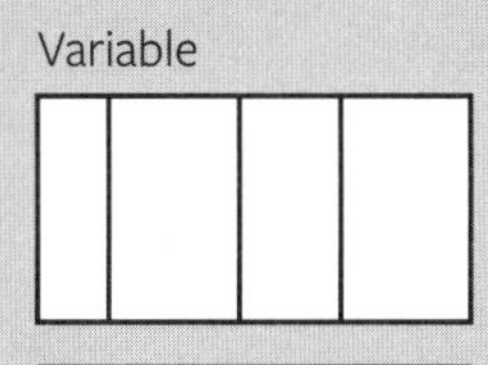

URBAN INTENSIFICATION

The principle of lot-based urbanism can be applied to the subdivision of large sites where redevelopment is occurring—housing estate renewal, formerly used sites or changes of use to housing. The resultant subdivision plan, also called a parameter plan, provides an easy way of developing a regulating plan with simple design codes. The whole of the Aylesbury Estate in South London, planned by Urban Initiatives in 2008, can be reduced to a 15-metre-wide (50 feet) lot subdivision plan with full design codes no longer than one page. Parameter plans can provide the basis for development control as can be seen in the DEFAULTS section on page 211.

Many of our earlier suburbs were subdivided using regular plot widths. With simple GIS techniques, these suburb plots can be subdivided into categories of plot widths. These plot widths can be used to develop typological building solutions, further plot subdivisions and infill strategies, which could involve the introduction of rear lanes to provide new frontage.

Two proposals by London-based architects show new ways of building in some of the capital's already developed suburbs. *Supurbia*, proposed by the architectural practice HTA Design, is a strategy for intensifying the three-quarters of a million privately owned semidetached houses in outer London. It envisages the use of 'plot passports', documents that set out a list of redevelopment options available to the householders in a specific area, allowing them to extend or redevelop their property. *Semi-permissive* is a strategy for intensifying London's suburbs proposed by the architects at Pollard Thomas Edwards. It would be implemented by a reform of the planning system to allow new, permitted development rights and to incentivise householders to become microdevelopers.

Macro-lots, an initiative by Camiel van Noten, examines strategic changes to existing lot subdivisions in failing low-density suburbs to create a new form of compact urbanism. It proposes combining multiple lots to enable new housing conditions, and a socioeconomic strategy, which strives for affordable homeownership as a collective interest. Local homeowners can decide to join the macro-lot on the basis that they are stronger together. By definition, a macro-lot cannot be imposed on people, since it is set up, maintained and expanded by its residents. The new context, obtained by reparcelisation, enables different housing typologies as an alternative to the existing housing stock. Van Noten suggests that the new subdivision of land, based on community land trust ideas, is the fundamental principle of the financial structure of a macro-lot, but there is no reason why it cannot be extended to other forms of ownership as well.

These strategies, combined with versions of parameter plans using the universal lot concept, could go a long way to initiating and accelerating Massive Small change. All of this could be incorporated into a simple neighbourhood operating manual.

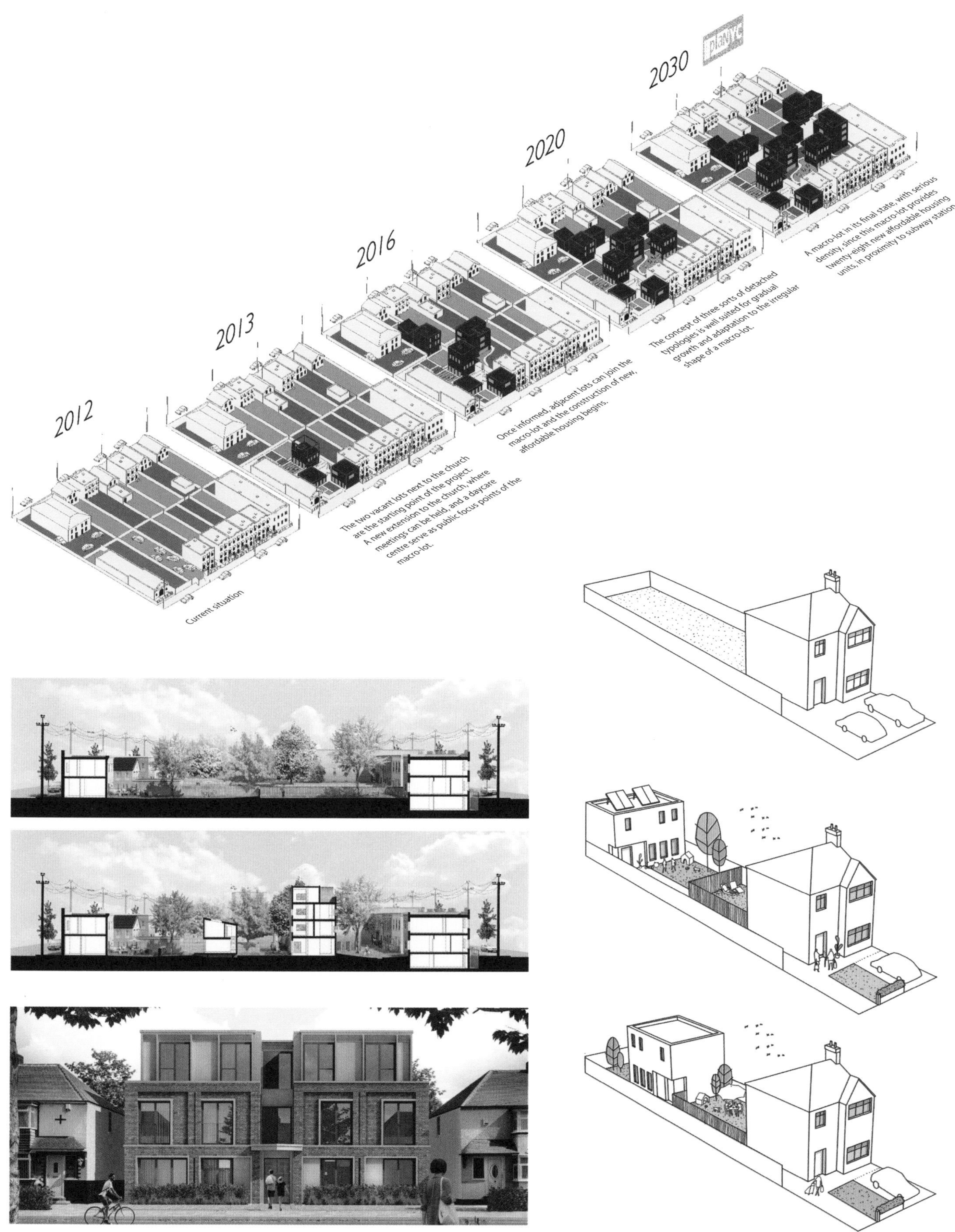

2012
2013
2016
2020
2030
planyc
Current situation
The two vacant lots next to the church are the starting point of the project. A new extension to the church, where meetings can be held, and a daycare centre serve as public focus points of the macro-lot.
Once informed, adjacent lots can join the macro-lot and the construction of new, affordable housing begins.
The concept of three sorts of detached typologies is well suited for gradual growth and adaptation to the irregular shape of a macro-lot.
A macro-lot in its final state, with serious density, since this macro-lot provides twenty-eight new affordable housing units, in proximity to subway station.

Opposite page: Plan of the renewal strategy for the Aylesbury Estate in London based on universal lot principles. **This page, top and middle left:** Camiel van Noten's Macrolots strategy, his graduation project for Studio Brooklyn, ASRO KULeuven, 2012. **Bottom left and right:** HTA's Supurbia initiative showing different ways of intensifying suburbs in London.

LOCALIA URBAN NEIGHBOURHOOD

A NEIGHBOURHOOD PATTERN EMERGES

In our Localia neighbourhood case study, we developed a generic tartan grid with subneighbourhood modules as our structuring elements for building the new urban neighbourhood. We now drill down deeper into the nature, form and arrangement of urban blocks. Having tested a range of options over a number of projects over the years, we have developed our way of looking at this challenge. It may help.

STEP 1. DIMENSIONING REGULAR URBAN BLOCKS

The easiest way of laying out blocks is from the centreline of the street. This means that the block becomes viewed with the street and not in isolation. There is always another side to the street. The street is also fundamental to the network layout and any tile-based gaming techniques developed. Localia, our imaginary urban neighbourhood, uses a 75- by 75-metre (250 × 250 feet) layout grid with a 6 × 6 grid square ward block.

→ Our experience has shown that the optimum length of an urban block in a neighbourhood context, measured from its centrelines, is approximately 150 metres (500 feet), so we combine two grid squares into one. If we offset the street dimension from the centrelines to give a 15-metre-wide street (50 feet), we have regular block dimension of 135 by 60 metres (445 × 200 feet).

→ The minimum length of the urban block should be no less than the width of the block, which means you can also start with the larger dimension and allow the block to be subdivided later if conditions demand. In other words, you can turn a larger residential neighbourhood block into a city centre block if required.

→ The optimum depth of the urban block allows the possibility of introducing a back lane or mews along the midblock—another example of scaleability.

STEP 2. DEVELOPING A LOT-BASED SUBDIVISION STRATEGY

We have adopted the lot-based principle to subdivide our urban blocks. As we are working on a 15-metre (50 feet) sublayout grid, we can create regular subdivisions for each block. These can be subdivided further into plots as necessary.

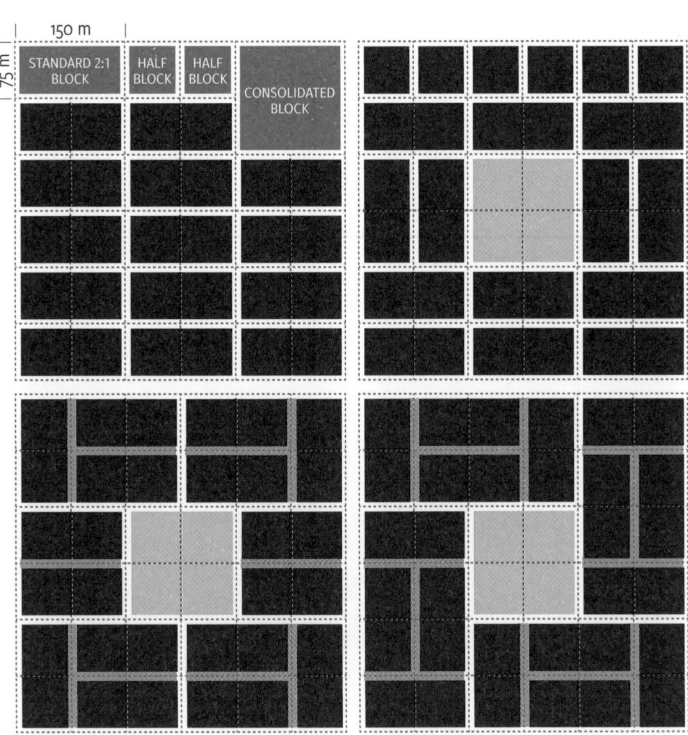

STEP 3. DEVELOPING A LANE BLOCK STRATEGY

A minimum 6-metre-wide (20 feet) rear lane can be introduced along the middle of the block, similar to the Boston Back Bay solution. This lane could be widened to 9 metres (30 feet) if necessary. These lanes are characterised in the following ways:

→ They are private roads with each property owning up to the centreline of the lanes.

→ Initially providing service access to the rear of properties, these lanes can become new frontages in the future as the neighbourhood intensifies.

→ They have narrowings at the entrances from the main street network. Sometimes a building is built over the lane to create a gateway to an internal, more semipublic space.

→ They have a drainage servitude imposed along their minimum corridor, which allows for the installation of sewerage and water utilities to serve the rear of the properties. For sites-and-services schemes and core housing solutions the toilet/ablution block could be located along the rear lane with direct access to the sewer system. We believe that locating the sewers and water along the midblock provides the most effective infrastructure solution, avoiding digging up streets.

Top: Evolution of the regular block showing how it can be split, consolidated and assembled into a variety of ward blocks with central green spaces.

STEP 4. DEVELOPING HALF-BLOCKS ALONG MAIN STREETS

A half-block can be used to allow the long blocks to be subdivided midway along their length and introduce more permeability to the spaces beyond. This is be done by:

→ Introducing a full street between each half block or a narrow pedestrian laneway

→ Converting half blocks can into effective, public open spaces at a reasonable scale to accommodate civic uses

→ Opening up a parallel route system to one or both sides of the main street to future-proof the main street in the event of excessive congestion or if it is temporarily closed for street markets, events and so on

STEP 5. DEVELOPING A CONSOLIDATED BLOCK STRATEGY

In addition to the internal public squares that accommodate local schools and play areas, regular blocks can be consolidated for other larger space-extensive uses such as higher-education colleges and hospitals. This could include two or more regular blocks as required.

STEP 6. DEVELOPING A WARD BLOCK STRATEGY

Based on Localia's six by six subneighbourhood module, we have developed a range of ward blocks by assembling our regular blocks and street blocks into the next nested level of block hierarchy. These equate to a superblock scale but are developed with the potential to take different block arrangements, including:

→ The ladder block, which involves a simple gridiron pattern of regular blocks arranged in a continuous fashion

→ The modified ladder block, using square blocks that provide for the downgrading of every second street

→ A combination of T blocks giving internal shared-surface streets

→ The Savannah-type model, with regular blocks arranged around a large internal public space

→ A modified Savannah-type model, made up with H blocks arranged around a public space

We have chosen the H-block arrangement around an internal public space as our preferred strategy.

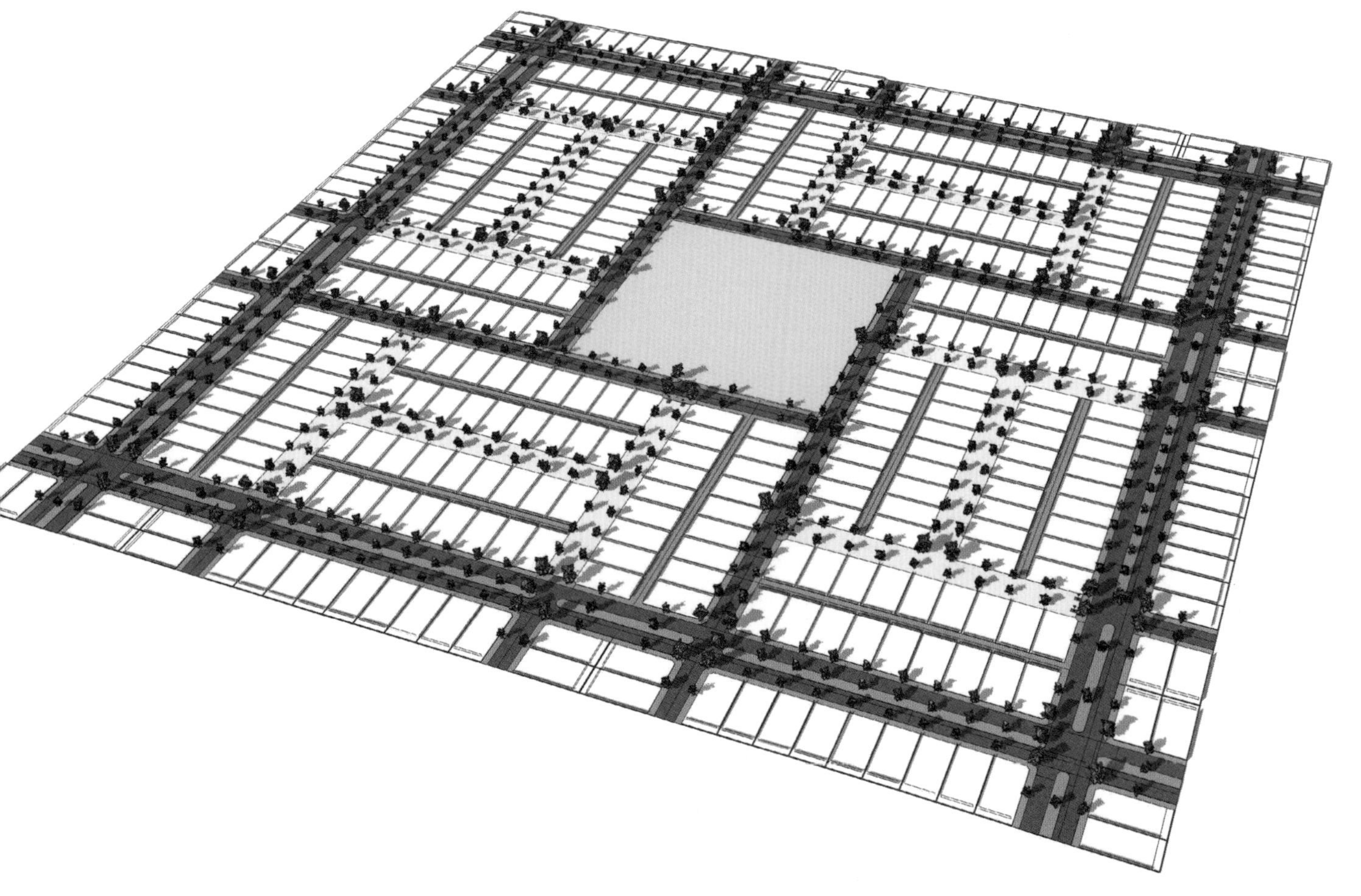

STEP 7. ASSEMBLING THE OVERALL BLOCK STRUCTURE

In Localia we see the potential for a four level hierarchy:

1 **Street level:** This could include street committees from residential streets to city streets, for example, main street trader groups.

2 **Street block level:** As our H blocks are made up out of 72 lots arranged around a shared surface space, we could have 200 to 600 households, or say, 1,000 to 3,000 people in this group. This gives us the potential to promote up to fourty-eight street block committee representatives to the next scale of democracy.

3 **Ward block level:** With four street blocks arranged around a central public space, with school and community infrastructure, we could have 800 to 2,400 households, or say, 4,000 to 12,000 people in this group. This gives us the potential to promote up to twelve ward block committee representatives to the next scale of democracy.

4 **Neighbourhood level:** Our ward block system defines the democratic structure of twelve councillors promoted to the neighbourhood council to join a few other special interest group representatives (business, culture, etc.). This is an efficient number to represent a community of say, 10,000 to 30,000 households and businesses, or 50,000 to 150,000 citizens.

We arrange regular or lane blocks to create smaller environmental cells, where the internal streets can be treated as shared-surface spaces, *woonerven*, or limited-access play spaces. The entrances to the shared-surface street can be 'necked' down to form a gateway to the quieter interior. We also apply the principles of boosters and reducers to shape the dimensions of our streets and blocks.

The scale of Localia lends itself to the combination of twelve ward blocks, some modified and others truncated as a result of boundary conditions or natural features. This structure of the neighbourhood and composition of blocks gives rise to a range of distinct social and economic groupings of people that can form the basis of the democratic structure of the community.

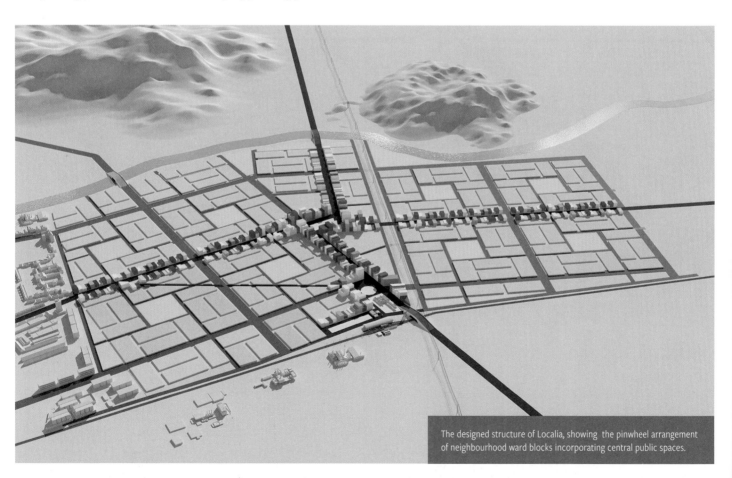

The designed structure of Localia, showing the pinwheel arrangement of neighbourhood ward blocks incorporating central public spaces.

INFINITE
ENABLING
COMPLEXITY
VIABLE
POTENTIALITIES
LIFE
SHAPING
ALIVE

PARTS &
LABOUR

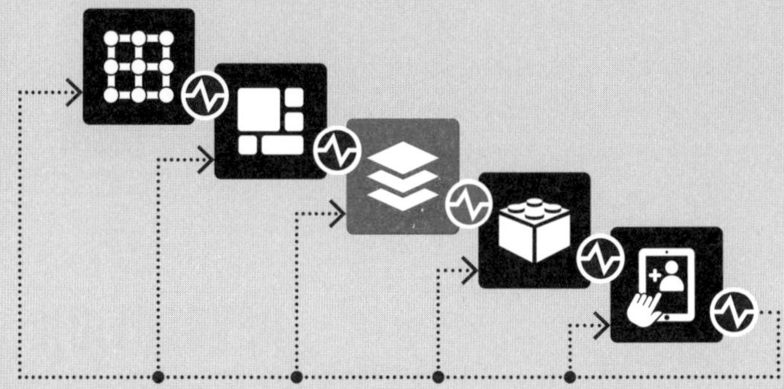

PLATFORMS

AS INITIATORS OF URBAN FORM

PLATFORMS, the third condition, are those enabling mechanisms that initiate and accelerate built form using the interrelationships between urban NETWORKS and BLOCKS as a starting point. They are the foundations that turn the two-dimensional into the three. They are catalysts for growth and change. Common platforms act as springboards for individual and collective action by people in forming their neighbourhoods. In this way they provide stability to the system, allowing varied individual responses.

There are different types of platforms: some which guide, some which progress, some which give clues and others that support. They include scaleable strategies for INCREMENTAL DEVELOPMENT, from initial occupation through to total development for a wider market. They all work together or in continuum to shape how the ordinary built environment grows, changes and comes together over time.

Platform *NOUN*

1 a catalyst that initiates and accelerates change

2 a framework for generating and regulating activity

3 the underlying supports to a complex process

SYNONYMS
springboard, seedbed, medium, foundations, infrastructure

SCOPE

This section includes the following platforms for responsive growth and change:

1 **Open building systems:** negotiated with local building industry, provides the springboards for innovation

2 **Codes, standards and regulations:** expresses the underlying urban rules that are applied to the development of the urban fabric and change over time

3 **Development tools:** introduces our DWELLER ADAPTIVE BUILDING SYSTEMS (DABS) approach. Elements include:
- → **Urban acupuncture projects:** targets pinpoint interventions in the urban fabric to catalyse change
- → **Responsive elements:** provides a simple kick start and goes on to accelerate development at all scales
- → **Scaling urban infrastructure:** focusses on starting small and scaling up, looking at the whole and using scale-free thinking
- → **Meanwhile uses:** provides a catalyst for urban change by road-testing potential uses, build new markets and give confidence to local revitalisation
- → **Demonstrating the possible:** through the use of demonstration projects, housing expositions, neighbourhood challenges and cooperative building projects
- → **Supporting platforms:** provides technical assistance, access to builders' warehouses, communal workshops, temporary accommodations and enterprise support

4 **Localia urban neighbourhood:** initiates development of the imaginary neighbourhood through the provision of responsive elements

THEORY

Radical processes of transformation are changing the cities and landscapes we inhabit. The traditional instruments of architecture and urban planning, are increasingly unable to address the new agenda. In our old top-down world, big catalysts were the flagships of regeneration—the cultural project, the new bridge or public space, even the new food store—big ideas that would trigger change and put a place on the map. But in most instances, flagships sink first and locations flounder.

In a bottom-up environment, this all changes. The catalyst is not a single end product but a mechanism that changes a market and impels and guides subsequent development—it is innovative and dynamic! Its purpose is the incremental, continuous generation of the urban fabric. It is anything that initiates and accelerates urban developments to deliver Massive Small change. It fuels emergence at the local scale. It is vital to building neighbourhoods.

Platform sharing and innovation

The building industry has much to learn from the car industry. The use of platform sharing has been one of the biggest revolutions in the family car industry in recent years. For many manufacturers, the car platform strategy has become important in new product development and their innovation processes. Family cars have to be responsive to market needs and to demonstrate distinctiveness while, at the same time, they must be developed and produced at low cost.

The automotive industry defines a car platform as 'a shared set of common design, engineering, and production efforts, as well as major components over a number of outwardly distinct models and even types of automobiles, often from different, but related marques'. The automotive industry reduces the costs associated with car development by basing products on a smaller number of platforms. This further allows different companies to create distinct models from a design perspective on similar underpinnings.

The rise of platforms and what this means for neighbourhoods

We have heard a lot about smart city products as a way of driving innovation, but how does this relate to the formation of neighbourhoods in an increasingly bottom-up world? Things are changing: we are now talking about platforms, not products, driving innovation. Apple, Uber and Airbnb are classic examples of this shift. Build a better platform, and you will have a decided advantage over the competition. So what does this mean for neighbourhoods?

Given the fact that a neighbourhood is an ecosystem, platform thinking comes about when systems thinking meets community. Sangeet Paul Choudary, in his book *Platform Revolution: How Networked Markets Are Transforming the Economy and How to Make Them Work for You*, shows us how these twin forces need to be reconciled.

> A platform is something that lifts you up and on which others can stand. The same is true in neighbourhood development. By building a common platform, other people can easily connect their efforts with yours, build products and services on top of it, and co-create value. This ability to 'plug-and-play' is a defining characteristic of platform thinking.

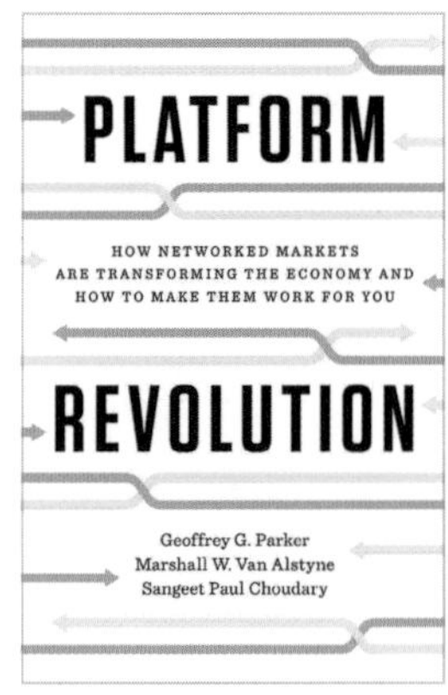

There are different forms of platform thinking. These range from John Hagel and John Seely Brown's focus on 'pull' to Geoffrey Moore's ecosystems. Where the traditional ecosystems push, these new platforms pull, relying on the power of networks to attract more users.

According to Choudary,

> While platforms require careful strategy and planning, a lot of platform evolution defies best-laid plans, and much of platform evolution depends on emergence. The platform manager can define the tools of interaction and the rules of engagement, but the definition of the end user experience is owned by the users.

Almost all platforms require a sense of community to some extent, but it is important to understand how important community is to the development of a neighbourhood platform. The problem is that one camp that understands systems thinking doesn't necessarily understand emergence and community, while the other camp that talks about community tends to talk about it in very flaky terms without understanding the role played by systems thinking. For platform thinking to work for neighbourhoods, it needs to reconcile its differences.

Could we build a neighbourhood platform?

What we need to imagine is what a neighbourhood platform will look like and how it will work. Could the invisible chassis become the underlying structure for this platform? More importantly, who owns the platforms and can governments build them or will they always be a private sector venture? We don't have the answers to this question. This is our challenge.

OPEN BUILDING

> *Open Building is an approach to the design of buildings that is recognised internationally to represent a new wave in architecture, but a new wave with roots in the way ordinary built environment grows, regenerates and achieves wholeness.*
>
> —Stephen Kendall

Most conventional buildings change in large and small ways to remain useful. This is the nature of emergence. We also know that the best buildings are those most able to provide the capacity to change functions, standards of use and lifestyle, and to improve parts over time. Long-life, loose-fit solutions always seem to trump those where form follows function.

John Habraken first articulated the principles of open building in his book *Supports: An Alternative to Mass Housing*. He argued 'housing must always recognise two domains of action—the action of the community and that of the individual inhabitant. When the inhabitant is excluded, the result is uniformity and rigidity. When only the individual takes action, the result may be chaos and conflict. This formulation of a necessary balance of control has implications for all parties in the housing process.'

The two domains in a neighbourhood development building include the act of building and the act of dwelling. The act of building separates out the collective part controlled by the community—the base building, which depends strictly on the regulations, structure and installations (called 'supports'). The act of dwelling is that which can be transformed and adapted to suit the user, such as the interior subdivisions, the separable units (called 'infill'). Habraken's support and infill separation is part of a broader reflection on our urban society.

Top: The Chimney Pots project by Urban Splash in Salford, Manchester, provides a typological approach to regenerating a Victorian housing terrace.

WHAT IS OPEN BUILDING?

Those advocating an open building approach recognise that both stability and change are realities in contemporary built environment. Buildings—and the neighbourhoods they occupy—are not static artefacts even during the most stable of times, and during times of rapid social and technological upheaval, they need adjustment in some measure to remain attractive, safe and useful. How then do we plan and implement a regenerative built environment?

Planning, designing and constructing buildings and neighbourhoods involves many people. They reach agreements and devolve responsibility—a normal characteristic of the culture of the development process. No one decides everything, and struggling to deal with the complexity brings its tensions. Since no single individual makes all decisions, the building adjusts to new needs and technical requirements. According to Habraken,

> We get to understand the importance of organising decision-making in such a way as to reduce excessive dependencies or entanglements among the parties involved. This helps in the avoidance of conflict between people and the parts of the whole they each control, and improves the chances of balancing common interests and the more individual interests of those who inhabit the space.

Thinking in levels

> *Our built environment is a live organism, a never ending changing process driven by rules and principles difficult to control and predict, which serves to our needs thanks only to its continuous adaptation and transformation.*
>
> —Israel Setién

Open building is the concept used to indicate some different but related ideas about universal solutions for the making of environments. It is Habraken's way of breaking down our problem mountains into problem molehills so that they are handleable.

The principal tool used by those working in an open building way is the organisation of the process of designing and building using 'environmental levels', which are the structures we have used to develop our conditions. The idea of environmental levels is not new, but the explicit formulation of the principle of levels is rather new, having been framed most recently in Habraken's *The Structure of the Ordinary: Form and Control in the Built Environment*.

Each level relates to the one below and above it according to certain rules, which include:

- → Distinct levels of intervention in the built environment, such as those represented by the base building and the fit-out, or by urban design and architecture
- → Users or inhabitants may make design decisions as well as urban professionals
- → Designing is a process with multiple participants also including different kinds of professionals
- → The interface between technical systems allows the replacement of one system with another performing the same function
- → The built environment is in constant transformation, and the changes must be understood
- → The built environment is the product of an ongoing, never ending design process, in which environment transforms part by part

The design professions, for their part, have evolved naturally in correspondence to the behaviour of environmental levels: urban planners, urban designers, architects, contractors and interior architects each operate according to a certain level of intervention. Environmental levels can be seen at work in different ways. For example, an urban street pattern defines lots and plots of land of varying sizes on which individual buildings are constructed. Some are demolished and new ones are built over time. The street grid remains constant and seldom changes. Often, several lots or plots are consolidated or subdivided further.

Economic forces, methods of construction and changes in social patterns often result in the intensification of the blocks, while in other situations, the opposite is true, and the blocks become more vacant.

If we look into the level of the individual building, we see the standard of intervention we call architecture. A building offers space for occupancy, providing form, services and safety for any of a variety of occupancies over time. The building is a stable spatial and technical 'offering', making itself available to each occupier to make their choices within the constraints of its base architecture. 'Shell and core' buildings are an expression of the 'base architecture' principles of open building, where the contractor moves to the next level by providing the full enclosure of the home with service connections and stair and lift cores, allowing for individuals to configure and fit out their own internal spaces.

Occupants can move in and out without compromising or disrupting the interests of the entirety. Sometimes, the entire façade of a building is removed and replaced, revealing yet another technical level, to some degree independent of the structure and interior layout. It is the formal recognition of these environmental levels that is an essential characteristic of the open building approach.

Above: *Support*, the title of the sculpture of monumental hands rising from the water by Lorenzo Quinn for the Venice Bienalle, 2017.

A system formed by subsystems

The open building approach sees the built environment in a dynamic way and develops methods of design and building that are compatible with it. Our built environment is sustainable to the extent that each part is transformed independently—part by part. In short, the architectural system is formed by subsystems, which are part of larger systems.

Open building is a practical solution to the condition of technical overcomplication in buildings that has resulted from the incremental addition, over the years, of new technological systems. The 'ownership' of these technological systems is by different trades who rarely cooperate, operating instead in their silos. These complications require all parties to reconsider their procurement and investment practices, their design approaches, and their regulatory frameworks.

Spontaneous settlements are clear examples of complex subsystems within a complex urban system. Their morphological characteristics combined with their development process are traditionally understood as chaotic and unorganised. And so are many emerging cities, traditionally known for their inherent chaotic and discontinuous spatial patterns and rapid and unorganised development process.

Underneath they display remarkable consistencies and conformities—that is the nature of emergent vernacular. They never fail to surprise.

From theory to practice

Changes in attitude and priorities are now taking the force of law. For example, in 2008 the Japanese government mandated the requirement for 200-year housing. It included new legislation and regulatory controls for use by local building-control officials. Projects approved under this legislation have preferential rates of taxation. In Finland, open building projects are employed by one of the largest residential development companies. In the Netherlands, we see the greatest use of open building systems, and this has led to remarkable efficiencies and quality outcomes in housing. In Poland, open building is known as the 'Warsaw Standard'.

According to Stephen Kendall, a longtime collaborator with John Habraken, open building approaches represent a robust and stable platform for:

1. **Clarifying confused decision-making that leads to conflict and the ineffective use of energies.** Recognising and working with (or refining and sorting out) levels of decision-making is fundamental. Technical solutions will follow. Sorting out such levels of intervention helps innovation of all kinds to flourish. Of course, there are many technical solutions available but, as we know, they are not widely applied.

2. **Sorting out 'who controls what'.** Although no single party can or should control the entire process, there is always 'control creep'. Settling these boundary issues to the satisfaction of all parties is key. In the office sector, there is no dispute about who builds the shell and core (base building) and who does the tenant fit-out. Everyone 'gets it' and things run rather smoothly. It's taken a long time for these boundaries to be clear in the office sector, but the same sort of agreement is now needed in the housing delivery process.

3. **Recognising the idea of capacity at each level of intervention.** Decisions at one level (e.g., urban design) should offer capacity for a variety of interventions at the next (building) level, and a building design should provide suitable capacity for variation and change at the fit-out level. Developing capacity is a hierarchical thing, not something to be integrated. Higher levels set the rules, but the rules need to enable variety at the lower levels, which we should not attempt to script (but only set constraints for and allow), and so the rules should be simple at each level.

This continuum of openness starts from self-building, where design choice is entirely open. The next step is the part-build stage with structured choices in the form of built infrastructure. In the last step, we find the full-build conventional housing provision, which provides a turnkey solution where everything is provided.

PLATFORMS AS FRAMEWORKS FOR ENABLING

Effective platforms allow us to develop a number of methods to enable delivery, phasing and diversity over time. These methods widen choice to a larger market—not just the big guys. Where land is subdivided using something similar to the universal lot concept, it allows different levels of entry and intervention by various players: individual, collective or institutional (public and private). This method accommodates the full range of procurement options, from individual self-build through to self-procurement to shell construction or full completion by any of a range of smaller local to larger building contractors.

For any scheme, there should be a proportion of land given over to each and every one of these activities. Local authorities could use parametric approaches to set and manage the percentage mix for each option, and this could be monitored and adjusted based on relative success and take up of any option.

In the United Kingdom, Urban Splash in collaboration with shedkm has introduced a new slant on delivering wider market choice through typological mass housebuilding. Their customisable two- to three-storey family homes, called the 'hoUSe' project, can be given different façades and internal layouts, and will replace the much-publicised Tutti Frutti self-build terrace proposals.

According to Tom Bloxham at Urban Splash,

> the 'hoUSe' concept enables purchasers to design their layouts. The internal planning is based on flexibility and adaptability. The houses are delivered as raw shells, with kitchen and bathroom 'pods' in place. The purchasers first decide if they want 'loft' or 'garden' living. Then a series of layouts can be selected which tailor 1, 2, 3, 4 and 5-bedroom homes with an open-plan or more traditional feel.

This is similar to the practice in Germany where purchasers can opt for a 'weather-tight' solution, which enables them to fit out their interiors or choose the 'key ready' option, which is the completed scheme.

All of these options point to the need for an 'enabling developer', who can operate across the full spectrum of choice—from the serviced site to the part-build and full-build options. The model of the enabling developer is being trialled by the United Kingdom's Homes and Communities Agency (HCA) to open up more custom-build (self-build) opportunities. The HCA is looking to maximise all the possibilities for custom homebuilders to access land that government is releasing as a cornerstone of its accelerated public land disposals programme. Where possible, HCA is using the build now, pay later model.

In all instances, the enabling developer could act as the infrastructure provider and land developer, especially since issues such as energy will need to be managed on a district-wide basis in the future. The enabling developer could also act as the neighbourhood developer to mobilise local social capital. This role could extend to being the site 'impresario', promoting the range of diversities of the site, or even becoming the 'town developer'. Its function could emerge from the skills of a contractor, a social housing provider, a local authority housing department, an estate manager or even a local energy provider. It is most likely to be a hybrid of these. In all instances, it demands a new breed of person or organisation to act in this role.

RIGHT TO BUILD

The UK Government recognises there are millions of people across the country who would like the opportunity to build their own home, either through self build or by working with a custom build developer that will give them the opportunity to design an individual home. If this huge demand were unlocked, it would lead to a significant rise in the number of new homes built each year and could lead to a permanent increase in housebuilding.

New 'Right to Build' legislation requires all councils in England to provide for sufficient serviced plots with planning permission to meet local demand for this market. Many are introducing local initiatives to meet local demand, whether through local plans, proposals for new settlements, working with custom build developers and community groups or by directly releasing land for serviced building plots.

The National Custom and Self Build Association (NaCSBA) has established a national Right to Build Task Force of experts to provide an enabling platform, which can help unlock this growing demand. The Task Force is government-endorsed and will support at least eighty organisations in this sector across the UK over the next three years. Support will be available to councils, community groups, housing associations and other organisations to deliver large, affordable housing projects.

'Right to Build' is the start. It just needs these starter conditions to be recognised to make it work better.

Opposite page: The 'hoUSe' project by Urban Splash in New Islington, Manchester, provides a typological approach to regenerating a Victorian canalside. **This page:** Camiel van Noten's Macrolots Initiative advocates a simple, enabling platform to accelerate the intensification of lower-density neighbourhoods in New York.

PART-BUILD OPTIONS

There is a range of part-build solutions that lie between serviced sites and full-build sites. Part-build solutions involve the standardisation and modularisation of the most basic primary structure of the building, which can be delivered most efficiently through mass housing or large construction methods if needed.

> *By defining construction processes instead of fixed building designs, it is possible to plan for future growth without eliminating spontaneous growth and feedback.*
>
> —Christopher Alexander

In terraced development, a part-build solution can be reduced to the 'party walls' concept, and in apartment buildings, it is in the cellular structure of wall and slabs: as shown in the 'urban warehouse' concept. A part-build solution constructs the elements of the building that should never need to change, no matter how much the building is adapted over the years. Everything else should be changeable and designed and built by individuals.

These unchangeable elements are also important because they address the most pressing concerns of the self-builder or small builder: setting the bounds of the project, limiting choice and starting up. These elements define the boundaries of the site, and therefore the relationship with adjacent sites. These elements are major determinants in defining the volume of the building by also defining the conditions for the front and back solutions. They also provide the essential structure that allows more domestic and traditional forms of structure to be utilised for roofs and internal walls and floors, all of which can be easily changed. In both instances, the contractor can proceed to the next level of part-build, which allows for infill and internal fit out by the occupants.

Christopher Alexander, in *The Timeless Way of Building*, provides a coherent theory which describes in modern terms an architecture as ancient as human society itself. This is something we need to rediscover. As he says, 'The mastery of what is made does not lie in the depths of some impenetrable ego; it lies, instead in the simple mastery of the steps in the process.'

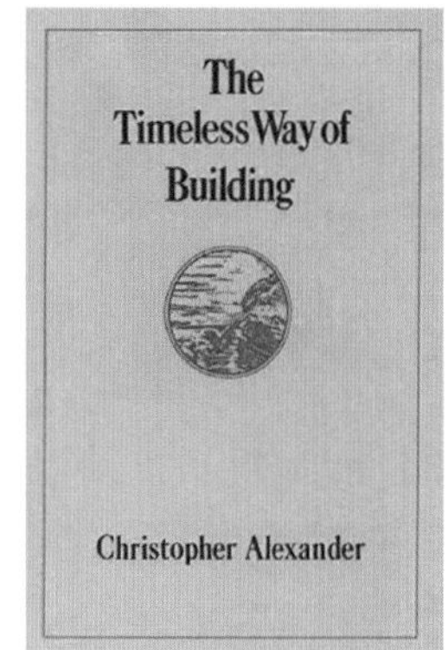

PARTY WALLS

For most types of starter housing at the medium-density urban scale, we need to develop party wall construction methods that use the benefits of mass construction but still facilitate traditional response—something that offers speed, consistency and regularity. These methods can be delivered using proprietary or conventional construction, but they must all have the same outcome: providing a volume of space. To achieve this volume, party walls need an element of modularity using standard heights and lengths for a range of medium-density housing conditions. We can learn a lot about this approach from kitchen design, which has standard sets of dimensions for its cabinets—tall and short, wide and narrow—that have become universal. If you don't like the standard items, you can fit your own doors, tops or appliances. Stoves, dishwashers and fridges all fit! The choice is well structured.

If the carcass of the cabinet fixes the volume, where you choose to set the height and number of the shelves is your choice, and this might change. In a similar way the party walls, in defining the volume of the building, should offer different internal responses. We know that most floors are fixed to deliver minimum floor to ceiling heights but what happens if we choose to trade off volume for floorspace? We just need the equivalent of the lug holes in the kitchen cabinet that offer simple choice.

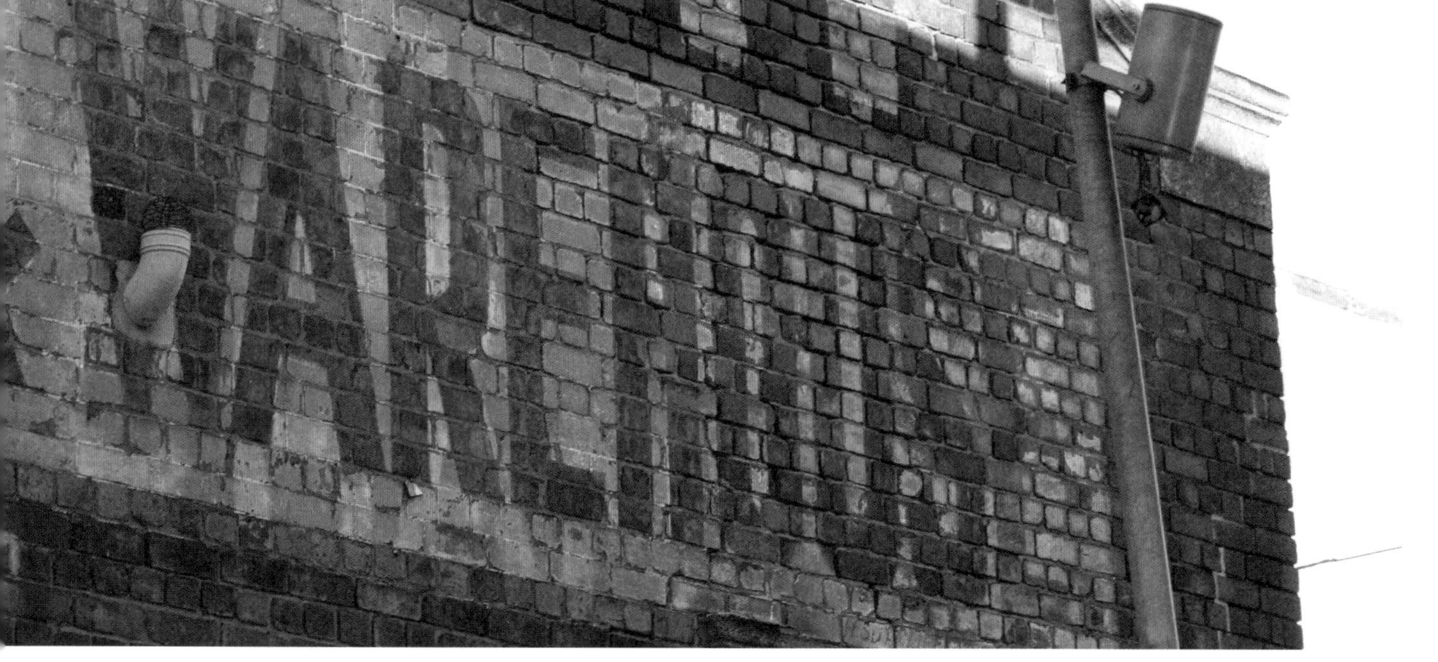

THE URBAN WAREHOUSE

If the standard Victorian warehouse is one of the most robust forms of urban building that can accommodate the widest range of uses, why do we not just build more of these and allow people to fit them out if they want?

Alex Lifschutz has been working with engineers at Arup to develop a system that can provide sustainable, adaptable structures that will last the test of time—the modern version of the urban warehouse. The recently prototyped system has an efficient storey height that is only slightly taller than the average for residential buildings but well inside standard office dimensions. This solution generates a floor to ceiling height accommodating offices, shops, restaurants and generous housing of all types (hotels, student housing, affordable housing, markets and loft flats). The system can support the highest loads for offices and therefore easily cope with housing of all kinds. The floor is fully accessible for services and deep enough to permit offices above apartments and vice versa, so that uses can be exchanged within and between buildings. Most importantly, the structure uses a minimum amount of material, can be recycled and encourages a green environmental system that utilises free night cooling. It is a classic, open, long-life, loose-fit solution.

We need more thinking like this, getting us away from our obsession with single use, form-based architecture that has not served us well. Like Japan, Holland and Poland we should be moving towards 200-year buildings that come with effective regulatory tools and with generous tax incentives.

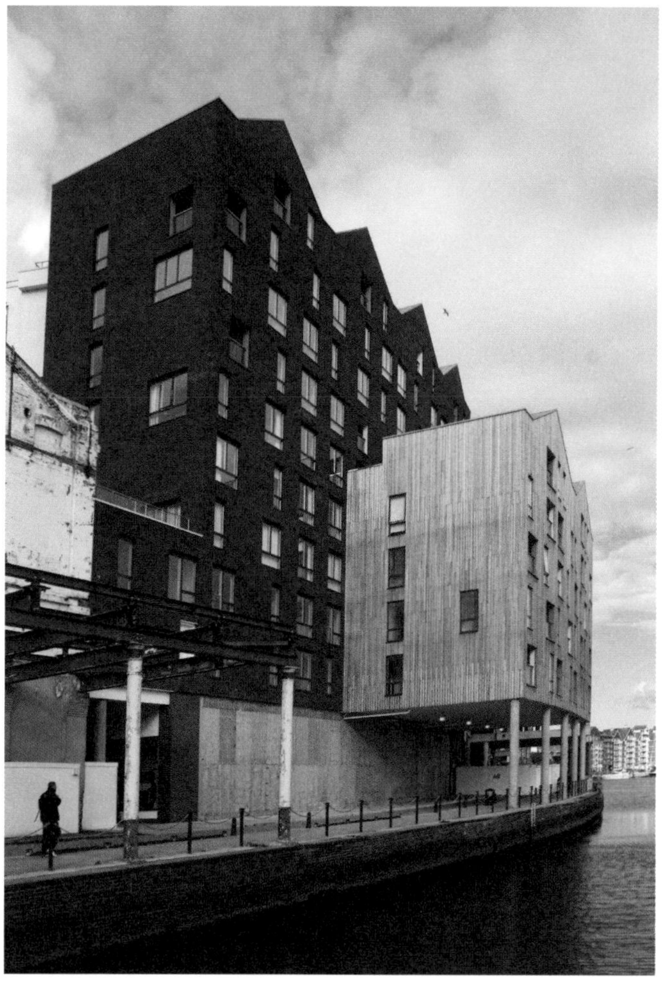

Bottom: John Lyall Architect's conversion of a former industrial warehouse into new waterfront housing and an arts centre in Ipswich, United Kingdom.

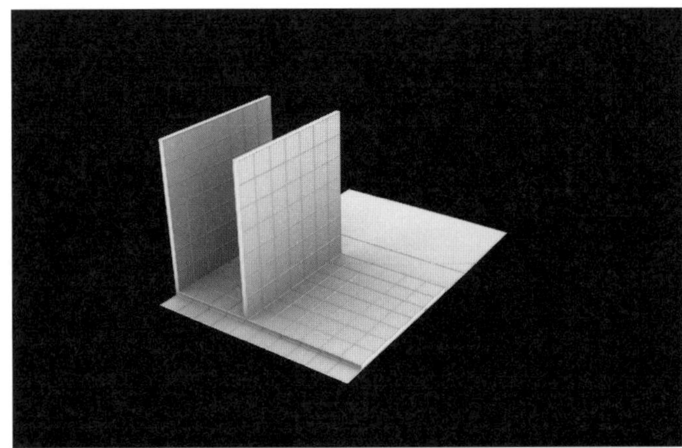

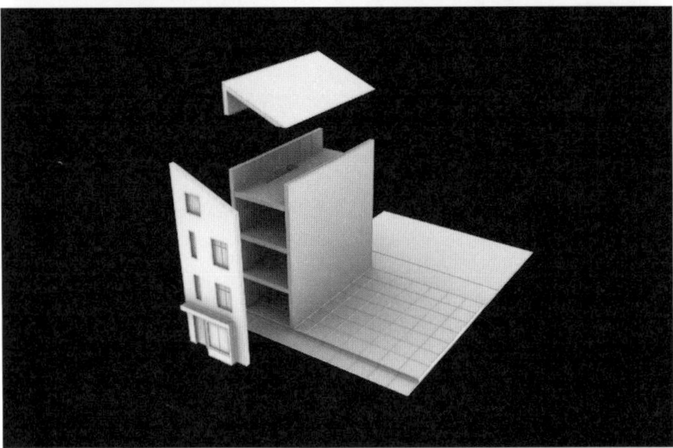

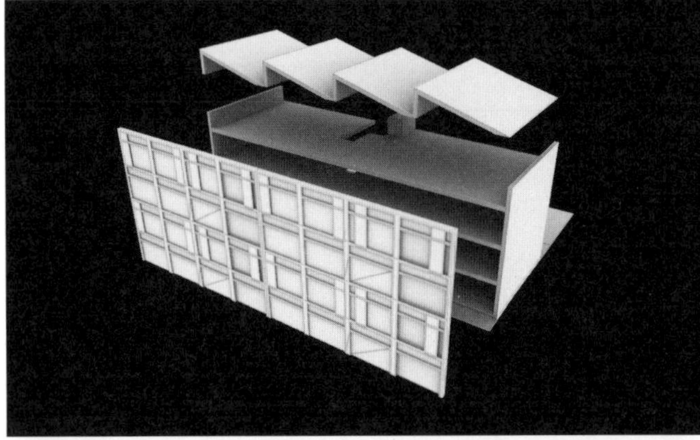

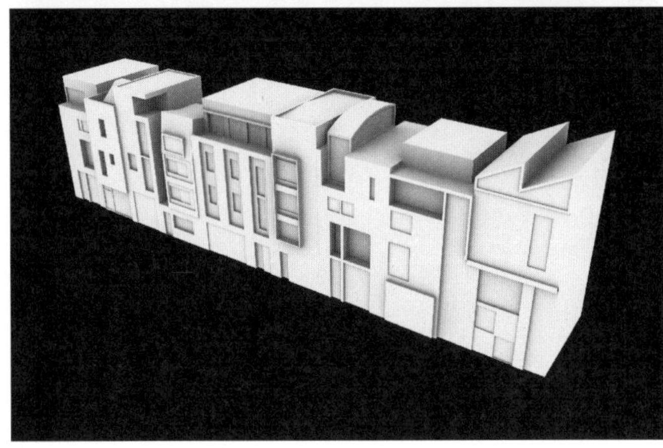

Above: A full spectrum of infrastructure options for arange of urban typologies, including party walls, walls and slabs, serviced cores, building envelopes—all contributing to the overall built form.

THE FULL INFRASTRUCTURE SPECTRUM

According to Brand's layers diagram, as noted in Setién's paper, 'Towards an Open and User-Driven Housing Architecture', these part-build solutions can be broken down further. The term *infrastructure* is used to make reference to the fixed and collective components of the building; the concept includes the following.

1 Infrastructure as a skeleton

In this first scenario, infrastructure is formed by the load-bearing structure and the access cores, with the rest of the components belonging to the infill. This separation allows one to design each house in an individual way and independently from the others, inside the infrastructure formed by columns, beams and slabs. Therefore, this scenario follows the original definition of support, as proposed by John Habraken. In this case, the internal partitions of each house, as well as the façade, are not part of the infrastructure, giving the architect a great freedom in the design of each house. An infrastructure as a skeleton is a construction able to accommodate houses that can be constructed, modified and demolished without affecting each other; in other words, we are talking about autonomous houses in a high-rise building. The reality is that there have been many collective housing projects where the interior of the units was freely designed; however, few projects have permitted the exterior walls to be freely located. The Next 21 building in Osaka (Japan, 1994) and the Ökohaus complex in Berlin (Germany, 1982) were carried out following these principles.

2 Infrastructure as envelope

In this second scenario, also called 'shell and core', the external enclosure becomes part of the infrastructure, acting as a common element representative of the whole building. This example can be found in speculative office buildings, which have operated for decades on the basis of these two construction phases. In the case of infrastructure as envelope, we tend to concentrate on four aspects of the project: the design of the perimeter and envelope; the relation between floor to floor height, and the depth of the floor plan; the position of the service and access core (lifts, stairs and ducts); and the structural system. The role of the designer then focusses on achieving the best optimisation of the space. This could include developing an open plan system, which enables diverse possibilities of internal subdivision. The Solids development in Amsterdam (The Netherlands, 2010) is an example of infrastructure as an envelope.

3 Infrastructure as services

In this third situation, also called 'serviced shell and core', the services (kitchen and bathrooms) become part of the infrastructural system along with the façade, access and structure. That is to say, the position of the services is fixed in the floor plan and therefore not controlled by the user. When our intention is to design a housing unit departing from the services as an essential infrastructural element, we should consider the way of grouping the services and their strategic positions in the floor plan carefully. Also, this consideration is vital to facilitating a smooth registration of the installations as well as the possibility of upgrading the equipment to meet the changing needs of users over time. Grouping together the service spaces enables a more efficient use of the installations since it allows for minimisation of the number of ducts needed, and it allocates them in an easy position for their registration and maintenance.

4 Infrastructure with open space

In this case, the infrastructural system has available open space that can be appropriated by the user over time, providing more flexibility in use. This open space is not common to all the building infrastructures, but its consideration is relevant to the study since it allows the possibility of extension of the house. This available space is not just any space, but areas that are suggestive and have potential for occupation, terrace roofs that allow extensions, courtyards that can be filled in, or double high spaces that allow later subdivisions. It can be external or internal, allowing for the possibility of internal (embryo house) or external (seed house) growth.

At the early stage, an open space is an unfinished space, but to ensure its proper functionality, the architect has to think of the different ways in which it can be appropriated and finished, designing it accordingly. The Elemental Chile project in Iquique (Chile, 2004) and the Evolutive house in Perugia (Italy, 1978) are two examples of infrastructures with open space.

SCALING UP THE BUILDING INDUSTRY

The building industry takes many forms. If what people build are shacks, then we have a shack-building industry. If what they build is formal or traditional, the industry takes on these qualities. If the construction is built by big developers or through many small companies, it takes on distinctively different forms. Building industry conventions take years to evolve and are deeply embedded in general building practices and applications of each specific country. They are rooted in place by their skills and resources. In the face of increasing pressures, we always seem to think that a total revolution will solve the problem.

The building industry is rife with individual patents and bespoke solutions, all vested in the control of individual companies or separate trades. Some solutions are tested but never get beyond the first scheme. Others never get started. The reason is that few of these have been able to move beyond the prototype to gain market penetration, and therefore they languish in the box of good ideas, never to see the light of day.

Right: The Empower Shack project, Cape Town, by Urban Think Tank.

Many believe that bringing a more production-based approach to housebuilding through modern methods of construction has the potential to influence the entire sector in a number of ways:

→ Reduce the time for on-site installation, as it is replaced by more factory-based production, where it is possible to control and manage the process better
→ Reduce build costs through reducing time spent on site by improving efficiency and reducing wasteful processes
→ Lessen the amount of material used and wasted throughout the production and construction process through the use of prefabricated, modular elements for load bearing and weatherproofing
→ Improve health and safety conditions, as less on-site activity is required
→ Enhance the living experience for residents

However, the majority of housebuilding is still based on a traditional, well-proven approach: on-site construction using traditional materials (concrete foundations, bricks, blocks, roof trusses, floor joists), construction techniques (delivery of material to site, as required, through multiple suppliers) and trades (groundwork, scaffolding for work at heights, bricklayers, carpenters, plasterers, roofers). Off-site construction is gaining ground, but it is still only used for a small number of developments. It is thought of as innovative, and builders have little experience with the systems and how to use them, so it has been unable to scale up its ambitions to make a big difference.

The secret lies in working with the building industry—formal or informal, traditional or modern—to progressively scale up their efforts. This is best done by defining standard best practice, modular coordination, and parameter-based building typologies and by developing the supply chains. Small shifts add up over time to making a big difference. Revolutions never seem to work.

CODES, STANDARDS AND REGULATIONS

Codes, standards and regulations are the hidden languages of making cities. As top-down systems of influencing and control, they dictate virtually all aspects of urban development. They are the expressions of the underlying urban rules that are applied to the elaboration of the urban fabric.

Codes, standards and regulations do have different meanings. A code is a model, a set of rules that knowledgeable people recommend for others to follow. It is not a law but can be adopted into law. A standard tends to be a more detailed elaboration, the nuts and bolts of meeting a code. Regulations are principles or rules based on and meant to carry out specific pieces of legislation (such as for the protection of the environment). Regulations are usually enforced by a regulatory agency, such as local government, formed or mandated to carry out the purpose or provisions of legislation.

In *The Code of the City: Standards and the Hidden Language of Place Making*, Eran Ben-Joseph examines the relationship between standards and place-making. 'The same standards for subdividing land, grading, laying streets and utilities, and configuring rights-of-way and street widths to accommodate cars have been adopted in many areas of the world regardless of variations in local environments.'

In analysing their impact on the modern city and its suburbs, Ben-Joseph argues that it is time for development regulations to reflect site-specific and localised urban design conditions.

Codes, standards and regulations were meant to bring order and safety to the city building process. But now, Ben-Joseph argues, these accumulated rules and their widespread application illustrate a disconnect between the original rationale for their existence and their actual effect on the human environment. We now have a separation of codes, standards and regulations from local conditions so, over the years, they have shaped neighbourhoods, generally in bad ways.

Codes, standards and regulations are different to norms, mores or conventions, which are bottom-up means of expressing the codes of urban society. Oliver Leech, in his book *Hidden Rules,* argues that these are far more important than codes or standards as they are the product of the city and its citizens:

> Communities are not built through standards, rules or codes; rules are built through communities and start shaping future development; either through limitations or through the genesis of a new way of building as a result of these restrictions. This new way might give birth to a new set of standards and so the city and its rules exist in a productive mutualism.

OPEN STANDARDS

In 1993, the music industry adopted the MP3 audio standard as the de facto platform for digital transfer and playback on digital audio players and devices. With this standard, it was possible to cut down a lot of useless digital data. MP3 was a platform that gave the industry a common voice and a common purpose. It was this standard that successfully drove the development and evolution of the Apple iPod to become an industry leader.

We need to define our open building standard that gives us the platform for the development and evolution of housing. We can call it the Popular Home Standard or PH3 Build.

High-level, principles-based standards can provide a framework for making choices about how we release the potential for people to make our towns and cities. Open standards can spur innovation directly by codifying accumulated knowledge and experience, and forming the common platform from which new solutions can emerge.

Standards developed using the open standard principles in information technology are developed through an open, participatory process. The benefits of this process are well documented. There is no reason why we cannot achieve similar benefits if we move to a 'cities' version of open standards. In fact, using a common terminology, we could adapt the IT sector's open standard principles to deliver our version:

1 **Cooperation.** Standards organisations respectfully cooperate; each respects the autonomy, integrity, processes and intellectual property rules of the others.

2 **Adherence to principles.** There is adherence to the five fundamental principles of standards development:

→ **Due process.** Decisions are made with equity and fairness amongst participants. No one party dominates or guides standards development. Standards processes are transparent, and opportunities exist to appeal decisions. Processes for periodic standards review and updating are well defined.

→ **Broad consensus.** Processes allow for all views to be considered and addressed, such that agreement across a range of interests can be found.

→ **Transparency.** Standards organisations provide advance public notice of proposed standards development activities, the scope of work to be undertaken and conditions for participation. Easily accessible records of decisions and the materials used in reaching those decisions are provided. Public comment periods are provided before final standards approval and adoption.

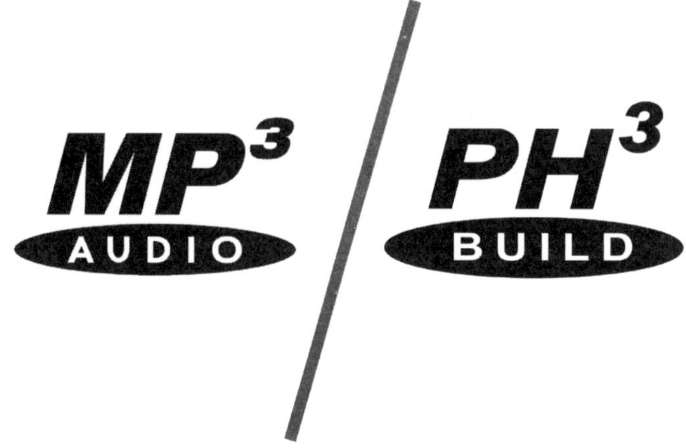

→ **Balance.** Standards activities are not exclusively dominated by any particular person, company or interest group.

→ **Openness.** Standards processes are open to all interested and informed parties.

3 **Collective empowerment.** There is a commitment by standards organisations to affirm standards that:

→ Are chosen and defined based on social, economic and environmental merit, as judged by the contributed expertise of each participant
→ Provide local interoperability, scaleability, stability, and resiliency
→ Enable local competition
→ Serve as building blocks for further innovation
→ Contribute to the creation of local communities, benefiting humanity

4 **Availability.** Standards specifications are made accessible to all for implementation and deployment. Standards organisations have defined procedures to develop specifications that can be implemented under fair terms.

5 **Voluntary adoption.** Standards are voluntarily adopted, and success is determined by the extent of the adoption.

SPACE STANDARDS

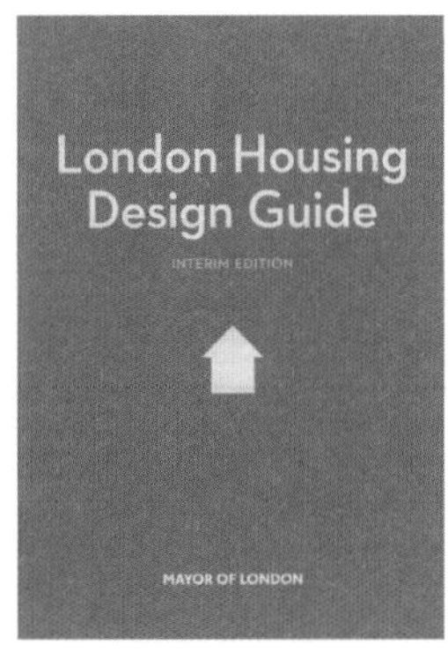

Within the context of promoting long-life, loose-fit solutions, standards should not be confused with defaults. Standards are written definitions, limits or rules, approved and monitored for compliance by authoritative agencies or recognised bodies as minimum acceptable benchmarks. The standard offer should also not be confused with standards, although there is some linkage.

Space standards are the eternal conundrum and, in a world where we are looking for long-life, loose-fit solutions, how do they apply? If they are slavishly applied, we will always end up with a home driven only by minimum space standards. Slavishly applied standards will limit future change. This is the inherent problem with the *London Housing Design Guide* that started as a Neighbourhood Design Manual and ended up as a restrictive space standards manual.

The Parker Morris standards were a means of giving the housing industry some fixes, but are they still valid in a rapidly changing social and cultural environment where not all requirements can be reduced to two-point-four person households? Families have moved on. We now have complexity in all its forms. If we moved to the quality of overall space criteria (and volume) as a universal choice rather than specific requirements for every room, we could open up choice as to how people used their space. If they choose to have smaller bedrooms and trade this off against larger living space, so what? One thing we have shown in our more robust housing forms is that interiors can change.

Standards can help frame or qualify standard offers. They should not alone determine them. In other words, standards can show that places will accommodate certain uses, but they do not need to be the only way these uses are achieved. Some of our best historical areas do not readily provide all the mechanics of ideal modern operating. Some of our best worker's starter housing is in small houses that break all the normal space standard rules.

If we applied standards to the letter of the law, then we would never be able to deliver the robust type of housing that the conversion of historical urban housing has given us in recent years. In a vernacular world, the home evolves to the pattern of living at the time. It is not phased by narrow limiting rules.

MODULAR COORDINATION

Modular coordination is a form of agreed standards that leads to greater productivity in the building industry. Through its ability to discipline the dimensions and coordinate the spatial qualities of a building and its components, modular coordination allows a more flexible open industrial system to take shape.

The benefits of practicing modular coordination are to provide a practical approach towards the following:

→ It facilitates cooperation between building designers, maufacturers, distributors, contractors and authorities.
→ It enables buildings to be dimensioned so they can be erected using standard components without restricting design.
→ It permits a flexible type of standardisation, which encourages the use of a limited number of standardised building components for the construction of different kinds of buildings.
→ It optimises standard sizes of building components.
→ It encourages the interchangeability of components, in whatever materials, forms or methods of manufacture.
→ It simplifies site operations by rationalising setting out, positioning and assembly of building components.
→ It ensures dimensional coordination between installations (equipment, storage units, other fitted furniture, etc.), as well as with the rest of the building.

A study undertaken by the Danish Building Institute in 1997 showed that use of modular coordination in the Danish building industry was the single biggest contributor to saving costs in residential developments. Achieving the highest level of coordination (and realising the benefits of this action) is a fundamental principle of a platforms-based approach.

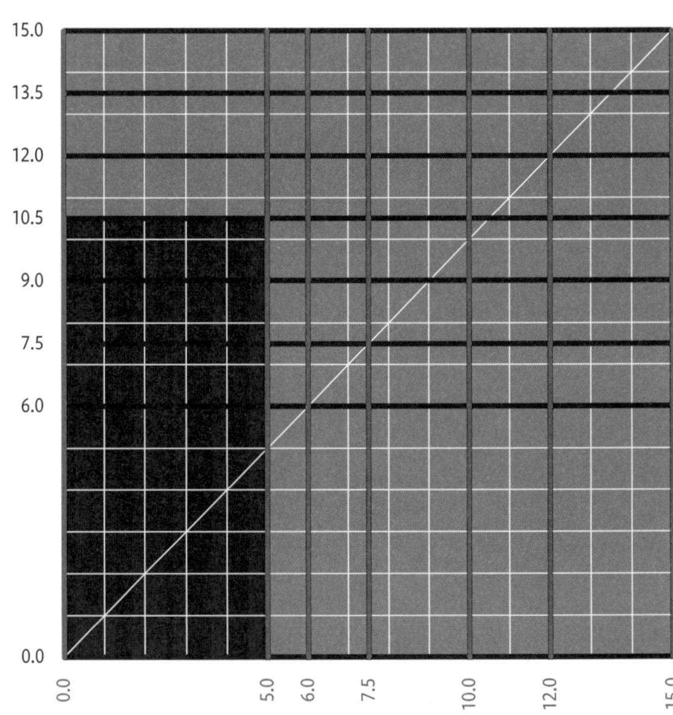

Right: The subdivision approach based on the universal lot method enables us to develop a modular coordination system that uses a regular grid and shows potential building widths and depths based on subdivisions of the 15-metre (50 feet) wide lot.

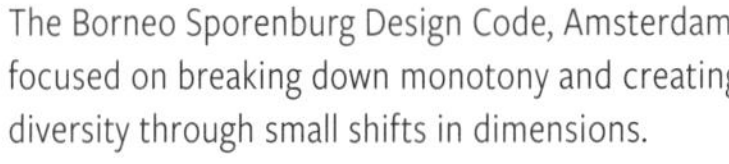

The Borneo Sporenburg Design Code, Amsterdam, focused on breaking down monotony and creating diversity through small shifts in dimensions.

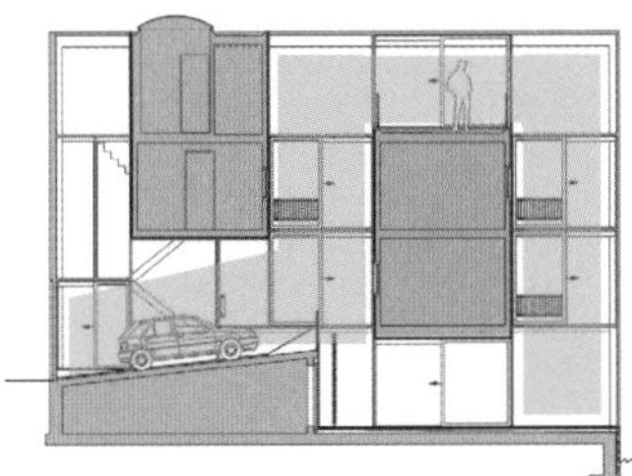

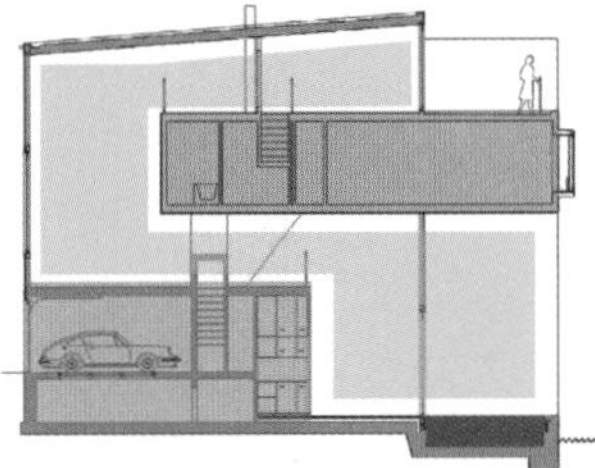

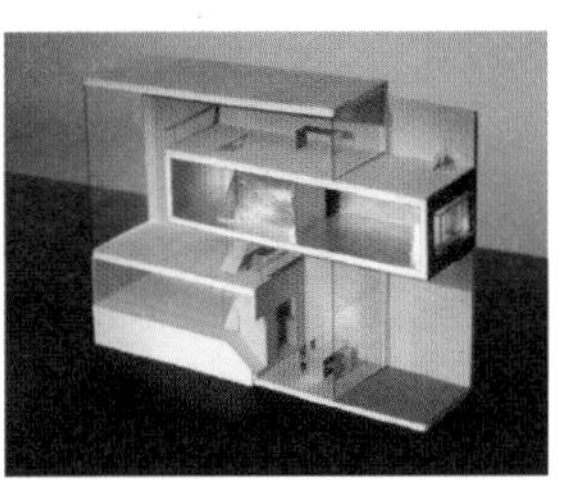

DESIGN CODES

According to David Walters in *Designing Community: Charrettes, Masterplans, and Form-Based Codes*, design code is:

> a set of specific rules or requirements to guide the physical development of a site or place. The aim of design coding is to provide clarity as to what constitutes acceptable design quality and thereby a level of certainty for developers and the local community alike that can help to accelerate the delivery of good quality new development.

A criticism commonly levelled at the use of design codes is that while they may help to determine the minimum acceptable standards of design, codes do little to encourage innovative architecture. In contrast, Carmona and Dann, in 'Design Codes in England: Where to Now?', suggest that design codes may foster innovation through the appointment of better quality designers because they help to raise the profile of design from the outset. Carmona and Dann also find that design codes can increase design quality by challenging traditional development processes, particularly in relation to housebuilding. A design code may be used by a local planning authority to extend permitted development rights and aid the speedy delivery of developments while retaining high-quality design content. All stakeholders have the potential to benefit from the use of design codes.

Design codes have the additional benefits over and above the standard permitted development rights, with the option of prescribing 'must haves' (for example, road widths and building heights) and allowing some leeway for meeting requirements.

One of the issues associated with design codes is that locally accepted typological solutions are often not available. There are ever-demanding pressures to return to first principles. Many aspects of development—street typologies, block patterns, open space solutions and subdivision principles—could be dealt with as neighbourhood-wide (or even city-wide) development orders. Design codes can be used as tools for large-scale development, but if we are looking to diversify the housebuilding industry and promote more local interventions, they also need to be evolved as mechanisms to guide small-scale, self-build or self-procured developments. There is no reason why local authorities could not adopt a borough-wide, pattern-book approach, offering a range of typological housing solutions that could be used off the shelf as default settings.

If you adopt the 'block/lot/plot' approach, the scheme almost becomes self-regulating and simple rules can be used to ensure richness and variety. The design code for Borneo Sporenburg in Amsterdam, an example of fine-grain development, is written on a single side of paper. The Aylesbury Estate in South London has followed a similar approach with a design code linked to plot and lot configurations.

REGULATIONS

According to UN-Habitat, regulations define all the desirable aspects of buildings and public spaces and determine city form. They can be consolidated in four main regulatory groups: construction, land uses, civic infrastructure and public health. Regulations are set by a variety of actors and represent the culture of the city and its time. They evolve through time, reflecting the changing needs of the population and, in turn, change the city. They evolve as places evolve and different concerns arise.

In Manhattan, the Tenement House Act of 1901 introduced height restrictions on residential buildings in response to the loss of light and air from taller, new residential development. Amongst other restrictions, this law required that new buildings be built with outward-facing windows in every room. It also defined the need for open courtyards, proper ventilation, indoor toilets and fire safety systems. Later, the 1916 Zoning Resolution looked at the regulation of the height and bulk of buildings and the area of backyards, courts and other open spaces. Building setbacks were introduced, and the maximum spatial envelope of buildings was regulated. It also proposed new land-use regulations, where districts were classified into three categories: residential, business and unrestricted use with specific use restrictions defined for each category. The 1961 Zoning Resolution further controlled land use and bulk of buildings, incorporating parking requirements and the need for open space. It introduced the concept of incentive zoning—allowing extra floors in return for developers incorporating plazas into projects. These regulations continually shaped the city as pressures for change arose.

In Barcelona, the 1861 regulation introduced new planning requirements to be incorporated into the general plan of the Eixample. This regulation controlled the image, health conditions and the construction of the new city extension. The document regulated maximum land coverage of 50 per cent, plot depth and width, building heights, courtyards and ventilation. It defined street dimensions as well as the proportion of the space destined to pedestrians. In 1891, a new ordinance was introduced that was specific to the Eixample's construction. It regulated building alignment to the streets: a maximum height of buildings for standard streets. This regulation resulted in a street cross-section of a building height to a street width ratio of 1:1. It required a perimeter block approach, with a maximum building depth for ventilation of courtyard surfaces. Subsequent regulations resulted in a continuous modification of the ordinances of 1891. As a result, the initial concept of the Eixample was progressively transformed as a consequence of the increase

Opposite page, left: Historic tenement housing has set the scale for normal development in New York. **Right:** Regulations for Barcelona's urban blocks protects the amenity of the courtyard. **This page:** Aerial view of Villa El Salvador shows the grain and pattern of the formal structure.

in building heights. In Barcelona, highly prescriptive regulations were not just shaping the city, they were designing it.

In comparison, the general plan of Villa El Salvador in Peru put in place a grid, and defined and assigned housing lots according to this general organisation plan. The grid served as a primary structure for the spatial layout of the city. Facilities, services and commerce were put in place later, and the grid was altered where necessary. The original organisational structure was not changed deeply by these additions and remains readable today. Housing was meant to be incremental and self-built. Formal, constructive and hygienic aspects of housing were not regulated. Today many of the lots are occupied fully, resulting in 100 per cent land coverage with poor public health conditions as a result of insufficient light and ventilation.

In recent decades regulations associated with the use of cars has had the biggest effect on the shape of our neighbourhoods, dictating our urban networks. The street in some countries has become the most highly regulated and controlled element in the city.

According to Philip Howard in *The Death of Common Sense: How Law Is Suffocating America*, regulations are destroying urban society in America, and this is also true in many other parts of the world. In some areas, regulations come so thick and fast they make no sense anymore. According to Howard, *health* and *safety* are the two most dangerous words in the English language. For example, London's plan to segregate cyclists through complicated cycle superhighways to improve cycling safety is killing more cyclists than ever. Good intentions have unintended consequences. Technocratic solutions never work in complex systems.

Today, environmental and heritage concerns and their resultant impact on building regulations exert a significant influence on the neighbourhood. The requirements for sustainable urban drainage, protection of nature and energy savings are affecting such issues as compactness, orientation and image of the neighbourhood. Requirements for full mobility for disabled persons are profoundly shaping the relationship between the building and the street and new requirements for such issues as recycling and cycle storage are adding to the complexity of this important interface.

This does not mean a full flight into mindless deregulation. In a bottom-up world, it just means simple rules. In the case of cycling in London, why don't we just say, 'Cycling first': give cycling priority on the street so vehicle drivers will know how to behave. In the case of neighbourhoods, if the simple rule was 'Respect your neighbour', people would work it out for themselves. Things would become self-regulating, and people would agree on what is important or necessary. Of course, it is important to have boundary conditions but also to always make these negotiable.

THE RESPONSIVE DESIGNER

HOW A HOUSING ARCHITECT'S LIGHT TOUCH MADE A BIG IMPACT

Daniel is an architect, born in Ghana and trained in urban design at MIT. He is burning with idealism and social concern. He works as a consultant to UN-Habitat and knows the scale of the problems caused by millions of people moving to cities. Reading Ayn Rand's novel *The Fountainhead* persuaded him that design could change the world.

He has visited new towns in the United Kingdom and social housing projects in the Netherlands to gain insight about how such change might be achieved. He has read about Hammarby in Sweden, though he has yet to visit it, and he thinks Passivhaus (a type of highly insulated house heated primarily by passive solar gain and heat from people, electrical equipment and other internal sources) sounds great.

Daniel admires the work of Alejandro Aravena of Elemental in Chile. Working on a housing project in Iquique, one of Chile's largest port cities, Elemental realised that the money left over from buying the land would allow them to build only half a house, so they concentrated on building the essentials: the overall structure, the kitchen and the bathroom. Given a well-designed framework from which to start, they would be able to infill and complete the house using the tradition and skills of self-building that squatter families acquire through necessity. This type of approach to social housing sees it as a public investment rather than a public expense. The houses gain value as they are added to over time.

Daniel's ambition has been to come up with a housing solution that everyone will adopt. He is excited by the WikiHouse project, which began as an experiment into the future of housing. Led by Alistair Parvin of Architecture 00 (zero zero), WikiHouse's aim is to create open production techniques by making the system freely available to all. The first full prototype was built in 2011. Since then, more and more people have joined and supported WikiHouse, with a growing global community of collaborators building prototypes, supporting development and advancing the WikiHouse system.

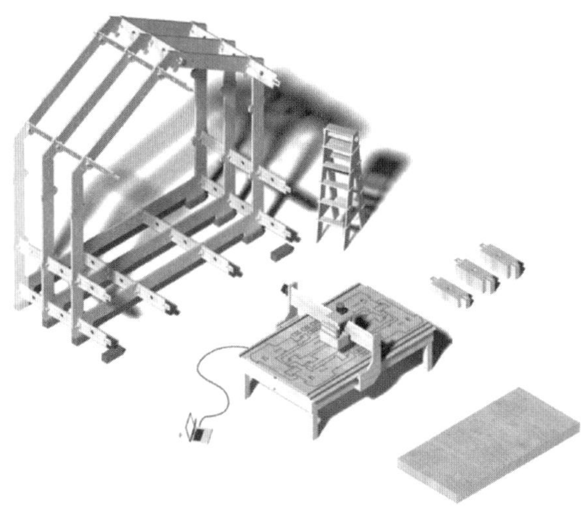

TRYING TO BREAK THE MOULD

Daniel has been working on the design of a kit house but has had limited success in convincing others that his solution will be the magic bullet. He makes a time-lapse film to show how easy the kit house is to build. Some people are impressed but his project does not get off the ground. Daniel hears that over 300 patents are lodged every year in the United Kingdom alone for housing innovations. Hardly any of them go beyond the prototype. Daniel financed his prototype with his own money. At least it provides a home for his mother.

In his role as a consultant to UN-Habitat, Daniel has worked on many low-cost housing projects in Africa. Most are in places where nobody wants to live. In most cases they are based on a single house or plot. It seems impossible to break this mould. The result is that the cities follow an American model of low-rise suburbs and high-rise centres. The densest form of development is seen in the informal settlements (such as Kibera, on the edge of Nairobi, which is said to be the largest slum in Africa), which use up all the available space.

The biggest problem facing informal settlements is poor sanitation and the risk of fire. Devastating fires are frequent, and the result is almost always that the shacks are rebuilt. Daniel hears of a shack 'reblocking' scheme being trialled in Cape Town. *Reblocking* is the process of rearranging and reconstructing the shacks in an informal settlement to make better use of open space and reduce the risk of flooding. This process seems to involve little more than rebuilding shacks with spaces between them, in a more regular pattern.

This might make it easier to install sanitation later, but Daniel doubts if it will do much to help the place become a more formal settlement.

Opposite page, top: The Elemental housing project in Chile. **Bottom:** Kibera, Nairobi, one of the largest informal settlements in Africa. **This page, top left:** The WikiHouse project uses open production techniques. **Top right:** Example of a shack-reblocking scheme in Cape Town, South Africa.

DANIEL SUMS UP THE ISSUES

Daniel realises that there are numerous issues that governments and urban professionals are not coming to terms with. Some of these issues require small realignments in policies and processes. Others demand fundamental rethinking. Some are unique to Africa. Others are universal. Whatever happens, these are the issues that governments need to recognise and address, if they are to succeed:

1. No matter how fast governments build, informal settlements grow at ten times the rate. Today's systems cannot cope.
2. The normal private-sector approach to mass housing has produced the poor living environments of many of the townships we see in sub-Saharan Africa. The informal settlements offer no chance of progressing to better, more formal housing over time. The system does not offer any third alternative.
3. People need an opportunity to look after the place they live in and to make it safer.
4. Governments should abandon the traditional view of housing as being a final product. Instead they should regard housing as a process of meeting individual needs: a process that government can help with a light touch. We need to develop systems that are self-regulating, not imposed.
5. Housing should be provided by methods that are interchangeable, scaleable and replicable: they should be capable of being applied in different circumstances and at different scales.
6. These methods depend on finding the invisible chassis that will enable these principles to flourish.
7. Top-down urban planning, design and delivery systems must evolve to offer a common platform with an equitable framework of choices (design options, procurement routes and entry levels to the system) for the individual, collective or institutional builder.
8. The message to Africa's urban policymakers is that the need is for policy coordination, not deregulation. They can unleash the potential for urban housing only by a coordinated push across a wide range of fronts. To do this, effective housing protocols first need to be elevated to the highest political level.

LOOKING THROUGH THE OTHER SIDE OF THE LENS

Daniel realises that he has been looking at the problem through the wrong side of the lens. People use their own efforts and creativity to solve their housing problems every day. Throughout Africa people are building shacks. Instead of coming up with an alternative building system, why not help them do it better? In dealing with informal setttlements on a daily basis, Daniel has to deal with the dangers of the spread of fire and disease. Both these issues relate to how the boundaries between properties are defined and how buildings relate to one another. In ordinary suburbs, spaces and distances are sufficient to avoid these dangers. In a more central urban district, buildings are likely to touch one another. In sub-Saharan Africa (unlike South America) there is no tradition of denser urban living, apart from the imposed western models. What is needed is a more compact form of urbanism. Building heights of even two or three storeys could have a major effect on stemming urban sprawl.

Daniel remembers the concept of open building devised by John Habraken, his old professor at MIT. 'We should not try to forecast what will happen,' Habraken wrote, 'but try to make provisions for the unforeseen.' To accommodate unknown future change, Habraken advised, we should introduce different levels of decision-making in the building process. These might range from urban infrastructure (such as roads and railways) to what he called the 'support' (the load-bearing structure, façades and roof), the 'infill elements' (such as the inner partitioning of buildings, which can be changed without affecting the basic building's structure or shape) and equipment (such as in kitchens and bathrooms) that is likely to be replaced every now and then. Daniel imagines people building their own urban neighbourhoods, districts and quarters by following some sort of code. He draws an imaginary neighbourhood, then rubs out everything apart from the basics—the street, plot subdivisions and the walls between sites. What he has left is what he starts with.

Places need a fundamental order, ideally based on how the land is subdivided. Daniel reads about the universal lot project that was pioneered for the international housing competition for Scotswood Housing Expo in Newcastle in the north of England. In it land is subdivided into regular development parcels. These plots can be subdivided further into smaller plots, or two plots can be combined to create a larger housing site. If he can define a framework for a choice like this, he has a starting point. He will create the conditions for people to occupy land efficiently and learn. But he recognises that this model is called 'site and services', and they have been doing it for ages. It breeds suburbia.

Daniel realises that the key to making urban places is building party walls between properties. This provides a stable structure and one wall for a shack to lean against. It prevents the spread of fire and defines the boundary. It encourages further development.

He develops the concept of the 'accelerator site'. After trying out numerous options, he chooses a 15-metre-wide (50 feet) plot as his primary unit. This enables families to occupy the whole plot, constructing a number of buildings in the form of a compound. Alternatively, the plot can be further subdivided into narrow-frontage plots of regular or varying widths. Daniel develops a pattern book that shows plots with a variety of frontage widths, depths and frontage treatments. The rear lane is a particularly good option, as mid-block services can be installed without having to dig up the roads. This service lane can allow the site to be intensified further at a later stage, providing access to new frontage development.

Working with his engineers, Daniel designs the accelerator party wall. Three metres (10 feet) high, it has projecting fins, three metres (10 feet) apart, to keep it stable. It can be two or more bays long. These walls, running along the side boundaries of the plots, can be built of bricks, blocks or rammed earth. Anyone can build one with a simple jig that will help them set out the key dimensions.

The most important feature of the party walls is that they are of a standard size, creating a common framework for all housing to develop from. When Daniel trials the system in his next project, the shack builders find that it works well at various scales of development.

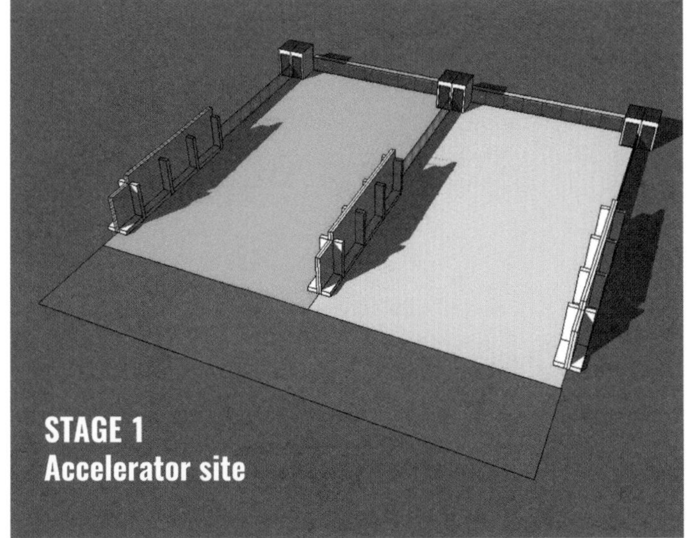

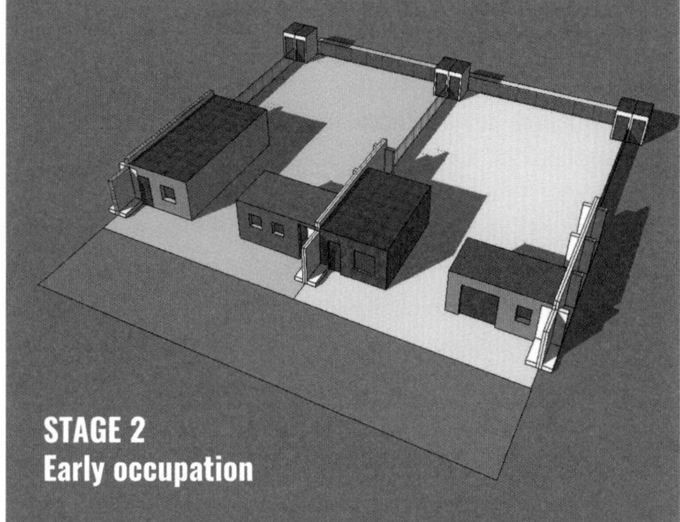

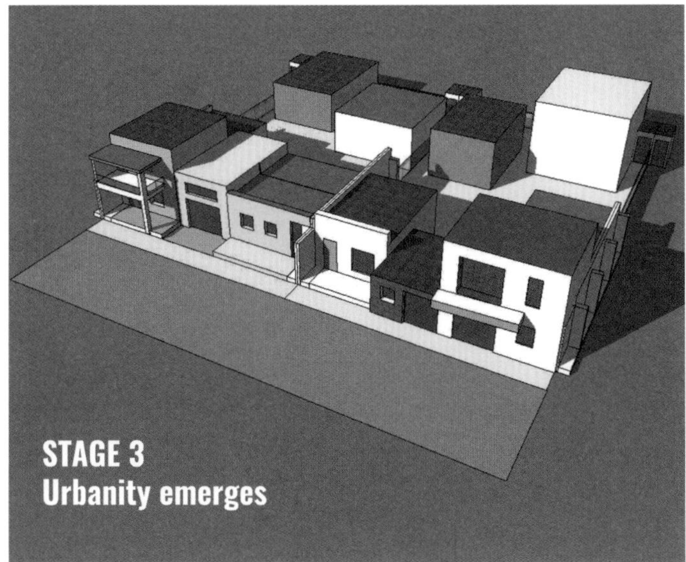

Opposite page, left: Model of Scotswood Housing Expo in Newcastle, UK. **Right:** Example of a spine wall under construction. **This page, above:** Development of the Accelerator Site concept shows how simple responsive elements can provide freedom within constraints.

CELEBRATING SUCCESS

Daniel writes to John Habraken, telling him of the success of the accelerator site project. He explains:

1 Early occupation starts with someone building their shack against the party wall, using the fins as support for the roof. Over time people harden up the street frontages of their buildings. Setting the first fin of the party wall back from the street line has left enough space to enable people to create new front porches, contributing to the social life of the street.

2 The project has allowed the shack-building industry to scale up its activities by giving it a common framework. The project now offers a materials package to prospective shack dwellers to help them get started.

3 The project provides a number of different ways in which people can enter the housing market and progress from being informal shack dwellers to becoming formal householders. Daniel has also worked with a number of housebuilders, who have developed their own range of standard housing types for the area.

4 In some cases the height of the party wall has been raised to create two-storey development. Daniel is working with his engineers to create the potential for three-storey development around some public spaces and next to main roads.

5 The project is used in combination with a range of starter-housing and full-housing solutions in a number of places, with some local authorities producing pattern books showing different responses to the party wall. Some pattern books show a toilet block attached to the spine wall.

6 Others show a completed room at the front of the site to allow early occupation. In other cases, the local authority has built the front wall to enclose the site. Others show combinations of these.

7 The accelerator site project has become known as the Nairobi Standard. It has proved simple to use, giving just the right level of help to trigger successful urban development.

> *We must define clear and simple boundaries within which people are free to organise and improvise. This means providing the enabling conditions within which endless potential solutions emerge. Structured choices enable the growth of highly responsive environments and provide a place's inhabitants with a full progression in life.*
>
> —Daniel O, Ghana

Dweller-adaptive building systems (also called DABS) are development tools that provide a set of special-purpose platforms to initiate and accelerate urban growth and change in a neighbourhood through a range of targeted physical interventions. They work alongside the final starter condition, ACTIVATORS, described on page 233, to mobilise and energise collective action and can be written in a simple operating manual. They include:

1 Urban acupuncture

> *Urban change that endures is often about carefully targeted micro interventions that can seriously change the energies and dynamics of a surrounding neighbourhood.*
>
> —Edgar Pieterse, Urban Age Awards

Urban acupuncture is an urban design approach that is similar to that of tactical urbanism or micro-urbanism. Micro-scale interventions appeal to community activists, enlightened civic leaders and cash-strapped governments, as they demonstrate proof of concept.

The term draws from Chinese acupuncture, a traditional medical practice, which makes a significant number of targeted pinpoint insertions into the human body to relieve stress, change behaviour and reenergise the patient. In the case of cities, urban acupuncture is akin to using subtle, physical, small-scale, tactical interventions into the city's neighbourhood fabric to transform the larger urban whole by relieving urban problems, changing methods and revitalising its built environment. This approach—coined by the Spanish urbanist Manuel de Solà-Morales, and championed by Jaime Lerner in Curitiba—dismisses massive urban renewal projects in favour of more localised and community-based efforts that, in an era of constrained budgets and limited resources, could offer valuable respite to urban dwellers. These can be either top-down-led or bottom-up-led interventions. Whatever form they take, they should be aimed at harnessing and directing community energy in positive ways to address the local urban problems for which they were intended. Their beauty is that they are often catalytic in addressing wider urban issues as confidence is built.

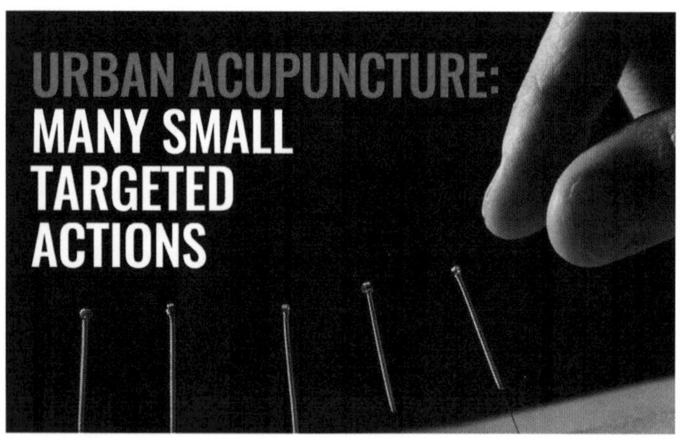

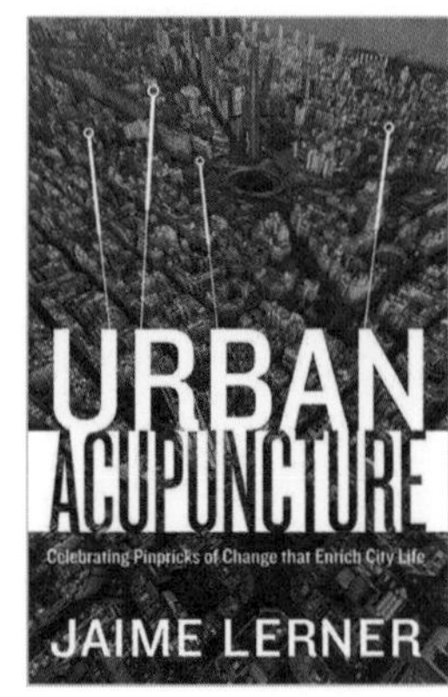

Unfortunately, the term *urban acupuncture* has been severely misused in recent years, and the temptation is to 'hammer in big nails' rather than use many pinpointed interventions. Do this, and you kill the patient and the catalysing effects of these actions. The secret lies in its subtleness and scale. Making Massive Small change demands many pinpricks.

Jaime Lerner, the former mayor of Curitiba, suggests urban acupuncture as 'the future solution for contemporary urban issues; focussing on very narrow pressure points in cities can initiate positive ripple effects for the greater society'.

The following are some examples of urban acupuncture in neighbourhoods:

→ **Street corner buildings** could become high-visibility sites to signal a change in urban quality and scale, providing local economic opportunity, a mix of uses and short-term accommodation for neighbourhood builders, amongst others.

→ **New urban housing typologies** could be built as 'show homes' to demonstrate how existing landowners can upgrade and intensify their properties.

→ **Small, public space interventions** could provide a new focus for urban life.

→ **Scale-free institutions** such as schools, daycare centres and libraries could start small and be scaled up over time.

→ **Local enterprise hubs** could provide managed workspace, communal workshops, and technical aid centres to assist urban change.

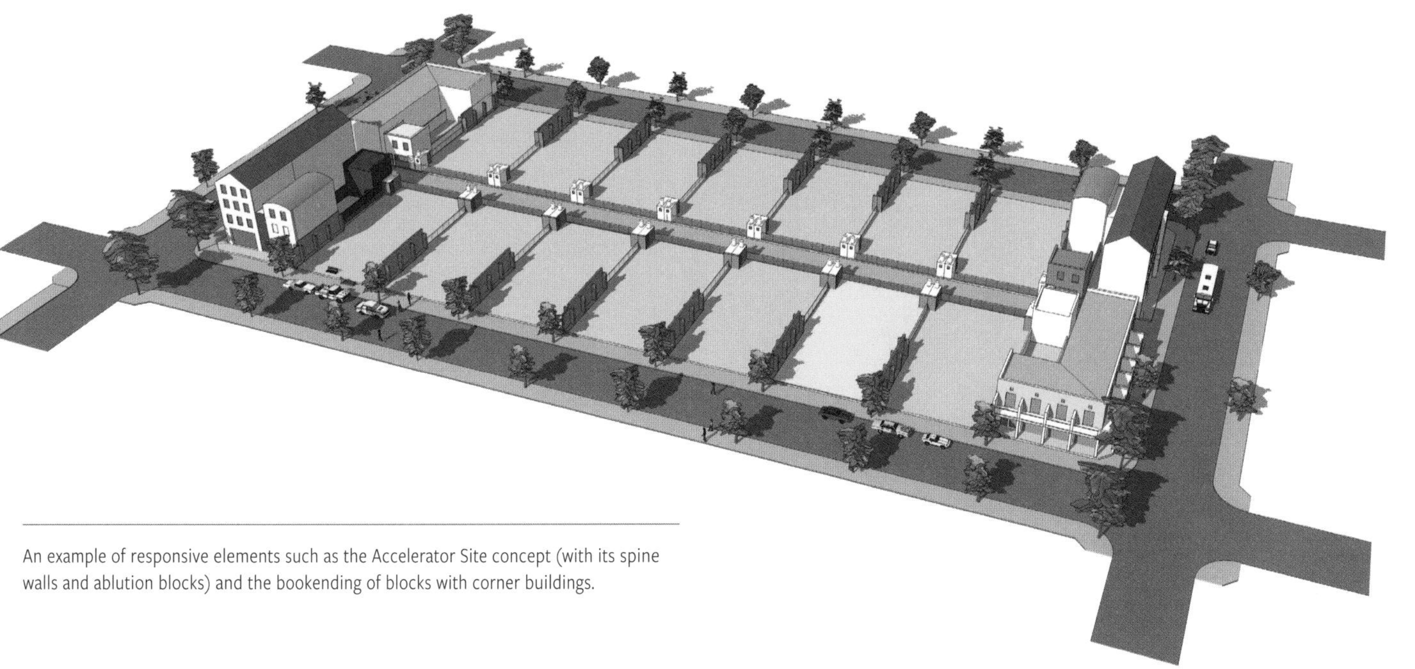

An example of responsive elements such as the Accelerator Site concept (with its spine walls and ablution blocks) and the bookending of blocks with corner buildings.

> *As with the medicine needed in the interaction between doctor and patient, in urban planning it is also necessary to make the city react; to poke an area in such a way that it can help heal, improve, and create positive chain reactions. It is indispensable in revitalising interventions to make the organism work in a different way.*
>
> —Jaime Lerner

2 Responsive elements

Responsive elements are targeted building interventions that provide a simple kick start to the neighbourhood building process and go on to accelerate development at all scales. Responsive elements are designed to create responsive action from the urban dweller and stimulate collective action that could lead to co-creating new conditions and influencing emerging patterns in urban development. Responsive elements are particularly useful in cash-strapped conditions and act like 'starter packs', facilitating early occupation of the neighbourhood or home. More importantly, they provide a means of moving development from a suburban to an urban condition, recognising that the interface between adjacent urban dwellers is the single most important thing to get right, particularly in those countries where there is not a strong urban tradition. The lot or plot, although providing the best constraints on development, does not alone ensure this.

> *When every action has a purpose, every action has a result.*
>
> —Greg Plitt

An easy way of demonstrating the importance of a responsive element is to draw an imagined neighbourhood and then start rubbing out things until you cannot rub out anymore before you destroy the essence of the place. What is left is then essential to triggering growth and change.

As regards platforms, examples of responsive elements at neighbourhood and house scale include:

→ **Colonnades** provide an early way of defining neighbourhood public space and street corners and create the preconditions for active frontage in the form of marketplaces, shops, local institutions and workspace to evolve over time.
→ **Spine walls,** also called party walls, built along the boundaries between properties create a common framework for housing to start and urban development to be accelerated. Early occupation starts with someone building against the spine wall. Over time people harden up the street frontages of their buildings.
→ **Frontage elements** provide the block enclosure, with street walls and front porches, to new development, ensuring the site can be secured. In combination with spine walls and service cores, they enable early occupation in informal buildings that can improve over time.
→ **Service cores** include building toilet blocks and washing facilities that can be incorporated in new development over time. The location of these is crucial to the future evolution of the house.
→ **Core housing,** also called starter housing, provides a minimum liveable space and can be extended incrementally according to the occupants' needs, as they are able. Core housing can be combined with spine walls and service cores. The Elemental project in Chile is an example of this.
→ **Shell and core,** a term borrowed from office development, provides the basic multi-storied structure of the building with its serviced core and access. As a responsive element, this enables future occupants to fit out their own space as needed.

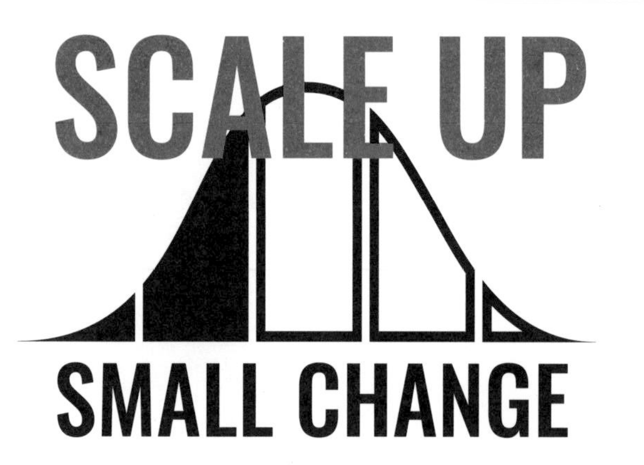

SCALING URBAN INFRASTRUCTURE

Urban infrastructure is the underlying base or foundation for a neighbourhood and, as such, provides one of the most important catalysts for progressive urban development. Infrastructure includes utility networks, movement systems, public spaces and social assets (schools, daycare centres, clinics, etc.). It is essential that the layout of NETWORKS and BLOCKS facilitate the early installation of this urban infrastructure, recognising that it can be scaled up as development increases.

PRINCIPLES

1 Start small and scale up

The temptation for infrastructure is to design a system based on a future end state that might take some years to materialise. Engineers still fall back on solutions that are supposedly known to be safe, and they are reluctant to learn by experimenting. It's too risky, they say. It seems easier to make a case for a big solution than for targeted local interventions that may have a far greater local impact. So, the large outfall sewer is still seen as the only way of solving drainage problems in cities, yet experience in India has shown that you can use natural or decentralised systems far more efficiently.

Recognising that roads are continuously dug up as conditions change, we need to start small and improve incrementally. Most systems can be added to. As places mature, and in some circumstances transition from informal to formal settlements, people's circumstances change and higher levels of services infrastructure become more affordable. As long as our networks remain open and adaptive, infrastructure can be upgraded. There are numerous examples of scaleable, modular infrastructure solutions that can act as platforms for urban growth and change.

2 Look at the whole

In terms of scaleable urban infrastructure, neighbourhoods offer significant advantages and opportunities for more sustainable forms of development:

- → They have a rich mix of uses, which makes it easier to balance loads and match the intermittent supply of renewables.
- → They have larger flows of energy, water and waste with which to work.
- → They can influence, through design, transportation choices and reduce vehicular use.
- → When designing at the neighbourhood scale, public spaces can be brought into play to temper the climate, absorb carbon, clean stormwater and sewer effluent, provide biomass for energy and even grow food.

If neighbourhoods can become their own micro-utility, supplying the bulk of their energy while treating and recycling their water and waste, a whole new form of urban neighbourhood is possible. In addition, if all of the energy can be generated locally and much of the waste processed on site, the cost and loss of efficiency in utilities and transport infrastructure can be avoided.

3 Scale-free thinking

Many of our neighbourhood facilities can start small and be scaled up. Schools can start in underused buildings, use underused facilities and use underutilised human capital in a neighbourhood. Jarmo Suominen at MIT Media Lab is focussing on new ways of developing schools as distributed systems by managing underutilised spaces and resources in a neighbourhood more effectively. The concept of a conventional learning environment was revolutionised when the students of Haukilahti Upper Secondary School started their studies on decentralised premises on the Aalto University campus in Otaniemi. The solution supports new ways of learning, increases the joy of learning and opens the school doors to joint operations and networking. It makes for more efficient use of space when the facilities are flexible and the rest of the environment is utilised in teaching.

Daycare centres can start in disused shops. Libraries can move around or be shelves in local shops. In Detroit, the function of the library has been shifted to space under seats at bus stops, with great effect. Post offices have already been devolved to local shops. There is no reason why these social assets cannot all remain as distributed systems.

Scale-free Schools is a design proposal by Architecture 00 in London for a new infrastructure of education in the twenty-first century. It focusses on what the changing roles of educators, new ideas for learning, emerging technologies and constrained resources mean for the infrastructure of learning and argues that the school as we know it is not the most efficient way of delivering education. Equally, we can question all of our other social assets. In an increasingly bottom-up world, we can see different opportunities for social development in a neighbourhood. We don't have to rely on formal models alone to start.

MEANWHILE USES

The potential of meanwhile or temporary uses have long been seen as motors of urban change, and it is only in recent years, through a range of successful cultural and economic projects, that we can assess their true effects as catalysts. We have seen the effects of the occupations by temporary artists' colonies in places such as Bushwick in New York, Temple Bar in Dublin or Maboneng in Johannesburg, and the regenerative effects they have had. We can also witness the success of the street market as a temporary event. Meanwhile, they thrive in places where things have stalled, and people do not know what to do. The uncertainty and openness attract and inspire others.

The urban catalyst project

Studies undertaken in Berlin and other European cities through the Urban Catalyst project have shown that although meanwhile uses are thought of differently, they are important to the urban development process.

> *Temporary uses are not considered to be part of normal cycles of urban development. If a building or area becomes vacant, it is expected to be re-planned, built over and used as soon as possible. Temporary uses are often associated with crisis, a lack of vision and chaos. But, despite all preconceptions, temporary uses can become an extremely successful, inclusive and innovative part of a contemporary urban culture.*
>
> —Klaus Overmeyer

The Urban Catalyst showed that through apparently spontaneous and unplanned temporary uses, viable patterns and mechanisms emerged. However, it noted that meanwhile uses do not emerge accidentally but are guided by different conditions and rules. Urban players act deliberately and follow their ambitions, as folllows:

→ **Citizens become temporary users to follow different aims.** Meanwhile users are motivated by the goal to claim vacant spaces and make them breeding grounds for the development of their ideas. They see this process as something different to formal processes that occur in highly regulated urban environments.

→ **Specific vacant sites attract specific meanwhile uses.** In choosing certain sites or buildings, users follow their own precise spatial criteria that allow their ideas to take root and grow.

→ **Meanwhile uses flourish with a minimum amount of investment.** These uses can recycle and use existing structures and spaces with minimal intervention.

→ **Meanwhile uses are mostly organised in networks and use clusters.** The clusters are characterised by their use profiles. A cluster is sustained by its complex internal networks, which means that temporary programmes often attract similar uses to the same or a nearby site.

→ **Meanwhile uses are initiated through many committed agents.** In many cases, temporary programmes only become possible through the determined action of these agents, who bridge the gap between users, the site owner and local authorities.

→ **Meanwhile uses are an urban laboratory for new cultures and social economies.** These programmes create a unique environment of experiment, where ideas can mature in time, leading to the foundations of many start-up ventures.

Without doubt, meanwhile uses is emergence in all its forms. They only require allowing it to happen.

Top: Cany Ash's Caravanserai project, developed on a vacant site in East London, was a succesful arts- and cultural-related meanwhile use, to support the 2012 London Olympics.

THE CREATIVE EDUCATOR

HOW A NEW TYPE OF SCHOOL HARNESSED COLLECTIVE INTELLIGENCE

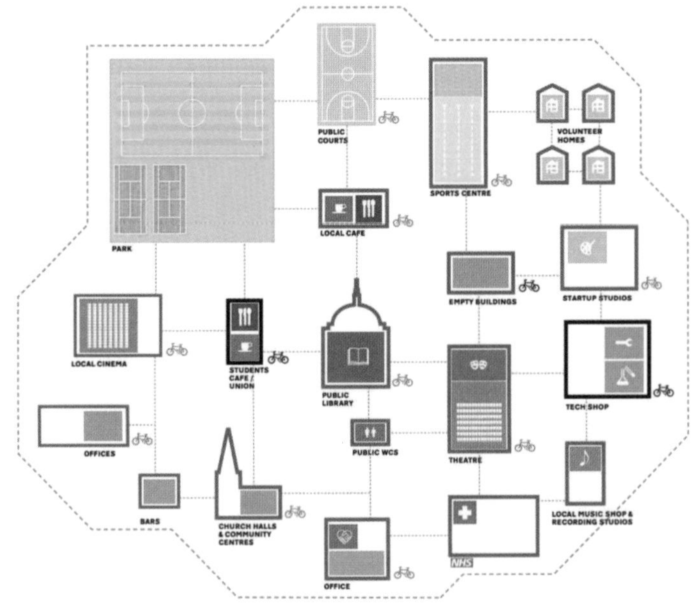

Formal education has failed to reach the grassroots in Andrew's neighbourhood. He has recently retired from his job as head teacher at a state school in the Easterhouse suburb of Glasgow, but he thinks he can still make a difference by educating underprivileged children in his community.

Andrew is a great believer in Ivan Illich's work on 'Deschooling Society'. This is well expressed in the view of the educationalist Ken Robinson that modern education is killing the creativity in children. In a TED Talk Robinson says that education has to develop on three fronts if it is to engage and succeed. First, it should foster diversity by offering a broad curriculum and individualising the learning process. Second, it should foster curiosity through creative teaching, which depends on high-quality teacher training and development. Finally, it should focus on awakening creativity through alternative processes that put less emphasis on standardised testing, thereby giving the responsibility for defining the course of education to individual schools and teachers.

> *Education doesn't need to be reformed: it needs to be transformed. The key to this transformation is not to standardise education, but to personalise it, to build achievement on discovering the individual talents of each child, to put students in an environment where they want to learn and where they can naturally discover their true passions.*
>
> —Ken Robinson

Robinson believes that much of the present education system fosters conformity, compliance and standardisation, rather than creative approaches to learning. 'We can only succeed if we recognise that education is an organic system, not a mechanical one,' he says. 'Successful school administration is a matter of fostering a helpful climate rather than a command-and-control attitude.'

Headlines about a broken Britain have become a recurring theme in UK politics. They capture a sense that community spirit has withered and died, that family relationships have fragmented, that a citizen's sense of responsibility has been eroded, and that crime is on the increase. The moral panic feeds off popular anxieties about dependency on welfare, the proliferation of young unmarried mothers, the isolation of the elderly and the doomed future of youth.

Some think Easterhouse is not broken, only because it never worked in the first place. Since more than 50,000 people were moved there in the 1950s and 1960s, mainly through slum clearance, Easterhouse has faced a severe lack of facilities and jobs.

While Andrew was principal at the main secondary school serving Easterhouse, he thought that things were at last getting better. But he was always battling to raise the confidence of pupils who sensed that they were trapped, with limited opportunities. Despite eventually being provided with bright new buildings, the underlying social problems remained. 'In our old school, every Monday I used to count the broken windows,' he says. 'There has been a significant shift in a sense of community ownership but there is a lot more work to do. It's not about just throwing money at the area; we need to change hearts and minds and give kids a sense of purpose.

'More important, families need a sense of purpose, too. It is no good if high-achieving pupils come back to a home environment where there is a dragging anchor of hopelessness. We need to build social capital at every level. The way we deliver education could be the way of catalysing this in the wider community.' This is something Andrew wants to tackle, but he wants to do it from the bottom up.

ANDREW SEES THE FAILURE OF THE SYSTEM

1 Education focusses on capital projects more than social development. Too often new buildings are seen as the solution.
2 Schools are treated as learning factories. You're either in or you're out of the system. Many young people fall out of the system.
3 The system does not take advantage of the latent social and cultural capital that exists in the neighbourhood. Below the surface there are educated, knowledgeable and skilled individuals who could help if given the chance.
4 Learning is separated from community-building, with little done to combat social breakdown and rebuild respect systems.

5 The potential energy and creativity of young people are neglected. Formal education can kill creativity.
6 The system fails to make learning a total experience; instead, it restricts learning to school hours.

ANDREW LOOKS TO A DIFFERENT MODEL

Andrew was heartened by the debate between young people during the Scottish referendum. They want a different society and he thinks he can help. He sees the problem of education in Easterhouse through the other side of the lens. Education could build social capital and transform the community.

Andrew has heard about the free schools project in England. Introduced by the government as part of the Big Society initiative, it enables parents, teachers, charities and businesses to set up their own schools. These non-profit-making, independent, state-funded schools are free for students to attend, but they are not controlled by the local authority. Getting such a school started takes a great deal of capital, and this is not quite what Andrew wants. But some of the principles could usefully be applied.

Andrew sees the video for Scale-free Schools, commissioned by Diarmaid Lawlor at Architecture and Design Scotland. It asks whether the shiny new institutional buildings of the boom times are really the most appropriate model for learning in the coming decades. Can we take their most successful elements and apply them in a smarter, more nimble way? What are the roles of the community in education and of education in communities?

Andrew wants Easterhouse to become a model Scale-free School. He knows that the place has many underused community assets. Parks are empty during the week; churches are closed for long hours; and the community centre, library and leisure centre all have space for more activities. If we used these, Andrew realises, we would no longer need to think of a school as a single building. The school could be:

→ a civic institution embedded in the community
→ part of the town centre of Easterhouse
→ adaptable to how its teachers and pupils want to use it

In other words, Easterhouse could become the school. It could form partnerships with its local businesses and organisations to help provide for the school. Less money could be spent on capital costs and more on operational costs. Andrew is inspired, but he is still talking about buildings. Could he take this concept further? He knows many people in the community who have skills that are locked up in their heads. Could you get older people to bring their experience to bear? Are there skills in the community that are lacking in the classroom? Are there services that could be provided that would keep money in the community and build the economy of Easterhouse?

Andrew hears about community asset mapping. This is a process where local people make a map or inventory of the resources, skills and talents of individuals, associations and organisations in their community. The knowledge is used to revitalise relationships and mutual support, rebuild communities and neighbourhoods, and rediscover collective power. Most communities have a considerable supply of assets and resources that could be used to build the community and solve problems. Asset mapping helps to identify them.

Andrew finds that Mrs. MacDonald was a pianist and has the only first-class piano in Easterhouse. Could a music school start in her front room? Mr. Williams was a cricket umpire at Lords. Could this be the start of a resurgence of Scottish cricket? Mr. Patel is the local pharmacist. Could he teach practical science? There are many other people with exceptional skills, and most of them agree to help.

This unlocks a totally different set of possibilities. Andrew starts the Easterhouse Community School with the local community centre as its base. Other buildings are used for classes.

ANDREW SUMS UP

A couple of years later he sums up what is special about about his school's project in Easterhouse:

→ The oldies have been mobilised. People with experience who were previously marginalised and lonely have become vital cogs in the community. They share their knowledge and there is greater respect between the generations.
→ Volunteering in the community by the children at the community school becomes widespread.
→ Kids walk between classes to different locations. The younger children join with others on supervised walks (called 'crocodiles'). Older people look out for them. Obesity levels amongst children fall.
→ The kids have their lunch (using Jamie Oliver's recipes) at the leisure centre. Local jobs are created and money is kept in the community. The good diet improves health further.
→ Different approaches to learning emerge outside the mainstream curriculum. Children are exposed to different ways of thinking. Confidence builds, as Ken Robinson predicted it would.
→ Easterhouse flourishes, transforming itself from a neighbourhood of social failure to social success.
→ It worked because it made everyone feel relevant and it grew out of the place. Educated people were not made to feel superior to those who struggled. Education became a social purpose and not just a way of getting employed, although many of our children went on to get good jobs. They were a different breed of kids. They were confident and organised.

> *I wanted to call what we created the School of Collective Wisdom, but that was too grand for the locals. My surname is MacAdam. They called it the Macadamy.*
>
> —Andrew M, Scotland

DEMONSTRATING THE POSSIBLE

The best catalyst for urban change is the example. Late adopters need to gain confidence by seeing the sense of the possible to change their behaviours. Processes of experimentation and learning that trigger bottom-up activity to transform places are vital. Therefore, this experimentation should be undertaken in public with the public. There are a number of ways of doing this, including:

1. **Demonstration projects.** These could show new methods and solutions to accelerating building activities; involve active participation by citizens in the building process; or provide in-situ training of building apprentices.

2. **Neighbourhood expositions.** These could include introducing show homes and open house days to celebrate successful local projects; showing examples of new urban housing typologies; providing cost breakdowns for prospective builders; and stimulating the local property market towards viability.

3. **Neighbourhood challenges.** Examples include local public space clean-up projects; ideas competitions; engagement with local universities and technical institutions to work with communities; and open bids to local government to fund catalytic projects.

4. **Cooperative building projects.** These could include local government supporting groups of active citizens working collectively to build social facilities (such as schools, accommodations and play spaces) and urban infrastructure programmes.

SHOW
WHAT
YOU
MEAN
WHAT
YOU
SHOW

BUILDING CAPACITY FOR SMALL-SCALE DEVELOPMENT

> *We are working toward a more generative real estate model, where local people can invest in their neighbourhoods and in that process, create new life and value that benefits their community. The kind of places we want to live in are built and maintained by people who love them.*
>
> —Incremental Development Alliance

Scale makes all the difference to neighbourhood building. The size constraints of small-scale developers limits them to a particular scope of project. They don't have the resources for large-scale developments, so they need to focus on small, simple buildings in a relatively concentrated area so they can easily keep an eye on things. Small-scale developers depend on the economies that arise from resourcefulness and relationships. It is these qualities that make them so adaptable in difficult times.

Building typologies for small-scale developers are those that span the gap between single-family houses and larger apartment buildings—ideal for intensifying suburbia or restructuring failed housing estates. They are also best suited for adapting neighbourhoods on a lot or plot basis, adding new homes without substantially changing the nature or scale of the street. Time has proven how important and practical these buildings are in stitching a neighbourhood together through thick and thin, generation after generation. These are the buildings that strengthen local economies and work for local markets.

To help build capacity in this sector, the Incremental Development Alliance, founded in 2015, provides a range of training workshops in many cities in the United States. The workshops take a big-picture view of neighbourhood-based development to help participants understand what makes a good viable project and how small-scale developers interact with urban professionals. They provide an opportunity for participants to bring an actual project in front of other seasoned small-scale developers. In small groups, participants work through exercises, applying them to their particular projects.

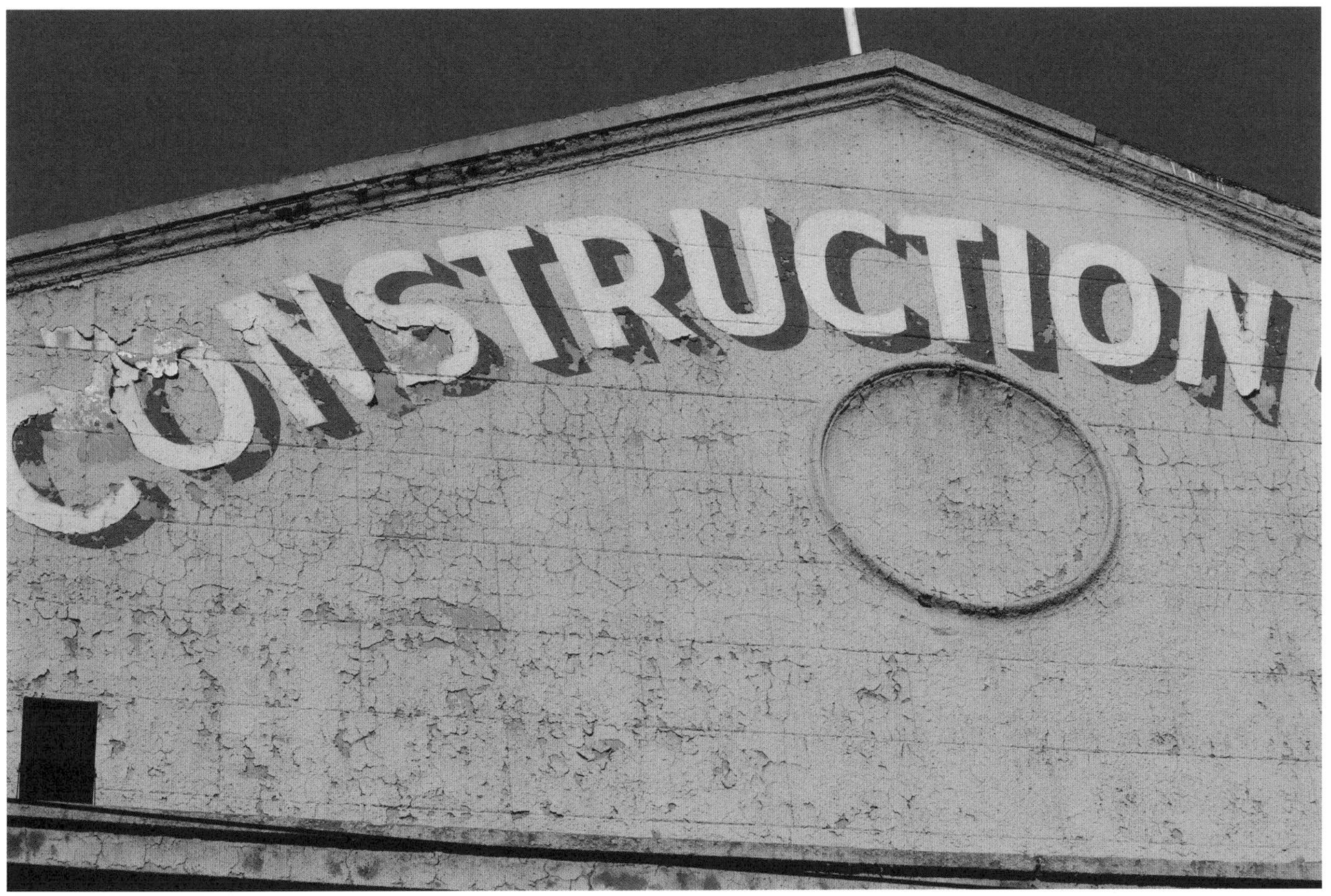

SUPPORTING PLATFORMS

Supporting platforms include a wide raft of neighbourhood support programmes that provide the infrastructure for initiating and accelerating neighbourhood building and social innovation. These include:

1 **Technical assistance** includes working with the local building industry and suppliers to scale up local activity; providing plan-drawing and building-approvals assistance to urban dwellers; and providing on-site training to self-builders and local contractors.

2 **Builder's warehouses** use the buying power of the public sector to provide cheaper building materials and components for local builders. This could include safe local storage facilities during the construction process and transport services.

3 **Communal workshops** could provide shared equipment, tool hire and access to brick- and block-making yards for people to invest their sweat equity, as opportunities arise.

4 **Temporary accommodation** provides social support to those displaced as a result of the construction process. This could involve local government building temporary shelters or housing people in spaces above corner shops—spaces that could later be given over to rented accommodations.

5 **Enterprise support** could involve apprenticeships in the building industry; development of local economic opportunities in the development supply chain; cheap accommodation in enterprise hubs; and business incubator support for local entrepreneurs.

Platforms provide the vital crossover point between the role of government and the responsive actions of people. Get these right, and the energy, creativity and goodwill of people will be released.

LOCALIA URBAN NEIGHBOURHOOD

TAKING THE FIRST STEPS IN DEVELOPMENT

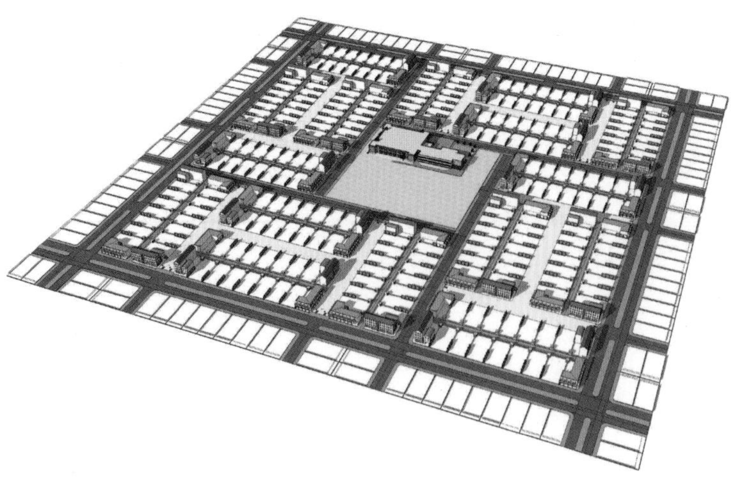

The local authority establishes a Neighbourhood Enabling Agency (NEA) tasked with ensuring that the full spectrum of entry-level housing choices is met for each of the income groups. They are not tasked with providing houses—their purpose is to release the potential of housing by providing the necessary starter conditions.

Armed with ward blocks comprising regular blocks that have been subdivided into 15-metre-wide (50 feet) lots, they have a structured framework for people to choose from a range of addressed plot and lot options.

It is on this basis they initiate and accelerate development:

The population demographics
The emerging population of Localia, our imaginary neighbourhood, has three main socio-economic groups:

1 **The formal settlers:** A lower-middle-income group of people in stable employment with the ability to raise limited mortgage funds. Their demand is for affordable housing.

2 **The precariat:** A low-income group who work in one or more short-term, gig-economy jobs. They can raise capital from local savings union, social housing grants or small starter loans. They are looking for co-operative housing schemes, social housing or starter housing.

3 **The strugglers:** A large group with sporadic income that lives on the edge of poverty and who primarily operates in the informal sector. They are looking for basic shelter and a foothold in the neighbourhood. As they are unlikely to get access to any form of formal borrowing, they are looking to invest their limited income and sweat equity (individually or collectively) in solving their own housing needs.

Step 1: The NEA establishes clear principles.

→ Everyone has different starting points and different endings. Some will move quicker and finish sooner. Some will start slower and take longer.
→ Everyone has the right to be supported at any stage in the process. This support can take the form of technical support, temporary accommodation or mobilising local help.
→ Everyone has the right to choose the path they wish to take to ensure meeting their whole-life housing needs.
→ Everyone is encouraged to self-organise, work collectively and share ideas to think and act small while still achieving economies of scale.

Step 2: The NEA mobilises the local building industry.

→ They develop a range of simple building standards that everyone can comprehend at every level.
→ They develop procurement routes based on small contracts that are renewed if standards are met.
→ They develop panels of approved contractors and subcontractors to enable people to make safe choices.
→ They develop local supply chains, including local block-making and reclaimed materials yards.
→ They develop and train local craftspeople to produce building components, such as windows, doors and staircases.

Step 3: The NEA develops a range of spine wall options.

→ They develop a set of standards based on a modular system that can be built by the full spectrum of building industry.
→ They show, by demonstration, how the spine wall could help the lowest level of entry to the building process and progress to a final outcome.
→ They provide a framework of starter options to assist people in their early decision-making and scale up growth and change.
→ They work with the building industry to develop typological solutions based on the spine walls.

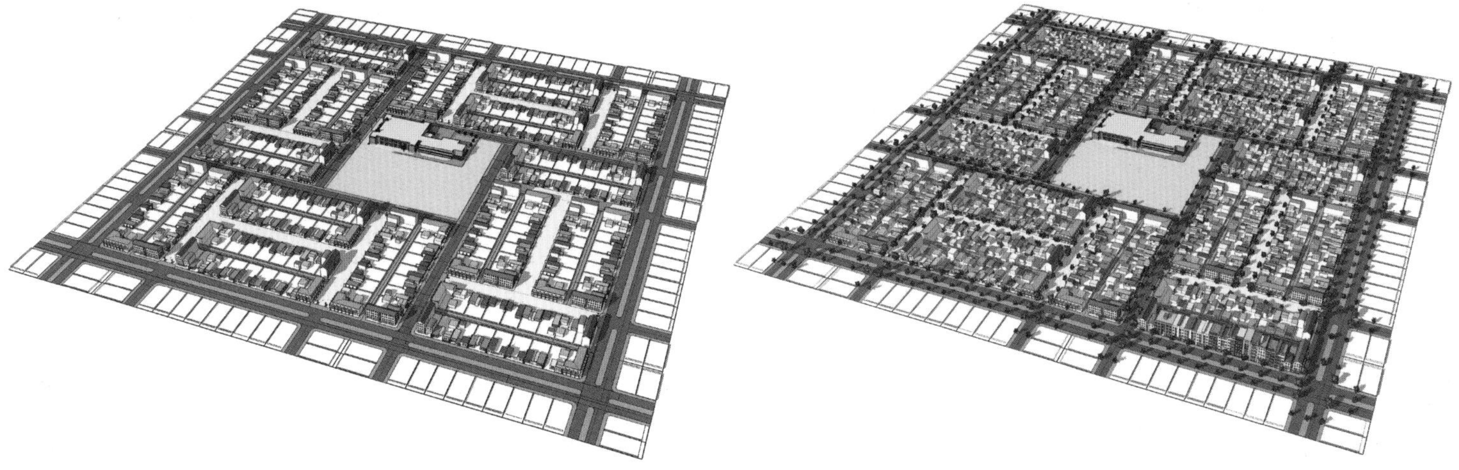

Step 4: The NEA develops a range of infrastructure options.

- → They offer, as a base option, a toilet building for each lot, based on a collection system. Water supply is initially provided on a delivery basis. Electricity starts with a minimum service to building street frontages.
- → They offer, as the next stage, a water supply system with standpipes within public spaces and shared surface street blocks.
- → They develop main road networks with a full range of services.
- → They work on an infrastructure plan to progressively work with local contractors and mobilised people to connect the base toilet blocks to a drainage system. Water supply is laid down the back lanes.

Step 5: The NEA develops a range of starter building options.

- → They put their initial efforts and resources on building a variety of long-life, loose-fit corner buildings of different heights. They offer hostel accommodation for a fixed period to those building their own houses. Ground floors become shops, enterprise space, and daycare centres.
- → They later convert the upper floors to social housing units or rental accommodation, or sell these spaces, depending on demand.
- → They develop starter school buildings that are initially used as building workshops, training institutions, technical assistance centres and storage facilities. As the community stabilises these buildings move towards being fully-fledged schools and community facilities.

For each of our groups there are different routes and different outcomes:

1. **The formal settlers:** They can purchase plots and procure completed housing from a range of sources. Local contractors develop their house types in response to spine-wall specifications and plot dimensions, some offering two- and three-storey homes. They can go on to intensify development by opening up additional accommodation on the back lanes. Others choose to follow the self-build route.

2. **The precariat:** They group to jointly build or procure their housing. The NEA offers narrow-fronted apartment options on four to six floors on the main roads. The scheme adopts an approach, based on the principles of the Berlin Townhouse project, to solve housing needs. The buildings become increasingly mixed use as people start their businesses.

3. **The strugglers:** They are encouraged to self-organise to jointly develop full lots as demonstrated in the Nairobi accelerator site project. Working with the shack building industry or building themselves, groups of families start early occupation on the sites and progressively improve their homes as time and economics allow. The NEA provides technical assistance to ensure basic standards are met.

Opposite: A ward block with starter elements—spines walls, ablution blocks and corner buildings. **Top left:** Early occupation of the ward block. **Top right:** Evolution of the area into a fully functioning neighbourhood.

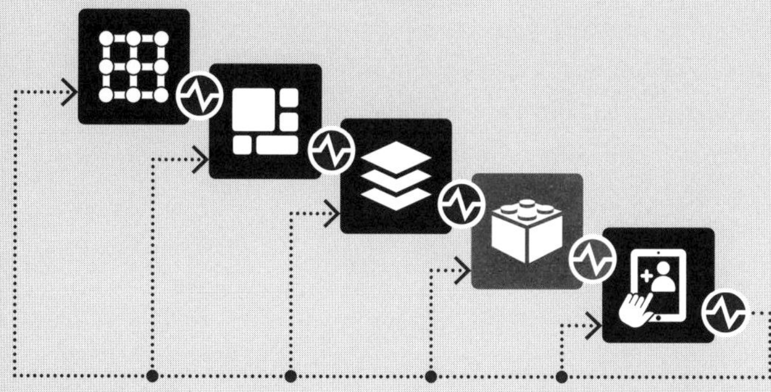

DEFAULTS

AS SIMPLE STRUCTURES FOR COMPLEX CHOICE

Defaults, our fourth condition, are enabling mechanisms that structure choice to create infinite possibilities. They build off our two previous conditions—blocks and platforms—and lead to the evolution of our building typologies at a variety of scales, to create an emergent urban vernacular fit for its time and purpose. Defaults are standard settings or choices that apply to individuals who do not take active steps to change them. They are a soft way of influencing positive choices, where development is more likely to turn out in a way proven to make good urbanism work from experience.

Default *NOUN*

1 The choices or presets that apply in the absence of active intervention

2 The standard options or types favoured by the conforming majority

3 The starting points from which changes can be made and choices improved

SYNONYMS
preset, standard choice, setting, fallback position, norm, normal

SCOPE

This section deals with three main theories that apply to creating defaults: structuring complex choices, the nature of conformity and the diffusion of innovation. It goes on to describe the qualities necessary for defaults to work and then considers six main topics:

1 **Towards an emerging urban vernacular.** It looks at developing a response relevant to our time

2 **Typological solutions.** It explores the use of pattern books in the past to structure vernacular

3 **The sweet spot of urban density.** It looks at medium-density, long-life, loose-fit neighbourhood solutions

4 **An open framework of choice.** It shows types of action and types of choice available to individuals, collectives and institutions

5 **Development tools.** It shows how the parameter book can be applied in forming neighbourhoods

6 **Localia urban neighbourhood—structuring complex housing choices.** It shows an imaginary example of this process at work

THEORY

Structuring complex choices

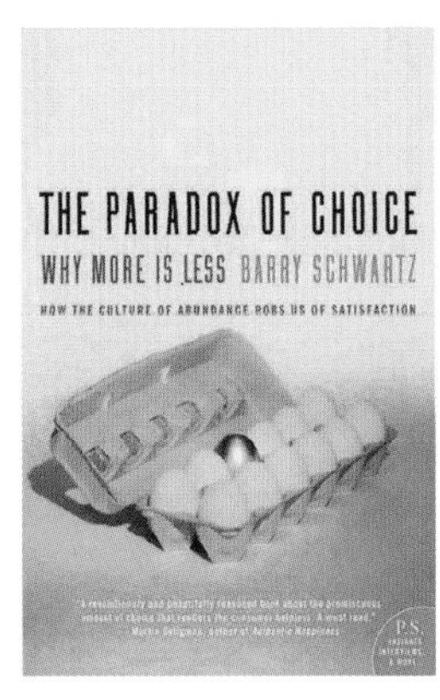

Are *flexibility* and *choice*, when used together, the two most dangerous words in the English language? Barry Schwartz, in his book *The Paradox of Choice: Why More Is Less*, has some interesting observations. As choice increases, the exercising of choice diminishes and with this comes the fear of choice. In other words, the question becomes: have I made the right choice?

Schwartz likens this to buying an insurance policy. As insurance companies offer more choices of complex products, prospective customers put off making any choice with the fear that they will make the wrong decision. As choice increases, take up reduces. Absolute choice is, therefore, no choice. What we are looking for is a limited choice with infinite possibilities...like a well-cooked meal that we can flavour! In urban terms, this is what society has always done. Some call it vernacular, and others refer to it as the prevailing norm: the rules in which urbanism can flourish at every level.

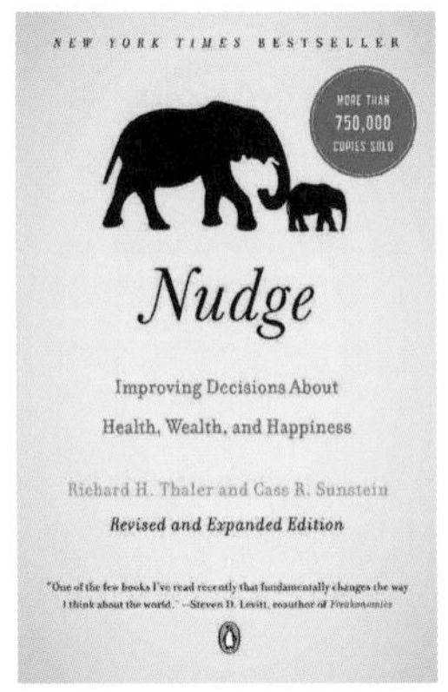

Choice architecture describes the way in which decisions are influenced by how the choices are presented and is a term used by Cass Sunstein and economist Richard Thaler in their 2008 book *Nudge: Improving Decisions about Health, Wealth, and Happiness*. They stress the importance of structuring complex choices and show that people adapt different strategies for making choices depending on the size and complexity of the available options:

> When we face a small number of well-understood alternatives, we tend to examine all the attributes of all the alternatives and then make trade-offs when necessary. But when the choice set gets too large, we must use alternative (simplifying) strategies, and these get us into trouble.

Using choice architecture, we can construct default choices and incentives to influence choice, and this can be applied to the design of urban environments.

> *Most innovative designers consciously reject the standard option box and cultivate an appetite for thinking wrong.*
>
> —Marty Neumeier

Behavioural scientists attribute this choice phenomenon to the 'status quo bias', the prevailing human resistance to changing one's behaviour, combined with another common phenomenon: the tendency to conform. Nowhere is this more true than in housing choice, and this fact is what has driven the volume of housebuilders' products over the years. So the real questions are:

- → What choices are available?
- → What are the pathways to this choice?
- → Having made a choice, how do I procure it?

These questions give rise to something more fundamental. What is the standard offer and, if I don't like it, how can I modify it or do something completely different?

The nature of conformity

> *Human behaviour is not so complex that it cannot be understood on the basis of just a few simple postulates, or by the operations of what we might regard as natural forces or herd instincts.*
>
> —Philip Ball

Conformity is a natural instinct in people. People conform for a number of different reasons, but it largely involves changing behaviours to 'fit in' or 'go along' with people around you. This influence might mean agreeing with or acting like most of the individuals in a specific group, or it could involve behaving in a particular way in order to be seen as being 'normal' by the same group. This nature of conformity is particularly prevalent in neighbourhoods.

The Neighbourhood Planning Act in the United Kingdom gives the potential for local design guidance where communities determine what they like or dislike, a condition that has many designers squirming. A report called 'What Home Buyers Want', by the UK's design watchdog the Commission for Architecture and the Built Environment (CABE), throws up many unsurprising facts. The survey by Mulholland Research and Consulting that underlies this report shows that most people want to live somewhere distinctive and with character—which is often expressed as a preference for old buildings rather than new. But it is a richer architecture that is wanted, and bland 'traditional' and minimal modernism are both unpopular. Individuality is desirable, within limits—a home should look similar but not the same as others in the vicinity.

Ted Stevens's experience at the NACSBA reinforces CABE's data, where the greatest call from its members was for standard plans, not 'grand designs'. Nicolas Boys Smith of Create Streets, in his research paper 'The Homes London Needs', is also clear that most people are looking for familiar typologies—what he calls street-based, popular homes—as an antidote to the bland models we use today. Developing local urban vernacular places more emphasis on local communities' stated preferences. It places more emphasis on designers to innovate within these constraints.

The tipping point

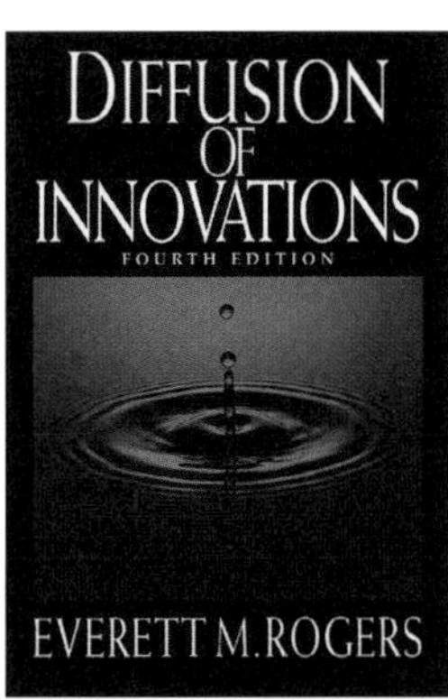

Behavioural research by Everett Rogers into the 'tipping point' for adopting new ideas has shown that when given a choice, most people tend to choose the new offer once early innovation has been accepted by the early adopters. If you look at Rogers' bell curve, presented and explained in his book *Diffusion of Innovations*, it explains this preponderance of conformity. The largest number of adopters of any process is the early and late majority and the 'laggards', accounting for well over 80 per cent of the total. According to Rogers, the 'early majority'—accounting for some 34 per cent of the total—rather than looking for revolutionary changes, are motivated by evolutionary changes.

They have three principles they follow:

1. When it is time to move, let's move together.
2. When we pick an innovation to lead us to the new paradigm, let us all pick the same one.
3. Once the transition starts, the sooner we get it over with, the better.

In the absence of continuous innovation, it is the early majority that the housebuilders fail to mobilise effectively. They are the group who will stabilise the next default settings. The next 34 per cent of adopters are the 'late majority'. They are doubtful, traditional and are very cost sensitive and require completely preassembled, bulletproof solutions. They are the classic conformers to which the default settings apply. The last 16 per cent of the adopters consists of 'laggards'. Laggards are sceptics who want only to maintain the status quo.

If you apply these statistics to bottom-up neighbourhood formation, it shows that developing the quality and content of the standard offer, once you have triggered innovation, will have a far greater impact than any other single factor in delivering successful places.

QUALITIES OF DEFAULTS

Defaults need a number of qualities to be useful. These are also drivers of change and include the following:

1. **Scaleability** is the capability of the urban planning, design and development system to enlarge the potential of a typical solution to accommodate rapid growth and change—increasing its total output under an increased load when additional resources are added. It implies a two-way process: the potential for scaling up or scaling down.

2. **Interchangeability** (also referred as interoperability) is a property of the planning, design and development system where one typical solution is capable of replacing the other without causing any need for alteration or adjustment to fulfil the same requirement. In housing, this could be seen as one house type replacing another within the constraints of the same plot or lot. It is just like 'plug and play'.

3. **Replicability** is the property of a building that allows it to be duplicated at another location or time with significant benefits in time and cost savings. This quality is particularly important to the development of normative housing, also called 'urban vernacular', where the lessons learnt can be reapplied. The outcome is not always an identical outcome, but it demonstrates the same broad characteristics.

These drivers work together to initiate and accelerate growth and change. In building urban neighbourhoods, these qualities of defaults can be explained through urban typology—the common characteristics found in many buildings and urban places. These features could be categorised in different ways, from their scale and intensity of development, to their degrees of formality or informality, to their underlying school of thought (say, modernist or traditional). The individual characteristics can be seen as patterns, which relate hierarchically across all levels (from small details to neighbourhood scale).

These qualities can also be seen as the outcomes of the invisible chassis—open adaptive NETWORKS, clear regular BLOCKS, and initiating and accelerating PLATFORMS.

TOWARDS AN EMERGING URBAN VERNACULAR

There is nothing wrong with the concept of the standard offer. We have been using it for years. We call it the 'norm'—a standard or model or pattern regarded as typical—and most societies have evolved their responses to doing things in a normal way. Most of the cities we love have these qualities, as *Monocle* magazine shows in its Top 25 Liveable Cities. In housing, we call it the 'popular home'. In urbanism, we call it 'vernacular', and we can take inspiration from it.

The formal characteristics of both vernacular urbanism and housing appear as a consequence of well-determined needs, easily coping with the demand of social, cultural and functional changes through the process of easy adaptability—which is the fundamental issue of sustainable urban living. In the last half of the twentieth century, the collective urban identity and legibility of much of the world's housing were lost. Recent housing has been mostly incoherent and arbitrary. However, a study of historical housing in many cities is a study of their urban vernacular. From the Georgian terraces of Islington to the brownstones of New York. From the hutongs of Beijing to the courtyard houses of Lima. And from the pension blocks of Paris to the townhouses of Berlin. Places have always developed their own vernacular. This quality evolves over time to reflect the environmental, cultural and historical context in which it exists. It is of its time, employing direct methods of building, using locally available resources, and being authentic.

Vernacular housing tends to have typological clarity that is lacking in much recent development. It should not be confused with historicist styling. We can criticise the lack of vernacular at the same time as a warning of 'the heavy-handed and superficial application of general "historicist" style'. The use of traditional design approaches such as Poundbury in Dorset, championed by Prince Charles, may have a lot to do with this fictionalising of vernacular. The real problem is that vernacular, which is an ever changing and a self-perfecting process, has stalled. Monopolistic practices in the control of land and delivery of housing in most parts of the world have given us a one-trick pony, and the challenge lies in how we can drive up choice and quality of the standard offer without just using the same old 'better design' story.

New housing that favours laconic, background architecture would offer coherence to our developing neighbourhoods and provide respite from the flashy, self-promoting, placeless architecture that sees every site as a landmark opportunity.

Mark Parsons, in his paper 'Towards a New Vernacular', argues that he has less of an issue with the space standards that house-builders are providing. In contrast, housing layouts, their street size and form, their public open spaces and the spaces between dwellings are imposed by government regulation. Highway and pavement widths, turning and car parking requirements and the cul-de-sac layout produce a suburban form or 'estatescape' of isolated architectural elements. The houses drown in 'a sea' of minimum widths and minimum standards. Add to this the planning requirements of minimum distance and minimum space, and you have it: the contemporary housing estate built as a cell unrelated to its surrounds. He says,

> Vernacular is relevant to our own time. The principles often prescribed to historical vernacular architecture are those that are applied, today, to the meaning of sustainability. Buildings of simple quality, reusable and adaptable, produced from materials that are freely available and economical to produce and use in construction. The historic architectural vernacular was created by the 'pressures' of their time; the availability of building materials and land; the cost of transporting and processing those materials into their required form; and the availability and cost of the craft skills necessary to put them together.
>
> Some of these 'pressures' should be re-imposed. Not by strict regulation of design or by trying to manipulate or impose a particular architectural 'taste', but by controlling the availability and source of construction materials. This could be achieved through offering tax and financial incentives for local sourcing, reusing materials and buying those which are both energy efficient and renewable; encouraging a move away from employment taxation towards taxation which targets construction materials which require large doses of non-renewable and polluting energy (the cost of labour more than anything else prevents the development of good building art and craft). This together with an emphasis on localised government; the provision of smaller housing estates; changes in highway design; and a rethinking of spacing standards could achieve more intimacy, a scale more in keeping with people and which we could happily live with, made up of houses which are truly distinctive and of their place and time. The new vernacular housing may well be very different.

What we do need is a vernacular that is relevant to our own time: a 'new norm'. The route to this is through establishing a regular urban fabric coupled with effective platforms that will enable this new urban vernacular, in the form of new typological solutions, to take root and flourish.

Opposite page: Making of Modern Street by Group 91 Architects, Dublin, shows the reinvention of the urban townhouse. **This page, clockwise from upper left:** Cape Town, New York, Jaipur, London, Istanbul, Mexico City—all showing their own distinct brand of evolved urban vernacular.

TYPOLOGICAL SOLUTIONS

> *About 2,500 years ago, Ionians in what is now western Turkey laid out the city of Priene with a grid of blocks measuring 36 by 50 metres (120 × 165 feet) each. A standard residential block hosted eight attached row houses, oriented southward with the porches facing the harbour. The stalwart, adaptable row house has persisted for millennia. It has remained a favoured form for architects for its simplicity and scale, an answer to a wide range of notions about what the city can and should be.*
>
> —The Urban Omnibus

The row house, in all its forms—the terraced house, townhouse or street house—has served us well since then and continues to be the most robust housing model we have today. The Making of the Modern Street project by Group 91 Architects in Dublin showed that the simple rules that define this typology could generate infinite possibilities to serve modern needs, without compromising great design.

Typology is the classification of (usually physical) characteristics commonly found in buildings and urban places, according to their association with different categories, such as intensity of development (from natural or rural to highly urban), degrees of formality and school of thought (for example, modernist or traditional). Individual characteristics form patterns.

Patterns relate elements hierarchically across physical scales (from small details to large systems). An emphasis on typology is necessary to match the physical development characteristics of a place within the appropriate typology for that location, as determined by local preferences taken in context with urban patterns as evidenced throughout history.

Places are defined by their building typologies: the London townhouse, the New York tram house, the Amsterdam canal house, the Tyneside flat and the Glasgow tenement. They are also defined by their patterns of development, which are also typological: the London garden squares, the Edinburgh burgages and the Beijing hutongs.

The big housebuilders use a palette of typologies...but badly. The main problem is that they are generally influenced by the need to keep the planners happy, based on loose and ill-formed constructs of character and distinctiveness. Thus, they become characterless and indistinctive. Designers would do well to work on evolving a range of typologies suitable to the requirements of a place. The big housebuilders just need a new palette as their default option.

Making the Modern Street project in Dublin shows how simple urban rules can generate infinite design possibilities to meet modern needs and aspirations.

Pattern Books

Pattern books have a long and architecturally respectable history, but they tend to be frowned upon by architects, who see them as a threat to the profession. Significantly, pattern books were the stuff of the building trade in the centuries before architects were professionalised. There was Palladio's *Quattro Libri* (1570), Colen Campbell's *Vitruvius Britannicus* (1715), Batty and Thomas Langley's *The City and Country Builder's and Workman's Treasury of Design* (1740) and J. C. Loudon's *An Encyclopaedia of Cottage, Farm, and Villa Architecture* (1834). These all provided templates for builders, creating not uniformity but consistency. Even more significantly, these pattern books were the inspiration for Georgian urbanism. The old 1978 Greater London Council's *An Introduction to Housing Layout* was a source of inspiration for many looking for standard house plans. Since that time we appear to have very little typological research other than what we can glean from our Dutch and German counterparts, who still see typology as a valid pursuit.

In the matter of putting quality back into housing, Pierre d'Avoine, who advocates, in his persuasive book *Housey, Housey: A Pattern Book Of Ideal Homes* (2005), a return to pattern books. D'Avoine is not advocating servile copyism but a radical reinterpretation of the idea. If design is to replace dogma, that includes modernist dogma, too.

The fundamental idea behind the pattern book is a reproducible formula, which can be shaped to suit different needs, be they physical, economic or cultural. There is a great opportunity, therefore, to introduce into the housing supply a wider range of choice by promoting new procedures for developing land in smaller parcels on a more individual basis. This action could be achieved by using standardised construction methods to deliver both 'desirability' and housing suitable for today's lifestyles—all within an affordable budget.

As regards affordability, Alex Eley, who co-authored the Mayor of London's *London Housing Design Guide*, pointed out that in 2006, in the English Partnerships' Design for Manufacture initiative, which aimed to create a sustainable home for £60,000 ($80,000 USD), the homes delivered offered an average of 76 square metres (250 square feet) of living space for this price. Other pattern book homes, for example the German Hebel Haus, deliver 108 square metres (1,163 square feet), with three bedrooms, for £47,800 ($64,000 USD).

Pattern-book housing is something the Americans have been doing for years with such products as the Sears kit house. Some companies specialise in particular housing solutions for specific markets—for example, one company only provides modular, workers' housing on small lots measuring 5 metres (16 feet) wide. Working in modular dimensions shows us that you can live well in small spaces, and buildings designed in this manner can be organised to fit a variety of situations and can be arranged in such a way as to solve issues of site constraints, orientation, individual needs, and desires.

Top: New Leyden in Holland achieves richess and variety within defined constraints.

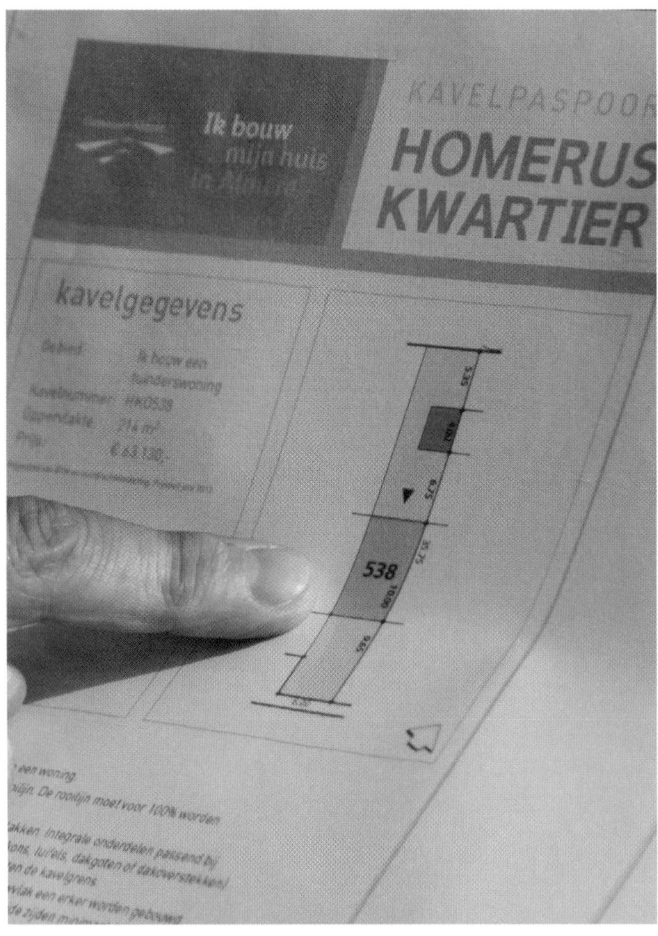

Plot Passports

Although Design Codes set out what form of development is permissible on a site, they can be quite technical, and sometimes they are difficult for private homebuilders to understand. 'Plot Passports' were developed to overcome this challenge.

According to the Right to Build Task Force—established by the National Custom and Self Build Association to help local authorities, community groups and other organisations across the United Kingdom to deliver large, affordable custom and self build projects—a plot passport is a simple and succinct summary of the design parameters for a given plot. They add value by acting as a key reference point for the purchaser, capturing relevant information from the planning permission, design constraints and procedural requirements in an easily understandable and readily accessible format.

Most are between one and four pages long and form part of the marketing material available for the plot.

The passport clearly shows the plot location, the permissible building lines and side spacing requirements, proximity constraints to neighbouring buildings and the part of the site where a new house can be constructed (ie, the developable footprint). There is usually also a building height restriction.

Passports are very clear about the number of dwellings that can be built (generally only one) and any other pertinent details, including car parking and access location, etc.

The choice of finishing materials, fenestration and roof shape is usually left to the plot owner. Most are kept as simple as possible so that people can evaluate the various potential plots and work out which suits them best.

Plot-, lot- and block-based urbanism shows us the importance of modular dimensions and their ability to spawn a number of permutations. The Popular Home Initiative also shows that we can build pattern books and plot passports that offer the widest range of choice that can be applied to default settings.

This page, top left: Plot passport for the Homerus Quarter in Almere, Holland. **Top right:** Examples of successfully completed housing in the Homerus Quarter, using the plot passport approach. **Opposite page, top left:** High density housing in the Kin Ming Estate, Hong Kong, China. **Top right:** Low density suburban housing in Arizona, USA. **Bottom:** Illustration of the target zone of 50 to 150 dwelling units per hectare based on standard building typologies.

LOOKING FOR THE SWEET SPOT OF URBAN DENSITY

In recent years we have seen the concentration on two dominant housing models: high-density (low-family) apartment living and low-density (high-family) houses. The high-density model has salved our conscience on sustainability but has not given us well-balanced communities, in many instances having the exact opposite effect. The low-density model, which primarily derives from our recent suburban traditions, has given us the worst conditions of urban sprawl. It has also poorly contributed to creating sustainable communities.

Medium-density typologies are well suited to achieving sufficient density for sustainable development and still giving us the critical mass and intensity needed for healthy neighbourhood formation. We now need to focus more on developing these typologies—similar to those in the best parts of many of our cities. This is what people today call the 'missing middle'.

Medium-density typologies are well suited to achieve high-family conditions. In numbers terms, we are looking at a target zone of 50 to 150 dwelling units per hectare. Within this density range, we are talking about housing typologies that conform to a typical party wall solution—a mews house, row house, terraced house, townhouse, small apartment block, or even mansion block—all buildings that fit within a typical two- to six-storey scale of development. This size would appear to be the sweet spot for the best forms of urban neighbourhoods worldwide.

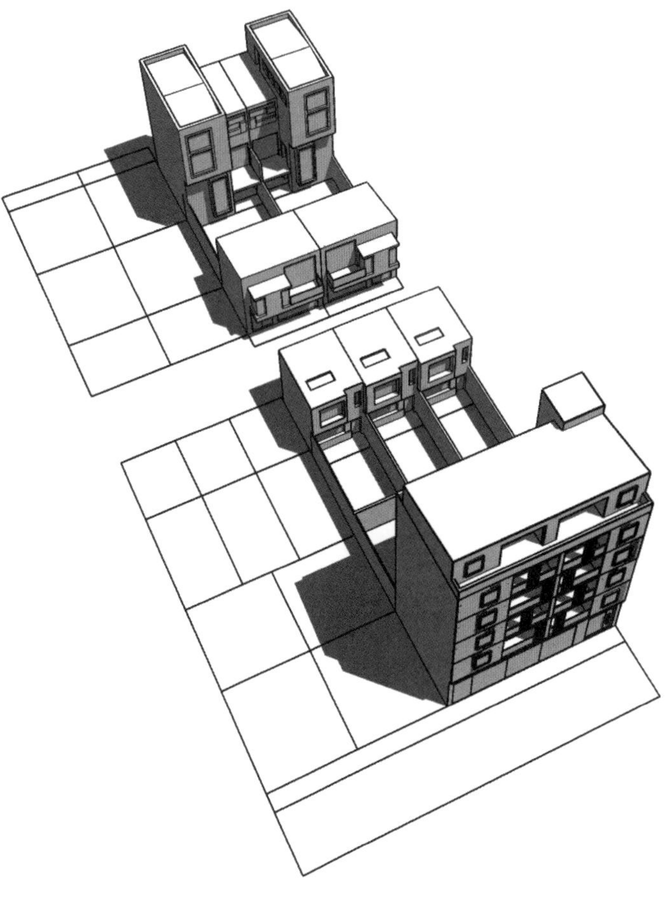

Streets

Blocks

Platforms

Defaults

Activators

LONG-LIFE, LOOSE-FIT

> *Without due attention to building in more of a 'long life, loose fit' way, the housing issue will continue to cause immense grief.*
>
> —Alex Lifschutz

'Form follows function' is a principle associated with twentieth-century modernist architecture and industrial design which says that the shape of a building or object should be primarily related to its intended function or purpose. This principle has also been extended to urban design. Where function does not change, form does not change. Herein lies the problem. Urban fabric is so carefully tailored to the programme of uses that it finds it impossible to adapt to other uses when functions do change. This is manifest in our endless suburbia that cannot transition into proper neighbourhoods; in our modern office buildings with their planned obsolescence; and in our bland identikit houses that can offer no more than housing.

Moving to a long-life, loose-fit approach—where space is universal—offers far greater possibilities for our neighbourhoods to evolve. The ultimate aim of course is to create a new generation of adaptable buildings that extends the life of its constituents and that in the future will be completely reuseable—something we believe is becoming increasingly real if we all embrace a circular economy. A circular economy presents an alternative to a traditional linear economy (make, use, dispose) in which we keep resources in use for as long as possible, extract the maximum value from them whilst in use, then recover and regenerate products and materials at the end of each service life.

The planned Scotswood Housing Expo project in Newcastle was an initiative developed by Urban Initiatives in 2010 that strictly built on the plot, lot and block subdivision principles described earlier. It looked to make long-life, loose-fit housing an essential component of compact neighbourhoods and provide a commonsense alternative to the outdated models that populate the national housebuilding industry today. It set a new benchmark for our housing challenge, ensuring the best possible outcomes in medium-density housing design, neighbourhood building and long-term management and maintenance, through a restatement of underlying values, through a clarity of purpose and a pioneering approach to innovation:

- → It embraced the needs of a complex and changing society, recognising the rapid social and demographic changes in society that shape new forms of urban living, social patterns and lifetime requirements, and posing new models of design, delivery and management for new housing.
- → It imbedded environmentalism as an integrated design requirement by promoting efficient use of land and taking the lead in innovative environmental design of new housing, avoiding unnecessary 'eco-clichés' and making a real difference to sustainable building and urban design.
- → It recognised the importance of building communities and explored the potential for making them well balanced through a range of social actions, management projects and programmes to foster an early sense of belonging in a community and build long-term stability in a community.
- → It searched for new housing models by exploring a new planning, design and delivery approach to buildings in the context of the plot, lot and block by promoting a flexible typological approach to these scales of development and combining the advantages of modern methods of construction with the benefits of repetition, rhythm and harmony that evolve from the traditions of good housing and urban design.
- → It looked to new ways of disseminating and influencing choice by developing pattern-book approaches to building design, allowing for easy interchangeability of units; use of modular dimensions, systems and practices; easy modification; and tailoring to the specific needs of a place.

Using the PLATFORMS approach, the Popular Home initiative allowed for the sourcing of common modules or parts to ensure quality and reduce build costs and complexities. It enabled units to be developed to different specifications and even levels of completion, while still using a conventional 'kit of parts' for each of the key modules of a house—allowing for standardi-

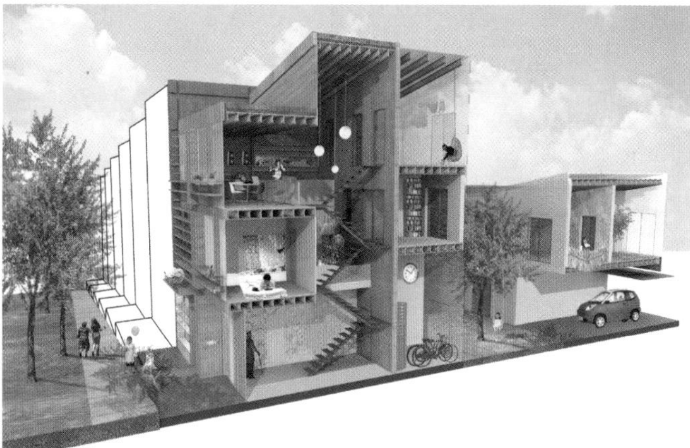

sation to ease building and achieve economies of scale. Initial work by a panel of architects tested lot configurations to see if any logical patterns emerged and, if so, whether house types could be developed as a number of interchangeable parts in the plan.

As stated previously, the 15-metre (50 feet) lot proved to be the most versatile and efficient dimension in accommodating many robust plan types for party wall solutions, while also offering the potential to be used in pairs to provide urban warehouse typologies. The project moved forwards on this basis. Working within the constraints of the 15-metre-wide lot, the architects developed a range of house types using party wall dimensions as narrow as 3.75 metres (12 feet) with others of 5, 6, 7.5 and 10 metres (16, 20, 25 and 33 feet) wide, accepting that two lots could be combined to give greater variation. These included narrow- and wide-fronted typologies for:

- → Mews and studio units for live–work use on back lanes
- → Terraced housing solutions, including two- and three-storey options with the potential for loft conversions
- → Semidetached housing and free-standing urban villas
- → House-over-house options and live–work units
- → Apartment and living-over-the-shop solutions

The project also recognised that we could use variable dimensions within the widths of the one or two lot combinations to allow for more bespoke solutions.

The volumetric / plot width normative approach allows for huge variation in architecture and house types, thoroughly tested by the panel of architects, but with sufficient standards to ensure that each place still works in urban design terms. The approach also lends itself to being effectively coded, with simple rules to achieve richness and variety within regularity.

This work led to an invited design competition run by the Royal Institute of British Architects (RIBA) competitions office in association with Newcastle City Council and English Partnerships. Many of the successful submissions made to this competition are illustrated here.

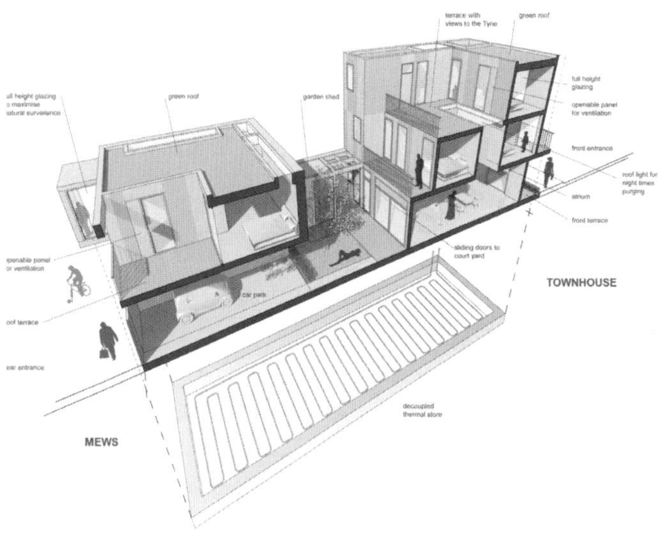

Opposite page: Model view of the planned Scotswood Popular Home EXPO Project in Newcastle, 2010. **This page:** Brochures and submissions made for the RIBA international design competition showing popular home solutions by a range of architects.

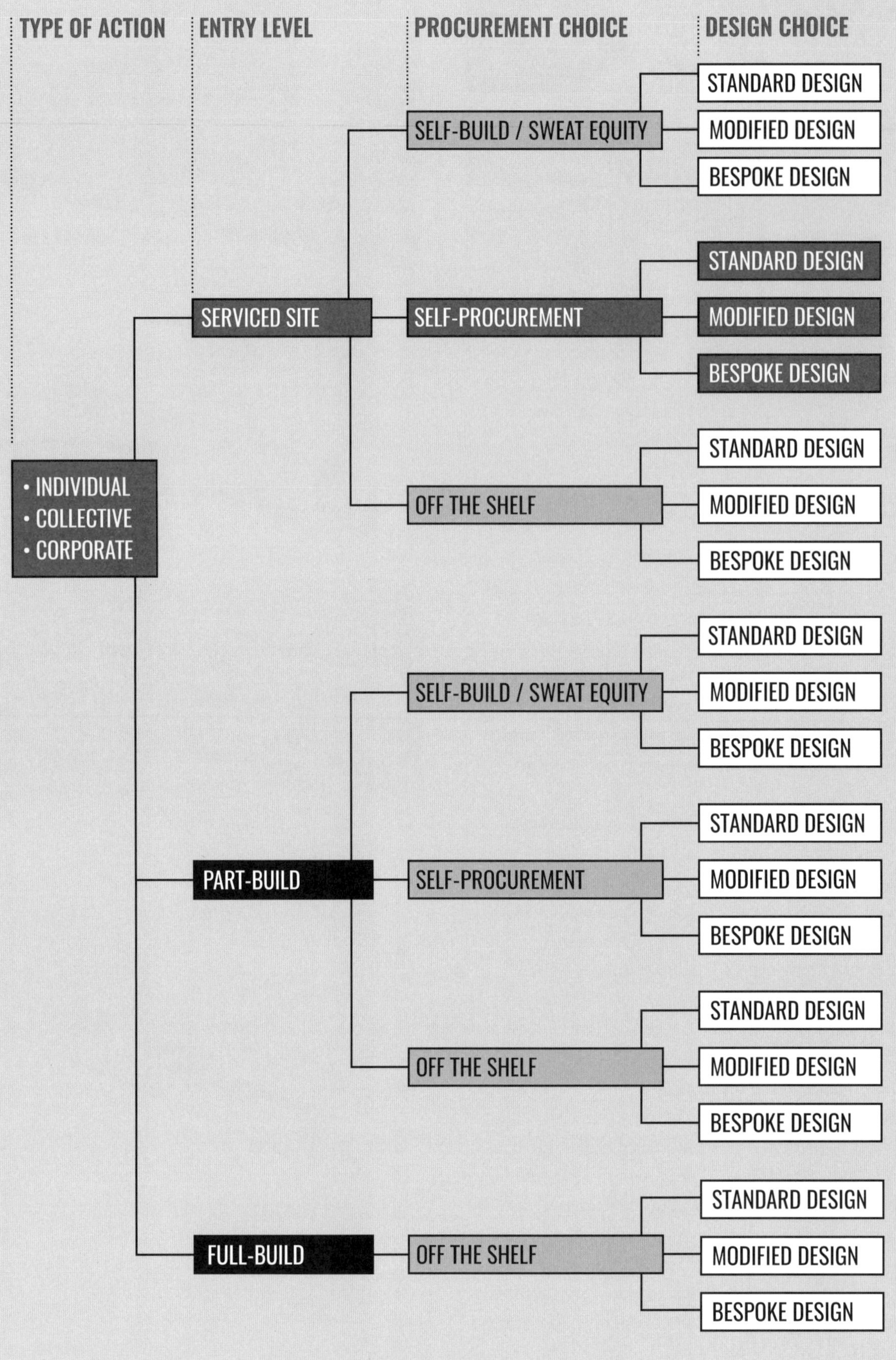
TYPE OF ACTION
ENTRY LEVEL
PROCUREMENT CHOICE
DESIGN CHOICE
• INDIVIDUAL
• COLLECTIVE
• CORPORATE
SERVICED SITE
SELF-BUILD / SWEAT EQUITY
STANDARD DESIGN
MODIFIED DESIGN
BESPOKE DESIGN
SELF-PROCUREMENT
STANDARD DESIGN
MODIFIED DESIGN
BESPOKE DESIGN
OFF THE SHELF
STANDARD DESIGN
MODIFIED DESIGN
BESPOKE DESIGN
PART-BUILD
SELF-BUILD / SWEAT EQUITY
STANDARD DESIGN
MODIFIED DESIGN
BESPOKE DESIGN
SELF-PROCUREMENT
STANDARD DESIGN
MODIFIED DESIGN
BESPOKE DESIGN
OFF THE SHELF
STANDARD DESIGN
MODIFIED DESIGN
BESPOKE DESIGN
FULL-BUILD
OFF THE SHELF
STANDARD DESIGN
MODIFIED DESIGN
BESPOKE DESIGN

PROVIDING AN OPEN FRAMEWORK OF CHOICE

We can assume that bottom-up pressures will widen the need for choice as systems become more open. This could lead to confusion as each community experiments with its ideas. Alternatively, we can choose to help delivery of these ideas with a range of default choices.

Three types of agents can be involved in building for neighbourhood formation or transformation. Each agent would focus on the plot, lot or block as a unit of delivery:

1 **Individuals** are single agents who wish to exercise total choice. The plot is the most likely choice for the individual, although the plot could be big enough to be a full lot.

2 **Collectives** are groups of individuals such as cooperatives. The lot or block is the most likely choice for these groups.

3 **Corporate agents** are formal organisations such as local authorities, estates, social landlords or building companies. They would likely take on a number of lots, blocks or combinations of these to comprise a full phase of development.

A rapidly changing market will have a significant effect on the need to diversify provision, and all of the alternative routes to delivering this continuum will take on more importance. Any platform must ensure we structure complex choices with the potential to offer the following three factors: entry-level choice, procurement choice, and design choice.

Entry-Level Choice

Each of the types of agents will have different choices to enter the building process at various levels of completion within the process:

→ **Serviced sites** are the lowest level of entry and could apply to the plot, lot or block scale.

→ **Part-build (facilitated self-build) sites** involve using contractors to build the overall structure and enclosure of the building with services and circulation cores, on the basis that the internal fit-out will be carried out by others.

→ **Full-build sites** imply a finished building will be undertaken by contractors.

Procurement choice

Any of the entry levels will trigger the need to choose the method of procurement to deliver the completed building:

→ **Self-build / sweat equity** could apply to physical involvement by an individual or collective to build out serviced sites and fit out and finish shell and core schemes.

→ **Self-procurement** could apply to the procurement of contractors by an individual or collective to build out serviced sites, and fit out and finish shell-and-core schemes.

→ **Off the shelf** implies that shell-and-core or full-build schemes are procured as completed products built through formal organisations.

Design Choice

Any of the above procurement choices will require that decisions are made about the preferred design route. These include:

→ **Standard design** involves the use of standard typologies from the parameter book.

→ **Modified design** could include adapting the standard typological approaches from the pattern book.

→ **Bespoke design** involves an individual personalised approach to the development of the scheme and could apply to self-build / sweat equity and self-procurement choices.

The entry-level choice framework provides the first point of entry to the system for the various types of action by the individual, corporate or institutional actors in the system. Serviced sites offer the lowest levels of structuring simple choices and open up the widest response. Full build fully determines the outcome. It is around the part-build option that the greatest opportunity is provided for a responsive environment or support structure that will enable effective action to be triggered by all the actors in the system.

All of these options point to the need for an enabling developer who can operate across the full spectrum of choice—from the serviced site to the part-build and full-build options.

THE CULTURAL EVOLUTIONARY

HOW A MODERN MAYOR USED OLD MODELS TO BUILD URBAN IDENTITY

Mayor Hao leads a city whose problems are very much like those of the city of Datong, which is featured in the Chinese film *The Chinese Mayor*. Datong's elected Mayor Geng had decided to relocate half a million people to high-density housing blocks to make room for an immense cultural project: the transformation of an extremely polluted industrial city into a newly erected cultural heritage site. It is a fascinating and shocking cautionary tale of how gargantuan construction projects are allowed to mushroom and then come to a sudden halt according to the whims of those in power.

The mayor of Datong was nicknamed Demolition Geng. His idea was to turn the city into a hub that could sustain itself through cultural tourism. As a former capital, Datong had a glorious past, though few of the ancient buildings have survived. Geng's solution was to build new, old-style buildings and a city wall that would re-create something of the city's ancient splendour.

The half-completed project ground to a halt, leaving Datong with crippling debt, a Herculean construction project that was not even half-finished, and thousands of people displaced. Mayor Geng has been 'relocated'.

Mayor Hao's city of Dangzou has had a similar recent history. Mayor Hao has replaced a former mayor whose ambitious schemes have failed. Mayor Hao has a reputation as a more thoughtful politician and administrator, and as someone who listens. He is wary of top-down initiatives that promise a great deal without having any clear route to achieving their aims.

Hao is concerned about the proliferation of faceless tall buildings that are commonplace in many Chinese cities today. They do not achieve the quality of life that traditional forms of development offered in the past. He calls them shoeboxes in the sky. He can do better for his people, imagining different forms of development that will make his city unique.

Hao loves the old form of neighbourhoods from his youth, and looks for a way to bring back the idea of the hutong, something he regards as a perfect social model. This has its roots in traditional Chinese ways of living. *Hutongs* are alleys formed by lines of traditional courtyard residences. Many neighbourhoods were formed by joining one courtyard house to another to form a hutong, and then joining one hutong to another.

The word *hutong* is also used to refer to such neighbourhoods. Since the mid-twentieth century, the number of hutongs in China has dropped dramatically as they are demolished to make way for modern high-rise buildings. More recently, some hutongs have been designated as protected areas in an attempt to preserve this aspect of Chinese cultural history.

Hao's biggest challenge lies in regenerating the historic urban core that fell into disrepair as its occupants anticipated a windfall profit from greedy developers eager to build their tried-and-tested apartment blocks. Things have changed since the market collapse in China. Regardless of this, Hao keeps returning to the singular urban dilemma of modernising China: the tension between sanctioning poor housing versus the consequences of rampant gentrification.

For him, the challenge is how to rebuild without requiring residents to move out; upgrade without relinquishing the sense of community; maintain a sense of continuity and history without parodying heritage; and ensure that development is cost-effective and affordable without inflating the housing market.

In the last five years, the historic centre of Dangzou has become the focus of a real and symbolic debate about new and old values: public versus private, progress versus conservation, land value versus social value. These hutongs in the very heart of Dangzou are slums. Eighty per cent of the historic centre is low-level sprawl, with many of the buildings in multiple ownership. It is a maze of shops, businesses and residential buildings, many constructed during the Ming Dynasty.

Previous municipal and provincial governments would offer sweeteners to residents to move out so that large-scale demolition and rebuilding could take place. The government is now tending to opt for pragmatic refurbishment, to the dismay of many occupants who were more concerned with being paid for their run-down homes.

MAYOR HAO IDENTIFIES A NUMBER OF MAJOR PROBLEMS

There are a number of serious flaws in the system that have to resolved:

1. He believes in building cultural capital, but he does not think that this can be done with fake buildings. He is determined to enable people to exercise their ingenuity in solving problems.
2. Development has been carried out at very high densities and with dull, monotonous design, with little sign of social or cultural life.
3. A way must be found to promote cultural life that does not depend on building major capital projects. Time is needed to allow new ideas to flourish. It won't happen overnight.
4. Dangzou's people, angry with being treated as pawns in a property game, want to have a say in the city's future. They are talking about how they want to live in a modern Chinese society.
5. Many of the demolished sites in the city centre stand vacant. These are the biggest opportunities to define a new way forwards.

MAYOR HAO SEES THE LIGHT

Mayor Hao visits London with a group of Chinese mayors as part of an Oxford-China exchange programme. He hears a talk on Massive Small at Oxford University and thinks that this could be right for Dangzou. The talk mentions the cultural masterplanning work of Dan Dubowitz. Dan is a radical incrementalist who believes that you start by starting. He recognises culture as an outcome. You cannot design for it, but you can create the conditions for it to emerge. Working with his new team, Hao identifies actions that can become catalysts for positive change, building social capital in areas devoid of urban life. Learning from Architecture 00's *Compendium for the Civic Economy*, he finds local ways of stimulating neighbourhood social action and mutual support.

He promotes new temporary uses in some of the large, desolate open spaces. These formalise over time into new street markets. Streetlife emerges. Hao creates community meeting spaces in some of the vacant ground-floor units. He introduces the concept of the roundtable, which brings the community together. People feel that they can achieve something and look for projects to mend the city.

Mayor Hao's first priority is to regenerate the hutong and remedy the damage caused by the demolition of so many sites in the historic urban core. He recalls that in Dashilar, Beijing, there is a similar hutong with a population density six times higher than the Beijing average, and more than three times that of Tokyo. Given these numbers, there are considerable opportunities to increase the residential densities in Dangzou without resorting to wholesale demolition of the area. The question is: how is it possible to retain people in the area without condemning them to remain in poverty and squalor?

Hao's project is to create what he calls a 'new cultural evolution', whereby the scale and density of the area are retained and expanded slightly, while providing new facilities that respect the historic setting.

Hao hears about the project in Dublin called the Making of the Modern Street, where a practice called Group 91 Architects explored new possibilities of the traditional model of townhouse. This gives him a clue about how the centre might be rebuilt. Dangzou needs to develop a new vernacular that will capture people's imagination. Hao is looking for a new way that is equally meaningful but without recreating the past. He knows that the traditional real-estate developers will resist. He has to create a new breed of urban pioneers who will change the market and redefine how Dangzou moves forwards.

He launches an ideas competition called Making the Modern Hutong. The project aims to create what he hopes will be a real cultural paradigm shift, by finding different ways of expressing the modern hutong. He gets his team to produce plans of each vacant site, with narrow lanes and subdivision into 30- by 30-metre (100 × 100 feet) plots, each being of a scale to accommodate the footprint of a traditional courtyard house. The brief for the competition calls for three- to five-storey housing based around courtyards.

Local people are invited to pitch for the plots, which are offered on a deferred payment basis. People come with their schemes. The results are breathtaking: Chinese architects, disillusioned with working on mega-

buildings, come out the woodwork and propose solutions that Hao never expected. They express a unique Chinese model of development with a strong regional identity. Some courtyard houses are a collection of many small units with doors opening directly to the internal courtyards. Some are larger units with smaller annexes. Others offer a mix of uses, with enterprise space, doctors' rooms, small workshops or even teaching space. They are the start of a new vernacular that will evolve over time as an acceptable model of development.

Existing courtyard houses are regenerated. Some are rebuilt on the basis of the brief. The population density of the area increases by 50 per cent, similar to that of the modern housing blocks, but feeling and looking much better. Within ten years a different form of culture emerges and people are talking about Dangzou as the 'new way'. The mayor earns the nickname Know Hao. He has found out how to release the energy of his constituents, and they have responded in the best possible way for the city.

HAO TELLS OF DANGZOU'S SUCCESS

→ Dangzou challenged the conventional way of developing cities. It went back to traditional, people-based approaches to find its way. The conventional real-estate model of investment is now dead in Dangzou. Investment has shifted to the new model.

→ Culture rests in people, not in buildings. The buildings should reflect the culture of the time and grow out of its needs. Dangzou is becoming the cultural centre because of this, not through some return to the past.

→ No city can heal itself just by putting up buildings. It needs to build its social capital at the same time. That is what makes neighbourhoods. That will not be done from a top-down vision, unless the purpose of that vision is to release action from the bottom up.

> *We must rediscover the art and process of urban evolution, harnessing the collective power of people and unleashing the potential of billions of bottom-up actions. The system must become the way. The way must become the system. That's when things work.*
>
> —Mayor Hao, China

The parameter book, a concept developed in the London Popular Home Initiative, provides the essential 'building blocks' for any typological-based strategy. These building blocks can start with a few typologies, and they can be added to over time. The parameter book can evolve as lessons are learnt. It can stand alone and become a valuable sourcebook for individuals, designers, builders and planners to inform best practice and policy.

Used in concert with a range of enabling mechanisms, the Popular Home parameter book can also be used to deliver all, or combinations of, our other planned outcomes:

→ Improving design quality through the continuous application of evolutionary design processes
→ Providing long-life, loose-fit solutions for all conditions
→ Easing the way through the planning system
→ Improving the costs, efficiencies and operations in the building industry
→ Widening consumer choice and opening up the market to more players

However, each of these outcomes realised in combination with one another could create an actual multiplier effect that could be compelling for housing delivery. The parameter book was provided to introduce into the housing supply a wider range of choice, by instituting new procedures for developing land in smaller parcels, on a more individual basis, using standardised construction methods that can nevertheless deliver 'desirability' and accommodation suitable for today's lifestyles, within a plausible budget.

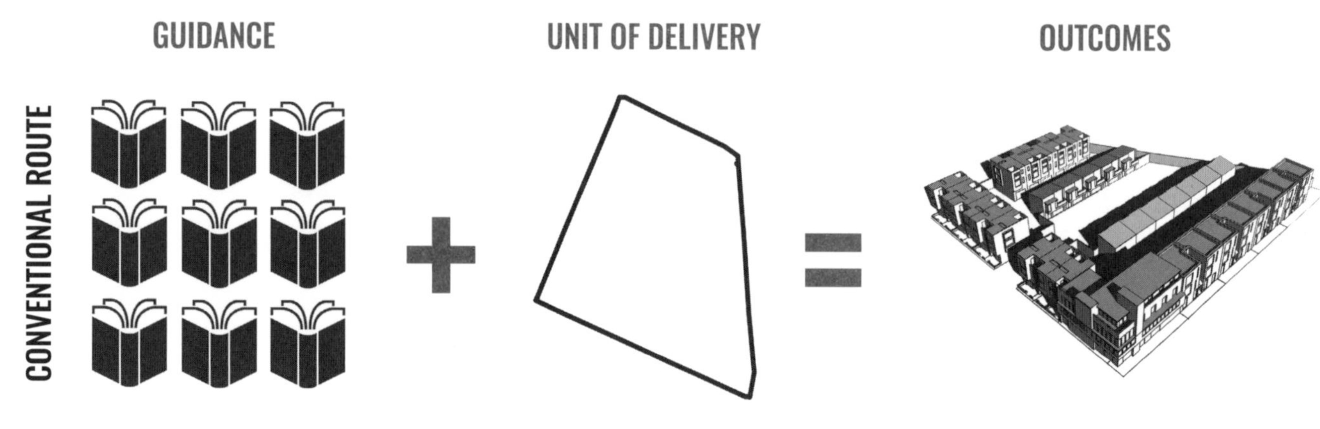

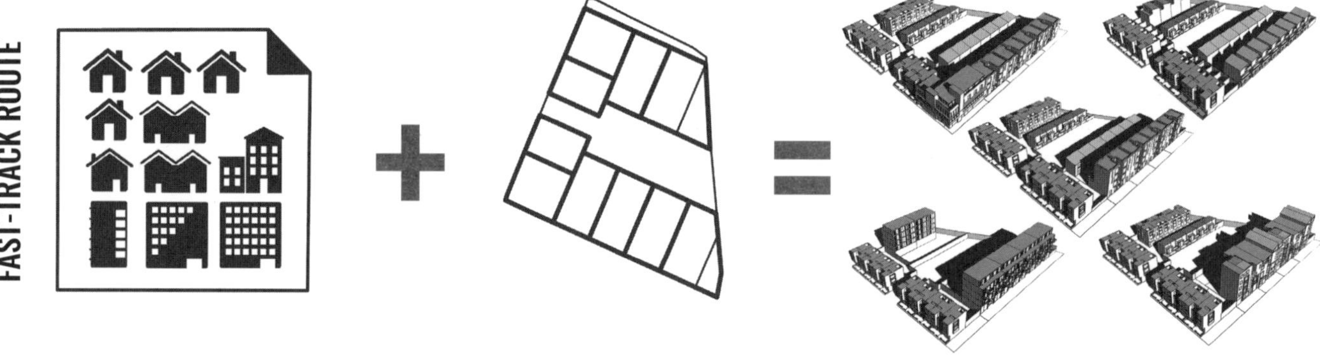

WHAT IS A PARAMETER BOOK?

The fundamental proposition behind the parameter book is a reproducible formula, which can be shaped to suit different needs, be they physical, economic or cultural. Using plot-, lot- and block-based urbanism it shows us the importance of modular dimensions and their ability to spawn a number of permutations. The London Popular Home Initiative also demonstrated that we could build pattern books that offer the widest range of choice that can be applied to our default settings.

The parameter book proposes a range of standard building types that will be acceptable for a typical range of housing conditions with which we are all familiar. These are homes that are suitable for bringing up families, homes with front doors and backyards, homes that accommodate us throughout our lives and allow changes to meet our needs.

Different internal and external layouts, garden design, type and façade can all be developed in adjacent units allowing architects to innovate. The parameter book enables internal growth and change within the long-life, loose-fit concept. It also allows for variation in street scene and building shoulder height to create visual interest. The primary house or houses are aligned along the frontage of the plot, with various setback conditions.

The parameter book will show a number of building solutions that:

1. **Offer a full range of individual, terraced housing solutions,** including row houses, townhouses, mews houses and multiple occupancy solutions such as houses that can be subdivided into smaller units and back again, maisonettes, small apartment blocks and larger mansion blocks
2. **Present a simple basis of providing for certainty with flexibility** by allowing the choice of a range of standard sizes with variable widths that can be freely interchanged with others as the market demands
3. **Allow for an infinite number of internal plans,** all based on long-life, loose-fit qualities that enable the homes to change over the lifetime of the occupants to meet their ever-changing needs, with the dimensions of these units allowing prescribed space standards to be met and even exceeded
4. **Allow for alternative architectural expressions** within a clearly defined set of parameters—for example, the overall built volume may be prescribed but not the treatment of the façades and roofs, which means that homes can be tailored to the specific character requirements of a location
5. **Allow for individual neighbourhoods to tailor their acceptable solutions** to those that work with the character, grain and pattern of places across their borough, which could include a palette of materials and details
6. **Provide the qualities of form to address the massing and scale of development** of the building type when placed on a site, with the building types seen as perspex boxes that provide the three-dimensional parameters for development for any given typology
7. **Contain the qualities of street interface** setback dimensions, on-plot parking criteria and utility provision (bins, cycle stores, etc.)
8. **Provide limits of deviation** for any aspect of the building type and the rules for dealing with modifications to the standard, in addition to showing how an application can go offline to follow the conventional planning process of special elements such as landmarks, important corners and irregular sites
9. **Provide the basis for standard type approvals** by local government building control to reduce costs and speed delivery

It is recommended that the town, city or metropolitan authority act as the 'holder' of the parameter book, providing regular updates and supporting research and feedback to the neighbourhoods. Each neighbourhood could choose to adopt the parameter book as is or adapt it to meet their individual requirements. The intention behind the initiative is to start small and add to the parameter book as new typologies emerge.

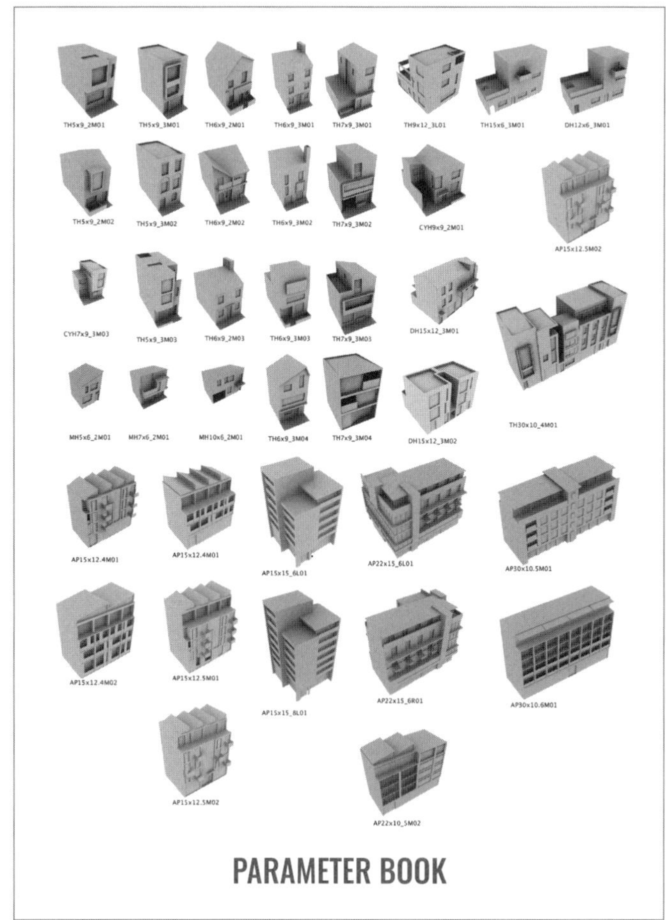

WHAT IS A PARAMETER PLAN?

A parameter plan is a means of breaking down larger sites into smaller regular development lots such that they can be populated with the standard housing types in the parameter book. This approach offers the following:

→ First and foremost, it is a constraints plan in that it deals with the site conditions such as immediate context, landscape features, boundary conditions, overshadowing issues, setback lines from adjacent properties, utility corridors, retained elements and so on.

→ Secondly, it is a regulatory plan like that used for preparing design codes. Overlaid on this are site access and layout issues, in particular, parking and open space locations, setback lines, potential special features, landmark locations and so on.

→ Thirdly, it provides a simple subdivision plan for a site with standard lot widths that can act as placeholders for a range of our pattern-book solutions. We are using a standard lot width of 15 metres (50 feet), which has proved to be the most accommodating dimension for our standard housing typologies. Each lot has a unique number on the plan with each lot identified as having either a 'normal' or a 'special' quality.

On larger sites, there will be a combination of blocks with lot subdivisions. In those instances, the choice of block typology will be a consequence of design. Block typology will include street typologies for a range of access conditions.

THE CHOICE MATRIX

The parameter book, in combination with the parameter plan, enables a simple choice matrix to be developed. The matrix relates the unique lot numbers on the parameter plan to the range of acceptable standard building types in the parameter book, so the local authority and applicant (individual, collective, or corporate agent) can agree to a set of structured choices that can be made. All will be acceptable, and different choices for each lot could be done as the project is being implemented. This gives us our certainty and flexibility.

How does this all help delivery and choice?

The importance of the parameter book is that, in combination with the plot, lot and block relationship, it allows us to develop a number of methods to facilitate delivery, phasing and diversity over time. These methods widen choice to a larger market.

Where land is controlled by the public sector, combination of the bits allows different levels of entry and intervention by various players: individual, collective or corporate. This method accommodates the full range of procurement options from individual self-build through to self-procurement, shell construction or full completion by any of a range of smaller local to larger contractors. All procurement options must allow for:

→ **The individual** building his home, operating at the plot scale

→ **A collective,** for example, three individuals, purchasing a lot for the development of a small scheme of three units

→ **A local builder** buying two lots, to build five homes every year

→ **A local housing association,** who wishes to build a small apartment building of no more than twenty units, purchasing two lots

SITE / TYPE	H001.1	H002.5	H003.9	H007.2	M010.5	M021.6	M002.1	A021.4	A056.6	A010.5	A100.5	A201.6
A1	●		●		●							
A2	●	●	●		●							
A3	●	●	●	●	●							
A4	●	●	●	●	●			●				
A5	●		●	●	●			●			●	
B1	●	●		●		●	●	●			●	●
B2	●	●		●		●	●	●	●	●	●	●
B3	●	●		●		●	●	●	●	●	●	●
B4		●		●		●	●		●	●	●	●
C1		●		●		●	●		●	●		●
C2									●	●		

→ **A national housebuilder** buying off-plan, as their normal course of practice to keep their cash flow going, for development of ten lots

For any scheme, there should be a proportion of land given over to each and every one of these activities, with the last option ideally being seen as a fallback position. Local authorities could use parametric approaches to set and manage the percentage mix for each option, and this could be monitored and adjusted based on relative success and take-up of any option.

OUTCOMES

There are three anticipated outcomes from the parameter book approach:

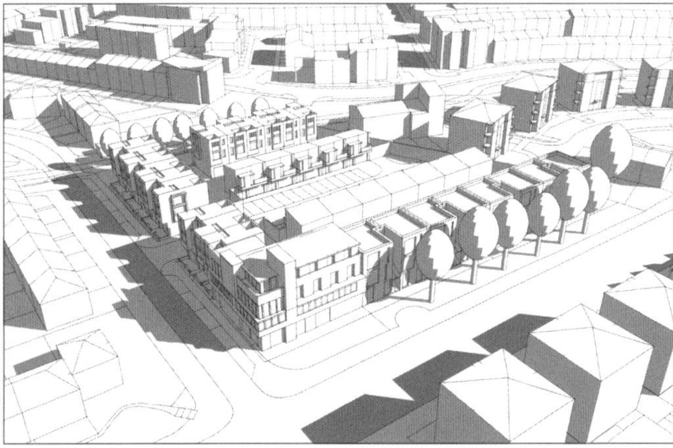

Outcome 1: fast-track planning

The parameter book, in combination with the parameter plan and the choice matrix, enables a standard planning brief to be adopted. Making use of standard planning briefs to provide the mechanism for developing quick development briefs for sites gives us a fast-track planning route, while still ensuring the desired outcomes.

Outcome 2: open building system

With the parameter book providing our building blocks, we can define the 'enabling mechanism' to improve the efficiency and operation of the construction industry. We believe that the formulation of a city-wide building standard will provide the mechanism for developing the basis of an open building system, thus overcoming the constant need of our fragmented construction industry to return to first principles.

Outcome 3: wider market choice

With the parameter book providing our building blocks, we can also define the 'enabling mechanism' to achieve wider market choice for a greater range of players—from the self-builder to the mass contractor and everything between. We believe that the enabling developer can be the mechanism to achieving our planned outcome.

The parameter book approach could be adapted to work in many places where traditional planning processes still hinder the housing delivery process. Where they don't, parts of this method can still be used to structure choice and accelerate action.

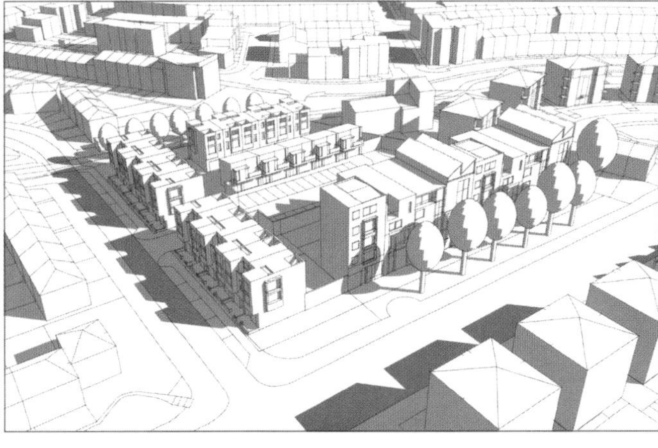

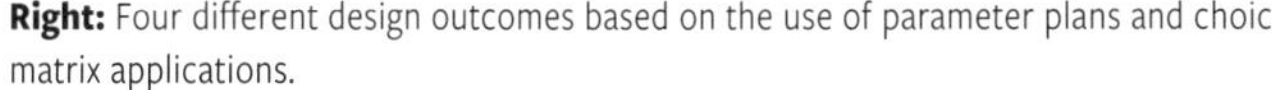

Right: Four different design outcomes based on the use of parameter plans and choice matrix applications.

LOCALIA URBAN NEIGHBOURHOOD

THE STRUCTURING OF COMPLEX HOUSING CHOICES

Localia is based on parcelling the blocks into universal lots and, as a general rule, uses the spine wall solution as a trigger to urban development. Some choices involve groups of people occupying the whole lot and parcelling up the land on a negotiated basis. Others have formal subdivisions into plots of varying frontages.

The local Neighbourhood Enabling Agency (NEA), tasked with releasing the potential of housing from a full range of sources—self-build, cooperative building groups, smaller and larger contractors—also assist local people in their housing choices. Demonstrated below, our range of different developing routes involving different procurement methods and densities of development. Each has the same starting point, and all can arrive at the same outcome within the limits of lot or plot subdivisions. All show the use of corner buildings as starter options. This is how they do it:

Step 1: The NEA develops a multi-level approvals process

→ They recognise that early occupiers of the site will come up with a range of different solutions to meet the needs. Through site visits and technical assistance programmes they assist these people in meeting basic standards that focus on preventing the spread of fire and disease. They issue simple certificates with the checklists to these occupiers showing that they have met these basic standards.

→ They provide incentives, advice and project management skills to enable people to progressively upgraded homes to meet full building standards. This is to ensure that anyone can start informally then move into a formal process, demanded by lending institutions, such that they may be able to raise finance for ongoing building works.

→ They introduce a planning approvals process, using a choice matrix approach, which gives automatic consent to anyone using standard plans on the specific plot type.

→ They develop a simple rating system that shows people are in the process of full standards, giving them targets to move to the next level.

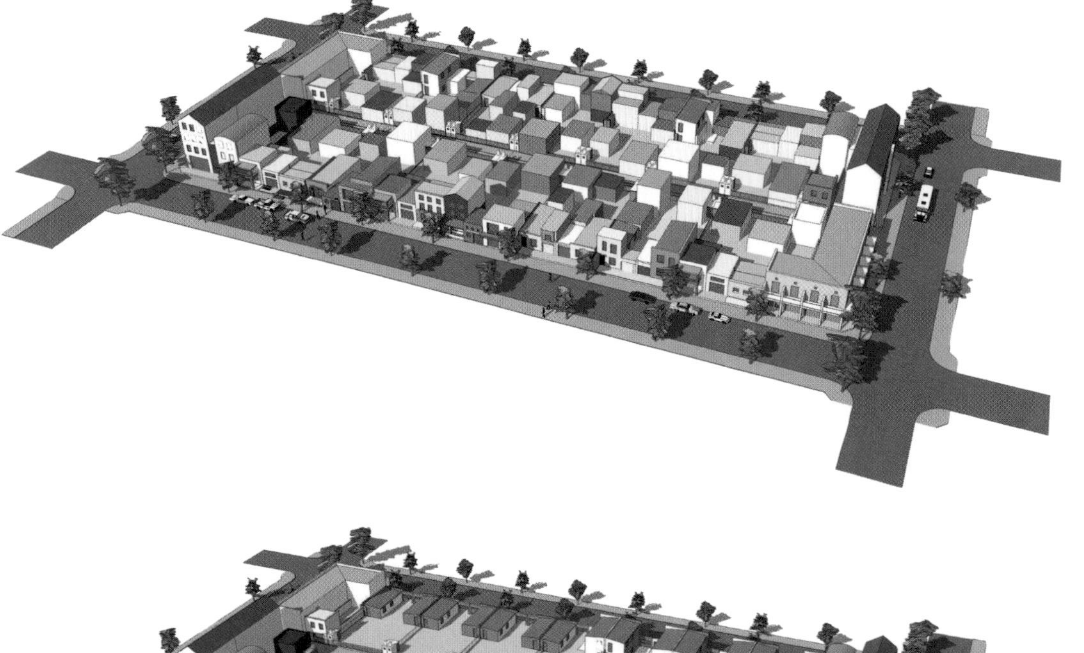

Option 1: The informal route
This involves people occupying the site early and finding different ways of the building. Vernacular emerges from the individual efforts of people to solve their housing needs.

Option 2:
The formal housebuilder route
In this example, housebuilders are invited to develop their responses to the spine wall solution. This could take the form of starter housing or full development. It could be single-storey or higher. Here we see a lot has been subdivided into two. A solution like this could be provided on certain blocks or distributed as a proportion of each block to meet affordable housing needs.

Step 2: The NEA develops a popular home parameter book

→ They start with a limited range of volumetric housing types for each plot subdivision option, to enable local contractors to evolve their solutions.

→ Working with the shack building industry and local contractors, they provide basic plans that show how are people can locate the temporary homes on the site, using the spine wall as the primary means of support to the starter home.

→ They develop packs of standard plans for people to adopt or adapt, within defined limits.

Step 3: The NEA shares, shows and celebrates different housing typologies

→ As different solutions emerge, they add these to their parameter book, providing a simple review of each house type in respect of how they meet people's needs, demonstrate innovation, reduce costs and improve energy efficiency.

→ They build show homes and encourage open days where people can visit successful solutions.

→ They introduce award schemes for individual buildings, lot developments and streets to incentivise others.

→ They develop an online platform to share these ideas with a wider audience, constantly evolving and improving how people can follow different routes to realising their dreams.

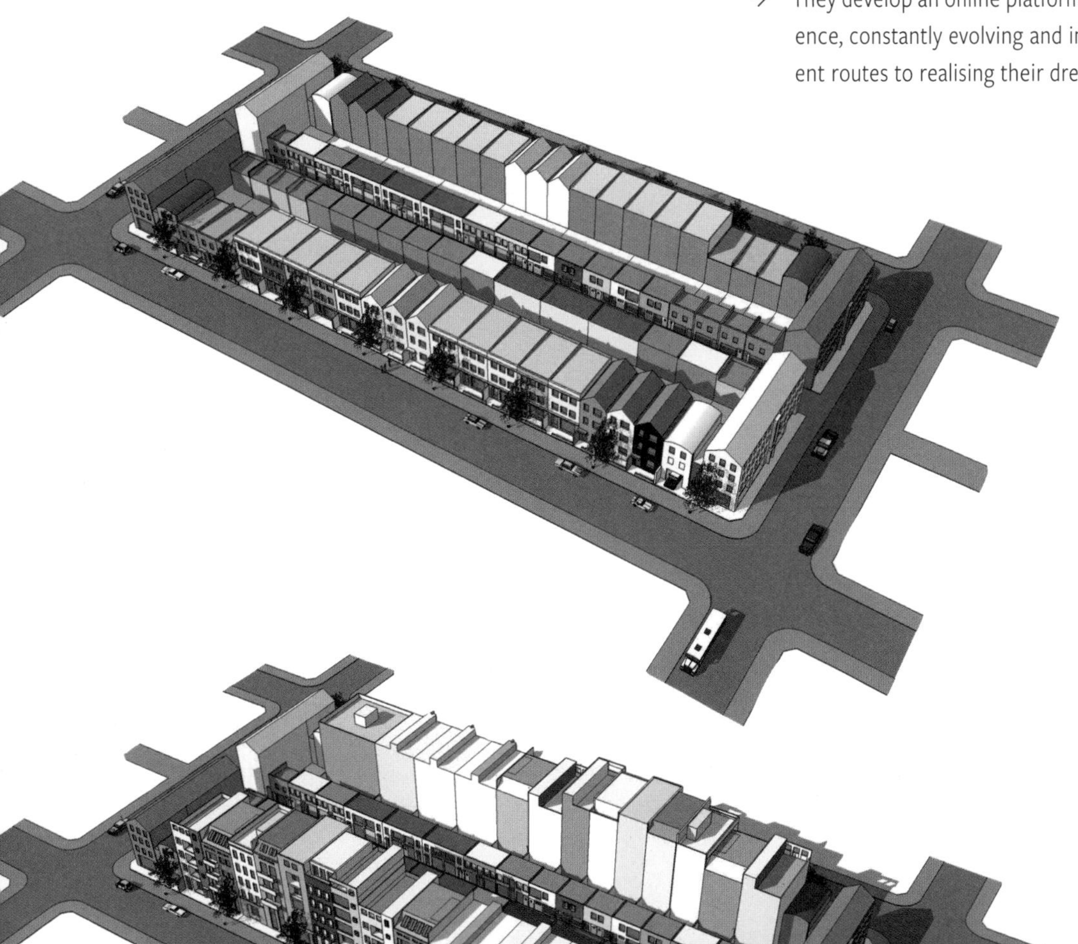

Option 3: The formal medium-density route
In this example, we see regular subdivisions of the lot. A range of 2- to 4-storey housing typologies has been developed based on different frontage dimensions—5, 6 and 7.5 metres (16, 20 and 25 feet).

Option 4: The formal higher-density route
In this example, we see regular subdivisions of the lot. A range of 4- to 6-storey housing typologies, including multiple occupancy townhouses and small apartment blocks has been developed based on different frontage dimensions—6, 7.5, 10 and 15 metres (20, 25, 33 and 50 feet).

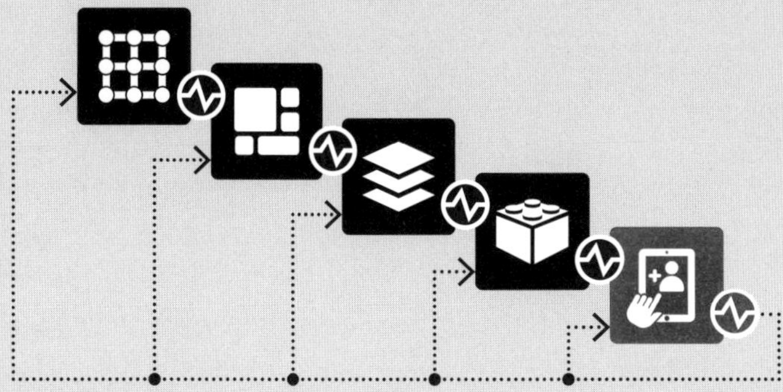

ACTIVATORS

BUILDING SOCIAL CAPITAL AT THE OUTSET

Activators, our final condition, are enabling mechanisms that trigger urban life and build social capital in a variety of scales, from the street to the neighbourhood. An activator has a greater purpose than to solve a functional problem or to provide an amenity. It involves the introduction of one ingredient to modify others. It is the stimulator of change working with all the other conditions to mobilise and energise communities. It positively catalyses collective action, opening up infinite possibilities for neighbourhood building.

Activator *NOUN*

1 An agent that catalyses collective action by stimulating or precipitating a reaction, development or change

2 A tactical generator of constructive social activism

3 A positive action that triggers an equal and opposite positive reaction

SYNONYMS
stimulant, trigger, generator, catalyst

SCOPE

This section talks about four theoretical concepts: activating collective intelligence, unlocking the social and civic economy, mobilising social activism and introducing 'innovativeness' into the system. It goes on to describe the qualities of activators and the importance of self-organisation in bottom-up systems.

Topics include:

→ **Asset-based community development:** as a methodology for the sustainable development of communities based on their strengths and potentials

→ **Shared visions:** built by creating a sense of commonality that gives coherence to diverse neighbourhood activities

→ **Participatory (bottom-up) budgeting:** as a means of directly involving local citizens in making decisions about how public money is spent in their community

→ **Activator programmes:** including innovative land-use strategies, people-activation strategies and implementation strategies—all set within the context of changing behaviours

→ **Development tools:** focussing on the use of NEIGHBOURHOOD CO:EFFICIENT, a neighbourhood gaming technique to engage collective civic action

→ **Localia urban neighbourhood—mobilising constructive community action:** showing an imaginary example of this process

THEORY

For the past decade, the term *social capital* has resonated strongly with communities across the world attempting to improve their residents' quality of life and overall well-being. *Social capital*, defined as 'the social networks and the norms of trustworthiness and reciprocity that arise from them,' is a powerful predictor of many social goods. It unlocks creativity and goodwill to trigger improvement in people's health and happiness, levels of economic development, functioning of schools, safe neighbourhoods and responsive government.

In our neighbourhoods, districts and quarters, an activator is a trigger for building a thriving urban society from the bottom up: it is anything that mobilises and energises the goodwill and creativity of people to deliver Massive Small change. It fuels emergence at the local scale. It is vital to building community.

Many of the methods outlined in this section require fundamentally different modes of behaviour, particularly by the public sector, in the planning, design and delivery of catalytic projects. In a constantly evolving programme of change, we need to set aside our obsessions with neatness and accept messiness as a precursor to emergence. Here we embrace the informal. We take flux as an emergent condition before maturity. We are prepared to turn a blind eye and give things time to settle. We now manage change better. We arm a place with its triggers of change. We monitor and adapt.

Despite the obvious fundamental contradiction between planned and unplanned, the informal and the formal are not contradictions. Saskia Sassen's studies on global economies and world cities show that informal and formal economies not only co-exist but also depend on each other.

While innovation comes more from informal contexts, formal settings normally ensure long-lasting, sustainable effects. We must formalise the informal. We also need to analyse and understand the unplanned patterns behind self-organised activities; deduct prototypes, models and tools from this investigation; formalise them; and make them available to all stakeholders. One the other hand, formal procedures of planning, administration and management have to be critically examined, and ways and strategies found for how existing practices can be de-formalised, de-institutionalised, adapted and changed.

Activators open up the potential for unlimited innovation in all its forms. Planning and design become more local, more personal and more exciting. We use our urban pioneers to initiate and mobilise change. Innovation is king. The others follow. There is a greater focus on experimentation in a range of locations. Planning and design become relevant again!

> *You can't use up creativity. The more you use, the more you have.*
>
> —Maya Angelou

Collective intelligence

Collective intelligence is referred to as shared or group intelligence that emerges from the collaboration, joint efforts and sustained competition of many individuals. It appears universally in consensus decision-making. It can be described as an emergent property of people and ways of processing information about their built environment.

Pierre Lévy defines collective intelligence as 'a form of universally distributed intelligence, constantly enhanced, coordinated in real time, and resulting in the effective mobilisation of skills.' He supports the claim that collective intelligence is necessary for the process of building democracy, as it is closely linked with knowledge-based culture, which is 'sustained by mutual sharing of ideas, and creates a better understanding of a diverse society involving different actors.'

Crowdsourcing of ideas has evolved from anonymous forms of collective intelligence and is growing towards credible, open source, collaborative intelligence methods that harness social networks.

Unlocking the social and civic economy

Wikipedia tells us that the *social economy* is the third sector amongst economies and lies between the private and public sectors. It includes organisations such as cooperatives, nonprofit organisations, social enterprises and charities. According to Wikipedia,

> A social economy develops because of a need for new solutions for issues (social, economic or environmental) and to satisfy requirements, which have been ignored (or inadequately fulfilled) by the private or public sectors. By using solutions to achieve not-for-profit aims, a social economy has a unique role in creating a stable, sustainable, prosperous and inclusive society.

Successful social economy organisations play a role in fulfilling governmental policy objectives by:

- → Increasing productivity and competitiveness
- → Enabling individuals and communities to form and regenerate local neighbourhoods
- → Demonstrating new ways of delivering public services
- → Developing an inclusive society for all its people and stimulating active citizenship

The social economy is a subset of the larger civic economy, which operates across a broader spectrum of interests.

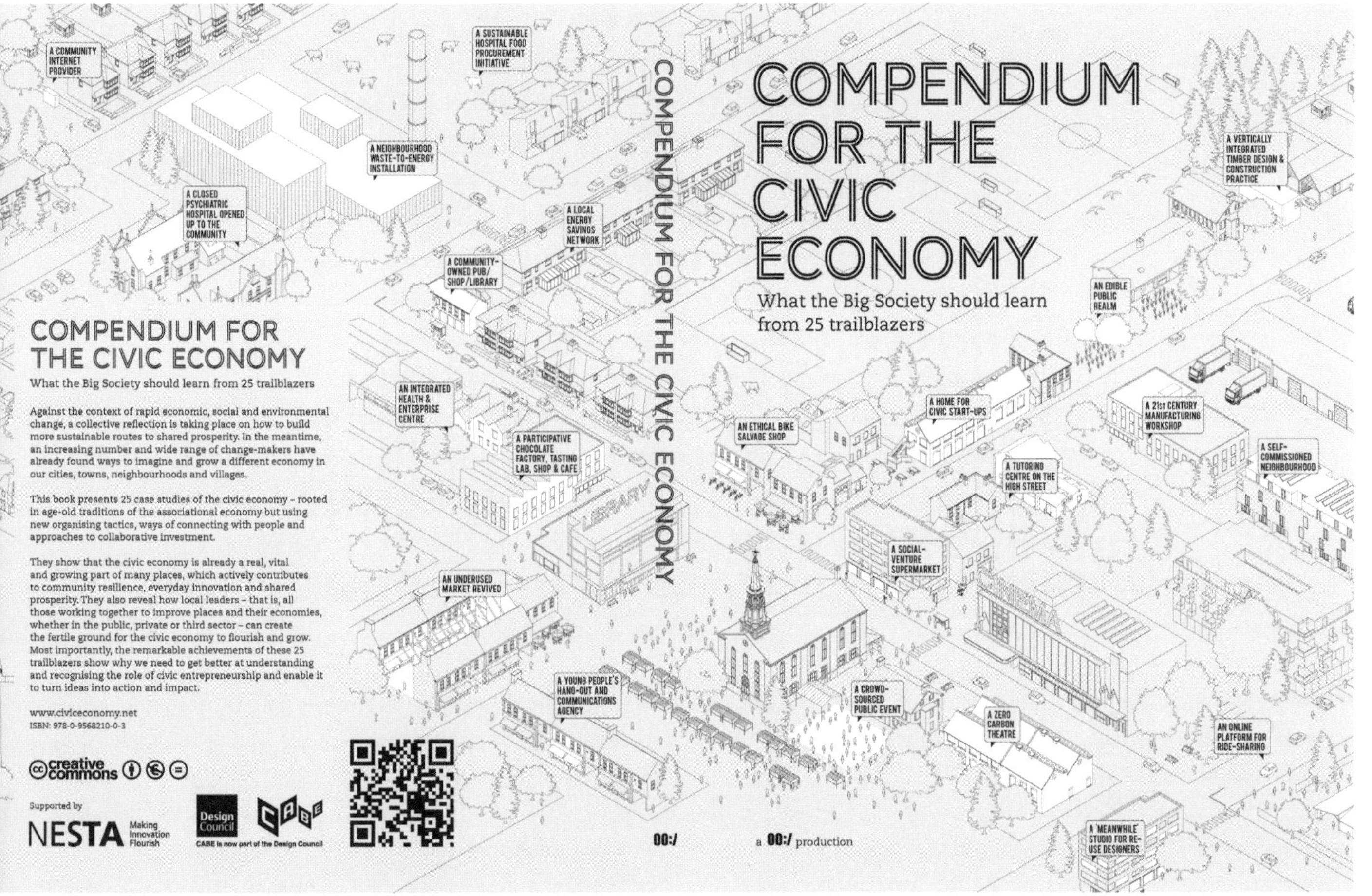

> *The civic economy is not the exclusive domain of any particular sector of the economy; instead, it bridges across the public, private and organised third sector as well as including the general public.*
>
> —Roger Murray

The civic economy has the potential to radically influence how neighbourhoods are formed. This potential is particularly important now that much of the urban regeneration and place-shaping practices of the past decade or so have failed to deliver the quality of place that people demand. Founded upon agreed social values and using collaborative methods to develop, produce, and share knowledge and finance, the civic economy delivers goods and services in ways that neither the state nor the market economy alone has been able to accomplish.

> *A civic economy is emerging, one which is fundamentally both open and social.... It's an economy which is fusing the culture of the web with civic purpose.*
>
> —Architecture 00

There is a lot to learn from the myriad of social innovations that are already showing us how the 'civic economy' can work to build urban society. This economy combines social entrepreneurship with the aspiration of civic renewal. It is already a vibrant movement, with many new projects, networks and behaviours changing the nature and economy of neighbourhoods across the world. From local food-growing projects to people's supermarkets, community waste-to-energy plants to cooperative utility services, these initiatives are having a fundamental impact on social interactions and economic opportunities in cities and their neighbourhoods. They are even influencing the physical shape and functioning of these places, changing the way they are designed, built and used.

The Compendium for the Civic Economy, produced by the Young Foundation and NESTA by Architecture 00, describes this new economy as bringing together

> a wide range of inspiring examples that begin to illustrate what places built upon a different economy might look like: edible public spaces, crowd-funded work spaces for social entrepreneurs, peer-to-peer car sharing websites, and town centre markets revitalised by a fresh approach to igniting good ideas. The list is growing—and its potential is enormous. This potential is a trend that goes beyond traditional divides between the public, private and third sectors. It is an attitude that questions all aspects of supply chains and makes them more equitable; an approach that enables citizens to be co-producers and investors instead of just consumers; and an opportunity to unlock and share the resources we have more effectively. This is the civic economy.

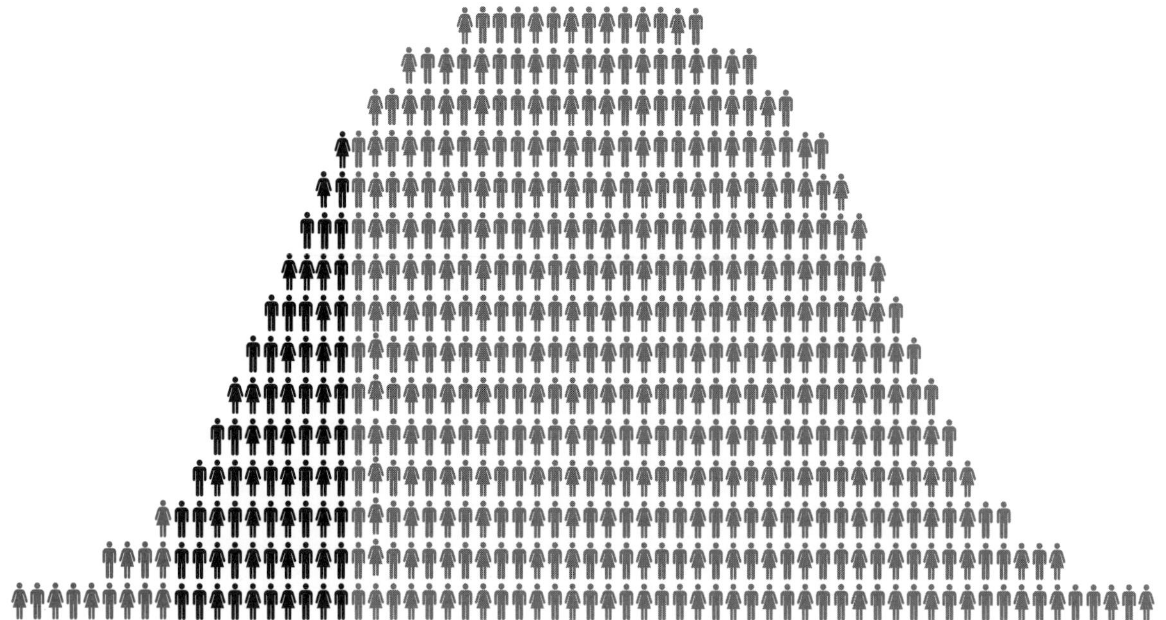

INTRODUCING 'INNOVATIVENESS' INTO THE SYSTEM

Everett Rogers' *Diffusion of Innovations*, discussed earlier, proposes that diffusion is

> the process by which an innovation is communicated through certain channels over time among the members of a social system. Individuals progress through 5 stages: knowledge, persuasion, decision, implementation, and confirmation. If the innovation is adopted, it spreads via various communication channels. During communication, the idea is rarely evaluated from a scientific standpoint; rather, subjective perceptions of the innovation influence diffusion. The process occurs over time.

Finally, social systems determine how and what happens, the roles of opinion leaders and change agents, the types of innovation decisions, and consequences of these.

To put this into action, we need to introduce 'innovativeness' into the system. The adoption process that follows, tracked through the diffusion curve, is a decision-making one in which an individual passes from the initial knowledge of innovation to forming an attitude towards the innovation. This attitude then leads to a choice to adopt or reject it, then to its implementation and the use of the new idea, and finally to confirmation of this choice. The process recognises the importance of the innovators and the early adopters in bringing the majority along.

1 **Innovators**

Innovators are venturesome, have multiple sources of information and show greater propensity to take risks. They are motivated by the idea of being a change agent in their community. They are willing to tolerate initial problems that may accompany new approaches and are willing to make radical shifts to solving such problems.

2 **Early adopters**

Early adopters are popular social leaders—visionaries in their market—and are looking to adopt and use new approaches to achieve a revolutionary breakthrough that will make a dramatic competitive advantage in their lives. They typically demand personalised solutions and quick-response, highly qualified support. In the context of a bottom-up agenda, we can take this thinking into working with communities to transform their neighbourhoods. We are not just talking about radical innovation; any shift from the status quo will involve some form of change. Many people in their communities will be the agents of change. They will be the innovators or the early adopters. We need to harness their energies in our bottom-up world.

Every community has latent assets—individual, collective and institutional:

→ Each community has its share of thoughtful, committed citizens who can be mobilised to help. Community development is strongest when it involves a broad base of community action.

→ Each community has its 3 per cent of innovators and its 13 per cent of early adopters. Tip the scales with this 16 per cent and change happens.

→ Each community has its leaders. Good leaders enable others to follow. They just need to be released to act in the community interest.

→ Each community has its fair share of skills—good thinkers, good problem solvers, good organisers and good doers. They just need to be unearthed.

→ Each community has its communicators—people who spread the word, people who share knowledge and people who tell stories. They need to be given the freedom to do what they do best.

QUALITIES OF ACTIVATORS

> *Don't get involved in partial problems, but always take flight to where there is a free view over the whole single great problem, even if this view is still not a clear one.*
>
> —Ludwig Wittgenstein

Neighbourhoods are classic self-organising systems. They form as distinct clusters: around uses, activities, community groups or even social classes.

Nobody tells people where to go; they chose to move to places that best serve their physical, social or economic needs. Every place forms its identity around its activators, and these are many and diverse: urban pioneers who made the first move, good schools, the best cheese shop in town, immigrant arrival points, old buildings looking for new lives. Creative quarters emerge around specific sectors (theatre, media, design professionals), lawyers establish their legal precincts, gay neighbourhoods are colonised, ethnic groups come together, young families gentrify declining areas.

You cannot design these places by zoning them, but you can create the conditions for them to emerge—and you can provide the activators to stimulate them. Catalysing any affirmative action, such as changing a market's perception of an area, requires an understanding of how innovation is diffused and ultimately adopted as the prevailing market view. It is now well accepted that a diffusion process in any social system follows a curved pattern in which the adoption of a new approach begins with slow change, is followed by rapid change and ends again in slow change as the product matures or new alternatives develop. People adopt innovations at different times and different rates.

These are the qualities that activators need to foster:

1 **Shared purpose** is an integrating force that enables people to work collaboratively to achieve urban society's goals, rather than developing their position at the expense of their fellow citizens. They must see the big picture.

2 **Social responsibility** is an ethical framework and suggests that an entity, be it a group or individual, is obliged to act for the benefit of society as a whole.

3 **Reciprocity** is a social rule that says people should recompense, in kind, what another person has provided for them. That is, people give back the kind of benefits they have received from another.

4 **Responsiveness** is the quality of reacting quickly. As a quality in a person, it involves responding with emotion to people and events. Responsiveness shows how much someone cares.

5 **Collective action** refers to measures taken together by a group of individuals whose goal is to enhance their status and achieve a common objective. It is enacted by a representative of the group.

6 **Cooperation** is the action or process of working together to the same end or towards a common effort.

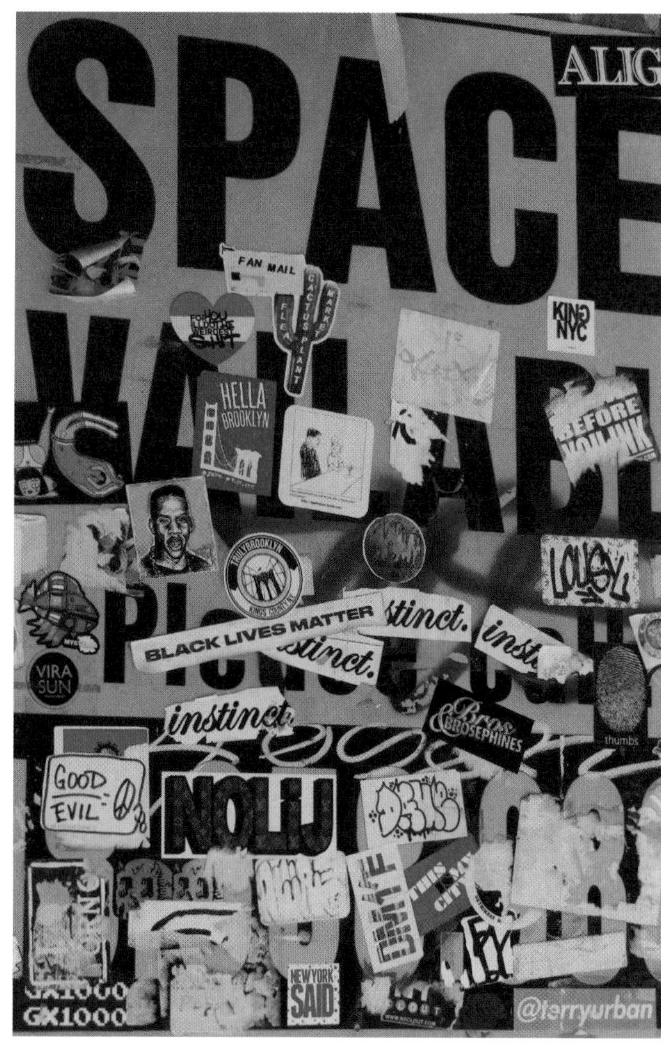

TYPE 1: ASSET-BASED COMMUNITY DEVELOPMENT

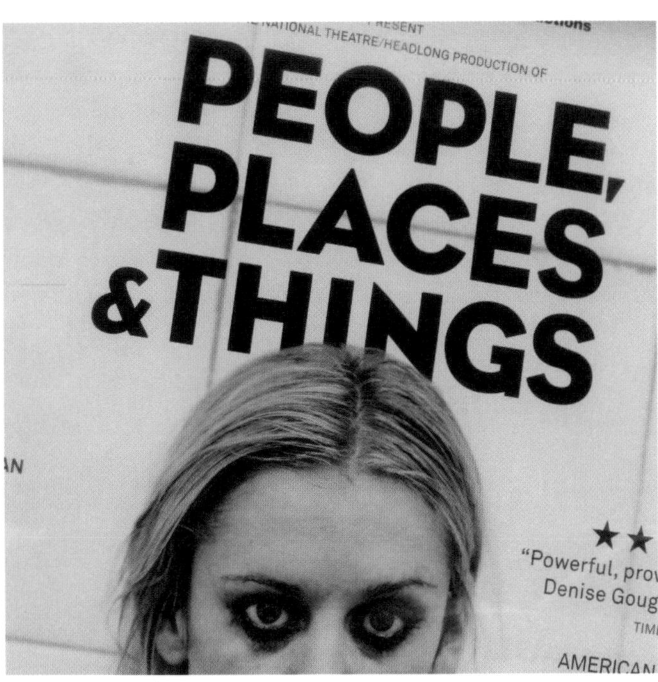

According to Wikipedia, asset-based community development (ABCD) is 'a methodology for the sustainable development of communities based on their strengths and potentials'. The ABCD approach was developed by John L. McKnight and John P. Kretzmann in their book, *Building Communities from the Inside Out: A Path Toward Finding and Mobilizing a Community's Assets.*

Community assets can be described as the collective resources that individuals and groups have at their disposal. How they can be deployed to meet the needs and aspirations of the community involves:

1 assessing the resources, skills and experience available in a community
2 developing opportunities for meaningful engagement by building supportive groups and networks
3 organising the community by making individual issues community ones that move its members into action
4 determining and taking appropriate action

Whereas traditional needs-based community development looks to local government to solve its problems, asset-based community development leverages the existing creativity and goodwill within the community to address these problems. Asset-based approaches are underpinned by attitudes and values related to personal and collective empowerment and activated within the context of positive change for the neighbourhood.

> *True values are not taught and declared; they evolve through the acts and interaction of the living, they are understood at a near tacit level by those who live them.*
>
> —Dave Snowden

Rather than building fragile reliance on top-down solutions (that often trap disadvantaged people in cycles of dependency), ABCD aims to expand capacity within communities by building their social capital. It understands that:

→ **Everyone has gifts.** Each person in a community has something to contribute to society.
→ **Relationships build a community.** People must be connected for sustainable community development to take place.
→ **Citizens must be at the centre.** Citizens should be viewed as actors—not recipients—in development.
→ **Enabling leaders activate others.** Community development is strongest when it involves a broad base of community action.
→ **Most people want to do the right thing.** Challenge notions of 'apathy' by listening to people's interests.
→ **Everyone must listen and learn.** Decisions should come from conversations where people are heard.
→ **Leaders must not be scared to ask.** Asking for ideas is more sustainable than giving solutions.
→ **Bottom-up self-organisation is critical.** Local community members create their hierarchical structures to lead.
→ **Institutions serve the community.** Institutional leaders should create opportunities for community member involvement, then step back.

ABCD looks to strengthen civil society by engaging people as citizens in community development, making local services more efficient and responsive.

This means the role of local government needs to realign to focus on facilitating and empowering rather than on delivering. Local government should not relinquish responsibility but should redeploy budgets and resources to enable bottom-up change to flourish. Empowered communities, with their resources and assets working for them, are in a better position to acquire additional external resources and put them to the most efficient and enduring use.

The ABCD approach has developed some different tools to activate communities. These are outlined on the page opposite.

1 Capacity inventory

This tool lists and develops an understanding of a community's abilities, including the following:

- → **Individual skills:** all skills, however specialised or varied, that could be used as trade-offs with others' skills—for example, digital knowledge, building, caring or professional services and so on
- → **Community skills:** the community work in which each person has participated—to determine potential future work interests
- → **Enterprise skills:** an individual's experience in business—to determine interest in starting a business
- → **Personal interests:** information on areas where someone could be mobilised to help in any way to advance the interests of the community

2 Community asset mapping

This tool recognises that there are five key assets in any given community—individuals, associations, institutions, property and connections—which can be sorted into three categories:

1. **Gifts of individuals:** such as youth, talents and skills, elderly, arts and culture, and benefactors
2. **Citizens' associations:** such as neighbourhood groups, places of worship, clubs and cultural bodies
3. **Local institutions:** such as educational establishments, business and industry, libraries and health facilities

Community asset maps are used instead of needs maps, which focus solely on problems in communities. Community asset maps, as an alternative, concentrate on the opportunities of community assets, abilities, skills, and strengths to build future neighbourhoods.

3 Time banking

Time banks are another example of using community assets to connect individuals' assets to one another in the collective interest of the community. They offer a unique way to help people develop their joint networks of support that underpin healthy communities.

The time bank is 'a mutual volunteering scheme, using time as a currency. Participants 'deposit' their time in the bank by giving practical help and support to others and can withdraw their time when they need something done themselves.' Neighbours and local organisations can share skills with one another, and earn and spend time bank hours or 'credits' in the process through a system of barter.

Time banking allows, for example, an hour of childcare to be equal to a proportional amount of time for home repair or even tax preparation.

4 Co-production

Co-production is both similar to and relies on an asset-based approach. It essentially describes an equal and reciprocal relationship between government and people that draws on the knowledge, ability and resources of both parties to come up with solutions that are practical, sustainable and cost-effective—it changes the balance of power from top to bottom.

According to the New Economics Foundation in their paper 'Co-production: A Manifesto for Growing the Core Economy', the essential characteristics of co-production exemplify asset-based principles:

- → Recognising people as assets rather than as problems—people are the real wealth of society
- → Valuing work differently—unpaid work such as caring is priceless
- → Promoting reciprocity—giving and receiving builds trust and mutual respect
- → Building robust and supportive social networks—relationships are the heart of people's well-being
- → Building on people's existing skills and resources
- → Facilitating rather than delivering
- → Breaking down the divisions between service providers and service users

Co-production is a useful tool for local or neighbourhood decision-making and works best when dealing with small constituencies, such as a neighbourhood or those affected by a particular service or service provider.

BENEFITS

The Glasgow Centre for Population Health, in their paper 'Putting Asset-Based Approaches into Practice: Identification, Mobilisation and Measurement of Assets', shows a number of potential benefits in taking an assets-based approach for individuals and communities. For those who engage, the potential benefits include:

- → More control over their lives and where they live
- → The ability to influence the decisions that affect them and their communities
- → The opportunity to be engaged how and as they want to be and to be seen as part of the solution, not the problem

This process may then lead to increased well-being through strengthening control, knowledge, self-esteem and social contacts, giving skills for life and work. Asset-based activities ensure that engagement with individuals is meaningful and empowering rather than tokenistic and consultative. This approach also strives to engage with people who would not usually get involved.

TYPE 2: BUILDING SHARED VISIONS

> *Few, if any, forces in human affairs are as powerful as a shared vision.*
>
> —Peter Senge

Peter Senge, in his book *The Fifth Discipline: The Art & Practice of The Learning Organization*, describes a shared vision as

> a force in people's hearts, a force of impressive power... At its simplest level, a shared vision is the answer to the question, 'What do we want to create?' A shared vision is a picture that everyone in the organisation carries in their heads and hearts.

So what does a shared vision do for a neighbourhood? It converts an abstract place into 'our neighbourhood'. It creates a sense of shared agenda and gives coherence to diverse activities. It allows everyone to work together. It creates a common identity and a strong sense of purpose. It encourages different ways of thinking and acting. It gives people courage, fosters risk-taking and promotes experimentation. Basically, without a shared vision, that vision you spent time creating is pointless and meaningless. And without a shared vision, the neighbourhood as a doing and learning collective cannot exist.

According to James Kouzes and Barry Posner in 'To Lead, Create a Shared Vision',

> As counterintuitive as it might seem, then, the best way to lead people into the future is to connect with them deeply in the present. The only visions that take hold are shared visions—and you will create them only when you listen very, very closely to others, appreciate their hopes, and attend to their needs. The best leaders are able to bring their people into the future because they engage in the oldest form of research: They observe the human condition.

APPRECIATIVE INQUIRY

> *We live in the world our questions create.*
>
> —David Cooperrider

Appreciative inquiry is a type of action-based research developed by David Cooperrider and Suresh Srivastva to build shared visions. They felt that the reliance on 'problem solving' hampered social improvement, and what was demanded was new methods of exploration that would help generate new ideas, tools and tactics to engage stakeholders in self-determined change.

According to Wikipedia, appreciative inquiry advocates collective inquiry into the 'best of what is, to imagine what could be, followed by joint design of a desired future state that is compelling and, thus, does not require the use of incentives, coercion or persuasion for planned change to occur.'

The model has been used as a process for valuing and drawing out the strengths and successes in the history of a group or community. The inquiry starts with gaining an understanding of 'the best of what is', continues with considering what might be and should be, and ends with 'a shared commitment to a vision and how to achieve it.' The process is not just about establishing facts but involves finding out where assets such as knowledge, motivation and passion exist in a community. The model is also a methodology for discovering new things, understanding complex processes and fostering innovation through the gathering of positive stories and images to construct positive interaction.

> *Let's come together to demonstrate the tomorrow we're working for; show how the world could be; make such a world feel not just possible, but fundamentally irresistible. Let us create a place where beliefs are made and unmade, and the limits of the tomorrow can be stretched together.*
>
> —Andrew Boyd

Some examples of appreciative inquiry include:

1 **Storytelling** as an informal and personal way of collecting information about people's experiences. Sharing and valuing different stories of past achievements is engaging and energising. Narratives can be a powerful vehicle for understanding and communicating the ways in which people and governments working together can activate community development. The book *The Radical Incrementalist: How to Build Urban Society in 12 Lessons* by the author was a way of showing how shared visions could be created to help build urban neighbourhoods through telling personal stories.

2 **The world café approach** is another technique that makes use of an informal setting for participants to explore urban issues through discussion in small groups around tables. People feel more comfortable and creative in a more familiar café environment and behaviours to stimulate more relaxed and open conversations flourish. Moving between groups, people cross-pollinate ideas and discover new insights into the questions or issues that are most important in their neighbourhood.

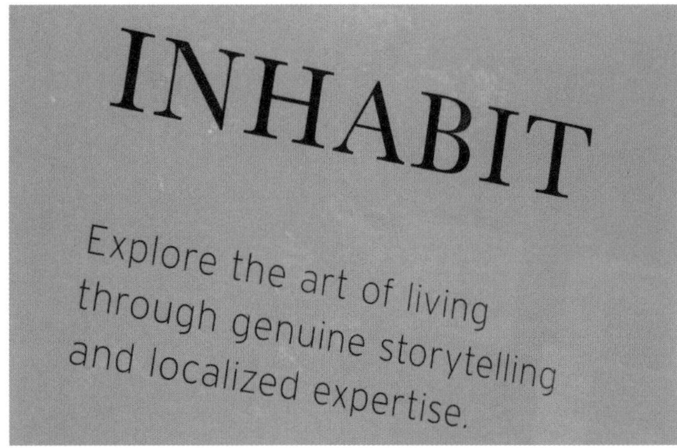

3 **Co-creation** involves curating meetings, festivals or events to help bring people together to work on an area of mutual interest, to help develop a vision for the future, and to work with others to make things happen quickly. Some examples of this form of appreciative inquiry include:

→ Open Space Technology (OST) is a method based upon evidence that meeting in a circle is the most productive way to encourage honest, frank and equal discussion, the open space referring to the area in the centre of the circle. This approach allows for a diverse group of participants to work together on a complex, potentially conflicting, real issue in an innovative and productive way. Open Space creates a progressive and dynamic conversation that is stimulated by mutual enthusiasm in a topic. It allows creative thinking around an issue when free and open discussions and collective decision-making are required. The process is very flexible and is driven by the collective will of the participants. This approach allows participants to develop ownership of the outcomes, supports the development of better working relationships and builds a strong sense of community.

→ Demo.B is a festival hosted by the Impact Hub in Birmingham, United Kingdom, with a series of open, co-curated events. With the help of local citizens, its aim was to explore, celebrate and actively demonstrate ways in which people could collectively build a better Birmingham together. Over three weeks Demo.B explored the nuances of a democratic city and how collective action could be accelerated through a range of themes—from citizen science to the spoken word—developing new models, ideas and ventures and inspiring people and communities to build a shared vision of a better world.

→ Civic Camp, a democratic, nonpartisan, public advocacy group in Calgary, Canada, enabled people to engage in the evolution of an improved social fabric and environmentally, socially and fiscally sustainable community. The underlying principle was that 'democracy is not something we have; it's something we make'. Civic Camp's role was to build a shared vision for the city from the grassroots upwards.

TYPE 3: PARTICIPATORY (BOTTOM-UP) BUDGETING

A budget is telling your money where to go instead of wondering where it went.

—Dave Ramsey

Participatory budgeting (also called bottom-up budgeting) is a means of directly involving local citizens in making decisions about how public money is spent in their neighbourhood. It is done through a process of open, democratic deliberation and decision-making, and a type of participatory democracy in which ordinary people decide how to allocate part of a municipal or public budget. It is the perfect tool for activating collective action. It is participatory governance in action.

Participatory budgeting has a number of goals:

1 To help local people shape local services to more effectively meet local needs

2 To allow citizens to identify, discuss and prioritise public-spending projects

3 To involve those left out of traditional processes of public engagement—low-income residents, noncitizens and youth

4 To involve local citizens in decision-making that is more in depth and meaningful than traditional consultation processes

5 To ensure that people have fair opportunities to have their say and make a real contribution

6 To increase transparency, accountability, understanding and social inclusion in local government affairs

According to Chris Harkins and James Egan in their paper 'The Role of Participatory Budgeting in Promoting Localism and Mobilising Community Assets', participatory budgeting offers a practical mechanism to:

→ Activate community assets and promote community empowerment, shifting power from the top to the bottom

→ Enable devolved decision-making and support collaborative working to move from an elected to a direct form

→ Deliver social and human capital benefits, including improved self-confidence in tackling community issues, enhanced negotiating skills and bringing together people from different backgrounds

→ Ensure more equitable public spending, increased satisfaction of basic needs, display greater government transparency and accountability, and increase levels of public participation

→ Build social capital by creating forums for local groups to meet, negotiate and make decisions together

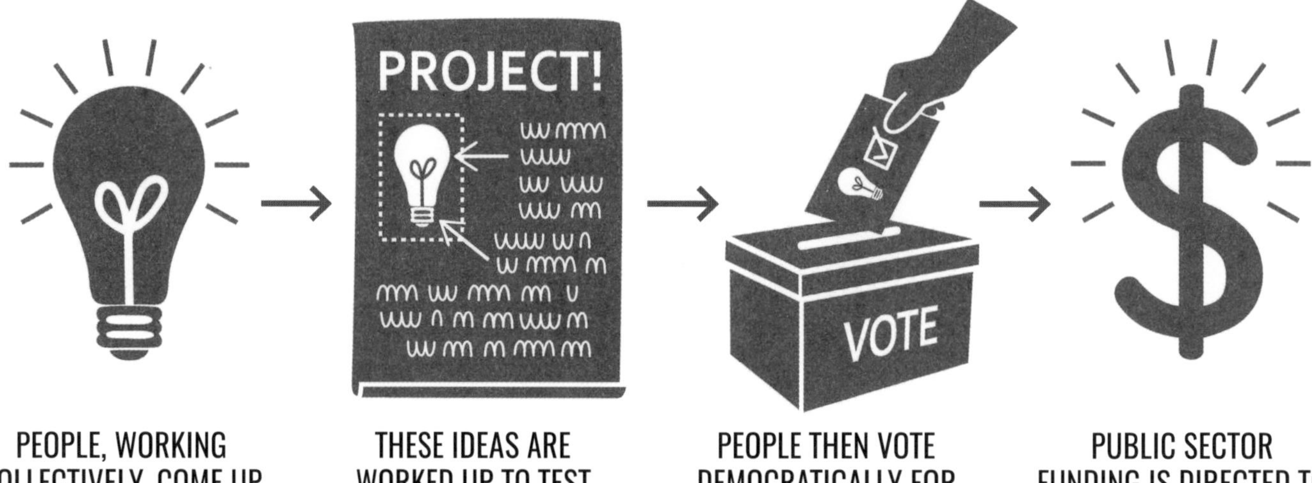
PROJECT!
VOTE
PEOPLE, WORKING COLLECTIVELY, COME UP WITH PROJECT IDEAS
THESE IDEAS ARE WORKED UP TO TEST PROJECT'S FEASIBILITY
PEOPLE THEN VOTE DEMOCRATICALLY FOR THESE PROJECTS
PUBLIC SECTOR FUNDING IS DIRECTED TO THE PROJECTS

From multi-million euro capital developments in the City of Paris to small-scale local regeneration projects in local communities in Scotland, participatory budgeting is based on opening up decision-making on public budgets—it's not just about money. It's also about stimulating new learning, volunteering and community activism.

—Jez Hall

According to Giovanni Allegretti of Coimbra University, participatory budgeting in different forms is being carried out in over 250 cities worldwide. In Pune in India, new forms of participatory budgeting are being used to drive slum-upgrading programmes. In New York, teenagers have become involved in participatory budgeting activities with the High Line community involvement project. The coastal city of Cascais near Lisbon deployed an SMS voting system to let citizens decide on the allocation of 1.5 million euros. Politicians recognise the extensive demand for participation in budgets. This recognition is reinforced by former Brazilian president, Lula, who argues that:

> People do not simply wish to vote every four years. They want daily interaction with governments both local and national, and to take part in defining public policies, offering opinions on the decisions that affect them each day. In short, they want to be heard.

Participatory budgeting is now gaining momentum in Scotland, with new processes developing across the country. Many local authorities are undertaking capacity-building programmes.

A new commitment in the Scottish government's manifesto states:

> Councils [will include] a target of having at least 1 percent of their budget subject to Community Choices budgeting. This commitment will be backed by the Community Choices Fund to help public bodies and community groups build on examples of best practice.

Participatory budgeting is not an easy process, but who said democracy was easy? It requires capacity building, it requires scale, and it requires continuity and commitment. It needs time to mature for trust to be built. It is our best shot at putting democracy into urbanism—from the bottom up.

Highline Park in New York provided an opportunity for all walks of life to become involved in participatory budgeting.

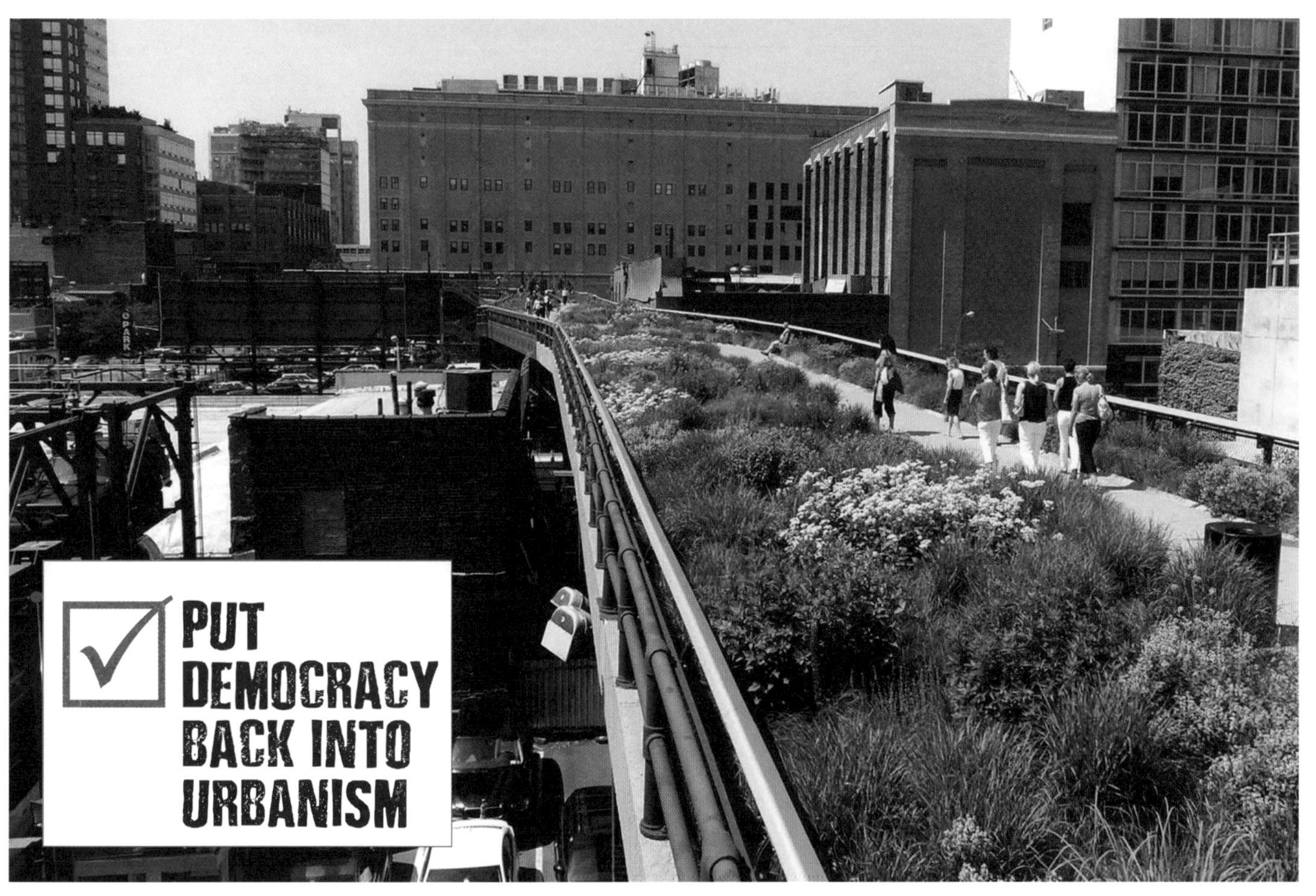
PUT DEMOCRACY BACK INTO URBANISM

TYPE 4: ACTIVATOR PROGRAMMES

There are a number of activators we can consider that could trigger positive change and increase the prospects of emergence. Some involve intervention; others involve standing back. Some can be used alone or in combination with one another. All are valid.

INNOVATIVE LAND-USE STRATEGIES

It is in the creative release of land that we can make a big difference in catalysing action. Where the old ways of defining a land use and marketing it for specific uses have failed, we can open up the door to new thinking.

Jeroen Saris, an urban strategist from Amsterdam, has developed an interesting model for urban development in which you should have at least a period of five years to open an area, attract people with ideas and forget about strict rules. Those are the ingredients for experiments and creative development. He says:

> Development companies should not only be focused on investors, but also on idea makers. Those idea investors should not be paid in cash, but in rights to use the space for a certain time.

Above: A streetmarket under the arches in Dumbo, New York. **Opposite page, top left:** Model of Scotswood Housing Expo, Newcastle, UK. **Top right:** Urban farming in New York.

Free idea zones

A free idea zone (FIZ) is a form of 'white land'—an unzoned part of the city—with 'fields' laid out that can be released incrementally. It is a zone where new ideas can be explored, often ideas that have not yet been fully formed and experimentation is deliberately encouraged as an innovative economic development strategy. It is emergence at its lowest level and works well in rapidly evolving economies, such as we have today.

For commercial development, a FIZ is an alternative to a traditional business park model, which rigidly lays out its wares for the market to accept. In a FIZ, new companies can bite off what they need and set up at little cost to develop their offers. These are the 'fertile fields' that facilitate a form of commercial squatting that can be formalised over time.

For neighbourhoods, a FIZ could be found in the small trading estates on their peripheries or former brownfield sites next to the railway tracks. In all instances, it says 'We are not here to tell you what to do...you tell us!'

Greyworld

Greyworld is a version of the FIZ but applied to existing underused urban fabric. It values *messiness*—a state that defies description but has many possible qualities for enabling emergence. Classically, greyworld is in old industrial buildings, in spaces under the arches or in low-grade backlands. Greyworld is an economic development zone, identified in a planning document as an area where the lowest rung on the economic ladder is protected at all costs. It implies a deliberate turning of a blind eye to any activity that may arise.

Staying away is a conscious intention, particularly in keeping planners and health and safety away so unpredictable things can happen. It is like formalising meanwhile uses with the express intention of keeping them there.

Test beds

This mechanism can be used to change market perception of an area and involves creative use of land to catalyse change. Creating test beds includes setting aside serviced land to accommodate demonstration projects and early wins, and they can take the form of:

→ National neighbourhood challenge pilot programmes

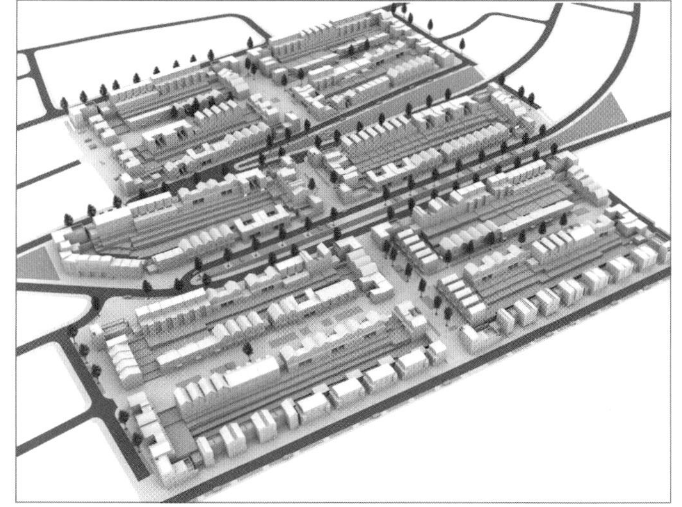

- → Ideas competitions where local people offer solutions that can be trialled as part of community development projects
- → Local housing expos by local builders to test new housing models, methods and materials
- → Show home projects, either temporary or permanent, that could act as benchmarks for prototyping and quality
- → Community self-build projects
- → *Grand Designs*–type projects, working with urban pioneers and early adopters
- → Incentive pricing of serviced land with special offers for first in, deferred land payments and discounts for early delivery

Sparks

Sparks are catalysts where specific higher-order generative uses or activities are introduced to trigger related activities—the civic infrastructure, public spaces and social, cultural and economic infrastructure. In other words, the activating 'sparks' for generating urban fabric and the local accretion of urban life.

1 **Civic infrastructure**—the town hall, library, courts and public offices—in combination with the civic square, are democratic symbols of urban society, which is why they are critically located in prominent places and look different. They should start as 'symbols', however temporary or incomplete, to build confidence in a place. They can be as multi-purpose as the community wants, but must be public.

2 **Public spaces**, at every scale, are the generators for public life and social interaction. Marketplaces and street spaces provide the lowest rung on the economic ladder for many to start trading small and interacting with communities. They should be freely distributed within neighbourhoods and along high-activity routes and nodes. They should be protected within the urban fabric. The publication *Start with the Park* by the Commission for Architecture and the Built Environment (CABE) shows the benefits of community ownership in developing and maintaining green spaces. Places that are 'owned' are places that are loved.

3 **Education facilities**, at every level—the daycare centre to the university—become the building blocks of local community and civic life. For many, education of their children is a way of breaking down spirals of poverty, so the school becomes a vital cog in economic regeneration. Inderpaul Johar's work on Scale-free Schools points to the need for a different approach to the provision of school buildings and services. Why can't the whole community become the school, with just a central core, activating underutilised buildings and resources to build a strong sense of community? In this way, schools can scale up or scale down to meet the community's needs over time and not treat learning as a 'factory' process.

4 **Health facilities**—from the clinic to the hospital—can start in temporary or mobile buildings and evolve as local demands increase. Many health functions, such as community health, can be distributed systems sharing other underutilised spaces.

5 **All other social, cultural and economic uses can start small and evolve.** In this way the corner shop and their spaces above; the emerging school or civic space; and the temporary-use building and religious institutions all become part of that vital first point of social, economic and cultural life. They need not be big or complete to start. Sometimes they just need organisation, some form of programming or even a simple booking system to release their full potential.

THE COOL CO-PRODUCER

HOW A SOCIAL ENTREPRENEUR PUT HIS CITY BACK ON THE MAP

Julian's friends call him a hipster. He is happy if people think he's a bit different. He goes against the flow. He has taken over his father's foundry on the edge of Katowice city centre. Mergen Odlewnia, a family firm for more than 150 years, makes cooking pots. The impact of globalisation and technological change have led to the business shrinking dramatically, like many other traditional mining and steel industries.

In his book *Shrinking Cities: A Global Perspective*, Harry Richardson compares Katowice with Detroit. Though not of the same scale of shrinkage, between 2002 and 2011 Katowice lost 4 per cent of its population and 23 per cent of its manufacturing jobs. The region has found it difficult to adapt from a socialist economy to a market-driven one. Although much has been done to turn the city around, Katowice seems to lack confidence and purpose, especially after losing its bid to become European Capital of Culture 2016.

Julian does not feel that Katowice has much to offer culturally. When the flight comparison website Skyscanner tried to recommend 'cool Katowice' as an alternative destination to the historic city of Krakow, the best it could suggest was a trip to the huge but uninspiring Chorzow Park. It came as no surprise when Wrocław was chosen as the Capital of Culture. Julian was disappointed, thinking that Katowice could have done for industrial Upper Silesia what Essen did for the Ruhr when it was one of three European Capitals of Culture in 2010.

Julian hears about URBACT, a European Union–funded exchange programme that has focussed on the role of cultural activities and creative enterprises in the regeneration of many European cities.

He learns about examples of industrial regeneration such as the Custard Factory in Birmingham, the Ruhr Valley in Germany, Kaapelitehdas in Helsinki, and Coroglio-Bagnoli in Naples. Katowice is part of the programme but regrettably has no examples to show. Julian finds out about other cities worldwide that are using old industrial buildings to create new cultural quarters. In the Maboneng District of Johannesburg, a desolate part of the city has been transformed into a place that is fashionable and buzzing. Shoreditch in East London is emerging as a new technology and fashion district. Something closer to home is happening in Berlin: Julian reads about Klaus Overmeyer's Urban Catalyst project, which focusses on temporary uses as a way of starting.

Julian is a socially minded person who wants to do something for his city that will endure. Although he likes the idea of operating in a market-driven economy, he has strong ethics when it comes to business. He has a very large amount of factory space with which to do something different. He wants to try temporary uses: perhaps a fashion market or a venue for music events. He would like to create a hub for the newest business start-ups. He reads an article in *VentureVillage*, which professes to be the most entertaining news outlet for digital innovation in Europe, reporting on the hottest business start-up hubs across the continent.

In 'Why Poland Is Ready to Hit the Tech Big Time', Maciek Laskus argues for Poland's start-up potential. 'While everybody talks about Berlin, our cities are rarely mentioned in startup discussions or publications,' Laskus writes. 'I believe that this is just about to change and you should keep a close eye on Poland.' Even the OECD says that although the Polish have a strong entrepreneurial drive, they are not reaching their full potential. More needs to be done to create the environments for small- and medium-sized industries to flourish. Like Laskus, Julian crunches the numbers. Of the 40 million people living in Poland, 22.5 million use the internet. That is more than in three nearby markets combined: the Czech Republic, Finland and Hungary. As Laskus writes: 'While Czechs, Finns or Hungarians have to be global, Poles have more options to build local tech companies and still do amazingly well.'

Cultural and creative industries have grown significantly over the past twenty-five years, now accounting for a significant part of the economy in many countries. Creative firms tend to need affordable and flexible work-spaces and leases, with good connections to both formal and informal networks. All these features are usually found in postindustrial spaces in inner cities, so Mergen Odlewnia is a perfect location.

Julian needs support from the government. But government is focussing on the Katowice Special Economic Zone (a collection of business parks) to support and accelerate the transformation of obsolete Silesian industries, and to create new jobs. It hopes to attract international investment for high-tech industries. Government agencies do not see Julian's project as a priority. Their systems are too formal to be able to respond easily.

Julian needs support from the banks, but they would prefer to invest in new international businesses rather than what they see as a failing local business. They think his project is too risky.

He needs the planners to help make his project a reality, but his innovative approach does not fit their inflexible policy framework. The planners' priority is to implement their masterplan, which involves the wholesale demolition of all the buildings in the area and installation of their replacement, which is a computer-generated vision of an idealised modern city. They have plans for smaller cultural initiatives that they hope will stimulate regeneration in the city centre, but there is little progress with this. The planners are not inclined to support Julian's vision.

Julian feels that the system does not work for him:

1 The system does not build on the social capital of those who have invested in the city for years. Yet the people of Katowice have always banded together to overcome the difficulties of changing markets, politics and social conditions.
2 The big investors are interested in large-scale, shiny new schemes. They rarely see the assets that are already in a particular locality.
3 The system tends to obstruct local people who have new ideas about how to solve their city's complex problems.
4 The city sees culture as big buildings and brands itself a 'city of gardens'. Everyone is looking for the 'Bilbao effect' to transform their cities. Katowice needs something different.
5 The system seems to be trying to command and control every outcome, as if maintaining old industrial space could ensure that the old industries will return.

JULIAN KNOWS THINGS HAVE TO CHANGE

Planners and policymakers increasingly recognise the potential role of the arts, creative and tech industries in regenerating former industrial space in cities. The Sentier quarter in Paris, for example, home to numerous internet start-ups, is now called Silicon Sentier. Dublin's Digital Hub, set up by the government in 2003 as a hothouse for ideas, entrepreneurs and technological innovation, is a cluster of digital content and technology enterprises. Old brewery buildings near the city centre provide much of the accommodation. In London, former industrial sites are becoming creative and cultural production spaces. The Truman Brewery in East London's Brick Lane is one of the best-known examples of an adaptive reuse of a former industrial space, with a market, retail spaces and low-cost workspaces for artists and arts venues. The area as a whole is known as Tech City.

Julian hears about Make City in Berlin. He signs up to what is Berlin's first festival for architecture and urban alternatives, bringing together architects, planners, civic groups and developers in a city-wide conversation on thinking and making cities differently. The city of Berlin is becoming a magnet for investors and a site for large-scale transformations of urban landscapes. Its free spaces are increasingly precious resources. In 2014 a referendum saw Berliners vote against the city government's masterplan for the redevelopment of the former Tempelhof Airfield. They insisted on playing a part in rethinking and reshaping the city.

Julian listens to a TED Talk in which Toni Griffin speaks about Detroit Future City and the role that local minority businesses will play in transforming its economy. Like Detroit, Katowice needs to build on its skills in engineering to allow a range of other businesses to flourish. Like Detroit, Katowice has to move on and find a new purpose.

Julian approaches a local civic leader who is looking for a new cause. They begin working with a group of local businesses and residents. They give their project a name: EMERGENZ, after the company's name, and which appropriately also stands for intelligence and thought. The vision is to create a place where new ideas for urban living and working can evolve.

'Cultural and creative industries are not merely consumption activities,' Julian writes.

> They also contribute to the employment structure of cities. They are associated with emerging lifestyle and living forms, such as live-work studios, which add to the rich mix of cities and accommodate a variety of uses. These so-called creative quarters are genuine examples of where Katowice should be heading: liveable, mixed-use, resilient and respectful of the city's unique heritage and urban fabric.

Julian and the group of local businesses and residents negotiate with the authorities in Katowice. After much haggling they come away with an agreement to work together. Julian wants the area designated as a free ideas zone (or FIZ, as he calls it).

He wants the council to keep the planners (and health-and-safety officials) away for a year so that things can grow from the lowest thresholds. He knows the theory that the sweet spot of creativity tends to lie on the fine line between chaos and order. That fine line is what he wants to create by making free space available and encouraging people and businesses to start and flourish. He calls this 'commercial squatting'. The local government, capturing the spirit of the initiative, gives temporary permission for the project for three years. It protects its position by calling it a pilot project.

Julian puts the old foundry buildings into a cooperative development trust (something he saw in Hackney in London), where all the trust's members share in the ownership of project. To get the ball rolling, EMERGENZ launches an Urban Pioneers programme (similar to a programme of the same name in Middlehaven in the north of England), inviting anyone who has an idea to locate at the site. He makes some of his business's resources available and puts in basic services with the help of an EU grant.

The first few businesses start up. Small manufacturers take advantage of some of Julian's factory equipment, artists use the foundry, and a baker sets up business to tap into the foundry's surplus heat. Julian sets up an energy-sharing scheme, which uses the foundry to heat managed workspace at very low cost. He launches a bond that allows people to share in any uplift in the scheme's value that results from their contributions. The place soon develops a real buzz.

Julian wants to be part of something bigger. Looking for inspiration, he approaches the Impact Hub. Part innovation lab, part business incubator and social catalyst, Impact Hub offers members an ecosystem of resources, inspiration and collaboration opportunities to grow ideas.

The idea is that a better world evolves through the combined accomplishments of creative, committed and compassionate individuals focussed on common purposes. Julian thinks that joining their diverse community of members and collaborators could inspire, connect and breathe life into the local seeds of new initiatives in Katowice.

Julian wants to be a hubmaker. He is invited to attend Impact Hubs' tenth birthday party in London to meet other hubmakers. Katy Marks and Jonathan Robinson tell of their early experience in setting up the first Impact Hub in Islington, at a time when their co-working model did not exist. The business model based on renting time not space was a response to the high rents of central London, and the need to nurture a large, diverse community, rich with ideas.

There is now a global community of eighty-two Impact Hubs across more than fifty countries on six continents. From Amsterdam to Johannesburg, Singapore to San Francisco, it is a rapidly expanding, diverse network of over 7,000 members. This model has now been replicated and adapted by many other organisations, but Impact Hub is distinct in that each hub is locally developed, designed and run, and has its own distinctive personality—supported by a truly international community. Impact Hubs are remarkable examples of how to scale up small change. Julian helps build the eighty-third Impact Hub, in Katowice.

EMERGENZ makes some strategic investments in the local property market and accelerates its programme. By rehabilitating derelict factories, upgrading underused commercial space and developing new local landmarks like the Foundry Theatre, it is able to establish space for nearly 250 businesses, shops, cafés, bars, restaurants, clubs and music venues in the heart of what is now a thriving quarter. All the space is made available at affordable workspace rates. Other converted buildings nearby house independent businesses owned by local people, cooperatives, social enterprises, artist colonies and cultural organisations, some of which are well known through Eastern Europe and beyond. Local ownership of businesses has provided for a stronger and more resilient local economy. These businesses are more likely to employ local people, and to buy goods and services from other local organisations. This delivers the desired multiplier effect of keeping money within the local economy.

The constitution of a development trust guarantees that EMERGENZ remains an accessible resource for local people. An asset lock ensures that the stock cannot be sold off, except to invest in improved commercial premises for local economic development. EMERGENZ is democratically controlled. It is therefore transparent and accountable to the community it serves and is made up of. All those who live or work locally, and believe in EMERGENZ's cooperative principles and ethos, can become members.

Katowice now sees itself in a different light. It does not need cultural capital status to put itself on the map. It has EMERGENZ. Most Polish cities might not work well for creativity-driven development, and the potential of their creative workforces is often neglected. Katowice is different. The officials now see policymaking as a creative practice. They favour open management of the city, developing a set of protocols to work with the creative industries.

JULIAN CELEBRATES HIS ACHIEVEMENTS

The emergence of cultural and creative industries in postindustrial spaces is becoming the bedrock of contemporary economic activities in the inner city. The challenge for planners and policymakers will be to regenerate postindustrial spaces while maintaining their mixed uses and productivity.

Julian presents his scheme at the Make City Festival in Berlin. This is what he tells the audience:

1. We must recognise that the city is a constantly changing organism, rather than mechanistic and capable of highly processed control.
2. Do not be obsessed with certainty. Facing an uncertain future, we need to come to terms with unpredictability. Our urban planners now know that they cannot predict and plan for utopian end states.
3. People are clever. They come up with ideas and actions that no one could have expected.
4. We need to create space that can be adapted easily to the needs of people at any point in time. The Impact Hub model gave us a toolkit for bringing people together and creating potential for change with a strong social purpose—without dictating the outcomes.
5. We have to use rapid and continuous feedback to understand how we can make many small changes in our surroundings.
6. It is difficult to control something as complex as a city with the blunt instruments we have today. We need to rediscover different ways of doing things. Experimenting is the best way to find them.
7. Something as complex as a city needs adaptive public administration that reacts to rapidly changing circumstances.

> *By adapting their environments to their needs, people shape the building blocks of urban society: the neighbourhoods, districts and quarters. Governments can release people's latent creativity to solve urban problems in ways that no one expected. They do it with simple rules, providing the essential conditions, and leading in a way that enables things to happen.*
>
> —Julian H, Katowice

INNOVATIVE PEOPLE-ACTIVATION STRATEGIES

The Sustainable Development Commission found that enabling communities to lead local renewal projects with a neighbourhood-scale approach is the most cost-effective way to ensure towns and cities are fit for the future and create the conditions for people to thrive. Through empowering community groups to come together to tackle issues of local priority, and to work in partnership with local authorities and businesses, multiple benefits can be delivered.

In fostering collective action by people, self-organisation and peer-to-peer working are encouraged at all levels. Bottom-up working depends on limited hierarchies with flat organisational structures that promote collaboration. Nobody should be too far from the top. Everyone should be close. Government can help foster this process.

Citizen engagement tools

> *The city is its people. We do not make cities to make buildings and infrastructure. We make cities to come together, to create wealth and culture. Buildings, vehicles and infrastructure are mere enablers, not drivers. They are a side effect, a by-product, of people and culture. The city's primary reason for being is to be found in its citizens. If we look there, we find that there is much more to urban life than efficiency.*
>
> —Dan Hill

Smart cities are alright but what about smart citizens? A lot is said about smart cities but, with the right skills, local communities can be smart as well. They should be able to create effective systems that will help govern and shape their development in new kinds of ways: the 'eyes on the street' that Jane Jacobs celebrated in her classic works on urbanism, now amplified by the communication capabilities and web-based tools of the networked age.

> *Just as the ants find their way to new food sources and switch tasks with impressive flexibility, our community tools should help us locate and improve troubled schools, up-and-coming playgrounds, areas lacking crucial services, areas with an abundance of services, blocks that feel safe at night and blocks that don't—all the subtle patterns of community life now made public in a new form.*
>
> —Steven Johnson

Social media allows active and engaged citizens to organise more effectively. In most parts of the world, the smart phone is now considered essential for urban life. Digital technology has spawned a wide range of citizen engagement tools from city-wide programmes to hyperlocal applications. In some instances, these tools have been developed to mobilise local action on reporting problems, such as potholes in the streets. In others, they are used to support crowdfunding initiatives. We have witnessed a raft of new platforms—Changify, Neighborland and Stickyworld, to name a few—aimed at helping citizens work together to change their city.

Priya Prakash, for example, is working on her Citizen Canvas, which she describes as 'a collaborative change and data-mapping tool for stakeholder teams that are involved in finding a shared vision for what a smarter city could be'.

Barcelona's Smart Citizen Platform generates participatory processes in neighbourhoods. It connects data, people and knowledge: the platform serves as a node for building productive and open indicators, providing distributed tools, and enabling the collective construction of the city for its inhabitants.

There is no reason why this technology cannot evolve into the new citizen's interface with the city, working in concert with a devolved planning system. It could be designed to harness the collective power of many small ideas and actions by becoming a mechanism for enabling bottom-up, civic-led activities. It could even be used to scale up larger infrastructure development projects.

Whatever happens, it must have the following qualities:

- → It must evolve into a common language for collaborative knowledge sharing and joint action by everyone in the system.
- → It must become a basis for cross-sectoral collaboration between all the urban professions and academia; between civic leaders and their agencies; and between active citizens and interest groups.
- → It must promote openness, shared working and joint ownership of ideas and solutions across the sectors.
- → It must be an open source, industry standard—available to all—to enable third party developers to expand on it.
- → It must operate as a simple feedback loop, enabling small changes to be rapidly evaluated and straw polls to be generated so that decisionmakers can change course if necessary.
- → It could evolve into a vehicle to promote a parameter-book approach that uses standard, default building types that people can use and adapt.
- → It must provide a forum for best practice so people can learn from others.

Shifting the focus from technology and the city to the role that active citizens could play in shaping their own urban environment, this highly distributed, bottom-up approach connects urban dwellers with information about their neighbourhood.

COLLABORATIVE PROCUREMENT

One possible way of getting people to self-organise is for cities to create the equivalent of a 'dating agency' that brings together people with common interests and ambitions. This action could be an ideal way of developing social capital in advance of any project. In the case of multi-tenanted or multi-owned buildings, people could choose whom they want to live with and how they develop a collective brief for their building. This model would work well where governments are looking to dispose of small sites to groups of people, such as *baugruppen*, described below. This process is actively used in places such as Berlin.

Vauban in Freiburg, Germany, has long been regarded as a good example of bottom-up urbanism. In Vauban the majority of development was by *baugruppen*: small owner-cooperatives, typically comprising fewer than twenty households who want to develop and own their own houses. Part of the attraction is the opportunity, in contrast to standard speculative development, to act as a catalyst by influencing the design of their residential environment before moving in.

As landowner and land developer, the Vauban council divided the land into small plots and allocated it preferentially to *baugruppen* and small and local builders, with bids also being assessed against criteria favouring families with children, older people, and Freiburg residents.

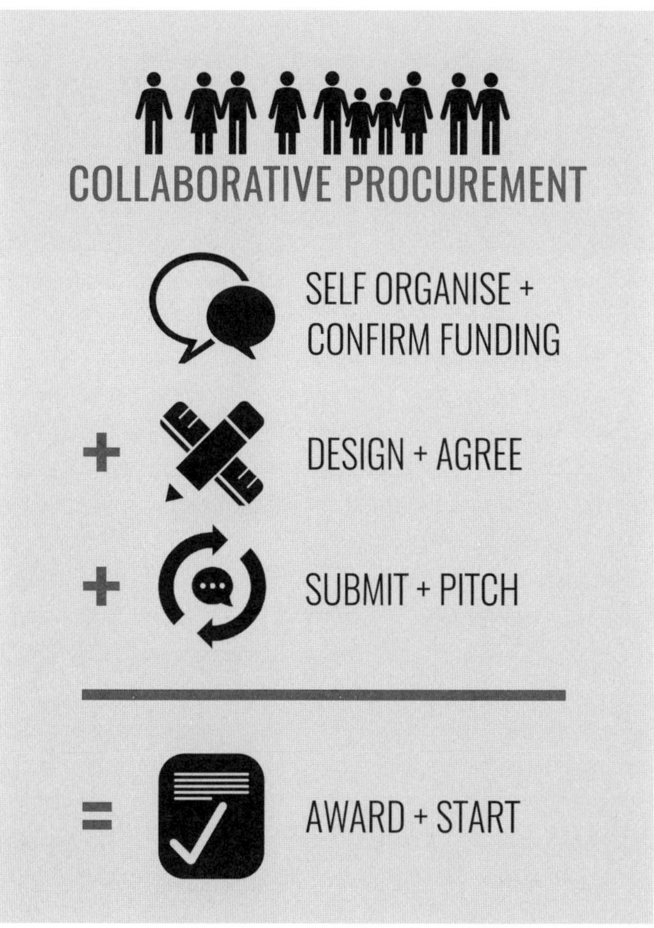

COLLABORATIVE PROCUREMENT
SELF ORGANISE + CONFIRM FUNDING
+ DESIGN + AGREE
+ SUBMIT + PITCH
= AWARD + START

Vauban's mandatory small plot sizes were significant because these allowed small developers to become involved: the largest public sector developer in the first new build phase, for example, built less than 10 per cent and the largest private sector developer built less than 13 per cent of the units. Compared to conventional housing developers, the *baugruppen* approach has several distinct advantages:

1 It engages active citizens in all aspects of urban planning, policy and development processes, soliciting their collaboration in providing rapid and continuous feedback. It enables them to take collective action to affect positive change at all levels.

2 It overcomes the producer–consumer gap inherent to speculative housing and the short-termist 'in/out' behaviour of conventional developers. Combining developer and owner roles means that the balance between upfront capital costs and longer term running costs makes energy-efficient and low-energy design more attractive. Overall costs are also lower since *baugruppen* appropriate the developer's profit.

3 The *baugruppen* promote community building, cooperation and common activities between future neighbours, and enable conflict resolution.

4 The small development plots and the large proportion of new residential development built by *baugruppen* (and designed by a wider variety of architects) generates a more architecturally diverse district, with the individually designed façades creating genuine rather than artificial diversity regarding visual character.

Baugruppen, however, needs support from the city planning department and independent consultants, and also more time to work up their proposals. Forum Vauban also formed a technical support unit.

Collective or participatory forms of housing are being advanced as alternatives to market-developed housing in many parts of the world. This model is thought to be more affordable than market housing; by one account *baugruppen* in Germany save up to 20% in construction costs when compared to developer-led housing (Hamiduddin & Daseking, 2014). While many cooperative housing projects are privately financed and subsequent resales are done on the open market, some cohousing groups do make special arrangements to ensure perpetual affordability for their members.

Collaborative procurement requires the local authority to put in place a simple process with a simple set of rules, providing clear constraints:

1 People organise themselves into groups and agree to work together within these rules, confirming their funding and programme.

2 The group appoints an architect, developing initial designs to meet their individual and collective needs and agreeing on their strategy to move forward together.

3 The group submits its application to the local authority and are invited to pitch to a panel who will assess their proposals on agreed criteria.

4 The local authority approves the scheme and gives the green light to proceed, subject to contractual matters being resolved.

Things happen quickly.

THE SMART TECHNOLOGIST

HOW AN APPLICATIONS DEVELOPER ENABLED SMART CITIZENS

Giuseppe grew up playing SimCity. He is intrigued by simulation games that show how one decision can lead to another. He plays Minecraft and Sugarscape. He studied mathematics and social science because he thought that they would give him the closest understanding of the complexity of cities.

Alongside his studies he pursues his interest in information technology (IT), working for a computer games company during his holidays and free time. He thinks he can build an app for designing a perfect city. 'All you need is a good set of metrics, a good understanding of social dynamics and an easy-to-use tool,' he says. 'Get those right and all you need to do is push a button.'

Giuseppe is headhunted by an international technology company whose focus is smart cities. Everything in the company's brochure is about smartness. A smart city, he understands, uses digital technologies or information and communication technologies (ICTs) to enhance the quality and performance of urban services, to reduce costs and resource consumption, and to engage more effectively and actively with its citizens.

Utopian urban visions help to drive smart-city rhetoric that has been promulgated most energetically over the past decade or so by big technology, engineering and consulting companies.

This appeals to Giuseppe. Some people call him a nerd or a techie: he sees himself not only as a smart thinker but also as an enlightened citizen. After a while he starts to have his doubts about his work, and about what smart-city visions might mean for the ordinary citizen.

Should the city be an optimised machine, with the citizens represented by contented and predictable pixels, or a melting pot of culture and ideas created by its unpredictable flesh and blood? Is the smart city an unnecessarily corporate, top-down idea? Giuseppe's mathematical background is clashing with his social science.

The metaphors of control rooms or dashboards, common to most smart-city visions, seem to Guiseppe to be hopelessly inappropriate for cities, even in relation to the urban systems that a city government might be trying to run. As Saskia Sassen points out, there is a tendency to 'make these technologies invisible, and hence put them in command rather than in dialogue with users'.

Giuseppe reflects on this dilemma:

→ His job is to work with big data to make better cities, but is he just using big data to justify corporate processes? He cannot see the real effects of his work on society. His approach professes to be collaborative, but it may be a different form of command and control.

→ Young, motivated urban thinkers are developing IT solutions to make our cities smarter. There are no limits to their ideas, but the urban planning systems are slow and indignant to change quickly.

→ He feels that advocates of smart cities have never really considered how they will affect how people live in cities.

→ He wonders if his work is just looking for a technological fix to apply to a bad system. Smartness should be an essential characteristic of the system, not a plug-in.

→ He thinks that the smart-city concept will be acceptable only if it emerges from the bottom up, led by citizens. But he knows that the system is hard to beat.

→ Perhaps a smart city need not depend exclusively—or even at all—on sensors and computers. Perhaps people are always the best sensors.

GIUSEPPE PURSUES HIS EARLIER DREAMS

Giuseppe leaves the big IT company. He decides to take a desk at Geovation Hub at the Urban Innovation Centre in London, a place that is part innovation lab, part business incubator and part meeting place. He will pursue his earlier dreams, now tempered with experience of what not to do.

He reads an article by Dan Hill of Future Cities Catapult, 'On the Smart City: or, a "Manifesto" for Smart Citizens Instead'. 'The city is its people,' Hill writes.

> We don't make cities in order to make buildings and infrastructure. We make cities in order to come together, to create wealth, culture and more people.... Buildings, vehicles and infrastructure are mere enablers, not drivers. They are a side-effect, a by-product, of people and culture.... The city's primary raison d'être is to be found amidst its citizens. If we look there, we find that there is more, much more to urban life than efficiency.

As Hill explains, 'We might argue that smartening the infrastructure enables citizens to make informed decisions, and this is certainly true. But...to see the city as a complex system to be optimised, made efficient,' is to see the city in very simplistic terms.

Barcelona's Smart Citizen Platform is the best example Giuseppe has seen for generating participatory processes in neighbourhoods, connecting data, people and knowledge.

Giuseppe wants to be part of this. He starts developing his own platform called CHASSIS (City-wide Highly Adaptable Space-Structuring Information System). Like the underframe of a car, it provides the invisible platform that everything is built off. It integrates with all the other citizen-engagement platforms and social networks for neighbourhoods, but Giuseppe hopes it will take local democratic decision-making to a much higher level. His ambition is that CHASSIS will become the new citizen's interface with the city, working in concert with the city's evolved planning system. It will be designed to harness the collective power of many small ideas and actions by becoming a mechanism for enabling bottom-up, civic-led activities. He realises that it needs to change behaviours and promote active learning at every opportunity, showing potential outcomes of decisions rather than fixed end states.

Giuseppe hears that the Greater London Authority is supporting crowdfunded projects. He thinks that his platform could act as the interface for these activities as well. His real interest lies in scaling this up to larger infrastructure projects. He realises that CHASSIS must become a common language for collaborative knowledge sharing and joint action by everyone in the system. It must provide a basis for cross-sectoral collaboration between all the urban professions and academia; between civic leaders and their agencies; and between active citizens and interest groups. Using this shared language, it must promote openness, shared working and joint ownership of ideas and solutions across the sectors.

Giuseppe develops an open source toolkit that anyone can use to share their ideas and actions. It operates as a simple feedback loop, so that decisionmakers can change course if necessary. It uses standard, default building types that people can use and adapt. It also provides a forum for best practice so people can learn from others. The toolkit becomes the industry standard platform, and numerous developers expand it with a range of plug-ins.

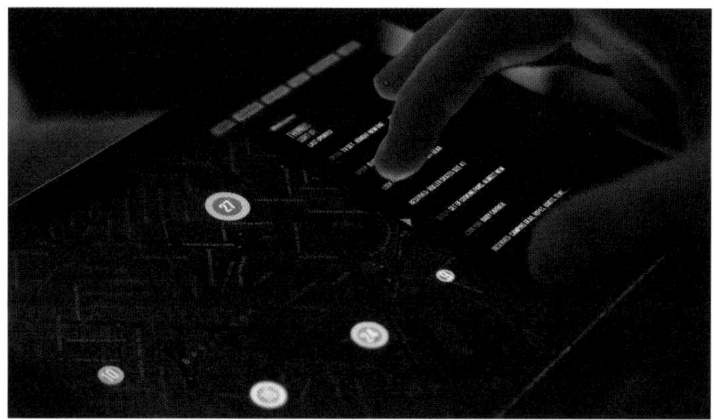

GIUSEPPE EXPLAINS HIS SUCCESS:

1. Earlier platforms took root in the cracks left by urban planning, city governance and market forces, but they only supported a few small, locally based community projects. They had a valuable role but were difficult to scale up.
2. Changing behaviour leads to changed attitudes. This is different to the thinking behind many smart systems. Those systems are all predicated on feedback loops delivering information to people, whose attitudes change as a result. Only then do they change their behaviour. With Guiseppe's platform, people (not systems) will create deep-lasting, evolutionary change through collective action.
3. Change happens through creating easy, accessible ways to try something different, and then scaling it up through social networks to show how effective it is. Easy-to-use digital platforms facilitate small change.
4. Shifting the focus from technology and the city to the role that active citizens could play in shaping their own urban environment, this highly distributed, bottom-up approach connects people living in cities with information about their neighbourhood; engaging them in all aspects of urban planning, policy and development processes; soliciting their collaboration in providing rapid and continuous feedback; and enabling them to take collective action to affect positive change at all levels.
5. Rather than just facilitating a stream of small projects to occupy the community while the 'big boys' in government get on with the important stuff, CHASSIS can be the vehicle for taking on urban governance models, or attempting to pay for large-scale infrastructure through crowdfunding initiatives. This process could include projects such as local energy generation, waste-water recycling schemes and public transport networks.

> *Smartness lies in trusting collective wisdom and avoiding the twin traps of reductionism and determinism. Technology is an aid to human intelligence, not a replacement. We must see the urban system as a complex network of interrelated spectrums, not polarities. The city is a constantly changing organism, not a mechanistic model capable of highly processed control. Technology can help, but it can't fix.*
>
> —Giuseppe P, Italy

INNOVATIVE IMPLEMENTATION STRATEGIES

We need an operating system that optimises the hardware of the neighbourhood—its land, buildings, infrastructure, networks and spaces—to run its software—the human needs of enterprise, social capital, shelter and marketplace; a system that recognises the necessity of innovation into new ways to deliver local services, provide new infrastructure and manage local change.

We know that we must move to new ways of providing flexible housing choice and tenure in our neighbourhoods. We also know that we can only meet our carbon reduction challenges if we address them at a community scale. Examples include:

1 Local economic programmes

A range of innovative approaches in diverse and complex neighbourhoods could build social capital and foster local economic development through micro-economic initiatives, community enterprise and links to training providers. These approaches should extend to development of local building companies; partnerships with local contractors and local building suppliers; and local apprentice schemes to ensure that the social and economic benefits of new housing construction and community retrofitting are realised locally.

The availability of affordable workspace is the single biggest catalyst for economic development at neighbourhood scale—the studios in the back lanes, spaces under the arches or over the shops, live-work spaces and local creative industries buildings. These spaces are where meanwhile uses and greyworld can play a significant role. The secret lies in ploughing the potential income streams for these activities back into other initiatives.

The success of local economic catalysts is well proven in the work of the Paddington and Shoreditch development trusts in London where affordable workspace is cross-funded by councils as part of planning obligations arising out of major development projects. These projects have resulted in an increasing cluster of new business start-ups: an activity that has a massive impact on the local economy. The demand for these spaces is so high it cannot be met.

This activity could be extended to more formal innovation hubs, enterprise centres, business incubators, accelerator programmes and mentoring schemes. In all instances, these should be coupled with adjustable business rates, which could be linked to turnover.

Small, independent shops can provide a hub for communities, providing local jobs, promoting local entrepreneurial activity and keeping money circulating in the local economy. The New Economics Foundation has done a lot of work on local incentives and planned activities, recommending new ideas to counter the impacts of the major food stores or national brands that dominate our main streets. The London Assembly's report on 'cornered shops' also promotes the concept of 'shop local'. There are now some schemes and initiatives where this principle has made a difference:

- → Local cooperatives and buying projects, for example, people's supermarkets
- → Community shops, which could include the local post office
- → Local loyalty cards such as the Wedge Card or the Brixton Pound
- → Local marketplaces, meanwhile uses and pop-up shops

There are opportunities where zoning legislation, building on the proposition for neighbourhood development zones, could promote a proportion of local independent shops on the main street to provide a balanced mix. France has excellent examples of this, where the local butcher and baker are treated as community resources and the cost of their business rates reflect this. In all instances, adjustable business rates and even devices such as tailored parking controls can be used to trigger different responses for local enterprises.

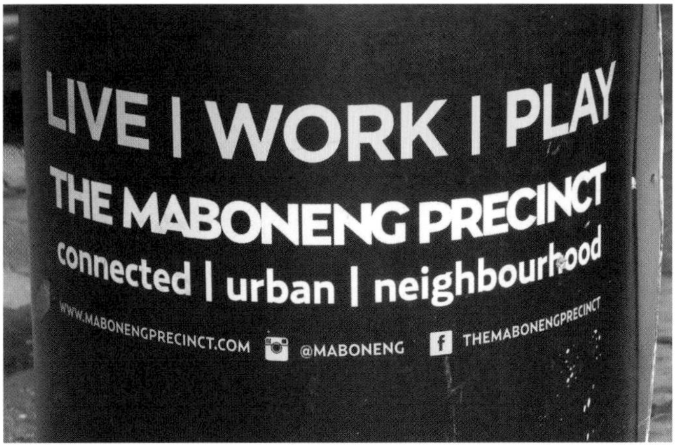

2 Arts- and cultural-led programmes

From policy-makers to urban guerrillas, the prospect of integrating design, cultural activities and neighbourhood building gives rise to a range of recurring aspirations:

→ The 'humanisation' of the built environment—where the urban fabric of society gives priority to people and public life, not roads or buildings.
→ The reconstruction of a civic identity and an expression of collective aspirations through a range of creative activities.
→ A creative interaction between culture and commerce, social and institutional life and a visible expression of national cultural consciousness.
→ Inspiring visionary ideas providing an impetus for cultural change and social participation without traditional social divisions.
→ The unpredictability and excitement that comes with emerging ideas and actions.

Arts- and cultural-led activities have formed the backbone of building successful urban societies in many great neighbourhoods in the world and continue to be the biggest single driver of innovation in our cities—the cultural quarters, the digital districts and the social enterprise hubs. We see these activities recorded in the artist colonies in Bushwick, New York; in the flea markets in Shoreditch, London; in the numerous festivals in Cork, Ireland; the cool streets of Woodstock in Cape Town; or the regenerated industrial neighbourhood of Maboneng in Johannesburg. Every place tells its own story. Every place has its own offer. Places come and go or take different forms. They cannot be replicated. Everybody is potentially creative but creativity is stifled. We just need to unlock the unseen possibilities in places and this is what creative people do.

Creativity must come from the place. It must be allowed space and time. Like neighbourhoods, you cannot design creative places, but you can put in the preconditions for culture to take root and evolve.

3 Neighbourhood management programmes

Processes could draw together all service providers in a single and focussed approach, ensuring effective and scaleable neighbourhood infrastructure and services are delivered. These processes could extend from maximising the use of community assets through local 'booking' systems to coordinating local procurement of goods and services to realise social innovation and good public outcomes for the neighbourhood. Critical to active collaboration is the need for innovative approaches around community mobilisation and the use of community charters, local agreements and new social contracts—'We will if you will'. As part of this programme, we should look to new forms of revenue to maintain the long-term future of 'software' projects that foster community action and responsibility.

Having a dedicated management team for the neighbourhood is one of the most effective means of triggering transformation of the area. The National Association of Neighbourhood Management sees neighbourhood management as residents working in partnership with mainstream service providers, the local authority, businesses and the voluntary and community sectors to make local services more responsive to the needs of their area. It is a process that recognises the uniqueness of each place, allowing the people that live, work or provide services in it to build on its strengths and address its particular challenges.

Operating in a defined area and at a scale that people identify with, and crucial to its success, is the neighbourhood manager: advocate, mediator, facilitator, influencer and negotiator for positive change. The role does not involve significant amounts of money—rather it involves using existing resources in a better way. This success is well demonstrated through the work of the Church Street Management Team in London, which has provided the catalyst to the development of its neighbourhood plan; its extensive public art and cultural programmes; and the management of its street market.

The role of neighbourhood management could be extended to the management of hardware projects, taking on the coordination of new housing and infrastructure programmes.

4 Community development programmes

Neighbourhoods are often recognised as the places where the dynamics of social cohesion are most tangible within the city. Within the overall urban dynamics, neighbourhoods have also been the breeding grounds for socioeconomic development projects, grassroots initiatives and social innovation, especially in the social economy. Not all triggers need to be hardware. Sometimes softer catalysts, such as empowerment of the community through neighbourhood planning programmes, civic leadership and capacity building initiatives, can have a greater lasting effect on neighbourhood transformation. This effect can be the result of:

→ Social enterprise activities
→ Greening projects and urban orchards
→ Social and cultural programmes
→ Neighbourhood watch programmes
→ Social network developments

One of the best examples of soft catalysts is access to seed finance at the local level: micro-finance to set up local businesses, community banks and credit unions, and local guarantee funds for community self-build schemes.

The catalytic effect of well-managed physical assets, such as community and faith centres, parks, and redundant buildings, are well recognised in the development of active communities and viable community-based enterprises. Asset transfer, a well-rehearsed principle in local politics, refers to local communities' ability to acquire land and buildings, either at market value or a discount, to deliver services that meet the neighbourhood's needs. Asset transfer is seen as one way in which local authorities, in particular, can support the development of the social economy, and thereby meet their wider strategies for renewal and improved delivery of local services.

5 Infrastructure development programmes

Upgrades to our physical infrastructure can tackle climate change, deliver reliable and efficient transport networks, improve health and well-being, secure a healthy natural environment, improve long-term housing supply, maximise employment opportunities and make our communities safer and more cohesive.

The provision of new local energy networks, district-wide heating systems, sustainable urban drainage schemes and retrofitting projects provides a ready catalyst for neighbourhood transformation.

'The Future Is Local', a report by the Sustainable Development Commission, shows that there is an unrealised opportunity in Britain to catalyse this potential by focussing on the neighbourhood as the optimum scale for addressing infrastructure reinvestment needs. At neighbourhood scale:

→ Engagement of residents can be secured through governance approaches most appropriate to each community and providing the supply chain and investors with a viable scale of project and structure of partner.

→ Efficiency measures become feasible at whole-street and neighbourhood levels that simply don't stack up at individual home scale, including most low-carbon and renewable energy technologies and transport.

→ Access to private investment is increased as neighbourhood scale provides 'critical mass', enabling scarce public money to be more effectively leveraged.

We now need practical solutions—the 'how' of managing upgrade works on a neighbourhood basis. These solutions will require building capacity at the local level; developing and sharing best practice nationally; and facilitating engagement by supply chain businesses, funders and policymakers wishing to see communities successfully taking ownership for changing the places they live.

6 Local delivery programmes

The development of innovative neighbourhood-scale organisational structures and delivery vehicles that can be adapted to the special requirements of a place as well as the community and local government are critical to the success of any neighbourhood project. Potential models focus on:

→ **Alternative approaches to long-term control of land.** This includes long-term investment models; risk-sharing and joint ventures with local government; as well as financing models that will ensure continued management, stewardship and maintenance of the neighbourhood are key. These approaches could include trialling community land trusts as collective ownership vehicles and other innovations around land release, deferred land costs, and private rental housing to stimulate the full range of responses locally.

→ **Development of flexible, targeted and incremental land-release strategies.** These could deliver serviced land to the market at a range of scales—the individual plot for self-builders and those seeking bespoke solutions as well as the lot (a collection of plots). These strategies could involve a small number of units to be built by small local builders and social landlords; the urban block that could open opportunities for larger local contractors and agencies; and the whole phase that could entice the national housebuilders. This process could allow the full range of catalysts and creative land-release strategies for a range of players.

→ **Development of funding, implementation and management packages.** These could include setting up local energy services and retrofitting companies to meet the low carbon challenge. Solutions could be delivered on a flexible and incremental basis, ensuring that the full benefits of a local approach are realised at the lowest thresholds of the community and that local government can share in its returns without exposing itself to undue levels of risk. Benefits include reduced cost and disruption, engaging communities, and unlocking smarter finance linked to long-term revenue streams.

→ **Development of a range of targeted funding programmes.** These could pioneer new thinking, processes and outcomes in the planning, design and delivery of our neighbourhoods. This idea involves initiating quick projects with a view to delivering tangible and measurable change immediately, while other more fundamental changes are being implemented by the government. This process means working with local communities to trial new ideas and accepts a willingness to experiment and make mistakes in the pursuit of developing better models.

Many of the land-release methods discussed in this chapter have an underlying context that behaviours will need to change. This includes changing or bending the rules on land sales by the public sector, on procurement rules and on the nature of ownership. Rigid procurement rules are an obstacle to a more flexible approach.

Public sector gap funding is not likely to be available for many, but improving financial viability and reducing risk can nevertheless be enhanced with the assistance of the public sector in a number of ways:

→ Payment for land could be deferred until the completion of the scheme or building. There is already an understanding in the public sector that land value can be deferred.

→ A long-leasehold approach could be adopted with a ground rent arrangement, which could be bought out by the developer or a succeeding owner paying a premium at any point during the lease. The ground rent could be inflation-proofed by regular rent reviews.

→ Land value could be converted into a share in the ownership of the property with the developer or succeeding owner having the option to purchase at a later date at then market value.

→ Promoting self-build for commercial or residential property has the potential to widen the benefits a developer can enjoy.

→ Build costs could be reduced by using the purchasing power of the local authority or other government agencies.

→ Financial guarantees could be provided to assist small local developers secure development finance.

→ Joint ventures could be considered with the private sector to share the risk and the profit.

→ The focus could be on smaller sites and developers could be prepared to look at anything from a single-house plot upwards. Nothing is too small.

→ The public sector could be proactive on delivering infrastructure and utilities.

We can make the biggest difference by using activators. We need to trial new methods and build up our toolkits in this realm. Experimentation (without fear of failure) is imperative if we are to change.

INITIATING AN URBAN PIONEERS PROGRAMME

Urban pioneers are Everett Rogers's innovators and early adopters. Their energy and initiative can be mobilised as potential agents of change in projects where the market is weak. This idea has its roots in the belief that many places will not be transformed into great urban living and working neighbourhoods, in the manner that we all want, if we follow the 'same-old, same-old' way. If we follow the well-trodden path of competitive dialogue with a master developer, we do not believe we will be successful. We therefore need to find a new way to work with local people to develop a new offer and boost the local economy by building their own homes and businesses.

We know that in addition to the recognised planning obstacles for the small builder or the self-procurer, access to affordable land represents the single biggest limiter to multiple small actions at the neighbourhood scale. This is where we need to be innovative. Land release does not necessarily mean land sale, or if it does, it does not mean freehold. If it does, it does not necessarily imply that payment cannot be deferred. It is now accepted that more flexible approaches are essential.

An Urban Pioneer programme can be used to stimulate a stalled housing market by initiating quick projects with a view to delivering tangible and measurable change immediately. This process involves working with the innovators and fostering the early adopters in local communities and the private sector at the local level, to trial new ideas and processes. It accepts a willingness to experiment and make mistakes in the pursuit of developing better models. Using Rogers's statistics, the innovators would need to account for 2.5 per cent and the early adopters 13.5 per cent of the total housing numbers. If we were looking for 1,000 homes in the future, we would need to find 25 innovators and 135 early adopters. An Urban Pioneer programme has eight phases:

PHASE 1. DEVELOPING A STARTER PACK

This stage requires providing a basic set of rules to start the process and the management to get it up and running and evolve it.

- → The Rules of Engagement—Set out clearly defined roles and responsibilities of all players.
- → The Project Programme—Agree on the main milestones and deliverables throughout the programme.
- → The Definition of Success—Clearly spell out the criteria to reward successful innovation.

PHASE 2. ESTABLISHING A HIT SQUAD

This stage might require an extension of the local authority operating as a dedicated neighbourhood-enabling team until a fully-fledged organisational structure is in place. It covers the key roles of all players:

- → The Project Initiator—Focusses on early wins and manages highly visible projects such as show homes, demonstration projects and active community participation in integrating new communities.
- → The Development Packager—Breaks the project down into bite-size chunks to enable a wider range of implementation strategies.
- → The Place Promoter—Provides the branding, communications and marketing functions for the programme.
- → The Supporter—Provides support throughout the process on such matters as legal, procurement and policy implications.
- → The Programme Coordinator—Provides the necessary client-side project management and costs control.
- → The Capacity Builder—Works with the council and neighbourhood team to raise standards, focus efforts and leave behind an intellectual legacy.

PHASE 3. DEVELOPING THE PROGRAMME

This stage involves developing the content and branding of the proposition to create a buzz around the project—developing an early plot 'parceling' diagram and loose design codes based on the agreed development framework for the neighbourhood and producing some early concepts to trigger interest. A steering group defines the ground rules for the project, the land-release strategy, the means of delivering the programme and the risk assessment and countermeasures. As part of this process, early market testing of this proposition is undertaken amongst the local creative community—working with local builders and developers to gauge its potential effectiveness. This phase sets the agenda for the longer-term transformational change of the neighbourhood and provides us with the metrics for measuring its success.

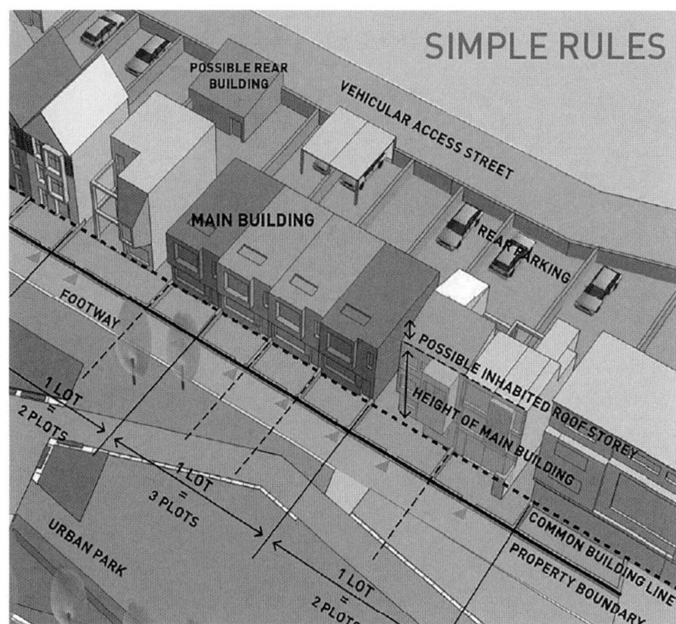

PHASE 4. PROMOTING THE PROPOSITION

This stage involves raising city-wide awareness amongst local individuals, collectives and organisations of the programme and inviting them to become the 'innovators' (the 2.5 per cent). Using the local press and television channels through the form of an ideas competition, interested parties express how they would take up opportunities to build their own homes or workplaces. Winners are offered plots or lots at zero cost or with some form of deferred payment and clawback conditions, provided they deliver to an agreed programme. The competition is judged on the basis of their innovativeness as well as the commitment and ability of the successful participants to deliver on what they promise.

PHASE 5. DOCUMENTING THE PROCESS

To diffuse innovation to a wider audience, the programme works with local media groups to produce a documentary of the process to learn from successes and failures in the pursuit of developing better models. This could take the form of a television series based on selecting a group of 'contestants' to participate in the programme and could be set up as a 'fly-on-the-wall' series. We look for an ideal cross-section of family and business groups who best represent the neighbourhood's social, cultural and economic diversity.

PHASE 6. BUILDING THE PROJECTS

This stage involves the innovators building their projects, possibly using a *Grand Designs*-type approach to bringing together the 'contestants' with local architects and builders to build their homes and business units in the neighbourhood, focussing on the principle of 'build local'. The projects should seek to demonstrate a broad range of responses from self-build to formal procurement, from individual to collective, from full ownership through to rental. In this way we will need to work with local social landlords, building societies and investors. Nothing should be exempt.

PHASE 7. MAKING PROGRESS

This stage will involve moving from the innovator stage to the second stage—the implementation of a further 13.5 per cent of the total scheme to accommodate the early adopters.

PHASE 8. MONITORING THE PROCESS

This stage involves establishing a basic set of rules to monitor the process and providing management with the tools to review and evaluate its success over time. It also includes:

- → Creating the mechanisms to share ideas to a wider audience
- → Setting up feedback loops
- → Redefining strategy on an ongoing basis
- → Reporting on progress and sharing lessons learnt

The Urban Pioneer programme gives us an ideal opportunity to allow new ideas to emerge from the bottom up. It demonstrates all the positive qualities of emergence at the local level and galvanises change. A programme like this is now being trialled in Middlehaven, Middlesbrough, in the North of England, a place that has suffered from trying all the big solutions and where there has been a significant failure of the housing market. It is early days but its outcome could be crucial for many stalled projects worldwide.

The Urban Pioneer initiative offers a strong brand and creates a buzz. It will promote more experimental and high-visibility projects that will capture the imagination of politicians and the wider community by addressing the issues of social inclusiveness, environmental concerns and cultural diversity, amongst others.

This page, top left: The layout of the pilot project for the Middlehaven Urban Pioneers project, based around an award-winning urban park. **Top right:** Extract from Middlehaven design code.

The NEIGHBOURHOOD CO:EFFICIENT development tool is a working method for enabling people and local government to collaborate to deliver positive growth and change. Developed over the years by Smart Urbanism, it is a tried and tested (and constantly evolving) tool for entering into new social contracts with the communities affected by new urban development, regeneration and renewal. It is pure localism at work, enabling neighbourhood teams to be truly involved in the planning, design and delivery processes by giving them the tools to take action and have genuine sway in their communities. It has two parts:

1 **PUBLIC PROTOCOL**, a neighbourhood planning toolkit, sets out the rules of engagement to build trust, understanding and commitment to collective action in any local change scenario. As such, it provides a full range of ideas, tools and tactics to build true collaboration between active citizens, civic leaders and urban professionals.

2 **The NEIGHBOURHOOD GAME**, an interactive gaming technique, is designed to narrow down choices in neighbourhood transformation and simulate potential outcomes. The technique is also grid-based, so it connects back to and works hand-in-hand with the CANVAS development tool, closing the feedback loop from the strategic to the local and from the individual to the collective. At a town or district scale, CANVAS is best suited to test the effects of primary growth strategies and public transport corridors. At a local scale, the NEIGHBOURHOOD GAME is best suited.

PUBLIC PROTOCOL

PUBLIC PROTOCOL is a practical guide setting out how successful community collaboration is achieved and is made available to communities at the start of any neighbourhood planning process. It spells out a number of ways of working with local communities through extensive experience in the field and is based on best practice internationally. There is no alternative to being well prepared when we start any community participation exercise. This guide shows what to do first, how to get the project up and running and what to do throughout the course of the project. It explains the tools we have to help and the extra things we can do to improve leadership and decision-making to ensure the best outcome for the project.

There are two types of community participation exercises:

1 **Consultation** is the simplest form. It usually involves presenting ideas or proposals about an area and asking for people's thoughts and feedback. In many instances it is a selling exercise.

2 **Collaboration**, on the other hand, is a longer-term investment. It involves working with people from the very start to develop a shared understanding of how we will do the job, what the issues are and how we can develop a shared vision. We know that effective collaboration works. We are aware it achieves better results.

It can also be difficult to achieve effective community collaboration, but from our understanding of self-organising systems, we acknowledge four basic principles of behaviour that are needed to promote open collaboration:

1 The first principle is **self-organisation**. Through the underlying mechanisms of decentralised control, distributed problem solving and multiple interactions, a community, without being told, can transform simple rules of thumb into meaningful patterns of collective behaviour.

2 The second principle is **diversification of knowledge**, which is primarily achieved through a broad sampling of options, followed by a friendly competition of ideas. Then, using an effective mechanism to narrow down the choices, communities can gain 'wisdom of crowds'. By adopting this principle, they can build trust and make better decisions.

3 The third principle is **indirect collaboration**. If individuals in a community are prompted to make small changes to a shared structure or idea that inspires others to improve it even further, the structure or idea becomes an active player in the creative process.

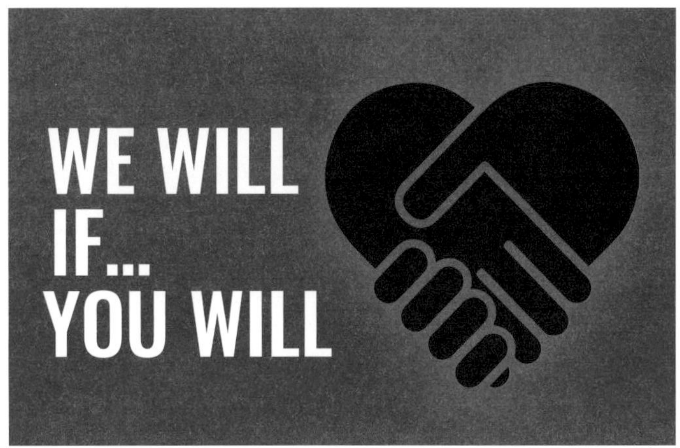

4 The fourth principle is **dissemination**. The basic mechanisms of coordination and communication can unleash powerful waves of energy or awareness that race across a community to evoke positive change.

Collaboration does not happen without seeding it. Language is used to both inform and baffle; professionals often use their language as their 'black box'. But language can also empower! The best way to equip a local neighbourhood team with the right skills is through capacity building—giving it the language that is used in the professional world (not dumbing down the process) so that it can shape ideas and proposals from the very outset. There is no substitute for leading from the front, armed with understanding and tactical acumen. Such is the way of thriving cities, towns and their neighbourhoods.

PUBLIC PROTOCOL spells out what to do before you start, including:

→ Building an active and engaged community representative and client group
→ Giving the project an agreed name (without the jargon)
→ Identifying community champions and community assets
→ Understanding local sensitivities
→ Testing initial ideas
→ Developing tactics for reaching the wider community

The neighbourhood planning toolkit of PUBLIC PROTOCOL comprises a range of techniques to ensure that we involve people in an imaginative and useful way. It includes:

→ **Building a Neighbourhood Futures Team**, a group of representatives from public, private, voluntary and community groups that come together as a combined team to act as project champions

→ **Agreeing on the core rules of community participation**, including how to build relationships, develop a common language, bring people up to speed on new thinking and engage difficult-to-reach people

→ **Developing a better understanding of the urban change process**, including use of design training workshops and site visits, reviewing local case studies, and implementing youth trainee programmes and Placecheck initiatives

→ **Using big ideas**, including public events, public exhibitions, temporary installations, expert panels and 'big ideas' teams to create a buzz around the project, although big ideas do not mean big solutions

→ **Committing to a way forwards** by writing community charters and celebrating this through public signing of the document by civic leaders and active citizens

→ **Working with the team** using workshop-style formats to take people through the various stages, from initial baseline studies to the preferred options stages

→ **Helping people make the best decisions** by thinking carefully about the critical link between development and funding, between the need to reduce our impacts on the planet and community needs, and between the type of places people want and what can be afforded—including the use of gaming techniques and other visual aids to support this consideration

→ **Involving the wider community** by getting to all parts, using community ambassadors, social media, drop-in centres and exhibitions, including getting feedback and reporting back

The underlying intentions of PUBLIC PROTOCOL provide the ethics, behaviours and rules for engagement for the NEIGHBOURHOOD GAME.

THE NEIGHBOURHOOD GAME

To achieve this collaboration, we have developed an interactive game as our effective mechanism to narrow down the choices in neighbourhood transformation and simulate potential outcomes. There are now a number of versions of the game—we know that it works. It's a great way to get people talking about specific issues that are important to them and introduce a friendly competition of ideas. It avoids the usual pitfalls of community involvement by encouraging those involved to think realistically about how their needs and desires will be delivered on the ground. Through this process, it structures and builds shared ideas that can be quickly disseminated to a wider audience.

We can use the game to sample options, thus enabling the team to understand the design and development process and how informed trade-offs can be made to ensure that the project is built. This is the right way of doing community collaboration, and real benefits will flow from using these approaches and techniques. Not only will we be able to meet the goals of neighbourhood development but also, more importantly, these approaches can help us to achieve successful regeneration in which communities are given the power to shape their own futures.

Metrics for measuring successful outcomes are agreed with the community in advance of the gaming process. They are free to come up with their own and to help rate how each is valued against the others. These metrics can be as simple as walkability factors and as complex as the importance of local energy production. Some metrics will be guided by policy and best practice. Others will be guided by community desires.

The NEIGHBOURHOOD GAME has the following qualities:

→ It helps to explore the relationship between many complex issues, such as urban resilience, the density of development, and its investment value, thus informing decision-making. It can be adapted to different places and different issues and can be played with a range of people, from active citizens to urban professionals or even civic leaders.

→ It can be used as part of community or neighbourhood planning events and is therefore ideally suited to a new localism agenda. For large-scale engagement, the tool can be used as a physical gaming board set out in a 'casino' format with a screen projection.

→ It works across a number of scales and allows grids to be tailored to specific areas. If a grid layout dimension is chosen to develop block sizes, such as in our imagined Localia case study, this grid should be tried.

→ It can assess the implications of new urban extensions, suburban intensification, housing estate renewal, and social infrastructure and town centre redevelopment.

How to build your own game

Anyone armed with a scaled plan (or aerial photograph), a simple spreadsheet application and some basic stationery can develop a game suited to their particular purpose. To simplify data entry, data is managed through a grid-and-tile system linked to a spreadsheet. The following are the components of the game:

1 **A game board** is based on a scaled aerial photograph or plan of the neighbourhood with a grid laid over it. At the neighbourhood level, smaller grid tiles of between 50 and 100 metres (165 to 330 feet) work best, so our Localia case study, which shows a 75-metre (250 feet) grid layout dimension, is ideal. A game board can be scaled to the size of a large table, still allowing people to gather around and be actively engaged. The board shows the following information:

→ Each grid square annotated with a unique cell reference to match the format of a spreadsheet—letters across the top and numbers down the side
→ Development constraints, such as retained natural and heritage features, flood plains and other barriers
→ Development opportunities, such as available land, links to wider area and public transport accessibility
→ Any other special features to help orientate participants and give them a sense of scale of the area

2 **Playing tiles** that match the grid size on the board are used to represent different land uses—their relative costs, traffic generation and requirements are linked to schooling, open space and local shopping provision. These playing tiles can be placed on the game board to explore where new development could occur, the appropriate balance of uses, the implications regarding delivery and funding. They include:

→ Types and densities of development for housing shown as density and type bands with numbers of units for each tile

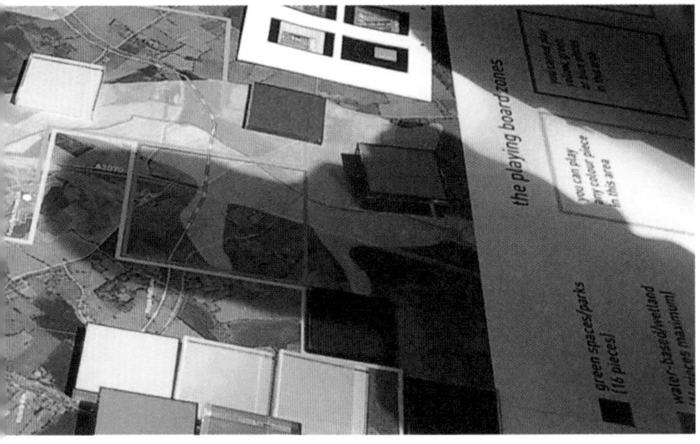

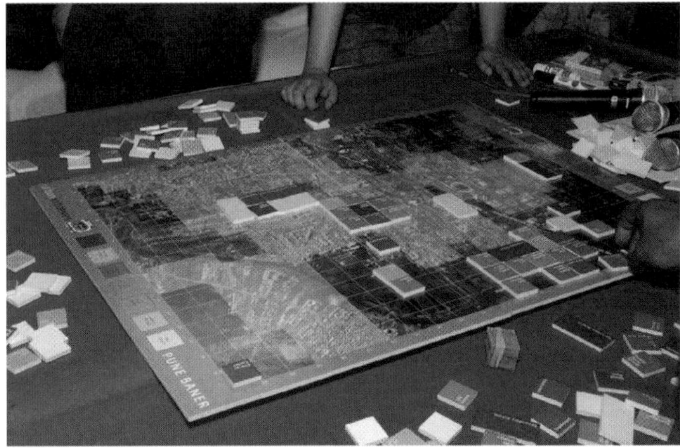

→ Types and densities of development for workspace or industrial uses shown as density and type bands with development areas for each tile
→ Types and densities of development for mixed-use development shown as density and type bands with development areas and number of units for each tile
→ Parks, education and local shopping tiles and any other special land uses identified

3 **An interactive spreadsheet** is loaded with a cell-format structure to match that of the game board. The spreadsheet is projected onto a screen as a live record of tiles played and decisions made. People then play different scenarios that have different outcomes and can see the results in real time. The interactive spreadsheet is loaded with the following data:

→ Values for each of the grid squares, which could include property values, measures of compactness, public transport accessibility levels, walking proximity, distance to local energy supply or any other metrics agreed in advance
→ Values for each of the tiles, which could include numbers, costs per tile, contributions to other uses and so on
→ A separate column that shows targets met, values created, rewards gained and reflects all of the metrics agreed in advance

4 **Unique pieces** introduce a tailored dynamic to the game. They include:

→ Pins that can be pushed into the board to block squares being played
→ Tiles that reflect rewards for meeting targets such as 'green dividends', cost gains that can be spent against special uses such as cultural facilities, allotment gardens or additional open spaces
→ Tiles that reflect savings as a result of collective community action, self-help, social enterprise and so on

5 **Simple rules** spell out the agreed metrics loaded into the spreadsheet, rules of engagement, roles and responsibilities of various players including the games-master, recording procedures and tips to maximise outcomes. The game uses PUBLIC PROTOCOL as its starting point.

How to play the game
Under the direction of a games-master, who observes the agreed protocols and works with the accepted metrics:

1 Participants are encouraged to think of different scenarios and play tiles and see results when the tiles' values are combined with the grid squares' values.
2 Participants are free to change the tiles around provided the spreadsheet is updated.
3 Participants are encouraged to play a number of games with different people leading different thematic scenarios, such as the 'most sustainable development scenario', or the 'least traffic-generating scenario'.
4 Participants can choose to change the values for different metrics to see the impacts of these changes.
5 The results of each game board are photographed alongside the spreadsheet and named for later comparison and debate.

The NEIGHBOURHOOD GAME does not design. It just shows the implications of decisions. It is a start and a roadmap. It exposes conflicts, but it offers mitigation. It is a live discussion tool where nothing can be hidden and no one can hide. It does, however, point a way to the professional team as to the thinking and values of the community and enables them to work up different options to be brought back to the community. The real value of the game lies in the metrics agreed in advance and in the decisions that need to be made by the community to make things happen. After people have been through this process, they understand what needs to be done. Trust and commitment to action are built. It is true collaboration.

LOCALIA URBAN NEIGHBOURHOOD

BUILDING SOCIAL CAPITAL FROM THE OUTSET

The emerging population of Localia is a vibrant mix of different cultures and ethnic groups with a range of different socio-economic characteristics. Many of these people arrive from rural areas or from places further afield. Some are skilled, others semi-skilled and others want to learn. Some are in groups, others alone.

Localia's Neighbourhood Enabling Agency (NEA) is tasked with ensuring that shared purpose, self-organisation and collective action are the primary driving forces for building social capital at every stage of the development process. This is how they do it:

Step 1: The NEA produces the first draft of a PUBLIC PROTOCOL for Localia.

→ They set out the simple purpose and clear principles for the development of Localia for all its new incoming residents. This is printed on large posters and available for all to see on the walls of NEA offices and technical assistance centres.

→ They identify the simple rules of engagement between the NEA and the people, showing how both can work together to achieve better outcomes.

→ They identify a range of community engagement tools and show how organised groups can use these to assist in building consensus and shared visions.

→ They establish tactics to deal with changes and conflicts, including easy appeal procedures and options for resolving these.

Step 2: The NEA starts a neighbourhood social network.

→ They invite all new incoming people to register their needs and intentions on a community database—initially on cards put on a community notice board and later on a social media network. Many people have access to smartphones.

→ They encourage new incoming people to make contact with like-minded people and organise themselves into groups with representatives.

→ They give self-organised groups an accelerated status in the site allocation process—as lot developers, as building developers and as others looking to procure homes adjacent to one another to take benefits of economies of scale.

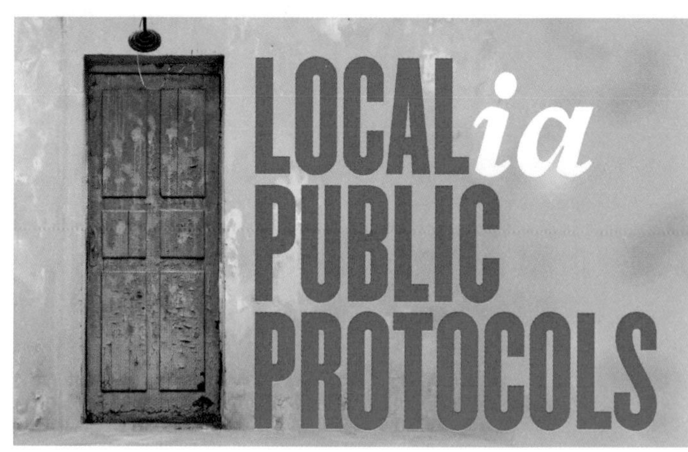

Step 3: The NEA enables a shared civic vision for Localia.

→ They hold regular sessions with groups, showing the sense of the possible, and invite people to use their creativity to take things further.

→ They provide a booking service for meeting space in corner buildings and schools, and encourage people to use these facilities.

→ They provide publicity and feedback, helping people to share ideas, actions and successes.

Step 4: The NEA asks people to help.

→ They encourage people to form voluntary groups and engage in established associations and institutions, to help undertake projects in the collective interest of the community.

→ They use their social network and community noticeboard to bring people together to share assets, skills and time, and show ways in which this can happen.

→ They provide access to civic leadership programmes and celebrate active citizenship through awards, etc. They build community champions.

Step 5: The NEA offers a range of activator programmes.

→ They introduce a free ideas zone (greyworld) centred on some disused industrial buildings near the station and allow people to start businesses and social enterprises.

→ They introduce a Sparks programme with temporary buildings around the main civic square to trigger the start of higher-order civic, education, health and cultural facilities.

→ They facilitate local economic, arts and cultural, and neighbourhood management programmes by making available space to interested people in the corner and school buildings.

→ They introduce an urban pioneers programme on sites along the main street to enable a richer mix of uses and enterprise. People compete for sites and win on the strength of their ideas. Innovation flourishes.

→ They manage street markets. They facilitate community orchards and local food production programmes. They organise energy saving projects and encourage neighbourhood watch programmes. They are open to anything.

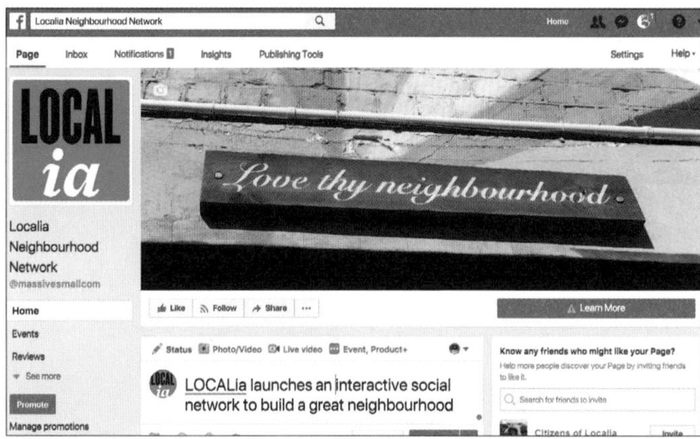

Step 6: The NEA introduces a participatory budgeting process.

→ They invite people to put forward projects and programmes that would trigger joint action by the NEA and local community.

→ They encourage people to help shape local services to best meet the needs of the local community.

→ They support collaborative working and activation of community assets to meet this goal.

→ They ensure more equitable public spending, transparency and accountability and increased levels of public participation.

→ They help share these budgets and show how targets have been met in the spending process.

Step 7: The NEA builds community

→ They hold ideas competitions and neighbourhood challenges to unlock the creative potential of people. They share outcomes and feedback.

→ They show by doing—building show homes, local expositions and live-action projects.

→ They hold world café events, citizenship workshops and community building programmes. They publicise local stories and celebrate successes. They create a buzz.

→ They enable temporary use strategies to allow people test ideas, explore new markets and prove concepts. Everything is possible.

→ They facilitate an annual Neighbourhood Day with street parties, exhibitions and cultural programmes. Everyone is welcome.

Step 8: The NEA lets things happen

→ Things started small and more things happened. Things changed. The temporary became permanent, and the permanent got better.

→ The neighbourhood grew and took different forms in different places. Everyone had a chance to realise their dreams.

→ Businesses started and flourished. People made local and bought locally. Money was kept in the community. Everyone won.

→ People were empowered and did things with the NEA that neither could have done alone. Democracy was put back into urbanism.

→ It was amazing.

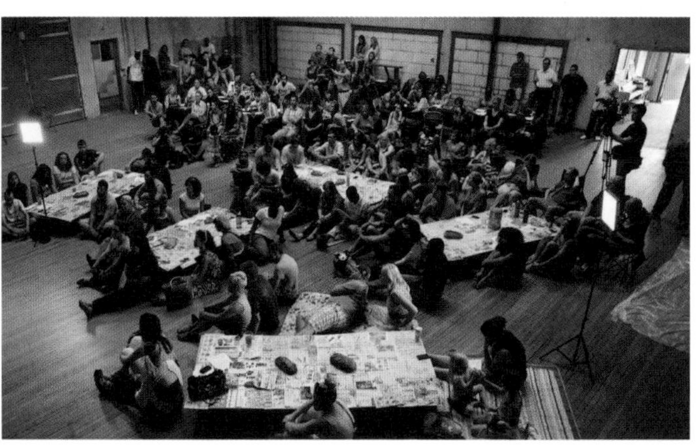

We have to be able to adapt to new situations. It's another form of the definition of intelligent behaviour.

—Hasso Plattner

FROM COMMAND-AND-CONTROL TO ENABLING **BEHAVIOURS** 2.3

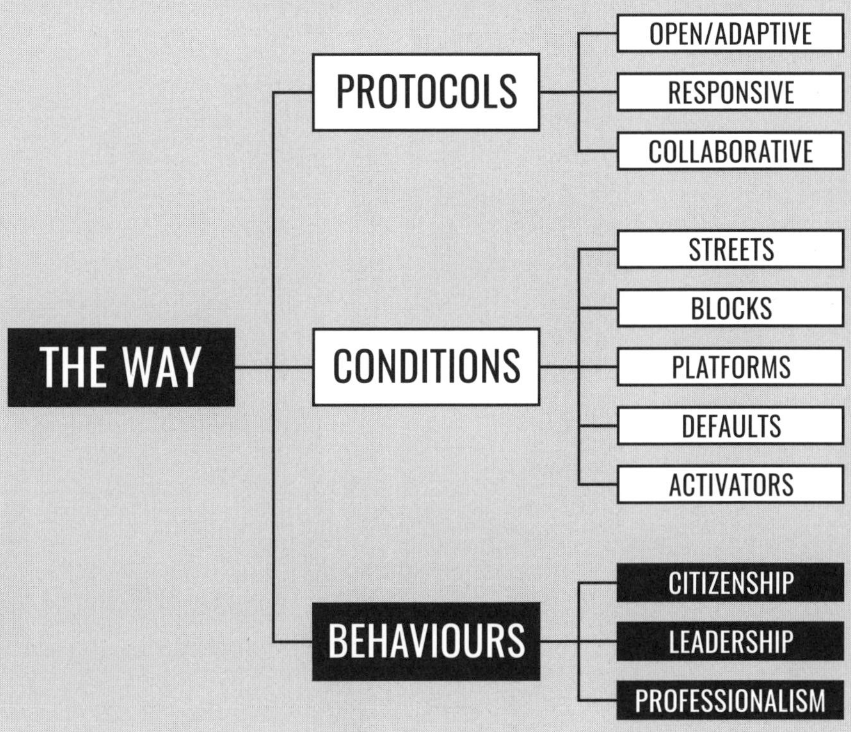

Behaviour *NOUN*

1 The range of actions and mannerisms made by individuals, organisations and systems in conjunction with themselves or their environment

2 The action, reaction or functioning of a system, under normal or specified circumstances

SYNONYMS
working, performance, operation, practice, conduct, functioning

Enabling BEHAVIOURS is the third enabling mechanism needed to evolve our top-down systems of urban governance to make a Massive Small change. To do this, we need to establish the appropriate form of leadership, management and ethics that provide the simple rules of engagement for all the players in the system—from top to bottom and back again.

Delivering any form of radical incrementalism requires a dramatic shift in the tactics we use today to govern this change. As governments and people face increasing global challenges from political, socioeconomic and technological change, the more traditional management response of increasing the effectiveness and efficiency of our existing operating models just will not work anymore.

MAIN STREET LIFE
REMEDS VIEW
CURIOCITY
SITUATION EAST
MAVERICK CORNER
FNB ATM
CASTLE
LITE
Responsibly. Not for Sale to Persons Under the Age of 18.

SCOPE

This section focusses on the nature of enabling behaviours and what it means for the tactics to be employed in our planning, design and development systems.

It introduces three main concepts:

1. Managing in the sweet spot of creativity and generative emergence
2. Managing through adaptive and collaborative leadership methods
3. Managing in the present, inventing the future

It does this in the context of our three main sectors engaged in building viable neighbourhoods:

1. Active citizens
2. Enabling civic leaders
3. Ethical urban professionals

Finally, it introduces The Massive Small Framework, a tool for all to work together to build a shared vision of a place.

A DIFFERENT MINDSET

Accommodating urban change by continually refining the current operational models has significant limitations. Here the effort is directed to the short-term fix, the catch-up effect and the retrofit nature of this activity, which attempts to apply yesterday's predictive (and often reactive) response to address the challenge of tomorrow's unpredictable problems. It has to change.

> *We need to put democracy back into urbanism by building a new social contract between the government and its citizens, based on trusting people to do the right thing. Governments can show the way by providing the protocols, conditions and behaviours to enable simple rules, emergent solutions and self-organisation to take root and flourish.*
>
> —Clause 1: A New Collaboration (Massive Small Declaration)

In his book, *The Wisdom of Crowds: Why the Many Are Smarter Than the Few*, James Surowiecki shows us how decisions taken by a large group, even if the individuals within the group aren't smart, are always better than decisions made by small numbers of 'experts'. This observation shows an enlightening way forward for pluralism, diversity and democracy.

THEORY

Enabling behaviours are distinctly different to command-and-control behaviours. Managing open, responsive and collaborative systems, more like living systems than static and mechanistic models, requires an entirely different mindset. Instead of relying on controlling every detail in our communities from the top down, many civic leaders today see the need to harvest the collective intelligence and collective wisdom of everyone. The process towards new insight and clarity can be messy.

In enabling bottom-up systems, traditional civic and professional leaders are less concerned with establishing a direction for the city and more involved with enabling activity that generates the best ideas.

Traditional management assumes that most top-down organisations are closed systems and that managerial hierarchies are the best way to maintain the equilibrium.

When things go awry, conventional wisdom favours elaborate command-and-control systems so that managers can apply the immediate corrective action to restore balance.

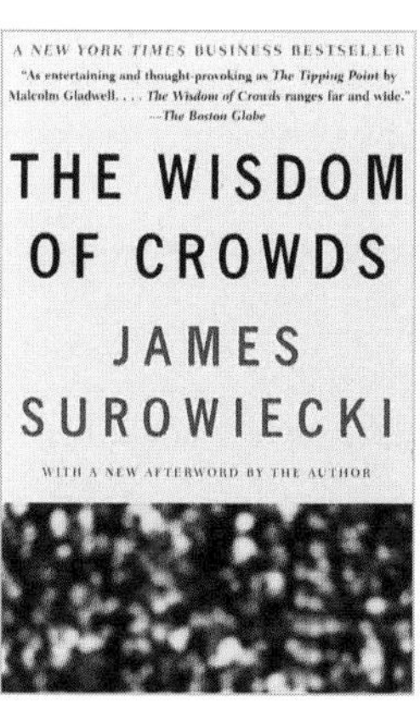

Managing complex adaptive systems

Rod Collins, in 'The Management Wisdom of Complex Adaptive Systems', presents a different view to the traditional approaches:

> New business models are showing us that the most efficient operations behave like complex adaptive systems where self-managing participants, following a set of simple rules, organise themselves to solve incredibly complex problems. There are no bosses or hierarchies in these open systems, nor are there complicated regulations to govern the collective behaviour of the individual contributors.

Because cities in the digital age are far more likely to be open systems, a management model that relies on hierarchies to maintain the equilibrium of the established ways will not get the job done, especially when managing innovation is the central business issue. Being innovative means knowing when to change and calls for the collaborative interaction characteristic of complex adaptive systems.

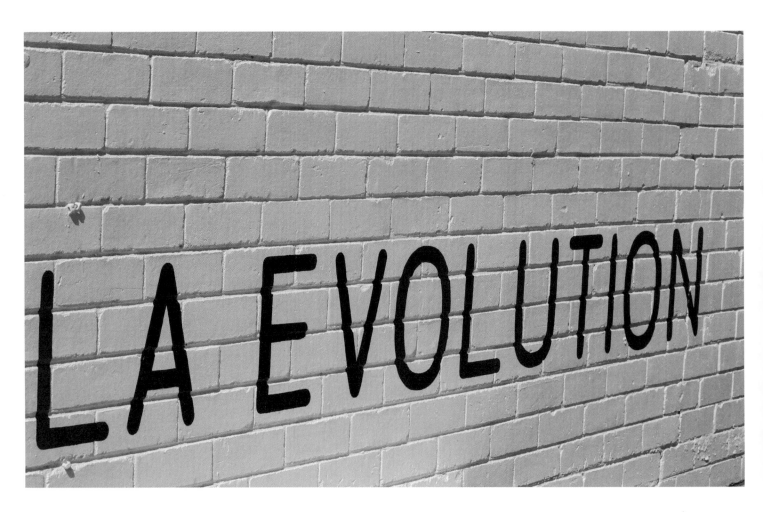

Agility is key

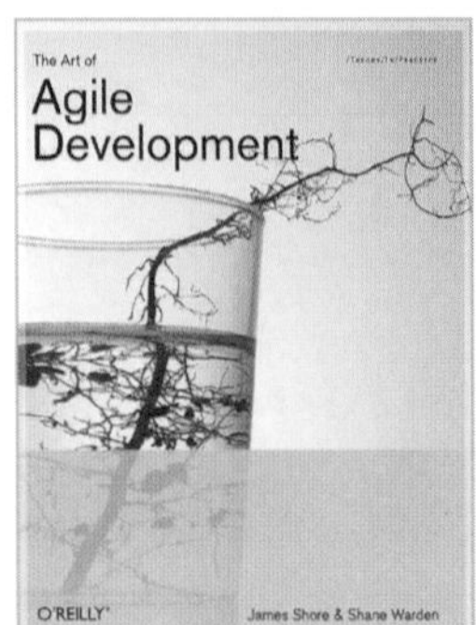

An iterative, incremental method of managing the planning, design and development of our urban environment in a highly flexible, responsive and interactive manner is the way, as demonstrated in Warden and Shore's book, *The Art of Agile Development*. Although its focus is on software development, we can learn a lot from the practical tips to start practicing agile development. Continuous strategy and feedback are more important than detailed long-term plans. New forms of technology, such as social media, interactive citizen engagement apps and smart citizen tools, will play a far more important role in managing this process. There will also need to be a greater reliance on trust between all parties, with open, transparent and ethical behaviours forming the basis of any enabling approach.

> *Agile does not mean laissez-faire—flexibility and freedom are based on the well-defined principles.*
>
> —Pearl Zhu

Trust and commitment

There is a natural tension between a desire to be open to the possibility of a different future (to be adaptive) and the need to reduce future uncertainty (to make decisions). The opportunity is to reframe management as a practice that enables outcomes rather than a process that gets results, to adopt an adaptive and collaborative style of running things (enabling management) that ensures collaborative learning and decision-making as the best way of co-creating more sustainable outcomes.

> *True professionalism and civic leadership must be built on trust and commitment to do the right thing and must be bound by commonly accepted behaviours. In signing up to these principles, urban professionals and civic leaders take their responsibility to the well-being and continued success of all the inhabitants of the city they have charge over.*
>
> —Clause 7: A Code of Ethics (Massive Small Declaration)

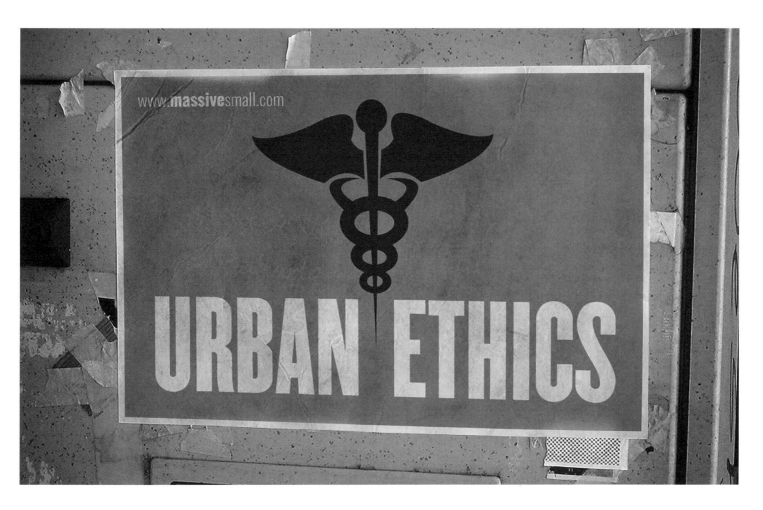

LEADERSHIP, MANAGEMENT AND ETHICS

> *We need people who dive deep, dream and dare do. We need people able to grasp the sublime and, therefore, that which is universally true for all. We need them to reclaim our humanity.*
>
> —Yasmine Sherif

Leadership, in this increasingly changing world, is about enabling the emergence of possible futures. Management, in this context, is about allowing the presence of those possible futures to navigate disruptive change successfully. Ethics, in this renewed social contract between government and people (and their intermediaries), is based on a system of moral principles that govern a person's behaviours in conducting any activity at any level, whether they are an active citizen, a civic leader or an urban professional.

Traditional command-and-control leadership and management approaches will always be found wanting in an environment where the future is increasingly unpredictable. Unfortunately, this directive style of doing things is still the dominant model for controlling complex urban environments.

Clearly, we need rigorous decision systems to structure organisational activity, but these systems need to enable, guide and support community interaction and decision-making, not stifle it. Just because decision-making needs to be clear (transparent and accountable) does not mean it cannot also be flexible (open and consultative).

> *Most leadership strategies are doomed to failure from the outset. As people have been noting for years, the majority of strategic initiatives that are driven from the top are marginally effective—at best.*
>
> —Peter Senge

Enabling management must have an adaptive capacity, a facility to synthesise (anticipate, analyse and successfully integrate) emergent change as a normal operational process. It must allow an adaptive capacity to flourish—this style of management must also embrace a collaborative decision system.

This system must enable and promote the emergence of other opportunities for change at all scales of government and community, while at the same time providing a useful framework for managing the response to this change.

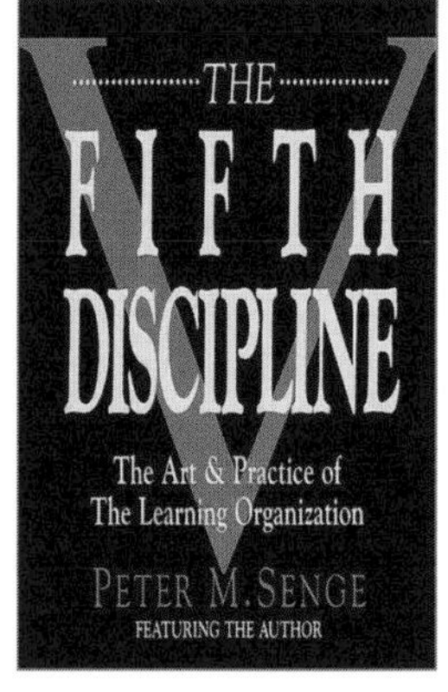

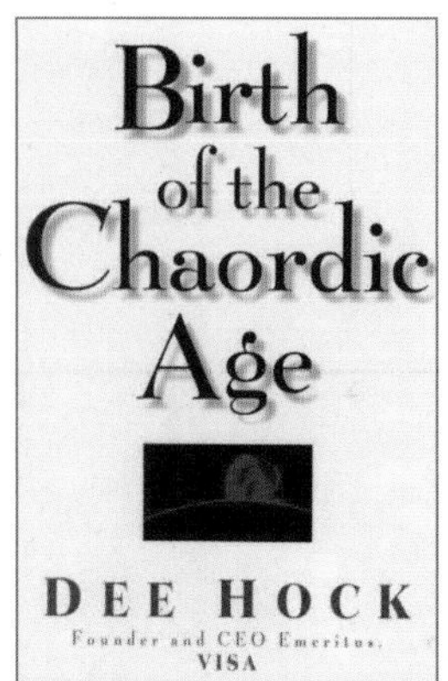

THE SWEET SPOT OF EMERGENCE

Dee Hock, in his book *The Birth of the Chaordic Age*, refers to the concept of the 'chaord', with chaos and order at two ends of a spectrum. On the far side of chaos is chamos—or destructive despair. On the far side of order is rigid conformity—or stifling control. When we move towards either of these extremes, the result is apathy or rebellion. It is on the path that lies at the midpoint of the spectrum, where chaos and order overlap, that leads us to new forms of collective learning and real-time innovation. A balance lies between two seeming polarities, which are in fact complements of each other. As we move between chaos and order, individually and collectively, we move through confusion and conflict towards clarity. He maintains that the greatest potential for creativity and generative emergence lies in managing the sweet spot of generative emergence. He calls this sweet spot the chaord.

> *At the edge of chaos is where life evolves—where things are not hard wired but are flexible enough for new connections and solutions to occur. New levels of order become possible out of chaos. In this space of generative emergence, we leave our collective encounters with that which not one of us individually brought into the room. This requires us to stay in a transformative shift, though we may want to veer toward either chaos or order.*
>
> —Dee Hock

By *chaord*, Hock means any self-organising, self-governing, nonlinear, complex, adaptive system or organisation, whether physical, biological or social, the behaviour of which harmoniously blends characteristics of both chaos and order. Loosely translated to neighbourhoods, it can be thought of as a community that harmoniously blends characteristics of co-existence and cooperation, or from the perspective of education, an institution that seamlessly blends theoretical and experiential learning.

These systems or organisations require a much different consciousness about the leader–follower dichotomy. According to Hock, leadership does not necessarily imply constructive, ethical, open conduct. It is entirely possible to induce destructive, malign, devious behaviour, and to do so by corrupt means. Therefore, a clear, constructive purpose and compelling ethical principles evoked from and shared by all participants should be the essence of every relationship in every institution.

He describes the difference between leadership and management as follows:

> 'Chaos/Order is the Place for Leadership. The practice of leadership resides in the place between chaos and order. When facing new challenges that cannot be met with the same way we are currently working, we need to learn new ways of operating. It is during these times of uncertainty and increased complexity, where results cannot be predicted, that leaders need to invite others to share diverse knowledge to discover new purpose and strategies and decide the way forwards.
>
> 'Order/Control is a Place for Management. The practice of management lies between order and control where activities need to be maintained and executed routinely so that a particular standard results. It is the place where "more of the same" is required. Therefore...predictability is called for and procedures and standards [need to be] clearly defined and adhered to.'

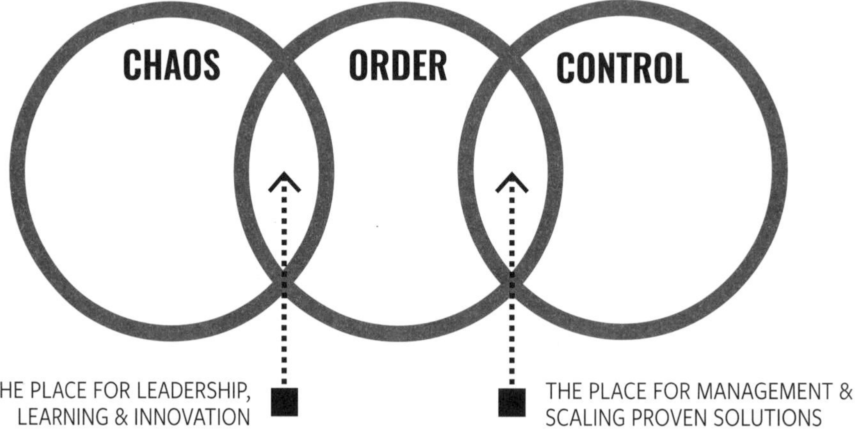

ADAPTIVE AND COLLABORATIVE LEADERSHIP

> *True leaders are those who epitomise the general sense of the community—who symbolise, legitimise and strengthen behaviour in accordance with the sense of the community—which enable its shared purpose, values and beliefs to emerge and be transmitted. A true leader's behaviour is induced by the behaviour of every individual choosing where to be led.*
>
> —Dee Hock

Engaging the whole stakeholder community

Change can only be achieved where the programme of urban change is recognised by all the stakeholders as an integral part of its future strategy.

For example:

- → To create a vision and strategy that is credible, it must be visibly and genuinely in sync with and relevant to community needs.
- → To successfully communicate the vision and get the buy-in of the community, the proposed change must make sense.
- → To establish an effective collaboration, it must be clear that the planned change outcomes will benefit all of the stakeholders.

Rather than responding to an engaging long-term vision and strategy for the future, many urban change programmes are concerned with managing discrete, short-term responses to environmental factors and stakeholder pressures. They are often reactive responses to 'correct' an unforeseen problem rather than being proactive in identifying and exploiting a continual flow of opportunities for change.

The benefits of these change programmes are often short term and focussed on quick fixes for particular groups of stakeholders, often at the expense of others. It is this limited focus and reactive approach to change that helps limit the potential for more proactive, holistic and enabling change. Rather, it could productively engage the wider community and give rise to an agenda of change that is critical for the longer-term sustainability of most cities, towns and neighbourhoods.

> *Collaboration is vital to sustain what we call profound or really deep change, because, without it, organisations are just overwhelmed by the forces of the status quo.*
>
> —Peter Senge

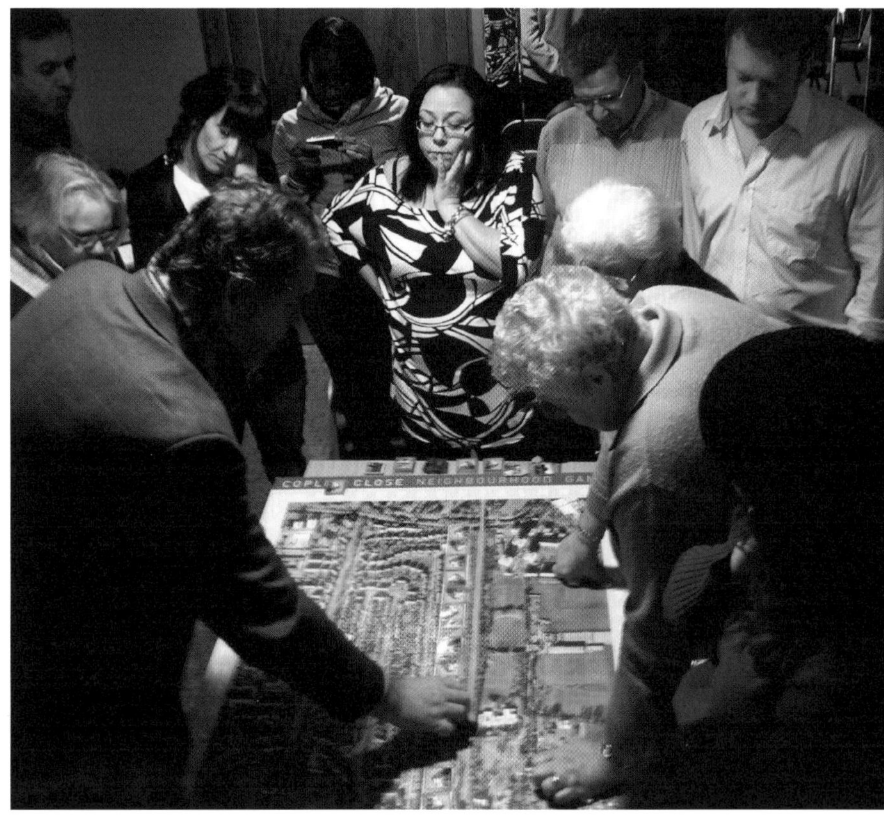

Principles for enabling management

> *Leadership exists when people are no longer victims of circumstances, but participate in creating new circumstances.*
>
> —Peter Senge

According to Tony Chamberlain in his book, *The Congruence Framework: An Opportunity to Rethink the Future of Organisations*, the application of enabling management could be framed according to the following fundamental principles:

Purposeful. It knows that the 'why' is more important than the 'how' to a committed community.

Inclusive. It appreciates the potential of its community and its connectedness and diversity.

Humble. It knows what it doesn't know and relies on the collective wisdom of the community.

Collaborative. It facilitates 'win-win' outcomes that sustain productive community engagement.

Caring. It is concerned with the collective well-being of its community, which is dependent on individual well-being.

THE PAST, THE PRESENT AND THE FUTURE

> *I think anyone's brief now is managing the present and inventing the future. That can be challenging because the present is this sort of dynamic, real-time thing that you're trying to get your arms around. And yet, at the same time, you've got to have your head up and looking into the future.*
>
> —Wendy Clark

Manage in the present, for the past is spent and done with and the future is uncertain.

—Marcus Aurelius

We know that mechanistic, hierarchical and linear models of leadership as top-down actions to influence and control the behaviour of those involved in urban activities are inadequate for the complex, interactive and interdependent dynamics of today's towns and cities. In complex adaptive systems, leadership is understood as a dynamically evolving influence pattern that includes elements of administrative, distributed and emergent leadership. Here leadership is an interactive and interdependent process from which learning, innovation and adaptation emerge.

Marcus Aurelius points a clear direction. Don't look backwards to move forwards. Apparently, this does not mean that we cannot learn from the past. It just means that we should not be held to ransom by the past. It also means that we cannot forget the future—but we also cannot plan that far ahead with any real certainty. What it does say is that we must fully embrace the present, something we are notoriously bad at doing in planning our urban environs.

The overexploitation of our natural resources and the increasing number of social conflicts following from their unsustainable use has created a wide gap between the objectives of sustainability and current urban management practices. It's hard to close this gap using the planning system we have today.

In evolving complex systems like cities, planning cannot be a static objective. Instead, planning is an open evolutionary process of improving the management of social systems through better understanding and knowledge. Therefore, urban management systems need to be able to deal with different temporal, spatial and social scales. They need to embrace irreducible uncertainty, multidimensional interactions and emergent properties.

Anticipating the future

Scenario planning is a well-developed, strategic planning method that some organisations use to make flexible long-term plans. It involves the adaptation and generalisation of classic methods used by intelligence agencies. It started out by generating simulation games for policymakers. These games combined known facts about the future, such as demographics and societal change, and imagined new social, technical, economic, environmental and political trends.

In applications, the emphasis on gaming the behaviour of opponents was reduced (shifting more towards a game against nature). According to Wikipedia, scenario planning is viewed as changing mindsets about the exogenous part of the world, before formulating specific strategies. Scenario planning may involve aspects of systems thinking, particularly the recognition that many factors may combine in complex ways to create sometimes surprising futures. The method also allows the inclusion of factors that are difficult to formalise, such as novel insights about the future, deep shifts in values, unprecedented regulations or inventions.

> *System thinking is a discipline of seeing the whole.*
>
> —Peter Senge

Systems thinking, when integrated with scenario planning, can offer plausible and dynamic future scenarios. The causal relationship between factors can be demonstrated, and action is taken to manage anticipated future needs

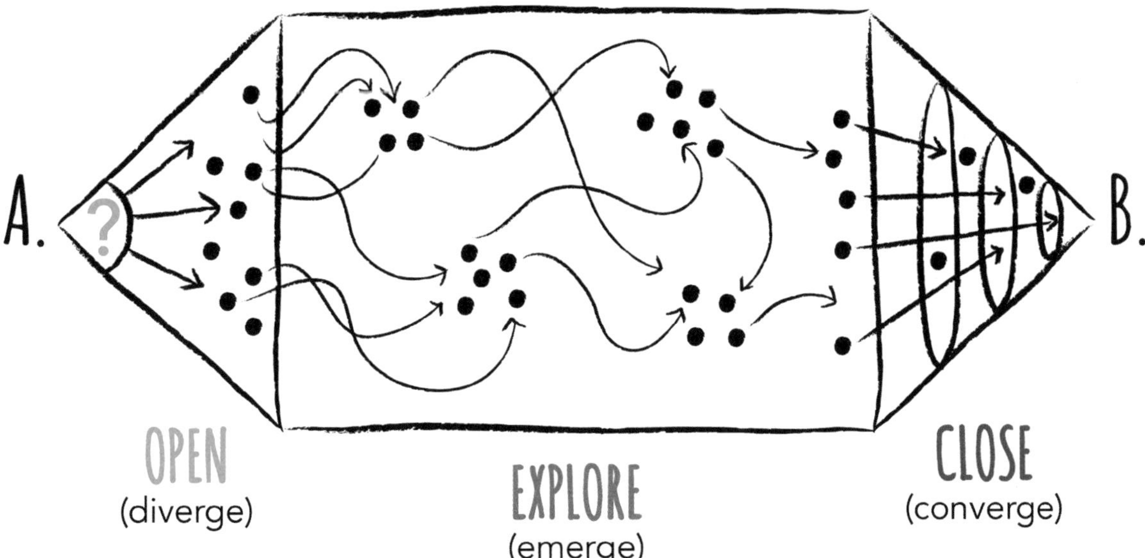

The 'divergence, emergence and convergence' decision-making process looks to open up the problem, explore through a number of scenarios and then close them down to a preferred strategy.

Divergence, emergence and convergence
Envisioning a preferred future and planning to achieve it can also be illustrated by the Participatory Decision-Making model, pioneered by Sam Kaner and shown in his book, *Facilitator's Guide to Participatory Decision-making*. The model has four distinct phases that work together.

Firstly this model reinforces the view that the future will not be an extension of the past, and, therefore, it can evolve in an infinite number of ways—and can be shaped.

Secondly, it looks to an exploration of the short- to long-term possibilities to inform decision-making.

Thirdly, it encourages change in the desired direction. One of the main features of the approach is that the future of cities should be explored, envisioned and planned in a collaborative and concerted effort by all stakeholders.

Finally, this new approach should provide enabling mechanisms for:

1 **Active citizens**
- → To envision their desired future, building upon shared values and needs
- → To actively participate in decision-making processes

2 **Civic leaders**
- → To challenge the thinking of people involved in urban planning processes
- → To channel the thinking of stakeholders into contemplating what future is desirable in the long-term perspective and the tasks that need to be addressed to achieve that future;
- → To discern the needs of communities, and to map the changing aspirations and ambitions of policymakers and decisionmakers
- → To develop mechanisms that would facilitate the collaboration of all stakeholders and communities in shaping the future

3 **Urban professionals**
- → To manage the increasing complexity of urban systems and the context within which they function, and to deal with the uncertainty of future change
- → To identify global trends and examine how they interact and what consequences they could have for a given urban environment
- → To anticipate and consider the short-, medium-, and long-term impacts of future change as well as consequences of their policies and decisions
- → To view cities as entities and examine various urban components in connection with other dimensions

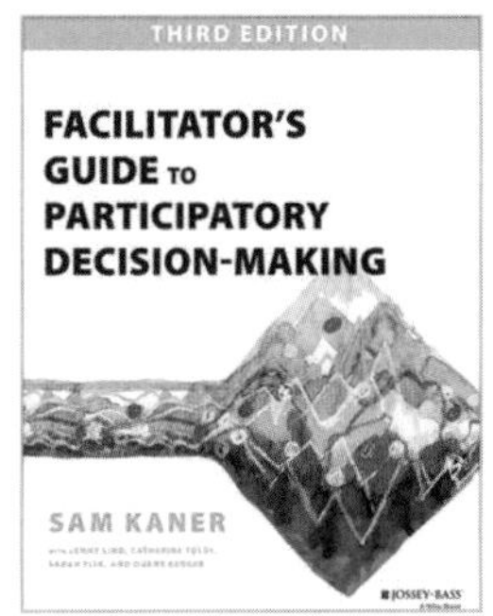

ACTIVE CITIZENSHIP

Civilisation rests on the fact that most people do the right thing most of the time.

—Lewis Mumford

An ACTIVE CITIZEN is anyone who gets involved at any level in their local communities and democratic processes, from neighbourhood to town, city and metropolitan scale. This involvement can be as small as a campaign to clean up a street, as important as educating young people about democratic values, skills and participation, or as big as taking on a demanding civic leadership role. They are influential, committed and take personal responsibility to act in the collective interest of people living in their community.

Enabling constructive citizen action

Social activism is intended to bring about social change by actively promoting solutions. If one feels strongly about a cause and is working towards a systematic change by fighting for change in society, then one could be considered an activist. The best form of activism is constructive, as it offers different alternatives. Social activism is commonly focussed on the concerns that directly impact the conditions and standards of those in society who are victims of them. Many societal problems have become a platform for social activist groups, including reaction to property developments, air pollution and forced removal of people.

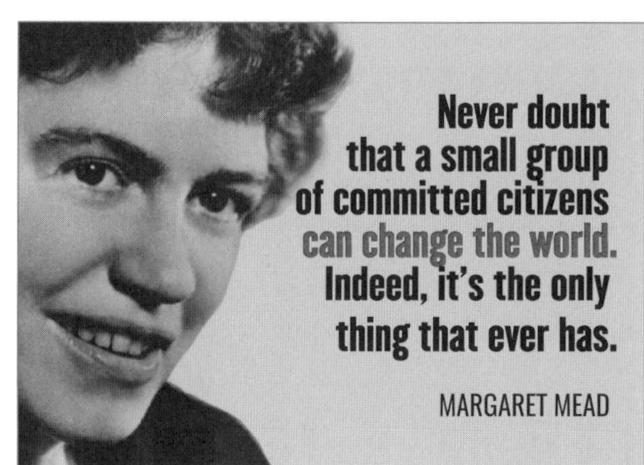
Never doubt
that a small group
of committed citizens
can change the world.
Indeed, it's the only
thing that ever has.
MARGARET MEAD

Since the days of Greece and Rome, when the word 'citizen' was a title of honour, we have often seen more emphasis put on the rights of citizenship than on its responsibilities.

—Robert Kennedy

Active citizenship has been described as the bringing together of rights-based and practice-based citizenship. The Royal Society of Arts in London, who have been spearheading an active citizenship project, take an alternative viewpoint to the established liberal concept of citizenship. They suggest that most liberal ideas of citizenship—from libertarianism to egalitarianism—see 'civic participation [as] a matter of personal freedom rather than a moral obligation' to act in the collective interest of the community. They think the capacity of citizens to contribute to tackling social challenges and problems is mostly untapped. According to Matthew Taylor, chief executive of the RSA,

> Current models for encouraging citizens to participate in civic life are geared around citizens influencing decision-making or service delivery, rather than individually or collectively making the change themselves. But this needs to change; participation must enable citizens to take action rather than just have conversations.

Active citizenship brings together knowledge, attitudes, skills and actions that aim to contribute to building and maintaining a democratic urban society. It is based on an accepted framework of universal human rights, the rule of law, cooperative values, social diversity and inclusiveness. Gaining this knowledge and developing and practicing these skills are all part of our shared social life. It starts at schools and continues until we pass on all of our knowledge and wisdom.

EFFECTIVE SOCIAL ACTION DISTURBS COMMON SENSE WITH UNCOMMON VALOUR.
JONATHAN JANSEN

KEY COMPETENCIES

According to a review of the UK government's Big Society initiative, the key competencies needed to allow active citizens to contribute effectively to building urban society are autonomy, responsibility and solidarity.

1. **Autonomy** is a much richer construct than just doing things alone. At its heart is the idea of self-determination and freedom from external influence, but it is used to 'reflect the psychological implications of subsidiarity, in the sense of taking personal initiative without state interference.' Autonomy is linked to our inherent creativity and goodwill. It is in the sense of people being self-authoring, creating their plans and working towards them for the sake of their community, rather than for financial rewards.

2. **Responsibility** is a competency where 'people take ownership of tasks that they might previously have assumed to be the responsibility of government, and often do so together with strangers.' An individual has to be truly responsible for something: ready, willing and able to respond to a given challenge in a given context. People need to take ownership of the consequences of their actions, especially when the link between the cause and effect is unclear.

3. **Solidarity**, meaning 'We're in this together', is a hugely complex idea, and is broadly about integration—the extent to which we feel we are on 'common ground with and have a sense of mutual commitment with the people with whom we share space, time and resources.' Solidarity underpins the shared norms required for social activism and productive outcomes. Strengthening social solidarity in our most culturally and ethnically diverse communities is still our biggest challenge worldwide.

In the absence of people claiming power, rather than being 'empowered'—not a prospect the authorities would in reality embrace—those in charge must resist the urge to reach for their clipboards. It is only when they come up with ideas that begin to grapple with the fundamental issues about the way we live our lives, and the way society is organised, that a public life worth participating in will truly emerge.

—David Clements

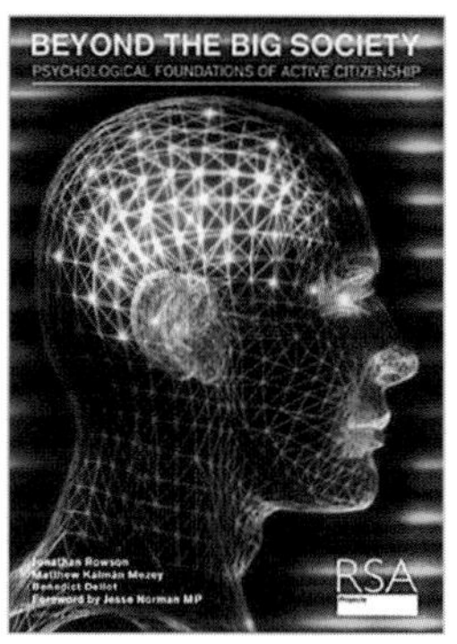

The distance between our dreams and reality is called citizen action.

—Anonymous

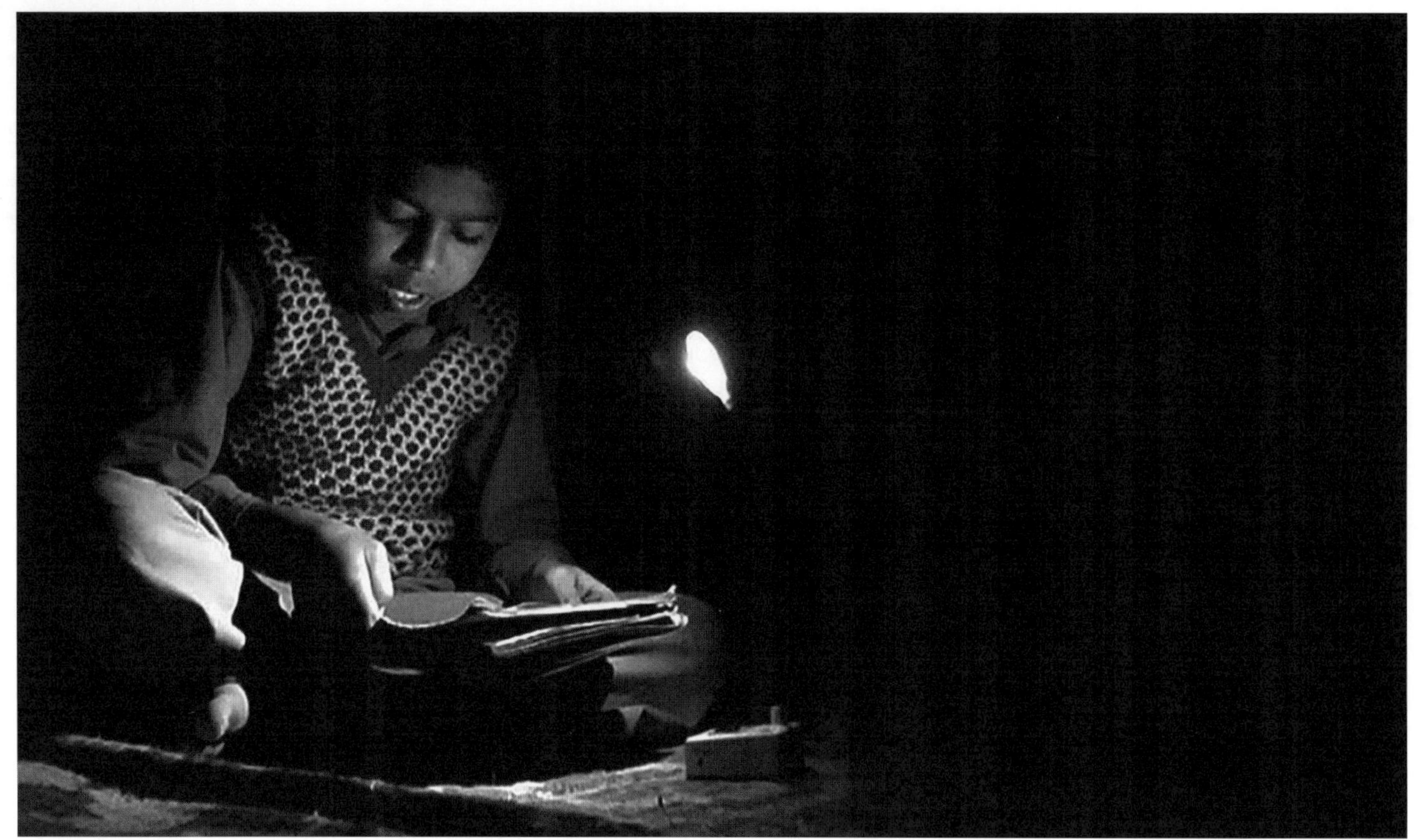

THE ENLIGHTENED SETTLER

HOW STREET LIGHTING GAVE CHILDREN AN UNEXPECTED CHANCE IN LIFE

Hector calls himself 'just a family man'. He lives in Julian Blanco, one of the informal settlements on a steep slope in Caracas, Venezuela. His family makes up part of a rapidly increasing population that lives outside the formal systems of urban society. In many parts of the world informal housing has become the norm. Even in well-developed countries, people are looking for ways to house themselves, rather than relying on governments' promises to house everyone in clean and decent homes.

Many governments see informal housing as a problem in isolation: a problem that needs its own special solution. Affordable housing, open-market housing and informal housing are treated as three separate staircases, each going to a different level of the metaphorical house and with no other way of moving from one level to another. People taking one route may want to transfer to one of the others when their personal circumstances change, through economic conditions, family changes, the cycles of life, or anything else. But it is rarely possible.

Informal housing is often part of a system that, while being meant to help the urban poor, ends up making the poor even poorer. Hector has seen the effect of this in his own barrio. The government has been so busy trying to solve specific problems that it has failed to realise that it is trapping people in their cycle of poverty by not allowing them to progress.

Most people in the barrio see informality just as one of the first stages in the maturity of their city. It is like a young child that will one day grow into an adult. Surely governments should do everything to nurture people in these early years so they can look after themselves in the future?

One-third of the inhabitants of the city of Caracas, Venezuela, live in informal settlements. The barrios, as they are called, provide a precarious way of life. They develop outside the framework of urban regulation, growing on invaded land and hazardous sites. Built by the people themselves, these settlements have become a permanent feature of Caracas's urban landscape. Their inhabitants are physically segregated and socially excluded from the formal city. They struggle to access basic services and infrastructure, and they face insecure property rights, challenged citizenship, rampant unemployment and high crime rates. They exert no power in the urban decision-making process.

The population density in the barrios has increased dramatically as continued migration from rural areas adds to natural growth. With declining economic prospects for poor people and a reduced rate of construction of affordable housing by the state and the private sector, barrios are the only option for many people. It is estimated that almost half of Venezuela's young people live in poverty in these marginal settlements.

Three strategies have been used to tackle these problems in recent decades. The first is to evict poor urban settlers and relocate them far from city centres. The second, the strategy of clean-up-and-redevelop, replaces informal settlements with new housing on the same site (though often this is housing that the poor cannot afford). The third is to upgrade the existing settlements, integrating them into the fabric of the city. A large number of projects have been undertaken as joint ventures between the government of Venezuela, the World Bank and other agencies, but new barrios are constantly forming.

The success of the upgrading process depends on the self-organisation and empowerment of the community, but these are hard to achieve. It is important to involve children and young people in identifying their own priorities for improvements, and help them to challenge the hazards of growing up in a barrio. Their own participation in the regeneration process can be a step towards eventually achieving full citizenship.

HECTOR HAS A PROBLEM

The government has made numerous attempts to integrate Hector's settlement, Julian Blanco, into the wider area by improving roads and steps. There is a basic water supply and sanitation system but the settlement is not electrified. Hector has struggled for ages to make things work. He used his own sweat equity to build a basic shelter for his family and improves it a little whenever he can afford to buy building materials.

At first Hector and his neighbours worked together to build their settlement. They organised themselves well. But as they became more settled they looked to the newly formed local council to take over the running of the place. Things began to change. What used to be done by people collectively became subcontracted to others. People became apathetic and social problems grew worse.

The settlement is now riddled with crime. Hector has heard that the government has received a report called 'Spotlight on Crime'. Written by a local university and funded by a large engineering company, the report claims that crime can be reduced by raising the level of lighting on the streets to the point at which the criminals will go elsewhere. Armed with this report, the government has raised funds from an international development bank to put in streetlights.

Hector has seen how the government has done this type of big fix in other parts of the city before. He is worried that this will be just one more top-down infrastructure project that goes wrong. New, tall floodlights will make the neighbourhood feel like a prison camp. The government is concerned that if it installs ordinary street lighting, people will tap into it to steal electricity for their homes. Putting fences around the base of the tall light columns is intended to prevent this happening.

Hector always knew that top-down systems would be needed as the settlement became more established. But those systems are not working, and local government is becoming increasingly remote from its people.

He sees the problem as a failure of the system on all fronts:

1 The system does not reflect any real understanding of local issues. There is no effective local democracy.
2 The system does not respond to the basic human dynamics that have been at work in this settlement since the outset. People have gone a long way to solve their own problems, but officials do not recognise this.
3 The system focusses on addressing the symptoms, not the root causes.
4 Abstract reports by vested interests come up with answers without understanding the questions.
5 The system looks for big solutions. It cannot cope with urban complexity that small, continuous, incremental change brings.

SO WHAT HAPPENS NEXT?

The government finally announces that it will install tall mast lighting in Hector's neighbourhood in Caracas to combat crime. Borrowing from the university report, it is called the Spotlight on Crime project. The community is enraged about the lack of consultation. Posters appear in windows. 'It's not darkness that creates crime but the lack of education for our children,' they say. Local people form a Shine a Light group. Hector is its spokesman. A delegation approaches the government to demand a different approach. The government says that it is too late: the contract has been signed.

Hector listens to a TED Talk by Alessandra Orofino, founder of Meu Rio, Rio de Janeiro's largest citizen mobilisation network. She talks about active citizenship and the role of communities in solving their own problems. Meu Rio is an online platform that allows the people of Rio to have a say in what is happening in the city. 'We think about our work as translating public policy issues into a language that is understandable to broader society and young people,' Orofino says. The site gives people an opportunity to act on things they think are important and allows both organisers and users to identify areas for change and action. Keeping an eye on the government has helped to inspire campaigns. Meu Rio has had remarkable successes in changing top-down actions and behaviours.

Hector is inspired: there is another way after all. He shares the knowledge with an old friend in government. The government reluctantly forms a working group, hoping that people will see reason and that opposition to the project will dissolve. The working group and the government agree on the basic rules of engagement. 'We will, if you will,' becomes the principle. They sit down together and agree how the funding for the street lighting project can be used to create the biggest impact.

The community organises itself around the challenge. Bonded together with a simple purpose, people use their own creativity to find a solution. They set up a neighbourhood watch, and crime starts to fall. Let's tackle crime by helping our children to learn, they say. Instead of shining a light on an empty street, let's shine it on a book.

This has become an issue worldwide. The organisation One Child One Light, in India, is lighting up a new possibility by making the most while the sun shines, literally. It has come up with solar-chargeable LED lights that are much more luminous and long lasting and can spark off a healthy spirit of enthusiasm for studying in children. The mission of this endeavour was to support every underprivileged child's right to education by giving a safe, clean and low-cost study light. The programme simultaneously aimed to eradicate the use of unsafe kerosene for lighting.

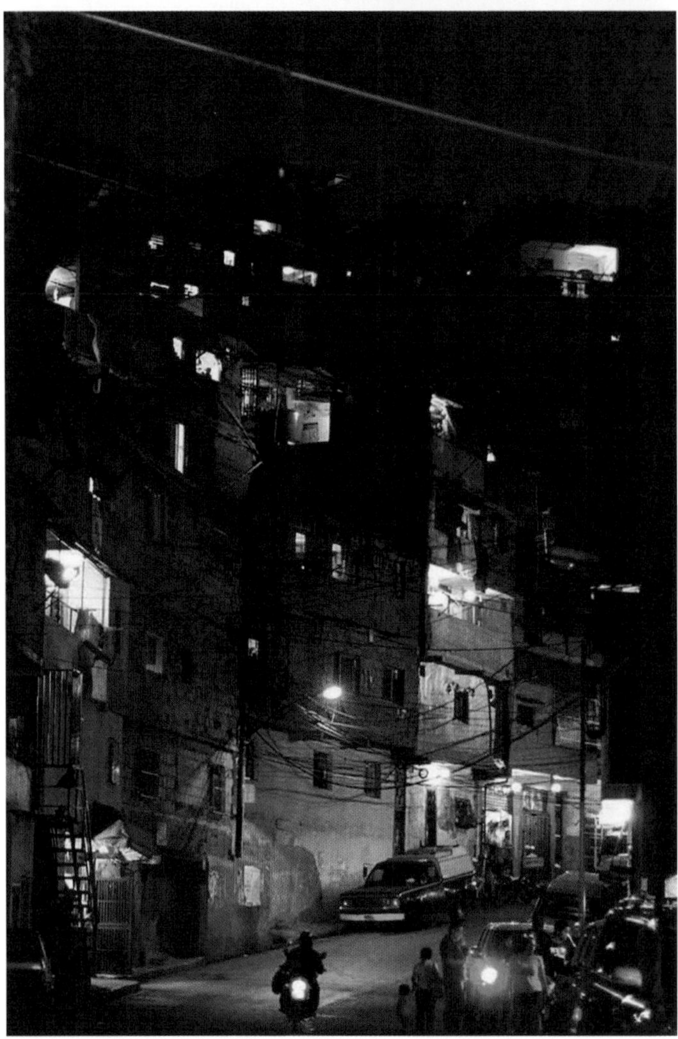

Top: Alessandra Orofino of Meu Rio, an online platform that has enabled thousands of citizens to become community activists. **Bottom:** Streetlighting in Caracas, Venezuela.

The local government replies that it can't be done. This is a street lighting project. A compromise is suggested. Let's try something different and see if it works on one street, the community says. We'll do the work ourselves and learn by experimenting. They hear about a type of electricity meter that can be mounted on the front of every building on the street. They agree to mount the lights on the fronts of the buildings and to light doorways first. This will provide all the street lighting that is needed. At the same time each house will receive one internal light free: a light to shine on a book. The children will be able to do their homework at night instead of only during the day. In the absence of good local teachers, online learning is now a possibility.

People are so excited that they start fixing up the fronts of their dwellings. They don't want their new light to shine on an unpainted door. Front windows are decorated. New plants appear in the front yards. A street party is held in the neighbourhood for the first time. Crime continues to fall.

The government is finally convinced. It rolls out the programme to other streets. Local businesses are offered the maintenance contracts for keeping the lights working. Some people pay for a smart meter to get additional lighting on a pay-as-you-go basis. Children do better at school, the local economy grows and crime falls to the lowest level in the city. The whole project comes out at a third below budget. Maintenance costs are slashed. As a result of every dollar spent by government, an average of $20 has been spent by local residents in upgrading their own homes.

Boosted by the success of their efforts, Shine a Light nominates Hector to join a group of active citizens to advise government on how they could work together to ensure full social progression from informality to formality, making the most of the collective strengths of both sides.

The work of the citizen's group is influenced by a paper published by the Cities Alliance. 'The Case for Incremental Housing' by Patrick Wakely and Elizabeth Riley argues that

> over the last two decades, the failure of standardised housing delivery models to respond to the sheer scale of need of the urban poor raises the question of whether the time has arrived to revisit the incremental housing approaches of the 1970s to 80s as a more realistic approach to meeting the housing needs of the urban poor....
>
> The basis of incremental housing was that the cost of housing could be reduced by recognising that poor urban families already build and extend their own dwellings incrementally in response to their needs and the availability of resources. The approach [of the 1970s to 80s] was to improve on this by providing appropriate legal and technical support. Over time the social and economic benefits of engaging communities and the realistic time needed for poor householders to build better quality buildings has become clearer. This learning provides the basis for re-making the case for incremental housing.

The citizen's group proposes a new social contract between government and the people. It is called the Caracas Compact.

THE CARACAS COMPACT

We, the citizens of Caracas, agree that government alone cannot solve all our urban problems and that we can meaningfully contribute to build a better urban society by working together. We propose that government provides the following clear rules of responsibility, engagement and behaviour to ensure that all our skills, resources and support systems are effectively deployed:

1. **Define 'The Caracas Way'.** We need a clear and simple set of protocols for all the people of our city to take positive action and solve their own problems. We must ensure that everyone has the same rules and rights. These protocols will evolve over time as we get better at doing it.

2. **Create a single housing staircase.** This staircase should be accessible to everyone, whether they are in the affordable, open-market or informal housing sectors. The first step should be set as low as possible and subsequent steps should be easy to take. Do not treat the building of informal housing differently: it is just the first sign of responsive action. Give it time.

3. **Provide freedom within constraints.** We need clear boundaries within which people are free to operate and innovate. Everyone must understand how it works. Structured choices must still allow for individual interpretations. There needs to be a rulebook with easily understood instructions and standards. Keep it simple.

4. **Facilitate early occupation.** We know that the people who move in first have the most difficult time. The essential elements need to be put in place that will stimulate action and allow people to start building their own homes. Technical support, temporary accommodation and access to cheap materials should be provided wherever possible. Infrastructure can follow. Nurture the early years.

5. **Focus on initial conditions.** Most places develop in ways that respond to their initial conditions, so a simple order of roads and subdivisions is needed to allow people to respond effectively. Start small: provide space for community infrastructure to take root and flourish.

6. **Foster local democracy.** We need to work through established democratic structures so that the community can express its collective interest. If these structures do not exist, we need to help people organise themselves. We need to develop ethical and enabling civic leadership, building accountability and responsibility at every level.

7. **Build trust.** We must re-establish the trust between government and people. This means being honest about where and what each party can deliver, honouring obligations and learning from failures as soon as possible. We must use intermediaries sparingly and keep communication simple. Trust people to do the right thing,

8. **Use infrastructure to build community.** Create social and economic capital at every opportunity by working with people on putting their local services in place and maintaining them. Ensure that government action leverages local community investment wherever possible.

9. **Build a pattern book of potential solutions.** We need examples to show and inspire people how they can progress from the early stages of site occupation to having fully developed homes. We need to work with both the shack-building and formal-housing industries to develop housing prototypes that are easy to upgrade.

10. **Monitor and review our actions.** We must not be fixated on a single, unbending, long-term vision. We need regular and continuous feedback from people on the ground. Use many small changes to make big differences. Evolve as necessary. Learn by doing.

HECTOR TELLS HIS STORY

Hector is asked to talk about the success of the Shine a Light project at the Meu Rio 'Our Cities' conference in Rio de Janeiro. He reflects on lessons he has learnt:

→ The project dealt with causes, not symptoms, and because of this it achieved a far better outcome than ever anticipated.
→ People are ingenious. They have natural instincts to solve complex urban problems, given the opportunity. They had an incentive to act in a way that achieved a positive social outcome. It was a simple solution and everyone could play a part in the process.
→ The community was bonded together by people feeling that it was their own project.
→ Every neighbourhood can build its social capital if something sparks the process.
→ The children in the barrio can now make the first step in improving their life chances through early education.
→ The neighbourhood is transitioning from an informal settlement into a real piece of town. 'But it could have been a prison camp,' Hector says.

> *Governments cannot tackle the increasingly complex problems of rapid urbanisation on their own. We have to mobilise people's latent creativity, harnessing the collective power of many small ideas and actions to make a big difference. You have to trust people to do the right thing.*
>
> —Hector C, Venezuela

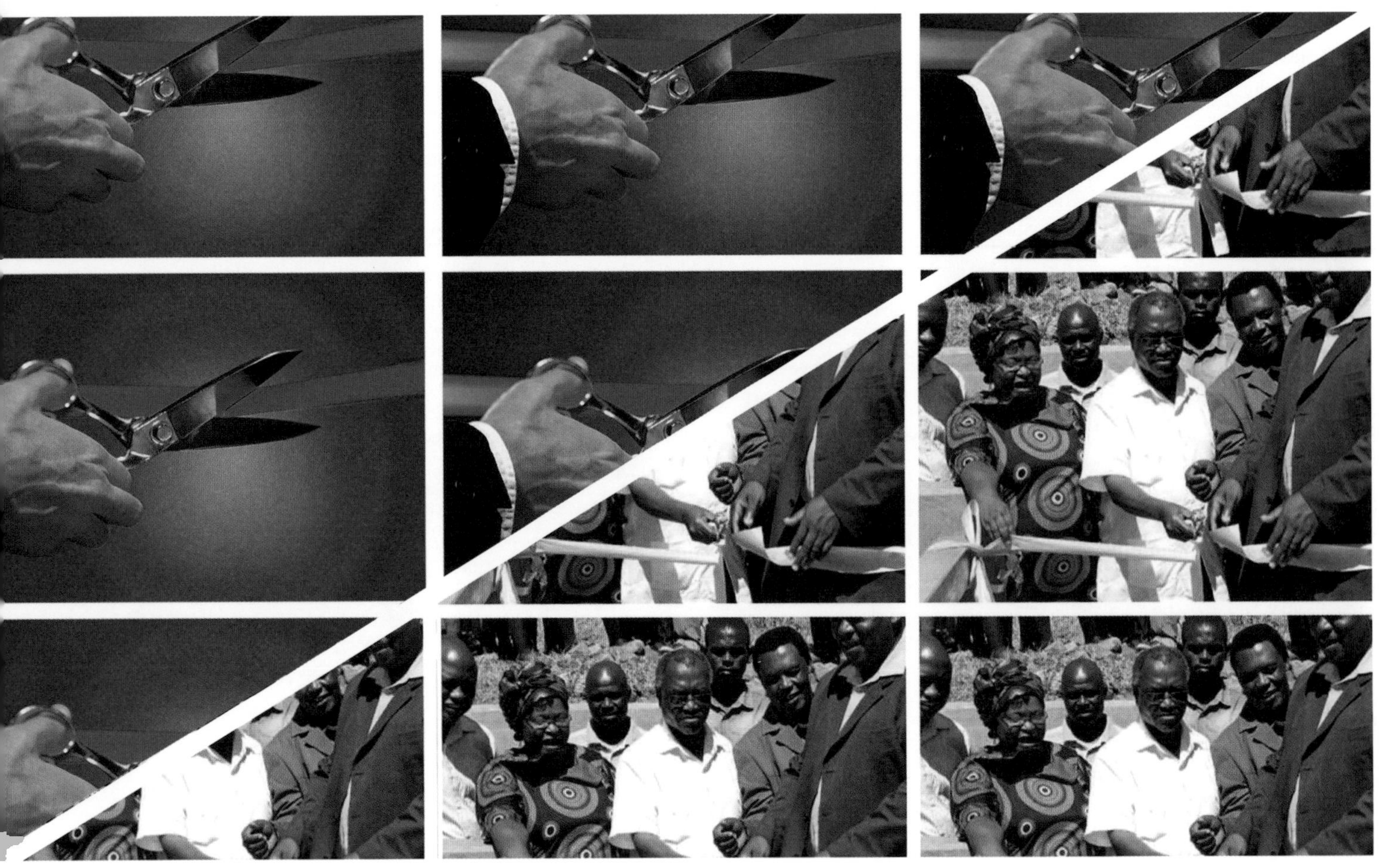

CIVIC LEADERSHIP

If you want to cut lots of yellow ribbons, you need to cut lots of red tape.

—Anonymous

A civic leader is any person who leads on local municipal affairs from an appointed local government executive, such as a city manager, to a democratically elected politician, such as a councillor. A civic leader could also be an executive mayor who straddles both worlds by being elected as the chief executive officer of the municipal government. In all instances and at all levels, a civic leader represents the sharp point of the top-down system.

The biggest issue in many citizen-engagement processes is a lack of effective civic leadership to help people learn to work together in constructive and collaborative ways, whether this leadership is internal to an organisation or found within local constituents. Many top-down systems are based on a traditional hierarchy. In an increasingly complex and dynamic world, there is a need for another, more constructive approach.

URBAN GOVERNANCE

Urban governance is the process through which democratically elected local governments and the range of stakeholders in cities—such as businesses, unions, civil society and, of course, citizens—make decisions about how to plan, finance and manage urban neighbourhoods. Urban governance is important for a number of reasons. It is critical in shaping both the physical and social character of the neighbourhood. It has an impact on the quality of local public services and how they are delivered. It determines how funds are equitably and efficiently shared throughout the neighbourhood.

> *Urban governance is about how residents access their local government and engage in local decision-making, as well as the extent to which local governments are accountable to citizens and responsive to their demands.*
>
> —Local Government Association

International experience tells us that, for the political economy of changing institutional structures, incremental, bottom-up changes tend to be more successful than top-down proposals.

Because formal structures are difficult to put in place, voluntary cooperation between local government and communities plays a much bigger and more useful role in urban governance. Notwithstanding the weakness of voluntary association, this form of local governance has steadily grown in popularity around the world. One explanation is that voluntarism is, according to H. V. Savitch and Paul Kantor in *Cities in the International Marketplace: The Political Economy of Urban Development in North America and Western Europe*, 'incremental, non-threatening, and capable of growing by trial and error'. Although, as the OECD noted in *Competitive Cities in the Global Economy*, these 'lighter and more informal forms of governance' can mobilise city-wide stakeholders around a shared vision, planning and resourcing for implementation might require a more formal arena for collaboration.

DEVELOPING A COLLABORATIVE CULTURE

Most thinking people believe that no individual has all the answers to the issues they encounter in their daily urban life. Solutions to urban problems today tend to be generated by the collective input from many minds. It is imperative for local governments to develop a collaborative culture that supports, encourages, and rewards constructive activism and cooperation.

This idea requires a major rethink on the roles of civic leaders to create a mutually supportive relationship, recognising the valuable contribution that active citizens and urban professionals can make in the process.

QUALITIES OF AN ENABLING CIVIC LEADER

Enabling civic leaders have a number of important qualities that cannot be overstated:

1 **They are passionate about finding ways to actively engage people in working on the issues that affect their neighbourhoods and themselves.** The aim is to motivate all in the community to become committed participants in making a difference to building social capital. Good leaders continually test their motivation and improve their awareness of how their personality and behaviour impact on citizens.

2 **They develop confidence in their abilities coupled with the humility to recognise that they have much more to learn.** Trust and respect play a significant part in the enabler's approach to working with others. Working in collaboration is seen as better, as this provides an effective way of demonstrating better value to everyone involved. When things are not going as planned, enabling leaders are not afraid to constructively confront those who adversely impact on the outputs of the team. Whatever action needs to be taken is done with concern for the collective and the individuals involved.

3 **Enabling civic leadership recognises that everyone is different and brings different talents to the table.** Enabling leaders also understand that most people are conditioned to see things from their own perspective and tend to ignore issues that do not fit their mindset. They know that the downside of a single-focussed process is dismissing ideas and opinions too early. Retaining an open mind means that you 'park' your ideas and opinions while considering the ideas and opinions of others. This shows your respect for other views as well as your willingness to be exposed to other perspectives that you might not have thought about.

4 **Receiving feedback, particularly when it is critical of your behaviour, requires some courage.** One of the real joys of being an enabler is the recognition that mistakes will happen, and this is acceptable, as they frequently provide great opportunities to learn. Openness to learning is linked to curiosity, and the enabling leader demonstrates this by being willing to explore new ways of doing things. They instinctively know that there is always a better way of working.

5 **Enablers understand that effective leadership involves a sense of duality with reasonable flexibility.** They need to constantly move from being the leader to a supporter and back again, all in a collaborative environment. Few leaders have all the answers in every situation. At times other team members have better leadership knowledge suited to the process. Good enablers can easily make this transition from leadership to supporting role when the team accepts accountability to provide the necessary leadership.

By doing the right thing, we have that special power to take people from devastation to hope.

—Naheed Nenshi, World Mayor 2014

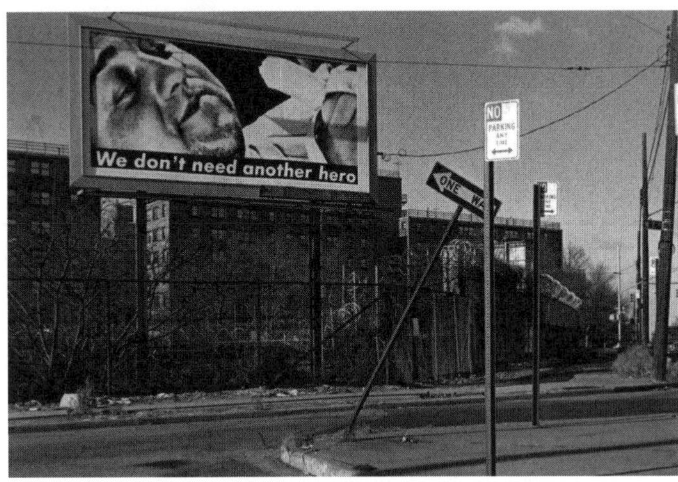

THE PERSISTENT ACTIVIST

HOW A STREETWISE CITIZEN RENEWED NEIGHBOURHOOD DEMOCRACY

> *To be in opposition is not to be a nihilist. There is no decent or chartered way of making a living at it. It is something you are, and not something you do.*
>
> —Christopher Hitchens

Bree has been told that she is a member of the 'precariat', an emerging class of society that lives without predictability or security. The Work Foundation describes such people as being usually in a series of short-term jobs, without recourse to stable occupational identities or careers, stable social protection or protective regulations relevant to them. The precariat is a growing class worldwide.

As a part-time worker for a charity, living with her daughter in a shared house in West Baltimore, Bree recognises this description of her standing. Having spent some years in squats in London and Berlin, she is an energetic activist and a vocal member of the Reclaim the Streets movement. She calls herself a 'radical incrementalist'.

Baltimore, victim of the urban decay that has blighted other once-great US cities such as Detroit and Cleveland, saw the collapse of its old industries and the communities that were associated with them. The shrinking of Baltimore's population to 65 per cent of its 1950s peak of 950,000 has left a landscape of more than 30,000 vacant lots and abandoned buildings. Many of the old row houses have been demolished and much of the land they stood on lies vacant.

The TV series *The Wire* shone a global light on Baltimore's problems: legitimate businesses departing, rising unemployment and a flourishing illegal drug business. Bree saw a rise in suburban poverty in the years after many people lost their homes in the subprime mortgage debacle. She saw the quality of life in her neighbourhood further eroded by the actions of government and big developers. The previous mayor had no effective solutions. He was too busy trying to attract far greater investment from major property companies, and sell off large chunks of land on the waterfront. He believed that trickle-down economics could fix local problems. In relying on the big players he ignored many small signs of life that could have emerged from the local community if given the chance. Bree knows that the community will organise itself in response to a challenge. It has done so successfully before. But it is frustrating not to have the support of local government.

Bree sees a number of failures in the system:

1 The system focusses on risky, top-down solutions that have little or no impact on the lives of local people. The only game in town is real-estate development. Most of the schemes seem to work only for the investors and the banks. Despite the global financial crisis, many think that things will return to how they use to be. Bree thinks that they will fail again.

2 The system focusses us on acting local but inhibits effective action or any global perspective.

'We need to renegotiate the social contract between government and its citizens—between top-down and bottom-up systems', Bree says. 'We need more democratic processes that will foster open and collaborative relationships'.

SOMETHING HAPPENS THAT GIVES BREE HOPE

In 2010 a new mayor, Stephanie Rawlings-Blake, elected on a ticket of social justice, launches an ambitious project aimed at bringing Baltimore's neighbourhoods back to life. At last the community has someone to work with. Faced with serious funding cuts, Baltimore has adopted a more targeted strategy. Instead of trying to fix the buildings themselves, the city implements its Vacants to Value strategy. This involves selling uninhabitable houses, facilitating private investment, offering incentives to homebuyers, and demolishing buildings in badly depressed areas.

The city teams up with the Reinvestment Fund, a social investor, to make best use of its community assets. The aim was to stem the effects of sluggish housing markets by creating suitable environments for local market growth. Concentrating its efforts on 'areas of strength' in 'middle-market neighbourhoods', the housing authority is focussing on rehabilitating 5,000 houses. The idea is to start the ball rolling so that the area comes to be viewed as attractive to private investors and becomes self-sustaining. The remaining 65 per cent of houses, in places where there is no market demand, will be demolished.

Rawlings-Blake makes it easier for communities to revitalise their vacant lots by providing technical assistance for citizens to redesign those lots for community use. The focus is now on three main initiatives for vacant lots in the city. The first, *Power in Dirt*, makes it easy for communi-

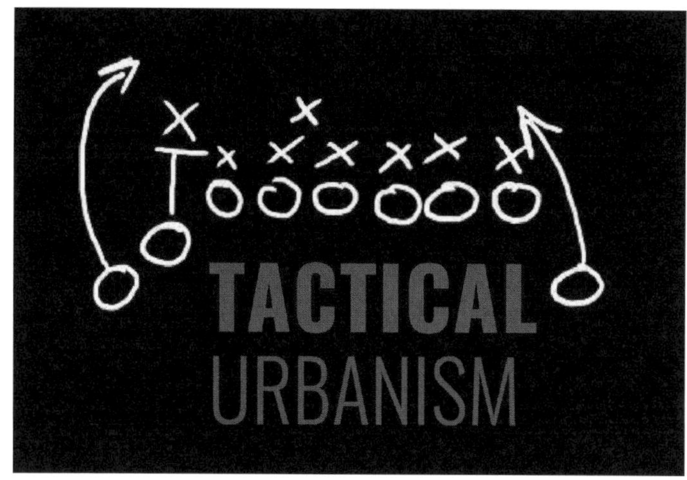

ties to adopt the city's vacant lots legally. The second, an urban agriculture programme, enables farmers to take part in developing a preselected 14 hectares (35 acres) of city-owned vacant land for urban agriculture. The third arranges the transfer of lots to land trusts for their long-term protection as open space.

Many cities have similar programmes, but Baltimore successfully streamlines the process, spreading the message to all parts of the city and making it user-friendly. The Power in Dirt initiative, by putting all of the city-owned vacant lots on a map for everyone to see, shows the city's willingness to be frank and open about those abandoned spaces that may not be redeveloped any time in the near future. It might not promote long-term system change, but it has been successful in mobilising citizens in the process of neighbourhood revitalisation. Some 800 community-managed open spaces are created. Power in Dirt succeeds in eliminating the barriers to revitalising blighted urban spaces. The idea is to start the ball rolling so that the area comes to be viewed as attractive to private investors and becomes self-sustaining.

Bree is driven by the need to do something with her community that goes beyond the urban agriculture story that seems to be the prevalent theme in most of the community-managed open spaces. People need jobs. They also need confidence. She finds out about an initiative in London called Caravanserai. It won London's Meanwhile Use competition for a temporary strategy on a large site in the heart of London's 2102 Olympics area. The architect Cany Ash, one of the people behind the project, describes it as 'an oasis-like trading post in the city' that creates lasting opportunities for the local community through a range of business spaces and participatory events. Her team see this as emphasising the relationship between enterprise and family life, with performance art, workshops, storytelling and food. Ash recognises that places like this form the foundations of urban society and culture. The project has finished but its spirit is carried on in many places. Bree would like to start something like this.

An article in *CityLab* discusses guerrilla gardening, pavement-to-parks and open streets. These urban interventions are quick, often temporary, low-cost projects that aim to make a small part of a city more lively or enjoyable. Projects like this have sprung up in many places in recent years. They have a catchy name: 'tactical urbanism'. These tactics are replicable across many cities, and have become worldwide phenomena.

Bree buys a copy of the book *Tactical Urbanism: Short-term Action for Long-term Change*, a book that describes how short-term action can lead to long-term change. Its lead author, Mike Lydon of Street Plans Collaborative, writes: 'Really, tactical urbanism is how most cities are built, especially in developing nations: step by step and piece by piece.' This is what Bree wants for her neighbourhoods as well.

Bree also hears about the work of Jason Roberts and his Better Block organisation in Dallas. She calls together a group of friends and they watch Jason's YouTube talk. One of Jason's projects has the slogan 'Let's go out and break every rule in the book this weekend'. It was inspired by his discovery that people can do almost nothing to improve their local street without taking matters into their own hands. Jason's principle is to start by starting. 'Don't wait, don't spent time mobilising people: they will come'.

Tactical urbanism and Better Block appeal to Bree's anarchistic streak. She wants to 'put democracy back into urbanism'. Working with Reclaim the Streets, she mobilises their support to have a Weekend Meet on every street in her community for a year. She gets a local graphic designer to produce signs and posters declaring her neighbourhood a Demo.B area (short for Democratic Baltimore).

She borrowed Demo.B from Birmingham in the United Kingdom, secretly liking the 'mob' element. Demo.B, in both Baltimore and Birmingham, focusses on how collective action on a range of themes can help to make the city more democratic. From citizen science to the spoken word, Demo.B aims to explore new models, ideas and ventures to inspire people and communities to build a better world. That's just what she needs for her patch. By the third Demo.B Weekend Meet, 150 people join in. By the tenth, 550 come. People are looking for projects. They are successful in adopting a vacant lot with a few adjacent derelict buildings, and they start their own Caravanserai. They improve building fronts with the support of a local paint supplier. A local school of architecture helps them build a number of temporary spaces: a stage, stalls and an outdoor meeting place.

Hearing about the success of participatory budgets in Paris, Demo.B lobbies successfully for a say in local budgets. The group now has limited

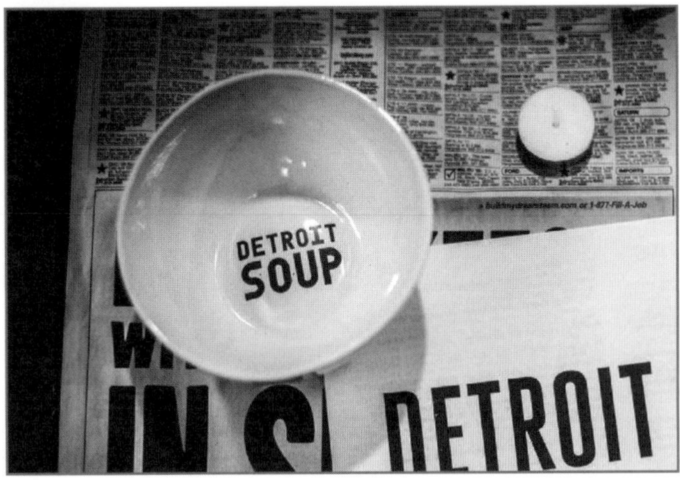

funds to direct to worthy projects. They hear about Detroit Soup, a social enterprise that raises funds for local causes. Detroit Soup is a micro-granting dinner, celebrating and supporting creative projects in Detroit. For a $5 donation, attendees receive soup, salad, bread and a vote. They hear four presentations on topics ranging from art, urban agriculture, social justice, social entrepreneurship, education, technology and more. Each presenter has four minutes to share their idea and answer four questions from the audience. At the event, attendees eat, talk, share resources, enjoy art and vote on the project they think would benefit the city the most. The ballots are counted at the end of the night and the winner goes home with all of the money raised, to carry out their project. Winners come back to a future Detroit Soup dinner to report on their project's progress. This becomes Demo.B's new model. The Weekend Meets become soup kitchens where local people pledge small amounts of money to match local budgets, and vote on awarding funds to local projects. New businesses start: several streetfood stalls, a cosmetics business, a bike repair business that starts a new apprentice scheme, a number of education-related ventures, a bookbinder and so on. A local, empty homes agency is formed where a local volunteer group, called DIY Force, is mobilised to help people improve their homes over a few days. Modelled on Concrete Action, a London-based housing organisation, moral and technical support is given to people with housing difficulties. This is crowdsourcing at its best.

Bree realises that Demo.B works well when it changes behaviours. There are still plenty of social problems to be overcome. Bree hears about an experiment in the United Kingdom that deals with antisocial behaviour. The British police used to serve ASBOS (antisocial behaviour orders) on youths who were creating a nuisance in their communities. All this seemed to do was to stigmatise the kids and put them further outside the system. She hears about a scheme that fights bad behaviour with kindness. It was inspired by a case where young boys were kicking a ball against the side of an old woman's house. Rather than call the police, she took out a tray of juice and biscuits. The problem disappeared and the same kids turned to helping the woman when they could. Respect had replaced revenge. Bree starts a similar social justice campaign that her friends jokingly call 'Give a dealer a cappuccino'.

Bree is obsessed with finding ways of releasing the collective power of many people working together to make a better world. She also has wider ambitions. She starts the Radical Evolutionary Party but realises that its initials are too similar to the Republicans. She changes it to the Radical Incrementalist Party. Her favourite slogan is 'Let's RIP', and her campaign poster for election to the mayor's cabinet declares: 'Let's do the right thing now, so we can rest in peace'. This appeals to her gothic streak. The community gets behind her. Her election campaign is successful and she is invited to become the new deputy mayor responsible for the Office of Neighbourhood Development.

Soon Demo.B is rolled out across the whole city. The latest buzz-phrase is *resilient cities*, yet too often building resilience is seen as overcoming crises, not laying the foundations for a better society. In many circles, *resilience* has just become another word to describe a top-down approach to what used to be called *sustainability*. Bree sees urban resilience as spreading the risk of any form of crisis by focussing on multiple small initiatives. If small projects fail, we can learn from them. 'Think local: act local' becomes the slogan. She and her supporters start community cafés with a focus on local life. Local credit unions are formed to keep the money in the community. Local businesses are given preferential rates to supply local goods and services to local government. Local small builders, using local apprentices, are used on all local capital projects. Five years later the Rockefeller Foundation gives Baltimore the title 'The World's Most Resilient City'.

Bree represents a new generation of civic leaders who see their responsibility to be the agents of urban change, building social capital and promoting self-organisation at every opportunity. 'Baltimore is a poster-child for showing how government and people can work together to do incredible things that neither could have done alone', she says. A proposal to shoot a new series of *The Wire* in Bree's neighbourhood is abandoned. The place is deemed to be no longer sufficiently dysfunctional.

ETHICAL PROFESSIONALISM

PROFESSIONALISM is reflected in the standards, aims or qualities that characterise or mark a profession or professional person. ETHICS encompass the personal morals and conduct of behaviour demanded of urban professionals.

Urban professionals exercise a specialist knowledge. In the urban context, they are capable of making judgments about places, applying this knowledge, and making informed decisions in situations that the general public cannot because they have not attained the necessary knowledge. How this knowledge is used—when providing a service to the public—should be governed and can be considered a moral issue. It's called professional ethics

SERVING THE MASTER

In a dominant top-down form of 'contractual' relationship (where the rules of the game have been established primarily by the forces of government and the big players) the urban professional is bound by a set of regulations that define necessary behaviours to undertake the work for the 'client'. In other words, they are told, 'follow these rules and you will be OK'. This relationship is like one between a master and a servant. It is reinforced by the codes of professional behaviour of different professional organisations that set standards of competence and conduct for members, establish educational thresholds, regulate members and improve their standing in the market, provide industry leadership and aspire to serve the public interest. They also confer on their members a badge of membership and status that demonstrates that they have attained the necessary level of competence and will be bound by a code of conduct. It is like an exclusive club with standing orders that reinforce the status quo.

The recent UK Edge Commission report, *Collaborate for Change*, showed that

> the standing and perceived value of the urban professions is being challenged, with detractors seeing in their conduct and practice a tendency towards protectionism, resistance to change, the reinforcement of silos and the preservation of hierarchies. This issue is now an international concern.

SILO SENSELESSNESS

Put an architect, a planner, an engineer, a surveyor and a landscape architect around a table. Do they provide a rounded view? No, usually they offer five specialist views. Each specialism is sustained by its language, its value system and its institute. Although there have been some attempts for the disciplines to learn to share common ground, too many professionals and their institutions just conform or revert to type.

As discussed in an earlier book by the author and Rob Cowan, *Re:urbanism: A Challenge to the Urban Summit,* 'the built-environment professions have become collections of increasingly specialised specialists. Such specialisms may be necessary, but their practitioners fail to collaborate, and their professional groupings make less and less sense'.

- → **Urban planners** may profess to be the generalists in the team, uniquely skilled in forging collaborations, but too often they are merely specialists in operating the planning system. For many planners, a concern with the physical form of development is what the profession escaped from when it discovered its new vocation in regulating land uses through socially inspired policy. For others, urban design is an escape from drudgery. A new incarnation of the profession is unlikely to be defined any longer by the statutory planning system. Planners have a broad range of skills and experience, and even now you cannot tell by the label 'planner' what you are getting. They need to be made relevant again.

- → **Architects** are no longer the omniscient generalists they might once have been. They learn the increasingly specialised business of designing buildings. 'Design and conquer' is still their mantra, relying on the cult of the single hero to show a new way forwards. How do you define architecture? The design of buildings? Tell that to the dozen types of specialist who may be part of the team designing a building of any significant size. Many architects profess to be urban designers but, for them, urban design is just about big architecture.

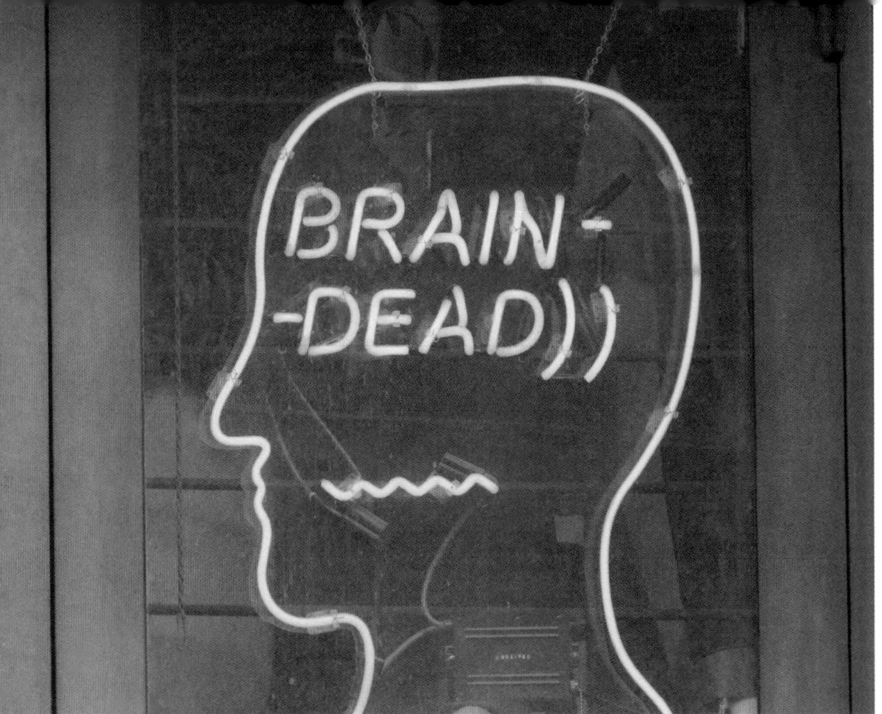

The hard disk has been corrupted even before the programme can be loaded.

—Re:urbanism

- → **Engineers** see the city as a problem to be solved through mechanistic models, rationalised efficiencies and safety factors. For many engineers, urban design is the consequence of meddling with matters that, unlike traffic volumes, drainage runs, road widths and turning circles, are distressingly unquantifiable.
- → **Landscape architects** resent being limited by their specialised role, but they rarely get the chance to think more widely. They are victims of context, chained to 'design by nature', seemingly limited to finding constraints.
- → **Building surveyors** engage in whatever specialism suits their particular niche. They pledge their allegiance to the market.

Despite the fact that all of these people are shaping our towns and cities, few will receive any training in how complex urban places work. Imagine if the medical profession trained its members to be specialists first. Some would become brain surgeons; some ear, nose and throat specialists; some paediatricians. A few would go on to do further training in the basics of physiology. Such people would be able to make the proud claim that, for example, they were not only an expert in brain surgery, but that they also understood how the blood circulated and what lungs were for. The idea is crazy, of course. Such a profession would have dead bodies on its hands. But that is how our built environment professions are trained. And that is why we have dead places.

URBAN DESIGN AS RETROFIT

Into this complex pot we throw urban designers, trying to provide the overview in an even more complex world. They, too, are victims of the system, increasingly called on to expand on complex urban policies by making them even more complex. Design codes follow action plans, character appraisals, tall building studies and 'place-making' strategies—all pointing to fixed end states that are out of date the moment the pen lifts off the paper. Masterplan follows masterplan in the pursuit of the ideal future. And so it goes on. In many ways, urban design is an extension of the same system with more bells and whistles.

For an urban designer, the world of professional labels is even more uncertain. Urban design is a professional skill, but it is also something else as well: the collaborative, multi-disciplinary process in which all the urban professions are involved. Urban design is never going to look like one of the traditional built-environment professions. But with any luck, none of the traditional built-environment professions is likely to look the way they do for very long either.

Urban design, with few exceptions, is a postgraduate course for the committed few. The starting point of urban design training is flawed. Professionals trained in a particular narrow viewpoint, some over a period of six years, are expected fundamentally to change their view of the world. Urban design training tries to retrofit architects and planners, drilled in anti-urban traditions, as good urbanists. The hard disk has been corrupted even before the programme can be loaded. Postgraduate urban design courses operate as little more than extensions to planning or architecture courses. Where both professions are being taught in one institution, the various departments squabble about whether urban design is a planning issue or an architectural one.

Trying to turn graduates into specialists is the wrong way to train built-environment professionals. Instead, we need undergraduate courses in urbanism that will broaden the students' interest into a real understanding of how cities change and are changed, and what they mean for the people who plan, manage, design, celebrate and live in them. On such a foundation we could train specialists who could work with other specialists and in the real world.

BREAKING THE MOULDS

The working relationships between professionals who manage the complex processes of urban change can no longer be understood in terms of simple stereotypes. Boundaries of the built-environment professions have their origins in history. They were always at least to some extent accidental and arbitrary. It's hard to move those boundaries once they have been set. However, many changes in professional practice and social, economic and technical conditions seem to demand it. The professions compete for territory over any areas of work that more than one profession sees as part of its specialism.

Where do the respective roles of urban planner, architect, urban designer, engineer, landscape architect and surveyor begin and end? An individual professional these days is likely to have a range of skills (based on his or her education, interests and experience) that conforms hardly at all to the remit of a single profession. There is no doubt that things have to change. All urban professions should start, like the medical professions, in understanding the whole urban environment—call it an undergraduate in urbanism. All urban professions should look at all aspects—the physical, social, environmental and economic aspects and the behaviours needed to bring these all together in a common platform. Bind this all with a common value system. Then specialise. Let urban design be a specialist generalist focussing on the whole view of our towns and cities. The medical profession has 'physicians' who focus on seeing the body and mind as a whole. Be like them.

ACTING AS A SERVANT OF URBAN SOCIETY

Professionalism is about success and influence, about having a reputation for excellence and being regarded as someone who exhibits these qualities under any circumstances in setting up completely different relationships with other actors in the system.

Leandro Valente, in an article on LinkedIn, identified ten golden rules that could be adapted to being a professional in service to urban society:

1. **Always strive for excellence.** This is the first rule to achieving greatness in whatever endeavour you undertake. This is the quality that makes you and your work stand out. Excellence is a quality of service that is unusually good and so surpasses ordinary standards; it should be made a habit for it to make a good impression on your bosses and colleagues.

2. **Be trustworthy.** In today's society trust is an issue, and any employee who exhibits trustworthiness is on a fast track to professionalism. Trustworthiness is about fulfilling an assigned task and—as an extension—not letting down expectations. It is being dependable and reliable when called upon to deliver a service. To earn the trust of your bosses and colleagues, worth and integrity must be proven over time.

3. **Be accountable.** To be accountable is to stand tall and be counted for what actions you have undertaken. This is taking responsibility for your actions and their consequences—good or bad.

4. **Be courteous and respectful.** Courteousness is being friendly, polite and well mannered with a gracious consideration towards others. It makes social interactions run smoothly, avoids conflicts and earns respect. Respect is built over time and can be lost with one inconsiderate action. Continued courteous interactions are required to increase the original respect gained.

If you don't stand for something, you'll fall for anything.

—Alexander Hamilton

5. **Be honest, open and transparent.** Honesty is a facet of moral character that connotes positive and virtuous attributes such as truthfulness, straightforwardness of conduct, loyalty, fairness, sincerity, openness in communication and operating in a way for others to see what actions are being performed. It is a virtue highly prized by employers and colleagues, for it builds trust and increases your personal value to all.

6. **Be competent and improve continually.** Competence is the ability of an individual to do a job properly; it is a combination of knowledge, skills and behaviours used to improve performance. Competency grows through experience and to the extent one is willing to learn and adapt. Continuous self-development is a prerequisite in offering professional service at all times.

7. **Always be honourable and act with integrity.** Honourable action is behaving in a way that portrays nobility of soul, magnanimity, and a scorn of meanness, which is derived from virtuous conduct and personal integrity. This is a concept of wholeness or completeness of character in line with absolute values, belief and principles with consistency in action and outcome.

Be more for what you are for, than more against what you are against.

—Anonymous

8 **Be respectful of confidentiality.** Confidentiality is working within a set of rules or a promise that restricts you from further and unauthorised dissemination of information. Over the course of your career, information will be passed on to you in confidence, and it is important to respect such confidences. You will gain the trust and respect of those confiding in you and increase your influence within the organisation.

9 **Set good examples.** Applying the preceding rules helps you improve your professionalism within your organisation, but it is not complete until you impact those around and below you. You must show and lead by example. Being a professional is about living an exemplary life within and without the organisation.

10 **Always be ethical.** Ethical behaviour is acting within certain moral codes by the accepted code of conduct or rules. It is always safe for an employee to 'play by the rules'. This is always the best policy, and in instances the rulebook is inadequate, acting with a clear moral conscience is the right way to go. This may cause friction in some organisations, but ethical organisations will always stand by the good moral decisions and actions of their employees.

SERVING THE PLACE

> *All institutions claim adherence to a code of ethics and an obligation to serve the public interest as a special quality that differentiates their members from those lacking a professional designation. There is, however, confusion between ethics and the public interest, and the latter is not clearly defined. Institutions should therefore resolve the confusion between ethics and the public interest, by clarifying and codifying a rigorous, shared understanding of expectations in respect of each at the individual, corporate and institutional level—raising awareness, providing guidance to members, operating a transparent sanctioning process, and moving from a tendency to exclusivity (centred on professional interests) to one of inclusivity (centred on the public interest).*
>
> —Edge Commission

As we move to an increasingly bottom-up response to urban development, the relationship between active citizens and civic leaders changes to a collaboration between bottom-up and top-down. Firstly, there is no clear master. Secondly, there is no system of trust. This is where ethics becomes critical, and all actors in the system should be bound by a code of ethics in the public interest.

Ethics at its simplest is a system of moral principles that affect how people make decisions and lead their lives. It is concerned with what is good for individuals and society and is also described as moral philosophy.

The Edge Commission, in the report *Collaboration for Change*, made recommendations on ethics and the public interest, building on shared experience internationally. This report included the need for a declaration of high-level principles and developing a national code of conduct and ethics across all the built-environment professions. We believe this should also be extended to civic leaders and active citizens as well as anyone involved in the urban process.

In the noble profession of medicine, our doctors are encouraged to go out and do the right thing, act responsibly, and make decisions that will be in the best interest of their patients. They are true professionals.

They abide by an ethos and have simple rules that guide how they behave. They are bound by oaths they swear and feel the full wrath of the law if they ignore their obligations. Although many follow the Hippocratic Oath—one of the earliest examples of professional ethics—the Declaration of Geneva is more commonly used. As currently published by the World Medical Association, it starts: 'At the time of being admitted as a member of the medical profession, I solemnly pledge to consecrate my life to the service of humanity.'

Just imagine if urban professionals operated like the medical profession...and why not? They are surely the physicians of our cities and towns—these are living organisms that need care and compassion. Just imagine if urban professionals swore a Hippocratic-like oath to serve the 'place'. If so, the Declaration of Geneva could be modified to read as shown opposite.

THE UNIVERSAL DECLARATION ON URBAN ETHICS

— 2018 —

At the time of being admitted as a member of the United Institute of Urban Professionals:

I solemnly pledge to consecrate my life to the service of urbanity.

◆

I will give my teachers the respect and gratitude that is their due.

◆

I will practice my profession with conscience and dignity.

◆

The health of urban society will be my first consideration.

◆

I will maintain by all the means in my power the honour and the noble traditions of the urban professions.

◆

My colleagues will be my sisters and brothers.

◆

I will not permit considerations of age, disease, disability, creed, ethnic origin, gender, nationality, race, political affiliation, sexual orientation, social standing or any other factor to intervene between my duty and urban society.

◆

I will maintain the utmost respect for urban life.

◆

I will not use my professional knowledge to violate urban rights and civil liberties, even under threat.

I make these promises solemnly, freely and upon my honour.

THE PRINCIPLED PLANNER

HOW AN ETHICAL PROFESSIONAL MADE PLANNING RELEVANT AGAIN

Maria is disillusioned. She has worked her way up the planning profession to become head of development management in a West London borough, but she does not find her job satisfying. She went into planning to make the world a better place. Her dreams are still tinted with utopian visions of what life could be like in a well-planned world. But she finds herself administering blanket policies and processes that are not working for urban society. Tackling the fundamentals of the planning system is the elephant in the room.

Maria reads an article 'For the Sake of Our Cities, It's Time to Make Town Planning Cool Again' in her favourite newspaper, *The Guardian*. Its author, Tom Campbell, writes: 'While the cult of the star architect has soared in recent decades, the figure of the town planner has arguably become comic shorthand for a faceless dullard. Yet the role is crucial to our urban future, and needs reinventing.'

The article discusses the crisis in the planning system and with planners. Although they are needed more than ever, the status of planners and city administrators has never been lower. Bold mayors might be in the limelight, but it is a very different story for the officers they preside over. The death of her profession's torchbearer, Sir Peter Hall, reminds Maria how the status of the town planner rose and fell over the course of his fifty-year career.

The government's austerity policies, which have led to local government funding cuts, pay freezes and redundancies of the last few years, have wrought their havoc, but a far deeper malaise has set in. 'The status of public servants in general has suffered over the last 30 years,' Campbell writes, 'but in the case of town planners, it has been particularly pronounced.

In an age in which financial success is championed and the entrepreneur installed in an ivory tower, it seems that there are few professions more derided than the local town planner.'

It is to be expected that socially minded town planners will be figures of fun, poked at by the neo-liberal, political right. In announcing a series of reforms intended to boost growth in 2012, Prime Minister David Cameron promised that his government was 'determined to cut through the bureaucracy that holds us back—and that starts with getting the planners off our backs.' Government-supporting think-tanks reinforce this view, publishing extensively on the planners' supposed controlling and interfering instincts.

Campbell quotes Andy Pratt, an economic geographer at City University, London, who thinks that there are real problems in the way planning is being taught. 'Like many others I know, I actually started out intending to be a town planner,' Pratt says. 'But I soon realised that all the interesting conversations about cities, regeneration, architecture and urban development weren't happening in the planning faculty. They were being had by people studying economics, urban studies and culture.'

He also quotes the city planner David Knight. 'Planners have become simultaneously under-respected and over-professionalised,' Knight says. 'Their training and practice too often leaves them able to communicate effectively only with other planners and professionals, working in an abstract language that alienates them from people. People are occasionally allowed into the professional planner's world, but in highly mediated terms dictated by the profession.'

The think-tanks trot out the standard old message: 'give people a far greater role in planning'. This is their way of saying that planning must get out of the way. What's new? Since 1968 it has been a legal requirement for authorities to consult the public on their local plans. Such consultations have become a standardised part of the development process and, as such, deeply disheartening. Consulting on complex top-down policies is not public involvement. Public endorsement is what is being sought.

Maria reflects, like Tom Campbell, that her profession has come a long way since the 1940s, when the Pelican edition of Thomas Sharp's *Town Planning* sold about 250,000 copies. It is no wonder that Sir Peter Hall, reflecting on a lifetime in town planning, concluded that 'planning and planners have steadily become residualised, returning to their marginal status'. But have they been marginalised by the system, or has the system changed and we have not, Maria wonders?

At work, Maria's biggest problem is the 10,000 unserviced, unfit illegal homes in back gardens in one part of her borough. The press calls them 'beds in sheds'. Maria realises that if this can happen in one of the richest parts of London, under a planning system that is still one of the most highly resourced, most highly regulated and most highly praised in the world, there must be something wrong with the system.

She takes the London mayor around to see the scale of the problem. He shakes his head and wonders what can be done. When 10,000 homes are built illegally in backyards, you may not be able to take enforcement action to remove them. There would be riots.

She realises that the system she worked so hard to maintain has fundamental flaws:

→ Everything that has been built in the past three generations has been through the planning system. Yet there are very few places good enough to show elected members as great examplars.

→ The planning system was based on a monocultural, traditionally employed, family model that is completely different to the culturally diverse, alternatively employed, dynamic family of today. Maria's own staff have a wide variety of social backgrounds, family structures and living arrangements.

→ Planning is based on the idea that people cannot be trusted and that the system knows best. But some of the finest examples of urbanism were created when cities evolved prior to the planning system being imposed. With all the guidance from government, quangos and design bodies, we have still not produced places with the qualities that previous generations achieved.

→ A great deal of the effort from Maria and her team is applied to the final stages of the development control process. Any planning negotiation seems to end up with the worst possible results. Desperate attempts to remedy this involve further work on assembling design panels, carrying out design reviews or obtaining other expert advice.

→ The aim of the planning system in England is to achieve 'sustainable development', as defined in the National Planning Policy Framework. Yet, by most definitions, much of what is built must be counted as being highly unsustainable. The houses might be constructed in a way that is relatively energy efficient, but their locations promote urban sprawl.

→ Planning has created a culture of stopping things. Maria has heard complaints that getting permission to do something is like playing against eleven goalkeepers. Policies were developed to keep the big developers at bay. Now those developers are the only ones who can play the game. When the system does not work for small people, the small people often break the rules—like those who build in back gardens in Maria's borough.

→ She knows that it is impossible to anticipate every outcome, yet the system still pursues its obsession with certainty. The best places have emerged from collective action over time, but the planning system does not work with complexity.

→ There is a schism between planning and people that has become deeply damaging. This has to change if the profession is to become relevant again.

→ Maria knows that fewer and fewer people are coming into the planning profession. She sees it as a profession that is given accountability without responsibility.

MARIA ACTS ON HER INSTINCTS

Maria hears a talk by Finn Williams, a young London planner, who has brought together a collective called Novus, producing 'a manifesto from the coalface of public planning'. With high ideals and established with the support of the UK Planning Officers Society, it wants to inject more radical thinking into the public sector planning profession.

Finn describes the manifesto as 'a platform for planners to think more provocatively about what they can achieve'. While aiming to raise the status of planners in society and persuading government that 'planning can be positive and bold', Novus is by no means unaware of the need for planners to raise their game, too, particularly in how they work with the public.

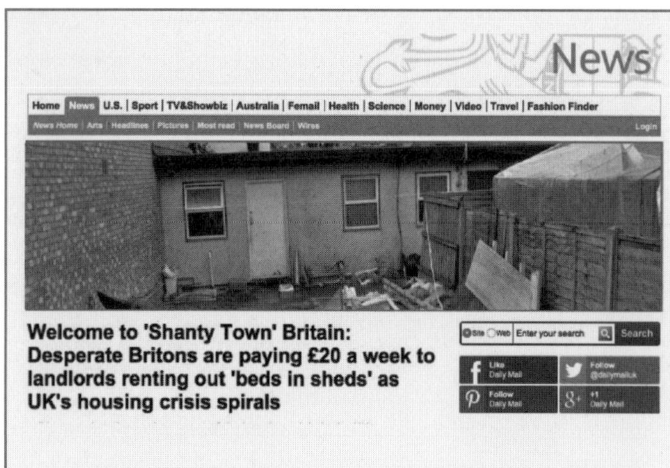
News
Home | News | U.S. | Sport | TV&Showbiz | Australia | Femail | Health | Science | Money | Video | Travel | Fashion Finder
Welcome to 'Shanty Town' Britain: Desperate Britons are paying £20 a week to landlords renting out 'beds in sheds' as UK's housing crisis spirals
Search

Maria also reads about Building Rights, a 'repository of planning knowledge; a user-generated forum where the rules of what is built and what is not are shared'. Described by its founder David Knight as 'a Mumsnet for planning', its explicit ambition is to make planning popular, and to build a wider community of expertise and interest in planning beyond the profession itself. According to the Building Rights campaign document (with a raised fist emblazoned across its banner),

> the proposal of Building Rights is not for a single revolutionary change to the planning system, but an incremental, micro-political one in which knowledge gradually shifts into the public domain through the actions of thousands of people, each of whom will be changing case law through their actions and, in knowing more about what planning is, becoming more able to demand more of what it could be.

At around the same time, Maria learns about the slogan of the president of her planning institute: 'Proud of planning'. It sounds like one of those throwaway lines that you see on so many campaigns that mean nothing. Words will not change the profession, she thinks: actions will. She realises that in an increasingly complex world her profession must become more relevant. In doing so, it must shift from pure top-down thinking to embrace more action from the bottom up.

Planners need to operate with different mindsets through some form of ethical professionalism, bound by commonly accepted behaviours. These behaviours should be defined by the collective adoption of a code of ethics equivalent to the medical profession's Hippocratic Oath or its Declaration of Geneva.

In signing up to these principles, urban professionals and civic leaders accept their duty and responsibility to the present and future well-being of the inhabitants of the city they have charge over. Maria stands for the presidency of her professional institute and lobbies to introduce a Hippocratic Oath for planners. Her slogan, 'Walk with the dreamers', comes from a poster on her wall identifying planners as being amongst those who want to leave the world better than when they found it. Her campaign is successful. Urban professionals are now bound by a code of ethics.

MARIA WANTS TO HELP CREATE A NEW BREED OF CITY PLANNER

She believes that part of the problem lies in who becomes a town planner, and how they are taught and trained. Students are narrowly instructed in current planning procedures, practice and regulations, with little scope to question the discipline, explore its history or critique its political undertones. It seems locked in a box with its past glories.

Urbanism is now the buzzword and almost every planner seems to want to be an urban designer. But too often the planning profession pushes such matters back onto its rigidly deterministic 'place-making' agenda. Local-authority planning departments have become less multi-disciplinary and more reliant on a small number of generalist officers, skilled not so much in the art of urban design but in managing processes.

Maria thinks that town planners must stop being taught along the lines of a technical profession. The best education lies in understanding complex adaptive systems, behavioural science and human dynamics.

They should be like the 'doctors of the city', not the managers. Planning needs softer skills in negotiation, community engagement, consensus building and enabling leadership.

How planners engage with people must change. People do care about the cities they live in, but rarely in a way that informs planning policy. Instead of telling people what to do, the planning profession has to develop the ideas, tools and tactics to create a more enabling system. The new system will be one where complex policies are replaced by enabling protocols that generate urbanism, rather than constrain it; where rigidly deterministic tools are replaced with an understanding of how conditions can be created to enable things to happen; and where command-and-control is replaced with enabling behaviours that release the latent creativity in people to solve urban problems.

Back at her day job, Maria hears about the work of the housing reformer John F. C. Turner. She likes his remark about informal settlements being cities in progress. Is her 'beds in sheds' problem just that? Perhaps people are simply using their ingenuity to solve a real problem. Perhaps they are building these sheds badly because they know they may be demolished. Would it be possible to create a framework that would allow informal development to happen? As history shows us, most places started informally and hardened up over time.

Maria's council decides to create a development control order that allows for development to happen in backyards. People are permitted to build in back gardens, provided they follow some simple rules. More people build in their back gardens and pressure is taken off housing delivery in the borough. Things go further when a new government issues a general development order that allows the demolition of an old interwar suburban house and its replacement with three or four townhouses or even a small apartment block, based on a parameter book of standard housing types. This means that poor-quality houses with shoddy rear developments can be replaced with better urban solutions that help to improve the whole area over time and open up the housing market to a wider set of players.

Maria convinces her chief executive to get the council to explore how active citizens, urban professionals and the council can work together to guide this change. They develop new protocols that replace outdated policies in the council's development plan. The system becomes more enabling than controlling, so Maria's department changes its name to Neighbourhood Enabling. Responsibility and accountability have been devolved to the lowest levels, fundamentally changing the scope and purpose of her team from being reactive to becoming strategic enablers. The planners are charged with going out and helping better urbanism to develop. They manage in the present, operating rather like the sound engineer at a concert, listening carefully and constantly making any slight adjustments they feel are helpful.

MARIA SUMS UP HER EXPERIENCE

Maria, now retired, still acts as an advisor to central government. She sums up her experience as follows:

→ Her staff were liberated from the tyranny of the system. Their behaviours changed. Bound by a code of ethics, they now work more like doctors, with a responsibility to urban society rather than to the system. They are given accountability with responsibility. They now feel that it is their role to make things happen.

→ She now knows that most people, given a simple set of protocols and structured choices, can generally be trusted to do the right thing. As Lewis Mumford wrote, civilisation rests on this fact. This is a dramatic shift from Maria's earlier professional life, where she tried to command and control every outcome, with little effect.

→ The formal role of planning in the system has changed. It now aims to help positive change to emerge by focussing on the preconditions that give rise to good urbanism rather than focussing deterministically on outcomes. Maria's team is now able to put the bulk of its effort into the start of the process. It focusses on ensuring that urban networks are open and adaptive. There is a new interest in the art of subdivision, with planners now more concerned with understanding the street, block, lot and plot as the basis for building the robust urban fabric that forms neighbourhoods.

→ Planners now see how important it is to develop frameworks through which open building platforms combine with open/adaptive networks to make the most of responsive urban fabric. On this invisible chassis, good urbanism can be built. The planners see the potential for parameter books to set out default conditions and structured choices. These will foster the development of a local urban vernacular.

→ Planners now see the opportunities for building local social capital in all they do. They regard the city less as a visual artefact and more as an evolving organism where people play an increasing role in collaborating with planners, rather than being consulted by them.

→ The changes that Maria introduced moved planning from blanket policy-driven approaches that restricted what people could do to protocol-led approaches that set out what people can do. The system has become more permissive, generating change rather than stifling it.

→ Planning has moved away from the ten-year, predict-and-plan approach, where decisions were made on the basis of large amounts of evidence about the past, towards managing in the present. Now plans are constantly updated, and their effects are monitored through rapid and continuous feedback loops. Directions are altered immediately in response to this feedback.

→ Planning has become interesting again. Planning courses now focus on managing complexity rather than looking for certainty.

> *True professionalism and civic leadership must be built on trust and commitment to do the right thing. Like any calling that fundamentally affects the lives of others, any member of the urban professions, any elected official and anyone in a position of authority in the city must be bound by a set of commonly accepted behaviours.*
>
> —Maria E, London

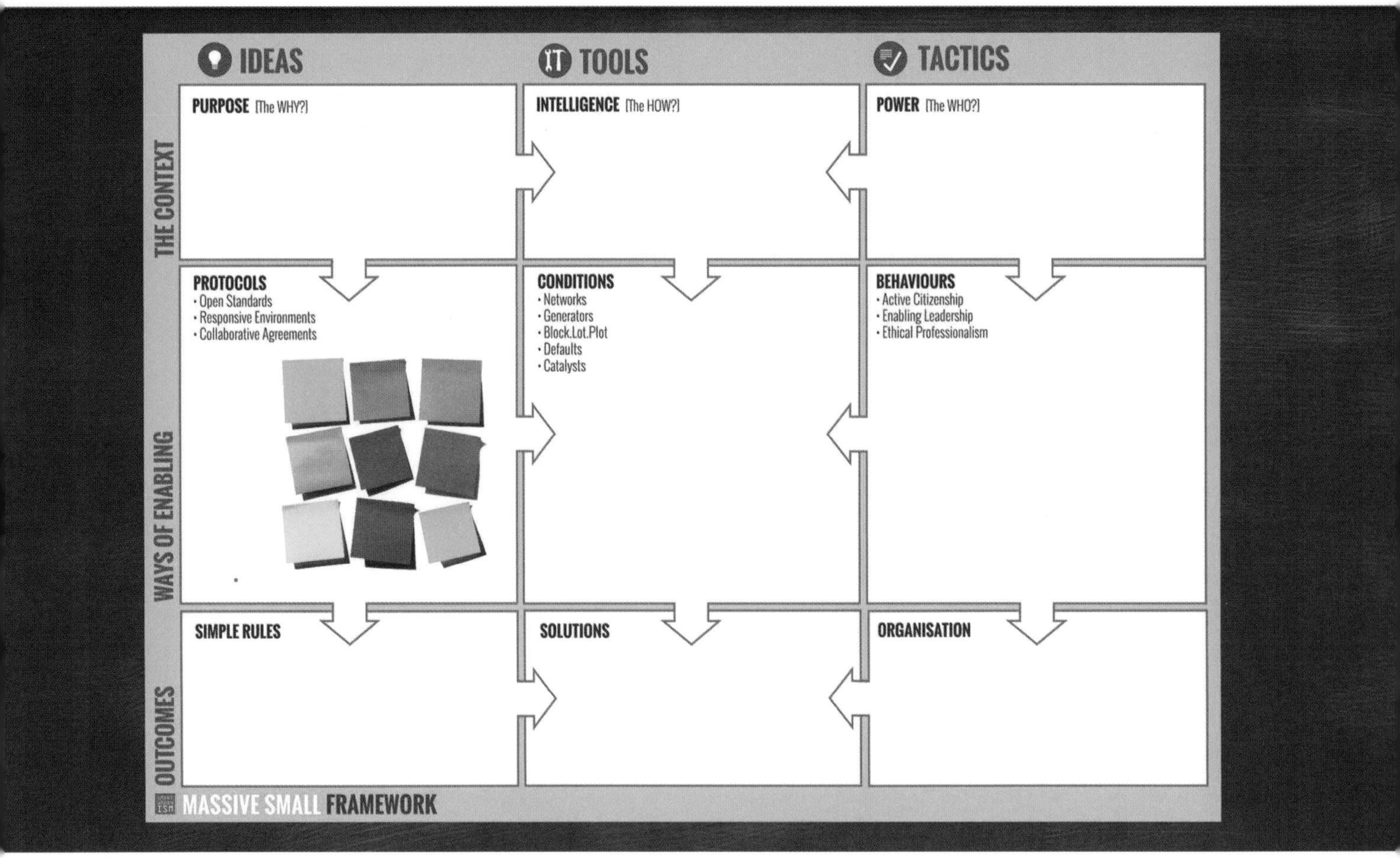

IDEAS | TOOLS | TACTICS

THE CONTEXT

PURPOSE [The WHY?]

INTELLIGENCE [The HOW?]

POWER [The WHO?]

WAYS OF ENABLING

PROTOCOLS
- Open Standards
- Responsive Environments
- Collaborative Agreements

CONDITIONS
- Networks
- Generators
- Block.Lot.Plot
- Defaults
- Catalysts

BEHAVIOURS
- Active Citizenship
- Enabling Leadership
- Ethical Professionalism

OUTCOMES

SIMPLE RULES

SOLUTIONS

ORGANISATION

MASSIVE SMALL FRAMEWORK

THE MASSIVE SMALL FRAMEWORK

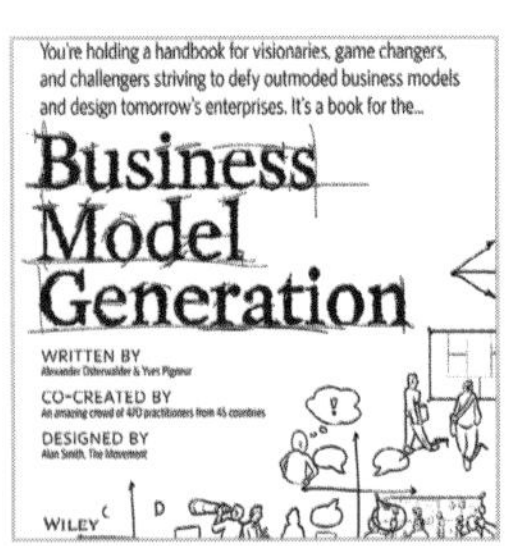

Co-creation is much more work than writing somewhere in a hidden corner and then publishing your content. The benefits outweigh the costs.

—Alexander Osterwalder

The MASSIVE SMALL FRAMEWORK is a visual framework for building collective action. It is our way of rapidly putting the Massive Small project into action, providing a simple model to show how engaged citizens, civic leaders and urban professionals can work together to reconcile the conflicts and potentials that exist between top-down and bottom-up systems. Within this context, governments need to put in place the enabling protocols, conditions and behaviours to allow bottom-up action to be released.

The framework is arranged in three primary columns: IDEAS, TOOLS and TACTICS, reflecting the primary organising structure of the sourcebook. Each column is broken into three sections: CONTEXT, WAYS OF ENABLING and OUTCOMES.

Prompts are given in each section to enable our groups to go through a process of understanding, clarifying and confirming their roles and responsibilities on the process.

USING THE FRAMEWORK

The framework provides a route map for participants to follow, showing how each column and section relates to the other:

DEFINING THE PROJECT

Before you start, you must have a clear understanding of your mission. The mission states the 'what' and 'for whom'.

For example: We want to take responsibility to build a pocket park for local children to use.

UNDERSTANDING THE CONTEXT

1 Simple purpose

What are you ultimately looking to achieve? Can you strip it down to its essence? The purpose explains the 'why'.

For example: We want our children to be healthy, active and socially aware.

2 Intelligence
What is the evidence, need, experience, example you can draw on? Or is it something rooted in what you all believe to be right? Intelligence explains the 'how'.

For example: We will start building the park by using what we all know and learn from experience.

3 Power
Where does the act of will lie to make it happen? What are the obstacles? Power explains the relationship between the parties.

For example: We want to work with the council, seek professional advice, but will do it ourselves.

UNDERSTANDING THE WAYS OF ENABLING

1 Protocols
What are the rules of engagement between all the parties that give rise to the project continuing? How can we deal with openness, responsiveness and collaboration to ensure the project will evolve?

For example: We will take the standard protocols in the sourcebook as prompts and modify these to get a clear understanding of how we can work together.

2 Conditions
What are the preconditions we need to meet to ensure that our project will be successful? These include how we are going to deal with:

→ Open/adaptive STREETS
→ Clear regular BLOCKS
→ Initiating and accelerating PLATFORMS
→ DEFAULTS to structure choice
→ ACTIVATORS to build social capital

3 Behaviours
How does each of the parties need to act? Where do accountability and responsibility lie in the context of:

→ Active citizenship
→ Civic leadership
→ Ethical professionalism

Refer to the content of this compendium for inspiration, templates and tested models to facilitate progress.

TESTING THE OUTCOMES

NOTE: These issues derive from a clarification of the CONTEXT applied to the WAYS OF ENABLING.

1 **Simple rules.** What are the simple rules the community can agree to that will deliver the project?

2 **Emergent solutions.** What are potential solutions that could derive from the simple rules in the context of the enabling conditions outlined above?

3 **Organisation.** What is the organisational structure we need to deliver on the emergent solutions in the framework of the agreed behaviours outlined above?

MONITORING AND REVIEWING FEEDBACK

Create a continuous feedback loop that enables you to go back to the WAYS OF ENABLING and explore alternatives until you have identified your starting position. Once started, review the project continuously to see how improvements can be made.

REMEMBER

The framework is a discovery mechanism enabling all the players to understand the full context within which they are working. It can be used with other citizen engagement tools and provides an overarching view of the whole system. Although it points to potential solutions, it recognises these as being emergent. Its primary purpose is to understand the complexities that exist in the system and show how these can be 'organised' by working together.

The Massive Small framework does not design neighbourhoods. It provides the structure to a healthy conversation about roles and responsibilities; actions and reactions; and desired outcomes and ways of getting there. Like Alexander Osterwalder's *Business Model Canvas*, it provides the building blocks for a range of activities. It can be customised to suit its purpose and used to illustrate potential opportunities and trade-offs. It can be printed out on a large surface so people can gather around—sketch ideas, discuss options and paste on Post-it notes or images. It is a visual process that can be used many instances of neighbourhood building.

THE CONTEXT

PURPOSE [The WHY?]

WAYS OF ENABLING

PROTOCOLS

- Open/Adaptive Environments
- Responsive Environments
- Collaborative Agreements

OUTCOMES

SIMPLE RULES

TOOLS

TACTICS

INTELLIGENCE [The HOW?]

POWER [The WHO?]

CONDITIONS

- Streets
- Blocks
- Platforms
- Defaults
- Activators

BEHAVIOURS

- Active Citizenship
- Enabling Leadership
- Ethical Professionalism

SOLUTIONS

ORGANISATION

MASSIVE SMALL FRAMEWORK

[*evolution not revolution*]

3

CHANGE

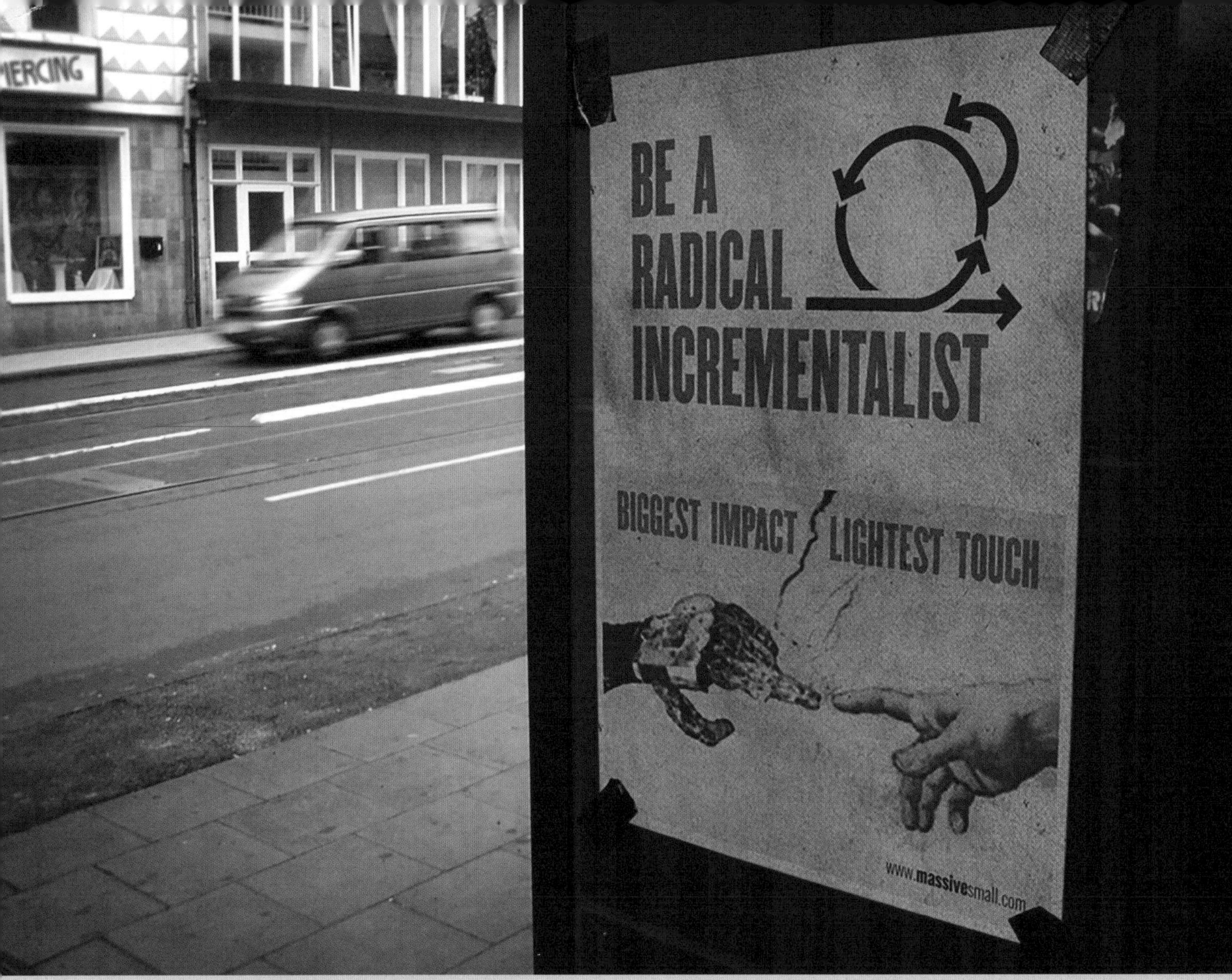
BE A
RADICAL
INCREMENTALIST
BIGGEST IMPACT
LIGHTEST TOUCH
www.massivesmall.com

Change *NOUN*

1 *Radical change*, also called *transformational change* or *disruptive change*, from accepted or traditional forms to new forms, involves favouring or tending to produce quantum leaps or extreme, fundamental, or system-wide changes.

2 *Incremental change* involves smaller adjustments, progressive baby steps or slower, gradual, evolutionary improvements towards an end result, in such a way that does not significantly threaten existing power structures and allows outcomes to be easily assessed.

System change is the emergence of a new pattern of organisation or system structure that brings about different outcomes. This part of the compendium shows how you could start the process by focusing on the basics of change, the leverage points of change, and the agency needed to bring about system change.

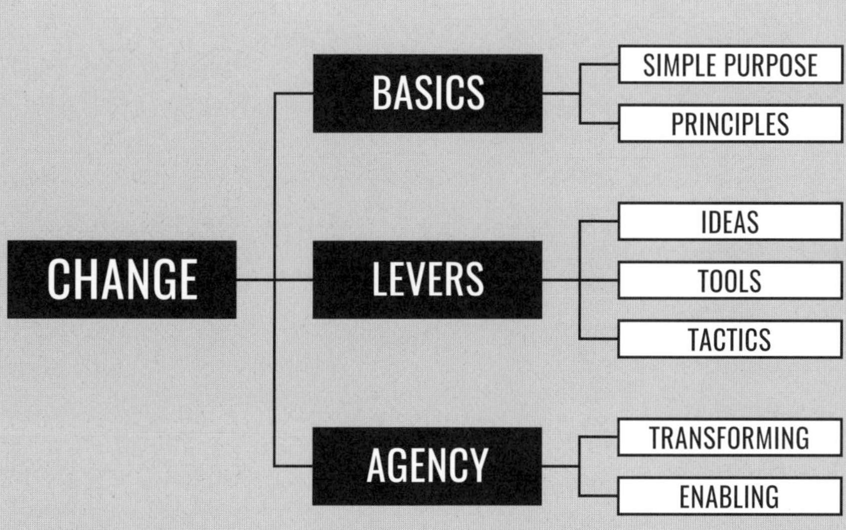

It is not the strongest of the species that survive, nor the most intelligent, but the one most responsive to change.

—Charles Darwin

THE BASICS OF **CHANGE**

3.1

Success at system change demands more than the best strategic and tactical strategies, the traditional focus of civic leaders, senior officials and their advisers. It requires an intimate understanding of the human side, as well—the overarching culture, values, people and behaviours that must be changed to deliver the desired results.

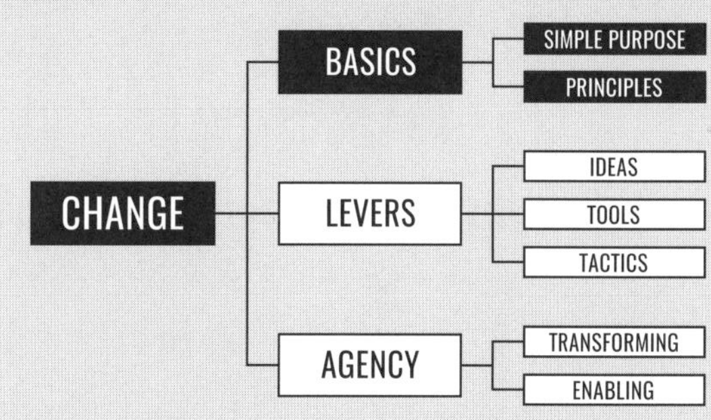

LOOKING THROUGH A LIVING SYSTEM LENS

> *Most top-down change strategies are doomed to failure from the outset. As people have been noting for years, the majority of strategic initiatives that are driven from the top are marginally effective—at best.*
>
> —Peter Senge

A great virtue of Peter Senge's work is the way in which he puts systems theory to work. Senge's book *The Fifth Discipline* provides a good introduction to looking through a living-systems lens, with systems theory providing the conceptual cornerstone of his approach. Senge's vision of a learning organisation as a group of people who are continually enhancing their capabilities to create what they want to create has been deeply influential in all aspects of change management. But as Senge realises, this process is easier said than done.

Firstly, Senge's view of initiating and sustaining change is more daunting than we imagine. And secondly, the task of making change happen requires leaders to change the way they think about organisations: 'We need to think less like managers and more like biologists,' Senge argues. This is why his approach translates so well to understanding system change in cities.

Cities are living organisms, not machines. That might explain why it's so difficult for us to succeed in our efforts to produce urban change. Perhaps treating cities like machines keeps them from changing, or makes changing them much more difficult. We keep bringing in mechanics—when what we need are gardeners. We keep trying to drive change—when what we need to do is cultivate change. This mechanical mindset is difficult to shrug off. It seems part of our DNA.

According to Senge, if you use a machine lens, you get leaders who are trying to drive change through formal change programmes. If you use a living-systems lens, you get leaders who approach change as if they were growing something, rather than just 'changing' something. Even on a large scale, nature doesn't change things mechanically: you don't just pull out the old and replace it with the new. Something new grows, and it eventually supplants the old.

We see the same thing at the level of behaviors: if new behaviors are more effective than old behaviors, then the new behaviours win out. That insight gives us a doorway into a different way to think about how systems might change: what if we thought of system change as the interplay amongst the various forces that are involved in growing something new?

> *Plan for what will be difficult while it is easy. Do what is great while it is small.*
>
> —Sun Tzu

Senge is a major protagonist for Massive Small change. Looking at nature, we see that nothing that grows starts large; it always starts small. No one is 'in charge', making the growth occur. Instead, growth occurs as a result of the interplay of diverse forces. And these forces fall into two broad categories: self-reinforcing processes, which generate growth, and limiting processes, which can impede growth or stop it altogether. The pattern of growth that occurs unfolds from the interplay of these two types of forces.

MANIFESTO

MAKING MASSIVE SMALL CHANGE

Our transformational goals for building urban neighbourhoods

We are committed to radically transforming the way we shape our towns and cities to deal with the challenges of a continuously changing and increasingly complex world. Government cannot do this alone. It must work together with people to harness the collective power of many small ideas and actions to build a better urban society for all our citizens and scale these up over time.

True urban society evolves only where compact urbanism meets human and social capital. If we can use the inherent creativity and goodwill that lies in people to build this compact urbanism, we will achieve even better outcomes.

We must focus on urban neighbourhoods as vital building blocks of socially diverse and mixed-use models of development for our metropolitan areas, cities and towns. Appropriately intense development with vibrant, connected and resilient public spaces, infrastructure and built form that can adapt to change over time are essential to deal with unpredictable future needs.

Government (at all levels) is best placed to provide the essential starting conditions that will release the potential for good neighbourhoods to emerge over time. We do not have to do everything—we will facilitate putting in place the essential urban structure, grain and platforms to create open/adaptive, collaborative and responsive environments. At a time when we need to do more with less, government must use its lightest touch to generate the maximum impact. Given support—and armed with the most effective ideas, tools and tactics—people can actively help to create viable urban neighbourhoods.

We believe that if we do this well, then government and its people, working together, will create far better social, cultural and economic outcomes that neither will ever achieve alone.

THE SECRETARY OF STATE FOR NEIGHBOURHOODS

UNDERSTANDING THE BASICS

Strategies for change themselves do not capture value. Value is realised only through the sustained, collective actions of all players in the system who design, implement and live the change. Long-term structural change is characterised by scale (it affects all or most of the system); by magnitude (it involves significant alterations from the status quo); by duration (it lasts for months if not years); and by its strategic importance (it will create significant shifts).

No single approach fits every situation, so ideas, tools and tactics must be adapted to a variety of situations. Here are are ten basics to consider:

1 **Address the human side of change.** Any transformation of significance will create people issues. New leaders will emerge, jobs will be modified, new skills and capabilities must be developed, and people will be uncertain and will resist. A formal approach for managing change should be developed early but often adapted.

2 **Change starts at the top.** Change is difficult for people at all levels, and the focus will be on the leadership team for strength, support and direction. The leadership must change first to challenge and motivate the rest of the players, 'talking the talk' and 'walking the talk'.

3 **Real change occurs at the bottom.** As change progresses through strategy, design and implementation, it affects different levels of government in different ways. Each of these layers must have enabled leaders who are aligned with the objectives of change, equipped to execute their mission and motivated to make it happen.

4 **Confront reality and demonstrate real faith.** People are inherently rational and will question the extent of change and their committment to making change happen. They will look to the leadership for answers. Articulating a formal case for change and providing a roadmap to guide behaviour and decision-making are critical to this.

5 **Create ownership, not just buy-in.** Change requires a distributed leadership that has broad influence over decisions both visible and invisible to everyone in the process of change. Ownership is often best created by involving people in identifying issues and crafting solutions.

6 **Communicate over and over.** The best-laid plans are only as good as people's ability to understand, adopt and act on them. The best change programmes communicate core messages—both outbound and inbound—through regular, timely advice that is both inspirational and actionable. Change leaders must take responsibility to tell a consistent story as part of this change process.

7 **Assess the cultural landscape early.** Successful system change picks up speed and intensity as it cascades down, making it critically important to understand and account for culture and behaviours at each level of the system. This means assessing readiness to change, bringing significant issues to the surface, identifying cultural factors that will support or inhibit change, and targeting sources of leadership and resistance.

8 **Prepare for the unexpected.** No system change programme goes completely according to the script. People will react in unexpected ways, areas of anticipated resistance will fall away, and the external environment will shift. Managing system change requires constantly reassessing impacts, efforts and the players' willingness and ability to adopt the next wave of change.

9 **Speak to the individual and the collective.** Change is a personal journey as well as an institutional one. It happens one person and one group at a time. People need to know how their work will change, what is expected of them during and after the system change programme, how they will be measured, and what success or failure will mean for them. Be clear on this.

10 **Have a simple purpose and clear principles.** This is probably the most important basic to get right. People will be captured by a compelling and shared vision for change. Clear principles give them the guiding framework within which they can work. As Dee Hock says, 'Far better than a precise plan is a clear sense of direction and compelling beliefs. And that lies within you. The question is, how do you evoke it?'

Starting with the right basics is the best way of starting. This means two things—having a clear and SIMPLE PURPOSE and having a clear set of PRINCIPLES. Here are some thoughts.

Those who initiate change will have a better opportunity to manage the change that is inevitable.

—William Pollard

THE MASSIVE SMALL DECLARATION

AN ANTIDOTE TO BIGNESS

This Declaration outlines the thinking, principles and behaviours needed to meet the future challenges of our towns and cities. Its ten clauses are mutually reinforcing: none should be considered in isolation from others. They will evolve as new challenges arise.

CLAUSE 1: A NEW COLLABORATION

We need to put democracy back into urbanism by building a new social contract between government and its citizens, based on trusting people to do the right thing. Governments can show the way by providing the protocols, conditions and behaviours to enable simple rules, emergent solutions and self-organisation to take root and flourish.

CLAUSE 2: RADICAL INCREMENTALISM

With the future uncertain and the past spent and gone, we must stop fixating on imposed end states for our cities. Instead, we must manage in the present. Focusing on catalysts and early beginnings; intervening in precisely targeted ways, and thinking regarding the collective power of many small ideas and actions will make a big difference.

CLAUSE 3: FREEDOM WITHIN CONSTRAINTS

We must allow for infinite possibilities by limiting choice. This means defining clear and simple boundaries within which people are free to organise, improvise and act. Structured choices promote the formation and growth of highly responsive environments, and provide a place's inhabitants with a full progression in life.

CLAUSE 4: EVOLUTION NOT REVOLUTION

Small progressive changes make a big difference. We must rediscover the art and process of urban evolution by unleashing the potential of countless bottom-up actions, all enabled by our top-down systems: balancing the roles and responsibilities of government and people, and building on their collective strengths. We must learn by doing.

CLAUSE 5: COLLECTIVE WISDOM

Smart citizens make smart cities. Data and technology should augment human intelligence, not seek to replace it. We must trust intuitive wisdom, avoiding the twin traps of reductionism and determinism. The city must always be seen as a constantly changing organism, not a mechanistic model capable of highly processed control.

CLAUSE 6: ENABLING LEADERSHIP

We must challenge and reform the rigid command-and-control systems that inhibit people's ability to adapt their place to their needs. This depends on new forms of leadership that can work at the interface between top-down and bottom-up systems, promoting self-organisation and building social capital at every available opportunity.

CLAUSE 7: A CODE OF ETHICS

True professionalism and civic leadership must be built on trust and commitment to do the right thing and must be bound by commonly accepted behaviours. In signing up to these principles, urban professionals and civic leaders take their responsibility to the well-being and continued success of all the inhabitants of the city they have charge over.

CLAUSE 8: A COMMON PLATFORM

Rational discourse depends on shared understanding. We advocate a common understanding and set of values to overcome our siloed thinking and help everyone in the system share knowledge and take joint action. Using this common understanding, we must promote openness, shared working and joint ownership of ideas and solutions across all the sectors.

CLAUSE 9: A WHOLE-WORLD VIEW

The total human habitat exists as a dependent sub-system of the environment. It can not be isolated from the natural habitat, particularly when global issues are increasingly felt locally. We must build the foundations for viable and resilient urban life, and a responsible urban society where people influence and shape their habitat.

CLAUSE 10: OPEN TO CHALLENGE

We must avoid the danger of group-think and the myth of the single hero. We must foster diversity, complexity and continuous change, embracing different perspectives and evolving as needed. Our thinking must embed analysis and self-correction at its very core, always being open to challenge. The focus is praxis: where theory meets practice.

SIMPLE PURPOSE AND CLEAR PRINCIPLES

DEFINING A SIMPLE PURPOSE

The first thing to do is for government to set a clear and simple purpose that will capture hearts and minds and galvanise action from the top to the bottom. It can do this by preparing a manifesto or going a step further by writing a declaration that can be signed by a wider set of actors in the urban process. Of course, it can do both. Here are examples:

Manifesto

Taking the concept of making Massive Small change and establishing it as an overriding collective vision for the development of our neighbourhoods, towns and cities could be a starting point. An example of a possible government manifesto that captures a simple purpose can be found on page 306.

Declaration

A simple purpose can be developed by adopting, adapting or recasting a version of the Massive Small declaration as a guiding instrument for urban change, and getting government, civic and local leaders to sign up to it. See page opposite. A copy of this declaration text can be downloaded from the Massive Small website.

People don't resist change. They resist being changed.

—Peter Senge

DEFINING CLEAR PRINCIPLES

Every place needs its own way of initiating and delivering system change, but they can learn from the experience of other places. These are some universal guiding principles we need to have at the back of our minds as we move forwards. They are a starting point and can be applied to most places—so they can be adopted in whole or part; adapted as necessary and even added to as new principles arise. They are not intended to limit, rather to prompt.

> *We need to design and facilitate change processes that build coalitions for change, create shared purpose and make systems work better for everyone, converting potentially controversial policy problems into projects of collaborative innovation.*
>
> —Innovation Unit

At the level of cities and neighbourhoods, system change necessarily happens with the public, in public. This interaction brings wicked challenges, but it has massive transformative potential.

According to the Innovation Unit, an independent, not-for-profit social enterprise based in the United Kingdom, this requires:

- → **Citizen engagement.** Re-imagining what relationships with citizens might look like, through deep engagement with citizens whenever and wherever possible, will be crucial to success.
- → **System leadership and governance.** Transformation requires strong leadership partnerships, but these are draining. Governance that supports the right behaviours can sustain change projects through tough moments.
- → **Shared vision and purpose.** Successful system change is owned not only by its leaders but by the people and organisations that are affected by it. Defining a compelling collective vision with a simple message is critical to generating this ownership.
- → **Learning.** System leaders elevate learning and connect it to system goals. This process enables leadership to be a learning conversation rather than trench warfare and supports those within the system to make change.
- → **Road mapping.** The management of change across complex, multi-layered systems can be extremely challenging. Making sense of this complexity requires an in-depth understanding of the mechanics and routes of change.
- → **Building a case for change.** Often innovators have an attractive future vision but fail to convince people that the status quo is unsustainable. But if 'no change' remains an option, there will likely be no change.
- → **Reinventing professions.** Radically different systems are impossible to achieve if the same people are asked to do the same things. Too often, strategies and practices are altered, but roles are left unchanged.
- → **Metrics and measures.** Without changing the outcomes that a system is working towards, real change is tough. And by its very nature, qualitative change demands new metrics.

Unlocking the creative potential of urban professionals, particularly in local government, has long been recognised as a vital component of civic leadership and management. Most urban professionals came into the profession to make the world a better place. Most have been stifled by the system. Endless compliance practices, relentless measurement against poorly aligned performance indicators, and responsibility given without authority (or vice versa) has killed initiative. Many urban professionals just do not feel valued anymore.

Whether generating novel ideas or coming up with innovative concepts for their cities, creative urban professionals can play a vital role in stimulating forward thinking and freshening up the urban outlook. But for that process to work, managers must provide the right platform for their subordinates to express their creativity.

'How Creativity Is Managed', a report by Robert Epstein, shows that to do this, they must develop the following managerial competencies:

- → Challenge their people by giving them difficult or impossible problems to solve, ambitious goals to attain, and the support needed to manage difficulties.
- → Encourage broadening of their horizons, which means providing people with training in subjects or topics well outside their comfort zones.
- → Support capturing of possible solutions that urge people to preserve their breakthrough ideas and give them the tools to do so.
- → Manage teams by assembling diverse groups that can use brainstorming and other techniques to maximise their creative output.
- → Model the core competencies of creativity by walking the walk.
- → Provide appropriate resources to enable creative functioning in a rich physical and social work environment that keeps people inspired.
- → Provide positive feedback and recognition to people who contribute new and important ideas.

More importantly, creative people must be trusted to fail. That is where real learning occurs.

Cities never fail to amaze. Every place has hidden assets, and these usually lie in people: a skill that can be deployed directly (or even indirectly) to solve a problem; a personality trait that can be used to galvanise others; a capability that can be bartered in return for a reciprocal favour. People like being asked to help if they can see a common purpose. People like feeling wanted and valued. It is a natural instinct in civil society to help. Don't be afraid to ask for help.

The former mayor of Calgary, Naheed Nenshi, was not afraid to ask his constituents. He started 3 Things for Calgary, an initiative that invited people to come up with three ideas where communities and local government could work together to make Calgary a better city. He was astounded at the response. It mobilised thousands of bottom-up actions. Mayor Nenshi was voted World Mayor of the Year in 2014.

Sir Howard Bernstein of Manchester in the United Kingdom, recognised as one of the most successful local government chief executives in recent history, kept up close relationships with the principal people in the city who acted over the years as his trusted advisors in all sectors. Many believe the culture of collaboration Sir Howard championed was an important part of his legacy: the deep and shared belief that people can do more in partnership than by working separately. He forged the Manchester family—a habit of making common cause, which worked across all parts of both the public and the private sector. He was not afraid to ask.

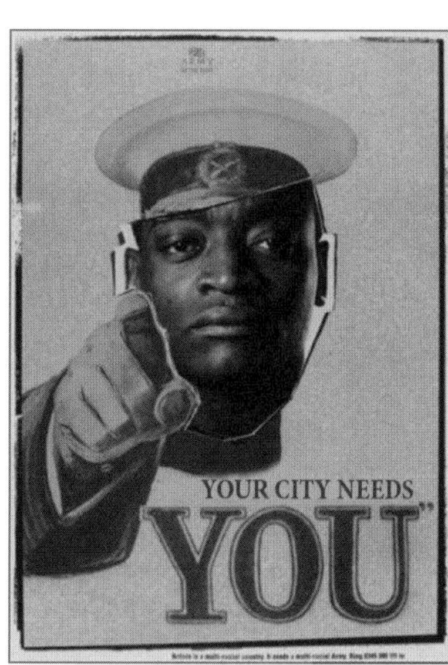

The most effective way to do it, is to do it.

—Amelia Earhart

Don't think too much before you start working, and don't work too much before you stop and start to reflect.

—Nabeel Hamdi

In our traditional top-down world, the instinct is to 'get an expert' and 'develop a strategy'. This tradition starts with a protracted brief-making exercise, follows with a lengthy commissioning process, continues with a prolonged study period and ends with a big comprehensive report. The report becomes the truth until the next report comes along, but the likelihood is that the report is out of date the day it is completed. And so it goes.

We do not need a new, big, cumbersome and protracted change management strategy or more complex policies to make Massive Small change happen—it just needs to start with our best shot and then evolve. Have faith that a small and dedicated team with experience in managing and solving complex urban problems and operating within a clear and coherent framework can be tasked with taking this shot.

The neighbourhood enabling model, with its enabling conditions and its developmental toolbox, provides us with a structured way of starting. It does this by breaking down the full system into distinct levels that allow a process of progressive doing and learning to evolve. Remember that the different levels remain mostly static or may change slowly—it is the developmental tools that act as 'switches' between each of the levels that are continually being reviewed and updated. By focussing on the switches between each of these levels we can evolve the whole system over time, using the switches to influence its upper level and informing its lower. These tools make systematic change more manageable.

It does not matter if the first attempt at change is not perfect at the outset. It is probably better if it's not. It needs time to mature.

Learning by doing, also referred to as experiential learning, is now an established approach in socio-economic theory by which transformational change, such as increased productivity in the building industry, for example, is achieved through practice, self-perfection and continuous minor innovations.

This approach is distinctly different from theory-based approaches, which pose hypotheses and seek to prove them. It's a far more straightforward and practical idea, but an incredibly complex process that's different for every situation. To understand how new ways will work, we need to try new things. We need insights from observers and onlookers and ideas from talking things through. We need rapid and continuous feedback; we need to learn from our environment and context.

> *The cycle of doing and learning, learning and doing, acting and reflecting involves a kind of 'activist pedagogy,' which is systemic to becoming skilful and wise. The purpose, given this setting, is to create their own knowledge, much in the same way as later, in practice, we would expect people to take charge of their own development.*
>
> —Nabeel Hamdi

This learning-by-doing approach needs, however, a well-structured framework to be effective. For example, projects require a conducive, enabling environment, where essential barriers are fluid, in order to get off the ground. This is where the neighbourhood enabling model and the approach to creating open, responsive and collaborative environments is critical. They are set up as continuous learning mechanisms.

So in urban transformation, new things can be tried by people and, as they gain acceptance, they can be instilled as the new normal. People just need the freedom to try. Any new system must, therefore, allow and nurture this freedom.

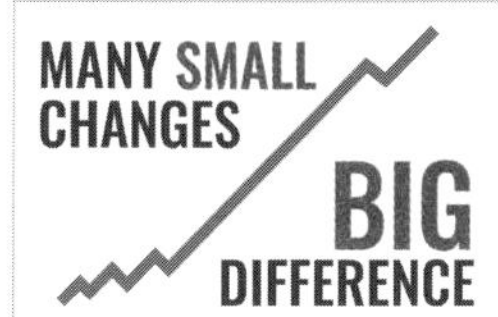

Haste is never a good idea. It is often quoted that 'Too much change too quickly leads to a Darwinian mess'. Move too fast, and nothing has time to sort itself out—equilibrium is hardly even approached before the equilibrium point is shifted. Moving too fast means that we are not consolidating our knowledge before we create another layer of disruption.

Some would argue that revolutionary change is just an extreme form of evolutionary change. Others would claim that revolution is a rapid, planned and deliberate action taken to modify the order of things, for example, a rebellion against an existing authority or government. Evolution could be an organic or planned progression of events. Progress is not necessarily rapid and could refer to natural development, the outcome of an idea or process. While revolutionary change is often required in a system, it can be a sign of poor management that has been unable to instil a culture of evolutionary change in the first place.

> *Small progressive changes make a big difference. We must rediscover the art and process of urban evolution by unleashing the potential of countless bottom-up actions, all enabled by our top-down systems: balancing the roles and responsibilities of government and people, and building on their collective strengths. We must learn by doing.*
>
> —Clause 4: Massive Small Declaration

Research across many disciplines, including economics and the behavioural sciences, shows that social systems improve most if they are allowed to evolve incrementally. In this way, actors and institutions can try things out, learn from their mistakes and improve their practice continuously over time.

This is best demonstrated in Hamilton, a mid-sized Canadian city, that focused its efforts on many small interventions to make a big change. As the head of the city planning department, Jason Thorne says, 'The cool little things are what get people excited and, in the aggregate, have the biggest impact'.

Rational discourse depends on developing a shared understanding of urban matters. This means building a common platform where learning is shared across the full spectrum of urban scales and with all actors in the system. It involves ensuring that all communication and debate is structured around the enabling conditions of the neighbourhood enabling model so that a common language for cross-sectoral collaboration and sharing is established, overcoming the professional and cultural roadblocks that occur when individuals or groups create their own operational silos. The developmental toolbox, as a shared set of gaming techniques and experimental models, plays a major role in testing new ideas, evaluating them and sharing the experience with others to help evolve the system.

> *To work our way towards a shared language once again, we must first learn how to discover patterns, which are deep, and capable of generating life.*
>
> —Christopher Alexander

Using this common understanding, we can promote openness, shared working and joint ownership of ideas and solutions across all the sectors.

The neighbourhood enabling model, with its enabling conditions and its developmental toolbox, provides us with the basis of a common platform.

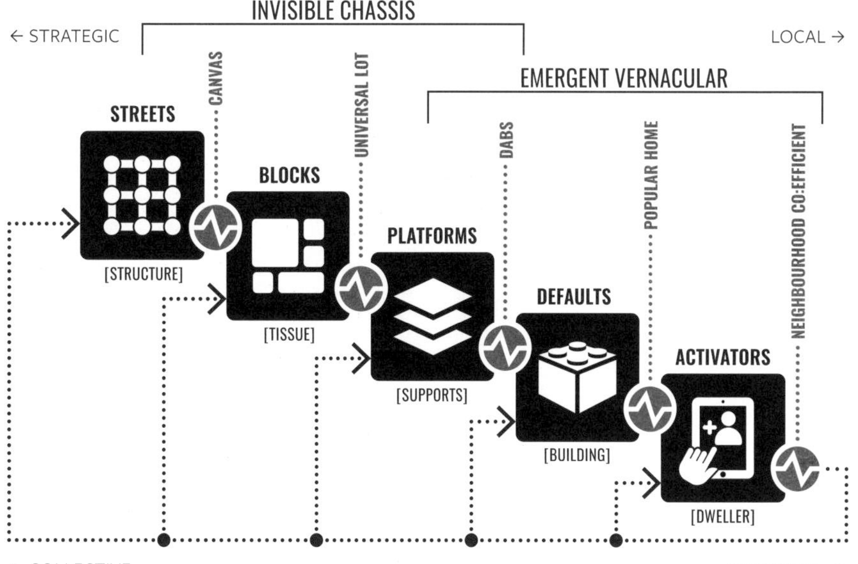

> *For the things we have to learn before we can do them, we learn by doing them.*
>
> —Aristotle

There is no such thing as a failed experiment, only experiments with unexpected outcomes.

—Buckminster Fuller

Current urban development models look to justify change by calling it a pilot project, as if this process of experimenting and learning is an aberration or just 'not normal'. In moving away from a system that focusses on fixed end states to one that sees trial and error, or emergent solutions, as the way forwards, we must recognise that at no point is the new system static. Evolution shows how a neighbourhood as a complex adaptive system is highly responsive to changing conditions. By its very nature, it is in permanent change, like a continuous experiment where we are always initiating, testing and accepting or rejecting outcomes as we learn about their success or failure.

> *Good reforms build on failed ones and learn from their mistakes. They are incremental and do not try to achieve 'whole-system' transformation all at once. They are based on existing best practice, rather than trying to reinvent the wheel. Start small at first and then grow, allow for trial and error, do not change all of a system at once but focus on driving through reform in those areas that need to change.*
>
> —Andrew Adonis

Within this context, failure is necessary to learn, so we must not be scared of it but embrace it. The secret is not to fail 'big' by focussing on big single outcomes. It is best to learn from many small failures because we can unpack these easier and try other options. This is evolution at work.

Intentionality seems to play a part in emergence in urban systems, especially in encouraging a particular kind of outcome. According to Richard Seel in his paper 'Emergence in Organisations', positive intentions can lead to positive outcomes, suggesting that it is possible to influence the broad general direction of emergence—although not to control or specify it. The intention, therefore, can be thought of as an emergent property created from the interactions of multiple agents within an urban system, which then feeds back into the system and influences its future development.

> *Emergence requires a kind of expectant waiting and sensitivity to the unfolding moment—a state often referred to in the literature on creativity.*
>
> —Richard Seel

Watchful anticipation is one of the most important and often overlooked drivers of urban change. Closing down too early can inhibit emergence, or at least prevent its full blossoming and subsequent influence on the continuing development of the system. Often driven by political imperatives, the desire for action in urban systems might be almost overwhelming, but emergence cannot be rushed.

System change is not immediate. It takes time to switch. You do not move from the old operating system on your computer to a beta version of a new system until the latest version has been well tested and the bugs have been ironed out. So is it with changing our top-down urban systems.

> *You never change things by fighting the existing reality. To change something, build a new model that makes the existing model obsolete.*
>
> —Buckminster Fuller

To implement the new system, a parallel running strategy can be applied in which the new system runs alongside the old system for a specified time. This should be long enough to ensure that all aspects of the new system are rigorously tested. Only when the new system is proved to be working correctly, will the old system be removed entirely, and then users will depend solely on the new system.

Parallel running allows results to be compared to ensure that the new system is working without any unintended consequences. If problems are found, the user can refer to the old system to resolve the problems and make modifications to the new system. In this way, operations can continue under the old system while the problems are sorted out. This approach also allows training of staff, helping them to gain confidence in the new system.

Because when we consider our urban systems we are not talking about a total operating system like a computer, it is possible to use a stepped approach to change from one system to another. If we adopt such an approach, it is important that we understand the shape of the new operating system we are migrating to.

So, a more effective way to shift our urban planning, design and development systems would be to put in place the organising structure of the neighbourhood enabling model and start small. This can be done by limiting the focus of initial change to evolving the tools in the toolbox—such as the universal plot, parameter book or the community toolkit—or on thematic issues such as temporary uses, suburban intensification or public space strategies. Either route can be employed.

A parallel running strategy should seek to:

- → Incentivise users to trial the new system by offering tangible benefits—speed, certainty and cost could be a few examples of doing this
- → Show improved outcomes—such as better community satisfaction, higher land values, better social outcomes
- → Stimulate small ideas and actions through local competitions (with or without rewards) and trialling these alongside other local initiatives

As some of these initiatives are proved to be working, there could be a phased shutdown of the old system to coincide with a phased switching on of the new system.

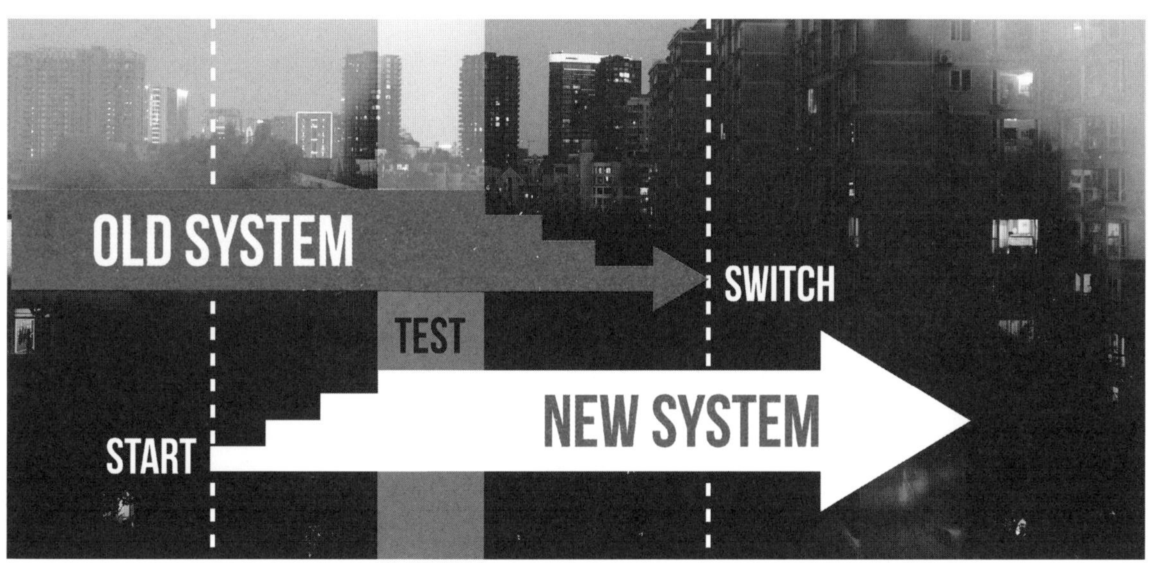

THE INSPIRING ENGINEER

HOW AN INFRASTRUCURE PROJECT BUILT SOCIAL CAPITAL

Shreedhar works as an engineer in the state department for slum upgrading in Mumbai. His job is to install basic services in informal settlements that have grown over time. He is given a budget, based on a unit rate per home, to install water and basic drainage into the homes. There is conflict in every project as some homes have to be demolished to make way for the service runs. Shreedhar needs the support of the police to get the job done.

The biggest problem he faces is that the pipes are being stolen, so his greatest cost lies in security from pilferage. Laying the pipes is the easiest part, but within a short space of time they are blocked and the system overflows, creating an alarming health hazard. People do not understand how the system works and maintenance standards are low.

Shreedhar has always thought that the role of an engineer in complex urban environments is far more important than just solving simple engineering problems. His profession tends to see cities in mechanistic terms, developing tools that focus on perfect end states that never seem to be realised. An example of this is the use of traffic modelling, which still forms the foundations in modern urban planning but does not work in places as complex as Indian cities. Nobody believes the models, yet the large engineering companies still persist in selling their wares on the basis that they deliver efficiency.

He has always admired Himanshu Parikh's work on slum networking in India. It seems that infrastructure projects can be used to build social capital and unlock community action. This is seen as part of a larger environmental upgrading plan of the whole area by establishing an innovative, low-cost, city-level sewerage network, and integrating this with new recreational areas and natural systems. Slum networking provides the preconditions for a better urban society and a greater degree of human dignity.

Shreedhar's own discipline still sees the large outfall sewer as the only way of solving drainage problems in cities, yet Himanshu Parikh has shown that you can use natural systems far more effectively. Other engineers still fall back on solutions that are supposedly known to be safe and they are reluctant to learn by experimenting. It's too risky, they say. It seems easier to make a case for a big solution than for targeted local interventions that may have a far greater local impact.

Shreedhar hears about Alan Baxter, a London-based engineer, through a Prince's Foundation for Building Community event in Delhi. Alan has taken a wider perspective on city building that sees engineering as a 'universal profession'. He calls his engineers 'urban designers' because he believes that they can have a far greater role in delivering good urbanism than engineers generally do.

In addition to his engineering practice, Alan runs a managed workspace for over 250 small organisations and practices in the field of urban development, who all seem to share common philosophies on how places are made. He helps start-ups and mentors others. He runs a regular programme of events that explore new ways of thinking. Shreedhar sees him as the model of how engineers should behave.

To widen his resource base, Shreedhar decides to work closely with Shack/Slum Dwellers International (SDI), a network of community-based organisations of the urban poor in thirty-three countries in Africa, Asia, and Latin America. SDI's mission is to link poor urban communities from cities across the southern hemisphere that have developed successful mobilisation, advocacy and problem-solving strategies. SDI provides a platform for slum dwellers to engage directly with governments and international organisations in adopting new strategies, changing policies and building understanding about the considerable challenges of urban development.

Shreedhar knows that what he is doing is very inefficient. This is how he sees the situation:

→ Local people are not allowed to be part of the solution, so they see the problems as being the government's. The residents need to become active partners.

→ The government should focus on creating the preconditions for these squatter settlements to become real urban places in time. It needs to install services and keep them running. At present it is spending up to four times as much on these projects as is necessary.

→ People do not see any incentive to work with the government to solve the problem.

→ Shreedhar does not have the power or responsibility to use his budgets effectively. He is just meant to follow orders.

SHREEDHAR TRIES SOMETHING DIFFERENT

Shreedhar is given the task of installing services in a part of Darawi, Mumbai's largest slum. He knows that when communities and authorities learn together and produce outcomes together, they are able to reach many more communities than the top-down initiatives that he has been engaged with. He hears about Renu Khosla's and Julia King's Centre for Urban and Regional Excellence (CURE) project in New Delhi that has enabled 322 households to retrofit toilets to their homes. It has been labeled the Potty Project. The toilets are connected through common shallow sewers to a septic tank linked to a simplified decentralised treatment system that treats the effluent before discharge and re-uses it. This turns waste into profit. The innovation has been not in the delivery of the infrastructure but in the way in which the project has retrofitted the system and engaged with the community. Because no two houses are alike, marrying the technology to the individual needs of each household has required a great deal of careful detailing, and close consideration of what exists and how to make it better. Much of this happened through street-level meetings and walking around the site.

Julia King describes the project as 'a charm bracelet of ideas and technologies'. Each charm on its own is not special: it is the combination of all that makes the whole unique. Every rupee spent on sanitation levers in nine more through people making improvements to their own homes.

Shreedhar approaches his superiors with an idea. 'Give me the responsibility to spend my budgets on this project in any way I choose,' he says. 'Don't tie me up with complex rules. Just give me a simple purpose. Let me release the potential of local people to help me.' The committee agrees to a six-month trial project. He asks SDI to help broker the project with the local community. SDI calls a public meeting and encourages people to organise themselves into representative groups. Street committees are formed, with one representative from each street on a central neighbourhood forum.

Shreedhar tells the forum: 'I have a budget to spend. I don't care how I spend it, but it must deliver water and drainage to every street. I know we can make this budget deliver far more if we work together.' The forum hears the problems that the project has faced and someone come ups with a slogan: 'The hole is greater than the sum of its pipes.'

A local signwriter puts up signs on every street where holes are being dug and pipes stacked. They have catchy phrases. 'Proper drains relieve stomach pains' and 'Clean water: healthy daughter' are the most popular. A billboard appears at a prominent entrance to the project neighbourhood. It shows a crude but effective printed plan of all the streets. Its drawings of identifiable buildings orientate people, and symbols point to problem areas. On one side of the plan is a pile of coins indicating the size of the budget. The other side shows coins spent. As work progresses, the completed streets will be painted red and the piles of coins will grow and shrink accordingly.

The community organises a hole-digging ceremony on the first street. Lines are sprayed on the ground showing the planned route of the underground services. Pipes are stacked in the street. Every able-bodied person present does some digging, symbolising a collaborative effort and their commitment to the project. The forum organises a pipe-signing ceremony at which the residents of the whole street paint their names, and sometimes small symbols, on the pipes. This symbolises their ownership of the project. Not one pipe is stolen.

The community puts in time digging ditches. One street after another gets new drains, clean water supply to standpipes in the street, and open stormwater culverts. As people begin to feel a greater sense of permanence about the neighbourhood, they respond by investing in their own homes, especially their fronts. Within months the street has been totally transformed.

They hear of a design competition led by the architect and urban designer Darshana Gothi Chauhan at London's University of Westminster. Building on the Indian prime minister's Clean India Mission, the competition aims to improve one hundred public spaces in Indian cities. The community works with a local architecture school to transform an important public space—the site of the project billboard—at the entrance to its neighbourhood. Confidence is high. Local people clean and level the area, putting in a new *kabaddi* pitch, a dance stage and a covered bamboo pavilion for local women. The local authority installs new public toilets. Pavements around the space are painted with kolam designs derived from magical motifs, and abstract designs blended with philosophic and religious patterns. Local traders return and take on the responsibility of looking after the space. The school of architecture submits this project as an entry to the competition and it wins the overall award.

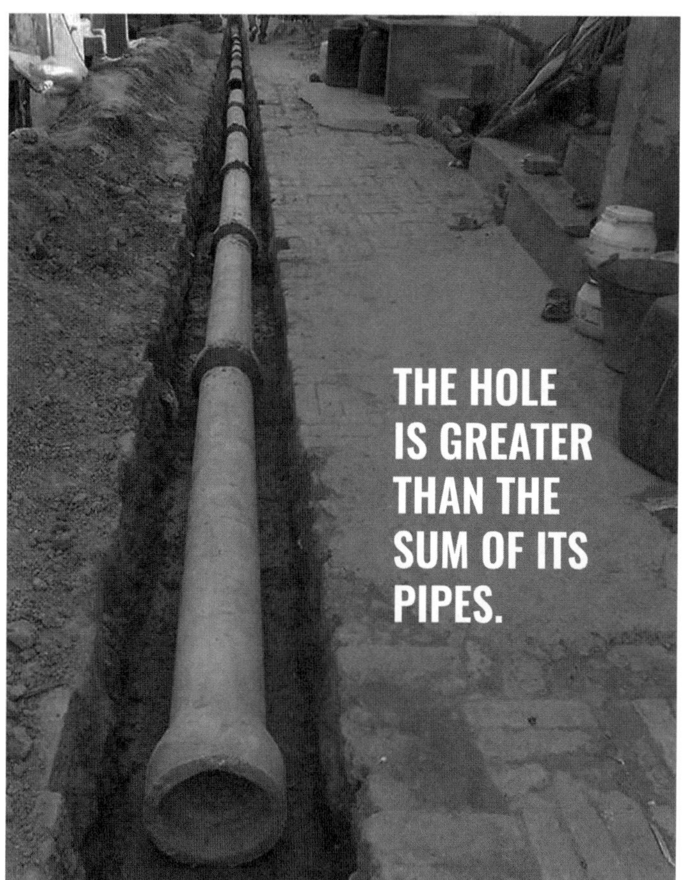
THE HOLE IS GREATER THAN THE SUM OF ITS PIPES.

Maintenance costs fall as the community learns about the rules for using the drains. Local drain cleaners are appointed to deal with any minor problems. Street cleaning becomes the community's responsibility. The job is completed well under budget, as the billboard shows. People vote to use the spare funds to build a community centre, the first in their neighbourhood.

SHREEDHAR REPORTS BACK TO HIS SUPERIORS:

1 The project's success has exceeded expectations.
2 It mobilised the community rather than becoming a cause of considerable conflict.
3 The community has a sense of ownership of the project and continues to maintain it.
4 Acting as an honest broker, the SDI helped to rebuild the lost trust between the community and the government. Making the whole process transparent encouraged most of the people to get involved.
5 When people see that there are plans to spend money in their area, they can be ingenious at finding better ways to spend it.
6 He has achieved not just a physical project but also a social purpose. He wants to share his experience with his profession.

'I think we have changed how we think about engineering our cities,' Shreedhar says. 'We have made the invisible visible. What is hidden in the ground is now imprinted in people's lives.'

CHANGING
PLACE
CHANGING
TIME
CHANGING
THOUGHTS
CHANGING
FUTURE

ACTIVATING THE CHANGE LEVERS

3.2

Change levers, also called 'leverage points', are places within a complex system (a business, an economy, a living body, a city, an ecosystem) where a small shift in one thing can produce big changes in everything else. Leverage points are points of power.

Donella Meadows at the Academy for System Change has identified some leverage points to help us understand and identify the indicators, and define the system structure or pattern that might change. As you go down the list, the greater the leverage and therefore the greater the impact you might have on changing the system.

Here is a simplified list of these leverage points:

1 **Structures**—these are changes in the physical structures of a system, for example, the way a transport, energy system or place is organised.

2 **Flows**—these are changes in how flows of information, finance or value might be distributed, are configured and relate to each other.

3 **Rules**—these rules dictate how the system is organised, so if they change they will have an impact on the flows, patterns and structures of the system.

4 **Power to evolve**—this is the power to add, change, evolve or self-organise system structure, so can we put in place the ability for the system to change, adapting to different responses to maintain the goal of the system. If a system is self-organising, it has the power to keep evolving itself.

5 **Goal**—changing the goal of the system, its purpose and function, will ultimately determine how the rest of the system operates.

6 **Paradigm**—this is a set of assumptions or a view about how the world works; a pattern of organising our thoughts, which informs everything.

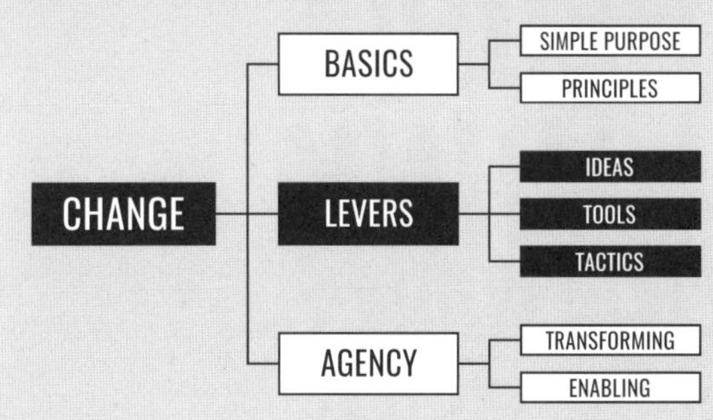

According to Meadows in her groundbreaking book, *Thinking in Systems*, 'Paradigms are the sources of systems. From them, from shared social agreements about the nature of reality, come system goals and information flows, feedbacks, stocks, flows and everything else about systems.'

She says paradigms are harder to change than anything else about a system, but there's nothing physical or expensive or even slow in the process of paradigm change. In a single individual, it can happen in a millisecond. 'All it takes is a click in the mind, a falling of scales from eyes, a new way of seeing. Whole societies are another matter—they resist challenges to their paradigm harder than they resist anything else.'

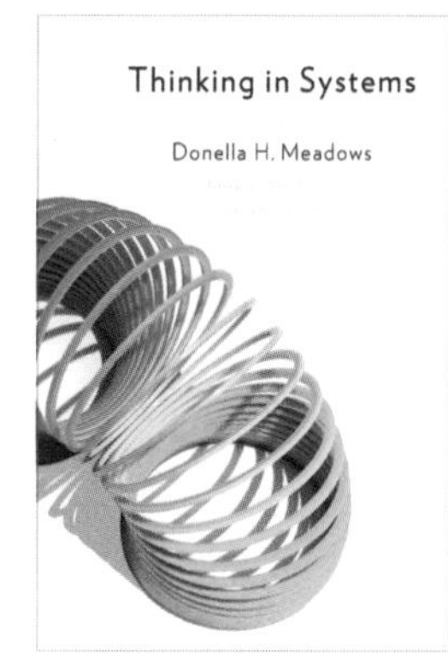

OUR THREE CHANGE LEVERS

For us, initiating system change means focussing on our three levers of change at all scales of government and community:

- Changing IDEAS (thinking and mindsets)
- Changing TOOLS (methods and applications)
- Changing TACTICS (leadership and management)

If we can categorise these levers, we can find a way to change a system. They are multi-faceted and act on each other. System change is unlikely to happen with just one of these levers, but it can happen with a combination of them all. To be effective, we need all of them to change.

This approach, with some obvious tweaks, should work in all countries (whether established or emerging) and in all sectors (whether formal or informal).

Managing bottom-up change is its own art.

—Kevin Kelly

CHANGING IDEAS

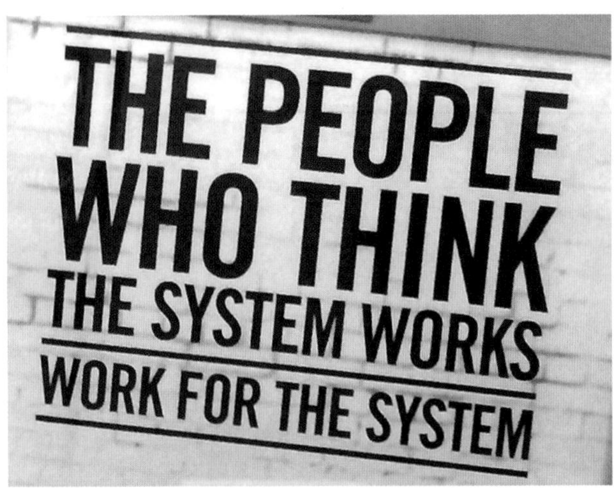
THE PEOPLE
WHO THINK
THE SYSTEM WORKS
WORK FOR THE SYSTEM

The most difficult thing to do is to change thinking and, with that, change mindsets. Even though many believe the existing system doesn't work, the default for many is the status quo. Transformational change, however evolutionary, is not easy.

Subsection 2.1, From Complex Policies to Simple Protocols, provides a starting point for changing top-down thinking through its three environments—*open/adaptive*, *responsive* and *collaborative*. The thinking behind these environments can be used at all scales of government to guide this change as a prompt to develop your way of doing things.

Here is how you can start

The world as we have created it is a process of our thinking. It cannot be changed without changing our thinking.

—Albert Einstein

AT NATIONAL SCALE

- Establish 'Making Massive Small Change' as the single national vision for forming neighbourhoods for all people in all places. Make it a rallying call to action. Give it a catchy term like 'Radical Incrementalism' or something similar.
- Make the vision easy to understand, especially by civic leaders, and communicate by making it the common language of everyone, so they can own and proliferate the idea. Spread the message and spread it again.
- Deploy Massive Small change as a proven, singularly superpowerful strategic instrument for accessible, broad-based and national economic opportunity and growth. Develop simple metrics to allow its success to be measured.
- Use it as a cross-cutting theme to integrate all national government departments, by concentrating impact of purpose, effort and funding to increase successful outcomes. Iron out the conflicts and cut red tape.
- Empower all departments, officials and civic leaders to enable this vision. Integrate the departmental silos and get them to move towards strategic and coherent project delivery. Promote cross-department working.
- Condense all levels of best practice and policy into this single collective vision. Always show what you mean and by example. Tell simple stories of successes and failures. Make it relevant to people's lives and experiences.
- Devolve responsibility for delivery of urban projects to the lowest levels of empowered urban society. Incentivise collective action at the local scale. Inspire a 'can-do' attitude. Show the sense of the possible.
- Unpack complex policies and develop simple PROTOCOLS that could expand or be incorporated in new national policies. Don't lead with national policy; continually evolve it. Write simple instructions.
- Develop an enabling leadership support programme for all civic leaders and urban professionals at metropolitan, city and town levels to embed this kind of thinking in everything. Show how they can do it everywhere.
- Establish an annual 'Neighbourhood' national holiday to relentlessly reinforce the Massive Small vision in the hearts and minds of all people through celebrations and other events, announcements and awards. Make it fun.

AT METROPOLITAN/CITY/TOWN SCALE

- Embed the Massive Small vision with its simple purpose at all levels of local government and evolve it to make it relevant to the particular qualities of the place. Empower all players to enable this vision.
- Make it feel unique and relevant. Call it 'The [Insert Metropolis/City/Town Name] Way' to reflect its fundamental interrelationship with the special qualities of the place. Build on the brand. Celebrate it.
- Make the vision easy to understand by all citizens and communicate it by making it the common language of everyone—so they can also own, evolve and proliferate the idea. Spread the message and spread it again.
- Use the vision as a cross-cutting theme to integrate all local government departments by concentrating impact of purpose, effort and funding to radically increase successful outcomes. Iron out conflicts and cut red tape.
- Devolve responsibility for delivery of housing and social infrastructure to the neighbourhood level. Promote local economic benefits from local action. Build capacity amongst local builders and suppliers.
- Condense all levels of local best practice and policy into this single vision. Make it accessible to all. Actively show how the enabling conditions are applied and how development tools can evolve. Learn by doing.
- Develop simple PROTOCOLS that could expand or be incorporated in new metropolitan-, city- and town-wide policies. Don't lead with local policy; evolve it. Write it in easy terms that people can understand.
- Develop an active citizenship programme focussing on a range of neighbourhood development programmes that look to build enabling leadership at all levels and collective action by communities in all places.
- Promote ETHICAL PROFESSIONALISM amongst all urban professionals and civic leaders. Build their capacity and change their ways of working and engaging with the public. Break down their traditional silos.
- Develop demonstration projects that show by doing. Promote neighbourhood events and exhibitions on a regular basis, showing results of action and progress, including 'Meet the Leaders' events, drop-in workshops, show homes, liason with non-governmental and voluntary organisations and so forth.

AT NEIGHBOURHOOD SCALE

- Tailor the Massive Small vision with its simple purpose for each neighbourhood and communicate the vision to all citizens with a 'sense of the possible'. Harness civic action to change.
- Show how the benefits of adopting the Massive Small approach are quickly evident to everyone, and how everyone can get behind it. Ensure that all own it. Get them to add to it and allow it to evolve.
- Show how the vision works for the individual, the collective and the institution. Promote a neighbourhood-based framework for action by all. Make boundaries permeable in order to not restrict creativity.
- Develop a set of open standards that clearly establish the boundary conditions within which people can challenge these ideas, evolve them and instil even further innovation into the system.
- Promote an understanding of co-creative approaches where top-down systems provide the responsive environments for bottom-up action. Always be open to challenge and don't tie it up in a web of complex policies.
- Identify clear rules of engagement to promote collaborative working between local governments, urban professionals and active citizens. Show the roles and responsibilities of all parties in the process.
- Use active citizen engagement programmes to help evolve current complex urban policies into simple PROTOCOLS that generate collective action and are clearly understood by all active citizens.
- Create an easily accessible platform that people can quickly grasp. Show how it is relevant to all by telling simple stories of how people have done this before and invite people to write their own. Share these stories.
- Promote an open, adaptive and collaborative leadership style with an agreed ethos at all levels of the community. Make this style and ethos publicly known at all levels. Walk the walk and talk the talk.
- Use rapid and continuous feedback to evolve these ideas and actions. Communicate these ideas and actions to a wider audience. Promote citizen engagement tools and social media as possible mechanisms for communication. Get people to share their experiences.

CHANGING TOOLS

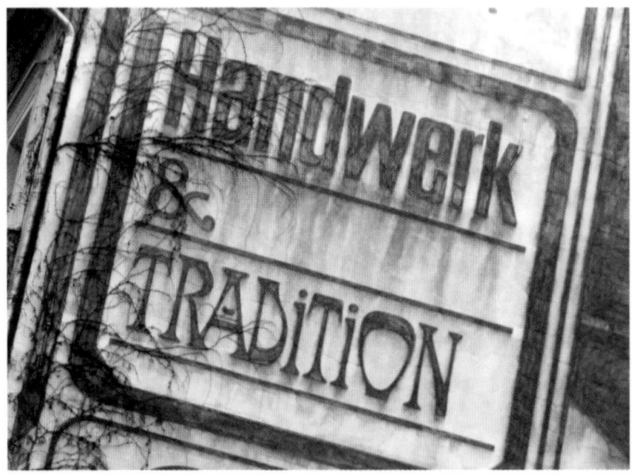

Communicating how change could be implemented in an organised and acceptable way is the stumbling block to most forms of system change. No politician likes giving away power.

> *Monkeys play by their sizes. Smaller tasks mostly come with smaller challenges. If you are willing to take step-by-step methods to solve bigger tasks, you will easily overcome challenges that attempt to stop you! Go, give it a try!*
>
> —Israelmore Ayivor

Subsection 2.2, From Fixed End States to Starter Conditions, which introduces the NEIGHBOURHOOD ENABLING MODEL, provides a starting point for changing top-down methods and applications through its five enabling CONDITIONS (or levels) as well as its development TOOLBOX (or switches) that allow each level to inform and influence the other. These conditions can be used at all scales of government to guide this change as a prompt to develop your way of doing things.

Here is how you can start

AT NATIONAL SCALE

Ⓣ Fix the five enabling conditions (levels) as the organising mechanism for all forms of policy and protocols at all levels of government to structure settlements, direct funding and galvanise this vision as a common way forwards.

Ⓣ Start with reforming the limiting convention of using tree-like road hierarchies for roads planning to become open, adaptive NETWORKS with hierarchical structures of main streets, boulevards, avenues and local streets.

Ⓣ Produce the structure and simple rules for a neighbourhood street design manual that can be adapted to local government scale and the particular requirements of a neighbourhood. Provide simple instructions.

Ⓣ Develop the toolbox at the interface of STREETS and BLOCKS—using something like CANVAS as a simple grid-based model for laying out neighbourhoods—and allow this to be added to and evolved as lessons are learnt.

Ⓣ Show various types of urban BLOCKS and their arrangements to act as possible templates to be adopted or adapted at the local scale. Produce a block layout manual with different 'tissues' for easy use.

Ⓣ Develop a simple, standard and regular way of parcelling land to allow further subdivision, opening up opportunities for all and providing structured choices. Develop the UNIVERSAL LOT as a land-parcelling principle.

Ⓣ Show examples of types of PLATFORMS based on open building systems that will help initiate the transition from site development to built form. Develop a generic building code to use as simple instructions.

Ⓣ Work with the building industry to develop something like DABS as a developmental tool that will act as a springboard for building innovation and allow this to evolve as important lessons are learnt.

Ⓣ Structure a starter set of housing DEFAULTS as parameters for a range of popular typological housing solutions for different urban conditions and allow these to evolve at regional and local scales.

Ⓣ Start working with a few metropolitan areas, cities and towns to test and evolve the NEIGHBOURHOOD ENABLING MODEL. Develop a sharing platform that allows local governments to learn from best practice.

AT METROPOLITAN/CITY/TOWN SCALE

🅣 Adopt the NEIGHBOURHOOD ENABLING MODEL as your best shot at galvanising action, structuring thinking and developing a local neighbourhood-based framework for action. Let it evolve. Give it six months.

🅣 Develop and disseminate the development tools—such as CANVAS and the UNIVERSAL LOT—and train urban professionals and local civic leaders in their use in preparing their neighbourhood plans.

🅣 Ensure that all the local agencies concentrate on early intervention and are not obsessed with fixed end states that never arrive. Establish the preconditions for a new urban vernacular to emerge.

🅣 Focus public sector effort on the first three enabling conditions that make up the invisible chassis—STREETS, BLOCKS and PLATFORMS—to help initiate the transition from site to final built form.

🅣 Work with the local building industry to evolve DABS as a generic open building code to maximise the effectiveness of the industry and reduce costs. Create a new breed of enabling developer to deliver parcelled land.

🅣 Evolve the standard DEFAULTS pattern book to produce a range of popular typological housing solutions for a range of urban conditions and uses and allow people to develop these over time.

🅣 Develop a popular home PARAMETER BOOK as a simple manual to return housing to a distributed system done by many. Let housing be incremental to make it even more affordable to all. Show individual successes.

🅣 Establish the principle of building social capital at every opportunity by developing a range of generic ACTIVATORS that will trigger social responsibility and collective action by local citizens in all forms

🅣 Initiate a development tool—something like the NEIGHBOURHOOD CO:EFFICIENT—that shows by example how these catalysts can be applied in different circumstances and allow this to evolve as lessons are learnt.

🅣 Create simple instructional manuals to guide municipal officials and support emerging property and construction-related businesses with readily available and directly understandable and useful information.

AT NEIGHBOURHOOD SCALE

🅣 Embed an understanding of the NEIGHBOURHOOD ENABLING MODEL within the community as the organising mechanism for all forms of collective action and integrated neighbourhood-based change.

🅣 Establish the use of standard DEFAULTS as a way of scaling up housing delivery at neighbourhood scale and define fast-track approaches to achieve planning approvals. Create the rules to break the rules.

🅣 Work with people to evolve a local version of their popular home PARAMETER BOOK as a local urban vernacular response to their neighbourhood that produces the best outcomes within local constraints.

🅣 Develop and deploy the use of ACTIVATORS to promote collective action through examples such as building groups (*baugruppen*), sharing economy, co-housing and civic action strategies.

🅣 Train and build capacity in the local community in potentials that arise from the use of the NEIGHBOURHOOD CO:EFFICIENT toolkit. Trial projects and programmes that enhance community assets.

🅣 Create a neighbourhood challenge fund to harness people's inherent creative abilities to solve their urban problems. Small-scale funds can be directed to co-creative projects by making the process competitive.

🅣 Build catalytic projects to benchmark development, provide exemplars and accelerate change. Employ temporary uses to test new ideas. Promote collective action through every aspect of urban development.

🅣 Promote the concept of scale-free institutions so schools can start and evolve, spaces can be shared, and all the assets in a neighbourhood can be deployed. Release the potential of community assets.

🅣 Evolve the TOOLBOX through rapid and continuous feedback from the local community. Use community engagement applications, social media and local press channels to achieve this outcome.

🅣 Engage the community in producing neighbourhood plans that will ensure the development of open/adaptive, responsive and collaborative environments. Embrace all ideas and actions. Allow ideas to evolve.

CHANGING TACTICS

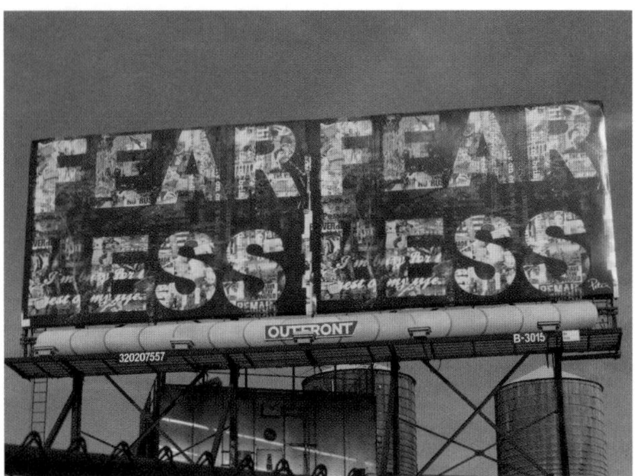

Transforming top-down leadership and management from a command-and-control model to an enabling leadership ethos requires a bold and brave move by governments—but it is the only way to organise complexity. It starts with a fundamental belief that most people can be trusted and the majority conform. It also recognises we must put aside our obsession with certainty and embrace unpredictable outcomes. It acknowledges that we need dedicated agencies and committed agents to accelerate and deliver this change. This requires different actions at different scales.

Subsection 2.3, From Command-and-Control to Enabling Behaviours, provides a starting point for changing top-down management and leadership approaches through its three sectors—*active citizenship, civic leadership* and *ethical professionalism*. The thinking behind these environments can be used at all scales of government to guide this change as a prompt to develop your way of doing things.

Here is how you can start

→ AT NATIONAL SCALE

- Create a senior government post for neighbourhoods, with responsibility for all planning, housing, community and local economic development, with single budgets that can be deployed directly to local neighbourhoods.
- Establish a small, dedicated transformation unit (TUNIT) as a permanent structure, answering directly to the neighbourhoods government leader, to support and accelerate this kind of transformational change.
- Get the TUNIT to set simple targets and realistic trajectories and ensure they are met. Provide the metrics to evaluate success and recalibrate targets and trajectories if necessary. Establish simple routines.
- Create a Neighbourhood Enabling Agency (NEA) as a delivery-focussed national agency with branches in all local and metropolitan authorities as the primary vehicles to coherently deliver the vision in areas of change.
- Demand an obsession with delivery and a capacity to deliver. The NEA must be like a hit squad that is focussed only on achieving results. Get talent and experience in there. Appoint wisely. Use staged contracts to ensure the agency delivers.
- Establish a state-owned citizen's bank to bypass commercial bank, inner-city 'red-lining' and high-risk aversion to certain areas. Create a focussed, no-security lending institution to include those currently excluded.
- Put all available government land into a central portfolio and make it accessible to local government for use in developing new neighbourhoods and urban extensions. This land is only to be released in smaller parcels.
- Replace public sector focus on megaprojects with a new form of radical incrementalism by people on the ground. Direct all funding to achieve initial intervention rather than providing funding for the duration of projects.
- Promote local economic development by promoting hyperlocal benefits—local procurement practices, local enterprise hubs, investment in local supply chains and maintainence of capital in the local economy.
- Get parastatal and charitable housing associations to play a bigger role in building neighbourhoods—enabling development and providing loan-guarantee funding, short-term accommodation during the construction process, community infrastructure, and shared ownership, amongst other aspects.

AT METROPOLITAN/CITY/TOWN SCALE

- Embed small TUNITS as local agents of the government's TUNIT as a permanent structure, answering directly to the civic leader, to support and accelerate transformational change at this scale.
- Get 12 to 20 people around a table to define the simple rules for places facing change. Have a draft of the rules published in a month. Tweak it and evolve it within six months. Foster urgency. Have first successes in one year.
- Protect and incentivise the small. Focus on the small guys. Make many developers, many small builders and many community makers. A multitude of small physically concentrated projects provides big opportunities.
- Give NEAS a clear role in facilitating change—assembling land and parcelling it; coordinating infrastructure; opening up new access to land; demonstrating possibilities and disseminating best practice. Release potential.
- Focus investment primarily on areas where the most significant potential of broad-based rapid economic access and growth can occur, where infrastructure already exists and where zones of change can be well connected.
- Maximise the potential for immediately visible change in these areas of possible change by focussing on replicable, scaleable and high-impact projects that will inspire action by all sectors.
- Identify priority zones, routes and public spaces where concentrated action and funding can be channelled. These areas could include a series of urban blocks, the main street, an urban park, amongst others.
- Allow the suburbs to intensify incrementally by allowing typology-based change. They are doing it anyway, despite government. Show a creative way of dealing with the backyards challenge.
- Enable and direct private-sector responses through precisely targeted grants and by demonstrating fast-track ways of getting planning consents for proposals that will achieve the desired outcomes.
- Concentrate funds and resources to make things happen. Develop a metro/city/town-wide housing association-type structure that offers 'staircasing' (shared equity schemes) for people starting up or scaling back. This structure could help derisk projects for commercial lenders, which will unlock much more finance.

AT NEIGHBOURHOOD SCALE

- Promote self-organisation at every level—from special-interest groups through to street committees, community organisations and neighbourhood forums. Make them proactive—doers, not stoppers.
- Actively collaborate with citizens, groups and nongovernmental organisations to help define and deliver urban renewal projects by working alongside them. Try, test, experiment and learn from this experience.
- Seed catalytic projects with small beginnings. Try and support temporary uses. Let things evolve. Manage in the present. Be nimble and agile. Develop simple rules to harness collective and spontaneous action.
- Promote small beginnings and scale these ideas and actions up to create big impacts. Start with a single action in each neighbourhood with visibly and experientially radical impact on everyone.
- Map and mobilise all community assets—physical and human. Don't be scared to ask for help. People like being asked to help in the collective interest. Start by starting. Learn by doing. Then share, share, share!
- Show how government and people can work together more efficiently. Incentivise and reward collective action. and recognise enabling community leadership. Offer prizes for innovation.
- Identify stumbling blocks and find ways to ease complicated processes. Promote automatic approvals. Cut red tape. Shift effort to making things happen. Make urban planning relevant to communities again.
- Establish citizen advisory groups providing critical feedback to TUNITS and NEAS. Use social media and public events. Publicise findings. Be open and transparent. Show how you are responding to findings.
- Engage citizens in participatory budgeting to show how best to provide public facilities and services. Link this to crowdfunding initiatives, 'services-in-kind' and community action to jointly deliver urban projects.
- Develop a new social contract between local government and citizens, clearly spelling out roles and responsibility and codes of behaviour. Use local community charters—'We will if you will'—to formalise this process. Get people to formally sign up to these charters. Communicate this process to the widest audience. Keep it simple.

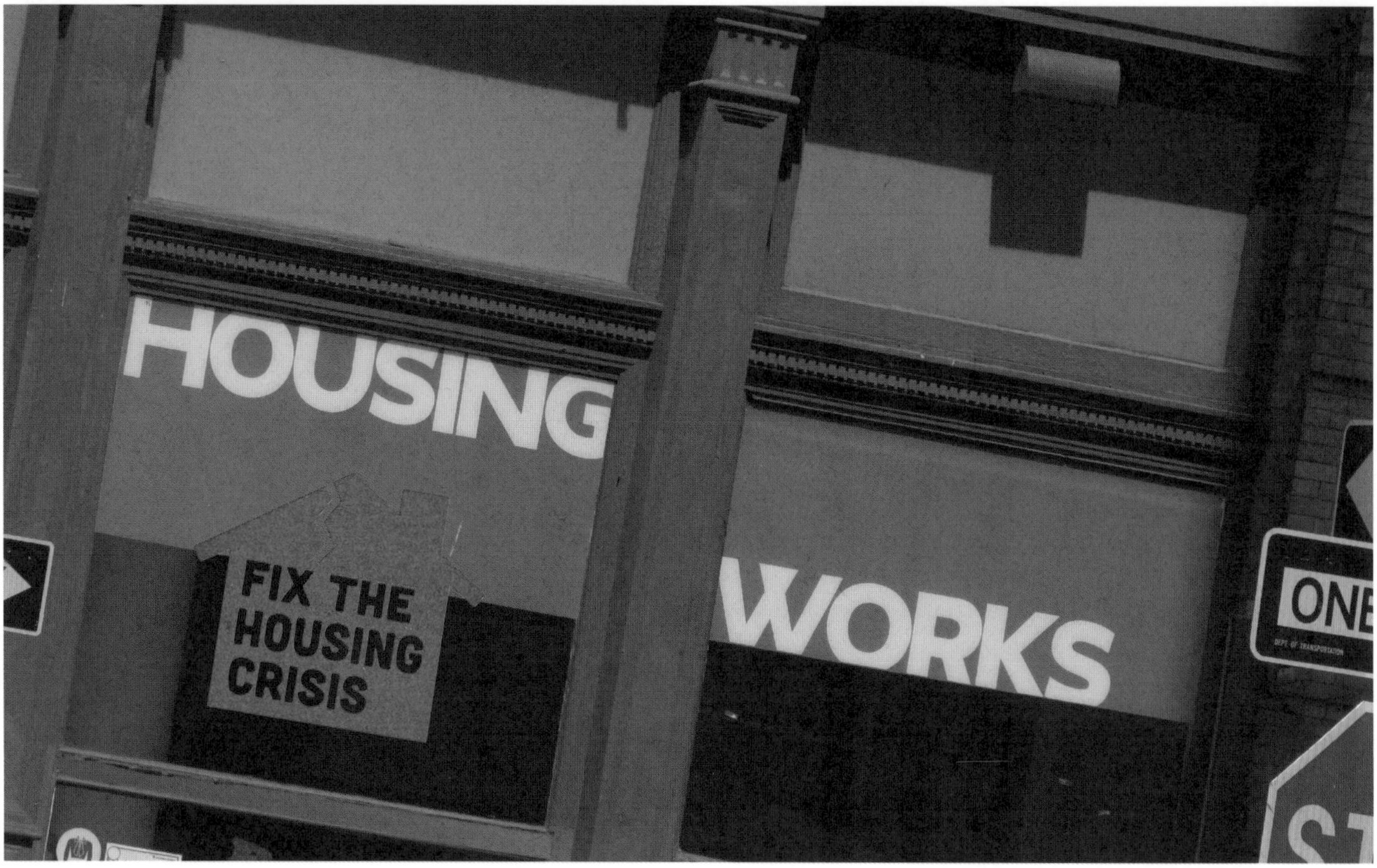

THE UPSIDE DOWN THINKER

HOW AN ASTUTE POLITICIAN HELPED SOLVE A NATIONAL HOUSING CRISIS

> *Always consider a brick in a wall, a wall in a room, a room in a house, a house in a street, a street in a neighbourhood, and a neighbourhood in a city.*
>
> —after Eliel Saarinen

Another day goes by and the housing crisis deepens. It is talked of as the United Kingdom's biggest policy failure. One new announcement follows another. The government has a new solution. The speechwriter works from the familiar template: 'We have a tech fix / a design fix / a financial fix / a policy fix' (delete as applicable). Those in charge, despite having been part of the problem for so long, are promoted to even higher levels of incompetence. Another industry body / think-tank / policy forum launches a new research paper / initiative / manifesto with a catchy title that tells us that the problem lies with planning/integration/fragmentation. Another expert tells us about the sheer scale of the problem, without providing any answers.

Another complex funding concept from the developer of the moment keeps us in a state of suspended animation. Another modern method promises to save the housing industry, though the industry does not see the need for change. Another conference wafts on, its speakers' interests deeply vested in the status quo. The crisis is not just in housing; it is also in our thinking.

Cecilia, a member of Parliament, has recently been appointed as housing minister. Some see this as a poisoned chalice: many of the seven previous housing ministers, all men, lasted for no more than six months in the job. Every top-down initiative failed. Targets were set and never met. Policies were repackaged but proved ineffective. Reorganisation followed reorganisation. The last minister tried to speed up the process by calling for more 'garden towns', as if we did not know that he just meant more suburbia with dodgy eco-credentials. The minister before him called for 'brownfield sites' to be developed without the need for planning permission. He also missed the point: deregulation does not get housing built.

The government pledged in a state of panic that it would scale up its housebuilding efforts by throwing money at desperate sites. Flip follows flop, and back again. Cecilia knows she has to act differently, but her special advisors and think-tanks trot out the same old concepts.

Cecilia realises that her special advisors and think-tanks are part of the problem. They have missed the point, probably because so few of them have real-world experience.

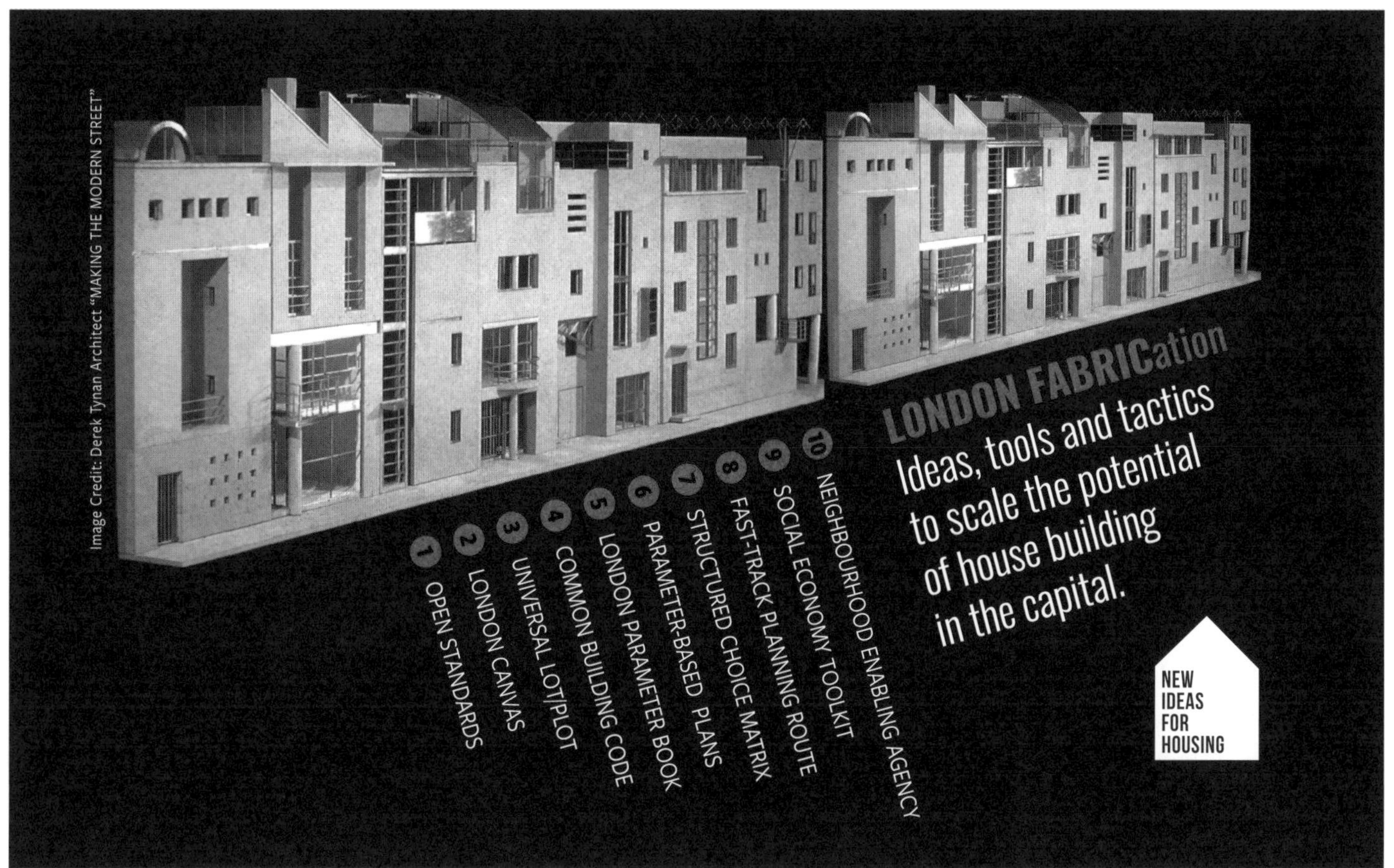

Image Credit: Derek Tynan Architect "MAKING THE MODERN STREET"
LONDON FABRICation
Ideas, tools and tactics to scale the potential of house building in the capital.
1 OPEN STANDARDS
2 LONDON CANVAS
3 UNIVERSAL LOT/PLOT
4 COMMON BUILDING CODE
5 LONDON PARAMETER BOOK
6 PARAMETER-BASED PLANS
7 STRUCTURED CHOICE MATRIX
8 FAST-TRACK PLANNING ROUTE
9 SOCIAL ECONOMY TOOLKIT
10 NEIGHBOURHOOD ENABLING AGENCY
NEW IDEAS FOR HOUSING

THIS IS WHAT HER ADVISORS SAY:

→ The private sector can solve the housing problem. Sell as much public land as possible to the biggest bidder.
→ Stop the government from interfering. Deregulate, cut red tape and bash the planners.
→ Build in far-flung places where relatively few people will object. Say you are building eco-towns or garden cities: no one will know the difference.
→ Say you are encouraging self-build, even if you suspect that few such schemes will ever get off the ground.
→ Focus on the funding mechanisms, even though you know that the prices of homes are well beyond many people's ability to pay.
→ Look for a technical fix. Learn from the Scandinavians, perhaps. Surely there must be new methods of construction that can solve the problem?
→ Ask the architects. Surely it's just a design problem?

Amongst other things, she is presiding over a housing agency whose job is to parcel up land and sell it to one of the big-ten housebuilders, who promise much but fail to deliver. She calls it her 'Homes and Communities Prevention Agency'. The housebuilders see it as their job to keep their shareholders happy (the housing shortage is sending their share prices soaring); they don't see it as their job to solve the housing crisis. The housebuilders are just as happy to sit on the land, watching the prices go up.

CECILIA REALISES WHY THE SYSTEM IS DOOMED TO FAIL:

→ The system treats housing as a numbers game, not as a matter of building neighbourhoods. The focus is too much on the technical aspects of housing and too little on the social dynamics of neighbourhoods.
→ The government looks to the housebuilders to solve the problem. But the housebuilders are a big part of the problem and government gets its answers from the very people who are creating the problem. It is a self-perpetuating cycle.
→ The government still puts its faith in big utopian visions but it has no intention of implementing them. They have neither the faith nor the act of will.
→ The problem must be self-inflicted: urban society did not have these problems three generations ago. What did we do differently then?
→ The system breeds adversarial positions between communities and government. Communities see housing development as a threat.

Cecilia knows that the old thinking will not solve the problems that it has created itself. That is what all her predecessors as housing minister found, too late. She needs to take a completely different approach.

It is coming up to six months since Cecilia was appointed housing minister. The system is as constipated as ever. Budgets have been slashed even further. Cecilia's department is being told to do more with less. She has to think differently and act differently, now.

CECILIA THINKS UPSIDE DOWN

Cecilia's new special adviser hears about a submission to the New Ideas for Housing competition called London FABRICation. This is something she should look at, he tells her. He has also heard about the London Popular Home Initiative through a colleague at City Hall. Cecilia reads about two proposals by London-based architects for new ways of building in some of the capital's already developed suburbs. Supurbia, proposed by the architectural practice HTA Design, is a strategy for intensifying the three-quarters of a million privately owned semidetached houses in outer London. It envisages the use of 'plot passports', documents that set out a list of redevelopment options available to the householders in a specific area, allowing them to extend or redevelop their property. *Semipermissive* is a strategy for intensifying London's suburbs proposed by the architects at Pollard Thomas Edwards. It would incentivise householders to become micro-developers. Cecilia finds the thinking behind both these proposals convincing.

She remembers hearing someone say that 'housing is not a problem to be solved, it is a potential to be realised'. She sees it as her job to realise this potential. She is determined to tackle the large national housebuilders' stranglehold on the industry. The market has to be opened up to much wider choice, allowing more people at every level to become involved in providing housing. This will include local contractors, small developers, self-builders and sweat equity (people contributing to the value of their home by their own manual labour). The government's role will be to facilitate this, allowing people freedoms that the present system stifles. The housing problem cannot be fixed by a few new policies: the system must be reformed.

Cecilia's team in the ministry prepares a plan of action. They recognise that the government can't do everything, and nor should it. First, they need to break down the full process into stages and find out where the government should put in its 20 per cent of effort in making the biggest impact at the earliest stages. To do this, they need to see the whole system as different levels of intervention, from the scale of a whole city and its neighbourhoods to the individual householder. This will identify where the government should lead and where others are more effective at doing so. A new agency will be set up: the Neighbourhood Enabling Agency (NEA). Its job will be to create the preconditions that will enable neighbourhoods to flourish from the bottom up. The agency will not be responsible for large-scale building projects. Instead it will focus on ensuring that the multiple actions of many small actors in the system are released.

'Focus on six' is one of the new agency's slogans, encouraging people to do things in multiples of no more than six. Many sixes add up to big changes. The NEA draws up new, open, responsive and collaborative protocols to allow this to happen. Cecilia's first instruction to the new agency is to stop selling public-sector land to the big housebuilders. Instead the agency works with all public bodies to create a land bank of small sites close to existing infrastructure. The priority is to create compact urbanism, so the agency will identify all remote brownfield sites and seek to trade them off for well-connected sites closer to existing settlements.

HOUSING IS NOT A PROBLEM TO BE SOLVED. HOUSING IS A POTENTIAL TO BE REALISED.

Using the principles of the Popular Home Initiative, the NEA ensures that all sites are subdivided using the universal lot concept. The lot becomes the NEA's unit of delivery. The agency can now release these to thousands of players, not just the few. The NEA establishes itself as the neighbourhood enabler in every local authority office. They draw up a parameter book of housing types, which are published on the government's Planning Portal. People adapt the house types to their needs, within a clearly defined set of rules. The agency sets up a choice matrix that enables local NEA offices to work with people to create a framework of options. Using local development orders, anyone who applies any of these choices using the parameter book with the universal lot is guaranteed planning consent.

The principle is rolled out to existing suburban development where development pressure has led to the building of ramshackle back-garden sheds used illegally for rental accomodation. Working with neighbourhood forums, the NEA identifies the potential for suburban neighbourhoods to be intensified. Anyone can replace their single home with three new terraced homes without applying for planning permission. The new arrangements allow instead for a more considered approach to intensifying them. The design of the new development varies in quality as architects and other designers get to grips with housing design. Gradually these suburbs begin to show the qualities that will lead them to become great neighbourhoods.

Cecilia convinces her government to think about transforming the overall system. Towns and cities are now seen as complex adaptive systems, not as mechanistic models. Urban professionals now think and act

differently. Citizens are actively engaged and civic leaders are inspired. Housing flourishes and neighbourhoods thrive. The crisis is now abating. Notwithstanding this, Cecilia sees the success of all her efforts in the following ways:

→ Breaking the system down into manageable levels means that her agency can create the preconditions for others to respond.
→ The housing market is flooded with opportunity, including many multiples of up to six. The opportunities are for many people, not just the few.
→ The small-scale, collaborative approach creates new opportunities to build social capital. Lively new urban neighbourhoods form. It is a scaleable solution that can be applied across the country. Innovation has returned to housing. People are learning by experimenting.
→ The government's new open standard for housing provides a common platform for construction across all scales. Innovation flourishes.
→ A common building code has been developed, based on open building standards and simple modular coordination for each housing type within the parameter book.
→ British Standards Institution approval has been sought and the common building code has been formally adopted as a common platform for all sectors.
→ The housebuilders have changed their purpose to become enabling developers, parcelling up land into universal lots and offering these to the wider market in the same way as government sites are offered.

If we are to release the potential for housing, we must challenge and reform the rigid command-and-control systems that inhibit people's ability to adapt their place to their needs. This depends on new forms of leadership that can work where top-down and bottom-up systems meet. We do not need to start again—we just need to begin balancing the roles and responsibilities of all people, building on their strengths. In some instances this means a far greater involvement by governments. In others cases, it means some simplifcation and streamlining to allow people to take greater responsibility in the system. Above all, this must never justify unbridled laissez-faire approaches and unprincipled deregulation.

—Cecilia H, MP, United Kingdom

800
600
1000
400
1200
200
1400
0
1600
kPa
WOODLANDS FIRE
WOODLANDS FIRE

TRANSFORMING AND ENABLING AGENCY

3.3

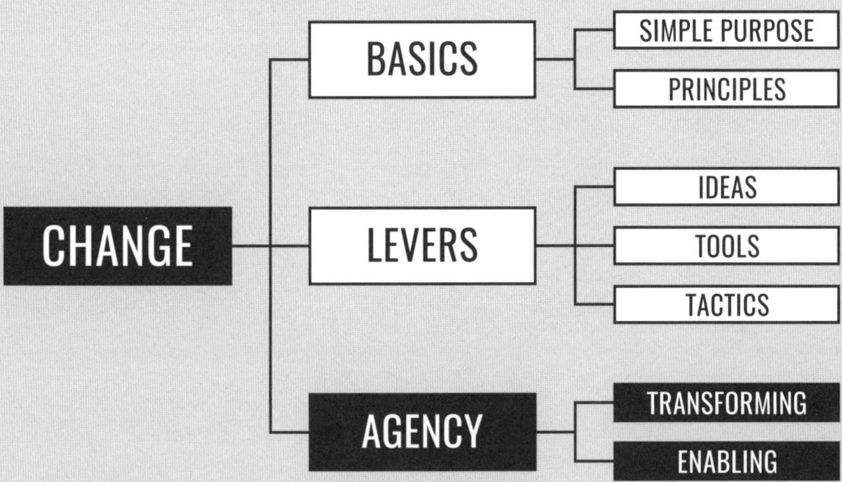

Delivering a government's transformational goal for building urban neighbourhoods, based on the 'Making Massive Small Change' manifesto on page 306, requires a government's systems to change. We suggest that government establishes two distinctive but closely interrelated change agencies, each working towards system change and accelerated delivery and both bound by a simple common purpose.

This approach, with some tailoring to specific contexts, should work in all countries (whether established or emerging) and in all sectors (whether formal or informal) in the global north and global south.

> **Agency** *NOUN*
>
> **the capacity of an actor to act and influence change in a given environment**
>
> **SYNONYMS**
> **authority, means, medium, channel, proxy, intermediary, go-between, mandate**

These agencies are deliberately kept separate for clear reasons. They require different mindsets, different rules of engagement, different hierarchies of responsibility and accountability, and different relationships within their national and local government leadership and their relevant departments. In an ideal world, these change agencies should be:

1 **A TRANSFORMATIONAL AGENCY**, whose purpose is to change the urban planning, design and development system into an integrated neighbourhood-based framework for action and to imbed the targets, trajectories and routines associated with this framework in nation-, metropolitan-, city- and town-wide leadership

2 **An ENABLING AGENCY**, which is a hands-on delivery agency whose sole purpose is to initiate and accelerate the development of urban neighbourhoods by delivering on the targets, trajectories and routines set out by the TRANSFORMATIONAL AGENCY (and the relevant authorities) in their integrated neighbourhood-based framework for collective action

A TRANSFORMATIONAL AGENCY

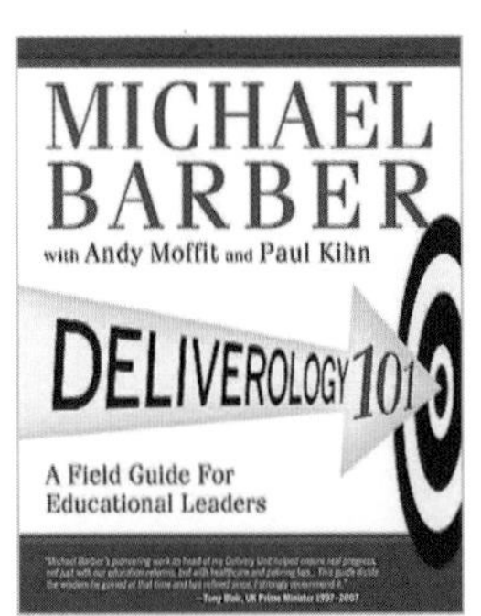

Sir Michael Barber, the author of *Deliverology*, makes a telling point: 'Don't depend on generic civil service reform because you don't have the time.' In other words, turning around the massive container ship of state, loaded with government's bloated policies, is incredibly difficult. The system is just too big to be agile. Turn too sharp, and it all topples over with disastrous consequences. More importantly, if you take on the whole system, you are doomed to fail, and besides, most politicians, schooled in their short-term thinking, will steer away from total revolution.

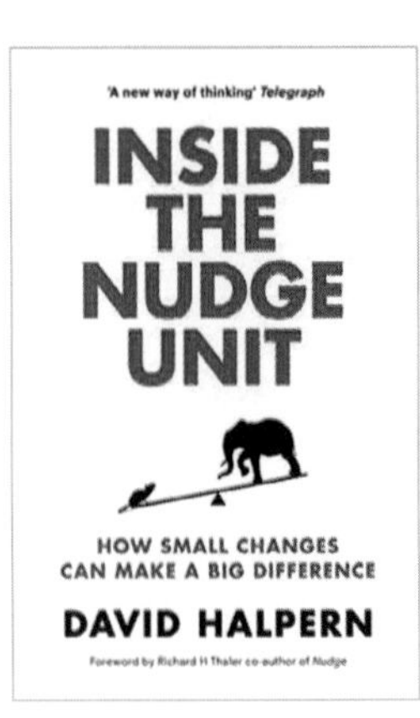

His solution is to create a small, dedicated unit, whose role is to constantly challenge performance and ask difficult questions, constantly pushing for faster progress, knowing full well that the tendency of any system is towards inertia. His solution is similar to a 'nudge' unit—as can be seen in David Halpern's book, *Inside the Nudge Unit*—where its role was in making progressive changes and 'fine-tuning the system'. This unit is not a delivery agency or project management group, which is short-term in nature, but is instead a permanent structure—operating as an extension of national and civic leadership. We have called it our transformation unit—TUNIT for short—a choice architecture agency.

A good example of this is the City Support Team, a dedicated unit within the National Treasury department in South Africa, whose role is to work with metropolitan and local authorities in realising urban change.

In our world, the TUNIT is tasked with delivering on the government's transformational goals and acting in a critical city support role. At the outset, it must embrace and embed the structure of the NEIGHBOURHOOD ENABLING MODEL—with its five enabling CONDITIONS and its development TOOLBOX—in every aspect of top-down system change in order to build a common language and platform for cross-sectoral collaboration that can be shared with all other agencies, including the Neighbourhood Enabling Agency. Once the structure is embedded in a clear framework for action, the new system can evolve as it learns by doing.

The TUNIT must operate at two levels:

1 **At the national level:** where it has a direct and interactive relationship with the top level of government leadership

2 **At the metropolitan, city or town level:** where it has a direct relationship with civic leadership

Barber points to three actions that we have adapted to focus on the transformation of national and local policy on urban neighbourhoods:

1 ASSEMBLE AN AGILE TEAM

The team should share the following key organisational and design attributes:

→ **Enabling leadership** should be derived from a respected full-time delivery leader who reports directly to the political head of the relevant government organisation, say, the Secretary of State for Neighbourhoods. Rather than exerting its authority, the delivery unit acts as an amplifier of the system leader's authority, providing a careful balance of support and challenge to those responsible for implementation.

→ **A limited size** will insure that the team is small enough to preserve flexibility, activate teamwork and promote vital group dynamics with a cohesive culture.

→ **Top talent should have five core competencies:** relationship management, problem-solving, analytical thinking, responsiveness to feedback and a delivery mindset (a 'can-do' attitude).

→ **The team should operate outside their system's line-management hierarchy.** This independence will allow the unit to be a 'critical friend' that delivers difficult messages but also sustains trust and credibility with all the actors in the system.

2 SET A FRAMEWORK FOR ACTION

Effective public-sector system reform means focussing on the most critical outcomes and avoiding 'firefighting' and involves the following tools:

→ **Simple targets** are a prioritised set of measurable, ambitious and time-bound goals. Reform must include setting targets, brokering negotiations with relevant public-sector agencies and ensuring prominence of these targets for the entire public-sector system.

→ **Realisable trajectories** are projected progressions towards these targets that create a tight link between planned interventions and expected outcomes. Trajectories serve as a tool for understanding a system's progress towards its targets and allow for meaningful debate as to whether targets are both ambitious and realistic.

According to Barber, two approaches can be used to help ground targets and measure trajectories:

→ **Benchmarks,** through historical comparisons, internal and external peer comparisons

→ **Interventions,** which require having some evidence of the impact of particular interventions and extrapolating these to the whole system

3 DEVELOP SIMPLE ROUTINES

One of the most essential functions of the TUNIT is to establish and maintain routines—regularly scheduled and structured opportunities for the system leader and implementation agencies to review performance and make decisions. Routines work because they create deadlines, which in turn creates a sense of urgency.

Barber recommends three distinct routines that vary in frequency, audience, format and type and depth of information they provide:

→ **Monthly updates** allow for agencies to engage in timely problem solving and course correction.

→ **Quarterly stocktakes** are used to demonstrate the civic leader's commitment to the delivery agenda and allow the system head to hold individuals accountable for progress on targets, discuss options and gain agreement on action needed. They also allow for best practices to be shared, successes to be celebrated and new protocols to be developed.

→ **Annual reviews** are in-depth assessments on the status of all the system's priority areas. These reviews allow civic leaders to compare progress across priorities, identify actions for relevant departments, and reassess the allocation of resources and attention based on each priority areas' need and distance to targets.

4 POST-IMPLEMENTATION REVIEW

After implementing system change, the post-implementation review phase will do the following:

→ Determine whether the targets and trajectories of the new system have been met; if the new system is running differently from the proposed objectives, the problems need to be determined, and further modifications to the new system should be carried out. This is to make sure that the new system is capable of doing the tasks it is designed for.

→ Ensure that the users are using the system correctly and routines are being adhered to; the reports should fulfil their purposes.

→ Make sure the system is maintainable and flexible; further improvement and additional features to the new system can be done based on the review.

→ Determine the flaws in the development process so that future systems can be improved, and users can avoid making the same mistakes again.

A nudge is any aspect of the choice architecture that alters people's behaviour in a predictable way without forbidding any options

—Richard Thaler

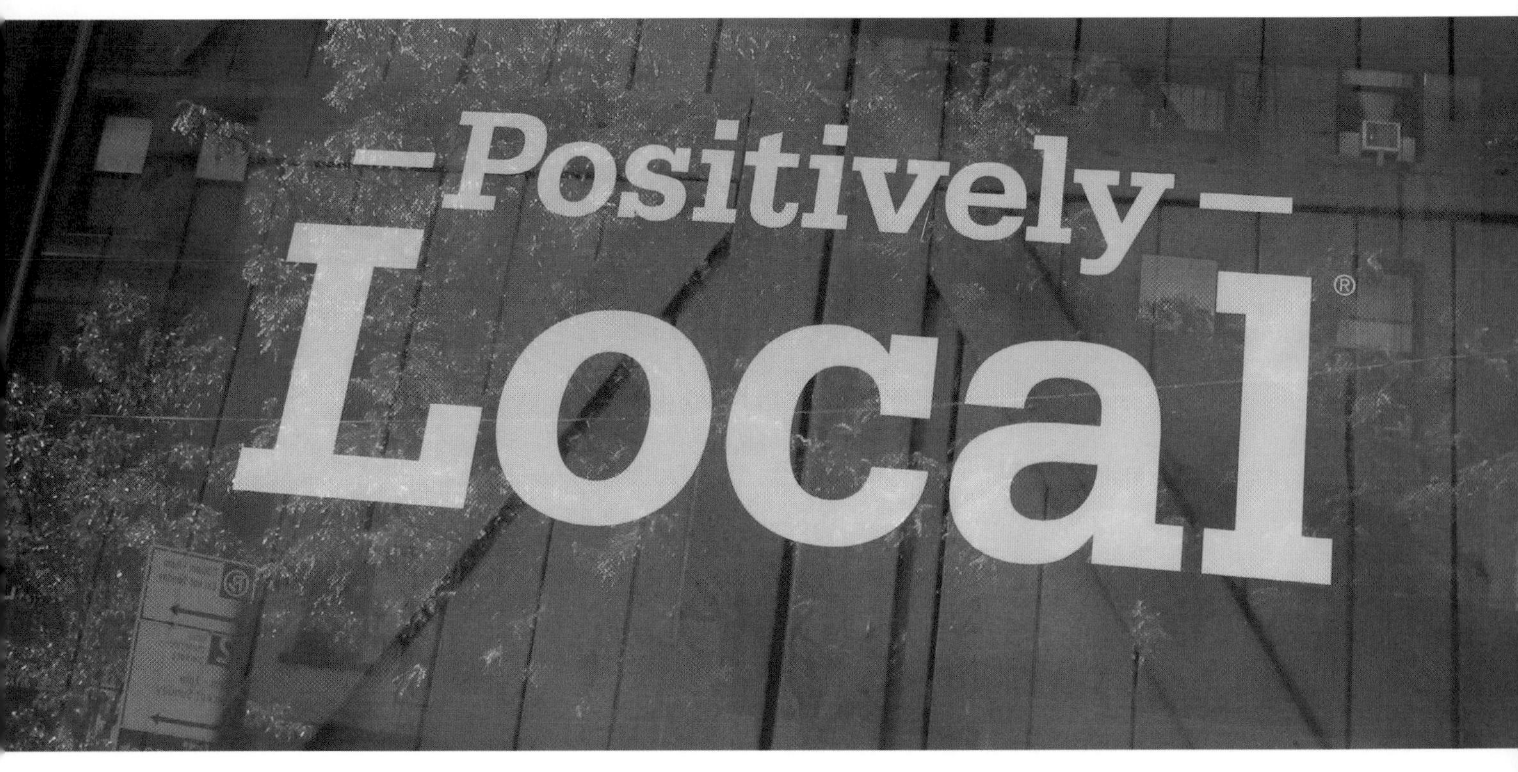

A NEIGHBOURHOOD ENABLING AGENCY

The concept of a neighbourhood enabling agency is one of a highly focussed, committed and agile organisation empowered by national and local government to make things happen. Its purpose is to deliver on the government's transformational goals for neighbourhoods within the framework for action set out at the national scale by the TUNIT and evolved locally to work best.

Its activities are characterised by the following:

- → It acts at the interface between government and people at all scales of neighbourhood formation.
- → It facilitates the formation of open, responsive and collaborative urban environments that build compact urbanism with high social capital.
- → It cuts away red tape and shows pathways to progress—promoting action, demonstrating by example and sharing this experience.
- → It creates essential enabling conditions for individual and collective response by active citizens.
- → It ensures that those active citizens have the tools, resources and authority to implement change.
- → It is 'can do' and 'will do'.

ROWING, STEERING AND CHEERING

The NEIGHBOURHOOD ENABLING AGENCY (NEA) does not do everything (nor should it). It plays different roles in different aspects of the enabling CONDITIONS outlined in the NEIGHBOURHOOD ENABLING MODEL, where the different levels move progressively from the roles of government to those of people. These roles can be seen as 'rowing' (actively implementing), 'steering' (directing and coordinating action by others) and 'cheering' (encouraging others to take responsibility).

Government's primary role lies in intervening early to ensure the first three enabling CONDITIONS—what we call the INVISIBLE CHASSIS—are effected. As the government progresses through the different levels of the NEIGHBOURHOOD ENABLING MODEL, its role diminishes, but this is counteracted by an increasing role of people in the later levels of the model.

The respective roles could work to complement each other in the following ways:

1 **On NETWORKS [rowing]:** Government is best placed to plan, design and develop all aspects relating to this enabling condition, although they could work with larger landowners who

are interested in providing an enabling developer role. This role could include providing or procuring the street networks, infrastructure systems and integration of services at the neighbourhood scale. Here the actions of the NEA are to act in an area-based role coordinating national and local government service functions to achieve an integrated approach to structural and infrastructural development.

2 **On BLOCKS [rowing/steering]:** Government is best placed to coordinate the delivery of development land and parcel it up to the local market. This role could include the acquisition of land and release of public-owned land to achieve an integrated and coherent urban fabric. Government could also work in partnership with private land developers to deliver on this integration and coherence. This role could also include working with existing homeowners in opening up new backland to intensify suburbs.

3 **On PLATFORMS [steering]:** Government provides a leadership role in steering the building industry and supply chains towards open building approaches. This role could include the design, specification and procurement of building structure from larger contractors best equipped to deliver major structural solutions; or with the local 'shack-building' industry in informal settlements; or developing starter packs—accelerator sites, basic service cores and corner buildings.

4 **On DEFAULTS [steering/cheering]:** Government plays a 'seeding' role in setting up the framework of structured choices through the development of a starter parameter book. This is further developed by people in response to their experience. Government helps to share this innovation and evolution with the wider community.

5 **On ACTIVATORS [cheering]:** Government can provide a starter catalogue of potential catalysts to trigger community action but is not best placed to take a significant role in developing these further. People are best suited to experiment, innovate and learn by doing. Government can, however, assist in communicating these catalysts to a wider audience.

OPERATING AT DIFFERENT SCALES

The NEA must not be an arm's length government agency working at the regional scale. The team will be much more efficient embedded in local government where they can take on a full, area-based, integrated role that currently lies in the domain of the traditionally siloed service departments. Ideally, the NEA should operate at three scales but in only two levels of governance. These are:

1 **Nation** (central government)

2 **Metropolitan, city or town** (local government)

3 **Neighbourhood** (agency)

AT NATIONAL SCALE

Here it acts as the top level of national government:

→ It provides an umbrella organisation for agents working at metropolitan-, city- or town-wide scale, assisting in the embedding, application and evolution of the elements of the NEIGHBOURHOOD ENABLING MODEL.

→ It plays a central coordinating role for budgets, allocation of resources and national-level infrastructure projects.

→ It plays a critical role in coordinating the assembly and release of publicly owned land for purposes identified for neighbourhood development.

→ It provides a common platform that collects experiences, initiates action-based research, works closely with the building industry, monitors and reviews successes and failures, develops best practice and shares this with others.

→ It plays an essential role in developing urban policy and protocols to scale up and improve neighbourhood development at all levels.

→ It provides the interface between the national TUNIT and local governments to review targets, trajectories and routines and take any necessary remedial action.

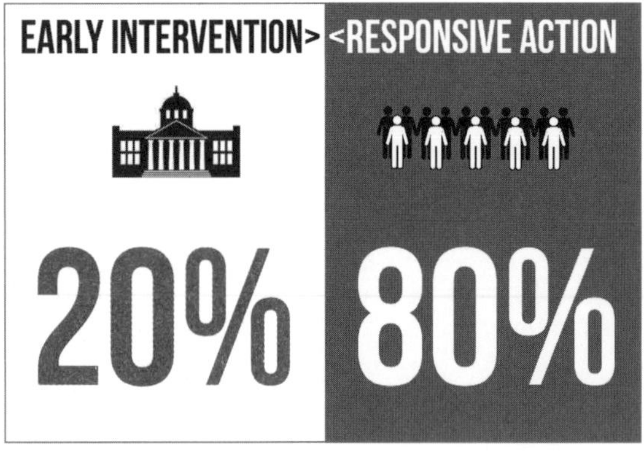

The primary mission of the NEA *is to identify and implement early interventions that will generate a massive responsive action from the bottom-up.*

—The Secretary of State for Neighbourhoods

AT METROPOLITAN, CITY OR TOWN SCALE

Here the NEA operates under the delegated authority of local government:

→ It provides an umbrella organisation for agents acting in the field that assists in the embedding, application and evolution of the structural elements of the NEIGHBOURHOOD ENABLING MODEL.

→ It plays a coordinating role for budgets, allocation of resources and local level infrastructure projects, and a lead role in the local support network of other local government departments.

→ It plays an area-based project role on thematic issues such as new neighbourhood extensions, suburban intensification and estate regeneration.

→ It plays an active role, working with other local government agencies, in planning, procuring and delivering NETWORKS as the precursor to viable neighbourhood development.

→ It plays a critical role in coordinating the assembly and release of publicly owned land for purposes identified for neighbourhood development at the local level. This includes planning, designing and delivering urban BLOCKS ready for release to individual, collective or institutional developers.

→ It plays an enabling development role to ensure implementation or procurement of the necessary services infrastructure.

→ It provides an interface with the local building industry and supply chains to provide and develop PLATFORMS for open building systems that work for all sectors.

AT NEIGHBOURHOOD SCALE

Here the NEA acts as a local agent of the metropolitan, city or town authorities working on the ground in local neighbourhood offices:

→ It provides a direct interface between local government, civic leadership and active citizens providing the essential citizen engagement role. This means it is the first point of contact with residents engaged in new urban development programmes or neighbourhood intensification.

→ It provides a close working relationship with urban professionals, building industry bodies, local government service departments, non-governmental organisations and active citizen groups on the application and development of the TOOLBOX.

→ It plays an active role in releasing and parcelling new development land using the UNIVERSAL LOT concept. This could also include working with street committees on opening up access to the rear of properties to facilitate backland development or working with housing estate communities on restructuring an area to deliver effective transformation.

→ It plays a direct and early role in building flexible-use corner buildings that benchmark development in the area. These buildings could act as local community hubs and accommodate such uses as meeting spaces, local enterprise space, secure storage, short-term accommodation, starter schools or daycares centres. These spaces could evolve into a range of uses, including local shopping, workspace, community infrastructure or affordable housing, and change as the neighbourhood matures.

- → It provides a facilitation role in helping people in the early stages of building or procuring their housing by providing short-term accommodation during the construction process, easy access to cheap (or recycled) building materials through bulk-buying deals and project management assistance.

- → It provides a technical assistance role by giving advice to prospective homebuilders, liaisoning with the local construction industry, maintaining lists of suppliers, helping with plan drawing and permissions, developing parameter book housing types and troubleshooting.

- → It plays an initiation role for new area-based projects by providing a range of demonstrator or starter projects to generate urban change. This role could include the procurement of serviced land, building structures (such as accelerator sites) and show homes.

- → It plays an interim role, in the case of unserviced lots, coordinating water supply and waste removal before second-phase infrastructure development. Here they work with local people and suppliers and install essential services, using this process to build local social capital and capacity.

- → It plays an essential role in communicating, developing and using ACTIVATORS to facilitate local community interaction. This role includes promoting self-organisation and collective action.

- → It plays an enabling role in neighbourhood management, participatory budgeting and fostering local democracy during the transformation process that could evolve into a more permanent structure as the neighbourhood matures.

- → It plays a direct role in managing budgets, reviewing targets and trajectories, recalibrating routines, monitoring local feedback on projects and sharing best practices and innovations.

The principles outlined above could be applied to any place and modified to suit local circumstances. They provide a template that can be adopted, adapted or restructured.

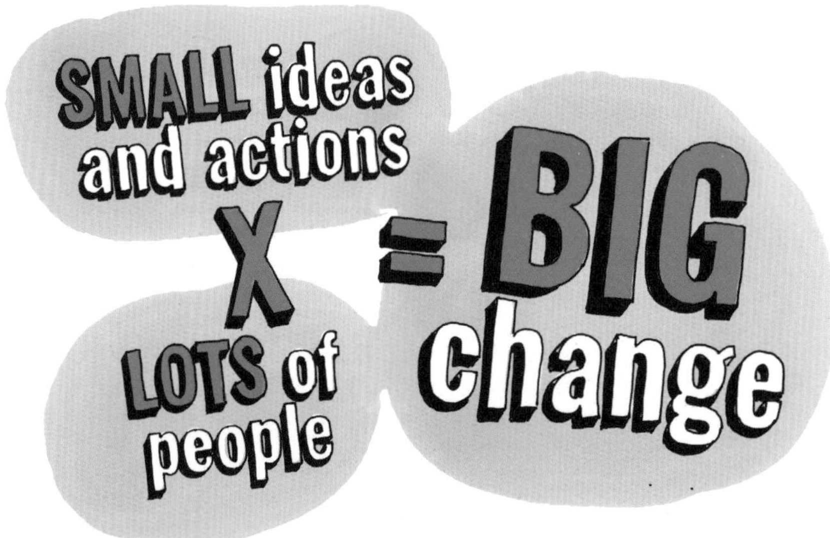

[the beginning, not the end]

EPILOGUE

BAKERI
est. 2009
FLOUR

This book is just the start and not the end. It can never cover the full range of complexity that neighbourhoods throw up. It is merely a glimpse into the sense of the possible. We identify the basic ingredients, show how they work together, and provide a way of bringing them together. The proof is in the baking. It will get better.

Every day new stories spring to mind. New books emerge and new networks spread new messages. New words of encouragement follow new ideas that are expounded by new difference-makers. The real temptation is to carry on writing, but in reality, it is important to draw this to an end at this stage and put this compendium out there for others to respond.

The inspirational case studies, the imaginary stories, the interesting essays and the hypothetical scenarios in this book are intended to demonstrate a possible way forward only. Hopefully they will prompt new ideas and new actions by others.

The most important aspect of this compendium lies in the organising of complex concepts into a clear and coherent structure. This means we do not have to go back to first principles—we can now build on solid foundations. Treat this as a 'line in the sand'. It provides a good boundary, but it does not mean that it can't be crossed. Cross it for a good reason. We welcome your open/adaptive, responsive and collaborative action and reactions.

A certain amount of opposition is a great help to man. Kites rise against, not with, the wind.

—Lewis Mumford

TEN THINGS TO DO

Success at system change demands more. Here is a final set of reminders. There will always be more.

1 Concentrate on the early conditions that give rise to successful neighbourhoods and build small catalytic projects that initiate action and stimulate new models for development.

2 Build an enabling form of civic leadership that cuts red tape and makes things happen.

3 Focus on the whole place, not its parts. It is easy to see things in isolation and treat them accordingly. Stop the dominant influence of single-focussed actions. Single-focussed actions can prevent good urbanism at the outset.

4 Foster inclusivity in the best traditions of urbanity, and build community in all its forms. Everything must be directed to helping people realise their dreams. Give them every support in this process.

5 Promote long-life, loose-fit solutions for housing for everyone, in all places and at any stage of life.

6 Provide a set of considered, structured choices that will evolve within the defined constraints and get better as we learn more.

7 Balance the spectrum of housing players to include the individual, the collective and the institutional. Open up many fronts and don't dwell on the big guys alone.

8 Derisk public investment by focussing on many small players; provide simple rules for engagement; and recognise that if a few fail, we can rapidly learn from our experience and make suitable changes.

9 Manage in the present. Use rapid and continuous feedback to assess the effectiveness of outcomes and make many small changes as needed.

10 Build trust and ask for help. Civilisation rests on the fact that most people do the right thing most of the time.

TEN THINGS TO NOT DO

1. Don't overconstrain. Focus on creating negotiable boundaries within which creativity, innovation and responsive action will flourish.

2. Don't be lured by the 'megaproject' as a cure-all. Recognise that megaprojects inevitablly fail to solve the needs of the community, and undermine social integration, financial sustainability and economic growth.

3. Don't be caught in the headlights of big numbers. Just focus on many small actions and see how quickly they add up to big numbers.

4. Don't impose restrictive rules and deterministic tools that stifle response. Sometimes unpredictable outcomes are better than we could ever imagine. Let people discover their solutions.

5. Don't be afraid to experiment. Try and try again. Many small experiments, by many actors, are more likely to find us many viable solutions.

6. Don't be afraid to fail. Recognise failure as an essential component of learning. It is essential to fostering a climate of innovation.

7. Don't see housing as a problem to be solved; see it as a potential to be realised.

8. Don't see 'good design' as the single conquering solution. It matters only as part of the system that promotes evolutionary design within clear constraints. This process is not just about design from first principles.

9. Don't be swayed by the big guys. They will always convince you that they can solve the problem. They never have.

10. Don't rush. This call is for a paradigm shift. It is not easy, but there is no alternative. Things take time to bed down. Sometimes time is the best tool we have.

STANDING ON THE SHOULDERS OF GIANTS

ESSENTIAL READING LIST

The inspiration for this work comes from some of our greatest urban thinkers whose thinking was ahead of their time. If committed urbanists read no more than these twelve books—viewing them as a collective body of work—they will be in a far, far better place.

1. Christopher Alexander, in his book *A New Theory of Urban Design*, points to seven principles for generative urbanism, showing how people have always pulled the order of their world from their own being.

2. Kirkpatrick Sale's *Human Scale Revisited: A New Look at the Classic Case for a Decentralist Future* carefully argues for bringing human endeavours back to scales we can comprehend and manage—whether in our built environments, politics or business.

3. Jane Jacobs, in her seminal work *The Death and Life of Great American Cities*, introduces the concept of organising complexity, advocating for generators of diversity to build urban neighbourhoods.

4. Lewis Mumford in *The City in History* not only deals with urban theories but studies civilisation itself, through narratives where culture is not usurped by technology but rather thrives on it.

5. Nabeel Hamdi's book *Small Change: The Art and Practice and the Limits of Planning in Cities* makes a compelling argument for the ingenuity of the improvisers and the long-term, large-scale effectiveness of many small-scale actions in urban development.

6. David Fleming's masterpiece, *Lean Logic: A Dictionary for the Future and How to Survive It*, is a dictionary unlike any other, stimulating exploration of fields as diverse as culture, history, science, art, logic, ethics, myth, economics and anthropology.

7. Leopold Kohr, in *The Breakdown of Nations*, shows why all bureaucratic planning is doomed to fail, protesting the 'cult of bigness' and promoting the concept of human scale and small community life.

8. John Habraken's book *Supports: An Alternative to Mass Housing* promotes architecture of 'lively variety' through insights in the field of user participation in mass housing, the integration of users and residents into the design process.

9. John F. C. Turner's influential work, *Freedom to Build: Dweller Control of the Housing Process*, argues that governments alone should not try to tackle housing problems but should give autonomy to urban dwellers to enable them to solve their own problems.

10. E. F. Schumacher's *Small Is Beautiful: A Study of Economics as if People Mattered* introduces his philosophy of 'enoughness', championing small, appropriate systems that empower people more, in contrast with phrases such as 'bigger is better'.

11. Ivan Illich, in *Deschooling Society*, provides us with a way of looking at all our formal institutions, positing self-directed education, supported by intentional social relations in fluid, informal arrangements.

12. Marshall McLuhan's *The Medium is the Massage* sounds the alarm with its one-liners and quick soundbites, showing how extensions of mankind, especially technologies, leave our urban society diminished not enriched.

All of these theorists flew against the wind. Their messages came at a time when few listened. Their time is now.

A certain amount of opposition is a great help to a man. Kites rise against, not with, the wind.

—Lewis Mumford

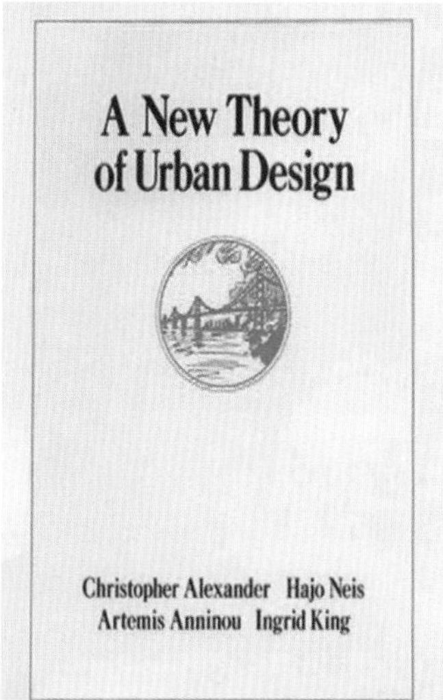
A New Theory
of Urban Design
Christopher Alexander Hajo Neis
Artemis Anninou Ingrid King

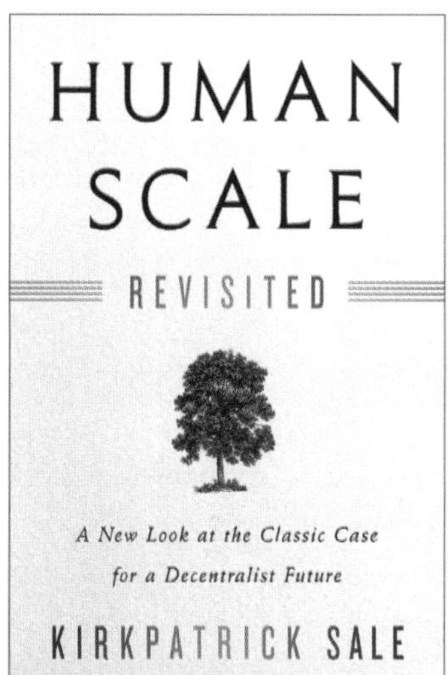
HUMAN
SCALE
REVISITED
A New Look at the Classic Case
for a Decentralist Future
KIRKPATRICK SALE

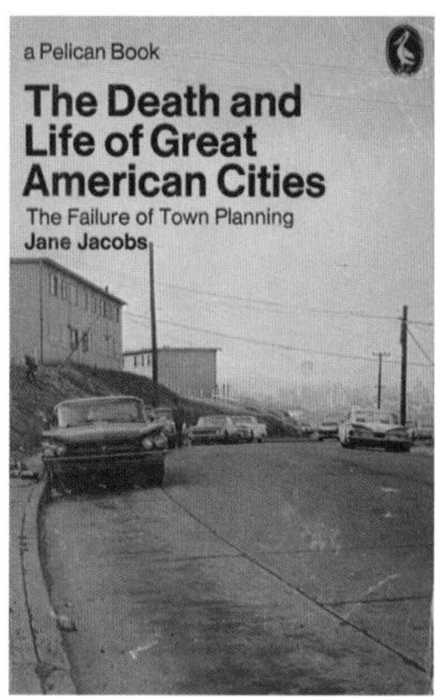
a Pelican Book
The Death and
Life of Great
American Cities
The Failure of Town Planning
Jane Jacobs

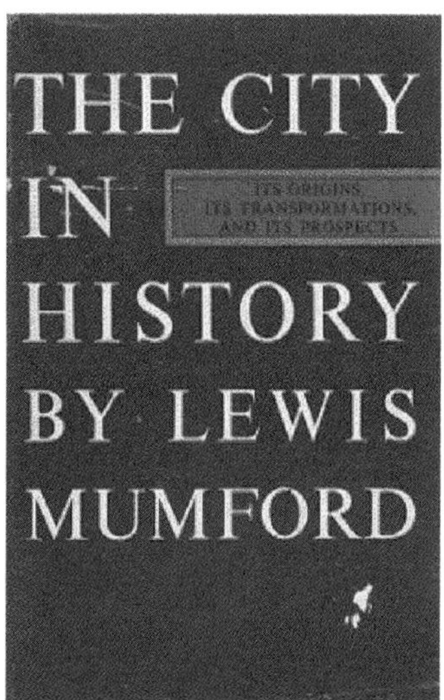
THE CITY
IN
ITS ORIGINS, ITS TRANSFORMATIONS, AND ITS PROSPECTS
HISTORY
BY LEWIS
MUMFORD

Small
Change
About the art of practice
and the limits of planning
in cities
Nabeel Hamdi

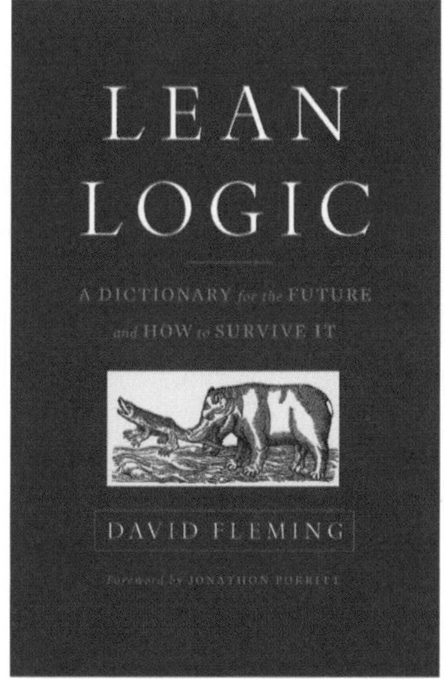
LEAN
LOGIC
A DICTIONARY for the FUTURE
and HOW to SURVIVE IT
DAVID FLEMING

"A teacher from whom
I have learned more than from anyone else."
—E.F. Schumacher, author of Small Is Beautiful
LEOPOLD KOHR
The Breakdown of Nations
With a new Afterword by the Author
and Foreword by Kirkpatrick Sale

HABRAKEN
SUPPORTS

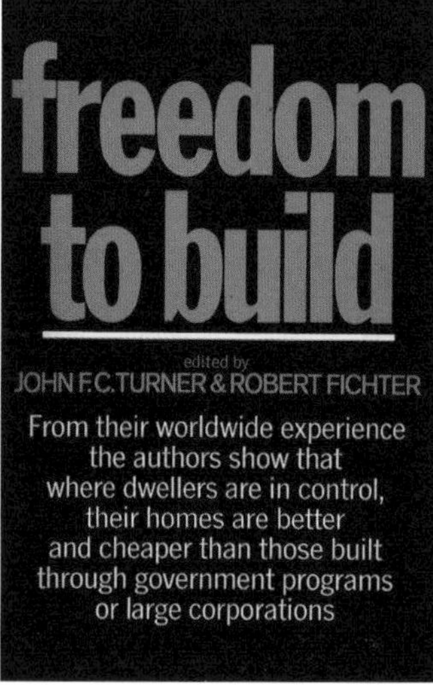
freedom
to build
edited by
JOHN F.C.TURNER & ROBERT FICHTER
From their worldwide experience
the authors show that
where dwellers are in control,
their homes are better
and cheaper than those built
through government programs
or large corporations

ABACUS
E.F. Schumacher
Small
is Beautiful
A STUDY OF ECONOMICS
AS IF PEOPLE MATTERED

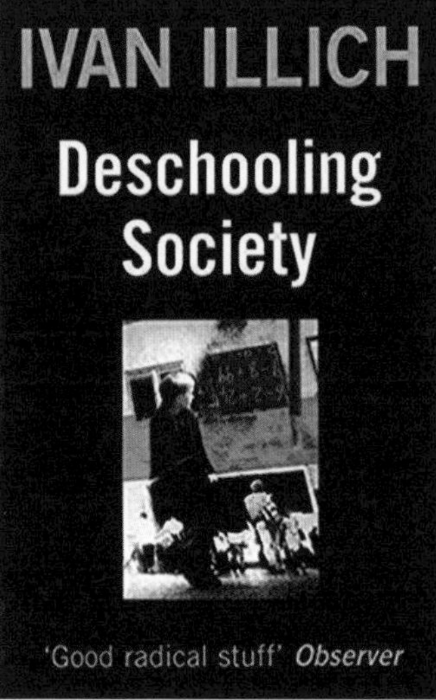
IVAN ILLICH
Deschooling
Society
'Good radical stuff' Observer

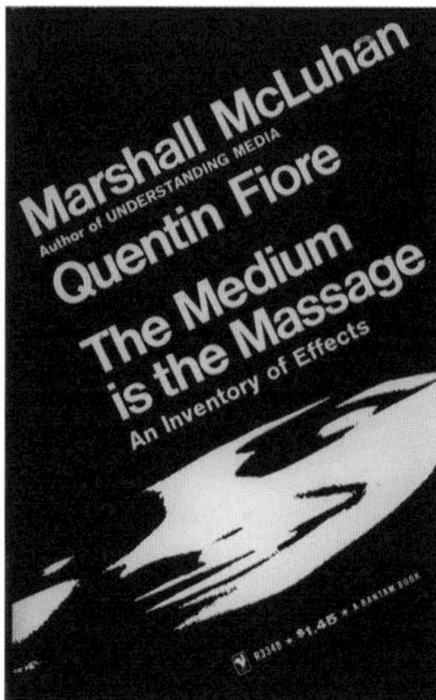
Marshall McLuhan
Author of UNDERSTANDING MEDIA
Quentin Fiore
The Medium
is the Massage
An Inventory of Effects

THE FINAL WORD

RSA

21st century enlightenment

Architecture+DesignScotland

THE PROJECT

The Massive Small project has evolved from small beginnings. It has been developed through a built environment research fellowship funded by the Royal Commission for the Exhibition of 1851 and hosted by the Centre for Advanced Spatial Analysis (CASA) at the University College London, to where it is today— a thriving community of interest. The focus of Massive Small is on what the 'new, new normal' for compact urbanism might look like in an increasingly complex world, and how our top-down systems of government can evolve to harness the potential of huge bottom-up community action. It has a simple purpose—to build a better urban society.

The project is run by Smart Urbanism, a London-based urban research and development collaborative that curates the popular Smart Urbanism (Massive Small) LinkedIn group. Established in 2009 as an independent social business and a short-life organisation, Smart Urbanism has access to an international network of enlightened urbanists, civic leaders and academic institutions. The Massive Small project aims to:

- → Show how people who shape cities can think and act differently to achieve better urban outcomes
- → Evolve new ideas, tools and tactics for delivering good urbanism by treating cities and their neighbourhoods as complex adaptive systems
- → Show how to create the initial conditions that will enable people to start small and then become increasingly effective in shaping their own urban environments
- → Show governments practical alternatives to inflexible, top-down planning, design and development systems at a time where they need to do more with less

The Massive Small project is now hosted by the Geovation Hub at the United Kingdom government's Urban Innovation Centre in London, and has established valuable links with other international organisations.

THE AUTHOR

Kelvin Campbell is a collaborative urbanist and avid writer. He is the chair of Smart Urbanism and the Massive Small Collective. After founding and leading Urban Initiatives—a successful urban planning and design practice—for over two decades, he decided to step aside and take a different perspective on urbanism, something he is passionate about.

Former visiting professor in urban design at the University of Westminster and chairman of the Urban Design Group, he is now honorary professor at the Centre for Advanced Spatial Analysis at the Bartlett, University College London, and teaches in the Masters in Sustainable Urban Development post-graduate progreamme at the University of Oxford.

In 2013, he received the Urban Design Group's Lifetime Achievement Award for his contribution to the profession and was later awarded the Built Environment Fellowship by the Royal Commission for the Exhibition of 1851.

Kelvin was lead author with Rob Cowan on *By Design: Urban Design in the Planning System*, the UK government's policy guidance on good urbanism. Together they have collaborated on and published numerous books and polemics including, *The Cities Design Forgot, The Connected City, The Councillor's Guide to Urban Design, Start with the Park: A Guide to Creating Sustainable Urban Green Spaces, Re:Urbanism: A Challenge to the Urban Summit*, and *The Radical Incrementalist: How to Build Urban Society in 12 Lessons*. Kelvin is also the author of *Massive Small: The Operating Programme for Smart Urbanism*, which is the beta version of this book.

Kelvin's philosophy has been shaped by his research background and his early experience in the study of informal settlements; tempered by his extensive practical experience in the planning, design and development of major urban design strategies worldwide; and, informed by his pursuit of alternative thinking about urbanism through education, professional practice and social concern.

THE INSPIRATION

> *If you are not part of the solution, you are probably part of the problem.*
>
> — Henry J Tillman

As an urban designer leading a great practice with some great people, we tried our best. We worked on amazing projects with some amazing people; we did some good things; and we won some good awards, but it wasn't good enough. We weren't making the world a better place. We were part of the problem.

Armed with the qualities of a seasoned contrarian and a rational optimist, I am a now a constructive activist operating outside the mainstream. I am also part of something far greater than someone just swimming against the tide. I am part of a collective body of people who are on a common path to show a different way. Good people have encouraged me to take Massive Small beyond being a good idea and make sure it can happen. That is what I am trying to do in this compendium. But it is a start, not an end.

This book is inspired by many, especially those above; those who gave us insight into their work on the cities as complex adaptive systems; those who supported the project; those who helped bring this book to light; and those whose actions and words gave us strength to carry on.

The Massive Small Compendium is dedicated to all those who are trying to make the world a better place, often against the odds—the millions of good people worldwide who struggle every day to house their families; to get on with life; to improve their neighbourhoods; to think outside the box; and to act as good citizens, civic leaders and urban professionals.

Sadly as we publish this book, my greatest inspiration, Christopher Alexander, is not well. I know that he would welcome this book as testament to his efforts. So will those other greats—Jane Jacobs, Lewis Mumford—as testament to theirs.

THE ACKNOWLEDGMENTS

My sincere gratitude goes to the Royal Commission for the Exhibition of 1851 and Architecture and Design Scotland, who provided financial support; to Mike Batty at the Centre for Advanced Spatial Analysis at University College London, who gave academic guidance; to Alan Baxter and the Geovation Hub for providing us with managed workspace; to the Royal Society of Arts and the Impact Hub for crowdfunding support; and to Kickstarter for giving us such an exciting ride.

We could not have done this without our Smart Urbanism LinkedIn community, who let us use their networks; our international volunteers (seen above), who spread the word; our endorsers of the Massive Small Declaration, who gave us weight; and our great Kickstarter backers, who gave us huge confidence, especially Larry Rosner from The Society Project and Priya Prakash of Design for Social Change (D4SC).

My special thanks go to Rob Cowan, a long-term collaborator and good friend; to Chris Freeman of Conduct Design in Berlin for his graphic design sensibilities; to Dan Dubowitz, our creative director; and to my son and operations director, Andrew Campbell, who developed the Massive Small Declaration, and produced many of the 3D graphics in this book. Further thanks goes to my colleagues at Urban Initiatives Studio, Urban Movement and all those who have remained good friends from the early days—Nicolas Baumann, Dan Hill, Diarmaid Lawlor, Scott Adams, Darshana Chauhan, to name a few. Thank you all for your sustained support over the years.

My sincere thanks also goes to Margo Baldwin of Chelsea Green Publishing, who gave a fervent vote of confidence in publishing this book; to Rose Baldwin who introduced me to Margo; and to Pati Stone, production director for Chelsea Green, in marshalling this book to the bookshelves.

Finally my deepest respect and gratitude go to my long-suffering wife, Louise, and my mother, Shirley. Both kept me fed, watered and content with life.

— Kelvin Campbell, 2018

THE SOCIETY PROJECT .ORG

Alan Baxter INTEGRATED DESIGN

IMAGE CREDITS

Unless otherwise noted, all photographs and illustrations are copyright © 2018 by Kelvin Campbell.

10 Courtesy Abbeville Institute: Leopold Kohr

13 [TL] Courtesy Piet Van Meerbeek (auto-suffisance.blogspot.be), Selfcity, Brussels
[TR] Courtesy UN-Habitat: Nabeel Hamdi

14–15 Courtesy Darshana Gothi Chauhan (University of Westminster) and National Association of Students of Architecture (India): Westminster Design Competition (South Asia)

17 Courtesy Hank Dittmar, Project for Lean Urbanism (leanurbanism.org)

22 Courtesy Jonathan Liebman, Propertuity, Maboneng, Johannesburg, South Africa : The Unfinished City Exhibition

28–29 Courtesy © Ross Fraser McLean Photography (facebook.com/RossFraserMcLean): La Estatua Monumental de José María Morelos, Isla de Janitzio, Mexico 2014

40–41 Courtesy Julia King (julia-king.com): Incremental housing in Savda Ghevra, Delhi

45 Courtesy Future City Cape Town (futurecapetown.com): Bad urban planning

48 [BL] Pixel Embargo / Shutterstock.com: Clenched fist

48–49 iStock.com/inok: Computer motherboard

52 Courtesy Creative Commons: Informal settlement, Mumbai

53 trekandshoot / Shutterstock.com: Suburban housing tract

54 [TR] Courtesy John Turner, photograph by Wolfgang Schmidt

56 Courtesy Academy of Urbanism

60 marekuliasz /Shutterstock.com: Same old thinking, same old results

61 [L] Courtesy Wikipedia: Ebenezer Howard's three magnets
[R] Courtesy Wikipedia: Voisin plan model, Paris

65 Courtesy Rakhi Mehra and Marco Ferrario, mHS CITY LAB: Incremental Development

66 Courtesy Indian Express: Connaught Place, Delhi

68 Alexey Laputin / Shutterstock.com: Graphic equalizer

69 Courtesy Wikipedia: Frederick Douglass, circa 1879

72 Courtesy Wikimedia Commons: *Creation of Adam* by Michelangelo

75 Charles Harker / Shutterstock.com: Guatemala City favela type housing near downtown

78–79 iStock.com/anactor: One-way sign

80 iStock.com/kadmy: Indian monk sadhu

85 [T] EG Focus, Creative Commons: Construction of Olympic Park, London
[B] © Jörg Zägel, Wikimedia Commons: Townhouses on Caroline-Von-Humboldt-Weg in Berlin, Mitte

91 [BL] Stephen Rees / Shutterstock.com: Line in sand
[BR] Courtesy Ohio State University: Keynote speaker Donald Sull at COE Summit 2017

95 sleaze / Superstock.com: Citizens count

99 "Protect forests like babies" poster, artist unknown

105 [TR] iStock.com/joxxxxjo: Adaptor plugs
[BL] iStock.com: Rubber stamps

106 Frank Lennon / Getty Images: Jane Jacobs

112 Courtesy Jason Roberts, Better Block Foundation: Reclaimed street

117 Courtesy NASA Goddard Space Centre Visualization Analysis Lab: Phoenix, Arizona

118 Courtesy Tim Stonor, Space Syntax: Map of London

119 Courtesy Nikos Salingaros - Adaptive Design Method: Pattern language and form language

120 Courtesy Google Earth: Florence, Italy

121 [TL] Courtesy Google Earth: Barcelona, Spain
[TM] ©Aerial Photography Solutions: Edinburgh New Town, Scotland
[TR] Courtesy Google Earth: Pink City, Jaipur, India
[BL] ©Hunter Photography: Savannah, Georgia
[BM] Courtesy Google Earth: Marylebone, London
[BR] Ekaterina Pokrovsky © 123RF.com: San Francisco, California

123 Courtesy Theo Deutinger Architects, Amsterdam (td-architects.eu): Grid city

126 [T] Courtesy Piere Grimal, *Roman Cities 1983*: Timgad, Algeria
[UM] Courtesy David Frandsen: Graaff-Reinet, South Africa
[LM] Iakov Filimonov © 123RF.com: Eixample, Barcelona, Spain
[B] Courtesy ©Land Cap: Marylebone, London

127 [T] Courtesy Google Earth: Ediburgh New Town, Scotland
[UM] Yehuda Boltshauser © 123RF.com: Tel Aviv, Israel
[LM] Courtesy Google Earth: Woodstock, Cape Town
[B] Courtesy Vistara, The Architecture of India Exhibition: Pink City, Jaipur, India

133 [LM] Courtesy Wikimedia Commons: Paris Boulevards
[B] DR Travel Photo / Shutterstock.com: Jaipur Avenue

134 [UM] Courtesy Eurarch, Wikimedia Commons: Dutch *woonerf*
[B] Courtesy 999 Photos: Melbourne, Australia

136 South African Protest Art (Source Unknown)

137 Courtesy Kempton Press: Tembisa, South Africa

148 [M] Courtesy Jordi Sanchez-Cuenca, Polis: Ecatepec de Morelos, Mexico City

149 Courtesy Graziano Gasparini: First map of Caracas, 1578

150 Courtesy Cris Toala Olivares, Iamsterdam: Amsterdam

151 Eric Nathan / Alamy Stock Photo: Woodstock, Cape Town, South Africa

152 Courtesy Vistara, The Architecture of India Exhibition: Nine Square Grid

153 [B] Courtesy Wikipedia Commons: Clarence Perry superblock

160 [L] Courtesy Etruxes Architecture, Graduate School of Design, Harvard University: Plan of Villa el Salvador, Lima

161 Klaus Ulrich Müller/ Alamy Stock Photo: Villa El Salvador, Lima, Peru
163 [B] Courtesy Google Earth: Savannah, Georgia
166 [T] Courtesy Jonathan Tarbatt: Homeruskwartier, Almere, Holland
168 Courtesy Nouvel Obs: Cite Balzac Vitry demolition, Paris
173 [T, ML] Courtesy Camiel van Noten: Macrolots strategy, his graduation project for Studio Brooklyn, ASRO KULeuven, 2012.
[BL, BR] Courtesy Scott Adams, HTA Architects : Supurbia, London
181 Courtesy Tom Bloxham, Urban Splash: Chimney Pots, Salford, Manchester, UK
183 Courtesy Ellen Curran: Venice Biennale
184 Courtesy Tom Bloxham, Urban Splash: 'hoUSe' project, New Islington, Manchester, UK
185 Courtesy Camiel van Noten: Macrolots strategy, his graduation project for Studio Brooklyn, ASRO KULeuven, 2012.
187 [B] Courtesy John Lyall Architects: The Mill, Ipswich, England
189 Courtesy Urban Think Tank: Empower Shack, Cape Town
193 Courtesy Nilay Karaköy, İlayda Genç, Cansu Nur Ürek, TED University 3rd year Architecture Students: Borneo Sporenburg Design Code study
194 [TR] Phant / Shutterstock.com: Barcelona Courtyard, Spain
195 Klaus Ulrich Müller/ Alamy Stock Photo: Villa El Salvador, Lima, Peru
196 [T] Courtesy Elemental Architects: Quinta Monroy Housing, Iquique, Chile
[B] Courtesy UNICEF: Informal settlement, Kibera, Nairobi
197 [TL] Courtesy Alistair Parvin, Wikihouse Foundation: Wikihouse principles
[TR] Courtesy Ashraf Hendricks/GroundUp News, Creative Commons: Shack reblocking, Cape Town, South Africa
200 [BL] iStock.com/YanC: A hand placing acupuncture pins on someone's skin
203 [T] Courtesy Cany Ash, Ash Sakula Architects: Caravanserai project, East London, UK
204 [TR] Courtesy Inderpaul Johar, Architecture 00: Scale Free Schools project
206 [BR] Courtesy Incremental Development Alliance: Workshop invite
214 Courtesy Derek Tynan, Group 91 Architects, Dublin: Making the Modern Street
215 [TR] pxhidalgo / 123RF.com: Jaipur, India
216 Courtesy Derek Tynan, Group 91 Architects, Dublin: Making the Modern Street, Examples of possibilities
217 Courtesy Christel, Bouwmeara Netherlands: New Leyden, Holland
218 [L, R] Courtesy Jonathan Tarbatt: Homeruskwartier, Almere, Holland
219 [TL] Courtesy Wikimedia Commons: Kin Ming Estate, Hong Kong
[TR] Tim Roberts Photography: Shutterstock: Suburban Arizona
224 Courtesy Zhou Hao: 'The Chinese Mayor', Zhao Films, 2015
225 Courtesy CFCCA, Kenya Hara Design Studio: Dashilar Hutong
238 Courtesy St. Ann's Warehouse: Poster for *People, Places, and Things*, play by Duncan MacMillan
243 Highline (source unknown)
245 Courtesy Jason Roberts, Better Block Foundation
246 Igor Golovniov / Shutterstock: Katowice stamp
248 Courtesy Impact Hub, San Francisco: Co-working space
249 [R] Courtesy Priya Prakash, Design for Social Change: Changify app
250 Courtesy Jonathan Tarbatt: Housing in Vauban, Germany
252 Courtesy Priya Prakash, Design for Social Change: Citizen canvas
253 Courtesy Smart Citizen Barcelona (smartcitizen.me)
259 [L, R] Courtesy Matthias Wunderlich, Urban Initiatives Studio: Middlehaven Urban Pioneers Competition
265 [BR] Courtesy Baratunde Thurston, NEAT: Detroit Soup public meeting
269 Courtesy Rod Collins
274 Ann Cutting / The Image Bank / Getty Images: Man sitting on mountain
275 Courtesy Sunni Brown (sunnibrownink.com): Open, Explore, Close
276 [T] Courtesy Royal Society of Arts Journal: Active citizenship
[B] Courtesy Smithsonian Institution, Wikimedia Commons: Margaret Mead
277 [B] Courtesy Nasief Manie, Netwerk24: Jonathan Jansen
278 Courtesy Dr. Ranganayakulu Bodavala, One Child One Light: Boy reading
280 [T] Courtesy Allesandra Orofino, Meu Rio, Brazil
[B] Courtesy Channel 4 News: Petare slum, Caracas, Venezuela
282 [T] (source unknown)
[B] Courtesy Arrive Alive (arrivealive.co.za)
283 Courtesy Future Leadership Institute: Naheed Nenshi
284 Courtesy Public Art Forum (contemporaryartsociety.org): We don't need another hero
285 [L] Courtesy City of Baltimore: Power to Dirt programme
286 [L] Courtesy Matthew Lewis, Detroit Soup (detroitsoup.com)
[R] Courtesy Chris Brooks, Baltimore Office of Promotion and the Arts (baltimorearts.org): Forever together
292 Elephant in Room (source unknown)
294 Courtesy BBC News: Beds in sheds, West London, UK
297 Courtesy Jason Roberts, Better Block, Dallas: Community consultation
300–1 Tsung-Lin Wu / stock.adobe.com: Evolution not revolution
302 Shutterstock.com: Outdoor poster mockup in the city
305 Courtesy Granger: Abraham Maslow
310 Courtesy Christopher DeLorenzo
311 Crown Copyright: Lord Kitchener Wants You
315 Courtesy BBC News: Beds in sheds, West London
317 Courtesy Julia King (julia-king.com): CURE project, India
327 Courtesy Derek Tynan, Group 91 Architects, Dublin: Making the Modern Street. London Fabrication
337 [L] Courtesy URBZ: Urban Typhoon Workshops, Khirkee, India

INDEX

D

J

K

L

M

N

O

P

Q

R

T